THE MORAL NECESSITY OF ATHEISM

NORTHWATER

CONSTANTINE ISSIGHOS

Northwater

Copyright 2018©. Constantine Issighos. Published in Canada. Printed in U.S.A. No part of this book may be reproduced or transmitted in any form or any means, electronic or mechanical, including photocopying, recording, and/or by any information storage and retrieval system except by a reviewer who may quote a brief passages in a review to be printer in a newspaper, magazine, or on the Internet without written permission in writing from the author/publisher. For more information please contact: issighos@gmail.com

NORTHWATER is an imprint of Awaqkuna Books Inc.

THE MORAL NECESSITY OF ATHEISM

Library and Archives Canada

ISBN 978-1-927845-08-0

Library and Archives Canada Cataloging in Publication.

Graffic Design: Sergio Gonzales Fansanando, Ica - Perú

ATTENTION: BOOK CLUBS, BOOK STORES, BOOK DISTRIBUTORS, PUBLIC or PRIVATE LIBRARIES, UNIVERSITIES AND COLLEGES: QUANTITY DISCOUNDS ARE EVAILABLE ON BULK PURCHASESOF THIS BOOK SERIES.

BOOKS BY:
CONSTANTINE ISSIGHOS

1) Prisoners of Our Ideals
2) The Magic World of In-laid Pictorial Tapestry
3) My Six-Sided Log Home
4) For God, Country and Drug Prohibition
5) The Moral Necessity of Atheism
6) Gustave Eiffel: Beyond the Tower Vol. 1
7) Gustave Eiffel: Genius of Iron Works Vol. 2
8) Gustave Eiffel: Art of Metal Structures Vol. 3
9) Gustave Eiffel: Art and Strength in Architecture Vol. 4
10) Gustave Eiffel: Magician of Iron Vol. 5
11) Gustave Eiffel: The Iron Lady Vol. 6
12) Gustave Eiffel: Genius of Harmonious Design Vol. 7
13) Gustave Eiffel: Visionary Engineer and Scientist Vol. 8

AMAZON EXPLORATION SERIES
CHILDREN'S BOOKS (50 pages).

1) Upper Amazon Voyage by River Boat
2) The People of the River
3) The Children of the River
4) Amazon's Nature of Things
5) Echoes of Nature: a Beautiful Wild Habitat
6) The Amazon Rainforest
7) Amazonian Sisterhood
8) Amazon River Wolves
9) Amazonian Landscapes and Sunsets
10) Amazonian Canopy: the Roof of the World's Rainforest
11) Amazonian Tribes: a World of Difference
12) Birds and Butterflies of the Amazon
13) The Great Wonders of the Amazon
14) The Jaguar People
15) The Fresh Water Giants
16) The Call of the Shamans
17) Indigenous Families: Life in Harmony with Nature
18) Amazon in Peril
19) Giant Tarantulas and Centipes
20) Amazon Ethno-botanical Garden

ACKNOWLEDGEMENTS

This book is clear, concise and persuasive. It is base on scientific evidence to explain the birth of the universe, life's diversity, organization, and beauty.

The author Constantine Issighos avoids the esoteric and metaphorical language used by philosophers and theologians and answers the question and meaning of our existence in scientific terms. Constantine presents historical evidence in simple terms, making the book richly entertaining and easy-to-read understanding of the atheist universe.

The The Moral Necessity Of Atheism addresses all of the historical evidence and role of the 1st century Roman Imperial Cult, the Jewish turncoat Josephus and others invention of the pacifist religion of Christianity to redirect the attention of the rebellious Jews in Palestine. As such, he questions the existence of Jesus. It provides proof that the cultural oral traditions of the Qur'an were not written by Mohammad. It shows how religion fuels war, foments bigotry, and abuses children, supporting his points with historical and contemporary evidence. In so doing, he makes compelling case that religion is man-made and that believing in God is not just irrational, but potentially harmful.

The author has demonstrated an impassioned, rigorous refusal of the "Holy Books" showing at their inconsistencies and cruelties that are riddle the Old Testament, the New Testament and the Qur'an in the Middle East or the "Bible Belt" of Mid-America. He bristles at the idiocy of the claim of the "intelligent design"---arguments which are based on reason, common sense, ethics, history and science. A comprehensive primer, the book addresses the scientific questions of the role of Laws of Nature, which are irreconcilable with the scriptures. The Laws of Nature and constants of the universe are carefully tuned to allow the eventual biological evolution of life. Never mind the myth that "Jesus died for us." The fact is that stars had to die in the universe for you and I to be born. Every atom in our body came from stars. In fact the atoms in your right-hand may have come from a different star than your atoms in your left-hand. The only way those atoms got into your body are that the stars were king enough to explode. It is also why every living organism on earth shares a commonality of DNA with humans.

The The Moral Necessity Of Atheism also answers ethical issues such as: humanist morality and the meaning of life, arriving at a controversial and well documented illustrated conclusion. Since 1859, after Charles Darwin rattle the religious industry with his revolutionary theory of human origins, the author has intensified the challenge to organized faith by advancing an evolutionary account of *proto-spiritualism* itself based on research in anthropology, *proto-cultural expression* evident in cave-art and social-psychology of caveman. The author demonstrates that religion first emerged not as a divine gift but rather as a thoroughly political and cultural adaptation for enhancing the power structural success of the clergy and tyrants in Mesopotamia and the Fertile Screen. Even more provocatively, the author argues that religion—like language—has subsequently evolved so as to ensure its own survival in a ceaseless adaptation of cultural strives.

The pious attitude projected in most faiths is an attempt to veil-over their harmful influence in society---through the myths that empowered apologists to claim that "Islam is a religion of peace," and the fanatical terrorists to commit their atrocities in the name of Allah. Remarkably bold, the author supports the use of social media for advancing religious doubts in faith-based Madrassas or western faith based schools.

The author questions the existence of any spiritual being---in our spiritless world--- and replaces religious blind faith with open-mindedness inquiry with plenty to think about in the pursuit of ideas. This book is a sequence to his *Prisoners of Our Ideals* which simple premise is met with enormous success. Hence, he maintains that religion is a form of mental illness, and it is both the cause and result of sexual repression. It is humourless and is grounded in mean wishful thinking that is utterly irrational. We cannot afford moderate lip service to religion and tolerate views of one religious group against another—an accommodation that only blind the rest of us to the real dangers of Biblical fundamentalism. The truth is that many who claim that their religion offered them deep love and forgiveness, only to become murderously intolerant of another's faith. Such hatred draws considerable support from their "holy books."

As such, it explores the fallacies, inconsistencies, and harm of religious doctrine and theist dogma. In its place, the author issues an appealing and compassioned invocation of atheist morality, reason and humanism as his arsenal against believers and sceptics. Perhaps the faithful won't change their minds---that is what faith means—but they would run out of refuge from which to hide. They are the prime examples of irrationality! The conclusion, then, is that both faith and irrationality must be abandoned and new ways of rational thinking about the origins of our atheist universe be adopted in its place. In the words of Bertrand Russell, *"I am as firmly convinced that religions do harm as I am that they are untrue."*

The reader will find this book and its illustrations an invigorating challenge and a pure joy to read.

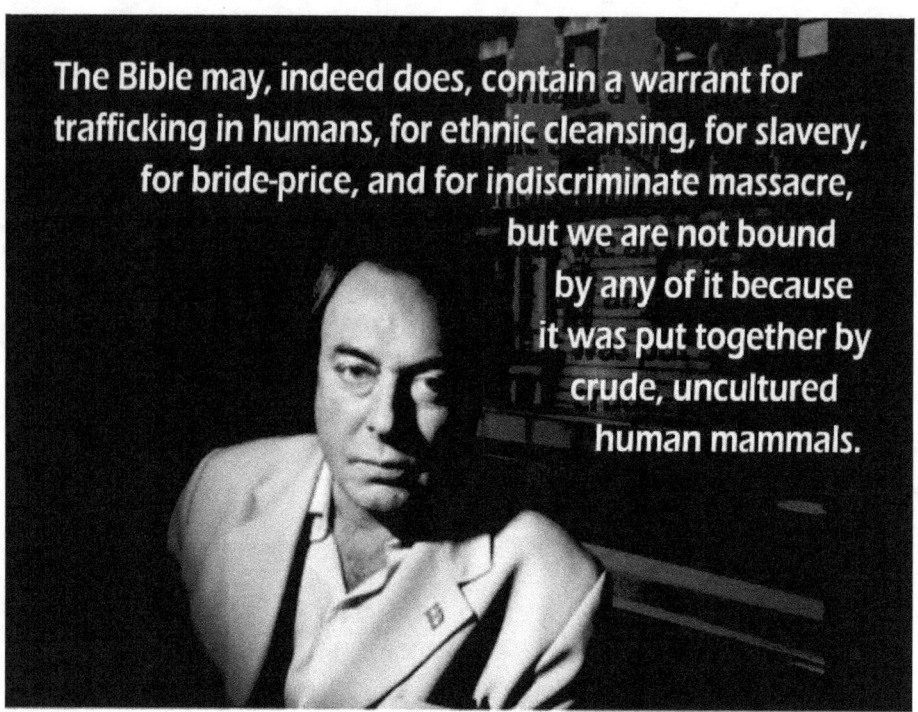

Christopher Hitchens 1949 - 2011

TABLE OF CONTENTS
THE MORAL NECESSITY OF ATHEISM

Page

Sub-Title	1
Legal Page	3
Books by Constantine Issighos	4
Acknowledgements	5
Quote by Christopher Hutchins 1949 – 2011	8

TABLE OF CONTENTS

Prologue	10
An Open Letter to my Readers	13

CHAPTER 1

In the Beginning of our Cosmos	35
The Governing Law of Nature	69
Evolution Not by God's Design	105
The Tall of Two Human Species	143

CHAPTER 2

Human Societies: From Palaeolithic to Neolithic Times	200
Pre-Historic Symbolism	250
Rome's Imperial Religion of Christianity	286
Christianity & Islam	345

BOOK II

CHAPTER 3

Natural Evolution of Atheism	456
Mythology of Organised Religion	504
Entrapment of Beliefs	539
Death & the Afterlife	609

CHAPTER 4

Faith & Reason	636
Religious Fallacies	660
The Plight of Children	690
Life after Darwin	724

PROLOGUE

This book is clear, concise and persuasive. It is based on the scientific evidence with explains the birth of the universe, and life's diversity, organization, and beauty.

The author, Constantine Issighos, avoids the esoteric and metaphorical language used by philosophers and theologians and answers the question and meaning of our existence in scientific terms. Constantine presents historical evidence in simple terms, making the book richly entertaining and an easy-to-read guide to the atheist universe.

The Moral Necessity of Atheism addresses all of the historical evidence and role of the 1st century Roman Imperial Cult, the Jewish turncoat Josephus Bar Mathias and others invention of the pacifist philosophy of Jewish "Christianity" to redirect the attention of the rebellious Jews in Palestine. As such, the author Constantine questions the existence of Jesus. It provides proof that the cultural oral traditions of the Qur'an were not written by Mohammad. It shows how religion fuels war, foments bigotry, and abuses children; supporting his points with historical and contemporary evidence. In so doing, he makes a compelling case that religion is man-made and that believing in God is not just irrational, but potentially harmful.

The author demonstrates an impassioned, rigorous refusal of the "Holy Books," showing inconsistencies and cruelties that riddle the Old Testament, the New Testament and the Qur'an whether in the Middle East or the "Bible Belt" of Mid-America. He bristles at the idiocy of the claim of "intelligent design"---arguments which are based on reason, common sense, ethics, history and science. A comprehensive primer, the book addresses the scientific questions of the role of Laws of Nature, which are irreconcilable with the scriptures. The Laws of Nature and constants of the universe are carefully tuned to allow the eventual biological evolution of life. Never mind the myth that "Jesus died for us." The fact is that stars had to die in the universe for you and I to be born. Every atom in our body came from stars. In fact the atoms in your right-hand may have come from a different star than your atoms in your left-hand. The only way those atoms got into your body are that the stars were kind enough to explode. It is also why every living organism on earth shares a commonality of DNA with humans.

The Moral Necessity of Atheism also explores ethical issues such as humanist morality and the meaning of life, arriving at a controversial, and well documented and illustrated conclusion. After Charles Darwin rattle the religious industry in 1859 with his revolutionary theory of human origins, the author intensifies the challenge to organized faith by advancing an evolutionary account of *proto-spiritualism* itself, based on research in anthropology, and *proto-cultural expression* evident in cave-art and the social-psychology of caveman. The author demonstrates that religion first emerged not as a divine gift but rather as a thoroughly political and cultural adaptation for enhancing the power structural success of the clergy and tyrants in Mesopotamia and the Fertile- Crescent. Even more provocatively, the author argues that religion—like language—has subsequently evolved so as to ensure its own survival in a ceaseless string of cultural adaptations of cultural strivings. The pious attitude projected in most faiths is an attempt to veil-over their harmful influence in society---through the myths that empower apologists to claim that "Islam is a religion of peace" and the fanatical terrorists to commit their atrocities in the name of Allah are not really Muslims. Remarkably bold, the author supports the use of social media for advancing religious doubts in institutions from faith-based Madrassas to western faith-based schools.

The author questions the existence of any spiritual being---in our spiritless world--- and replaces religious blind faith with open-minded inquiry, with plenty to think about in the pursuit of ideas. This book is a sequel to Constantine's *Prisoners of Our Ideals* a simple premise which has met with enormous success. Hence, he maintains that religion is a form of mental illness, that religion is both the cause and result of sexual repression. It is humourless and is grounded in mean wishful thinking that is utterly irrational. We cannot afford to give moderate lip service to religion and to tolerate views of one religious group over another—an accommodation that only blinds the rest of us to the real dangers of Biblical fundamentalism. The truth is that many who claim that their religion offers them deep love and forgiveness only becomes murderously intolerant of another's faith. Such hatred draws considerable support from their "holy books."

As such, this book explores the fallacies, inconsistencies, and harm of religious doctrine and theist dogma. In its place, the author issues an appealing and compassioned invocation of atheist morality, reason and humanism for both believers and sceptics to consider. Perhaps the faithful won't change their minds---that is what faith means—but they would run out of refuge and places to hide. They are the prime examples of irrationality! The conclusion, then, is that both faith and irrationality must be abandoned and new ways of rational thinking about the origins of our atheist world be adopted in its place. In the words of Bertrand Russell, *"I am as firmly* *convinced that religions do harm as I am that they are untrue."* 5

This book takes the reader into a grand journey from the "Big Bang" to Neanderthals and cave-art, to Fertile Crescent to Roman Imperial Cult, and the late birth of Islam. The astute reader will find this book and its illustrations an invigorating challenge and a pure joy to read.

AN OPEN LETTER TO MY READERS

"Any animal whatsoever, endowed with well-marked social instincts, would inevitably acquire a moral sense or conscience, as soon as its intellectual powers had become as well developed.... as in man."

Charles Darwin: Descent of Man

The nature of this publication will be best understood by a brief narrative of how it came to be written. To begin with, I'm not just an atheist but I'm also a confirmed positive-atheist, one who has dedicated a large part of my life exposing religion's crimes against humanity. I deplore what religion has done to our humanity. I have seen its effects around the world, especially with Catholicism in South America, in the Muslim world of the Middle East, and the religiousness of the Orthodox Church in Greece and in the Eastern European societies. During my travelling about the Amazon Rainforest of South America, I collected notes on pre-historic pagan animist spiritualism in various tribal communities that I encountered, the environment in which they lived, and their culturally defined social norms. This was done without any interest in publishing on the subject beyond my series of children's books, *The Amazon Illustrated Exploration Series.* During my travelling, I discovered that the Amazonian tribes are the nearest living examples of pre-historic humanity, its animist religions and the foundational basis of its socio-cultural community. My notes seemed to be sufficient to indicate the need to write and enlighten my readers on the socio-cultural progression of humanity's pre-historic tribal settlements, and beyond, with the aim of demonstrating the historical development of atheism.

This means that I shall explain The *Moral Necessity of Atheism* by taking a materialist view and explaining the non-theistic nature of geology, biology and of human societies. It is based on reason and evidence rather than on primitive mythology and religious superstition. My experience with the Amazon's tribal and indigenous communities revealed to me a close resemblance to humanity's Stone Age and of Neanderthal, Cro-Magnon and Homo sapiens narrative of social progression. I witnessed that the existing Amazon tribes held the socio-biological living evidence to that narrative. I also want to trace the origins of humanity's man-made theism and its progression from Animism to organised religion. My analysis is based on biological evidence of humanity's inclination to theism. It is based on a non-theistic historical dialectical materialism and my presented biological evidence is based on the scientific explanations of human evolution put forth by Charles Darwin (1809-1882) and Alfred Russell Wallace (1823-1913).

I acknowledge that the present day Amazonian rainforest and the Arabian Desert tribal communities are descendants of biological natural selection and natural adaptation in those regions, including other parts of the world. This especially holds true when we look at the natural selection in their gene propagation, survival and mutual protection of their tribal members. There are also universal moral human characteristics shared among populations on various parts of the world, which may have been historically interrupted, but not altered in their essence. The evidence can be witnessed where the tribes may allow their elders or newborn to perish due to famine rather than risk the survival chances of the whole. Such humanist based moral decisions were taken on the basis of right and wrong survival instincts of the whole---rather than on the basis of moralistic "good" or "bad."

Through a historical development of tribal survival instincts, pre-historic men adopted and developed a sense of morality, of what is right and what is wrong, or conscience. As such, pre-historic men adopted an internal faculty which directed them to follow one instinct rather than another. The one instinct men followed would be the right one rather than the wrong one. This holds true in multiple cases where moral decisions or choices needed to be made. Man's adapted faculties alone were in control within the biological history of human moralities, and within those which were actually evolved under necessity and with time. The propulsion of biological evolution, even moral evolution, is propagated by natural selection. The evolution of human moralities is also based on combined social instincts which were used for the survival benefit of the group. These combined social instincts may have varied from one geographical area to another, but not necessarily from one community to another--especially of those who shared the same physical surroundings. One probable explanation is that, having nearly similar social structures, habits and constitutions, men tended to form nearest kindred and solidarity in the social adaptation of their moral instincts.

The historical evolution of man-made social morality is fundamental if we are to explain the existing differences between humanist and religious morality. It must be said that the existing humanist morality has evolved simultaneously with man's natural evolution and social adaptation which was brought about by the survival of human-species from Neanderthals of 40,000 years ago to Bronze Age and present day Homo sapiens. It evolved on the basis of social characteristics passed along hundreds, if not thousands, of generations of humanoid species. This social process was man-made and not theistic. It evolved millennia before pre-historic man invented Animist religions--and much later the "Sky-God"--that were adopted by a succession of inherited social habits.

Humans today are capable of great technological and scientific marvels and constant innovation. We became this wonder-people from a loose band of nomadic hunter gatherer cavemen scattered in the present day Amazonian Rainforest and African Continent, and eventually around the globe. These nomadic tribal people did not know how to cultivate the land for crops or navigate the seas and lacked the ability to read and write. They led a simple and isolated existence in small communities. They had no knowledge of the workings of the universe above their heads or the manifestations of the physical environment around them. Archaeological evidence is ample and conclusive in favour of the principles of their gradual social evolution and the non-theistic manner of development of such human communities. Archaeological excavations have not found a shred of theistic involvement in the human evolution that marked our survival on earth.

Once men began to form communities they learned to share food and shelter, take care of the old and young, the sick and the weak, as well as the females. Men provided protection, leadership and means of subsistence for their immediate families and beyond. They fished and hunted and later cultivated lands for food production, and used agricultural produce as a means of exchange with others. They defended their families and their communities by killing their enemies and conquered more natural resources to meet their ever increasing necessities of life. This is how strong communities became stronger at the expense of weaker communities who either amalgamated or perished in the process. Through such socio-exchange activities, humans developed a sense of moral direction as a guideline for themselves, their offspring and their communities. Their moral direction became an all-inclusive, intended mimetic process that was not legalistic, theistic, natural, heretical, or qualitatively "good" or "bad," but rather man-made out of humanist necessity. This is a Darwinian natural order, a state of affairs which humans have recognised to exist outside the moral perimeters of their individual consciousness.

The Darwinian evidence of natural selection and adaptation confirms that they are governed by the physical laws of nature alone. This is an inclusive process experienced by every living plant, animal and human in every geographical region on the planet earth. Out of such process of adaptation, and by the variable manifestations of our physical surroundings, we have determined our social instincts, including our habits and thinking process. The physical conditions of our surroundings have in turn directed our social and moral structure and behaviour. The Darwinian order, of the Laws of Nature, does not interfere on behalf of humanity, nor can they be temporarily suspended, nor do they interfere to save us from tsunamis, earthquakes, hurricanes, floods, sickness or epidemics. Miracles are not part of the natural order of things, for miracles could not suspend the natural order of things on behalf of anyone, including man!

Humanity's social behaviour evolved out of life's material process. It does not include a theistic or mystifying speculation and superstition, nor illusions and delusions, pre-suppositions, unverifiable beliefs and wishful thinking. One's imagination, or ideas in their heads, does not alone influence one's material surroundings. Take the Laws of Nature upon humanity's living functions, which includes our biological process of birth, growth, decay and death. Any "suspension" of these Laws of Nature is nothing more than a delusional belief which leads on to "life after death," which derives from our fear of death.

It is my long standing conviction, expressed in this book and my previous book *Prisoners of Our Ideals*, that all religious orders and cults, past or present, large or small, are man-made inventions set up to worship an illusion in the sky, to enslave humanity for the sake of power and profit for the clergy. My positive-atheism does not consist in disbelieving; it consists in professing the lack of reason and verifiable evidence by those who believe. It is near impossible to calculate the physical, ethical and moral damage done by religious delusions, myths and superstitions in our human society. Religious mental disorder, generated by delusional beliefs, has corrupted and prostituted the otherwise naïve mind of a believer by exhorting him to believe things that he does not understand. Such a man can become a true creator of human tragedies, a religious perpetuator with unneutered religious convictions, a man who has prepared himself to commit accusations, offences and crimes against humanity. The salvation for his moral confusion can come from one and only one Sky-God---if only that God was not *"a jealous God,"* a *"capricious God,"* or a *"vindictive God."* Can you conceive of any other kind of man or God more morally destructive than this?

Every religion and cult---since the dawn of history---has publicly expressed in *sotto voce* that it alone has some special messages from God, who communicated those to certain individuals. The Jewish religion had Abraham and Moses, the Christians had Jesus and the Apostles, the Muslims had Muhammad and the Mormons had Joseph Smith---all self-deluding and fraudulently claiming that God was exclusively available only to them.

As an atheist, I maintain that objective morality does not require a supernatural theistic or non-theistic foundation of any kind. Yet, religious followers believe that there cannot be goodness in the world without a supernatural entity. This falsehood attacks our sense of humanity in our deepest integrity, in that, we are nothing, that we have no moral principles, no humour and no irony unless we are the property of a celestial dictator and yearned for his rewards and feared his punishments. It attacks humanist essence in its core, including our sexuality and our individuality by projecting in us a sense of shame, guilt and fear.

These religious claims are still the source of immorality, misery and unhappiness. Christianity projects a monopoly on morality by claiming it alone has taken actions or made moral statements that an atheist (like my self) cannot make, such as, *"love your enemy,"* or *"turn the other cheek"* and (Rome's Imperial morality) *"Give to Cesar what belongs to Cesar."* I do not support that these are moral claims, in that, should we love the suicide bomber or turn the other cheek when they attack and kill school-girls for want an education? I claim that we humanists and atheists must dislike "martyrs" and have accomplished their defeat. It is positively immoral to claim that *"I love a suicide martyr"* and would be defeatist and cowardly, anthropocentric and dishonest to do so.

Religion is like the old general store which has a little of this and little of that of everything and for everyone *"Seek and you shall find."* Its goods are in a form of metaphors, parables, and patterns which humans can use to support any explanation, for we are pattern-seeking mammals. As humans---or mammals--we are programmed to look for patterns as part of our evolution. Patterns are optional foundational structures of given explanations, regardless of whether those are valid or invalid. In other words, when we cannot come up with a good explanation, because of our ignorance of the subject, we then come up with a bad explanation rather than none at all. Patterns offered by religious explanations are providing us with rather lazy and believable half-baked answers to complex issues. These patterns offer a kind of mental "comfort zone" that does not demand us to be critical, analytic, and investigative towards an issue. The only requirement religious pattern-seeking has is for us to believe, for this is the core element of religious faith. To be thinking critically is to perceive patterns in science, art, philosophy and politics, human rights and in all possible areas of human life.

One of the core religious pattern-beliefs is "life after death." Bear in mind that we do not know, or we may not even say, that there is not a heaven to receive all the devoted Christians. We may say that the Laws of Nature operate without the "life after death" assumption, or we can take one strep away from the laws of physics, or of the observable laws of the universe, that could lead us to believe that there is such a place as heaven, where humans can live a "life after death." As atheists we do not seek false patterns to answer even our most improbable questions. We may say that there is no such a thing as "God," we may even look for any indication to support that assumption, but all the Laws of Physics do not provide evidence to support the existence of a "force" or a "God" who has created the cosmos. We can therefore affirm that there is not an intervening God who answers Jewish, Christian or Muslim prayers, who can read our thoughts, who knows with whom you sleep, what kind of foods you eat and is at your disposal to forgive your sins. To take the issue of religious patterns, further even if Jesus existed, even if his mother was a virgin, even if he was born on December 25th, even if he was resurrected; it still would not prove that Jesus was the Son of God.

So, why do religious people believe in such nonsense? It is because humans are pattern seeking mammals; it is part of our brain's evolution to look for patterns. If we cannot find any, our minds make up one or many---preferably those that are easy to imagine and easy to justify. It is very appealing for us to be lazy in our thinking process, not recognizing the fallacies we promote to our children by our unwillingness to educate ourselves to think critically. The Biblical verses are the most destructive ones which have directed us to *"Seek and you shall find"* any answer you want, in the ready-made patterns of this primitive and delusive book. Seek for an explanation of God's destructive powers in tsunamis, earthquakes, famines, epidemics, blasphemy and religious wars; and you shall find many delusive pattern-answers to please God. This may include human or animal sacrifices, a virgin girl's body thrown into a dry-well or the decapitation of an opposite religious believer or non-believer. As a believer, you are free to commit any atrocity you desire, and a holy-book will be there to provide you with a religious pattern to justify your actions. Remember that those who make you believe in absurdities can also make you commit atrocities.

Religious patterns are not only evident in today's modern societies. Although not monotheistic or theistic in the classical sense, the indigenous tribal communities of the Amazon Rainforest are humanity's surviving examples of primitive spiritual patterns that, in their essence, are no different from organized religion. The Animist mode of patterns is also part of the tribal men's evolution seeking to explain the world of the jungle or in prehistoric cave-art. When the Amazon indigenous had no scientific explanation of the jaguars' spots, they came up with one pattern-explanation related to the spiritual powers of the jaguars, and they painted their face with jaguar spots. When the Amazonian rain-storms are in their full force, the tribal men burn aromatic herbs to appease the spirits who control the rains. In the peaceful night on the Amazon River, the Pink Dolphin is transformed into a young man who tends to visit and impregnate the first young village girl it sees. In reality, because of this myth, the Pink Dolphin is well protected by the indigenous tribal inhabitants. They not aware of course that it is not possible to suspend the Laws of Nature---turning a dolphin to man—so one false pattern-explanation is as good as another, except they are not true.

Of course there are no evil or good spirits, no absolute truths and no celestial dictator called the Sky-God. Everything humanity has accomplished is because of our own innovation, our sense of moral balance between good and bad, right and wrong. Are we perfect mammals? Of course we are not, for our biological programming in our brain is still developing and still experimenting and adapting by natural evolutionary process. Human species were not at all evolved to believe in God or be born religious or mystical. Our brain is biologically programmed to look for patterns in life and assign meaning to them. When there is no pattern our brain invents one rather than having none at all. For example, the ancients were looking at the stars and galaxies but they had no scientific explanations for it, so they invented a shortcut pattern-version: the Zodiac astrological constellations. Christianity has derived and built its myth around the Pagan astrological structure of the Zodiac constellations. In the case of the medical science of proven drugs, those who are looking for another pattern-source of "drugs" find one in Homeopathy. In this case, an ill person sees in it a pattern-meaning (homeopathic cure) where none exists. Religious devotees see symbolic rituals and attach pattern-meaning to them, as if symbolism was a reality, and attach a meaning where none exists. Symbolism is converted to tangible reality. Patterns in our brain do not differentiate between reality based patterns and symbolic patterns, for it are up to us to know the differences between reality and illusions in all facets of life. For instance, like ourselves, our ancestors were biologically programmed to look for patterns in life and assigned meaning to them. When they were faced with a real life threatening situation, they attached a pattern-meaning of "danger" to it and defended themselves or ran away. What happened when the situation of "danger" was non-existent? Instead of ignoring their brain-attached false pattern-meaning of "danger," they assumed a danger and acted in accordance with their false pattern-meaning.

Attaching pattern-meaning is an all consuming task of our brain. It is biologically programmed to do so in all situations; from love affairs, family affairs, friends, work and community related true or false situations and religion. For example, you may be in love with a person, believing that and here is where you attach a pattern-meaning, this person is also in love with you. Your brain creates a pattern-meaning based on your wish, which may be true or false. In the case of a religious person who is terminally ill, he would worship and light candles hoping for a miracle-cure; based on pattern-expectation, that the Laws of Nature would be suspended on his behalf.

Believing in the existence of God is not just a single idea in the mind of the believer, for the pattern-meaning of the term "believe" represents some kind of truth. From this point on, any theistic claim can be made possible and believed. That is, from the theory of evolution (which theists called intelligent-design), to the Big Bang theory; all are due to God's genius.

We should be cautious of an argument that forwards a pattern-explanation that explains everything, which more likely explains nothing. For example, let us take the religious pattern-explanation that "Man is made in God's image." Humans are one (1) chromosome away from chimpanzees. Our human commonalities with other creatures on earth; such as, family, solidarity, kinship and community building; are much closer with those than that "we are made in God's image." Anthropomorphically we are Apes (primates), for if we were made "in God's image," what image are pigs, scavengers and hyenas are made of? This pattern-argument build in the Christians' brain that "we are made in God's image becomes meaningless because the pattern-image of God does not exist.

Other non-existent patterns are:
- There is an absolute truth.
- There is a salvation
- There is a Second Coming
- There is a supernatural dimension
- There is a Big Brother in the sky watching you
- There is a rescue coming from the void (unseen)
- There are miracles capable of suspending the Laws of Nature.

Human beings are as other species are. In the world of nature, we are on our own as we have been for hundreds of thousands of years. Along the way, our humanist morality was built by us, as part of our social order, which is stolen by religion for its own devious purpose.

We behave the way other primates behave in the natural world because we humans are not yet very highly evolved mammals. We live in a rather unstable natural or social environment but we are able to adapt. We do however; have mammalian instincts, which is also a human-dimension for social bonding and solidarity. It is also our moral stand towards one another that perpetuates our existence, for morality could not be imposed upon us by the Sky-God who does not exist. It is a false pattern-meaning to make the Sky-God the responsible entity for our existence and behaviour. In our daily lives most of us behave morally in front of others. But we do also behave morally when no one is looking at us. Why? It is because its part of our biological evolution process, which is programmed in our codes of behaviour and in accordance with the material conditions we find ourselves. In a peaceful environment most of us behave peacefully. In war or conflict conditions we---as primates---protect ourselves and others against our opponents. We see this similarity with other primates in nature; say in the Amazon Rainforest, where territorial disputes often occur. Morality, or lack of it, is based on human conditions; in civilised society we will behave better, as it directs us to behave accordingly. Religion therefore does not make us behave better but rather it entices us to be in opposition to all "others" that hold different pattern-beliefs than our own. We can see this religious animosity in Muslim countries where false-pattern beliefs motivates one group to go against another, one false pattern-belief of "ethnicity" against another's' or man's false pattern-superiority over woman's "weakness" and so on. Most of those false pattern-beliefs are perpetuated by the Holy Books of a number of old or new religious cults including the Jewish, Christian, Muslim, Hindu and sub-groups of those.

It is important for us to understand humanity's secular moral system. Our understanding should be based on the realisation that other people have brains, minds and feelings just like our own, and such recognition is part of the building blocks of our non-theistic moral system. Religion teaches us to be satisfied with irrational answers invented in the Arabian Peninsula by superstitious tribesmen, ignorant of the reality of our cosmos. For instance, if you have a religious book which tells you how the world began, or what the relation between the Sky-God and yourself is, it tends to curtail your natural curiosity. It cuts off our core source of wonder from the extraordinary lovingness of the physical world we live in. In the question of morality, it seizes our brain from its rational thinking process; and when this happens, all other things follow especially by distorted or misdirected morality. Furthermore, some of us prefer junk-explanations of false-patterns rather than non-explanations.

Again, our brain is biologically programmed to look for pattern in life, even when no patterns exist, because our brain does not have a "blank-space" between two thoughts. There was a historical time when this was the best we could do; when we did not know of our cosmos and universe, when we did not know the powers of the bacterial over us, when we did not know that we do not have a dominion over them, when we did not know that the Earth is round and that the Earth revolved around another spherical planet like the Sun, that some natural phenomena are terrifying and even lethal, and that asking questions would lead us to philosophy, science and attempts to interpret cosmology and biology. Until such time, when the relevant answers were found, our brain filled the gap missing between answers with false-patterns in a form of random opinions, wishful thinking, magical solutions, superstitions and beliefs, sense of fear and all-round ignorance. True enough, pagan religion was our first attempt at interpreting cosmology (trying to make sense of where we are in the universe), culture or our first attempt on philosophy. But religion gave us the worst false-pattern explanations we could come up with for this was the best we could do. This was the time when humanity was in its infant stage of development, full of ignorance and superstition, and under the totalitarian control of the intoxicated by power and wealth, the military and priestly castes.

These aforementioned points should be regarded as humanity's mental catharsis, and an atheist manifesto of intellectual independence. Some people ask me what difference it makes whether a person believes in God or not. I say to them that how religious beliefs affect them and their families really makes a huge difference in their lives. Its the difference between been right and been wrong, its the difference between truth and delusions, its the difference between *believing* that the earth is flat, and *knowing* that the earth is spherical, its the difference between believing and knowing, its the difference of knowing that the earth is not the centre of the universe, knowing that the earth is only a spec in this vast space which contains multiple suns, galaxies, and many planets, some of which are many times larger in size than earth, its the difference between knowing the *material* conclusions of life rather than believing in religious *delusions*, it's the difference between verifying dialectical knowledge and having a blind faith in religion, it's the difference between humanist progress and Medieval Dark Ages.

This is the essence of this book, to discover the material origins of humanity's esoteric-beliefs which led to the eventual creation and adaptation of religious thoughts and to discover that God in the sky had nothing to do with the invention of religion, for it was man who invented him and not the other way around. The history of *pagan spiritualism* and organised religion proves that it can pervert man's concept of life and of the universe, and has turned man into a *helpless-creature* before the universal powers of the *Laws of Nature*. If you believe that there is God, that you were created, that you were ordered not to eat the fruit from the tree of knowledge, that you disobeyed God's order, that you are a fallen angel, that you were born in sin, that you will forever be punished for your sins, that you will devote the rest of your life praying to a capricious, vindictive and jealous God---and in this case---your solace is of your own delusions. On the other hand, if you know that the universe is still a mystery to be discovered, that you are a product of Natural Selection and Evolution, that you were born without knowledge and your intelligence comes from your material experience, that you dedicate your valuable time to improve your friend's, your family's and your community's lives with a hope of securing mutual happiness, then that also makes the difference.

If you believe that you were created, then God has made the gravest mistake, for it is inconceivable that a celestial power wasted so much time and energy in order to create such an inferior living being. As such, you are full of sins and ills; the main cause of the world's misery and suffering, which is an essential part of human life. As a disgraced Angel, who has failed to control and prevent your sins, disease and sorrows have affected you and others. Was this also part of God's plan, as a punishment for your disobedience, for you to spend the rest of your entire life's destiny attempting to free yourself from your original sins? Is your religious obligation to make yourself as miserable as possible by praying, fasting and practicing masochism, sadism and misogyny and other forms of torture? Is such a delusion causing you to insist that others close to you must be, under pain of punishment, as miserable as yourself? Mother Teresa believed that the more you suffer on this earth, the closer you are to God. Is this also your fear, that if others fail to be as miserable as you are, this will trigger God's wrath for more severe punishment and chastisement? Is this why human misery, guilt and the sense of escapism have become such an integral part of religion?

The inevitable result is that you spend your entire life, not on the essentials of living a happy life, but paying for the priests' and bishops' comfortable living so they can raise their voices to God in a frenzy of fanaticism. You spend your hard earned money not to advance your family and possibly help your friends, but to pay for the cost of building churches, temples and religious schools to lie to and indoctrinate your children. Your time and energy is wasted to cleanse your sinful soul, which you do not possess, to save yourself from future punishment which exists only in your deluded imagination.

Religious delusions or hallucinations take many forms. In India's religious circles, for example, some devotees do not wash themselves at all; believing that the filthier they are, the holier they are, while others wash only their fingers. Some stand up and never sit down, some sit down and refuse to stand up. Some cut their hair short and some never cut their hair, some people (like in Africa) amputate their children's genitals---female genital mutilation (FGM). Some amputate their own genitals (castration) and others amputate their breasts, some fasten and others gorge themselves, some never stop talking while others remain silent all their lives. Some remain virgins and some are promiscuous, some are pedophiles while others promise to try not to touch children inappropriately. Some stand on their heads and some brand themselves with hot irons, some continue flogging themselves with chains while still breathing. Catholic convent nun's cut-off their hairs to make themselves un-attractable to the opposite sex, monks swear never to touch a woman, and wear ropes around their waist as a sign of enslavement to their dogma. Ascetic monks, who live in *Meteora caves* in Greece, are praying for salvation while wearing rags and depending on others to feed them. With no exaggeration, there is not an insanity or delusion that has not been introduced by religion. All three monotheistic religions have made so many lunatics, in peace and war, that they could provide the psychiatric institutions with a stream of delusional clients forever.

Atheists and humanists do not subscribe to the concept that man is a depraved human being, or that there is a dictatorial and jealous God, or that there is a hell and that man will suffer the penalties of eternal torture. We do not subscribe to the notion that we should make ourselves as miserable as possible in a false hope of securing some happiness in the "afterlife", nor that physical or mental illness is God's punishment for sins. Illness is a natural process and consequence of life that only by understanding the nature of the illness, are we able to protect---when possible---ourselves from its deadly effects. The use of prayers—instead of medical treatments---is responsible for spreading epidemics that have on a number of occasions, almost wiped out entire villages and cities. This is true, for I witnessed it myself; in isolated villages in the Amazon Rainforest and the Sierras Mountains of Peru, where villagers paid for the Shaman's prayers instead of using the money to purchase medicine. These beliefs tend to perpetuate the suffering of the ill and prayers have no more effects on curing illness than on ensuring the health of a believer.

Priests, Rabbis, Imams and holy men of all sorts are facing similar natural causes of life and do not enjoy God's exception for their religiousness. They suffer similar ills and sensations; they are subject to the same passions of the body, the same doubts of the mind and are the same victims of dreadful circumstances, just like every other member of the human race. They commit similar offences, just like other mortals, and especially because of their religious calling, they are involved in the frequent embezzlement of church funds. They are not immune from the passions of the flesh and this is the reason so many priests are in jails in the USA, Canada, Ireland and Australia for pedophilia. In Muslim countries, such as Iran and Afghanistan, young boys are part of the sexual prerogatives of the Imams. In fundamentalist

Islamic countries such as Iran and Afghanistan imams can legally purchase a young girl as *"temporary wife"* for a fixed payment to the girls' parents (a form of pedophilia and forced prostitution) for a month or two, because the religion of Islam permit them to exploit the girl's poverty.

Religious men and women of the cloth often live above the living standards of their flocks, just like "Mother Teresa," who received millions of dollars from the USA and Europe; and used the money to build religious institutions around the world, rather than to feed and provide medical care to the poor of Kolkata. She used the donations to travel in style to Ireland, in USA and other European countries in order to promote and finance anti-abortion, anti-contraception and anti-divorce campaigns rather than feeding the poor and providing them with curative medicine in the Third World countries where she built more than 500 religious institutions.

All these people of the cloth are not free from the rules of life, morality, and ethics and from humanists' and atheists' scrutiny. They can not hide themselves from the forces of intellectual integrity, social media and the laws of society. Their claims that they are anointed and are the vicars of God are fraudulent and hypocritical, for if they can not fulfil their promises of salvation while their followers are alive, how can they fulfilled them when their believers' are dead. If they are impotent here; where they have a chance to demonstrate their powers, how can they fulfil their promises in the afterlife? The mythical and delusional "after life" exists only in the clergy's dishonesty and in the believers' deluded imagination.

The illusions of life are many and varied; some mentioned in my book, *Prisoners of Our Ideals,* show that things are not always what they seem to be and it is well known fact that appearances are exceptionally deceiving. This is the reason why, for some people, it is difficult to understand the religious deceptions of claimed miracles and why it took human beings so long to comprehend the true conditions of the Laws of Nature and of the natural process of biological life. Religious deceptions matter in cases of great importance as well as in matters of low level consequence. There is no "Big Brother" in the sky to tell us what is true and what is false or to warn us of life's dangers. We must find whatever the truth is, and whatever the pitfalls of life are, for ourselves after trial and error of many personal experiences. In short, there is no messenger or voice in nature to warn us how to avoid deadly consequences.

The first piece of self-deception was during pre-historic man's initial development of consciousness. During this early state, his inability to think of any concept of life derived from his own primitive, limited intelligence. Pre-historic man, until the Middle Ages, could not conceive what the earth and the universe were, except as having been created by God. Man could not conceive the real causes of his suffering in life except that those must be the results of some disobedience to his Creator. Primitive as man may have been---as a Neanderthal, Cro-Magnon or as Homo sapient---man did not inflict punishment on the innocent. Any evil act could only come from a merciful God and his vengeful representatives among us. Protestants against Catholics, Christians against Jews, Muslims against Christians and Jews, Shiites against Sunnis, Hindus against Buddhists, and the list can go on. The results of such religious conflicts are, first and foremost, the killing and infliction of suffering on the innocent in Africa and Arabia. All this is happening in the name of a man-made religion; including from biblical instructions for committing genocide, enslavement and self-infliction, from an imaginary God.

As an illustration of primitive man in this respect are the delusion man experiences when he believes that the Sun rises and sets. As a matter of fact, the Sun is stationary and it is the earth that orbits around the Sun as *Galileo (1564 – 1642)* so courageously declared, at the cost of his freedom. Although we no longer believe the Sun delusion, the religious concept of it is still very much with us, when we refer to the "sun-rising" and "sun-setting" in our every day language. There is a delusion that the Sun shines and it rains from the clouds to make the flowers bloom and, for the religious, this is the beauty of God's nature. It is nothing of the kind, for poisonous plants and unruly weeds are also fully nourished by the warmth of the sun and the moisture of the rain water.

Is this then evidence of the ugliness of nature? Evidently not, for both are the inevitable consequences of the material environment where vegetation thrives. It could not be otherwise. Is the elephant one of nature's masterful pieces? Is the elephant's physical structure, beauty and grace a work of art? No, it is not, for the elephant's bodily structure is the result of millions of years of Natural Selection and Adaptation to the environment in which it still survives to this day. The long trunk, as well as the long neck of the giraffe (to feed on leaves of tall trees), is the result of Natural Adaptation. The fact that certain animals survived for millions of years, and still thrive today, is proof that they are equally as favoured by nature as man. To the natural world, the blossoms of flowers, plants and unruly weeds are identical and the aroma of the one is equally alike as the stems of the other, for both are nurtured by nature. The sun does not necessary shine to bring us light or warmth but also to bring ultraviolet rays to sustain other life form on earth. In nature, for matters that are of importance to man, is of very little consequences to nature. Life's process functions on a non-preferential basis, for nature does not favour one life form over and above another.

In nature, it is the survival of the most adaptable species to its environment, and not the strongest, the most desirable or the most intelligent that survives. The conditions are in favour of the wild and carnivorous animals, for they thrive by killing other forms of life which they live off. When conditions favour man, he kills and lives upon the forms of life he considers they exist solely for his necessity and for his pleasure. When conditions are favour viruses like cholera, influenza, Ebola or HIV then we have what is known as an epidemic. While germs and viruses are invisible wild animals, they are forms of life that thrive and adapt on upon the soil of the human body. In the case of viruses which are drug-resistant, we are witnessing the viruses' natural evolution of adaptation. The viruses are adapting to and resisting the drugs that are given to defeat them. This virus adaptation is most vivid against HIV drugs. When the virus of HIV is resistant to the drugs, by the natural evolution of adaptation, the doctors stop drug administration until the resistance of the virus is reduced to its original state. You see, when the virus has no need of strong adaptation, its defence is reduced. At this point the HIV drugs are re-administered to the patient, and the HIV virus is controlled by the on-and-off administration of drugs. The knowledge of these defence mechanisms protects us from the invisible enemies to health. It is not necessary therefore, to moralise upon their differences as being "good" or "bad" wild animals in nature because, as forms of life, they are all identical. Who are we to say which one of the wild animals in nature are the better in the overall scheme of life? Humans and wild animals, invisible viruses and germs are all part of nature which does not favour or discriminate one over the other. Nature provides all of us with sunshine, water and air to sustain us in the environment which we live. To nature, the night is just as important as the day, so is the environment in which humans and wild animals lived. They all are following the same laws of life, that is: birth, growth, decay and death. Some live at night while others live in the day, some are "cute," some appear as "monstrosities," and this is proof that there is a lack of religious "intelligent-design" in nature as far as man is concerned.

When we come to a realise that we are not God's chosen life form, that we were not especially created, that the universe was not made for our own benefit, and therefore we are all subject to the same Laws of Nature as are all other forms of life; then and only then, we will recognise that we must rely upon ourselves and ourselves alone. Whatever benefits we enjoy and devote our time and energy to help ourselves and our fellow human beings, it strengthens us to face the difficulties and problems of living. The recognition of a problem is the first step to its solution, for we are not fallen angels, nor were we created perfect. On the contrary, we are the product of millions of years of purposeless Natural Evolution and we are the descendants of all the strengths and defects of our primitive Neanderthals and Homo sapiens ancestors. The most important things for us to recognise is for us that we are born without knowledge and that the acquisition of knowledge is a difficult process. We teach our children to learn how to talk, we send them to school to learn about science, math and Natural Evolution, to learn that the Laws of Nature cannot be suspended, we teach them our language, we teach them of our moral humanist values and the *Golden Rule "do as you want others to do you"*, to take care of the environment because the Earth is the only home we will ever know, and to be truthful and brave. As parents we know that the child's brain needs the same kind of training as any other part of the body. It requires exercise for its development. Nourishment of the brain is just as necessary as nourishment of the body's limbs. Educating our children in humanist knowledge, science and biology are the primary tasks of civilisation.

We do not lie to our beloved children about a celestial dictator who isn't there, and of hell and fire; that we were born sick and sinful and we are now ordered by God to be cured; that there is a God who watches them every moment of their lives and in the afterlife; that our children will never be free from such a jealous god; that there is a heaven where they will go to prey to God and listen to harp-music all day long, day-in and day-out. We do not lie to our children by telling them that, if they commit crimes, they can absolve their sin by simply confessing to a priest and giving a donation. Moreover, just like some foods that has been adulterated and no longer contains any nourishment for the body, so there are truths which have also been adulterated by religion and superstition and they are valueless as nourishment for our brain's intelligence. As Thomas Paine *(1737 – 1809)* said, *"The Church knows that an educated man is a un-believer and that is why the Church continues to adulterate education with religion and superstition."* To maintain its dominant position, the Church must keep people in mental shackles, a form of perpetual slavery. Both senses of fear and superstition are a contagious diseases and the ignorance of man produces natural fear of the elements of nature because what man cannot understand, he attributes to God whose primary purpose is to punish and harm man. Under this spell it is almost incredible that man even advanced from his primitive state of ignorance. His fears produced such fantastic monsters in the religious clouds before he even required the first elementary knowledge of the cosmos. Man's ignorance made him easy prey for the priests, mullahs and rabbis, and his gullibility was such that he believed everything he was told, and soon he became a slave to these liars and hypocrites. Whatever the priests had told him, it was claimed to be from God, who made a special revelation called the Bible, and that it was necessary for man to believe everything it was said in order to save his soul. Man was told that if he disobeyed its commandments he would suffer eternal punishment in hell, where the fire never ceases and where his skin will burn and fall-off, re-burn and fall-off again and again. Man was also told to interpret the Bible the way the priest did and what the priest revealed from that text of the Bible was that man was a corrupt and a sinful being and, in order to be saved after death, man had to give a substantial part of his hard earned wages to the priest to pray for him and to speak to god on his behalf---for a punishment for which man was already doomed.

These were evil schemes of fraud for which the priest was living off the hard work and sweat of others. On a personal level, I remember, as if it was yesterday, when my grandmother Angelica was taking me to a Greek Orthodox Church every Sunday morning. I was listened to the sermons given by the well-fed priest, in a *soot-voce* telling the villagers (among other threats) to repent their sins or God would punish them after death. I always wondered what possible sins my grandmother could have committed for, in her 92 years on earth, she had never travelled more than 50 kilometres from her village; when our family visited her, she would cry as she killed one of her chickens to serve us for dinner. Now, I have asked myself many times, what possible sins could my grandmother have committed to deserve the priest's threatening her with hell and fire every Sunday?

In the past 5,000 years, while priests and their politico-military class gained more power and wealth, they also began to spend it acquiring arms for the protection of their property. As a result, when a lord or a king took power of a state, the priests were well-protected by becoming a deterrent force to others. It is incredible that such non-sense as religion was imposed upon humanity and, what non-sense would be, had it not it was been so tragic, that believers could not bear that they could not live without the priests and, because people have wanted hope for so long, for so long there were, and still are, plenty of hypocrites to be found to take their place. One only has to travel to the Americas to witness the heavy-feeling of religiousness and sense the peoples' fear and superstition of anything theistic or magic. Priests and Shamans, charlatan healers and imported religious fundamentalists from the USA make false claims that they stand between the sinful helpless and God's wrath because they are appointed by God with a celestial authority and the power to intervene.

Throughout history, men fell on their knees before their own masters, and the priests convinced the ignorant to also turn hypocritical and in servitude. The religiousness of the ignorant prevented them from seeing: that as long as there is one person suffering an injustice, as long as there is one person that bears an unnecessary sorrow, as long as there is one person who is inflicted with an undeserved pain, the worship of God is a moralising humiliation; that as long as there is one mistake in nature, as long as there is one wrong permitted to exist, as long as there is hatred and antagonism among our brothers and sisters in this world, God's existence and goodness is a moral impossibility. This simply means that injustice upon earth renders the justice in heaven impossible.

We must recognise that as long as mankind anywhere in the world loves God more than our fellow mankind, the love for one's God, saints or spirits is a wasted love, which is often translated into hatred for others. Al Qaida, Al Shaba, the Islamic State of Iraq and the Levant (ISIL), Boko Haram, and the Taliban are Muslim religious affiliated armed groups, with Islamic motivations of their love for Allah, which are aimed against the innocent of other monotheistic religions mainly in Africa, Arabia and Asia. The most meaningless term in the human language, is the term "God"! The reason for this is that the subject represents so much human abuse. There is no other term, in any human language that is as meaningless and incapable of explanation as the term "God." It begins and ends with nothing; it is the beginning and the end of ignorance, it has as many meanings as the numbers of existing illusions and delusions combined, each person has his or her own particular opinion about what the term "God" means, a term without premise, without foundation and without substance, a term without the validity of all things to all people, which makes it meaningless and indefinable. It is the most dangerous term used by the unscrupulous who are using it as a bluff-card for the religious indoctrination of the ignorant and ill- educated, it is a poisonous term that has paralysed the brains of human beings and turned them into grovelling slaves, it has turned good men into lunatics who go from door to door trying to explain---to the unlucky who just happen to open their door---what God is and what he is supposed to do when he is on duty, it has made man prostitute the most precious things in life: his own dignity and self-respect, his independence and his enquiring mind, for in the "name of god" means in the "name of nothing."

I admit that it is difficult for me to understand the minds of those who, having been demonstrated the evidence presented by biological science, by humanism and atheism, still prefer to remain under the shadow of religious superstition and in ignorance. It is difficult to deny the material evidence which shows that, once the human brain is poisoned by religious superstition, it is near impossible to escape the paralysing fear which destroyed its ability to think clearly. It may be said that fanatic religious faith stultifies the brain and it is a great obstacle to the path of intellectual progress. The more religious a person is, the more he steeps into ignorance and superstition and the lesser his sense of moral responsibility. The more knowledgeable and intelligent a person is, the less religious he is, as most serious scientists are. **In** theocratic dominated countries, like Saudi Arabia and Iran, the people may be technologically advanced but socially underdeveloped, living under religious cultural restrictions, misogyny and heavily oppressive totalitarian religiousness. By the same token, in the nations whose people are the most enlightened; and where their constitution is based on secularism of separation of Church and State, they are the most socially progressive, such as in the northern Scandinavian countries. This shows that, when people are intellectually free, the social progress they make is immeasurable. When men learn to guard their intellectual freedom then progress will come to the entire world in the fields of science, un-adulterated moral laws and social altruism.

When anaesthesia (inhalation of nitric oxide) was discovered by the English scientist *Joseph Priestley (1733-1803)* it was a celebration of human altruism which benefited millions, but not the inventor. When it was used in operation rooms, it elevated man from an unbearable pain and that relief of man's pain was the most morally humane act of altruism since the dawn of human history. Yet, the religious faithful opposed the used of anaesthesia on the grounds that God sent pain as a punishment of sin. The use of anaesthesia was considered a sacrilege by the Church. Imaging for a moment; being in the operating room, and listening to a priest telling you that you must obey God and refuse your pain relief. What a monstrous diversion! This single example should convince all of us (whether one believes in God or not) that no fundamentalist believer would have bothered to discover anaesthesia by going against God's orders. He would have been in mortal fear of his God's wrath for interfering with His divine plan to make man suffer for eating from the tree of knowledge. The core of the matter is; in this one instance, a man's altruism seeks to relieve another man from his suffering, disease and mental torment. The believer maintains that pain is ordained by God and therefore he must accept it, as a penance for living. Fear of God's wrath has been a stumbling block of progress and alleviation of human suffering. The believers' only true love is their love for suffering.

When doctors in Africa attempted to administer anaesthesia to women during childbirth, Protestant and Catholic clergy became abusive towards the doctors for daring to violate God's command that *"in pain shall bring forth children,"* that is, for not bringing children into this world in accordance with an idiotic message in the Bible. The discovery of blood's composition has also been responsible for saving countless human lives. Blood was also feared by the religious and ignorant cleric, and a taboo was placed on it for no one to touch it, as if it was contaminated. This idiocy still continues today under the Jehovah Witness dogma which does not permit the transfusion of blood from one human to another who needs it.

During the Middle Ages, even medical students' surgical training on a deceased human body was prohibited by the Church, and even the study of simple human anatomy was not permitted. An order was placed on morgue-houses on pain of excommunication so that they would not dare permit medical students to receive a dead body for their studies of human anatomy. As a result, a black-market of stolen dead-bodies was thriving, to meet the demand of medical research across England. The study of the human anatomy in our contemporary times of the 21st century has brought us incalculable information, thanks to the brave medical student examples of the 16th and 17th centuries. The scientific exploration of the human anatomy has resulted in the emancipation of the medical mind from the shackles of superstition, paganism and religious dogma. However, for a number of centuries, the Church and its religious fanatics prohibited the dissection of the human body under the penalty of hell and fire, and under the idiotic threat that said that, if your body was dissected, God would not be able to recognise it on the day of resurrection. Such has been the paralysing effects of religion that have prevailed over the minds of man.

The discovery of the chemistry of food and applications to a nutritious diet has contributed more to human health than all gods, demons and clergy, and all the ceremonies, with all the lit candles and all the wasted prayers and donations combined. Preventive scientific based medicine (not homeopathy) has accomplished enormous results in bring prolonging the lives of people. Hygiene and its applications have saved millions from diseases and premature death. Man's medicine has reduced the premature death of infants and youngsters and childbirth deaths, by a large percentage, in today's underdeveloped countries.

Charles Darwin's discoveries and 1859 publication of his On the *Origins of Species* penetrated, what was regarded until then, God's secrets about the so- called "creation of man." Other biologists before Darwin touched the issue of origins of species and natural evolution, but it was Darwin's braveness that brought into the open the truth about the biological origins of man. Since then, we have realised that we must rely on our own effort and ingenuity to solve our problems whether it concerns our biological origins, heath, social or political affairs. We must no longer be afraid of natural phenomena and attribute them to God's desire to punish us for our sins. The lightning in the sky is no longer regarded as the Greek God Zeus' temperamental attitude or of other Gods in our own times, because we now know how to produce lightening by technological means.

In this book, I take the issue of religious illusion and delusion beyond philosophical and linguistic perimeters and confront them with biological evidence, socio-scientific evidence, dialectical-materialism and reason. This book, *The Moral Necessity of Atheism,* is in a number of ways, a continuation of my *Prisoners of Our Ideals* which deals with how the idealism of religious faith distorts our reality, the gravitational preference we have for ideals vs. material reality, and how symbolism and metaphorical concepts are propagated by others to control our lives and the things that inspire us. The book's narrative has a cosmological beginning, the formulation of human societies, and the invention of a new religion, Christianity, under the guides of Josephus Bar Mathias (the Jewish turn-coat) the Roman Imperial Cult, and more.

As much as possible, I present here Paleontological evidence to show how pre-historic man's Animism created the mythical concepts of supernatural entities, leading to Neolithic religiousness that is still followed today. I present scientific conclusions and provide intelligent sources for the delusions of religion, secular idealism and the moral bankruptcy of theism. I am hoping to establish that, through the history of bloodshed conflicts and the social and economic crimes committed in the name of God, religion must be regarded as a Crime against Humanity.

As you read this book, you must also bear in mind that we cannot possibly know that there is not a God, a force, an intelligent designer or a prime-mover, for it is not within our scientific mental-campus to know that. This question is for philosophy and theology to deal with, not for science. As we scrambled through the entire Laws of Nature, however, we can say that the Laws of Physics appear to operate without that religious assumption. There is no possible way to step way from the Laws of Physics or the Laws of Biology or the observable creation of the cosmos, and lead you to assume that there is an intervening personal God who answers your prayers and who knows everything about you, and so on. From this point on, anyone who says "I am a deist and I do not think that the cosmos is an accident, there must be some kind of active supernatural force," I'll say that, "no one can disprove your claim, but the proof of it, is in your court."

Now, it is difficult for me to imagine a society totally free of religion, but why do we have religion in the first place? Biologically, we are pattern-seeking mammals, it is part of our evolution, and we have looked for patterns since pre-historic times when the Neanderthals, Cro-Magnon and Homo sapiens lived in caves while trying to interpret the natural events around them. Our pre-historic mammalian ancestors viewed living creatures of the environment and explained them in their cave-art in supernatural pattern-form, and allocated qualities to them that no animal has ever possessed. We are biologically programmed to give meaning to patterns when valid meaning and reason does not yet exist. Our brains need to fill up any mental-gap that exists in order to complete our pattern-seeking requirements and find answers. Since animals did not possess supernatural powers, our pre-historic ancestors simply invented them through their biological pattern-requirements. Our pre-historic ancestors did not have a reality-based answer they invented pattern-meaning "opinions," "beliefs," "assumptions," or "wishful-thinking," to add to their belief-systems during their life span, because they simply did not controlled their ideas or thoughts. Again, our ancestors were as we are, biologically designed to look for patterns in life, and if we cannot find good information or an explanation, most often we come up with a bad one rather than none at all.

I cannot imagine that, what the world would be like without religion, for the simple reason because, in one way or another, it has been with us for so long. Although the numbers of atheists and humanists are larger than ever, let's say from a hundred years ago, religion still influences our lives and, in some parts of the world, is more oppressive than ever. As for those like me, who are literally millions without religion, we still live in a religious world where it is difficult not to notice its existence. This is, for obvious reasons, because some of the fundamentalist developments that create media attention, such as "creationism" and "suicide" bombers are in the front row of religious exhibitionism. The homicidal violence in parts of the Muslim world against the ideas of the "Godless" western world does not help to diminish racism or the distortions of the cultural values imbedded in those ancient civilisations. Unavoidably, atheists cause tension among Christians and secularist idealists by rejecting the delusion of the soul, a concept which occupies a prominent role in the industry of religion, popular psychology and new trends in daily cultural media. The materialist rejection of the existence of the soul is, at the same time, the rejection of the mythology of religion.

CHAPTER I
IN THE BEGINNING...

According to the tribal Biblical myth of *Genesis 1,* in the Christian and Jewish Holy Books, the world and everything in it, including men, was created by God in 6 days and the 7th day God rested. By the 6th day, God saw his creation and it was very good, and there was morning and evening. Following the creation of man (Adam) and a woman (Eve), the Bible describes a line of their discordance, and added the ages of these people which led to the conclusion that the Earth was about 6,000 years old. The originators of the Genesis myth never expected that one day, in the future, this age would be in strong contrast with scientific evidence which shows that the Earth is about 4.5 billion years old. They were confidant that the ignorant and ill-educated tribesmen of the Middle East would have no means of discovering the distortions of the cosmos presented in the Bible. Knowledge was the prerogative of the elite and the temple priests, the philosophers and scribers of the time. For thousands of years, the Jewish Torah and later the Roman Catholic Church had maintained an anti-scientific policy against anyone who dared to challenge the myth of Genesis 1. This included Galileo, and other prominent scientists who dared to challenge the Biblical delusion of the Genesis.

The enterprise of creating myths and *allegories,* superstitions and unfounded explanations of our cosmos were in the center of the pagan and religious cults then, as it is still today. The numerous scribers who wrote the Gospels were no more educated than the Taliban warlords today, and keeping the lower classes, even more ignorant, was their means of social control. Today, the Genesis 1 myth has been totally and utterly refuted, but other religious distortions, about life in general, are still at work, well financed and politically connected! What a non-sense!

Let us take this issue from the beginning relating to the Universe, our planet Earth and the appearance of life on it. This is a brief scientific history of the world starting from the *"Big Bang,"* the appearance of the first humanoids on Earth, how the planet prepared the conditions for the rise of Man, how the Stone Age tool-making is the ancestor of the Industrial Revolution, and how the first seeds that sprouted in the valleys supported life. All these issues would demonstrate that everything in our geological and biological world is connected, including the paths that led to human development. It took the Universe 13.7 billion years to unfold the secrets of our own galactic planetary system. Let us begin then.

13.7 billion years ago: there was a little something, a spec of *energy* which was smaller than an atom, and at this point, cosmic history as we know it, is about to mysteriously begin. For causes which we may never know, the universe suddenly erupts and, in a split of a second, this tiny atom becomes as big as a galaxy. This explosion, the *"Big Bang,"* was made of pure energy that would forever exist, that would be all the energy needed to power the stars, that would fuel everything that lives, all the energy that we would ever consume, from the beginning of time and into the future. This was the cataclysmic birth of the Universe; an ever observable expansion of the universe, cosmic background of radiation, abundance of chemical elements and the superior Laws of Nature. Was the universe then created out of nothing? Was there a universe rather than nothing? The term "nothing" in the 21st century has a relative meaning, for it is not absolute, for a "nothing" still contains invisible particles---hydrogen, helium, lithium-- within its nothingness. The important elements of our existence, such as carbon, nitrogen and oxygen, were created because the stars exploded and "stardust" was created and absorbed by all living matter. The protons inside our body are exactly where most of the mass of our body comes from.

According to Dr Lawrence Krauss, one of the most amazing realizations for the study of cosmology in the 21st century is that quantum mechanics combined with relativity "allow something to come from nothing," such as energy. When we apply quantum mechanics to gravity, a truly remarkable thing is about to happen; that even space itself could be created out of nothing. There has been a revolution in cosmology in the last decades. We now understand that the dominant energy in the universe resides in an empty space. That understanding has changed everything, for it helps us point unambiguously to the possibility that the universe arose from nothing. Religion and theology, and to a large extent philosophy, contributed almost nothing to our fundamental understanding of the universe. This is because questions such as "what something is" and "what nothing is" or if there is or not "a thing in itself" is really scientific questions, not philosophical ones. Cosmological science made it possible to verify that the universe did not need God, that God is redundant. This is a dramatic concept, since science does not require that there should be a God, for it is also possible that there is no need for such assumption. This is also a central possibility which makes our understanding of the universe totally different since from what it has been for more that 5,000 years of religious mythology.

About 350 million years later, after the Big Bang, the first *hydrogen atoms* would be used by the universe to create everything in the world that surrounds us. A hydrogen atom is an atom of the chemical element hydrogen. The first hydrogen atoms blasted through the universe, spreading out unevenly, which allowed gravity and heat to sculpt, mould and work to create more hydrogen atoms. In those pockets of more tiny hydrogen atoms, gravity began its work, and the first galaxies were beginning to form. This process eventually begins to reveal the timeless secrets of the universe. Throughout the universal time and space, the Laws of Nature and gravity demonstrate that when matter and energy were drowning together in one place, more complex things emerged. Gravity is a natural force that attracts a body towards another physical body having mass. For instance, plural gravities form a counter multi-gravitational attraction between planetary bodies, such as the earth and moon, or other planetary bodies near their surface.

13.4 billion years ago: inside the forming galaxies, *gravity* begins to squeeze together clouds of gas and dust causing pressure and heat to violently rise. When the temperature began to increase to 19 million degrees Fahrenheit, hydrogen atoms were bound together, creating a new chemical element called *helium,* which radiated and generated an additional burst of energy. As such, the first stars were born, adding more energy and light to the universe. But something was still missing from the universe. There were millions of stars but there was not a single *planet*. In order to form planets, and eventually life, the universe would need more than just hydrogen and helium. You see, stars are chemical element-factories, for they fuse hydrogen to helium, convert helium into *lithium,* all together forging 25 elements for preserving life, including *carbon, oxygen, nitrogen* and *iron.* But there were still elements such as copper, gold and uranium which were still missing because their weight was far too heavy to be made in the stars. Those elements needed to be created in another way, for stars did not have enough energy to create them. But if the element-factories were not powerful enough, their massive explosion into the universe was caused by the second "Big Bang," the *supernova* which provided the extra energy needed to fuse heavier elements. For instance, a supernova is a star that suddenly increases greatly in brightness because of a catastrophic explosion that ejects outwards most of its mass. In the firing thrust of their own destruction stars create *uranium, gold* and all the rest of the heavy chemical elements that would fill our world, including *copper*. These planetary elements form part of the library-list of chemistry, set in the life of our material universe.

You see, supernovas are absolutely necessary for life on earth to exist because most of the chemical elements are in our bodies and the bodies of every living thing on earth. We have *iron in* our blood, and old bits of supernova floating around through us. In short we are all star-dust, and the heavy elements such as *bronze and tin* were found and created the Bronze Age and the Iron Age. The elements contained in the multi-vitamins we consume include *zinc, copper and selenium;* all the chemical elements that originally were created by the supernovas. These supernova elements would become the seeds of life on earth and perpetuators of human history. But before there would be life on earth, the universe needed to build us a suitable home by assembling the right material, in the right place, all at once. The kinds of material which would be assembled would determine the kind of home-planet that could be built to sustain life on earth.

5.4 billion years ago: for a long period of 8 billion years, the element-factories of supernovas would continue their work; stars would explode and be re-born, each generation containing very final stage of more chemical elements than the last. This represents the final very stage geological evolution for some stars. Celestial events are huge releases of tremendous energy, as the star ceases to exist, with about 10, to 20 times as much energy produced in a single supernova explosion as our Sun releases every second. Finally, enough elements gathered for the next step on the path of creating life on earth. Earth grew from a cloud of dust and rocks surrounding the young Sun. Earth formed when some of those rocks collided. Eventually the force of gravity attracted other rocks becoming the Earth. A new star is born, our Sun. It is so massive, gathering 99.99% of all the gas and dust of our solar system, yet enough still left behind for gravity to build some other bodies, like planets. The third one from this massive star would be our home! Do you realise then that "God" had nothing to do with it?

4.5 billion years ago: by the time *Earth* emerges, two-thirds of the history of the universe has already passed. Earth's surface is divided into a few dozen plates of rocks, one of which sometimes ploughs under another causing an earthquake. This *plate-tectonic* process would eventually form the first continent, nicknamed "Ur." The first *Sunrises* sweep across this lava burning planet, an Earth spinning so rapidly that a day lasted only 6 hours. This planet was made of massive scenes of red-hot floating lava and volcanic rock. Within the burning volcanic rock, the chemical elements are in a chaotic state. Something needed to bring order into this chaos, and once again, this something was gravity. This means that lighter materials drifted towards the surface of the Earth and formed a solid crust, while heavier materials sank towards the center forming a molten iron and nickel core. This liquid metal created a magnetic field which reached into the outer space, like a force-field which protected our Earth from the sun's charged particles. Soon this magnetic field would allow life on Earth to grow, and would later guide the explorers to navigate around the globe and connect the two halves of the world's *Equatorial* hemispheres. Yet, for all these to unfold, the Earth would need a critical physical partner.

In the distant past, around 4.5 billion years, an object as large as Mars smashed into Earth at twenty thousand miles per hour, and our planet absorbed much of the impacted matter. A spread of molten debris was scattered off into space. Within a short time from the moment of the impact, gravity gathered this scattered debris and moulded it into a second sphere; a disproportionately large nearby Moon that would orbit around the planet Earth. The formation of the Moon was an incredibly important event in Earth's history and its climate today. The Moon's gravitational influence keeps Earth's spin axis, gravity and climate steady, thus saving us from wild environmental changes. The impact of the collision with the Earth caused it to tilt on its axis, thus giving the planet a key ingredient of life, the four seasons of *Winter, Spring, Summer and Fall.* You see, the seasons are caused as the Earth, tilted on its axis, travels in a loop around the Sun each year. Summer happens when the Earth's hemisphere is tilted towards the Sun, and winter happens when the hemisphere is tilted away from the Sun. Having the four seasons is very important in the evolution of life on Earth. The constant stability in the Earth's tilted axis is also very important for maintaining environmental and biological life on Earth. The Moon's power of gravity has slowed down the Earth's rotation speed which eventually would increase our day from its initial 6 to 24 hours.

4.4 billion years ago: it is still too hot on Earth for water to exist. However, there is vapour water-steam in the Earth's atmosphere. For life to begin in some parts of the Earth however, rainfall must take place in those regions where the Earth's crust is cooling down. For the next millions of years, as the planet cools down, rain begins to fall forming puddles, lakes, rivers and eventually oceans. The Laws of Nature related, connected and supported each event and condition to reach its final objective.

3. 8 billion years ago: by this time our planet has a rotating Moon, a tilted axis balance and a steady rainfall which covers the Earth's entire surface with water. But the planet Earth is not yet a hospitable place; for it to be so, oxygen and fertile lands are needed to sustain bacterial life. Beneath the surface of the primeval oceans however, a biological revolution is taking place. Six simple chemical elements (including hydrogen from the Big Bang, oxygen, carbon and nitrogen created by stars), have combined to form one of the key substance that would make all of the Earth's biological life, as such, including humans. The most spectacular is the *DNA,* for within its spirals, it hides the secrets of life!

Seven hundred thousand years after the Earth stabilises, life begins under the oceans on the shoulders of tiny organisms such as *bacteria,* forming a global empire of bacteria. In fact, these formed a zoo of bacteria on our bodies. These beneficial bacteria far outnumber harmful varieties, helping to prevent the establishment of colonies of pathogenic bacteria. The first organisms were simple cells, like modern bacteria, but some of them became much more internally complex. You see, without bacteria there would be no life as we know it; no plants, no animals and not even protists, *eukaryotic organisms* that are unicellular like most algae. These eukaryotes organisms developed lots of specialised equipment within their cells. They also had a new source of energy, sausage-shaped objects called *mitochondria* that were once free-living bacteria, but which were absorbed in the process called *endosymbiosis*. Every plant and animal you have ever seen is a eukaryote.

Without exaggerating, each one of us has more bacteria crawling on our bodies than there are people living on our planet Earth. It is estimated that the human body contains about 100 trillion cells that are not human at all, for only 10 of those are actually human. The rest are from bacteria, viruses and other micro-organisms. Without these bacteria we would be dead! For billions of years micro-bacteria will have Earth all to themselves. Like our infant universe, the first life, in the form of bacteria, was small, simple, single-cell, but full of possibilities. The secret of how it exploded into all the incredible forms of life we see around us today; including vegetable, humans and the animal world, goes back to the beginning of time. As we can imagine, all the energy needed to maintain life on Earth was already created by the first Big Bang 13.7 billion years ago; and all living micro-organisms since then, needed to grab their share of this energy in order to survive. The more we harness this energy, the more we use it, the more complex we can become. Almost our entire entire share of the Big Bang's energy is beamed to us by the Sun.

2.5 billion years ago: some very special micro-bacteria in the ocean figured out how to consume the Sun's *photosynthesis* energy to live. All life needs energy to survive, but unlike green plants today, the first photosynthesising organisms did not release oxygen as a waste product, so there was no oxygen in the atmosphere. In doing this continual photosynthesis, organisms also created the most important waste product in the history of the world: *oxygen.* For the first half of Earth's history, there was an atmosphere that had hardly any free oxygen. But then some bacteria began harnessing sunlight to make sugar from carbon dioxide and water, just like green plants today. These microbes pumped out enough oxygen as a waste product to create the oxygen-rich atmosphere we have today. Soon, the chemical element of oxygen would re-make our world, but first it had one more important task to do. Earth's 1.2 billion year old oceans were full of iron particles and it is common knowledge what happens, under the Laws of Nature, when iron meets oxygen: it creates rust. As such, rusted iron in massive scale was collected at the bottom of the seabed. Millions of years later these massive deposits of iron rust would rise above sea level to become the major source of iron and steel, ready to be harvested by the modern Industrial Revolution. Today's most famous iron and steel structures such as the Statue of Liberty, the Eiffel Tower, the Panama Canal Locks and Brooklyn's Bridge, among others, are the direct link to the first life forms on Earth.

Once there was no more iron in the sea to rust, these ancient micro-bacteria had a new mission to complete. They created so much oxygen that it filled the oceans and escaped into the Earth's atmosphere. From then on, we have a very different planet in comparison to the rest of the planets in our solar system. With oxygen in the Earth's atmosphere, life now takes a giant leap forward because, for the first time, some micro-bacteria learned to live on oxygen. This means, that every human breath we now take is a ritual of 2.5 billion years old. Oxygen is a game-changer and, by taming its power, life has found a better way to energise itself. It was many times more efficient than anything that was used on Earth before. What life did with all this new energy will be the legacy that leads to us.

2 billion years ago: during this period of time life, in general, becomes more complex. The Earth's skies become bluer and so do the oceans that reflected them. As Earth's crust began to cool and the mantle started to harden, large solid continents appeared, and so Earth became a place that we, as we are familiar with it, call home! Of course, nobody knows when life began on Earth. The oldest confirmed fossils, of single-cell organisms, are about 2 to 3 billion years old, but life may have begun a bit earlier than that, but not while huge rocks were still bombarding our planet Earth. What about multicellular life? For the first time, life was not made up of single cells. Now cells were teaming up to form larger organisms with characteristics like mouths, limbs and sense organs. It is difficult to say when this happened: there are fossils of large organisms or those may simply have been colonies of bacteria dating back 2.1 billion years. Different groups of organisms probably evolved multicellularity independently, with vegetation managing it before animals.

550 million years ago: as the planet Earth celebrated its 4 billion year birthday, oxygen levels have risen from next to nothing to as much as 14%, and life on Earth was about to take a biological wild ride! The *Cambrian Explosion*, biology's version of the "Big Bang," accelerated organisms' size and complexity, with oxygen leading this expanding acceleration. The Cambrian radiation was a relatively short evolutionary event, beginning around 542 million years ago in the Cambrian period, during which most major animal phyla appeared. The name refers to the sudden appearance in the fossil record of complex animals with mineralised skeletal remains. It is within this breathtaking stand, of roughly 30 million years, that most of Earth's animal species evolved. About 542 million years ago the first bony fish evolved in the seas. These bony fish are our direct ancestors! Although, these *vertebral fish* do not look anything like us, they evolved the body parts that would make our body parts possible; including the spine and mouth, the jaws and teeth, to represent the modifications that evolved later from the original fish body parts. For the first 4 billion years of Earth's history, plants and animals have lived and reproduced in the seas. But all this begins to change. With oxygen comes the *ozone layer*, protecting us from dangerous radiation. Plants make the first move followed by animals.

400 million years ago: animals are also ready to take their first giant biological leap forward. Among the first to show are the *amphibians* whose descendants would include us. The most incredible moment in evolutionary history could have been when the first amphibian walks out of the ocean and begins walking onto land and takes its first gulp of air. It is kind of like our great, great, great, great grandpa coming out of the ocean and seeing this fantastic world for the first time. This amphibian could live on land protected, with ponds and greens to feed on, and with plenty of space to walk around. Eventually, humans would conquer every imaginable forest, mountain and desert terrain; but before humans could do that, our amphibian ancestors had to cut-off their ties to the ocean.

Mating season and, like modern frogs, these amphibians had jelly-like eggs that would dry out if left on open land. But some amphibians eventually solve this problem, for they evolved a new form of egg, with a hard shell that keeps the moisture in. The amphibian could have been more than 500 miles from the ocean and still have moisture in that single egg. This allowed them to carry the ocean with them onto the land, and this signals the evolution of a new biological evolution: of the amphibian evolved into walking *four-legged reptiles*. In this way, the four-legged reptiles carried with them their hard-shell eggs and thus they began to colonise the land by laying the eggs further and further away and finally cutting ties with the oceans.

300 million years ago: biological life flourishes in tropical lands such as the Amazon Rainforest of today's South American Continent, Western Canada, Africa's savannas and other swamps, places where Mother Earth was cooking-up a surprise. As plants died in the tropical lands, they were buried, compacted and cooked. Energy created by the Big Bang and radiated by the Sun to plants on Earth, was now locked beneath-ground as *coal*, nature's gift to the human race millions of years into the future.

250 million years ago: An environmental apocalypse evolves with the largest spike of volcanic activity ever taking place since the early days of the planet Earth. The atmosphere is chocked with poisonous *carbon dioxide,* and Earth's almost entire animal life which was developed by the biological Cambrian Explosion, is now dead on its tracks. More than 75% of all land and 90% of marine life on Earth was made extinct in this worst dying-off event: the *Permian Extinction*. In fact, the Permian Extinction is a natural re-occurring event on the planet Earth throughout its history. This was the largest mass extinction recorded in the history of life on Earth. It is a natural occurrence, regardless of what animals or plant-species become extinct. This is because the Earth's natural world does not act in favour of one species over another, including man, nor does it recognise their actual existence. Whatever biological life was formed on Earth, it was outside the scope and purpose of the natural world. In the last 500 million years, several times these apocalyptic events have wiped-out most of Earth's dominant species. These events may look catastrophic (and they are) but, simultaneously, it allows new species to take over, perhaps because they are more adaptable to the new environment than those that become extinct.

New creatures appeared, like the *Dinosaurs*, which would roam the planet Earth for the next 150 million years. During this time, hardwood forests also appeared, and after 4 billion years, the Moon's gravity settles Earth into a 24 hour day. At the start of the Dinosaur's era, Earth's continents begin to drift apart and away from *Pangaea*—one mass land. But now they begin to break apart; with Africa separating from South America, the vast Atlantic Ocean becomes wider to become one of the defining barriers of Earth's environmental history. The undisputed dominant animals during the Dinosaur era were the *Triceratops and T. rex* Dinosaurs. However, there were some important creatures surviving and multiplying among these giant dinosaurs; little mammals feeding off the eggs laid by these mammoth dinosaurs and leading a reptile life. During the whole 150 million years of Dinosaurs' size and dominating of the Earth's food sources, the rest of living mammal creatures remained no larger than a small cat. During those millions of years, all small, medium and large size animals on Earth were the dinosaurs.

65 million years ago: the biological deck is about to be reshuffled, for 6 mile wide asteroid rock crashes on Earth causing extensive geological damage, creating a dust-cloud which blocks the sun, temperatures plummet and every creature that weights more than 25 to 30 kilograms becomes extinct. This new Permian Extinction includes the small, medium and giant dinosaurs, and thus the dominance of dinosaurs on Earth was over. One may say that the greatest gift the dinosaurs gave us (mammals) was their dying, because when they became extinct, it gave mammals the time to rise. From that point on, it does not take very long before the first true *Primates* appear. These mammals have something very distinct from all the extinct reptiles. Like their later versions (the humans), these mammals have evolved forward facing eyes allowing for acquired distance vision and flexible hands with five fingers, which means they could grasp things and organise their ability to hold food and manipulate parts of their environment.

50 million years ago: Natural Selection and Adaptation is now in full swing and our primary primate ancestors are evolving on a planet that is warming on to a much higher temperatures, such as in certain geographical areas like as in the tropical jungles of South America. By this time, the African and South American continents are almost fully taking their final shape. But in Northern Africa, modern Egypt was still submerged under the sea. On the floor of that sea lived tiny shell creatures. Their hard shells were made of *calcium* and *carbon* which was piled up at the sea bottom for millions of years where they formed into *limestone*. This limestone would be used by future generations of *Natufians in* the Levant Region and the *Egyptians* to build their cities and pyramids. If you look closely at the pyramids today you can still see evidence that in fact, these 4,000 year old pyramids are made with 50 million year old seashells.

10 million years ago: Earth is evolving into the world that most of us would recognise. The Colorado River was carving out the Grand Canyon, mountain ranges like the Himalayans have risen and, as they are so tall, they disrupted weather patterns. The Himalayas were setting the stage for a colder planet. The Isthmus of Panama emerges connecting North and South America, cleaving the connection between the Atlantic and the Pacific Oceans and causing the disruption of currents leading the world towards an *Ice Age.* With Earth getting colder, our primate ancestors are hanging on in the tropical zones. But a new creature is coming in that threatens to destroy them.

7 million years ago: our primary ancestors are living safe in the trees but their "comfort zone" is about to be invaded. This newcomer would have a profound effect in more on human history than any other living thing on Earth. It appears strange to think that this newcomer is no other than, *the grass* (Phocaea). The grasslands appeared almost simultaneously around the world, with the African savannas, the Eurasian step lands, the North

American Prairies, the great grasslands of Argentina and most ecoregions of the Earth, except in Antarctica. In eastern Africa grasslands invaded the traditional woodland of our ape ancestors. Trees and shrubs became absent, temperatures varied from summer to winter, and the amount of rainfall was less in temperate grasslands. With fewer trees now, and greater gaps between them, our ancestors that lived in trees, had to adapt or become extinct.

As more and more apes were in the same trees, with less food left, they began to look for other sources on the ground. Looking for food from one area to the next and separated by large gaps of grasslands, our ancestors gradually came down from the trees, extending their food sources to what was available in the grasslands; a stark new habitat. It was a new landscape that was better suited to primates that walk on two legs, keeping their heads above the tall grasses to watch out for predators. Standing on two feet was a revolutionary biological advance because it frees our hands, hands that we would need to shape human history beginning with hunting-gathering, building shelters, making stone-tools and defending ourselves.

One must remember that the Human species (Homo sapiens or the Wise man) is the latest version of a long biological development of Natural Selection, Evolution and Adaptation. We were not all of a sudden appeared on Earth the way we are biologically structured today. There were a number of other pro-human species (hominoid) before us that were extinct due to *Natural Selection and Evolution* that did not favour their adaptation and survival. Methods of Adaptation were not strong skills of theirs and nature did not favour them over other species. In fact, as harsh as it may sound, the truth is that the Earth's Natural World and the Universe are not aware of the existence of any plant or animal life on Earth, including the mammal species. The Natural World is governed by the universal *Laws of Nature* which we are obligated to obey and follow if we are to adapt and survive its changes. These Laws are permanently ingrained in the nature of things. In other words, the Laws of Nature can not be suspended---temporarily or permanently--on behalf of or in favour of any life form on Earth. There are millions of species; from micro-bacteria to fully grown animals like the Dinosaurs, that have gone extinct ever since the beginning of time, and that process of extinction continues uninterrupted today.

For our purpose however, let us concentrate on the *genus Homo* and the emergence of Homo sapiens as we are today. The genus Homo produced various species, of which only the Homo sapiens (Humans) have survived. At any given moment in historic biological evolution, there were more than one species of Homo on the planet, until very recently with the total extinction of the *Neanderthals*. For instance, these are the fossil forms of Homo.

Beginning about 6 million years ago, the Human Family Tree consisted of the *Ardipithecus Group*; about 4 million years ago the *Australopithecus Group;* then about 2 million years the *Paranthropus Group;* and between 2 and 1 million years ago the *Homo Group*. Each group consisted of several branches of its own kind. For instance the Homo Group consisted of:

Homo erectus (upright man) was the first human species that migrated out of Africa around 2.0 million years ago, colonising most of Eurasia and parts of Southeast Asia. Remains have been found 1.8 to 1.0 million years old in Europe and Asia (Georgia, Spain, Indonesia, Vietnam and China).

Homo naledi recently discovered in South Africa on an ancient burial site about 2.8 million years old, estimating the existence of this Human species as recently as about 100,000 years ago.

Homo habillis (handy man) the archaeological findings of cranium confirm that this genus Homo lived from 2.5 to 1.8 million years ago.

Homo antecessor lived in Europe from Spain to Georgia 1.2 million to 700,000 years ago. It could be the ancestor of the *Homo heidelbergensis*.

Homo heidelbergensis (heidelberg man) could be the direct ancestor of the *Homo neanderthalesis* in Europe who lived 600,000 to 250,000 years ago. Remains have been found in Germany, France, England and Greece.

Homo sapiens idaltu (elderly wise man) is an extinct sub-species of Homo sapiens that lived about 160,000 years ago in Africa.

Neanderthals (Homo neanderthalesis) inhabited parts of Eurasia and parts of Spain and France about 700.000 years ago until their extinction as recently as 25.000 years ago. *Mitochondrial DNA* analysis confirms their interbreeding with Humans.

Cro-Magnon in 1868 there were several human remains found in the rock shelter near Dordogne, France. Among these bones there was a cranium and mandible of a male about 50 years of age. This particular specimen is known as the *"Old Man of Cro-Magnon"* who lived in the *Upper Palaeolithic* period 40,000 to 10,000 years ago. The question of the inter-breeding relationship of Cro-Magnon to the earliest form of Homo sapiens, as well as of the Neanderthals, is still unclear. It appeared that they were flourishing during the Stone Age before their extinction. However, there are still some modern human groups that are thought to have retained a close relationship to Cro-Magnon types, at least in their cranial morphology, such as of those of the *Dal people* from *Dalecarlia,* Sweden. In this list of *genus Homo*, you would find no evidence of the existence of the Biblical mythological characters of Adam and Eve!

2.6 million years ago: early pro-humans or hominoids walked on Earth. Rocks are loaded with the element *silicon* created in the cores of the stars billions of years before. Silicon is the second most abundant element on the surface of the Earth. One of its chemical abilities is to bond with oxygen to form *crystals* that combine into solid rocks. These rocks can be chipped and shaped without shattering. Hominoids started shaping rocks, breaking *crypto-crystal silicon* to make sharp edges, to use them for cutting, carving, hunting and as weapons. This means that, by having a slightly modified stone, the hominoids now had a "hammer," with a crude cutting edge, and could now do a number of more things than previously. This slightly modified stone-tool, as an extra bit of technology, allowed humans to persist and eventually reinvent new technology. Silicon launches the first technological revolution: *the Stone Age*. Millions of years later, it powers the first hand held device; another chemical ability of silicon would make it the height of technology: *the cell phone*.

Once again, the next step of becoming fully human relies on a little known secret of our home planet. In the known universe, Earth may have a special power, its ability to *sustain fire*. Other planets and moons may have lightening and lava, but only on Earth do we have two critical things we need for fire to burn: a) a vast fuel supply in the form of plants and forest and b) an atmosphere full of oxygen to fan the flames. If sustaining a fire was not a possibility, there would be no humans on Earth. Our ancestors, the Homo sapiens, have made our world with fire. Our ancestors, had fire under control some 800,000 years ago; it is a skill that connects humans to the very beginning of our existence. We must remember that all energy was created by the "Big Bang" and all human life is in competition for its share of this energy. Using fire to cook is like having an external stomach to break down foods, create more calories, giving us more energy, which in turn allowed us to support bigger brains. Fire is also the ultimate gateway technology, and soon humans would use fire to create pottery, fire to heat shelters in the cold winter seasons, make metal into weapons, water into steam power, and fire as engines' internal combustion energy. In short, if there was no fire, there would be no metal; no fire no rubber; and fire is transforming technology thus into a world full of possibilities.

200.000 years ago: the modern human physiology is fully taking place. The *larynx*, or the voice box, which was located high up in the throat of our ancestors' descends lower. It also contained the *Hyoid-bone*, a crucial bone necessary to articulate vocal language. This made it more possible of uttering complex sounds; we begin to communicate with members of the same and neighbouring groups. For the first time, information can be transmitted and shared amongst individuals and across generations. As such, Homo sapiens gained an advantage over any other creature on Earth.

Hunters could describe dangerous situations, a new food source or clean water pond and can now communicate this new information to other hunters. **Language** helps humans go from go alone to being in a network with other humans and, based on others' personal experience, our broad life's view is advanced by the use of language. One can borrow on others' personal experience and can communicate such information to future generations. This is a powerful advantage over other creatures that do not have language. As a species, humans became smarter, more communicative and more adaptable; and thus they became major players on this planet. According to the Darwinian Theory of Evolution, it is not the strongest or the most intelligent species that survived on Earth, but the most adaptable.

100,000 years ago: men can move, we have capable hands and affirmative tools, we can communicate and control fire and we are finally ready to expand out of our African home. We begin to follow a path millions of years in the making, beginning from present day Kenya towards the Middle East, Palestine and the Levant. The shifting continents linked Africa with Eurasia, creating the largest continuous continent on Earth: the Afro-Eurasia. This continent is 33 million square miles; more than twice the surface area of our entire Moon. For early humans this means that more than half of Earth's land can be reached by crossing deserts, swamps, forests, mountains and valleys on foot. Homo sapiens' dispersal was a crucial factor because we were one of the few primates that lived in more than one continent simultaneously. This means we better adapted to the kinds of environmental things that caused other hominoid-species; such as the *Homo naledi* of South Africa or the *Neanderthals* of south-west Europe, to become extinct. Just as the world begins to open to humans, the planet turns on us; an *Ice Age* begins and this new environmental condition would put Earth's mammals and human strength to an ultimate test.

50,000 years ago: by this time the ice glaciers of the North Pole have reached mid to southern Europe, while humans in South Africa continued their land journey, arriving in China and Australia and, by 40,000 years ago, humans had reached the Mediterranean coast of Europe. By 20.000 years ago, with the Ice Age nearing its end, the marching of humans reached the edge of the frozen tundra of Siberia. Despite the difficulties caused by the Ice Age, humans endured, adapted and survived tremendous odds by continuously moving while looking for new sources of food and means of better shelter, and developing the last skills we would need to be truly human. The clues lay in the cave evidence of symbolic designs and the expression of symbolic thoughts. By taking an intellectual leap, humans begin to think beyond their immediate physical surroundings and of their survival as mammals. When we now look at these cave arts see humans expressing to other humans in the future a bonding symbolism of their humanness. From that moment on, human history was marked as being different than any other species on Earth.

At this stage of the Ice Age, with vast amounts of frozen water locked in ice, the sea levels plummet 150 meters, and the last spread of crossing barriers to man were erased. Humans were advancing across the frozen landscape, from the tundras of Siberia to the North American Continent on foot. In less than 3,000 years after crossing the Barrier frozen tundra, some human groups reached the South American continent. From the beginning of time, billions of years have passed in preparation that allowed Humans to finally emerge and spread out across the planet; and human history, as we know it, has truly begun. Now, as we humans take our place at center stage, it is important to remember how small a slice of history we actually occupied. This means that we humans have been around for only a brief period of time in the recorded history of the universe. The stars and our revolving planets have carried out the slow work of organising the universe's chemical elements, and this was the only way that was made human history possible. Humans faced the adversity of the Ice Age and other Permian Extinctions head-on and, rather than dying-off slowly or becoming completely extinct, we have adapted to live under different climatic conditions. At one point, the human population decreased to near extinction levels of 10,000 in the entire Earth. We had to become even more adaptable and skilful to find new food sources, better shelter protection and increase our technology and intelligence. Eventually we occupied the entire globe from coast to mountain top and from tundra to desert.

About 20,000 years ago, the Ice Age begins to retreat and the sea levels to rise, and Earth's human population now was trapped into two separate unconnected hemispheres: the Eurasia and the Americas. Each section of humanity was left to make the best of it under this new geological condition. As the glaciers receded, they carved out lakes and rivers and coastlines and the world's map as we know emerges. In Africa, the increased rainfall causes Lake Victoria and Lake Albert to overflow and form Egypt's Nile River. In Eurasia other rivers emerged to form the Tigris-Euphrates river systems in Mesopotamia (present day Iraq) and the Indus River in modern day Pakistan and China's Yellow River to the North and Yangtze River to the South. In South America the landlocked tributaries and the Maranon and Ucayali Rivers overflow to create the great Amazon River that drains into the Atlantic Ocean to the north. These river valleys became important to how human history unfolded now that the Ice Age has retreated. These are the rivers valleys where fertile soils would allow the first seeds of human civilisation to be planted.

With temperatures warming after the Ice Age, plants and animals are more plentiful, and man can choose to stop moving as a hunter-gatherer. Permanent settlements begin to be built along the river banks and populations grow. With more population to feed, our ancestors have to get innovative, for they had to find a way to increase the food production they can get from the surroundings. A new discovery needed to change the planet and the path of mankind. We learned to cultivate seeds and the seeds we planted came from the same plants that, millions of years earlier spurred our Natural Selection and Evolution from *Ape to Man.* The undeclared hero of human history, *the grass,* which was ignored by hunter-gatherers for thousands of years, now produces some of the most important food sources on Earth, including wheat and sugarcane, rye and barley; the types of grass including all of the other cereal crops. Together they formed a staple crop which our civilisation depended for its subsistence and it forms also the majority of our calorie intake. It all goes back to the Big Bang, which is central to the story of all life on Earth, and our competition for the energy which was created at the beginning of time. Just as oxygen gave us an edge, just as fire allowed us to consume more calories, switching to agriculture was an energy revolution. You see, a hunter-gatherer needed 10 square miles of territory to provide him with enough food for sustenance and with enough energy from wild plants and free range animal-meat to survive.

On the other hand, a farmer can harvest the Sun's energy with efficiency, and reduce his land volume to 10% of the hunter-gatherer. In the warming after the last Ice Age, agriculture begins forming in Africa and *Mesopotamia* and more places around the globe. But, by the fortunes of Earth's geography, no place of the ancient world has a better concentration of plants and animals to be domesticated than the Middle East irrigated *Fertile Crescent.* In the Middle East there was this remarkable conversion of species that seems to be attestable to the domestication of plants and animals; such as, cows, pigs, sheep and goats, two varieties of wheat, barley and lentils, figs and olives, all concentrated in this small geographical region. Unlike the Fertile Crescent of the Middle East, in the desert of sub-Sahara Africa and in the Americas, there are very few wild species that could be easily domesticated. This was a critical difference, for the people who are lucky enough to share plentiful plants and animals would become more powerful and get a massive head-start into the modern world. Until 500 years ago, the people of South America, who had a poor plant supply (mainly corn and potatoes) and the llamas as their meat source protein, had developed a socially weak;

primitive empire of the Incas, while simultaneously the people of Europe and Middle East were advancing in science and letters, with armed and naval forces which conquered the world.

One animal which gave man an unbeatable edge is the *horse*. It is a little known fact that the horse was first evolved in the American continent but died out, along with many other large animals, around 12,000 years ago. There were at least 3 species of Ice Age horses of various sizes—some as small as ponies and as large as Clydesdales—evolved in North America for the last 40 million years. These powerful potential allies disappeared before they could be used by the indigenous people of the Americas. Fortunately, before their total extinction from the Americas, large numbers of them crossed the Bering Straights back to the grasslands of central Eurasia. This was a narrow escape that had a profound effect on human history. Around 8,000 BC, nomadic people in central Asia learned to tame them for the first time. As time went by, domesticated horses would be harnessed across Eurasia, advancing everything from work to travel and transport to warfare. Perhaps no other animal had a bigger influence on the course of human history; and the circle won't be complete for another few thousand years when the explorer Christopher Columbus used them on his second voyage to the Americas on September 24, 1493. These horses would be the first to set their hooves on the Americas' soil since their die-offs 10,000 years before.

10,000 to 6,000 years ago: Domestication of plants and animals set the next stage for the development of the human history. Like the clouds of interstellar dust, gathered by gravity to bring material to form the stars, a type of gravity is at work in places like Samaria, located in the fertile lands known as Mesopotamia, which gathered a large population and spin offs of power and innovation known as the *First Agricultural Revolution*. This was a wide-scale transition of a number of tribal groups and cultures, from a nomadic lifestyle of hunting-gathering, to one of agriculture and settlements, allowing the ability to support an increasingly larger population.

At this point of our narrative, it is important to notice that God was totally absent from the cosmological, geological and biological evolution of the Universe in the last 14.5 billion years since the Big Bang. The appearance of God (*Theophany* in Greek) started at the approximate time of the Agricultural Revolution, about 6,000 years ago, when man was asking questions about who or what controlled the cycles of nature, the Sun's daily motions and of the Stars, the passing of the Seasons, what or who caused floods, rains, dry spells and storms, what controlled the tribes' fertility, its domesticated animals and its crops. Living during the Age of Agricultural

Revolution, people had no scientific knowledge of how to answer or resolve these questions. But the need for answers was so important that some responses were required, even if they were merely based on false pattern-meaning. Some priestly and tribal leaders within the communities started to invent answers based on their personal pattern-meaning which created the first mythology of religious belief system.

Agricultural evidence indicates that the domestication of various types of plants and animals formed the world's first historically verifiable revolution in agriculture, starting in the *geological epoch of the Holocene:* the development of major civilisations and transition to urban living. It led to the diffusion of many crops and farming techniques across the *Neolithic Mesopotamian* world. It was a period of major transition from the pre-agricultural period, characterised by the *Palaeolithic diet*, into an agricultural period, characterised by a diet of cultivated foods, and a further transition into living longer by an advance in social changes. Some of these Samarian settlements can be called *"our first cities."* One of them, *Uruk,* had around 50,000 inhabitants living in less than a square mile, a population density that rivals a modern city. Humans had become more efficient at deriving energy from cultivated foods; a land size that once could only have supported a single hunter-gatherer now supports thousands.

But changes in diets also increased new dependencies; because once human population moved into agriculture, they became depended on a very short list of species for their calories. In the case of the Middle East, this was wheat and barley. Wheat and barley seeds had to be gathered at the same time, and then planted and harvested at the same time. This meant that the population had their food for the entire year arriving during a singular harvesting time. This also means that there was a need for the establishment of a social organisation that would record the collection and storage of seeds, plan and organise the necessary labour force to cultivate and harvest, then store and distribute the crop.

In these first cities, the care of crops which were most important took the forefront due to human needs for food. To keep track of them our ancestors developed writing and; in order to protect their crops, the first army was created and, to administrate it we have the beginnings of politics. Under the circumstances, the city dwelling people needed an administrative body which would govern their obligations from one citizen to others and towards the hierarchy of the state. In the words of philosopher *Thomas Hobbes*, citizens need a *Leviathan* or a *"common power"* under which they would be governed. Planting seeds had set man into a new path, settlements were grown into cities, but to take the next step, from cities to civilisation, humanity would need the help of a surprising creature: *the donkey.*

5,000 years ago: after wandering the Earth for more than 100,000 years, mankind settled down into settlements, villages and towns. We clustered near rivers along the Tigris-Euphrates Rivers of Mesopotamia and the Nile of Egypt, the Indus, the Yellow and Yangtze Rivers, and civilisations were about to escalate. But first these settlements had to muster one thing: *trade.* The more they exchange goods from other lands the greater they grow. It appears that long distance trade and communication was a necessary prerequisite to allow the growth of urban civilisation. The first civilisation arises on the back of a creature with a lonely reputation in the modern world, the donkey. The donkey transportation was the means to an interstate, high-speed highway of its day, a tradition that still holds presently in a number of mountainous regions of the Mediterranean, the Middle East and South American countries today. Their ancient travel routes would lay the groundwork for the modern world, moving not only timber, spices and bronze, but also new populist ideas and stories, myths and beliefs. The civilisations they connected would be the first to be described in the Jewish Bible. The donkey caravan routes converged in the Persian Gulf which would link up with ships carrying goods to India. In this sense, they brought together populations into a greater material and cultural exchange of popular pagan beliefs.

It is important to understand how the world works today. Just like the first human civilisations, we also trade and network across the globe. By 4,000 BC, humans had gone from humble huts to extended towns and cities. In Africa great pyramids arise on the banks of the Nile, the first stone monuments arise in Britain, and back in Mesopotamia, man-made Temple Mountains called *Ziggurats* climbed ever higher towards the mythological sky-gods. To construct and cement these massive structures together, the builders of Mesopotamia used a substance that leaks from seepages from the Tigris-Euphrates Rivers; it is called *bitumen,* used as asphalt (or black-tar) in modern highways. It was the first petroleum product used by mankind. While bitumen is highly priced, the seepages of bitumen from the river were considered not as favoured material because it cached fire easily; the ancients called it *naphtha* and we called it *gasoline.* This was the first indications of the vast oil fields that, one day in the future, will turn this beneficial product of the ancient civilisations into modern private wealth and states' warfare.

The legacy of these first civilisations can be seen in surprising ways. The Samarians introduced the art of writing and likely invented the *wheel;* which eventually led to another invention, the chariot with the horse that would change the course of history. Combining the invention of the wheel with the domestication of the horse that had occurred among the nomadic tribesmen, along with the invention of the chariot, and we have a formidable mobile war machine.

1500 BC: the chariot-driven clashes of upcoming imperial armies would eventually use copper and tin (the metals they would need for bronze tools and weapons). Likely the stars made an alternative metal, *the Iron*. Now metal smiths made a crucial discovery that, by working at higher temperatures, it would be easier to mould and sharpen a knife or a sword. The stars also helped by providing a multiply larger amount of iron than any other metal on Earth. Humanity enters the *Iron Age*. History has been taking humanity on a wild ride, from the initial blast of the Big Bang, to the formation of Earth and its first creatures, the rise of Man, the Ice Age which spread mankind around the world, then stranded us on different continents, leaving us to survive with what was available to us, and a world that still remains a divided place.

This brief article has demonstrated that the Laws of Nature, Energy, Gravity, Physics and Chemistry (among other geological events) have created the Universe and our planet Earth. There was no theistic Grand Designer who created the universe by his intervention as a divine being, because the main force behind the cosmic formulation was gravity. In other words, in the creation of the universe, a Grand Designer was "not necessary." The recognition of this evidence alone is a great achievement for the humanists and atheists of the world. That is, the fact that Man---who is a mere collection of fundamental elements of nature---is now able to understand the Laws of Nature that govern us and our universe, is a great triumph. This stands in contrast to the religious myth that the Earth was carefully designed by a divine entity just to please us human beings. Nothing could be further from the truth. In the words of cosmologist Stephen Hawking, *"Spontaneous creation is the reason there is something rather than nothing, why the universe exists, why we exist."* Humanity is indebted to the cosmologists, physicists and astronomers for discovering the strange nature of cosmic reality, and for explaining why the forces of Natural Selection have apparently been fine-tuned to permit the biological evolution of complex organisms and creatures such as human beings. Our Universe and its Laws of Nature appear to have a function that is tailor-made to support life, and if we are to continue to exist, it leaves little room for their suspension in favour of man. This is not easily understood by those whose view of the world is based on a *Master, on a Miracle or on Mystery*. The poverty of religious fallacies allows an unimaginable existence of a universe. The strange reality of nature just happened to be fine-tuned within the exact perimeters of the Laws of Chemistry (hydrogen, oxygen, carbon) and additional key atoms and elements in order to generate laws that allow those chemical entities to interact in ways that build up more complex chemical combinations. So, please continue reading this book, in order to understand our world. But if it is a Sky-God or Celestial Designer, Miracles or Magic you are after, my advice to you is to steer clear.

2000 to 1000 BC: The people of the regions in ancient Mesopotamia lived their daily lives in similar ways. The civilisation of Mesopotamia placed a great value on the written word. With the gradual rise of more complex civilisations in the river valleys of Tigris-Euphrates in Mesopotamia, knowledge became too complicated to transmit directly from person to person and from generation to generation. To be able to function in complex societies, leaders needed some way of accumulating, recording, and preserving social activities and cultural heritage. So, with the rise of trade, leaders, the governing classes and temple priests came to the invention of complex writing, by about 3200 BC. This was done in order to have some kind of control in recording the affairs of society. Once writing was invented, the scribes seem dedicated to the recording of every facet of the lives of the people; from the names of the kings, to contracts for wheat sales to the sales of slaves.

Because firsthand experience in everyday living could not teach the nobility and the upper classes such skills as writing, reading and arithmetic, a place devoted exclusively to the tutoring of those skills had to be invented. This invented process took a considerable time to develop because ideas, theories and social changes do not come from the void! Rather these are social products of trial and error tribulations of many past generations. By this time, peoples' socio-political status was determined by whether they were "citizens" or not. The populations of the cities were divided into social classes which were hierarchical. These classes were the King and the Military Nobility, the Priests and Priestesses, the Upper Class, the Lower Class, and the Slaves. The lower classes and slaves were not regarded as proper citizens. The legal definition of "citizen" applied only to the upper social classes above the "property-less" or lower classes. They were the only class who had the right to hold property, and slaves. The lower classes were the field and house workers, manual labourers, artisans, mercenaries and anyone whose family did not belong to "who's who" in the community. For obvious reasons, the lower classes and slaves formed the majority of the population.

Education in the ancient world was first developed into a conscious method that led to a movement to educate upper class leaders and citizens rather than the lower classes. It was a system of education that tried to harmonise naturalism (material reality) on the one side and supernaturalism (pagan religion) on the other. The material-reality of the creation of the Universe was not known, although there were attempts by naturalists ("scientists") of the day. The best they could come up with was the "interpretation" of the Cosmos by means and formulation of the pagan astrological *Zodiac Signs*, and not the material origins and make-up of the universe.

The tutors, the scribes or teachers were highly respected and served at court, in the temple and in tutorial places, where as scribes would teach the boys of the upper classes the art of writing and reading. These tutorials were supported by the fees paid by the members of the upper class whose sons attended the tutorials. Private tutors were also held in high regard and were paid well by wealthy families of the cities to tutor their sons to excel at their literacy work. Private tutelage was mostly run by the temple-priests who were considered men of exceptional intelligence, virtue and character. Only boys of the upper classes were considered intelligent enough to be able to master literacy. This paradigm remained in place for many centuries and future generations of the ancient world. Women, members of the lower classes and slaves were excluded from attending tutoring. They were simply regarded as unintelligent; the issue of equal rights was non-existent. The Priests and Priestesses held a prominent socio-political position because they were property holders. They were the official predictors and interpreters of pagan *signs and omens* for the nobility, the army generals and the rich who could afford the high price of their services. They also served as *healers;* they would take care of the business of the temple as well as officiating at ceremonies. As a dominant and influential class, they were in close contact with the emperor or the king and nobility in order to serve both their political agendas of the day. Of course, the priests and priestesses also had their own long-term agendas, whose goals were to preserve their influence and the benefits they derived from it. The premise for their existence was to keep society under their religious hold and influence, which always coexisted on par with their social position.

In the ancient societies of Mesopotamia, Greece, Egypt, Persian and Iraq, religion was an integral part of peoples' lives and part of one's daily existence. The temple-priests had convinced the citizens that it was the Gods who provided them with food, with all their needs and comforts and, in return, they had to obey them, offer money, and volunteer their labour in the services of the pagan Temple-Gods. People believed that the Temple-Gods were the originators of the universe and mankind who remained their supreme masters and guided their existence. In other words, they lived a life with infinite obligations towards the Temple-Gods. All aspects of their existence were imbued with a sense of the supernatural, the mysterious entity at work, and like everything else, it was dictated by the temple priests. They had convinced the people, including themselves, of the delusion that they were the direct representatives of the Gods on Earth.

The upper classes included the merchants who owned their own trade markets and caravans, the store-keepers and scribes who kept private or public records, tax collectors and accountants, private tutors and architects, shipbuilders, military men, and astrologers (from the priests' class), and all followed along the same line of thought. Within the upper classes there were also women who were brewers and tavern-keepers---and also doctors and dentists. But, before those occupations were proved to be very lucrative businesses, most were taken over by the temple priests as *healers*. The lower classes were made up of those occupations which kept the cities in their daily operation: farmers, artists, musicians, construction and canal builders, bakers and basket makers, butchers and fishermen, clay pot and redbrick makers, metal workers and carpenters, jewellery makers and goldsmiths, perfume makers and prostitutes, mercenaries and sailors. Any member of the lower classes, with recognisable exceptional skills, could climb the social ladder and could own property and hold the same esteemed positions as those of the upper classes.

The lowest social order was made of the slaves who were men or boys, women or girls. Men who were captured in war would become slaves. One could also become a slave in a number of other ways: selling oneself into slavery to pay off a dept, or being sold by a family member to relieve a debt, being sold as punishment for a crime, or being kidnapped and sold into slavery in another region. Kidnapping was a common practice among the desert tribesmen and the Mediterranean pirates. Beautiful women, strong men and young girls tended to bring the best prices. Slaves had no rights, had no single ethnicity, nor were they solely sold for manual labour. Slaves were housekeepers and maids, landscapers and gardeners, managers of large estates and agricultural production, tended horses, sheep and goats, and were employed in whatever capacity their masters saw they had the skills to perform.

In such societies of the ancient world, leisure was the main pastime of the lower classes, re-enacting telling stories and beliefs associated with their limited life styles. This means that their daily activities were focused around their household and their extended families. Their observation of the universe and its events were left to be dealt with by the temple-priests and the "wise men" of the court of the King. Anything that was assumed by myths and distortions about the origins of the cosmos was trickled down the social scale as a form of belief-system rather than as knowledge. Street orators would then adopt and modify such myths with further distortions of their own imagination or illusions. The variation of illusions depended on the degree these myths were acceptable to the lower classes. There was a whirlwind of fantastic and magical events that were peddled as true, and people believed them because they simply had no means, by reason or evidence, to refuse them. The most fantastic of the myths of the day was the *Epic of Gilgamesh*, due to the fact that it contained a legend of a flood which has close similarities to the Biblical account of the Noah's Ark. Eventually, it became customary to believe many of these well reversed myths, for no one would dare question their validity. This gave religious justification for the temples' complete authority over the people of the upper and the lower classes. The world events were interpreted in terms of mythology rather than historical facts, or a mixture of both (thus the need for etymology). The Roman Empirial Cult and the ancient "historian" Josephus Bar Mathias were the most elaborate typological mythic scribes in the Neolithic times which gave us the mythical creation of Jesus Christ. More later.

The wise man of the upper classes also portrayed celestial events through elaborate temple-ritual re-enactments; with symbolisms presented as reality, signs and omens, bringing the original celestial figures down to earth to become legendary "ancestors" of those who were telling the stories. By this identification, with the magic behind the celestial events of the Gods, the dominant classes would become the special children (or relatives) of the mythic creator, and the creator himself would receive the honour of being metamorphosed into a legendary First-God of the land. Temple activities were re-enacted the world over, as the dominant classes re-lived cosmic events on earth. Through these temple activities, two primal instincts stand out: an illusionary escape into a perfect paradise, and a profound fear of an apocalyptic celestial catastrophe, motives which fuelled peoples' collective state of permanent anxiety.

The material world was conceived to be *lesser or secondary* and was bound to a divine entity which was *primary,* and every household, village or tribe had its own god or gods. Everything that happened on Earth was not related to geological causes or Laws of Nature but had a divine dimension to it. Even famine, physical or mental sickness were the results of the wishes of Gods rather than the results of natural causes. The overriding purpose of one's life was to serve the temple-Gods by tending the sanctuaries and burning incense at their altars. To some extent, this meant that the entire economic life of the lower classes in the village or city-state was geared to the service of the temple and the dominant classes. In short, religion was polytheistic---of lesser Gods---with one chief God who was re-invented from time to time, but always referred to as the "Sky-God" in the Samarian region. Life's meaning and purpose, therefore, was placed on the *metaphorical* and *mythical* side, and the real natural world was reduced to a supportive role of that delusion!

There is a need here to say something about the literary value of mythology; if it is taken as a literary work, a story-telling or as literary fantasy. The question then, is whether a myth is true or not, is not relevant, because we assume that a myth is an invented pattern-meaning story. Let me explain! Human beings were not evolved to believe in the existence of mythological figures, or born religious, or inclined to mysticism. Our brain is biologically programmed to look for patterns in life and attach meaning to them. Otherwise a blank mental space should be in the mental-gap instead of filling it with whatever our brain decides. As youngsters going to elementary school, we were given pages with printed words and blind-gaps to fill with the correct words: i.e. pattern-meaning. Now our brain is not biologically evolved to maintain mental-gaps between a question and an answer. The brain would rather fill the mental-gap with an invented pattern-meaning; it cannot do either wise unless we keep repeating the pattern-meaning *"I do not know"* in order to fill a mental-gap. Our brain would rather invent a pattern-meaning than have no meaning at all. We also must be aware that our brain does not differentiate between *a true* or *false pattern-meaning*. For instance, we attach the pattern-meaning to a real *danger situation* and we behave accordingly. What happens when the pattern-meaning of "danger" is false due to a false alarm? At one moment we believe the danger really exists and behave accordingly---and our brain followed its biological function of creating a pattern-meaning for our personal protection, in the same way as if the danger was false.

Did our ancient ancestors were aware of this inherited biological pattern-meaning of our brain? Probably not. So when an ancient scribe or a philosopher looked at the stars and wondered if there was a relationship between man and stars, that philosopher had no evidence to support any true pattern-meaning, so myths were created to fill up the mental-gap between the question and answer with mythological tale. Myths depict unlikely events that bend or suspend the Laws of Nature which carry a metaphysical explanation of the universe. As such, religious myths often offer non-human characters, i.e. Gods, Goddesses, supernatural beings, first people, intelligent designer and so on, and forming settings of another world---someone like this one but different. Myths seek to answer life's meaning and purpose by using metaphoric narratives to build a belief system which is the core of all mythology. Homer's Iliad, Odysseus adventures, the Old Testament and the New Bible, the Family Robinson and Treasure Island are stories, legends and myths built with the help of metaphors and symbolic meaning to create a great literary value. As literary works, they should be read but not believed as religion.

What happens when a myth is created and obliges people to believe and act upon it as if the described or prescribed event is truth? Is the metaphorical description of Genesis 1, a religious mythology or a material event that can be scientifically proven? Is there verified evidence connecting Genesis 1 to the origin of the Universe? Are the characters of Adam and Eve the only full fledged human-beings on Earth, and no other? Yet all evidence shown here confirms that the universe turns against creationism. Are the supernatural animals depicted in the pre-historic caves of Spain, France and Greece, (created by the human species of the Neanderthal, Cro-Magnon and Homo sapient cave-artists), *Animist* myths? Does the metaphorical term "believe" an investigative term? Can the term"belief" stir us towards verifying something that is not based on reason and evidence? A belief may appear mystical or genuine to the believer, but every serious scientist would confirm that personal beliefs are not sufficient enough to constitute evidence or truth. Having the intellectual dynamism to differentiate between myth, on the one hand, and scientific verification on the other, makes one know reality from delusion. Never mind the myth that "Jesus died for us," the fact is that stars died in the universe for you and I to be born. Every atom in our body came from stars. In fact, the atoms in your right-hand may have come from a different star than your atoms in your left hand. Those atoms only got into your body because the stars were kind enough to explode! The subsequent chapters attempt to show that tragic delusions in human history get justified by religious beliefs of leaders who started them in order to meet their religious objectives.

THE BEGINNING OF OUR COSMOS

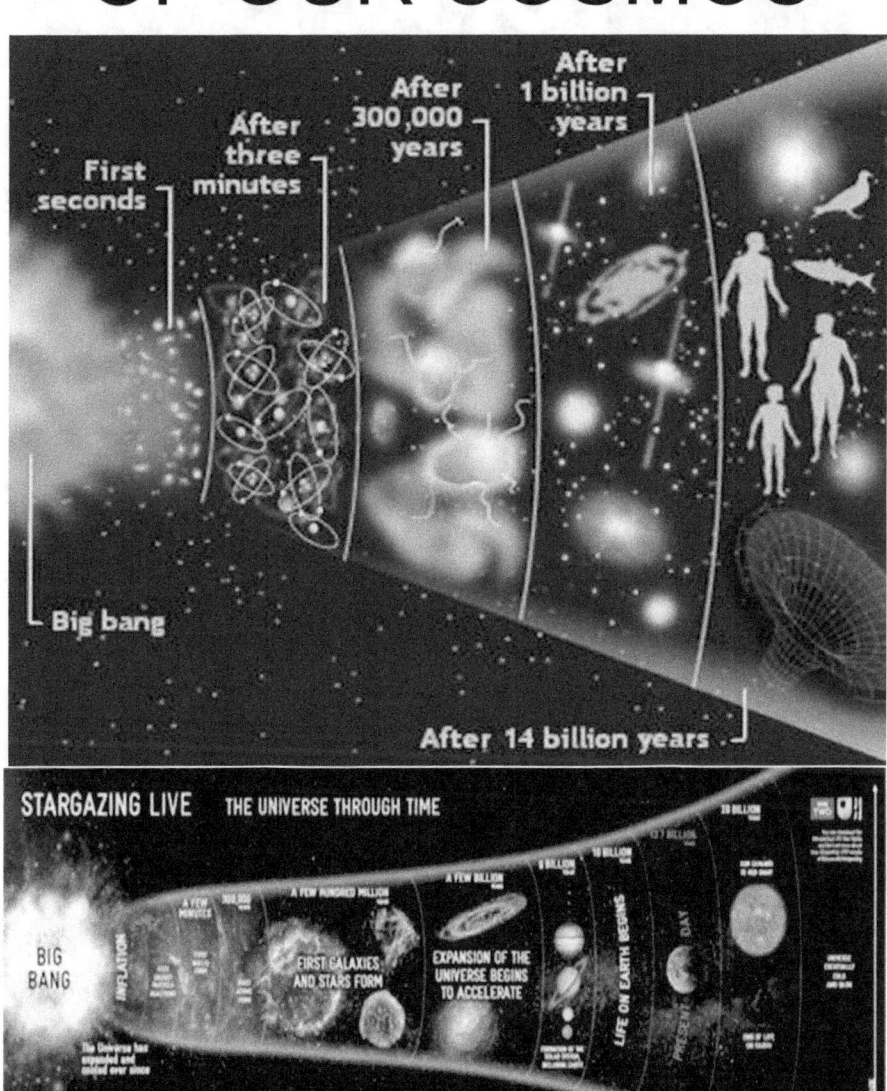

THE LAWS OF NATURE

NATURAL LAW

NATURAL:
Inherent; having a basis in Nature, Reality and Truth; not made or caused by humankind.

LAW:
An existing condition which is binding and immutable (cannot be changed).

You cannot hide from the laws of Nature

- Menander -

THE LAW OF UNIVERSAL GRAVITATION

Explore the Law of Universal Gravitation by explaining the role that gravity plays in the formation of planets, stars, and solar systems and in determining their motions.

Gravitation causes dispersed matter to coalesce, thus accounting for the existence of the Earth, the Sun, and most of the macroscopic objects in the universe. It is responsible for keeping the Earth and the other planets in their orbits around the Sun; for keeping the Moon in its orbit around the Earth; for the formation of tides; for convection, by which fluid flow occurs under the influence of a density gradient and gravity; for heating the interiors of forming stars and planets to very high temperatures; and for various other phenomena observed on Earth.

GRAVITATIONAL FORMATION OF PLANETARY SYSTEM

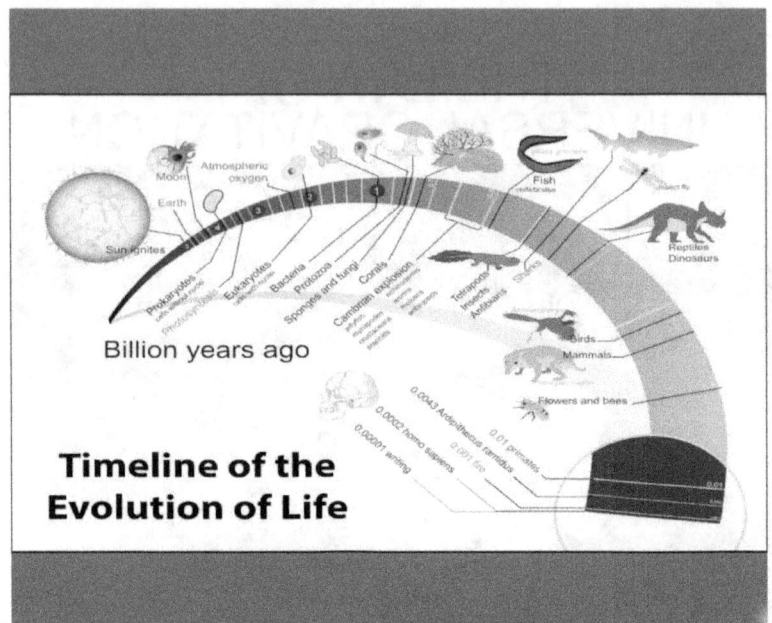

THE CAMBRIAN EXPLOSION

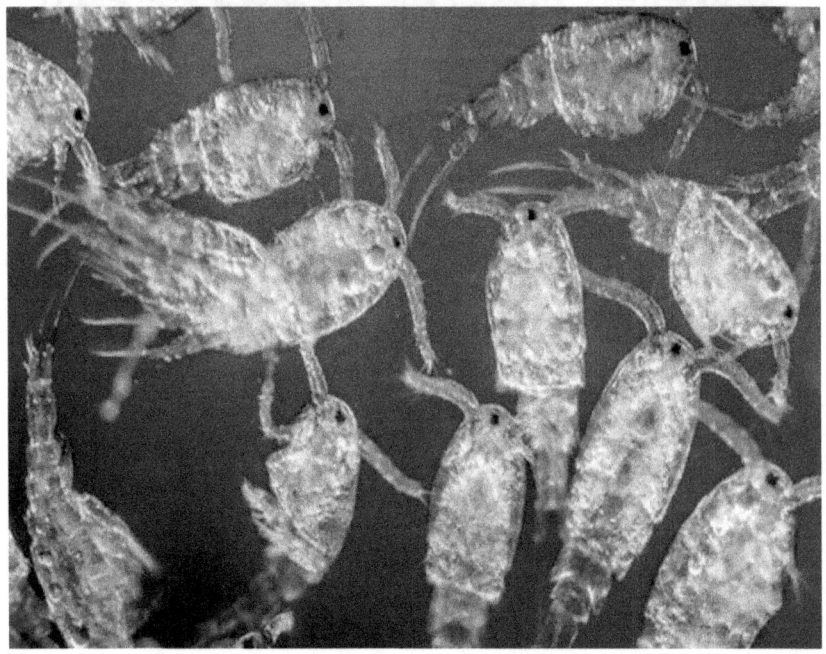

THE CAMBRIAN EXPLOSION

THE CAMBRIAN EXPLOSION
MICROSCOPIC LIFE

REPTILES & BACTERIA

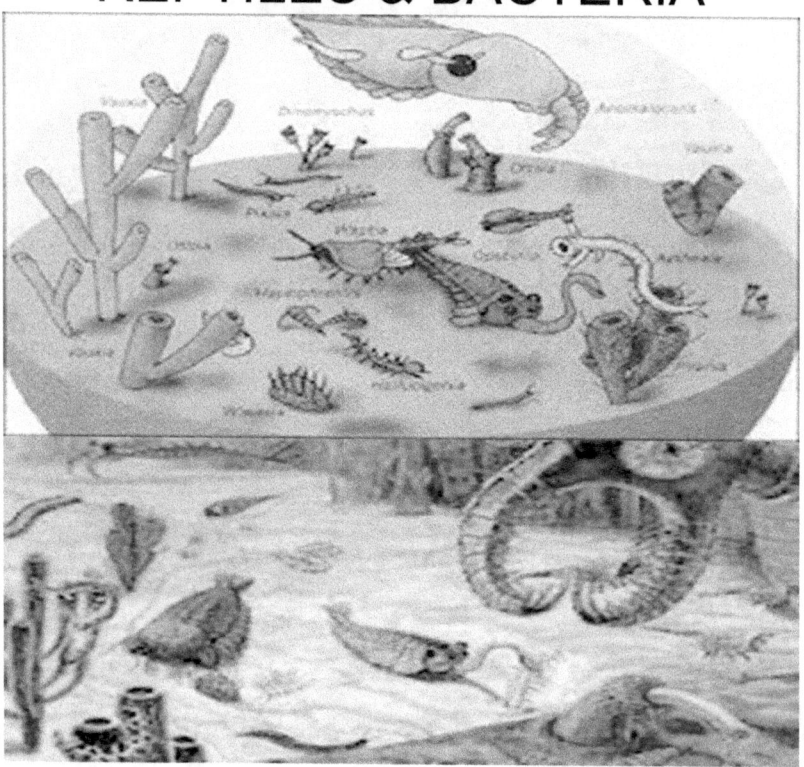

THE CAMBRIAN EXPLOSION
FOSSILIZED CRICKET

FOSSILIZED ORGANISIM

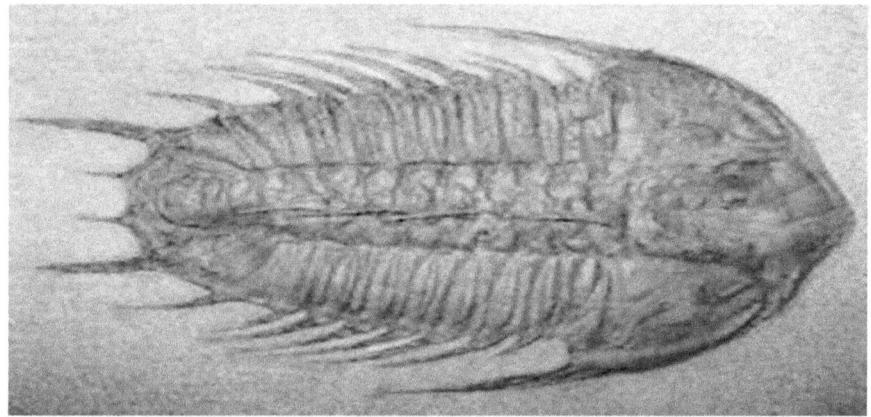

FOSSILIZED OPABINIA

CAMBRIAN PREDATORY MICROSCOPIC ORGANISMS

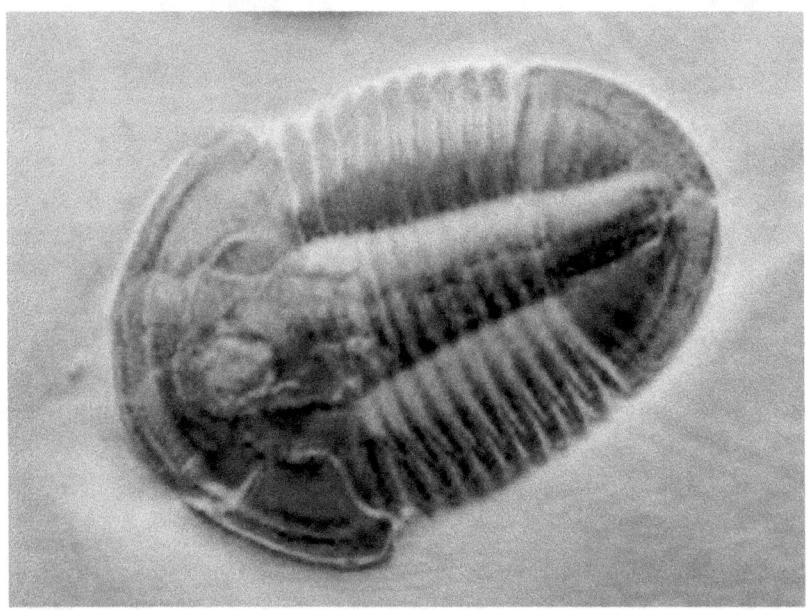

THE GOVERNING LAWS OF NATURE

Laws of Nature regulate, in physical governing terms, the world on the basis of how it functions and how the entire universe follows the same principles, and that these entrenched Laws of Nature never randomly change. In other words, the Laws of Nature are the core physical principles which govern the phenomena of the world. These laws are not written in legalistic, philosophical or metaphysical terms, nor do they depend on our social approval or disproval of them. They are not moralistic, negative or positive in their essence, nor are they mysterious, theistic or magical. They are not governed by strong beliefs, by wishful thinking, by magic or by logical arguments.

The Laws of Nature function independent of the human mind, theistic illusions and society's delusional descriptions of an event. For instance, a Laws of Nature identifies the explosion of a volcano which is caused by earth's internal pressure. Every time a volcano erupts it is because the Laws of Nature---imbedded in the earth's internal pressure--- results in a similar event, i.e., the eruption of a volcano. With few exceptions, the Laws of Nature are descriptions of why some natural phenomena occur and when they occurred in material terms. Heavy rains could result in flooding, and knowing this Law of Nature measures may be taken to prevent damages but we cannot prevent heavy rains from taking place. Environmental and geological sciences can explain natural phenomena through the Laws of Nature and by explaining those, humanity can behave accordingly. Hurricanes, tsunamis and earthquakes, gravity, the speed of light and others remain constant and are natural phenomena; so are diseases, bacteria or the death of a living organic matter including a human being or an animal. Curing a disease via medical sciences prevents the natural or recurrence of them.

Laws of Nature do not create natural phenomena but only provide humans with an approximate description of them. Therefore the Laws of Physics (in Laws of Nature) is a pattern that nature and our universe is governed by and obeys without exception. These descriptions are based on scientific evidence or proposed theories in biology, human evolution, chemistry and geology, cosmology and space science. They can also be computed, documented with numbers and measured in mathematics. Can the Laws of Nature temporarily or permanently be suspended on behalf of our human innate (mental) beliefs, wishes or desires? The human mind's beliefs have no external powers to impose any changes to the Laws of Physics or to suspend the Laws of Nature temporarily or permanently. Miracles of resurrection for instance attempt to suggest that the Laws of Nature (birth, growth and death) can be suspended by raising the dead from their graves. Humanity should recognize that we are only a tiny aspect of the universality of the cosmos. We are not the center of the cosmos; and if we continue to behave as if we are, then the environmental consequences upon us will be terrifying if not lethal.

Religion is the Mother-Load of all delusional patterns, false evidence and irrelevant claims about humanity, morality and relations to our cosmos. Most of its claims about the existence and power of a Sky-God include events that supposedly resulted from the suspension of the Laws of Nature. These claims have not been proven in the last 3,000 years nor can we expect them to be verifiable. We are referring to verifiable and observable physical events where such Laws of Nature were temporarily suspended by Gods' will and power, and that their suspension was terminated afterwards. Needless to say, religious beliefs or mental causes can alter personal "feelings" or state of mind, leading to a belief in the existence of God or events caused by God. In dialectical reasoning and science however, personal "feelings" resulting from beliefs in God do not count as evidence. Faithful devotees believe that God can influence events on earth or in a person's life, but the term "belief" is not an investigative or scientific term which can be used to verify a truth.

Observable evidence, not irrational beliefs in "miracles," can verify the improbable violation of the Laws of Nature. Using language, one can present logical arguments in support of miracles, but the Laws of Nature do not function in accordance with the mind's logic and a person's linguistic skills. When the Earth was regarded as being flat instead of round, the logical argument was that one can fall off the earth's edge into a void. The argument may be logical but the pattern-explanation is non-existent and therefore false. Religion is "creeping-into" scientific narratives of natural events, and adopting impressive sounding terms, legalisms and pseudo-scientific expressions to re-gain their once held privileged social position. Self-delusional believers like the writer Frank Turek, uses terms like "aerodynamics," the "Big Bang" and a slue of astronomical definitions to support biblical religious beliefs that were made up by illiterate Middle East desert tribesmen some 2,000 years ago.

In this case a simple question needs to be asked: had Arabian Desert people known that no human or Sky-God could ever suspend the Laws of Nature, would they have invented and followed their superstitious or religious myths? Taking into consideration their lack of knowledge of the Laws of Nature; what other choices did they have, but to invent illusive pattern-meaning explanations about the world where no such patterns existed. Now we know that the human brain is biologically programmed to see patterns in life; and in absence of real ones, the brain fills up the gap with invented patterns that do not exist. Because of the demand placed upon the human brain to generate patterns, it tends to take shortcuts in order to meet that demand. For the human brain, one pattern is as good as the next; the task of analysing them depends on our cognitive experience. The cognitive experience of the tribesmen was not better than their imagination, and their brains were available to generate as many delusional and non-existent patterns they needed. In short, they believed to be true everything they thought, and because they thought of a pattern, it must be true!

Today, religious devotees recognise their predecessors' ignorance and are adopting modern methods to continue with their self-delusive task of finding a connection between the Laws of Nature and the Sky-God; and, of course the latter being the leading cause. Those people have turned the Laws of Nature on their heads by insisting that these laws are God's ways of governing our world and the cosmos beyond. In other words, the Laws of Nature concept is a "belief in God" and not materialist Laws of Physics. Physical or materialist Laws of Physics apply to the physical or material conditions of our earthly natural world and our cosmos. Those laws are not subliminal (mental concepts) nor are they speculative to be manipulated by an irrational application of language. They do not operate on the basis of human desires or wishful thinking. For instance, when a natural event, such as a tsunami happens, geological scientists are interpreting the event on the basis of the Laws of Nature (Laws of Physics) as the physical or material causes of the event. Any assumption of celestial causality of such events is purely delusional. These devotees are following the same old track of requirements perpetuated by ancient, ignorant tribesmen who were eager to believe but were not cognitively capable of investigating.

The whole existence and perpetuation of religion is based on such a core requirement: the obligation of believing rather than investigating. If you do not believe, then religion is powerless. Creationists are manipulating and distorting the core scientific reason for scientists to investigate the Laws of Nature and Space in order to "prove" the existence of God's work in the universe. For Christianity and Islam, stealing, borrowing or plagiarising from other religions, philosophies and now from scientific sources, is a normal shameless task. They still envision the universe as following the Biblical laws in order to prove that God is the creator of the laws of physics. They believe (with no evidence) that God made the universe to operate in according to divine reason. How do they know this? It is the "I believe," presented as their own whims in the works of their monotheistic God that justifies their delusion. The universal Laws of Nature are suspended—only on behalf of Christians--- because pantheistic societies do not believe in one fixed God, (some do not even have a creator of the cosmos), for their gods are inconsistent and temperamental in the things that they have made. In according to this dogma, the Christian God is an orderly God who created an orderly and predictable universe whose laws of nature are orderly and well-placed. This is the main contradiction of the advocates of the dogma of religious delusion.

In fact the Universe is not orderly or fixed and the Laws of Nature are not of specified origins at the moment of their occurrence. The universe is not fixed; it is not orderly, for it is expanding at rapid speed and planets explode and destroyed every second. For instance, on a clear night, it can be seen that the *Andromeda Galaxy* is in a collision course with our galaxy. According to cosmologists, in approximately 4.5 billion years the two galaxies will collide. Well, some kind of orderly God, some kind of orderly God's laws of nature, some kind of orderly universe; whose God intentions will be to eventually destroy his orderly creation. In the last 3 million years 98% of the life forms on our planet have gone extinct, including 60 – 70 early humanoids and at least 2 fully develop *genus Homo* (human) in the last 40,000 years. Human population on earth was once reduced to a mere 10,000 and we have survived because of our adaptability to climatic conditions and availability of food sources. Our fellow travelers, the Neanderthals and Cro-Magnons were not as lucky. The Laws of Nature that caused their extinction are what they are, and cannot be suspended or be dressed up with good, bad, moral or religious characteristics. The question behind scientific pursued is legitimate and for many of the physicists, biologists and cosmologists, who laid the foundations of modern space discoveries, there is a clear answer: that the Laws of Nature in biological life or in the universe cannot be suspended on behalf of man.

The origins of explaining the idea of the Laws of Nature lie in the ancient Greek period from the 6th century BC, pre-Socratic era. Philosophers' tasks of this period were attempting to explain the natural phenomena taking place in the cosmos and their occurring causes. The traditional explanation of natural events was related to the capricious attitude of the Greek Gods, instead of explaining those as being natural phenomena caused by natural events. For instance, a thunder in the Sky was attributed to God Zeus's bad mood rather than climatic changes. Eventually it was discovered that natural phenomena were caused by natural occurring events which had nothing to do with God Zeus's capricious behaviour. Eventually eclipses were explained and were even predicted based on information collected by the *Antikythera mechanism* about the sequence of their occurrences. The Antukythera is a complex clockwork mechanism which was used by ancient Greek astronomers as an analog computer designed to calculate and predict astronomical and calendrical phenomena.

Pattern analysis of natural phenomena however, gave way to random speculation and not one of these Greek philosophers thought of putting their speculative claims about nature to the rigor of testing them. This was the time when the physical world was regarded as being mundane and studying it was a worthless effort that would only arrive at a worthless knowledge. Instead, the study of ethics, law and morality and how to live well were worthy studies of the philosophers. Some Greek and Egyptian philosophers were even more disparaging about the physical world, for they regarded it as being the shadowy reflection of the pure world of abstract thoughts. They wrongly assumed that we get true knowledge from the pure world of abstract thought, for ideas in the mind had far more value that the manifestations of the physical world. Eventually the gravitational balance of the world shifted from the material world, to the man's mental thoughts. Hundreds of years later, successive philosophers encapsulated Laws of Nature within their philosophical scheme and the idea of associating them with paganism, for the interpretation of star-positioning with human relations brought about the Zodiac Signs. The mythological characteristics of the pagan Zodiac Signs were adopted and shared among a number of pre-Christian religions and star-positioning was later used to form the structural base of early Christianity. Much more later.

In the eventual conflict between Christianity and Paganism in the 4th and 5th centuries AD, science paid a heavy price for its association with paganism, resulting in the destruction of the Alexandrian Library and the banning of the study of natural phenomena throughout the Roman Empire. Eating the fruit from the metaphorical *Tree of Knowledge* was clearly prohibited by the early Christian theocracy, imposing such a dictatorial decree throughout the Roman Empire. Only much later did Thomas Aquinas (1225 – 1274 AD) claimed that it was acceptable to nibble at the forbidden fruit, provided the scientific reason remained the handmaid of the Christian autocratic faith. Aquinas provided rational arguments for the belief of God and his "science" crept in, along with the rest of his philosophy, once the Papacy theologians argued that Aquinas posed no threat to the authority of the Church. However, everything in our cosmos, every plant and animal, every particle of material substance or energy, is bound by laws to which they must adhere. Those laws are precise; not random and not monolithic, but mathematical in nature and cannot be suspended, (temporarily or permanently) on behalf of any biological entity like man's wishful thinking, desires, magic or imaginary celestial entity.

Laws of Nature must be in just the right sequence in order for our universe to function as is. Within the universal body there are varieties of Laws of Nature (not sub-laws) with their own applicable and precise task in various parts of our natural world. For instance, the Laws of Chemistry, the Laws of Physics, the Laws of Natural Selection, the Laws of Gravity, the Laws of Mathematics, and the Laws of Planetary Motion; all are but few examples of physical properties that are governed by their own laws. The universal totality of the number of Laws of Nature is immense. Whatever changes occur within the physical properties that are governed by the Laws of Nature are due to the infinity process and variations of Natural Selection or Geological principles. The Laws of Nature, which includes multiple parts of our natural world and planetary universe, function in consistent or uniform ways. They do not arbitrarily change and they apply to all naturally occurring phenomena. We now know that the Laws of Nature are not fixed as *"things in themselves"* and unattached from other laws and principles in our natural world. They function in relation to and as part of other laws of our cosmos. This is why our earth's biological life can depend that the Laws of Nature would apply consistently throughout the time.

Evolution occurs when biological species change from one kind to another. The principle of Natural Selection ranks with Newton's laws and the Laws of Thermodynamics as one of the most powerful explanatory principles in the history of biological science. The principle states that living organisms evolve by deferential survival in a world in which only the fittest spread their genes into future generations. By fittest it means the best adapted organisms into a prevailing environment; and environment includes both the organic and non-organic environment. Natural Selection therefore depends on populations of different genetic individuals of the same species. That is, different genotypes created by continual mutations of genes, which changes in genes from generation to generation. For that to occur there must be hereditary variation among individuals, for there would be no alternative choices for natural selection to make. Mutations in genes result from naturally occurring radiation and from errors in copying the DNA from one generation to the next. Natural Selection displays no purpose, preference or inherent direction. This means that Natural Selection is just what happens, for it is not a law such as the Laws of Physics. It is a principle that revolutionised our understanding of the evolution of every organic life on earth. Based on the most advanced biological understanding, however, it is the human selection that has one major difference from its natural counterpart: *purpose and direction.*

The Laws of Physics describes how the universe operates. There are many different Laws of Physics describing how light propagates, how energy is transported, how gravity amongst planets operates and how mass travels through space, and much more. In the core of calculating planetary physics lie certain mathematical formulas. For instance, Einstein's mathematical formula $E=mc^2$ can be derived from the principles and equations of special relativity. This formula shows how an object with mass (m) will accelerate (a) when a net force (F) is applied to it. It is amazing how every planet in our universe consistently and precisely obeys these rules. Cosmic scientists are intensely working to find answers to many questions related to the Laws of Physics many to be derivative principles from other Laws of Physics.

Biological life requires a specific chemistry. From human to animal and vegetable life, the Laws of Chemistry are powered by chemical compositions and actions and depend on the consistency of these Laws of Chemistry to operate in a uniform fashion. The genome information that is part of any biological life is stored on a long molecule called DNA. The Laws of Chemistry give different properties to the various elements beyond the human life. For instance, each element is made of one type of atom, and compounds are made of two or more atoms that are bound together in the universe. When given enough activation energy, the lightest element of hydrogen will react with oxygen to form water. Water, in turn, has some interesting properties, such as the ultimate ability to store a large amount of heat energy.

The properties of various elements and chemical compounds are not arbitrary. Chemical scientists have organised them into a Periodic Table based on their physical properties. Substances in the same column on the Table tend to have similar properties. Periodic Table elements in the vertical column have similar outer electron structures. Thus, the outer most electrons determine the physical characteristics of an atom. It should be noted that the Periodic Table did not happen by magic. Atoms and molecules have their various properties because their electrons are bound by the Laws of Quantum Physics, and because chemistry is based on physics. The precise Laws of Quantum Physics make all such manifestation possible. It took billions of years for Natural Selection to create the Laws of Physics in just the right sequence that the Laws of Chemistry would come out as they are. This inter-process of Natural Selection did not need or have to depend on an "Intelligent Design," or a "Superior Mind," or a "Celestial Designer" (God) to bind it together with activated sequence.

Mathematical laws and principles include the rules of addition, the transitive property, the communicative properties of addition and multiplication, the binomial theorem, and much more. As is the case with other laws, the Laws of Mathematics can be derived from other mathematical principles, but, unlike the Natural Laws of Physics, the laws of mathematics are man-made and abstract. They are not attached to any specific part or planetary function of the Universe. Since mathematics is not attached to any part of the physical world, they are man-made or a human invention and are used as theorems or axioms in our understanding of the Laws of Nature. The way we choose to express mathematical theorems is through symbols we may derive from different sources (or to different course). In other words, we use mathematics as the means of benefiting from the theoretical understanding of certain physical events.

Orbital scientists have discovered that the planets in our own solar system obey a variety of Laws of Nature. The planets orbit in ellipses and not in perfect cycle, with the Sun focusing on the one side of the planet's ellipse. That some planets' orbit is at times closer to the sun then in other times. That planets' orbit sweeps out equal space areas in equal times, and that planets' orbit speed increases as they get closer to the sun within their established orbit. Orbital scientists have discovered an exact mathematical relationship between the planet's distance from the sun and its orbit time period. This mathematical formula also applies to the orbits of the moon around the earth and other moons or planets. As with the Laws of Chemistry, the Laws of Planetary Motion are a derivation of other Laws of Nature and could be derived mathematically from certain Laws of Physics---especially from the Laws of Gravity and Motion based on Isaac Newton's (1642 – 1727) discoveries.

David Hume (1711 – 1776) states his scientific opinion of the subject whether a "miracle" can suspend the Laws of Nature (i.e., death) on behalf of a religious wishful thinking or performed by an illusionist or by falsehood, *"A Miracle is a Violation of the Laws of Nature; and as a firm and unalterable Experience has established these Laws, the Proof against a Miracle, from the very Nature of the Fact, is as entire as any Argument from Experience can possibly be imagined. Why is it more than probable, that all Men must die; that Lead cannot, of itself, remain suspended in the Air; that Fire consumes Wood, and is extinguished by Water; unless it be, that these Events are found agreeable to the Laws of Nature, and there is required a Violation of these Laws, or in other Words, a Miracle to prevent them? Nothing is esteem'd a Miracle, if it ever happen in the common Course of Nature...There must, therefore, be a uniform Experience against every* *miraculous Event, otherwise the Event would not merit that Appellation. And as a uniform Experience amounts to a Proof, there is here a direct and full Proof, from the Nature of the Fact, against the existence of any Miracle; nor can such a Proof be destroy'd or the Miracle render'd credible, by an opposite Proof, which is superior."*

Miracles, resurrections from death, life after death, hell and heaven, are a transgression of the Laws of Nature and we have no compelling evidence in the existence or even belief of such miracles. Our assumptions about the suspension of the Laws of Nature derive exclusively from ancient biblical texts or from the testimony of others who claim to have seen or have performed miracles. Testimony can never be counted as a probability, let alone as proof of the existence of miracles. David Hume argues that we should treat such claims as less reliable than our evidences against them which come from their contrariety to the Laws of Nature. Our experience of the Laws of Nature is founded in the human knowledge that the Laws of Nature are constant. Since a miracle, by definition, is a violation of the Laws of Nature; any claim in favour can only be credible if it is more forcefully probable than the Laws of Nature. Those who believe in miracles are doing so on the basis of faith, not of reason and evidence. There are rational grounds for trusting someone's testimony about witnessing miracles, or of the suggestion that miracles are founded in the bible which are probably fabrications of the tribal authors of the Arabian Desert. The same can be said about the existence of God as celestial designer which also requires the suspension of the Laws of Nature.

The core base in the claim of the existence of an intelligent designer, as a creator of the universe, lies with the Greek philosophers of *Socrates*, in ancient Greece. The primary argument for the existence of God was that; since individual beings in the universe are either the products of intelligent design (*gnomy* in Greek) or a mere luck (*tyxi* in Greek), we then ought to believe that we clearly are the products of a powerful God. It was envisioned then that, because the universe is so complex, it had to have been literally created by an intelligent designer. It is now customary for religious propagators to update their creationist arguments under the label of the *"Argument from Design."* This Socratic philosophy influenced the creationist assumptions of the monotheistic religions in many ways. In the monotheist Christianity, this assumption was included by *Saint Thomas Aquinas (1225 – 1274 AD)* as the fifth claim in his *"Five Ways"* for "proving" the literal existence of God.

The non-creationist arguments of the Greek philosopher *Aristotle (384 – 322* BCE) in ancient Greece, does not reject creationism in its simple sense, but dismisses the literal cosmic "creator" who has physically created the universe and who maintains the natural order of our cosmos. For instance, the contemporary "Intelligent Design" religious movement in the USA has updated the creationist argument for an intelligent designer who has the power to intervene (suspend) in the natural order. The aim of the intelligent designer's intervention is the suspension of the Laws of Nature on behalf of the believers. This argument throws away the Bible "out of the tribal window" and tries subliminally to substitute its primitive beliefs with "theistic science" which seeks scientific confirmation of miraculous suspension of the Laws of Nature in the history of life of our cosmos.

These propagators do not recognise that the Laws of Nature guaranty only that stars and planets and biological life will emerge, not as primitive or intelligent life. Scientists support that modern science is atheistic, and contrasts any religious notion that supports theistic explanations for natural phenomena.

Even in ancient Greece the distinction between science and religion, was established in which science cannot be used to explain religious claims. To imaging a thing (God) into existence does not constitute evidence or can we assume that other peoples' imaginary mental experiences---which include dreams, illusions and hallucinations---actually exist. Mystical and other shamanistic experiences can be explained by esoteric forms. For agnostics, the intelligent design argument is built upon a faulty analogy as, unlike man-made objects, humans have not witnessed the design of the universe, so humans cannot possibly know whether the universe was the result of design.

I claim that this deist or agnostic "fence-sitting" analogy of intelligent design is faulty. How can this be demonstrated? How can we answer the agnostics' uncertainty whether or not nature is a product of an intelligent design? The Laws of Nature provide the basis of comparison by which we distinguish between a designed object and a natural object. Any comparison has to be based on the characteristics of a designed object which differs from natural characteristics. The religious claim that the natural world and its Laws of Nature were designed is an attempt to dismiss the fundamental base which differentiates the characteristics between man-made objects and natural objects. At the time of Charles Darwin, the Laws of Nature were treated as if they had a purpose which was absolutely central to the philosophical thinking in 1862. Darwin was so fascinated by the biological evidence of his findings that he was impelled to call the structure of organisms *"the metaphor of design"* which the religious propagators of "intelligent design" have misinterpreted to mean not a metaphorical but a "literal design."

The metaphor of "design" simply means that organisms, because of their complexity, give the appearance of having been designed. We now know that the Laws of Nature and Natural Selection theories impel biological scientists to routinely refer to the design of organisms and other characteristics with those terms. In other words, speaking of the apparent design to which the biologists refer to would properly be, *"as if"* designed. Simply put Natural Selection and Evolution processes selection and adaptation of life forms under its functionality of the biological world. It carries no meaning, morality, sentimentality and no purpose in a fundamental causative manner. The perception of purpose in biology is in its mimicking of such purpose; but upon closer inspection of its true function, the issue of "design" becomes questionable.

It is false to assume that Natural Selection and evolution of life on earth was adapted over millions of years with humanity in its center. In fact, since the formation of the planet earth, more than 95% of all life forms have gone extinct, and Natural Selection still continues unobstructed while it is unaware of our existence. Indeed, if anything, geological, biological and astronomical science confirms this point, the Laws of Nature of the Universe confirm, and the astronomical observation continues to demonstrate, that our planet earth is no more significant, within the millions of stars, than a single grain of salt in the salt mine. A human-centered universe is probably very appealing to religious faithful, but nothing in our advanced understanding of cosmology and Laws of Physics requires us to believe it. In fact, we have begun to understand the improbability of physical organisms and cosmological organisations that were created by a celestial design.

Darwinian rational scientists have successfully refuted the usual arguments that design is founded in the intricacy of biological life. They have convincingly established the fact that the complexities sufficient for life have over billions of years, from the primeval chemical stew, a pre-existing composition of particles and the Laws of Physics. In other words, life's DNA of every plant and animal on earth was assembled by a combination of chance and the Laws of Physics. Without the Laws of Chemistry and the Laws of Physics, as we have discovered them, life on earth would not have evolved in the span of 5 billion years. In the Laws of Physics, a nuclear force was necessary to bind protons and neutrons in the nuclei atoms; electromagnetism was necessary to bind atoms and molecules together; and gravitational force was necessary to keep the resulting chemical nutrients for supporting life, as part of the earth's land and water surface. These natural forces acted by allowing the formation of protons and neutrons in stable hydrogen and deuterium atoms. These atoms have been around for billions of years and, by joining together with protons, they produced chemical elements in stars.

Equally, gravity was necessary to gather together available atoms into stars and, by compressing the stellar cores by million of pounds per square inch, it raised the core temperatures by millions of degrees. This high degree of temperature caused a nuclear reaction, and the elements of the chemical Periodic Table were synthesised as the by-product. If gravity had not been weaker than electromagnetism, our earth would not have lived long enough to produce the elements of life. Only the fact that the gravitational force was many times much weaker prevented this (produce the elements of life) from happening. Is it not clear then that a celestial intelligent designer was not responsible for the activation of the natural forces which gave birth to our solar system?

Religious propagators of intelligent design submitted the so-called *anthropic coincidences* as evidence for a universe that was created with humans as the main objective. Many have made this claim publicly in debates before university students and in other forums about the existence of God. Within the various debates they stated that the great age of the universe is, in fact, a sign of God's plan for humanity which was needed to allow life to evolve. This indicates that they have accepted evolution, but that does not rationalise why it was humanity and not bears, antelopes or scavengers that was God's final objective. Furthermore, given the self-centered human inclination, convincing religious faithful that God designed the universe with the Jews, Christians or Muslims in mind, is as easy as convincing a child that sweet candies are good for their teeth!

We have additional scientific explaining to do about the Laws of Physics and the formation of the stars and planets, after we biologically explain how life evolved by Natural Selection on earth. Religious advocates are lacking the honesty and dignity to recognise that human life evolved naturally on earth with no outside interference, that the existence of stars and planets, quarks and electrons, and the very Laws of Nature themselves were never presented in the Bibles as evidence for intelligent design of the universe. The most common answer still given by religious propagators when asked to present evidence for intelligent design is that they reply to your *"question with a question"* of their own rather than present their evidence or rational answers. They reply, "How can the world around us happen by chance?" This is a "dead-end" question which the most brilliant exposition of the case of Natural Evolution would not answer. It is because the Laws of Nature do not work on the basis of human logic or arguments. Do you really believe that the very existence of the universe is determined by our thinking or believing process? Not at all! This is because the pre-existence of the Laws of Physics and values of physical and chemical constants had to be evidently in balance for life on earth to have evolved.

Science works on the basis of probabilities, not on dogma. For instance, if a scientific explanation or theory is proven wrong by the admission of new evidence, the old theory is discarded in whole or in part. Before addressing the question of how the Laws of Nature have come about, we need to provide a response to the arguments from probability. According to statistical theory, the probability for the universe existing with the Laws of Nature it has results in balance and unity. This balance and unity of its properties confirms the universe exists with 100% probability. On the other hand, a small probability exists that other universes may exist that support some kind of life. The degree of probabilities can be debated among cosmic scientists. The probability that one of our planets (Earth) in our universe supports life is 100% probable. Some cosmological theories propose a thesis that does not require more than one universe to exist. If such probability is possible then ours is the only universe; and that our universe happened by chance, we have no basis to conclude that it required a miracle for some form of life to exist.

When we are examining evidence for or against intelligent design, it must be understood that I'm following a customary practice of science. I'm seeking a scientific explanation about our universe that has for centuries been attributed to a theology of a celestial God. Fundamentalist believers will be calling you and me nasty names, such as "atheist," secularist," or worse, and will accuse us of undermining faith and morality. As with any scientific investigation, however, we must openly declare our commitment to the scientific process and confirm to ourselves and others that we will accept wherever the conclusion of that process may lead us. If that conclusion is verifiable evidence for the existence of a celestial intelligent design, then so be it! However, if we cannot find such conclusive evidence, then we must not feel compelled to soothe the sensitivities of believers. We should not lie to ourselves, or them, that the religious prejudices have a scientific merit. We must present our reasons and scientific evidences forcefully whenever anyone claims scientific knowledge for beliefs that clearly fail the objective test and methodology of science. We must emphasise to others the need to pursue these issues in an open, objective and rational manner, and we must count all possible ways of how life may have developed. We must question the religious claim which violates the Laws of Nature; in particular the Laws of Physics, that science requires a celestial miracle to produce a universe.

We still need to answer the question whether the Laws of Physics require the existence of an intelligent design? Did the order of the universe require a pre-existing intelligent design to do the ordering? Was there nothing before there was something? Can something be created out of nothing? Some of these questions are best left to theologians and religious philosophers to answer. I am just wondering if God is *something,* then, itself, must have come, uncreated from nothing, and I will leave it to theologians to explain how a creator God solves the problem of *"something from nothing."* In physical terms, creation ("something from nothing") violates the Laws of Thermodynamics.

The Laws of Thermodynamics requires the constant conservation of energy and that any change in energy level must be compensated by a corresponding inflow and outflow from the system itself. Here is an interesting point: if the universe started from "nothing" thermodynamic energy conservation would seem to have been violated by the creation of physical matter. However, cosmologists' best estimates today estimate that the total energy of the universe is zero. That is, within a small *zero point energy* that results from quantum fluctuation---with the *positive* energy of physical matter balanced by, it's opposite, is the *negative* energy of gravity. Therefore, since the total energy of the universe is zero, no energy was needed to produce the universe and the Law of Physics was not violated, because of the corresponding inflow and outflow of energy from the system. Our universe started out in a condition of maximum disorder---the Big Bang's total chaos. This means that the universe had no order at its earliest definable instant, and so, if there was a celestial creator, it had nothing to create! It is senseless, and one cannot ask, much less provide an answer to, "what was there before the Big Bang," since this can not be logically defined because the concept of "time" before the "Big Bang" is meaningless. You see, language is inadequate to define the mathematics of Einstein's relativity of time as the forth dimension of space-time, the speed of light, the co-ordinates of time and space that are inter-changeable, that is, the time which is intertwined with space and came into being at the instant of "when" or "where" space-time came into being. So where the order of the universe did did come from, if it did not exist at the "beginning" of the "Big Bang?"

Where did the Laws of Nature come from, if not from some pre-existing lawgiver? Cosmologists now are beginning to unravel how the Laws of Physics could have come about *naturally,* as the universe spontaneously exploded in the "Big Bang." For laymen like you and me, we first have to confront our prejudice that is built into the concept of the Laws of Nature. Throughout our religious history we have been taught the notion of God-given Laws of Nature. This notion has been deeply engraved in our "religiousness" thinking and by out cultural process of learning about the "Force," the "Supernatural Being" or the "mind of God." We must remember that our descriptions and prescriptions of our cosmos are expressed in human linguistics. As such, the concept of Laws of Nature is a logical expression and invention of humans by which we govern ourselves. They represent our imperfect attempt at a "short-cut" method of identifying, with a single term, complex observations we make with our senses and linguistic limitations. For instance, the identity-term "Laws of Nature" contains, within itself complex aspects of our universe-mechanics and structures, which we summarise and identify by a single term: *Laws of Nature*.

This is not to say that we subjectively determine how our universe works or behaves; in a chaos or in an orderly manner. There are a few religious scientists however, with subjective religiousness-thinking, who maintain intelligent design governs our universe. Most cosmologists and scientists do not deny that an objective, ordered universal reality exists, independent of our senses, linguistic abilities, personal beliefs, feelings and wishful thinking. We simply have to recognise that our logical linguistic concept of "Laws of Nature" may carry with it, certain illusional-baggage (metaphysical) that is tied to our traditional "religiousness" and pre-scientific thoughts.

Scientists are learning that several universal and profound Laws of Nature are, in fact, linguistic statements about the simplicity of nature which needs little explanation. For instance, the "Laws" of energy (momentum, and angular momentum conservation), simply reveal the homogeneity of space and time. The primary law of thermodynamics---conservation of energy---results from there being no unique moment in time. The Copernican principle that there is no preferred position in space simply reveals a conservation of energy. Our universe is a gallery of analogous assumptions of simplicity. A homogeneous universe is one with a high level of symmetry, in the simplest of all possible universes that did not happen by accident. In short, in our universe there are many existing conservation laws which need no explanation beyond the mathematical symbols used to represent their corresponding symmetry. Any deviation from the corresponding laws would represent a departure from simplicity and homogeneity. Other force laws and principles that give structure to the universe, appear as spontaneously broken symmetries, accidental, uncaused events that occurred in the first second of the "Big Bang" as the expanded universe cooled. Other, more complex and less universal, Laws of Physics codify what all human experience testifies, that people grow older, not younger and that the dead do not rise: i.e., cannot be miraculously resurrected. The various aspects of the Laws of Nature can be very difficult to explain and to understand by laymen at anything more than the minimal and descriptive level. Nevertheless, we should not leave the field of the Laws of Nature open to those who demonstrate their determination to propagate the false hypothesis of intelligent design with no commitment to scientific truth. We can question that creation of "something from nothing" violates the Laws of Physics by those who attempt to force their religious beliefs into our lives through the back door of "intelligent design."

There are many beliefs currently held that violate the basic age of earth, its geographical features, its life forms and the integrity of our universe. The earth, its life forms and the rest of the universe are believed by most Jews, Christians and Muslims to be about 6,000 years old or just about at the beginning Age of the Agricultural Revolution in ancient Mesopotamia. But Natural Evolution shows that our cosmos evolved over a period of 14.5 billion years, driven by undirected natural forces without any input from God or intelligent designer. Some even suggest that God may not have created life on earth, for it may have been some other super-intelligent life form---some species of extraterrestrial---who visited earth billions of years ago, set evolution in motion, and injected their own designs into various life forms. In Peru, South America, there are cultural beliefs that maintain that we all have come from outer space and that the *Nazca Lines* confirm such claims. In the city of Ica, Peru, there is the *Dr Javier Cabrera Museum* which perpetuates this idea (in *Ica Stones*), but the evidence presented is questionable.

Many past Christian theologians and philosophers appeared to have abandoned the Bible all together in support of the concept of intelligent designer, a notion that does not appear in any biblical writings. They include Mencius Felix, 3rd century, Basil the Great, 4th century, Moses Maimonides, 12th century and Thomas Aquinas, 13th century. This is an exhibition of extreme "intellectualism" taken by philosophers in support of purposive design in both physics and biology. By refusing to own the Biblical uttering of creation they are falling into their own linguistic trappings of extreme verbalism. If we add them altogether, then the probability is one: that of uncertainty about the Laws of Nature, Cosmic-Science and Charles Darwin's Natural Selection, Evolution and Adaptation.

Almost everything that distinguishes our knowledge of the universe from earliest centuries can be attributed to science, which achieved its most impressive level by successive pioneer scientists in the last 400 hundred years. In the 16th and 17th centuries, new conceptions of science profoundly influenced philosophy, methods and results in astronomy and physics and were tested by the traditional mental environment of the time. Centuries before, scientists were absorbed in the theology of the medieval world of the Italian Renaissance. The world of the pioneer scientists however, was still influenced by Socrates, Plato, Aristotle, Luther and Thomas Aquinas, and, above all, by Newton, Hume and Charles Darwin. It must be said however, that four great pioneer scientists, Copernicus, Kepler, Galileo and Newton were at the forefront in the creation of modern cosmological science. The early Polish astronomer *Copernicus (1473-1543)* was devoted to astronomy. He came to conclude that the Sun is at the centre of the universe, and that the Earth has a twofold motion; a diurnal rotation, and an annual revolution about the Sun. Fear of reprisal from the ecclesiastical censure led him to delay publication of his discovery but allowed his scientific views to become known. His book, *De Revolutionibus Orbium Coelestium* was finally published in the year of his death in 1543. This book escaped the official Catholic condemnation until the time of *Galileo Galilei* when the Roman Catholic Church became must less liberal towards scientists with the revival of the barbaric Inquisition.

Kepler *(1571-1630)*, was the first important astronomer after Copernicus to adopt the heliocentric theory and discover the three Laws of Planetary Motion. His first law states: the planets move in elliptic orbits, of which the Sun occupies one focus. The second law states: the line joining a planet to the Sun sweeps out equal areas in equal times. The third laws states: the square of the period of revolution of a planet is proportional to the cube of its average distance from the Sun. This means that the first and the second laws could be proven in the case of the planet Mars. The discovery of the third law, which all the astrologists agreed upon, states that all planetary motions are circular, or compounded of circular motions. Where circles were found doubtful for explaining planetary motions, epicycles were used, i.e., a curve traced by a point on a circle which rolls around another circle. For instance, imagine taking a cart-wheel and securing it flat on the ground. Then take a smaller cart-wheel (with a nail in its centre with its point touching the ground) and lay it also flat next to the larger wheel. Then roll the small cart-wheel round the big cart-wheel. The mark of the nail in the ground will trace out an epicycle. This shows that the moon's orbit, in relation to the Sun, is roughly of this sort; approximately, the Earth describes a circle round the Sun, and the moon meanwhile follows a circle round the Earth. This was an approximation of Kepler's observation of the inexact system of epicycles.

Galileo *(1564-1642)*, is the most notable of the founders of modern cosmic science, with the possible exception of Newton. There is something coincidental or "odd" about Galileo's birth, for he was born about the day the great artist Michelangelo died, and he died in the year in which Newton was born. Galileo is important as an astronomer, but above all, as a founder of dynamics, for he discovered the importance of *acceleration* in dynamics. The principle of "acceleration" means change in velocity, whether in magnitude or direction. This means that a cosmic body moving-uniformly in a circle has, at all times acceleration towards the centre of the circle.

Galileo was the first astronomer to identify the *Law of Falling Bodies*. This law, taking into consideration the concept of "acceleration," is of the utmost simplicity. It demonstrates that, when a body is in a freefall, its acceleration is constant and is the same for all bodies, heavy or light, large or small. Only the resistance of the air may interfere with its acceleration. What Galileo proved was that there are no significant differences between large and small bodies of the equal material. Before Galileo, it was assumed that a large piece of lead would fall much faster than a small one but he proved that this was not the case. Measurement in Galileo's time was not an accurate task but he did arrive at the true Laws of Failing Bodies. Centuries later and following Galileo's footsteps, Gustave Eiffel's experiments with aerodynamics led him to drop structural bodies from the Eiffel Tower in his experiments for measuring air and wind resistance. For part of my series of books, *The Eiffel Illustrated Exploration Series Vol. 8,* I had the good fortune, in 2014 to visit the *Eiffel's Aerodynamics Laboratory,* in Paris, France. I had the chance to view the well-preserved high drop-instruments used by the French structural engineer in 1912. Eiffel's experiments helped in the development of his wind-tunnels to test the aerodynamics of airplane wings, the road safety of motor-vehicles and the structural balance of sailboats. It was Galileo who introduced this immensely productive method, in-so-far as the resistance of air interference is concerned.

The *Laws of Inertia* explained a puzzle which Galileo was able to unravel in his quest for aerodynamics. This law states that if you drop a piece of lead from the top of a tower, it will fall at the foot of the tower. The puzzle lies with the earth's rotation, for the lead ought to have slipped away during the fall. But this does not happen. The reason being is that the lead retains the earth's velocity, before being dropped, as everything else on the earth's surface. However, if the lead was dropped from a much higher tower, there would be the opposite effect to that. This means that, since the top of the tower is further from the centre of the earth than the bottom (which is moving faster), the lead should fall slightly to the east of the foot of the tower.

It is a common knowledge that Galileo was condemned by the Roman Catholic Church's anti-scientific Inquisition, first in secrecy in 1616 and then publicly in 1633 and spent the rest of his life under house arrest. By this year the Inquisition in Italy had control over the State and thus was successful in putting a drastic end to science, which did not revive there for centuries. As such, Galileo was forced to recant his findings and promised never again to openly declare that the Earth rotates or revolves around the Sun. In countries which were following the Protestant dogma, however, as anxious as the clergy were to suppress and harm science, they were unable to gain control of the State. The Protestant Church's attempts failed to prevent scientists from adopting the heliocentric theory, resulting in considerable damage to the Church's reputation by exposing its idiocy.

Newton *(1642-1727)*, achieved a complete scientific triumph based on the groundbreaking preparations already set by Copernicus, Kepler and Galileo during their life times. Starting from the three *Laws of Motion*; (of which the first two were due to Galileo), he proved that every planet, at every moment, has acceleration towards the Sun, which varies in according to the distance from the Sun. Following the same formula of acceleration, it explains the moon's motion and the failing bodies on the Earth's surface which is again related to the moon's according motion. Based on the *Laws of Acceleration,* Newton was able to discover the *Law of Universal Gravitation:* which states that *"Every body attracts every other with a force directly proportional to the product of their masses and inversely proportional to the square of the distance between them."* From this formula he was able to deduce the motions of the planets and their moons, the orbits of comets, the sea level tides and even the minute deviations from elliptical orbits of planets.

These scientists were remarkable, not only in astronomy and dynamics, but in many other areas connected with science. In the area of scientific instruments, the telescope was invented in 1608 by Lippershey, but it was Galileo who made serious use of it for scientific reasons. It is probable that Galileo invented the thermometer; his student Torricelli invented the barometer and other instruments were greatly improved, largely by the work of Galileo. Due to those inventions, future scientific research became far more exact and extensive to include sciences other than astronomy and dynamics.

Gilbert *(1540-1603),* did his research on magnets, and *Harvey (1578-1657),* discovered the circulation of the blood. *Leeuwenhoek (1532-1723),* discovered spermatozoa or unicellular organisms, as well as bacteria. *Robert Boyle (1627-1691),* is regarded as the "father of chemistry" who discovered that in any given quantity of gas at a given temperature, pressure is inversely proportional to volume. The advances in pure mathematics were great indeed and indispensable to the work in the physical sciences. Co-ordinated geometry resulted from the combined work of several 17th century mathematicians including *Descartes*. The differential and integral calculus, invented by Newton and Leibniz, is the core-instrument for almost all higher mathematics. Formulas were used in Newton's book, *Principia* in 1687, which made it possible to calculate the orbits of certain comets; that they were obedient as the planets to the Laws of Gravitation. Although these are the most notable theoretical achievements in pure mathematics, there were still innumerable others of great importance. The reign of the Laws of Nature had established its hold on the scientists' curiosity and imagination, surpassing the populist notion of magic and sorcery. In fact, the mental outlook of these innovative scientists was completely modern, living and functioning among the few who were still largely medieval. The first thing to note is the removal of the philosophical beliefs of animism and spiritualism and of the man-made mythology of the astrological Zodiac Signs and Calendar from Astronomical Science and the Laws of Physics.

The ancient Greeks considered the power of movement a sign of life. Living matter such as man and animals move themselves, while dead matter could only move when impelled by an external force. The energy of a living matter, in Aristotle's thought, had various functions, and one of them was the movement of the living body. As for the rest of the world, Aristotle's various "external forces" or "movers" were all divine or theistic spirits, and were the ultimate source of all the movement of the bodies in the heavens. As such, any animated body would soon become motionless; thus the operation of the spirit on matter had to be continuous if motion is not to cease. Aristotle's spiritualism was dismissed by the first Law of Motion which states that lifeless matter, once set moving, will continue to move forever unless stopped by some "external force."

It is true that science and religious beliefs, at times, were a mixed bag of facts and religiousness, but eventually, things that resulted from science created a profound change in the perception of man's place in the universe. In the medieval beliefs, the earth was the centre of the heavens and everything that had a purpose was concerned with man. In Newton's perception, the earth was a minor planet, not an especially distinguished star. In comparison to the universe's vast distances, the earth was a mere pin-point. For Newton, the planets were originally hurled by the God's hand, and once this was done, the *Laws of Gravitation* kicked in, and from then everything went on its own without further need of divine intervention. Although most of the 16th and 17th century's men of science were models of religious piety, the Creator's existence was doubtful and it was not clear that the world had a beginning in time. Such an outlook, suggested that the scientists' work and wonderings were disturbing the Church's orthodoxy and the theologians were quite justified in feeling uncomfortable. There were many who still believed in the glory of God, but no one could let such beliefs intervene in an astronomical calculation. The world might still have a purpose, but purposes could no longer be part of the scientists' explanations.

The triumphs of science revived human pride in its ability of seeing the natural cosmos as it is. The dying ancient tribal philosophies had been obsessed with the sense of sin, hell and fire; characteristics of the oppressive Middle Ages. To be humble before the Sky-God was prudent, for God would always punish human pride by floods and tsunamis, earthquakes and forest fires, invaders and crusaders, comets and diseases. It was widely propagated by the Church that only by being greater and greater in humility before God, could humanity avert God's threatening calamities. But it became near impossible for men of science to remain humble since they were achieving such scientific triumphs. Even amongst them, they still shared a comfortable wishful thinking that surely, the almighty Creator of such a vast universe had something better to do and think of than sending proud scientists to hell and fire for minute theological discrepancies.

There were, however, many other reasons for the men of science and the scientific-minded to be self-satisfied for creating a culture of knowledge. The world had ceased to be a menace. Comets had been humbled by the giant Halley, and the earthquakes, although they were frightening events, were still such interesting phenomena that seismologists and geologists could hardly ignore them. When all was said and done, these added triumphs of science convinced the scientists that they were prominent members of society, and not the miserable sinners that some still proclaimed themselves to be in Sundays' sermons.

There are some concepts in use in modern theoretical physics that differ from those used in the 16th and 17th centuries. For instance, the concept of "force," which was subliminally related to theistic power, has now been found to be superfluous. According to Newton, the "Force" was the cause of change in motion, whether in magnitude or in direction. The force was conceived as a sort of sense that we experience when we push or pull an item across the floor. For this reason, the force was considered an objection to gravitation; that it acted from a distance, and that there must be some independent medium by which the force was transmitted. This notion of "independent-medium" transmitting force added nothing more than a subliminal theistic intermediacy between acceleration and configuration. Since the Newtonian times, modern scientists have discovered that planets have, at all times, acceleration towards the Sun, which varies due to points of distances from it. The modern scientists merely state the calculative formulae which determine acceleration and distances without the need to use the term "force" all together. With no pun intended, the "Force" in Newton's time, was the faint ghost of a theistic view of the causes of motion. Eventually, and very gradually, this ghost has been exorcised.

The essential purport of the first two Laws of Motion is that the Laws of Dynamics are to be stated in terms of accelerations of the orbits of the "heavenly" bodies. This means that the Laws of Motion in this form (orbits of bodies) could not be more than an approximate; that planets do not move across the sky in exact ellipses. This is because of the interference caused by the manifestations of other planets. In fact, for the same reason, the orbit of a planet is never exactly repeated. During Newton's time, the Laws of Gravitation, which dealt with accelerations, were very simple and was thought to be quite exact, and this miscalculation lasted until it was amended by Einstein. This still remains as a Law dealing with accelerations.

Finally, in this brief article, we have seen that the period of history which is described as "modern" has a progressive outlook which differs from the medieval period in a number of ways. Two issues however, stand as the most important in the western world: a) the notable declining authority of religious institutions, and b) the ever increasing authority and prominent social position of science and scientists. On the social level, our culture in contemporary times is more humanist or non-theist, than clerical. In society as a whole, its governmental and NGO institutions have increasingly replaced the Church as the dominant authority that controls education and culture.

For centuries, mentally ill or disabled persons were regarded as living under God's curse, and I wished that everything could have been explained in another way according to the Laws of Nature. We have seen why the Laws of Nature are so powerful. For instance, the game of football (or soccer) is governed by two sets of laws 1) it is the man-made rules such as penalties, goals, off-side, the size of the field or the ball, which all players must obey, and that can be changed only when the governing body decides, and 2) the other set of laws that apply to the game are fixed, immutable, and they govern what happens to the ball once it is kicked. The force and angle of the foot-strike determines exactly what happens to the ball. The Laws of Nature are a description of how things actually work in the past, present and future. In soccer, it shows exactly where the ball would go and there are other laws that work simultaneously and they govern everything that it is going on in the field, from the energy that the kick has produced in the player's muscle, to the rate that the grass grows beneath the players' feet. But what is really important is that these physical laws, as well as being unchangeable, are also universal. These laws apply not just to the fly of the ball, but to the motion of single or multiple planets and everything else in the universe. Unlike laws made by humans, the Laws of Nature can never be broken or temporarily suspended, and this is the reason they are so powerful but, from the religious point of view, very controversial too.

The rejection of the Churches' authority, which is the negative characteristic towards it, began long before the ecclesiastical authorities enjoyed the positive characteristic. This negativism was translated as the acceptance of scientific authority in the modern sense. The first serious surge of science was the publication of the Copernican theory in 1543 which was later improved by Kepler and Galileo in the 17th century. It was then that the long fight between science and religious dogma began, in which Church traditionalists and their alliances fought a losing battle against new knowledge. The legitimate authority of science is very different from the Church's authority since it is intellectual, not governmental. No penalties of Hell and Fire were imposed upon those who challenged it; no moralistic arguments influenced those who accepted it. This scientific authority did not, like the Church's authority, describe and prescribe a complete system covering human morality, human hopes, and the past and future history of the universe.

So far, we have presented the *theoretical science*, which is a proposal to understand the world of *practical science* which, in turn, is an attempt to *change* the world, sometimes for the betterment and other times for the determent of men. The practical importance of science was first recognised in connection with war Galileo and *Leonardo da Vinci (1452 – 1519)* were contracted by the central government based on their claimed ability to improve artillery and the structural engineering of fortification. From that time onwards the involvement of men of science in war industry has steadily grown greater. The scientists' part in developing new medicine, machinery for industry and agriculture, first use of steam and electricity, computers and communication technology came much later, and began to have a political importance near the end of the 20th century. The Industrial Revolution developed the science of metallurgy and steam engines which, in turn, implemented its findings in the development of railroad machinery, and better structural buildings such as bridges, viaducts and rail tracks. The new steel railway system and marine navigation transported agricultural goods, mining raw material and people which, in turn, expanded the horizons for exploration of new markets.

Emancipation from the oppressive authority of the Church led to the growth of individualism, sometimes even to the point of anarchy. Discipline, intellectual, moral and political, was associated with personal choices, not with dictatorial religious or puritanical philosophy. The freedom from mental shackles led to the astonishing display of genius in art and literature. Meanwhile, practical science as technique was building up in practical men a quite different outlook from any that was to be found among theoretical scientists. Practical science conferred a sense of power; man is now much less at the mercy of the Church than he was in former times. But the power conferred by practical science and technique is social, not individual. Scientific technology requires the co-operation of a large number of individuals organised under a single direction. Its tendency is against anarchism and individualism, since it demands a well-knit social structure. Unlike religion, practical science is ethically neutral; it assures scientists that they can perform wonders, but does not tell them what wonders to perform. In this way it is always transient, and the purposes to which scientific knowledge will be directed it depends largely on chance.

THE LAWS OF NATURE CANNOT BE VIOLATED

THE LAWS OF NATURE

NATURAL LAW

NATURAL:
Inherent; having a basis in Nature, Reality and Truth; not made or caused by humankind.

LAW:
An existing condition which is binding and immutable (cannot be changed).

You cannot hide from the laws of Nature

— Menander

COPERNICUS
MODERN COSMOLOGY

MODERN COSMOLOGY

"Accordingly, since nothing prevents the earth from moving, I suggest that we should now consider also whether several motions suit it, so that it can be regarded as one of the planets. For, it is not the center of all the revolutions."

Nicolaus Copernicus

ISAAC NEWTON

FATHER OF ATHEISM

ARISTOTLE (384 – 322 BCE)

- Plato's student
- Contribution: origin of laws came not from gods, but from the laws of nature
- Believed that justice should aspire to equality
- True meaning of law is through human reasoning—guided by observations
- **Rationalism**: observation and human reasoning

Aristotle (384-322 BC)

"THE ORGANIC MATERIAL, AS THE LAWS OF CHEMISTRY STATE, CAN NEITHER BE CREATED NOR DESTROYED."

LAWS OF CHEMISTRY

LAW OF CONSERVATION OF MASS	LAW OF CONSTANT COMPOSITION / LAW OF DEFINITE PROPORTION
LAW OF MULTIPLE PROPORTION	LAW OF RECIPROCAL PROPORTION

LAWS OF CHEMICAL COMBINATIONS

Law of Definite Composition

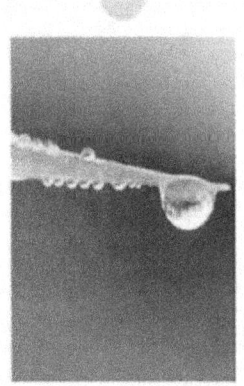  

A drop of water, a glass of water, and a lake of water all contain hydrogen and oxygen in the same percent by mass.

NATURE OF THE UNIVERSE

There is no justice in the laws of nature, no term for fairness in the equations of motion. The Universe is neither evil, nor good, it simply does not care. The stars don't care, or the Sun, or the sky. But they don't have to! WE care! There IS light in the world, and it is US!

— Eliezer Yudkowsky —

SELF-PRESERVATION IS THE FIRST LAW OF NATURE.

Samuel Butler
English Author
1835-1902

KEPLER'S PLANETARY LAWS

KEPLER'S 1st LAW

All planets orbit the sun in elliptical paths with the sun at one focus.

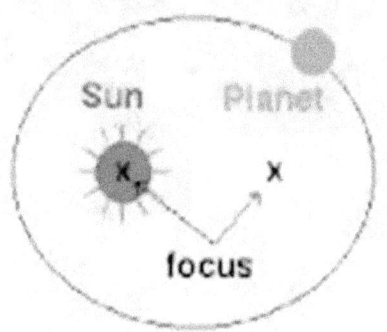

KEPLER'S 2nd LAW

A planet sweeps out an equal area of space in an equal amount of time.

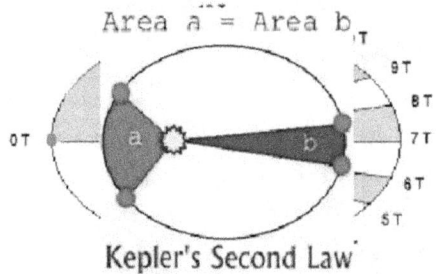

Kepler's Second Law

T = any unit of time (hour, day, week, etc.)

LAW OF AERODYNAMICS

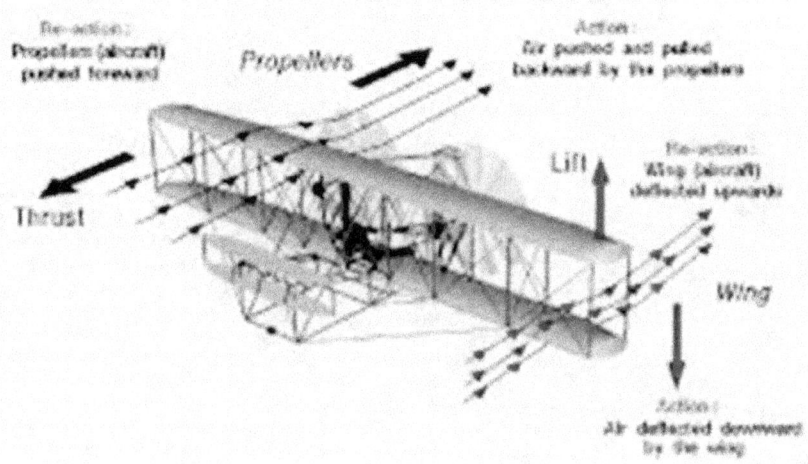

Kepler's laws of Planetary Motion

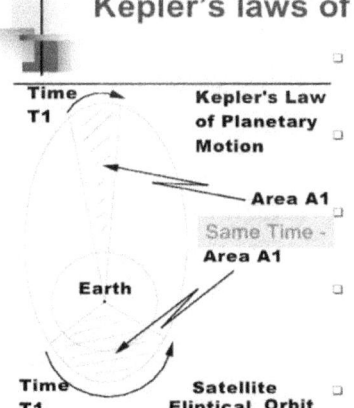

- In the early 17th century, Kepler discovered the three laws of planetary motion:
- The orbits of the planets have the same physics as earth satellites.
- 1. The law of orbits: Planets move in elliptical orbits with the Sun at one of the foci.
- 2. The law of areas: the line from the Sun to a planet sweeps out equal areas in equal times.
- 3. The law of periods: The square of the period is proportional to the cube of the ellipse's major axis.

101

LAW OF PLANETARY MOTION

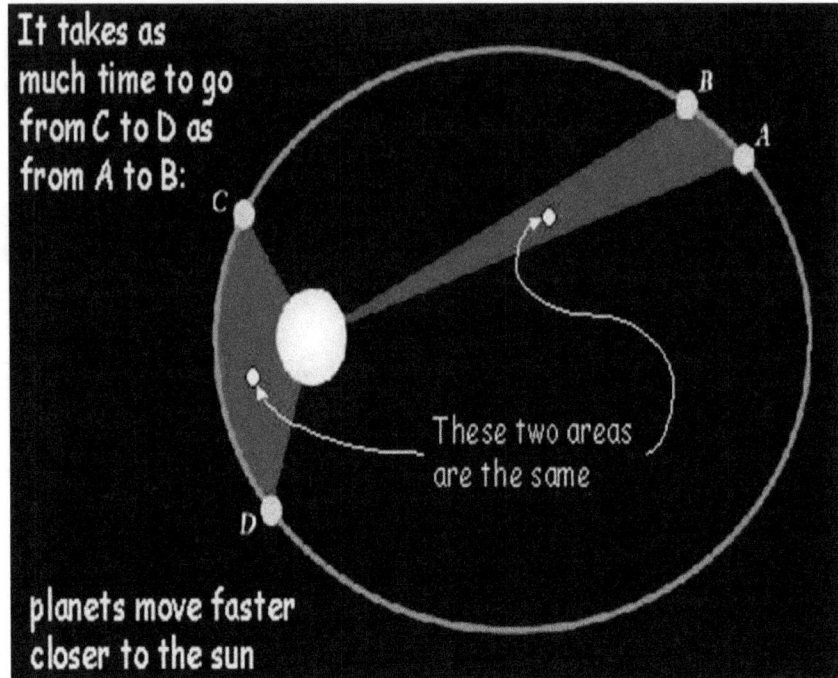

LAWS OF ECOLOGY

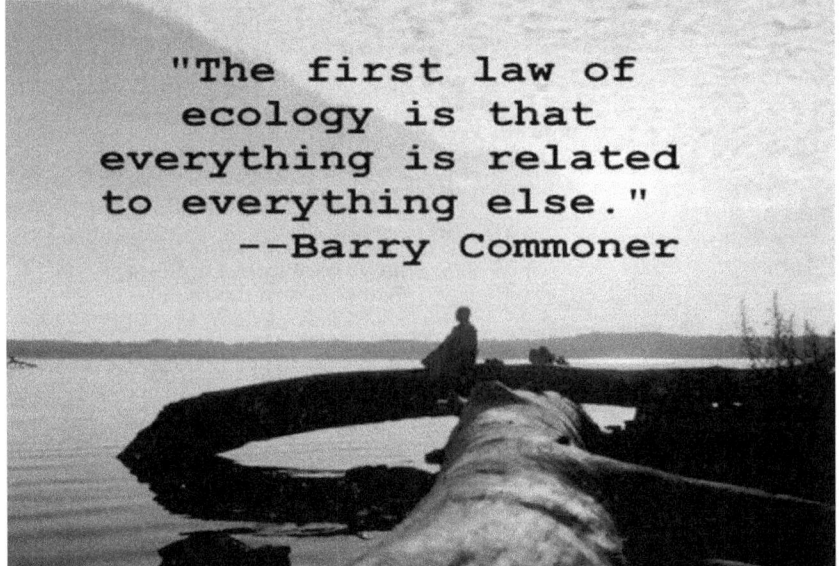

FATHER OF NATURAL EVOLUTION

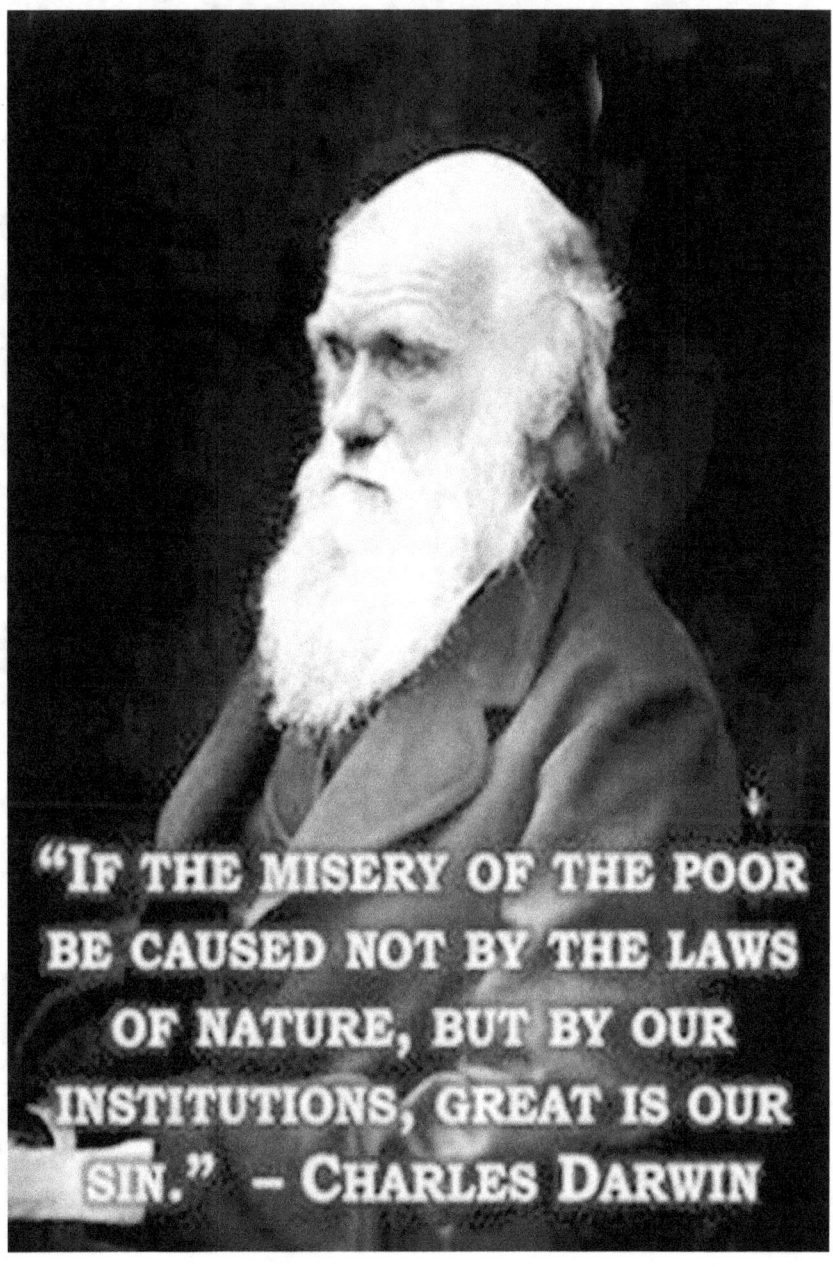

EVOLUTION
NOT BY GOD'S DESIGN

Let us begin with the question of *"What is Evolution?"* Simply put, evolution is the gradual biological change, a change in groups of living things, including humans, over time, and a continual process that connects all forms of life on Earth to one another. It is a Darwinian definition called evolution which is a "descent with modification" from a common ancestor. Darwin discovered that the evolution of living species has been occurring, without a preference of one over another, for billions of years. This natural occurring process of living things is responsible for the dazzling diversity of life on Earth, including the billions of extinct species. This is a biological fact, based on the mechanisms of constant evolutionary change, such as Mutation and Natural Selection, which biologists pursued to theorising, studying and explaining.

In scientific terms, "theorising" means the most logical, best-tested, and best-substantiated evaluation of an observed phenomenon. For instance, the Theory of Evolution by Natural Selection explains how all living things—man, plants, animals, microbes—change over time. As such, the scientific theory, in whatever field of science, is also predictive—it can tell what is likely to happen. But we must be careful here, for a scientific theory is different from a scientific hypothesis. Hypothesis is a scientific "concept" that has yet to be fully tested and verified.

At the beginning, 3.5 billion years ago, the shape of life on earth was a single cell and, as life formed, the fist primitive animals emerged. The shapes these live forms took were, in large part determined by whether they would live or die. Body shape makes an animal what it is, how it influences and interacts and adapts with its environment; the way it interacts with other organisms and with its own species. Adapting to its environment may involve speed or mimicking the shape and forms of other organisms to avoid been attacked. Successful defence mechanisms have to evolve so other predators are discouraged from pursuing them. Fish and sea life creatures may instantly change their appearances to blend with their immediate environment and land animals may have adopted fur-colours to avoid detection from predators. All these have to do with survival of the species which includes Adaptation and Natural Selection.

Let us begin with the basic question: what is Nature and Natural Selection? Natural Selection selects animal breeding; what kind of animals will survive and what kind of animals will be extinct. How Nature does selects? In a cruellest way! True enough, most of the world is cultivated and controlled by humans, but there are still vast areas where nature is still in full control. I have lived in the Amazon Rainforest of South America for a number of years and have seen the animal world at its natural ways (see *The Amazon Illustrated Exploration Series*). It is, undoubtedly one of the wildest places in the world where the dominant Natural Selection can be witnessed.

As night folds, the animal world becomes active on the principle of "kill or be killed." It is a cruel and predatory world and the total amount of life suffering in a single night is immeasurable and beyond contemplation. Animals are taken apart and eaten alive by other animals whose teeth are sinking into their flesh. Thousands of animals are dying from starvation or disease or feeling a parasite devouring their flesh from within. There is no dominant central authority and no safety-net for the small or weak animals; for most of them life is 'nasty, brutish and short', to use Thomas Hobbes' terms. Food shortage and disease, among other factors, controls the animal population. The more animals produce offspring, the more struggle for survival they encounter. It is simple a matter of economics, a struggle for resources.

Nature is an arena of permanent pressure and, in each case, the chance for animal survival and perpetuation is small and most animals die young. What are the odds that are the change for survival are not just by chance? All species vary, even if only slightly and stay alive either because of sharper teeth, of running faster than its prey, or because of camouflage or better eyesight and sense of smell. These tiny variations in each animal are a crucial key to their chances of survival. When and if an animal survives, it tends to pass its variations to its offspring which, in turn, also may survive and reproduce. Nature's struggle for survival means that animals without their helpful variations tend not to reproduce. Their lives' destiny is survival and the finishing line is reproduction. This process is the core essence of Natural Selection and the key to Evolution.

Most of us who live in a civilised world, natural selection appear orderly and harmonious and the brutal reality of nature is somewhere "out there." But daily Natural Selection is scrutinising every living animal variation, even the most minuscule; and in all geographical areas of the world. As such, Natural Selection rejects that which is unfit and preserves that which is fit to survive and reproduce. We in the cities see nothing of this slow process until we visit the "wild" in close range.

Mammals like the Human species originally evolved through hundreds of variations of chimpanzees, apes, humanoids and anthropoids; all in the struggle to survive, from their beginning of some 125 million years ago.

Our body form, once established, never changed but shared similarities in bone structures with other mammals: the structure of the neck, the head on top, the backbone, arms and legs (or 4 legs) and all with unique or even bizarre variations. Longer necks help to feed from taller trees, thinner skins for warmer climates and, as such, life forms become specialised. Gradually, very gradually, as successful variations are inherited, Natural Selection scalps life into different shapes and better adaptation to the environment of their immediate surroundings. This process is called the Origins of Species.

Natural Evolution continues and species are adapting in their environment by the presence of other species. In the Amazon Rainforest, the cougars are finding it harder to hunt because the animals are getting better at escaping the cougars' claws. The cougars therefore are adapting to hunt on land and river-shore fishing when they have no other choices. Camouflaging to escape being hunted and venomous stings is all part of the strategy of defence mechanism for survival. This is the silent war of nature.

Human beings are not immune from the silent war of nature. We are at perpetual war against viruses that cause diseases and epidemics, most of which are lethal. This is an advanced stage of engineering of life, in unexpected places on the war of nature, which is been fought in all of the most inhospitable environments of the world. In some African countries such as, Kenya, Uganda and Malawi the spread of AIDS is in epidemic proportions, especially in cities' slums with large numbers of sex workers. Hundreds of sex workers have died from AIDS complications, yet there are some sex workers who are immune to AIDS virus, even though they are practicing unprotected sex. Those immune sex workers believe that God is on their side or they are simply lucky to have avoided catching the AIDS disease. The fact is that neither God's work, nor Luck, has anything to do with their immune system. The odd of survival nears the level of impossibility for these sex workers to still be alive. Something else is at work! Medical evidence shows that strong genes that were passed on from past generations strengthen their chances for survival, and those with weaker genes simply die of the disease. The survivors will transmit their strong genes of resistance to their descendants so future epidemics of HIV will not affect them. Africa's HIV epidemic will force Natural Selection and favour women with genetic resistance to the disease. In short, this is the unstoppable power of Natural Selection; confirmed and absorbed by modern medical and biological science.

Natural Evolution theories of the mid 19th century explained how the diversity of life on earth evolved spontaneously without the support or interference from any Sky-God. Natural Evolution evidence, however, went directly contrary to Biblical myths and superstitions invented by tribes of the Arabian Peninsula some 4,000 years before Charles Darwin's theory of the *Origins of Species by Means of Natural Selection* (or *the Preservation of Favoured Races in the Struggle for Life*). It also went against the historical institutional power and influence of the clergy, the land oligarchs, the political elites, the military brass, and any delusional story of "intelligent design" later invented and adopted by creationists.

The *Origins of Species 1859* publication made it possible for the rest of humanity to read about the natural laws that explain life itself; and that alone, with evidence to support the claims made, has turned our world back on its feet. It is now possible that we no longer feel the necessity to believe in the existence of anything supernatural or any celestial entity. We became free to choose the truth, and completely revolutionise the way we view ourselves, our material world and our biological origins. Based on that understanding, in the early 20th century, scientists and evolutionists discovered the relationship between genes and cells. Genes, being a long string of code in the cells for all living things, are passed on in their entirety to the next generation of offspring. This means that when animals reproduce, their genes are copied and put in the sperm or eggs for a task applied to them by natural selection. The genes of every cell, of every living thing, can be counted and measured that make up the DNA. The decoding of the human DNA in the year 2000 has provided scientists, and the entire humanity, with more solid evidence of Natural Selection than Charles Darwin could ever have imagined. All living organisms in the entire planet Earth are closely or distantly related to one another; from monkeys to cabbage to lions and eagles. What is so fascinating about DNA is that it turned biology into a computer science where we can see the similarities and differences between living organisms or their common ancestor. Thus, evolution through Natural Selection has been, without a doubt, a triumphed proven fact. In legal case is closed or is it?

Religious people are accustomed to living their lives on the basis of entrapping themselves in the subjective notion of "belief." It is either you "believe" in something or you don't "believe" in something. The objective and verifiable truth is irrelevant! This emotional entrapment of "believe" is so strong and so deeply felt that it blinds them and prevents them from broadening their scope of knowledge in most areas of life. The question of Evolution by Natural Selection vs. Biblical Creation is supported or rejected by arguments based on "believes." It is either you "believe" in Evolution or "believe" what the Bible says about Creation. In a worst case, you may "believe" in Evolution (or part of it) and also "believe" in the Bible's delusion that God created the world. **Verifiable** truth and evidence, fossil discoveries, biological explorations, DNA gene prognostics and reason are not enough to overcome the dreadful state of mind some people live with. Escaping from freedom (to use Erich Fromm's term) and submitting themselves under the delusion of a "believe" denotes their human intelligence. The industry of religion is there to provide them with as many "believes" their hearts desire, because it also needs their donations and perpetual support. As for the rest of us, we hope that one day the religious people will see the elegant reality of life, of plants, birds, insects and humans that were entangled and evolved in the grandeur of life. Let us also hope that they'll be brave enough to ask questions about what they were brought up to believe and be inspired by a life without God. There were, in ancient epoch's people who believed that God created the cosmos; in an orderly and harmonious way, rewarding good behaviour and punishing bad deeds, and at times when God behaved in mysterious ways, it was because humans could not interpret God's intentions. You see, if we could reason with the religious believers, there would be no religion!

Lucky for us, Charles Darwin's Theory of Evolution by Natural Selection drove a wedge into such primitive, misleading, comfortable and delusional mythology about creation. Darwin's theory brought us a harsh and disturbing truth; that humans are part of the Natural Selection, and do not have dominion over other animals, over nature and over the sky above us. We originate from anthropoids: we are the 5th Ape!

What does it mean for humans to be evolved; with our sense of morality and understanding of the meaning of right and wrong? We must defend our humanist ethics at all cost, because the industry of religion has attacked Natural Selection and viciously accuses Evolution of being barbaric; that atheists want to live in a primitive State of Nature. This is further from the truth, for we want to educate our children of the ways nature really is, rather than how it can be metaphorically. The pitiless wars in nature, the struggle for survival, and the human civilization may share some similarities, but those similarities are separated from our civil and liberal values, ethics and morality. In the corporate world, cut-throat competition and the survival of the fittest may be similar to the struggle for survival in nature; but that is because humans neither are nor are developed, as yet, to the highest level of harmonious co-operation for the utilisation of natural resources. So let us dare to look at the deep and dark site of Natural Selection and the hopes for humanity.

As for the similarities, we know that Natural Selection is the driving force of our evolution, but this does not mean that civil society ought to run based on the set of principles governing Natural Selection. Evolution by Natural Selection is a system by which, for hundreds of thousands of years, in a struggle for existence, successful variations of species were adaptable to have survived to reproduce. This resulted in life forms which became specialised such as the giraffes or the apes, the orangutans, gorillas, chimps and the humans. Visiting Africa, the Amazon Rainforest, or any zoo, you see an unmistakable truth, that we share human variations with these apes. This would confirm that all life on earth is related and that the African ape variations are our closest evolutionary relatives.

Africa is the birth place of the human species, and Kenya is where it all started, sometimes between 5 and 6 million years ago. Natural Selection took place when a common ancestor's offspring followed two separate lines of evolution; one leading to present day chimpanzees and the other to the human race. This ape-like, mutual grand ancestor was neither a chimpanzee nor human. During hundreds of thousands of generations, Natural Selection selected 60 to 70 humanoid or anthropoid species that eventually became extinct. Fossil records chart the extraordinary life journey of our human ancestors; by the gradual variation in the growth of their cranium size and by their evolutionary struggle for survival. About a million years ago, all other cranium variations of humanoids or anthropoids gave way to a largest size cranium of the human species. It was Natural Selection (not Adam and Eve) which carved out the evolutionary chart to the rise of the human species. As a result, *genus Homo* is the upright walking apes with the big brains that out- thought the competitions from other anthropoids and survived to tell the story.

Yet, religious people are horrified about what natural evolution reviles of our origins; the idea that we are related, far cousins of present day chimpanzees and that our ancestors were not Adam and Eve. It is a challenging of what this tells us of the implications of such delusional beliefs on human society. They cannot comprehend that humans are apes in according to our biological origins as species. It horrifies them to believe that God had nothing to do with the rise of the human species, for if they confirm evolution through evidence, this will destroy their belief in God.

It is however important for us to investigate the dark side of Natural Selection and to investigate what is means to have evolved in nature's brutal struggle for survival. We are the 5th Ape, in the lines of closely related extinct apes who we competed with for survival, and solidified our own human origins. But apes have only occupied a brief moment in the origins and evolution of life forms. For instance, sharks have been on earth for more than 300 million years, as well as other forms of life. We are amongst the hundreds of thousands of other life forms that appeared and went extinct; all part of Natural Selection. It is a religious delusion to believe that we have dominion over other life forms, which was biblical definition of what it meant to be human. We had only to shine the light of science over to confirm the origins and history of man.

Natural Selection is a life's journey not a destination to arrive to; it does not have goals to accomplish, nor does it have grand schemes of morality or purpose to teach us. It never had and it never will, for it function as a continuing biological process; timeless, spiritless and irrevocable. It is a harsh, unguided process which favours those that can pass on their genes to the next generation. Human beings have no dominion over Natural Selection for we are no more than just another of its products.

Archaeological cranium evidence of humanoids, in the process of becoming human, was discovered in Kenya, and estimated to be 2 to 3 million years old. Its cranium size and body size is much smaller than ours; a kind of chimpanzee on hind legs, who was on its first step to becoming a human. This cranium named the *"Torcana Boy,"* was our common linear ancestor but was neither a chimpanzee nor human. He is our common linear ancestor (our cousin) between us and the chimpanzees. We humans are the African Apes, originated from humble biological beginnings, which survived, procreated and spread across the world. How lucky humans are to have survived against all the odds of the pitiless wars in nature. Natural Selection's principle of *"survive or be extinct"* was monitoring our every challenge and tribulation. This is the *state of nature,* where only the fittest and the most adaptable survive and the rest perish. This is, in fact, the dark side of Natural Selection, but it is not morally-vicious, it is not vindictive and it is not capricious. It is simply selective and supporting of those species that are able to adapt to such ruthless competition in such a state of nature. You see, it is not the most intelligent; it is not the strongest but the most adaptable species that survives. The sooner we realise this, the sooner we humans will get off our pedestals and recognised that we are part of the animal world that Charles Darwin discovered we belong to. So what does this mean for contemporary man and his society? First, we must understand what this brutal glory of the state of nature really is! Is it a kind of state of nature in harmony with itself? Is it there to favour and to serve man in his peculiar ways? The short answer is no, because we humans are one of the many players living and competing within this state of nature. There is no God or Gods to guide us to a better understanding of the cosmos around us! We are here to serve our own selfish-gene interest, and so are others selfish organisms working for their own survival.

When living in the Amazon Rainforest, I was fascinated by the high trees that form the *"Canopy of the World"* as I wrote in my children books the *Amazon Illustrated Exploration Series*. The upper part of these huge trees is dense; very little sunlight passes through to reach the ground. Yet this canopy supports a diversity of life, from monkeys, birds, spiders and varieties of plants and trees. Most of these animals living in the upper canopy have never set foot on the ground. There is plenty of sunlight and rain for all that share the upper space of the jungle. Plant seeds germinate in the canopy and produce flowers that other species pollinated. As such, plants and trees are struggling to get to the sunlight and all varieties of life forms are exploiting each other to survive.

As you are walking on the ground under the canopy and looking at the wonders of nature, you may notice that there is a choking-fig plant that crawls around a huge tree trunk. The top of this plant is already in the canopy where the sunlight and water temporarily supports it. The plant's seed was germinated in the upper canopy and, as it started growing, it began its long journey to reach the ground, looking for nutrients. As it was descending, it continued to wrap around the big tree-trunk. When its roots finally reach the ground, it now has the strength and nutrients to survive by wrapping itself around the big tree trunk for support. Natural Selection's brutal struggle for survival takes place before your eyes and the end result is the eventual strangling death of the big tree and the survival of the choking plant. This brutal struggle of evolution is the driving force for survival of all life forms which exist in the state of nature. Knowing this truth, we must not unleash the worst of human nature on each other, on the environment or on knowledge of ethics and morality.

If the state of nature has evolved the way it has, does this mean that human society has to follow the brutal examples set by Natural Selection? Does this mean that the entire world's poor or disadvantaged must perish, that all the sick and handicapped people must be left to their luck? Would this create a natural selection among us in a form of *Social Darwinism,* where the economically and politically strong will survive at the expense of the middle or lower classes?

The truth is that there is an area within our social structure where an intense competition exists, and where most of us regard as natural, acceptable or even indispensible: the corporate world of cut-throat business practices. The social effects of such practices have dripped downwards and have changed our social contract status of citizenship into corporate-entities who function under the directorship of the corporations. Most of us have become *registered* corporate-*entities* by holding membership cards of cash-rewards, discounts, reward-points, credit-card holders, frequent-user rewards, air-mile rewards, gold-card holders for hotels and airlines; all part of their business schemes built to entrap us as their exclusive corporate-entity of rampant consumerism. Certain corporate businesses such as the Oil and Energy Multinationals, Banks and Financial Institutions, Insurances and Mortgage and the IMF have recognised that they are part of Social Darwinism; that the strong must survive and the weak must perish: *Thatcherism* or neo-liberals. This unrestrained capitalism is justified and is denying the rights of the poor and the weak citizens of our society. This corporate behaviour is even practised between rich and poor nations: where the poor receive huge loans that they cannot repay, and thus are forced into a perpetual *Austerity* against social programs, while their own corporations become stronger, more profitable, and people's hunger and suffering more evident. The old oil, auto and rubber barons of the early 20th century were not at all ashamed for been Social Darwinists: the oil tycoon Rockefeller in 1912 said *"I thank God for giving me my money."* They believed and still believe that business should model after nature; of the brutal jungle scrimmage for survival, competing one against the other with the aim of eliminating the competitor. This is their sense of humanity's progress as competing corporate apes, under Social Darwinism.

Other forms of Social Darwinism that applied to human affairs were the attempt to control the base of evolution, by accelerating the process of elimination of the weak among us. This accelerating process of elimination was institutionalised in the early 20th century under the infamous *Eugenics* program. The Eugenics of Social Darwinism in the many parts of the world attempted to control evolution by sterilising the poor in the Third World, in Nazi Germany and by the Imperialist powers of the times. This was the base of scientific racism; where doctors in Fascist countries sterilized women and where the Imperial powers of Britain and others exterminated millions of Africans and Chinese under variety of Eugenics programs. Once, I happened to be visiting the South China coastal province of Whampoa where the British colonial power was controlling the population by poisoning the water-wells resulting in the deaths of tens of thousands of innocent people. The racist ideology of the time was that African Blacks and Third World poor were fallow brothers; they were also regarded as lesser brothers that needed to be eugenically controlled. In such a hierarchical order the white man was on top and the ethnic weak man at the bottom of the scale of Social Darwinism. The aim was simply to stop the weak from procreating and multiplying through the compulsory sterilisation and murder of anyone who was classified as unfit to live. In Nazi Germany, millions were exterminated under the horrific Eugenics program. But it is wrong to blame the Charles Darwin Theory of Natural Selection for the atrocities committed under the false version of Darwinism. Neither Hitler's genocide nor the Bosnian and Rwanda war criminals of the 1990's, nor the *British Eugenics Society of 1937* were Darwinists. Eugenics under any version is not Natural Selection! Ethnic cleansing or the barbaric elimination of the weak is not Darwinism. Darwin exclaimed that nature is the breeder and in control of Natural Selection, not men's dark, tribal, barbaric and racist ideology of Eugenics. There is a great injustice done to the name of the scientist who discovered the Origins of Species.

We are, however, attempting to control natural selection in other spheres of life: from genetic engineering of pigeons to beautification of flowers, increase the strength and long lasting quality of agricultural products and human gene-cells to cataloguing the human DNA among others. Anything to improve man's quality of life, and provide better health service to millions of Third World peoples is a welcome site. Natural Selection, I am confident, will let us know if we went too far in our own controlling desire in the natural selection process. So far, no virus epidemic was ever caused by medical procedures or experimentations under controlled environments. The criminal offence of chemical warfare should be focused on the war industrial complex and far right-wing politics where profits, not humans, are placed first. When you look around you, can you see the obvious paradox that the existing social co-operation, kindness to each other, and even morality, could have ever evolved from the mindless brutality of the state of nature?

In the state of nature, evolution of life on earth has been driven by brutal struggle for existence. Yet one can also witness signs of kindness among members of the animal world. Monkeys are grooming each other, a baby elephant is protected by the whole group of elephants, a warning sound is given when a predator approaches near non-predatory animals, a mother carries her cubs to a safer den and stands alert, or an adult hunter teaches cubs the art of hunting for survival and a female gives milk to another's cub, a vicious crocodile carries her tiny baby crocodiles in its jaws to a safer place for cuddling for warmth and comfort. A mother that just loses her cub to a predator may remain standing there for hours waiting for her baby cub to return.

These animals may also display acts of altruism by giving something to another without expecting rewards in return. Why would these animals display such acts and manners of kindness? The question is, how did altruism was evolve in the animal world, which includes the human species? Were there instincts which formulated the animals' instinctual behaviour, that were part of the dynamic strategy of survival of the group? Was the evolutionary growth of the brain (with all its manifestations, to recognise kindness, danger, help or negotiating acts of behaviour, guilt or sexual lust), developed by Natural Selection instinct value for survival? The physical world that we lived in (not religion) has triggered emotions in us, such as, moral acts of trust and sympathy, love and caring, phobias and gratitude. Fear has an evolutionary basis as a defence mechanism, and our moral emotions can be analysed the same way, as being part of our defence mechanism to support the survival of our group.

We do, in fact, have a natural evolved sense of morality, which is inherited in our genes, for preserving and perpetuating our existence. We do things for others without regards to ourselves or at our cost. In such cases the individual aim for survival does not appear to be the sole reason. Sexual selection of partners of the opposite sex selectively breeds; this prevails which members of the species would survive, and who will prevail in winning the sexual favours of the opposite sex. This means that there are twofold ways for an individual to pass his genes to the next generation; first to survive and second to be sexually attractive to the opposite sex. We do anything possible to attract the attention of the opposite sex, sometimes even at our expense, by competing with others. We are constantly trying to make ourselves attractive; show our unique personal qualities and physical attributes. Bodily attributes are the mobile advertising-board of neon-sign which sends messages to the potential opposite sexual partner. Natural Selection therefore combines survival and passing the genes to the next generation. Women are more prone to selective breeding by looking at potential partners of the opposite sex to give them the "right-kind" of children that their male partner projects. Natural Selection through sperm-bank donors; at least in the developing world, may sound like another form of consumerism; are giving women the choice they are seeking for the next generation of gene carriers. It is a high-tech Sexual Selection of attractive, intelligent and kind males to impregnate females and to pass on those genes attributes to their children. Of course, and without a doubt, this is another form of Eugenics, where choice of specific selective breeding is advanced by artificial means of science and consumerism.

As familiar as it may sound, how animals (including humans) evolved to become altruistic; the science of genetics could provide answers to the wonderings of altruism. We now know that genes are coded instructions that build every living thing on earth, including the human brain and its functions (the mind). These genes give rise to the family traits, down through the generations; of your kind of height, colour of hair and eyes and other visible attributes. As such, all living things are survival entities whose core goal is the perpetuation of their genes under Natural Selection. As vehicles of our genes that are part of us, we are discarded once we have completed our innate task of passing on the next generation of coded genes through reproduction with our opposite sex. This is a natural process repeated for millions of years and will continue into the next survival age. Our presiding generations become immortal through Natural Selection, each generation slightly different than the previous one, some better equipped to run, better physical strength or with even bigger brains and higher intelligence.

There has been a whole misinterpretation of the concept of the "survival of the fittest." It simply means the survival of the fittest genes, the kind of gene that looks after its own interest, for otherwise it would not survive. This is the self-interest gene, preoccupied with its own survival, in competition but not necessarily against other organisms (although exceptions exist). In order for this self-interest gene organism to be accepted by other self-interest gene organisms it must behave in a socially acceptable manner, a kindness in an altruistic way, in order to form a social bond with others. Altruistic behaviours of friendship, social co-operation, mutual assistance and gratitude do not diminish our self-interest for survival. That is the meaning of the phrase the "survival of the fittest" by means of adaptation, not by means of hostility towards others. In the aim of preserving ourselves, we are seeking to co-operate with others who will provide us with the kind of self-serving social support of a civil society, or in animal group solidarity of kinship in the state of nature. The self-interest gene organism, such as man or animals, builds group kinship of family, which is an all-inclusive entity that provides support, perpetuation of genes, caring, friendship, acts of altruism, protection and offspring as vehicles to gene immortality. We see altruism in parenthood when the parent jumps into the river to save the child or where a parent feeds the child first before herself.

In reciprocal altruism exist in the cases where the old saying applies *"you scratch my back; I'll scratch your back."* In the snow-belts in Canada, a neighbour who has a snow removal machine will remove the snow from their neighbour's driveway and, in return, this neighbour will reciprocate the favour by cutting the other's grass and cleaning away leaves in the summer. We see acts of reciprocal altruism also with chimpanzees in groups where they groom each other by returning the favours. Humans are also known to have sacrificed themselves for others, or in austerity, to share food with extended family members, and with others, such as the Syrian refugees arriving in the Greek islands, which may or may not be able to pay back the favour. The self-interest gene organism (or the Selfish gene as Richard Dawkins calls it) gives rise to altruistic individuals who will survive because they are nice to others and others to them. In the strong desire for selfish individualism of the *"me-me"* generation does reciprocal altruism work!

In the state of nature we see the intense competition for survival amongst animals and humans living in it. In developing countries we see the ruthless "dog eat dog" lifestyle striving for success, while we also see people be kind and decent to each other. Why is this apparent social contradiction so evident? Is it because it is in our own best self-interest to also be reciprocal altruistic individuals as a means of survival? Is this a good enough genetic reason behind altruistic kindness? In the state of nature, of the Amazon Rainforest, we see monkey's exhibit empathy and moral concern that goes beyond the *"tit for tat"* altruism of *"you scratch my back and I'll scratch yours."* For instance, in a fight between two monkeys, the one who loses receives hugs and grooming from his peers as a consolation for his defeat! African apes and chimpanzees exhibit similar acts of empathy and moral concern as the monkeys do in the Amazon Rainforest of South America.

It is not my intention to romanticise nature, but it has so much altruism in it, that humans should imitate it. We are an inseparable part of that nature, with genetic instructions for moral behaviour, ethics and empathy towards others.

In nature, however, there are two *"complimentary-opposites"* (and variations of them) that are mutually inter-related. Some of these complimentary-opposites are more profound than others because of their physicality, and others, based on humanist adaptation, vary with time, geography and social norms. For instance, we see Night and Day, Light and Darkness, Man and Woman which are more profound "complimentary-opposites" because of their direct physicality to nature; as well as Cold and Hot, Wet and Dry, and so on. This reality has existed for billions of years which also include their own variations of it, such as, not-too wet, not-too dry, not-too cold and not-too hot. Even in the profound "complimentary-opposites" there is an impregnation of given precedence on each opposite because; in the reality of the Natural World nothing exists in its absolute. Complimentary-opposites (CO) are life's equilibrium; a kind of balance that tilts on one side and again on its opposite side. For instance, we organise our daily lives during the Day and re-organise it during the Night. We behave in according to the CO's equilibrium (scale) of either day or night. When the day-scale tilts we behave one way and when the night-scale tilts we behave in another way. The variation of CO's exists in between the day and night scale, until the balance or equilibrium is completed in one or the opposite side. Needless to say, such profound complimentary-opposites are not aware of the effects they imprint on our lives, and have no directive intentions to govern our lives. It is simply the magnificent functions of our universe.

A man and a woman are also profound complimentary-opposites each has its own biological functions as per Natural Selection as part and parcel of the Origin of Species. As male and female organisms, do both exist in their absolute? Are there variations within them? Of course, they have such variations, for each organism carries within a degree of precedence of the opposite sex in their hormones, in their DNA and in their psychological make up. It is not an exaggeration to point out that even Natural Selection does not exist in the absolute, for there are variations in the human organisms that are nature's mistakes rather than intentional manifestations; for example Intersex is a female with male genitals, chromosomes and gonads that does not allow a person to be distinctly identified as male or female. In the animal world, however, hermaphrodite organisms have both reproductive organs and this is a normal biological condition. Natural Selection and the State of Nature manifest conditions under the Laws of Nature where all living things behave according to their own make-up. All contain their own complimentary-opposites (a sort of Yin and Yang) and variations of them. The question on variations now is, can a person (any one of us) be Good and Bad, Moral and Immoral, Giving and Taking; each with its own variation of Goodness and Badness, Morality and Immorality?

Throughout our human history philosophers tackled the question of morality in humans. There is valued presentation in support of one or the other complimentary-opposite. In my book, *Prisoners of Our Ideals*, I go deeper in explaining the concept of complimentary-opposites. In the USA political and corporate leaders identified with Darwinian Natural Selection; where the "survival of the fittest" prevails and the weak perish in order to justify their own "Social Darwinism" inequalities. Accordingly, man is brutal by nature and therefore it is within his nature to be competitive, selfish and predatory towards one another. In the so called capitalist societies, the upper dominant classes have no doubt of the social validity of Social Darwinism. Their support of Social Darwinism gives them the comforts of life as entitlements given to them by Darwin's Natural Selection. They see or ignore the suffering of the disadvantaged, the poor and the non-predatory classes as being a natural state of nature and ignored it. Competition is the name of the game; from the little guy to the big guys, all competing for the bigger slice of the pie. It is simply built in our genes, so they claim, to be predatory, to survive in the "dog eats dog" world.

The complimentary-opposite argument, mainly supported by the left-wing, is that Man is good by nature but he is turned bad by social conditions or by natural circumstances as in the animal world. But is this enough to explain the kindness of humans we see all around us or even in chimpanzees in Africa or in the monkeys in the Amazon Rainforest of South America? Is this a mere veneer, glossed over to hide man's true nature of nastiness, that we are not inherited-kind but we are kind to make a good impression to others? However, human empathy is proven to be genetically part of us. Human empathy is not a variation of *Good or Bad* in us, for empathy is a profound, self-promoting, evolutional gene and variations are simply circumstantial elements surrounding human empathy. Expressions of human empathy in India may be offering a bowl of rice to the poor, but in Greece or in Canada it may be offering money to a poor person to purchase his own food. Those acts are circumstantial variations but the human empathy remains intact in its core value of altruism.

The best argument in support of human kindness, empathy and altruism goes beyond the limitations of closed kinship set by Natural Selection. We live in villages, towns, cities and mega-cities where the genetic root of our empathy and altruism is very much alive. When it comes to humanity, something special is happening, for we went beyond kinship empathy in a scale-up world. We live in large, anonymous, populations of strangers, not with familiar kinship of our genes, but among people who will not reciprocate our altruism. Still, we see acts of kindness to help others in distress, an internal ancestral urge of consolation to others. Most of us no longer live in small groups of kinship extended family and we have adapted living among strangers, but our ancestral, hard-wired self-promoting gene guides us towards self-preservation projected onto our fellow human beings. This is the human antidote to the darkness of Social Darwinism. By being kind to others, by showing empathy and acting altruistically, we help and strengthen ourselves to survive in this dog eats dog world. Sometimes we find the strength to extract ourselves from the nastiness of the state of nature and to rise above our brutal origins and live by our recently acquired civilised humanist values. Other times we fail, for this is the complimentary-opposite that leads us to wars, genocide and designed Eugenics. We should also remember that we humans are the only species who were able to escape from the brutal force of the Natural Selection that created us. It was us who, *without religion,* amassed the strength to free ourselves and did so by the force of our genes for kindness, empathy and altruism.

As such, we humans are on our perpetual guard to eliminate the process of elimination, for we build social cushions for the disadvantaged, for the mentally ill and for those who made the wrong choices in their lives. We provide medical care by skilful practitioners, public defenders against governmental and police abuse, community kitchens for those who cannot feed and take care of themselves, and social left-wing activists and human-rights guardians for all of us. We can see the best of our humanist altruism; not in high-class glamorous Hollywood settings, but in the cities' poor neighbourhoods, in the home-shelters for the down-on-their-luck people, and in the re-training schools of our nations. We care for the most vulnerable of our society by exhibiting the best among the pinnacles of our human civilisation. A society running on autocratic, ruthless Social Darwinian principles will be a cruel place to live for both the comfortable and the less. Natural Selection gives us big enough brains to empathise, to imagine ways for eliminating the ruthless state of nature, and to create a much gentle society for all to live.

We are in control and purpose of our lives, for Natural Evolution has no purpose and benevolence, no planning, no morality or empathy, no goodness or evilness, no theism or deism and not the slightest sense of altruism. However, we are not alone, for we have each other, about 6 billion human-others on earth, with hundreds of thousands of villages, town, cities and mega-cities where each one of us can find kindness, empathy, comradeship, kinship, friendship, personal and institutional help, love, sex, entertainment and create innovative altruism to help others in agricultural, technical or social projects. We have to take care of the productivity of our environment near us and in the far places; the lakes, rivers and the corals of the seas. We are at the point of understanding that our self-promoting gene has built communities of kinship with others who share similar self-promoted genes. In short, we can tame the barbarity of Natural Selection and of the state of nature, because our evolved brains empower us to rebel against such brutal force. So let's grow up and be brave and take care of our only home we will ever know; for us and for our future generations to come.

Let us now turn our attention on those who deny Natural Evolution in the name of the industry of their religion.

They are denying Charles Darwin *Origins of Species* with elaborate schemes of delusional beliefs. They are ignorant of the knowledge that the theory of Natural Selection has turned our attention towards discovering the unwavering truth of the reality of our cosmos. Biological science, since 1859, has proven that Natural Evolution is true, along with subsequent discoveries of cosmological evidence of the age of our planet Earth which is about 4.5 billion years. The irony is that those who have the skills and the mental capacity to build their religious industry must also be capable of seeing the proven fallacies they are spreading to their followers. So why do they falsely believe that the earth is 6,000 years old and that Natural Evolution does not exist? Why are they so firmly against the biological evidence of our genetic make up and denying, through dubious arguments, the proven facts? What are they afraid of by not telling the truth?

When I was a boy I realised that while my mother was very religious my father; been a seasoned socialist partisan of WWII, was an adamant atheist. At home, my mother made sure that I prayed before dinner, before going to bed, attended catechism (religious classes) every Saturday and went to church mass every Sunday. In school, there was daily one hour of religious studies of every chapter and verse of the Old Testament. I learned all about the biblical wars and genocide, the rape of women, slavery and God's commands, human sacrifices and the slaughtering of innocent children. I believed that all such events did happen and were justified because this was God's will. My brother, Anastasios and I were submerged in these totalitarian beliefs, and not once were we encouraged to question God's orders or claims. My father never interfered with my tiresome schedule and not once ever taught me about the fallacies of religion. Of course, at that stage of my life, I also didn't know how to ask my father the right questions about religion. Then, at the age of twelve, I came across a book by the German philosopher, *Friedrich Nietzsche (1844 – 1900) 'Thus Spoke Zarathustra"* whose hero, Zarathustra, declared that *"God is Dead."* To this very moment, I still remember vividly the jolt that I felt as I read this simple phrase. I also remember asking my self---*how someone dare can say that god is dead! How can it be possible for God to die?* For days upon days, I struggled to find logic and reason about the justification of such a declaration. When I ask my father if god is dead; and over my mother's objections, he took me for a long walk and slowly and without malice my father explained to me the fallacies of religion, and Evolution by Natural Selection. After many questions and long walks, I finally understood the meaning of being a humanist and an atheist! I became an atheist then, and I remained so all my life, and gradually I became an anti-theist! And I have my father to thank for it! My brother, however, still remains a devoted Christian to this day. He was not lucky enough to escape from religion! The mental illness of religion is so imbedded in him that he is too afraid to live without its delusions.

Charles Darwin's 1859 publication on the *Origins of Species* caused such a shock to the public that brought about the overdue schism between science and religion. Darwin's Theory of Evolution by Natural Selection is the most profound, provocative, controversial and far-reaching visionary idea in human history. Darwin's ideas were not based on philosophical or theistic arguments, speculations and oratory skills. In simple terms he explained Natural Selection based on biological evidence, recorded fossil samples and hundreds of confirmed investigations performed by other scientists in field excavations from around the world. Biological and related sciences have now the necessary evidence to prove that evolution is true. Scientific evidence is more than a collection of fossils and logical claims of truth. No one can claim the existence of absolute truth, and that is the base of all science. Scientific-truth is a claim which has so much proven evidence to support it, that it would be mere idiocy to deny it. Just like it would be an idiocy to deny that the earth is round that diseases are caused by bacteria, or to deny that the Sun would raise the next day. Darwin's argument for the validity of Natural Selection is a supreme achievement of the human intellect, more so than algebra or calculus because it shows us where we came from. It is a human need to ask, who are we? Where do we come from? How do we get here? Why do we look the way we do?

The story of our human evolution is just a small chapter within a much larger story: the evolution of all living things. Evolution shows us that we are much more connected with the rest of the world that we could ever have imagined, and with the rest of the animal life. We can recognise our connection to our closest relative, the apes, but, when we know how to look, we can also find it in other land and sea mammals, birds, reptiles, even in insects. The more biological scientists dig in fields, the more we see that everything in life has evolved from a single starting point. You see, the '*Tree of Life*' has been branching for more than 4 billion years. We now have the means to follow its branches back to its original roots. We look back on Earthly time and find certain 'sign-posts,' certain key events, the great transformations that led to evolutionary steps for biological changes.

In the history of our planet great transformations have opened the door for new ways of life and new forms of lives. You see, 50 million years ago, certain land mammals evolved to sea creatures like the Orca or Killer-Whales and, long before that, fish grew legs and colonised the land. Whales are the largest living animals and like humans, Whales and Dolphins took their present forms relatively recently. Whales are so different that it is difficult for biologists to compare them to other living things and thus Whales remain by themselves as a branch of mammal evolution.

At the dawn of animal life itself the first skeletons appeared and these wrote a few chapters in the life-story: our story. Part of discovering life on Earth, is to understand each chapter. By understanding each different chapter we can begin to see unity of life, the common history of all life on earth. Great transformations are part of the hundreds of thousand of years of human history, but, compared to the age of earth, we humans have just arrived in the 'neighbourhood.' You see, 95% of Earth's 4.5 billion years was occupied by bacteria or single-cell organisms. As such, all animal life appeared on Earth in the last 5% of that time, and all of human history appeared in less than 1% of Earth's time. We came quite late on the 'circle-dance' of life, yet we have been shaped by the same geological and biological atheist-forces that helped shape all life on Earth.

To understand how we fit-in we must look back before our own origins and see how other life-forms were evolved. Mammals appeared on Earth about 200 million years ago. Land mammals like humans, elephants and lions, for instance, are warm-blooded and give birth to living young and they breathe air. These characteristics are all forms of adaptations for mammals living on land. But Whales and Dolphins are mammals too, yet they live in the sea. They are mammals that live in the water and they give birth to living offspring and they breathe air. But we know that mammals evolved on land, so it is a real puzzle how whales originally evolved. To understand how that happened, we will begin to understand how the great leap of biological transformations took shape and begin to solve their mystery. Whales have very large and complicated brains, like humans do, and, in that sense they are our alter-egos; they live in the sea, we live on land; they dominate the sea while we dominate the land. How did whales get to the sea from the land?

The answer lies in the fossils of primitive land mammals found in Pakistan during a 1978 geological excavation. A bone fossil of a skull was found that geologists could identify as being similar to the skull shape of the wolf. It contained a distinctive walnut-size bone structure, which is part of an animal's inner ear, which shape could only be found in the ear of the Killer-Whale. The question is what is the ear of a whale doing in the skull structure of an animal that resembles the wolf? Biologists wondered what was the missing link? This was one of the first fossil evidence ever found about one of Darwin's daring claims: that whales have evolved from land mammals. To confirm this claim, biologists needed to find more fossils, ones that would demonstrate the whale's transitional forms. But, since political violence broke out in Pakistan, biologists had to look somewhere else: in the Sahara Desert of Africa.

The Sahara Desert is one of the driest places on earth, but 40 million years ago things were quite different. The Mediterranean coast was further inland from where it is today in a place called the Valley of the Whales. Scattered across this barren place geologists found heaps of fossil whale bones, some big vertebrae dated 40 million years old. Geologists believe that this specific area was naturally protected and this is why so many whale bones were concentrated in one spot. Some even suggest that the *Basilosaurus* whales came to this protected lagoon to die or came to give birth to their young. Now if whales evolved from land mammals, they did so long before these Basilosaurus whales existed.

Digging further, geologists discovered an amazing find, whales that had legs, a characteristic which the Basilosaurus had, but modern whales have long lost. The discovered complete set of leg bones was small but unmistakable with a knee cap and even toes. It was concluded that whales were once four legged animals and, over millions of years, the front legs became fins, their bodies lost fur and familiar lines of shape, they lost their nostrils on top of the head, as whales adapted to breathing in water. Whales and Dolphins may look like fist but they do not swim like fish. Fish swim by flexing their spine from side to side like sharks. But whales, dolphins and otters and other sea mammals swim by undulating their spine up and down. This undulation of the spine is in the same way that all four-legged land mammals like dogs and horses use their spines when running. Since these discoveries, the list of transitional whales has grown. This evidence is in line with Darwin's insistence that the evidence of Natural Evolution is all around us. You see, Natural Evolution does not invent new things. Rather Evolution is tinkering with all sea and land living things by using the 'old' to create the 'new.' It does this every time with every animal group during its evolutionary history, if we choose to look for it.

Land animals were also products of much earlier transformation. Hundreds of million of years ago there were no animals on land because all our ancestors lived in water. At some historical time, life shifted from water to land. It was the moment when fish crawled out of the water and on to land. If the animals had not made the transition, you and I would not be here today. It is important therefore to understand how, when, and possibly where, that transformation took place. The first life forms to leave the water really started something. Their descendants eventually evolved into today's reptiles, birds and mammals. The common ancestry of the mammalian creatures is still identifiable in their bodily structure even today. Just like humans they all have bodies with four limbs or four legs.

I refuse to sympathise with the shock religious people must have felt when they were told in 1859 that it was Evolution and Natural Selection, not God, that was responsible for life's existence on earth. I do not seek the establishment of an atheist utopia or an atheist kingdom on earth. I do not seek the abolition of spirits or personal spiritualism, for these illusions or self-delusions alleviate peoples' anxieties (like simulated but otherwise medically ineffectual medicine i.e., placebo). So is drug use which makes drug users momentarily 'happy' but how damaging are those drugs to them? I often wonder how it is possible for the clergy and the commercial peddlers of religious delusions to lie to children for profit. My task as a writer is not to turn away from the delusions of religion or refuse to question religion. Whatever my "weaknesses" are in understanding believers they are based on two undertakings which are not difficult to carried out a) my refusal to lie of what I know about religion, and b) my resistance to the Churches' theistic oppression of believers.

Fundamentalists are denying Charles Darwin's Theory of Evolution by claiming that it is just another theory and because it is a theory, other theories are just as good as the theory of evolution. This is not so, for a scientific-theory of evolution is more than a hypothesis; for it is a coherent group of scientific propositions that explain facts about life on earth. Medical theories about the evolution of diseases are about knowing the facts that generate such diseases and at what point bacteria are transmitted from one person to another or from animals to humans.

Furthermore, for every scientific theory and evolutionary dispute over evidence, which may or may not be conclusive but were investigated under intellectual honesty, there is no further agenda beyond the validity of the facts presented. There is always a dispute amongst evolutional scientists, for they do not take things on faith. In the Theory of Evolution there is no dogma and no stone-tablets, for scientists go where evidence leads them with impartiality, even handiness and objectivity, to search for the truth and not at all in support of religious interest. For a scientist, in whatever field of science, objectivity means that, when uncomfortable evidence of truth arises that contradicts his claims; he is obligated to retract them in order to meet the objectivity he so rigorously seeks.

You see, wrongness in scientific proclamations or in philosophy of social facts is something we all secretly or openly dread. But we all understand that we are fallible and we leave little or no room for being wrong. For a genuine scientist or a social thinker however, realising that he could be wrong can be devastating, but proven wrong by your own peers often feels identical to being right. For instance, this is a narrative about an elder statement and visiting professor of the Zoology Department at Oxford; who for years taught his students that the *Golgi Apparatus* in the interior of cells was not real. That is, until a visiting American cell biologist presented in-class convincing evidence that the *Golgi Apparatus* was real. At the end of the lecture, the old professor strode in front of the class, shook the American by the hand and said, with complete sincerity, *"My dear fellow, I wish to thank you. I have been wrong these fifteen years."* *Golgi Apparatus* gathers simple molecules and combines them to make more complex molecules, which either stores them or sends them out of the cells.

So, the Darwinian "theory" of Evolution is many things; primarily that a) evolution happens and it gradually evolves, b) that genetics of population evolve over long periods of time, c) that one species splits into two or more species---branching from a common ancestor, d) that all species on earth are linked to a common DNA ancestor---all the 9 million large or small species on earth, and e) that most evolutionary change was caused by a natural selection process which, in turn, produced adaptation.

The Darwinian Theory of Evolution shows that simple forms of detectable traces of life originated on Earth hundreds of millions of years ago (3.6 billion); and, at some point in the evolutionary process, more complex forms appeared. The fossilised evidence we see more recently closely resembles the ancestors of the life forms that existed further in the distant past. During the evolutionary process within lineages and when those lineages happen to split and then evidence can be traced showing the gradual changes in the fossil of the branched species. In museums of natural history, such as, the Smithsonian Museum and others, often we can see lineages divided into two or more in the fossilized marine records, and traced common ancestors in those fossils. Land fossils of animals in Western North America reveal the evolution of horses---reduction of toes to a single toe---from twenty five million years ago to present, by tracing gradual evolutionary changes to the modern horse. Some lineages which happened to split were discovered long before modern science, in that, the reptiles which lay eggs and birds which also lay eggs share structural commonalities, which evolution split into separate species. As such, scientists are able to find transitional forms that connect modern life groups to their common ancestors. This is the so called "missing-link" that creationists insist that evolution does not have and therefore they wave their bibles as proof of creationism.

They do this because they are ignorant of the evolutional requirements of the "link." In the evolution of reptiles to birds, for instance, you are not required to show the "link" but you are required to show that three hundred million years ago there were only reptiles (but no birds), and that there exist fossils of early birds, or ancestors of early birds, with reptilian characteristics and other similarities i.e., in their circulatory system and egg-laying. In fact, there have been a number of fossil discoveries of half-reptilian and half-bird such as, the *Sinornithosaurus miltenni* discovered in China in 1980's with an estimated age of about 125 million years; after dinosaurs were existence but not birds. These fossils were from feathered-reptiles with bird-head characteristics but reptile bodies and feet; the kind you see in the *Jurassic Park* movie.

In human embryology, the unborn babies are hairy at about the age of six months and then the hair falls off before you are born. This is understandable because we are evolved from hairy apes, but we are born naked of hair because we evolved into humans. One must note that the gene-hair does not just disappear with evolution but it simply fades away with time, while still partially doing what it is supposed to do, grow bodily hair. So the hair-gene does no longer fully function as it was originally intended to function because it has been mutated. You see, Natural Selection and Evolution does not have clear cut-off links from one stage of evolution to the next because evolution is a continual process, not a "stop-and-start" again function. The creationists are asking for false-link requirements to support their dubious biblical myths of creation.

So why can religious people not accept natural evolution? The evidence for evolution is convincing; they admit this much, but they themselves are not convinced. Why someone will find the evidence of evolution convincing, but yet not be convinced, is beyond clear comprehension. But let us try! There is an internal struggle in the minds of religious people between the psychic comforts of believing in creation vs. dealing with the reality of the material truth of evolution which is devoid of any artificial psychic comfort zone. Based on these peoples' psychic need, the industry of religious enterprise is now offering "intelligent design," claiming that evolution was created by an intelligent being which is God. With this, now we have a pathetic religiosity mixed with linguisms of "science" to create a new God not of primitive biblical origins, but a God who is scientifically educated, who engineered life, and who is now called "intelligent designer." The Bible, of course, has no reference to God as an intelligent-designer of creation; it contains no reference to any structural design of animal or human organs, for God's reference to life on earth is only magical. This is a newly invented concept supported by a linguistic term; as in "theistic-evolution" which is a self contradictory or self-negated term, for it is either Natural Evolution or it is Biblical Genesis. Have creationists abandoned the cruel, tribal, Arabian Peninsula, primitive roots of their religion?

The cause for refusing to recognise Natural Evolution is called: Religion. Why there is a strong opposition to Evolution in the USA and not in any North European country, is because the industry of religion is quite powerful in the US. Creationists have the money, the legal and political power, to try to impose their creationist agenda on society, and they do so in a number of cases. In a legal case brought by creationists as reported in the Pennsylvania newspaper, *The Patriot-News* in 2008, a Judge ruled that Intelligent Design was "NOT SCIENCE" on the front page. Without exaggerating, every creationist is also deeply religious, and every religious person is also a creationist. They do not believe in evolution because it contravenes the Bible or the Qur'an. It is not that religious people are not aware of the evidence of evolution, or that they are idiotic. They simply prefer a belief system they are taught to follow since childhood, rather than reality. This affects their views on the origins of our species and that we are not the special objects of creation. It is repulsive to them to think that we used to be hairy and walked on our knuckles, and thus preventing them from understanding evolution.

Evolution demonstrates that we are primates, descended from other primates, and that we are one branch in the tree of life and that we are not more special than other animals. Creationists see Natural Evolution as being without meaning or purpose and that life under evolution has no morality. Because of such beliefs and others, religion is against evolution. It is true that Natural Selection and Evolution not contain religious beliefs or philosophical arguments on meaning, purpose and morality. But are those reason enough to be against Natural Evolution; that goes on uninterrupted and with or without their approval? In short, anti-evolution and anti-scientist are high on the disapproval rates among the faithful, and the industry of religion is more than content to keep the masses obedient to their dogma. Of course, the more you study Natural Evolution the less you tend to believe in God's creation and this happened to Charles Darwin whose evidence on Natural Selection finally convinced him otherwise. This also happens to too many who get their religion in their childhood first and before they investigate (if ever) evolution. In such cases, religion builds a mental-wall, a blockage against any investigative initiative into Natural Evolution. Devotees are determined not to accept evolution no matter what undisputed evidence is presented to them.

Thus, Charles Darwin's *Origins of Species* of 1859, still fuels clashes between scientists convinced of its truth and rejectionists who reject its theories of life without a creator. He explained the concepts of "the struggle for existence" and "natural selection" and the complex relations between our closely related species—Neanderthals, Cro-Magnon and Homo sapiens or other animals---and their habitats—caves, hunting and fishing or grazing--in order to explore how natural conditions might have as similar effects as human selection. The process of species change is very slow and complex, and this is the reason they remained wrapped in obscurity. Darwin appreciated the complex relationship of any species with its environment and how it is that some species have greater success than others, as in Homo sapiens vs. Neanderthals, in perpetuating living offspring. This means, that various conditions of life cause organisms with particular physical variations to survive---this is called Natural Selection. Yet, creationists place beliefs above facts in a fruitless attempt to reject Natural Evolution.

This can be seen in the 2006 Time Magazine surveying religious people with the following question: *"If science found a fact that contradicted the tenets of your faith, what would you do?"* Well, 65% of Americans would reject the evolution fact in favour of their religious faith! The difficulty is that people must reject their faith if they accept evolution as a fact. The suggested solution is to loosen the grip of religion in their minds, or those parts of religion that fundamentalists fanatically maintain. On the other hand, the more dysfunctional society is, the more religion is accepted as a means of escaping that dysfunction. Like a radical philosopher once said: *"Religion is a form of protest against an unbearable reality."*

A century's long search in the genetic-engine of living things confirms that, in so many ways, evolution is simpler than we originally thought: its engine is made of tiny numbers of powerful genes. We first thought that all the diversity of living things would involve all sorts on novel creations all starting from scratch. But now we understand that this is not the case. Evolution works with existing common groups of gene information and uses them in different new ways and in new and different combinations, and without having to invent anything fundamentally new other than new combinations. The commonality of form in all animals is now understood. Animals resemble each other because they use the same set of genes to build their bodies; as set of genes inherited from a common ancestor that lived long ago. What we see now among all the animas is just variations on the body plan that existed 500 million years ago. Therefore, one inescapable conclusion we can draw from the *Tree of Life* is that all living branches share these genes, and at the root base we could find the last common ancestor of all animals. We can deduce that all living things must have had and shared these genes.

NATURAL EVOLUTION

AND THE

ORIGINS OF SPECIES

NATURAL ADAPTATION

Darwin's Observations

- Darwin made many observations along his stops on the Beagle
- **Darwin's observations included the diversity of living things, the remains of ancient organisms, and the characteristics of organisms on the Galapagos Islands.**

Darwin was amazed by the tremendous diversity of living things. Scientists now have identified more than 1.7 million species of organisms.

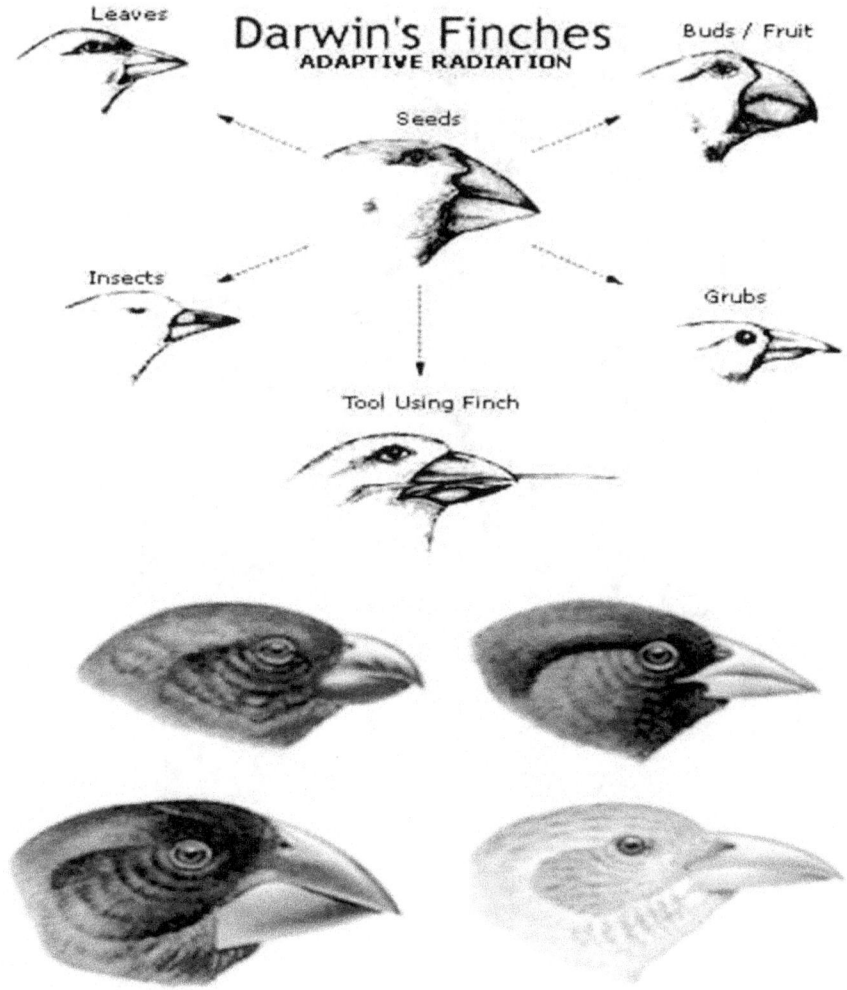

131

CHARLES DARWIN

HMS BEAGLE SEA VOYAGE TO GALAPAGOS ISLANDS

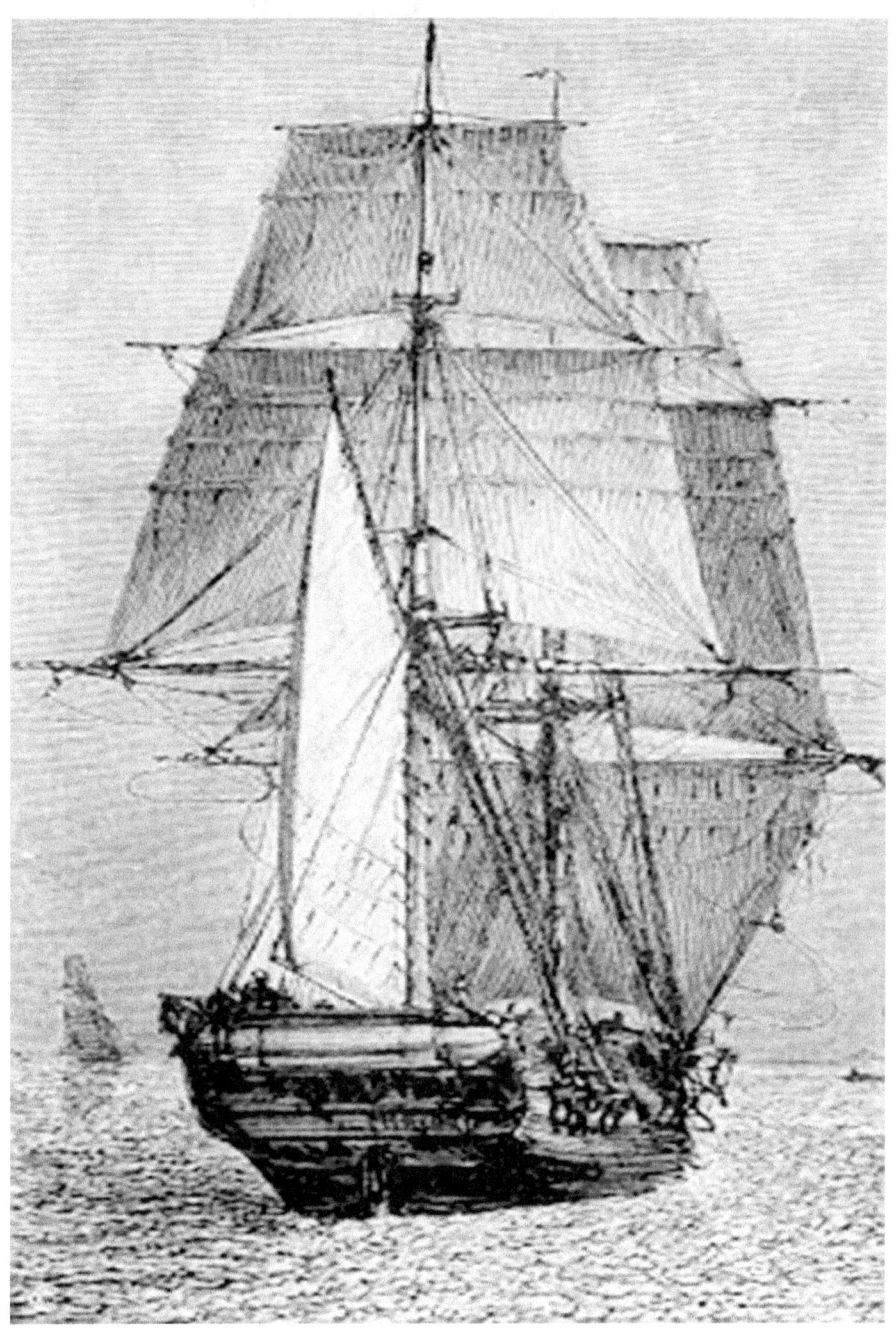

DARWIN RECORDINGS OF NATURAL EVOLUTION

GALAPAGOS ISLANDS LANDSCAPE

ADAPTATION OF SPECIES

GALAPAGOS ISLANDS

GALAPAGOS ISLANDS

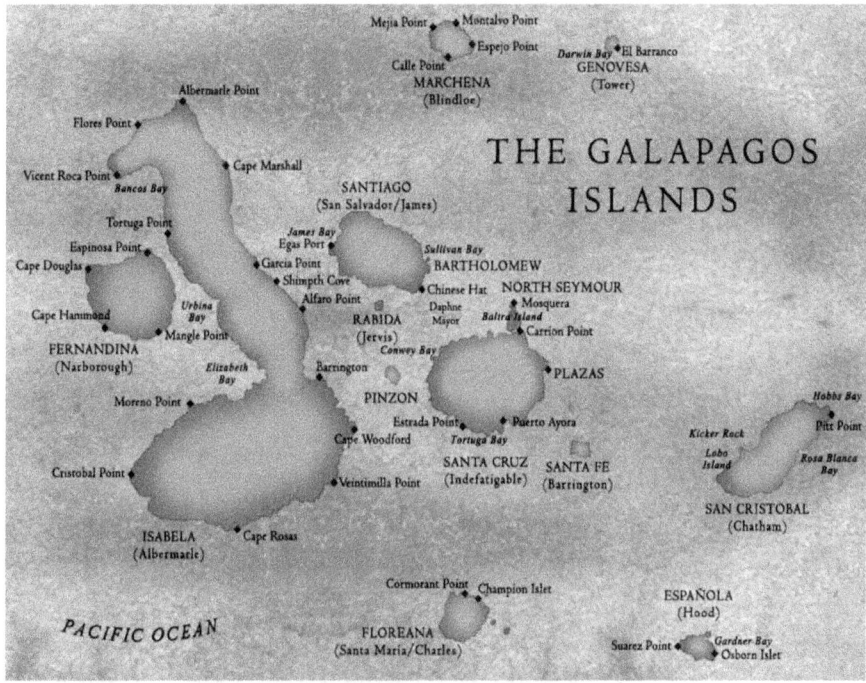

DIVERSITY OF LIFE

ON DARWIN'S "ORIGINS OF SPECIES", 1859

NATURAL SELECTION & ADAPTATION

NATURAL SELECTION & ADAPTATION

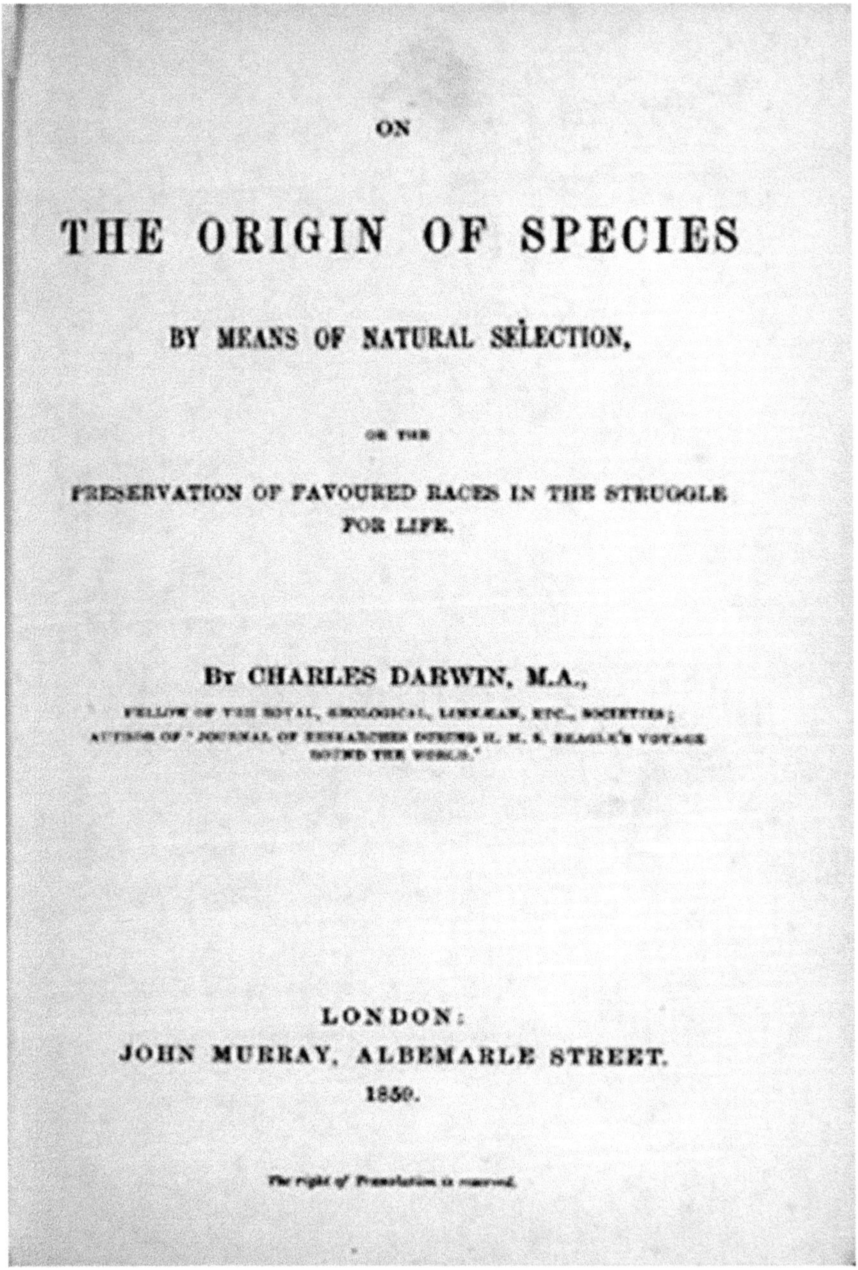

ON

THE ORIGIN OF SPECIES

BY MEANS OF NATURAL SELECTION,

OR THE

PRESERVATION OF FAVOURED RACES IN THE STRUGGLE FOR LIFE.

By CHARLES DARWIN, M.A.,

FELLOW OF THE ROYAL, GEOLOGICAL, LINNÆAN, ETC., SOCIETIES;
AUTHOR OF "JOURNAL OF RESEARCHES DURING H. M. S. BEAGLE'S VOYAGE ROUND THE WORLD."

LONDON:
JOHN MURRAY, ALBEMARLE STREET.
1859.

The right of Translation is reserved.

DARWIN'S ORIGINAL NOTE OF THE TREE OF LIFE

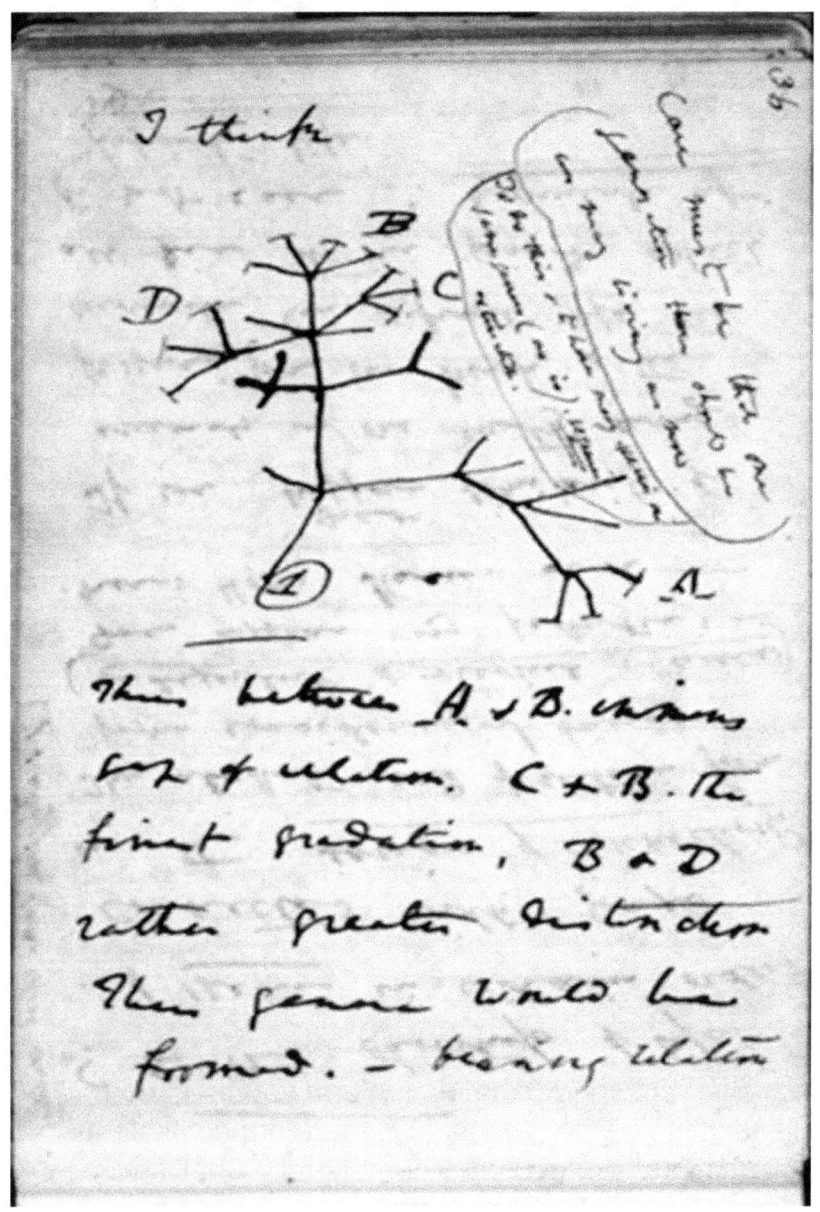

November 1880
CHARLES DARWIN'S LETTER TO FRANCIS McDEMOND, BARRISTER AND COMMITTED CHRISTIAN CONFIRMING HIS ATHEISM

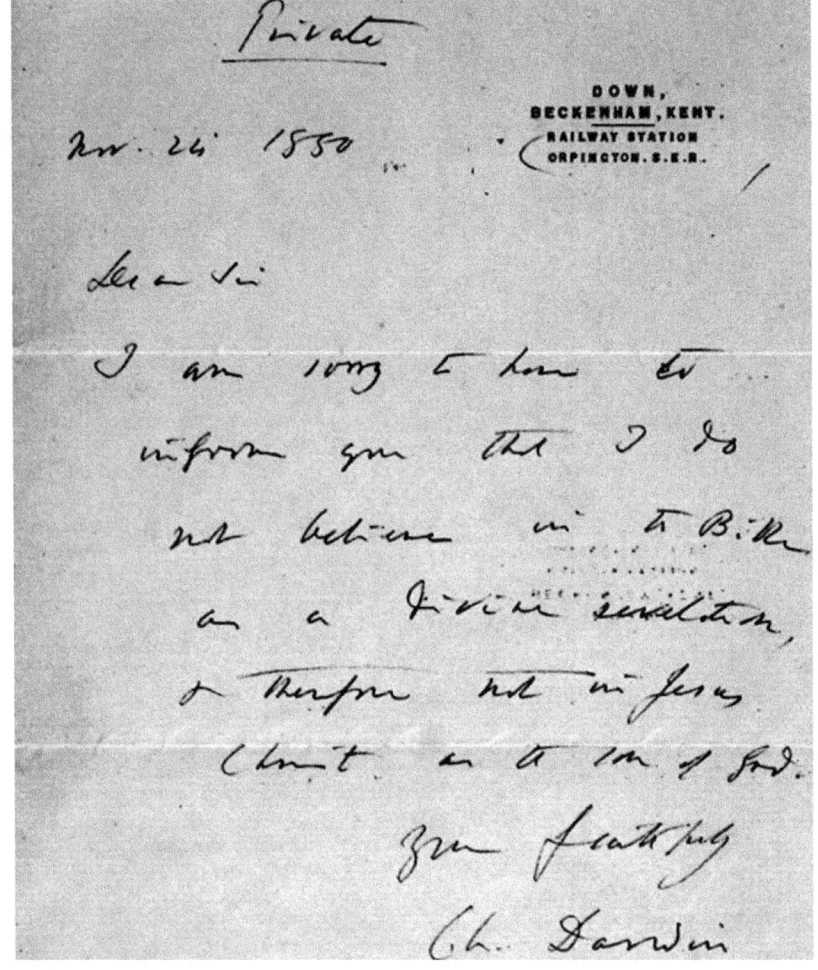

Dear Sir, I am sorry to have to inform you that I do not believe in the divine revelation & therefore not in Jesus Christ as the son of God. Your faithfully Ch. Darwin.

THE TALE OF TWO HUMAN SPECIES

Religious false pattern-meaning explanations about the origins of humanity, which were given in the Torah, the Bible and in the Qur'an, were based on centuries' old primitive myths and superstitions. During the past centuries, and until 200 years ago, we had no definite answers on the fundamental questions: where do human species come from, and how old is the human race? For centuries philosophers, naturalists and materialists all over the world pondered and speculated with these questions but found no proven scientific answers. Myths therefore were built to narrow the gap in historical, geological and biological evidence. That is, not until 1859 when the very first scientific research and propositions about the origins of species were offered and started a biological scientific revolution that has changed the world. It was found in the narrative offered by Charles Darwin of the *Origin of Species by Natural Selection of 1859.*

The subsequent archaeological evidence dated about 100,000 years ago, upon which the human race had imprinted, confirmed Darwin's theories of human evolution. For instance, in our ancestral remains in pre-historic caves of Greece, Spain, France and Croatia in Eastern Europe and in the desert fields of Palestine and Kenya, archaeologists found that they were inhabited by human species closely related to Homo sapiens. Such evidence confirmed Darwin's theory of the biological origins of the human race. That is, there were species of human groups that survived nature's forces, and others were extinct because they could not adapt to their environment. For these human groups, life's simple task had to do with the survival of their members under harsh environmental conditions. The Biblical claim that God created Man some 6,000 years ago leads to the question: who then created the other humanoids that were extinct some 100,000, 40,000 and to 10,000 years ago? These human species such as the *Neanderthals* and *Cro-Magnon* had primitive arts and culture, animist spiritualism, social organisation, decorative burials, a form of vocal communications, and moral obligations to protect their young, the old and the sick.

The following narrative is based upon the accumulative evidence and knowledge presented by renowned biological scientists including Charles Darwin. For the sake of clarity, reference to 'humans' or 'human species' or 'Homo sapiens' includes the Neanderthals and the Cro-Magnon; the early Humans that were biologically not much different than we are today.

Some 40,000 years ago the European Continent was still covered by the Ice Age which meant that much of it was under thick layers of polar ice. During the winter months temperatures plunged to 30 degrees C. bellow zero, similar to the Icelandic and the Canadian Arctic today. The people living in such cold regions had adapted to it the best they could and based on their biological and social instincts of adaptation. Imagine: it is the first light, the daily routine has already begun, and the young hunters are a formidable team. A hunter and his young son, driven by instinct to survive, have killed a wild pig for food. They used its skin to protect their bodies, and utilised its bones for spears and needles to mend, and much more. The valleys are covered with wind-swept tall grass and the dense forest offered refuge to red deer, wild pigs and other animals. Limestone caves provided shelter for the people of the regions of Southern Europe, where the Ice Age was not as severe. These are the *Neanderthals,* the first human species to adapt to this harsh environment and frozen continent. The members of this small clan are well-equipped for survival with long spears and well-proven co-ordinated hunting strategies. For countless generations they were Europe's remarkable kingdom of mysterious people.

In some ways the Neanderthals were very similar to Homo sapiens, yet different. A second group of human species were the *Cro-Magnons* who were very much like us. The name Cro-Magnon is taken from a cave where *Luis Lartet (1840 – 1899)* a prominent geologist and palaeontologist, found the original skeletal remains in 1868 near the village of *Les Eyries*, France. In caves, Cro-Magnon human skeletons were uncovered in five archaeological layers. In the uppermost layer, human bones were found to be between 10 and 35 thousand years old. The Neanderthals and the Cro-Magnon were not separate species from each other, just different in anatomical forms. Amazingly, all these early Human species actually overlapped in Europe for a few thousand years, and DNA evidence today shows that they interbred! However, Modern Man (Homo sapiens) is a forerunner of both the Neanderthals and the Cro-Magnon because Homo sapiens were living in Africa hundreds of thousands of years before migrating to the European Continent. There they found the Neanderthals and the Cro-Magnon living at the end of their existence by few short thousands of years later. Unlike the Neanderthals, the Cro-Magnon people were very similar to Homo sapiens and it is pointless to separate them from us.

About 45,000 years ago, *Homo sapiens* arrived in the European continent from Africa and found a frozen continent. As hunters and gatherers they were challenged to find food, keeping them warm and able to provide food and shelter for their dependents. They had to adapt in order to survive. But nothing could prepare them for an astonishing discovery; for they thought they were the only people alive on earth. As they made their way though the Middle East (present day Palestine) and into Europe they found that they were not alone. Another people inhabited the rock shields; very similar to Homo sapiens, but different. They must have come via separate routes (perhaps through western Africa) into this continent. These Neanderthal people did become fellow travellers in our own great journey as Homo sapiens. Following Darwin's Origin of Species in 1859, a number of excavations began to take place in order to discover the missing link between us and the origins of our human ancestors.

In 1856, in the Mettmann valley near Düsseldorf, Germany, contracted labourers were digging for limestone, containing a vital mineral which was then used in the local chemical industry. In the process of digging, workers discovered a part of a human cranium of unknown origins. It was later discovered that this cranium belonged to an ancient hunter, a tribal leader, a family man, a father and a member of a human-like surviving species, the Neanderthals. The cranium housed a large brain which had developed by Natural Evolution, perhaps a bit larger than the Homo sapiens' brain. Since the first discovery of a cranium in 1856, over 300 Neanderthal craniums and skeletons have been found throughout the European Continent and the Middle East, but none in Africa. Why?

From the initial and subsequent discoveries, the craniums and skeletons were problematic, for none of them fit with anyone's' traditional idea of our ancestors, the Homo sapiens. These skeletons tell the same story of short, powerful ape-like men who had adapted and perfectly evolved for the icy European environment they lived in and as cave dwellers. This living environment was a harsh place to exist because of the last stage of the Ice-Age with temperatures fluctuating from one extreme to another. Under these extreme conditions there was very little gathering of vegetation growing to maintain life. The only dietary solution was in the hunting of animals and consuming a high-protein meat diet. Under such environmentally strenuous circumstances, Neanderthal man had to be resourceful, able to cover long animal-tracking distances and be a good hunter or he would not survive.

The tools found with the skeletons and burial sites confirm that they had developed highly sophisticated stone-tool technology for spear hunting, as weapons just as the Homo sapiens had, and as carving tools for animal meat and skin. Their spears had to be strong and well-maintained, for if these failed the hunter could be killed by the animal he was aiming to hunt. Their hunting for meat suggests that they were able to support family groups up to 20-25 members.

Hunting therefore was their most important activity if they were to survive as a group. It involved organised group solidarity, leadership and hunting techniques, such as rubbing their bodies with animal droppings to prevent detection and the ability to blend with the environment. As time went on, animals became rarer and more difficult to detect without the Neanderthals knowing the reasons for their declined numbers. Each time, they had to go further and further to hunt for food and to support the groups' daily consumption of much needed high-protein meat. What they did not know was that they had a competition for hunting and dominating the environmental resources coming from new comers called Cro-Magnons (Homo sapiens).

It was in the Middle East that Homo sapiens first came into contact with Neanderthals, on their way through Palestine. Archaeological evidence of Homo sapiens caves and burial grounds were discovered on lime stone regions in Palestine. The cave contained the remains of 12 human skeletons. Within these skeletons there were stone tools along with bones estimated at being 100,000 years old. These were the oldest Homo Sapient remains outside Africa. Then something extraordinary was discovered! The new discovery happen within a few hundred yards from the burial grounds near in a place called *Tabun*. The remains found in the near new caves were very different from the Homo sapiens. The bones of the Tabun skeleton belonged to a female which was buried at the same period around 100,000 year ago. These were two different burial cemeteries; with two complete different human remains, yet so near to one another. Their differences were in the cranium structure, with Homo sapiens a bit smaller (like modern man), and the Neanderthals female's a bit larger. Archaeology had to answer the question whether these two human species lived side-by side, for how long, and what their relation was.

In Spain, on the site that is called *Gran Dolina*, in the *Atapuerca Mountains, in the Province of Burgos,* archaeologists discover a treasure of bones belonged to a human-like species named *Workingman* of about 850 thousand years old. This humanoid species were meat-eaters, lived in groups and travelled following herds of animals. The features and style of their teeth revealed similarities of another humanoid called *Agasta* that lived in Africa about a million years ago. Among other things they used fire for their needs. Agasta humanoids were part of the great family that we can trace other species including Apes, Workingman, Neanderthals, Cro-Magnons and Humans. Agasta was also a stone tool maker and the first humanoid to explore the world. As such, they began their great migration out of the African Continent along the Nile River, through the Middle East and Europe and South East Asia. As such, they populated a number of regions with their offspring.

Over the next hundreds of thousand of years, their descendants adapted to the harsh temperatures of Europe and, since they were the only humanoid hunters around, they were also able to survive. Evidence confirms that about 300,000 years ago these migratory groups began to organise their life style activities, using caves as their habitat against harsh temperatures, and for protection for their families and building fires for warmth and cooking. When they were outdoors they constructed temporary shelters using timber wood covered with animal skins. Their "burial" grounds were in caves with deep shafts where bodies were thrown into. This was also a ritual burial site with a mixture of bones and layers of clay. Some of the buried craniums had signs of severe blows on them which indicated ongoing scrimmages against other humanoid groups. Unconfirmed evidence suggests that they are most likely the direct ancestors of Neanderthals, going back from 100,000 to 1 million years ago.

There is no evidence of Neanderthals in Africa or Asia, for most confirmed evidence comes from within Europe. This brings us back to the 1856 discovery of a cranium, in the limestone caves of the Mettmann valley, Germany. Was the cranium a missing link between Humans and Neanderthals? Evidence wrongly concluded in 1913 France suggested that the Neanderthal was a stooped creature with bent knees and thus a semi-idiot. The evidence that was analysed was misinterpreted, for this particular Neanderthal was suffering from severe arthritis, and this was the cause of him stooping and with bent knees, and not because he was a brute or too primitive. This was far from the truth! But the false-story persisted for a long time.

Harsh environment and terrain were suitable for species that were innovative, with stamina and adaptability and who were born and raised under these conditions. The Neanderthals were this species. For 40,000 thousand years Humans also roamed the frozen grasslands of Europe, and Neanderthal people were facing a similar life struggle to survive. They travelled from Spain and France in the West to the shores of present day Turkey's Black Sea in the East. Like the Humans, Neanderthals used caves and overhangs as their habitat; they used similar stone-tools, they gathered food and used fire, as Humans did, for heating and cooking meat and vegetables. Their powerful jaws were used to hold onto leather pelts while striping the fat from it with their stone-tools. They were shorter than Humans, but lot stronger, and could lift and drop a human like a fallen branch. Their short size structure was built in order to reduce evaporation and preserve body heat; a balance of adaptation to a harsh cold environment. Thus, biological adaptation was a key to their survival.

They buried their dead and decorated their burial grounds with bones, feathers and wooden spears, as Humans did. They felt the loss of a close member of the group and celebrated the new seasons and events in the sky, as they thought what these phenomena meant. They probably celebrated celestial "deists" of their own making and painted invented protective signs of Animist spiritual powers derived from the animals they hunted. They were biologically programmed, like the Humans, to look for pattern-explanations, to interpret the cosmos and their physical surroundings by giving a pattern-meaning to them. When real pattern-explanations did not exist or could not be found or were meaningless to them, they tended to invent pattern-explanations of their own making which were not necessarily true. This was done, and humans still do, to fulfil any missing gap between not-knowing and knowing something reasonably to be true.

Despite the misinterpretations, the Neanderthals were not brutal or crude cave men and women. Equally to Humans, they successfully adapted to life on earth and for thousands of years we were fellow travellers. As time went on, the Neanderthals made their way to warmer climates of the Middle East; while simultaneously, Humans were roaming the Mediterranean coast along the Nile River and towards the land of present day Palestine. From the burial evidence gathered in a series of caves in Palestine, humans and Neanderthals lived together in the Middle East some 100,000 years ago.

On the outskirts of Nazareth, in northern Israel, lies the oldest human burial cemetery chamber in the world. This was an established burial cemetery dated about 100,000 years. The interesting thing about this burial site was that there lay a body of a mother whose child was placed by her feet. Biological analysis of both skeletons found in the cave confirms that they were anatomically indistinct from our own. Were they the second or third branch of anthropoid species that were extinct within a measurable distance of our own human evolution? We do not know if they were destroyed by us or died out from other causes. They used stone tools, collected shells for decoration of their graves; they probably had language ability, maintained burial rituals with gifts and patterns of life similar to modern human symbolism. These people were entering into pattern-explanations of abstract thoughts and symbolism which marked signs of theistic beginnings long before the Biblical verses of Genesis 1 were written. These were not unique qualities of the Homo sapiens. We were not the only ones burying our dead, for the Neanderthals had developed their own burial rituals, the initial stages of language communications, group solidarity and organised leadership for planning ahead. We know for sure that the Neanderthals could speak to one another, perhaps with limited vocabulary. This is confirmed by the discovery of a tiny bone called the *hyoid*---under the base of the tongue--- its primary function is to enable man to speak and to communicate with enough verbal skills to plan ahead.

In the Cabara caves in the slopes of Mount Carmel, in south west Israel, a man's skeleton was found belonging to a Neanderthal, buried some 60,000 years ago. The skeleton was the most complete that was ever found in a shallow grave as was the typical style of Neanderthal burial. This burial was intentional, with distinct outlines of cemetery boundaries, and a unique Neanderthal practice of removal of the cranium after a period of death. They tended to leave behind the bottom jaw intact while removing the upper part of the cranium. The purpose of this ritual is still unknown and not easy to determine. Some archaeologists however, maintain that this ritual was related to the *"voyage of the dead"* into the mysterious void. Just like Humans, the Neanderthals also lived in a world of symbols—as pattern-explanations—described in wall-arts found in caves. A child's intentional burial was found to contain parts of deer, ostrich bones and eggshells as offerings to a ritual; as a sign of loss and grief and a sense of bereavement, in a symbolic way, just before the grave was covered. Since both Homo sapiens and Neanderthals were not aware of the reality of the cosmos, they interpreted the real world through man-made symbolic ritual offerings, imaginary pattern-explanations and habits. This was the beginning of adapting of theistic illusion, supported by mystical pattern-explanations of convenient choices of understanding and symbolism. Thus symbolism became reality; one indistinguishable from the other.

The Neanderthals were showing signs similar to human, in that, a moral attitude towards others was felt present. They cared for the old and the sick, their females and their children. Evidence of a man's severely broken arm that must have needed someone to provide him with food, concern, support and constant care for his injury. This moral attitude of anthropoids ---both Homo sapiens and Neanderthal--has been preserved for thousands of years and, as such, it exposes the present religious falsities on the monopoly of moral claims. What makes it interesting is that the Homo sapiens and the Neanderthals lived parallel to each other and so near to present time. Neandrethals migrated and lived in the Middle East region for at least 60,000 years, at the same time as Homo sapiens. Have we shared similar burial practices, stone tools and symbolism? Is it not also tempting to imagine that both shared and had much more in common? Were Homo sapiens and Neanderthal, sexually active with each other? Were there permanent unions that resulted in giving birth to new offspring? One can assume that people who lived so closely together shared parallel life existence and behaved so similarly that they must inevitably be related. Yet these are confirmed different humanoid species. However, our common ancestor is the Homo Agasta (or Ergaster) of Africa from 2 million years ago. From that time on, our journeys took us onto separate paths of different continents; the

Neanderthals roamed Europe and the Homo sapiens evolved in Africa and Palestine before migrating into European Continent.

In 1859, the British biologist Charles Darwin published his *Origin of Species* suggesting that all living things, including Homo sapiens and Neanderthals, came from earliest simple forms of common ancestry, through the biological process of Natural Selection and Evolution. The gentle time slope of evolution confirms that life on Earth evolved steadily and slowly, carving its way through for more than 4 billion years. Natural selection, and not a celestial-designer (God), was the "sculptor of life." It was in the same year of the publication of the Origin of Species in 1859 that public interest was aroused about the vital question about the origins of the human race: where we came of from and how we evolved from early to modern man. Little did we know then that, during the 4 billion years of life on earth, more than 95% of all life forms on Earth disappeared over time, including other species of humanoids or anthropoids. This conclusive evidence of humanoid existence was unravelling for the first time in the limestone caves of Mettmann in 1856.

Early man evolved biologically over a long period of time. For the first time in our modern history, geologists and biologists began asking the right questions about the origins of man. If humans have evolved from simple life forms, the implication to the religious as well as to the scientific minds was disturbing. If humans were not created by God in Genesis---to the dismay of the Church---then we could only be descended from ape-like man. This scientific confirmation also impacted the scientific psyche profoundly, in that, the evidence of our common dissentience made humans an inseparable part of the animal world of primates. The Charles Darwin 1859 material discovery, of the origins of life on Earth, is still deeply felt by the "creationists" whose views are mostly expressed as such, in the digital insanity of TV televangelists in the USA and those who hide their religiousness behind 'intelligent design.'

Charles Darwin stayed away from the religious-scientific controversy, but the new generation of young scientists and biologists were not afraid but eager to find answers to Darwin's *Theory of Evolution* and contribute towards it. Inspired by the discovery of the Neanderthal cranium 3 years earlier, the theory of evolution became the most important topic in the scientific circles. Reason and evidence was needed, not belief and faith, if the natural evolution of man was to advance beyond its original theory. Scientific attention turned to an ancestor that will link humans to the apes. An ape-man was the missing link and the upcoming scientists, eager to make a name for themselves, went to great lengths and visited every corner of the earth to find it.

By the end of the 1800's biologists became consumed with the idea of finding the missing link between the apes and man. Reason and evidence steered biologists to seek a possible link between the Neanderthal man and Homo sapiens. Travelling back in time, Neanderthal "foot prints" were made about 300,000 generations or about 40,000 years behind Homo sapiens. This was the progression of the narrative to find the origins of the Homo sapiens and his fellow traveller, the Neanderthal, from ape to man.

The first life-chapter to this narrative was written about 40,000 ago in the caves of northern Germany where the cranium of the Neanderthal man was discovered. Since then, evidence has placed our ancestor's home in Africa. In British East Africa, in 1915, there was a discovery of stone-tools which lead to revolutionised the human origins. What was the defining factor of the first human ancestor; were tools, and not his upright walking. The missing link was in fact, the tool-maker and therefore the beginning of humanity and stone-age technology. His remains were discovered in 1960 in Tanzania, Africa. Our ancestor was then named the *Homo habilis*, literally the Handy man or the Working man.

With this discovery there was also additional cranium evidence found nearby which showed that Humans existed side by side with Homo habilis for nearly a million years. Since the time of Charles Darwin's profound discovery of the Origin of Species in 1859, the single line ancestor link between the Homo habilis and Humans ended with the most advanced mammalian ape (yes we are Apes) on earth, the human being. Somewhere in the middle had to be the link between the two. What is amazing was that the two species lived side by side and this has changed how we view human evolution. It should be noted that Natural Selection does not favour one species over another, for only the survival skills of each determines their existence. They were evolutionary formed but, in time, they disappeared while others continued to form biological links closer to humans. A number of other competing human-like species appeared to occupy the earth at the same time with humans.

In the European Continent, the Neanderthals were trackers and opportunistic hunters, for they hunted any forest animal that was a convenient hunt for their survival. They also exhibited advanced human skills in their solidarity that was more than mere ape-like social skills. They consulted one another and arrived at common consensus on mutually based self-interest. The question still remains whether those evolutionary advanced skills originated with them or with possible human contact. Scientists long held a view that Neanderthals became human by a crucial large leap of evolution forward.

If this is the case, Neanderthals should have identical DNA to humans. Evidence from two sets of DNA---one Human and the other Neanderthal bones---revealed that there were vast differences between them. They were both human but they were definitely not our direct ancestors at all. These two groups were separate human species who, by historical and biological coincidence, shared the same geographical space and time. Were there any consequences created by the arrival of the humans in the mist of the Neanderthal evolution? Some 40,000 years ago, humans arrive in Europe and such a migratory move appears to have a direct but not an exclusive, cause of dramatic events for the Neanderthals. Yet, within a mere 20,000 years the Neanderthal people were all dead and gone. As anthropomorphic species and fellow travelers, they became extinct. Why?

Neanderthal evolution did not prepare them for this new threat. Physically the late comers were not well adapted to the European cold climate but Cro-Magnon (early humans) had other advantages. They evolved in new ways of living together and with an innovative way of thinking and planning ahead. Their numbers were small but they were always scouting for new territories, such as the fertile valleys of South Western France. These lands were perfect for human habitation as the Ice Age weather in this region was becoming warmer. As for habitation in this region, the only problem was that the Neanderthals were there first. The geographical terrain of limestone cliffs was ideal for sheltering both Neanderthals and Humans hunters and gatherers. But there was a major difference between them of how they utilized nature's resources. Salmon fish and reindeer were migrating each year in nearby rivers and migratory plains, both Neanderthals and Humans made their fishing and hunting in close proximity to one another. Humans were organising their effort of hunting reindeer and elk and fishing salmon while nomadically migrating about and finding temporary shelters. In this migratory way, humans stayed close to their seasonal food sources. As such, they were not short of meat protein, leather for body protection and sleeping comforts.

It was a migratory existence, without the security and comfort of permanent habitat, in exchange for a paramount abundance of food sources. Their innovative thinking and adaptability led them to experiment with the preservation of their abundant of food supplies. They processed their food supplies by smoking or drying them and thus preserved their meat-protein throughout the on-and-off seasons. Through this method human groups managed to support their hunters, their families, their children and the old and the sick. With such a social distribution system, group solidarity remained high and at an utmost important level for the survival of the whole community.

Their migratory life-style expanded their views of the physical world and knowledge of it. They began to understand every vegetable and animal species in the occupied landscape. Since they were biologically programmed to look for pattern-meaning in their surroundings, they learned to plan ahead and anticipate real pattern-meanings of benefits and dangers and take precautionary measurer with increased success. Constant migratory change encouraged stamina, innovation and flexibility. Evidence of their adaptation can be seen in the improved style of their tools used to hunt elk and salmon fishing. Seeking the best quality of stone material for sharper tools and weapons, they travelled further and even traded with other human groups at distant horizons. Their realism and innovation encouraged them to experiment with new things such as producing qualitatively better tools and weapons.

The blades and spear points were secured by using fibres and natural resin for tighter grip thus adding an efficient weapon for their protection. As they migrated often they would have encountered other groups of human, they would exchange information, ideas and build new alliances with. As such, new and old communities were mutually supported in their collective effort for critical survival, and simultaneously forging the beginnings of a successful means of social adaptation.

In contrast, Neanderthals were living with and being driven by inflexibility and predictability. From evidence gathered from their permanent homesteads in South Western France, their tools had hardly changed in the last 40,000 years. Their food sources came from within a 50 klm radius of their settlements. Therefore, their food supplies came from whatever they found within such short distances or from migratory herds passing through. Their meat diet did not include year round migratory salmon, elk and reindeer, but only wild cattle. Cattle, at whatever numbers, tended to be part of the local landscape. Hunting such large size wild beasts caused the Neanderthal hunters great bone injuries in their upper bodies. Such a remote and narrow self-sufficient life-style tended to drive them "inwards" instead of "outwards," causing further social and cultural isolation from other Neanderthal groups.

One other group that Neanderthals came into contact with were the modern Homo sapiens living near by. It appears that the two species lived side by side in a harmonious co-existence. From this co-existence some Neanderthals learned to better modify their tool design and territorial conflicts between the two groups were non-existent, even though the two human species shared the same landscape. Estimates placed the modern Humans and the

Neanderthals combined population at less than 10,000 and fewer than 500 families scattered over the entire European Continent. Since they were living side by side for thousands of years it is hard to think that they did not co-habit in heterosexual relationships.

A skeleton of a 4 year old boy in Portugal shows an intriguing instance of inter-breeding; a mixture of Human and Neanderthal characteristics. But this offspring died without leaving descendents. There is no surviving evidence that shows major Neanderthal DNA mixed with human genes and whatever might have been the cause, human genes displaced Neanderthal genes. The only thing Humans needed was a better adaptation to European climate and landscape and an estimated mere 10 thousand years to overtake the Neanderthal genes. In a recent article in *Science,* by *Ann Gibbons, February 2016,* US geneticists discovered genes of Neanderthals behind modern diseases of the skin, immune system, heart, blood, even psychological, such as depression. When our Human ancestors migrated from Africa to Europe and Asia, before 40 to 50 thousand years ago, evidence strongly suggests they intermixed with Neanderthals who already lived there. Thus, in according to the geneticist *John Carp,* assistant professor of biology at Vanderbilt University, Tennessee; prefacing research in genetic correlation, the current human genome carries traces of those ancient intermarriages. The new design is based on genetic analysis of 28 thousand adults in which the researchers identified Neanderthal genes. Among other things, it was found that the DNA of Neanderthals significantly increased the addiction to *nicotine,* but another gene assists *blood clotting*, thus helping close wounds; and other genes have a favourable effect in enhancing the reaction of modern immune systems against pathogenic microorganisms. However, there are certain Neanderthal genes in our bodies which helped us to adapt to the hostile European and Asian environment, but today those genes no longer offer any advantage or impose a detriment.

It was in the Siberian Peninsula however, that the Neanderthals made their last survival stand. Gradually, and as the Ice Age was receding from southern Europe, they were pushed into a harsh and ragged offshore mountain range, isolated caves and overhangs of the Siberian landscape. Archaeologists still find their remains here and there that linger-on. From all the evidence gathered in the Northern European Continent (Germany) we can confirm that the Neanderthals were extraordinary people and far from being evolutionary failures. They survived for more than 150,000 years through the Ice Age. For much of the time, Neanderthals shared the elegance of our cosmos with us. They may have been a different human species but they were still part of the family of anthropoids: our family. Both Humans and

Neanderthals were fertile recipients to sperm by either group. With their extinction we became the only human beings on earth and custodians of our future. We should all acknowledge that our extraordinary journey as Homo sapiens formed us as the only survivors of a number of full-fledged anthropoid species that became extinct in the last 4 million years. These human species were not from the delusional Adam and Eve biblical line of procreation and inheritance.

HUMAN AND NEANDERTHAL SYMBOLIC ART

This is the day that cave miniature sculptures and wall drawings were born, for there must have been a moment of time, in our anthropoid history, when we were able to draw and sculpt what we saw in our landscapes; and gave a visual pattern-meaning of what they symbolised. But the first obstacle to overcome and appreciate pre-historic cave art, is our own lack of understanding; for pre-historic men were not mere savages, but capable of designing beautiful and symmetrical cave art. The world's oldest Neanderthal or Homo sapiens cave artwork engravings are dated back to 40,000 years. These caves were found in Spain, France and Eastern Europe depicting large animals; which the pre-historic artists imitated nature's beasts without understanding the results of their end meaning of their symbolism.

In Eastern Europe, Hungary and Romania in particular, a simple art engraving was found which contained an attractive symmetrical design on the object-tool. This means that the Neanderthals were highly skilful in producing aesthetic designs. In Altamira, Northern Spain, near the end of the 19th century, a cave gallery was discovered which contained a number of Neanderthal, high quality, artistic figures of painted animals on its walls. In the high-society's artistic circles of the 19th century, however, these cave artworks were rejected as being nothing other than of the early "savages." What had happened in the pre-historic Stone Age times that lead to the creation of such artistic symbolism? To begin with, let us state that the modern Human and Neanderthal people were not biologically evolved to have souls, to be born religious, to believe in God or be mystical. However, our brain is biologically programmed to look for patterns in life and assign meaning to them. When the Stone Age people saw a dangerous situation they attached the meaning of "danger" to that situation and took precautions to protect themselves by fight or flight. Therefore, the pattern-explanation could be given on the reality of a dangerous animal or the pattern-explanation can be given to the "power" of the animal by giving it extra-large bodily mass. Our brain assigns shortcut-patterns to things or situations, which have and give quick-meaning based on past real experiences, illusions or delusions and basic assumptions. This is a kind of free-enterprise of ideas and meaning of patterns which our brain utilises many times per day, since time immemorial.

What happens when an assumed pattern-meaning is non-existent? The short answer is that our brain would create a shortcut pattern-meaning rather than leave the mental space "blank" with no meaning at all. For example, a Stone Age cave artist saw a powerful beast roaming while hunting for its next meal. The exhibited muscular power of the beast attracts the artist's attention. How does the cave artist transform the pattern-meaning of the beast's power onto the cave-walls or sculpture? Would it be based on his brain's invention of pattern symbolic-meaning? If the artist's expression was a symbolic pattern-interpretation of the beast's "power" then that beast would be given a "soul," a "spirit," a "good" or "bad" of non-tangible and non-existent meaning of illusionary qualities. Then, why stop there? Why could the cave artist brain not create a pattern-interpretation of "wings" attached to a horse and show this illusion flying around in the sky? This is the beginning of man-made Animist religion and the beginning of humanity's struggle with theistic, pagan or secular delusions.

What happened in pre-historic caves' space and time that lead to the creation of such symbolism? This is the story of when the pre-historic world invented its first images for whomever the cave artists were, their brain's pattern-meaning search was accepted as logical and created illusive images of real life's animals. Looking at this cave art at 20/20 we see a splendid cave art gallery. But did the cave artists know, or could they distinguish, the literal power of the animals they painted from the illusive supernatural "powers" the artists 'gave' to the same depicted animals? Was this illusiveness the pre-historic groups' stepping stone, gradually leading to man-made *proto-spiritualism* and an Animist religious worshiping of things that do not exist?

These Alta Mira cave images in Spain appeared to be of standing, running or sleeping animals, such as horses, oxen and long extinct animals. In other caves there are breathtaking images of natural representations of small and large size animals. These pre-historic cave artists' revealed confidence and skills that matched near anything painted from the modern world. In fact, the famous Spanish painter *Pablo Picasso*, after viewing these cave paintings, said *"We have learned nothing."* When analysing the dates of these cave paintings, it was discovered that human species began to create artistic representations of the material world late in their evolutionary development, perhaps within 35,000 to 40,000 years ago. As their migratory style of life increased---following their animal food resources---so did their "explosion" of pattern-seeking meaning of creative images of the world around them; but only of animals in different poses. The assumption is that the cave artists were primarily focused on animals, not any animal, but some in particular which represented strength and power, such as horses, bulls, wild boars and reindeer. By now the artists' fascination was directed by their brains' pattern-meaning of the animals' spiritual, illusive or supernatural, but not realistic interpretation. Why?

The Homo sapiens, as the Modern Man, also are biologically programmed to look for patterns even when patterns do not exist. This is because our brains keep feeding us short-cut information of the world around us and whom most of us use. Pattern-meaning does not differentiate between reality and illusions or delusions, for its task is simply and constantly, to provide us with "something" mental rather than "nothing" mental at all. In the case of Altamira, what was the fascinating appeal with these animals to the minds of the cave artists? Were the paintings about hunting? Since this was the first imaginary, man-made animist-spiritualism, was it also made in a hope of having an eternal hunting success?

Animist spiritualism of hope became the social and cultural bond of the community of hunters and gatherers, and the beginning of an illusive birth of man-made religious flow. This was also the beginning of the symbolic, but illusive, separation of the existing physical world from the spiritual world of illusion or delusion which included the "spiritual-strength" and the "spiritual-powers" of the depicted animals. This perhaps explains that, while the cave artists projected their own delusion in the magical strength and powers of the large animals in their artwork, they were consuming smaller animals as part of their hunters' regular diet. Is this why no bones of large animals were found in the caves? Was it regarded an animist-spiritual sacrilege to kill and eat large animals similar to those depicted in the caves? Did this practice of abstaining from killing and eating "holy-animals" reduce the intake protein diet of the Neanderthals? As we see in contemporary India, "holy-cows" roam the streets while millions starve because it is forbidden to eat. Abstaining from consuming "holy-animals" is a confirmed Animist religious practice because these animals are worshiped as "deist" in multiple religious ceremonies and by various old and new spiritual cults. Did such Animist spiritual beliefs, of abstaining from consuming large size animals, in part also contribute to the ultimate extinction of the Neanderthals? Did the cave artists of the Stone Age give the animals they depicted a magical potency of spiritual powers which co-related with to practiced symbolic rituals? Did both Homo sapiens and the Neanderthal promote a delusional, transient, subliminal road into the world "beyond" the real? Was it because they were re-creating their hallucinatory encounters with the animals, with which their artists revered and painted. Early cave artists' paintings in Spain and France were predominantly depicted the animal world. They looked at the animals and, by the process of pattern-meaning; they were given illusionary zoological powers and elevated their status in a supernatural illusionary form. Human beings however, were not as yet depicted with a supernatural strength and power, either in relation to the animals that were depicted or independently of them.

No pattern-meaning was invented yet by the Homo sapiens' brain to entice the cave artist to take a giant-leap into the world of illusion that included humans with or without the appearance of the animals. It appears that, since the animal world was not as familiar to them, the cave artists had the freedom to speculate on the unknown and mysterious parts of the animal-kingdom. It was in that mysterious part of the animal-kingdom, where cave artists felt no restrictions from reality, that the horizon of illusion and delusion encountered no limitations. On the other hand, the human communities were very familiar to the artists. They themselves lived, ate and slept with their equals in the community of humans. The simplicity of life involved a mere hunting and gathering and not much else. There were no powerful men equal to giant animals, there were no mysteries surrounding man in their group. There was no space to create supernatural human beings comparative to the world of animals in the forest. In time, artists created a limitless horizon which gave them a pattern-meaning into something beyond the narrow world of their humanity. They took a small-leap into an illusive world which now is integrated in their depicted paintings of animal parts onto the human body, such as wings or half-man and half-horse.

In South Africa, cave paintings depict a figure of a man with animal hoofs instead of feet. They are cave paintings of strange new images of animalistic creatures. These illusive spiritual paintings of a man include bodily parts of animals, as some kind offered gesture, to appease the supernatural illusion of the animals they are worshipping. Such primitive Animist conceptions offered pre-historic communities a misguided relief from their inability to observe the elegant reality of the natural world. As such, their life's emphasis was misplaced on the side of the spiritual rather than of the material or physical world which, after all, sustained them. Through their rituals and habits the physical world became irrelevant and meaningless and it could only play a secondary role. The superior meaning of life became the fantastic, the mystical, the ritualistic, the symbolic and the all inclusive supernatural, a system of delusions which it is still followed by religious followers of various contemporary sects and cults. In short, pre-historic man was not developed enough to be able to control his thoughts; an inability to differentiate between the mentally-fantastic from the material-real. The false pattern-meaning of idealism has been passed-on to generations of believers of 'spirits' of a non-existent idealised world. Artistically of course, these cave paintings today have a cultural value but creating 'culture' was not the reason why pre-historic cave artists were painting.

A radical philosopher of the early 20th century once said, *"Knowledge begins from ignorance"* and the pre-historic communities and the cave artists, although skilful, were ignorant of the manifestations of the natural world. They created an illusive pattern-meaning in their minds for some kind of supernatural protection against the harsh elements of their environment. All were living under an equally irrational fear of their environment and the cosmos. But because the cave artists, and much later their Shamans, were in an influential social position, they were able to spread their own misguided interpretations of cosmic events, drastic climatic changes, and the role of the Laws of Nature, superstitions and fears. Group leaders made sure that their influence was integrated into the social life of the habitats. Habitually, all communities of hunters and gatherers, fishermen and inhabitants visualized and conceptualized their world by seeking pattern-meanings of stability, comfort and protection which could only have derived from the illusions of the Animists' spirits. Nature and its laws functioned as they were for billions of years without temporarily could be suspended, and without giving preference to one kind of species over another. Humanity then, as it is now, has always been on its own, depending on its own survival instincts and abilities, learning about its environment and changing it to meet its necessities.

For the next few thousand years this was humanity's infantile state of development, where increased numbers of human communities worshiped imaginary worlds while they went on about their day to day lives. Cave artists, group leaders, ritual performers and shamans, pretenders and self-deluded laymen could not accept the differences between material reality and delusions cloaked in religious robes and habits. Their beliefs about the material reality were fogged by their fear and superstition of it. Ignorance and contempt were directed against reality for not matching their delusional, pattern-meaning, expectations of a perfect world of magical thinking and illusions. Constant ritualism reinforced beliefs that animal-spirits, ritual-performers and group leaders had direct contact with a vastly illusive spirit world and could make things happen. These claims were incorporated in peoples' psychic and daily lives and were obediently followed until 10,000 years ago. When the animalistic influence was declining it was because it was slowly being replaced by a well organized and well managed religiousness. **This** was the time when human communities came to deal with larger questions about hereditary power and authority, life after death, family values, war and hostilities, concepts of good and bad, right and wrong and morality in general. Those questions were materialized within the early human societies because humans are biologically programmed to deal with them and have done so for hundreds of thousands of years. What was different this time was that those questions were given answers based on the political and religious agenda of the upper classes, the priestly and the military classes under the influence of their intoxication of power. Still some animists' spirits remained intact among the lower classes in their belief that they were responsible for fighting diseases promoting fertility and predicting the future. All such beliefs were pattern-explanations programmed in the human brain, needing them to be produced on-demand--in a short-cut mode in order to meet peoples' expectations.

Rituals have held an important role from Stone Age to Agricultural Revolution and in the Neolithic Age to symbolise natural processes such as harvesting, healing and floods. They also reinforced beliefs of unsubstantiated recognition of evil spirits, evil Gods (Satan) and good spirits, like of long dead "wise men" or lesser gods. Humanity's primitive cultural processes built a mimetically thinking process based on a whole slue of wishful pattern-explanations, half-truths and pseudo-science. It reinforced a pattern-system of unquestionable obedience and blind faith. Yet nothing of the above came from outside the human realm of cultural parameters. There were no capricious Gods, Devils or Saints, no animist-spirits, no supernatural human-souls and no earthly representatives of the Sky-God to impose upon us the powers of a celestial dictatorship. We've done it ourselves and some of us are still doing it! So let's get rid of this nonsense and free ourselves from it. Let us not escape from freedom. This total celestial dictatorship is the envy of Saudi Arabia and Iran, the imams of the Taliban, the ISIL, Boco Haram or Al Shibabs' theocratic system of oppression.

We are part of a natural world which has its own governing laws, the Laws of Nature, with its own system of gradual or sudden environmental changes and an ever-expanding universe that has consumed billions of stars and galaxies. This is the Material World we live-in, which is made of material stuff, with billions of living organisms, with a long list of extinct species, including humanoids like the Neanderthals and the Cro-Magnon. With one exception; the Human mammal who has survived all! Human beings have lived and adapted on earth for millions of years and have survived on the basis of natural law and the processes of *Birth, Growth, Decay and Death*.

Recent discoveries revealed that Natural Selection and Evolution has brought the Neanderthals mush closer to Humans, as genetic evidence revises our human family tree and reveals their presence within our genes. Language and communications were present; as tools were made for better hunting results and cutting of animal parts to desired size. Scientists find, deep in our human history and genes, as they are decoding the generic DNA make-up of Neanderthals, similar verbal communication genes that are present amongst these pre-historic hunters. A new evidence of Neanderthal mental capacity reveals that they were not idiots, but an ancient human species still evolving under Natural Selection and Evolution. At the time of the first discovery of Neanderthal skeletons, more than 150 years ago, scientists of the time did not notice that the stooped skeleton was infected by severe case of arthritis, and thus it was mistakenly put in a wrong position. This gave the wrong impression that the Neanderthals were not fully walking upright and they must have been hairy and stupid. This was far from the truth! They were not mere brutish cavemen. Scientists however, revealed that the only thing Neanderthals were lacking, that was developed in the Human Species, was the capacity of brain power.

They survived the harsh European climate for at least 300 thousand years and most men died from hunting injuries under the age of 30 at best. If the story of Neanderthals is a murder mystery, they disappeared when humans began to populate the best of caves, cultivated the best fertile lands and hunted in the same hunting grounds as our fellow travelers had for thousands of years. They were slowly disappearing as humans were appearing on the scene. Natural Selection, Evolution and Adaptation favoured the survival of the most adaptable and, in that cruel environment; the Human species were the fittest to survive. We did not wipe them out, for it was simply that our brain outlived them, as opposite to their physical strength and endurance.

Now new discoveries in genetics and archaeology are challenging the misleading traditional view of the Neanderthals as lacking even a limited sort of cultural coherency. But Natural Evolution of the Neanderthals in their cultural environment will show otherwise. The Neanderthal technology of stone-tool making shows their mental capacity in the style and method of stripping-out the central part from a large stone to extract the most flat, sharpest and largest cutting tool. It takes time to chip away small pieces to get to the central part of the large stone, and it takes one single and accurate stroke to get the final waffle piece out intact. This piece has a sharp edge around its perimeter for cutting meat in a number of ways.

Because this stone-flake is very flat in its edges, it could be re-sharpened a number of times. It took archaeologists years to perfect such stone tool-making technique. It was thus revealed that it takes, planning, judgment, manipulating, chipping away unnecessary flakes of stones in order to get to the final objective. In this process there is a goal objective present, not just sculpting away a stone. This is not a hit and miss process, for experiments in morph-metrics revealed shapes and angles that Neanderthals used with precise strokes to turn a raw block of stone and get into the precise core of the stone. They were engineering their rocks to get the right products that had specific properties. Sculpting tool-stone in this manner was an art form of a kind. This process of stone-tool making was much more complicated than what humans were making. This was Neanderthal's stone-making complexities and it is a testament of how intelligent they must have been.

Neanderthals natural adaptation in their environment progressed even further, specifically in the flint spearhead technology. At the base of the flint spearhead a black mass paste was used, most likely as a glue to secure it in its case at the tip of the wooden shafts. Their combined technique of the spear-shape, fastening with leather-strings and securing them with a gluing substance turned the hunting shaft into a robust weapon. Such a gluing substance was probably used in many aspects of their lives, in building structures, in clothing and in foot-wearing or fastening bodily decorative ornaments. The glue was not a sap from a pine tree, which was easy for Neanderthals to find and use. Further detailed chemical analysis revealed something different; that this type of glue material was a man made pitch from birch-trees which was produced by heating birch-bark. Without exaggerating, this was the world's oldest known synthetic manufactured material, and this makes Neanderthals the inventors of the first industrial process. This was natural adaptation at its best!

Still, the question arises how primitive human species could have invented such process called *dry distillation,* where birch-bark is processed to produce the kind of glue they needed. There were a number of steps needed; from cutting, rolling, drying, and pit-digging to carefully heating the birch-bark without burning it and collecting the manufactured glue. Communication and co-ordination of activities must have taken place amongst the Neanderthal members of the community to reach their objective of synthetically manufacturing glue. Now, since language is very difficult to excavate, some other method is needed to conclude of the Neanderthals' linguistic capacity. How did they communicate these complex ideas? Could they share with us that linguistic capacity that humans usually think of as unique only to them? Some new genetic, scientific method was needed to shed light on this question; by comparing genetics to the rest of our family tree, an answer could be found. What was needed was looking at specific genes where we can expect us and our closest relatives to differ; such as the gene that is fundamental for the development of language, called *Fox P2*. This is a very interesting gene which is directly related to the unique human characteristic for the development of language and speech.

The Fox P2 gene is found in other species, although the human Fox P2 is distinctive and, by comparing it with the potential Neanderthal version, we can shed light on what makes human language special. In such genetic investigation and experiments, what was needed was the genetic blueprint of both the Neanderthal and Human: their *genomes*. A genome is a particular genetic recipe for species, made up of distinct sets of chromosomes which are responsible for making every species different from others. Within the chromosomes there are genes which determine our bodily characteristics, such as how many fingers and hands or legs we should have; and every part of this unique recipe is encoded with just one molecule DNA. We are now aware that human genome has been completely decoded and human DNA information is available for genetic research.

But no scientist has ever attempted to decode the Neanderthal genome. That is, not until *Dr. Svante Paabo, of the Max Planck Institute, in Leipzig*, attempted to achieve an appeared impossible task. This was an attempt to map out the DNA in a nucleus of a 30,000 year old Neanderthal cell. The right kind of specimen of bones was found in the Venditive Cave, of Croatia, containing ample genetic possibilities in 3 bone fragments of separate females. Of all the bone fragments that were found, these were the best preserved specimens for decoding the genome and for retrieving the strands of DNA. In this process a major problem arose showing the bones' DNA contained specimens and contaminations from other organisms which colonialised these specimens over the last 30,000 years. A clean-up task was needed to remove the rogue bacteria DNA from the samples and preserve the purity of the Neanderthal specimens which was successfully completed. The result was that the specimens contained 5 times the concentration of DNA from the original estimates. This concentration made the task at hand much easier for reconstructing the genome. It should be noted that the DNA molecule's intertwined strands are held together by 4 key chemicals represented by letters. These chemicals bond together as pairs, always *C to G* and *A to T*. These sequences of letters are the building blocks of repeating units which spell out the genome's unique recipe. It was critical for their sequence to be in order and precise, for just one letter out of place (in a billion of pairs), and the genome would be inaccurate.

The Neanderthal DNA sample, however was in fragments; resembling a giant jigsaw puzzle, that required it be put together in correct sequence of C to G and A to T, with each piece fitting in precise order. Doubts and despair were in the forefront of the minds of all those genetic scientists who were involved in the project of decoding the Neanderthal genome. Their efforts of the scientists would take 4 years before they finally were able to put together the final piece of the puzzle in its correct sequence. The origins of our species, Natural Selection and Human Evolution are something that humanist and atheist very much care about. It is such an incredible technical achievement to investigate a 30,000 year old DNA and added to that, this was about the closest extinct human ancestor that could also tell us about our own evolution and biology. The end result is that science decoded the extinct Neanderthal genome from 30.000 years ago. It was Natural Selection and Evolution, not God or some absurd "intelligent designer," that built an incredible sequence of genetic complexities in the genome of our human ancestors: the Neanderthals.

The decoding of the DNA of the Neanderthal genome has provided a scientific opportunity to compare it to human DNA. Among other comparisons, scientists investigated the language gene Fox P2. The question is, would an identical gene be shared by Neanderthal and Human organisms? Would the Fox P2 be shared? The answer is yes! It is confirmed that both Human species shared an identical Fox P2 gene! The Neanderthals had an exact version of Fox P2 genes as humans did, and the same chemical letters in exactly the same order. As such, the Neanderthals had the same communication skills, but the kind of language they spoke, is unknown. Did they have a spoken language? Yes they did, and while how extensive and complex their language was, is not known, they could not have survived the way they did and for so long a time, without it.

The Neanderthal decoding revealed that they and humans shared more abilities then previously thought. On the other hand, did we humans have enough commonalities with the Neanderthals to interbreed? If they and humans interbred successfully, then traces of their DNA would be found in our own DNA. Most scientists at the time believed that this was highly unlikely. As a matter of genetic principle, when two different species interbreed they produce infertile offspring. For instance, when a horse and a donkey interbreed their offspring (mule) is infertile. Now that the Neanderthal genome has been mapped out, this question could be answered. It was important to take DNA samples from contemporary humans of different ethnic groups, such as *Orientals, Africans, Whites and Asians* and then compare this modern DNA with the Neanderthal DNA.

Scientists focused on only a small amount of the Human and Neanderthal genome; of variable areas where the order of DNA sequence varies from one individual to the next. In this case, if interbreeding had taken place, DNA letter-sequences typical to Neanderthal would show up in the human DNA strand. On the other hand, if there no interbreeding had taken place (or infertile sperms) there would not be any Neanderthal DNA in the variable areas. The general expectation was that negative results would show in all human DNA genome samples, regardless of ethnicity. If there were positive results, then the Neanderthal genome should match with every human ethnic group on earth.

However, that was not what scientists found. Instead, they found that the human African DNA matched to European human DNA more often than from the Neanderthal one. The Neanderthal DNA was closer to the Europeans' than Africans' DNA. It was concluded that the Neanderthals were more often closer to the Europeans and Asians, than with the Africans. This means that, somewhere along the times of co-existence, Europeans and Asians picked up Neanderthal DNA. Subsequent experiments re-confirmed the validity of this data again and again. In other words, this was not a fluke statistic or an accidental mistake. Does this mean that we have a little Neanderthal ancestry in the contemporary genome in us? Was the world ready to be convinced of this fact? Were creationists ready to accept that God did not make the Neanderthals but only made Man "after his own image"? Was there another God who created the Neanderthals? Were the authors of the Old Testament mythology not aware that there was another extinct human species that lived some 30,000 years, before the originators of contemporary religious industry compiled their absurdities about Genesis 1 and Adam and Eve?

The presence of Neanderthal DNA genome in humans is small (1% to 4%) perhaps because our fellow travellers did not interbreed more often or because they were extinct far too soon? But the implication of finding small amounts of Neanderthal DNA in humans is staggering. One explanation is that, after migrating out of Africa, humans must have interbred with Neanderthals and that it was their offspring fertile who inherited Neanderthal DNA. They were genetically close enough to have children with our species. This means that their offspring continued breeding with other humans and they became an incorporated part of the whole human race.

They also had some kind of spoken language, they buried their dead, and they decorated the graves with symbolic artefacts and had some kind of animist spirituality. Scientists continue investigating Neanderthal revelations about their skills that were discarded by archaeologists as invalid long ago.

But the most important question is: why are humans are still here and the Neanderthals are not? When humans began to co-habit the same geographical areas, this marked the beginning of the end for Neanderthals. Some 10,000 years after the first appearance of humans in Europe the Neanderthals were gone. The popular belief among scientists is that humans drove them into extinction by out-competing them for scarce resources or by simply killing them off. But the most recent evidence points to a different possibility in that it had something to do with Neanderthal inter-breeding with humans outside the African continent, including the harsh European environment and shortage of food.

Was this inter-breeding happening sporadically or more frequently? Scientists compared the Neanderthal DNA genomes that are now available, to a larger number of human DNA genome samples. This included more than a thousand individual DNA genomes of different ethnic groups from around the world. The aim was to discover whether ethnic populations from around the world had also inherited small doses of Neanderthal DNA as was discovered in Western Europe. But this is not what was discovered.

The intensity of DNA numbers were found in China, in Tuscany, the UK and Germany. Even among them there was variable relative presence of DNA numbers in their populations. Different groups of humans from around the world had fewer presentence of Neanderthal DNA genomes than from other parts of the world. China had less than Europe. In Southern Europe there were more people with Neanderthal DNA than Northern Europe. China had the smallest numbers of humans with Neanderthal DNA, with some individuals having less that 2%. In Tuscany, Northern Italy, however, this DNA presence rises to 4%, which means these people have the highest number of Neanderthal DNA than any other group in the world. This may explain that, during Europe's Ice Age, South Europe was most densely populated and was a hot-bed of inter-breeding between Neanderthals and Homo sapiens. South Europe such as Greece was then a breeding ground for Neanderthals and, as humans began participating in inter-breeding for a long time, they got more Neanderthal DNA than the Orientals or Africans. This also means that there were not just sporadic sexual encounters between Neanderthal and Human, but many resulting in offspring. Natural Selection and Evolution played a decisive part in the whole process of survival of the species.

This conclusion dramatically represents how Humans and Neanderthals interacted in Ice Age Europe and leads to a new assessment of how Neanderthals became extinct from the European Continent. Most of the time, however, an extinction of a species is not a sudden event, but rather it is a much more gradual process. This Natural Selection process may take place over thousands of years, which eventually will lead to the disappearance of the species. Some genetic scientists believed that the Neanderthal DNA was absorbed by a dominant DNA over a long period of time. That dominant DNA genome was of the human species. The ratio of the two species was 10 to 1 in favour of the human population, and the theory is that Neanderthals were not killed to extinction by superior warriors but were genetically overpowered and were simply bred out. Natural Selection and Evolution in the process of interaction and absorption with humans, led to the disappearance of our human cousins, the Neanderthals. The Darwinian theory of the Laws of Nature placed the Neanderthals at the losing end of it, resulting in the survival of the fittest process. Whatever the degree of their DNA survival, success maybe counted by their inter-breeding with the human race; Neanderthal DNA has survived within the human DNA genome to this day.

Has the small degree of Neanderthal DNA within us played any significant role in the make-up of the human genome? What, if any, of the Neanderthal DNA has contributed towards the genetic strength of the human species? Does the small presence of 1% to 4% of the DNA within us make a significant genetic contribution towards our well-being? Investigating closely at Neanderthal DNA that we have inherited, scientists discover something intriguing. Neanderthal DNA, in locations fundamental to the human immune system contains genes that appear to be vital to our ability to fight off diseases! Such locations are called *Human Leukocyte Antigens* (HLA) which make the cells that attack diseases and bacteria. This confirms that, since the Neanderthals lived in Europe for hundreds of thousands of years, they must have developed an immune gene system to fight off diseases. This was lacking in Humans when we arrived in Europe. In this new environment our immune system could not recognise and fight off bacteria and diseases which it never encountered before. Neanderthals give us a survival kit which helps our immune system to fight diseases. It was because of our inter-breeding with the Neanderthals that their genes were beneficial to both species.

Case in point, in a type of blood cancer linked *mononucleosis;* it was found that HLA could reduce the chances of contacting this deadly disease. This is a life-saving legacy passed on to the human race from the inter-breading offspring of the Neanderthal. This is the kind of legacy which saves lives, even as you read this, and also goes to the heart of who we are today! In this case, Natural Selection and Evolution was at its best! The above interpretation is scientifically justified. However, religious believe that God created Man in his own image; if this is so, then under whose image was the Neanderthal human species were created? Neanderthals were humans. They buried their dead, used tools, had complex social structure, employed language, had controlled use of fire, practiced religious ceremonies, used complex syntax in their spoken grammar, and played musical instruments. We know from their fossils that Neanderthals engaged in all. Pristine evidence of Neanderthal humanness came to light when a small flute was discovered next to a small child's skeleton in Slovenia. The small flute was made from a high bone of a cave bear, where four precisely aligned holes were punctured on one side of the four-inch long bone. This, and many other cultural evidences, strongly supports Neanderthal humanness. Their anatomical differences are extremely minor and can be, for the most part, explained as a result of a genetically isolated species that lived a rigorous life in a harsh cold climate and environment.

Other extinct remains of fully human species---the third so far-- were found in a cave; known as the *Rising Sun in the Cradle of Humanity,* about 50 km of northwest of Johannesburg, South Africa called *Homo naledi*. It is assigned a *genus Homo* in 2015 since its original discovery by the archaeologists of the Witwatersrand (Wits) University in 2013. The 15 individual fossils, which included women, children, adults and elderly members of this human species, were found in a room, deep underground, in a cave network. This room had been isolated from other chambers and was not open to the surface. What is important for us to understand is that the fossils were found practically alone in this remote chamber, in the absence of any other major fossil animal. The characteristics of the findings seem to confirm a ritualised burial behaviour, traditionally thought to be uniquely of the Neanderthal or Human sapiens trait. The remains tell us something about the Homo naledi's social behaviour with their deliberate burial ritual, a ritual that scientists believed only the Neanderthals and Homo sapiens practiced. According to a team member, the paleoanthropologist John Hawks, the way the remains were laid suggests a social and emotional basis of group behaviour. It demonstrates recognition that a member of their group was special in some way and in the way it was buried.

The Homo naledi species, though biologically related to humans, appears to have several important features that make it distinct. The Homo naledi has fingers that are more curved than modern humans, suggesting it was adept at climbing, and the most complete foot samples are on the smaller end of what is found in modern humans. The species has a lower foot arch and the whole skeleton showed Homo naledi was able to walk upright, as well as climb trees. At the time of writing, it was difficult to estimate the age of the remains because of the lack of fossil records from other animals directly related with the find. The age of the remains will be released after further research, but preliminary estimates suggest that the Homo aledi may have lived around 3.3 million years ago and walked the Earth recently until about 100,000 years ago. The remains were unveiled, for the first time in South Africa in September 2015 before the world's leading scientists and the public. This is our newest link to the evolutionary chain, as our closest relatives and newest human species. According to *Lee Berger*, the lead paleo-anthropologist the Homo aledi walked upright just like an ordinary human being, with their feet like our own, standing at 5' tall with the head the size of a human hand fist, with perfect line-up teeth and with high shoulders.

There a number of European pre-historic museums which forge interactive links between nature, heritance, the scientific study of the two, and examines the past to understand the existence of our human fellow traveler, the Neanderthals. Thanks to original, attractive and educational experience-enactments the European Neanderthal Museums provide exhibits to generate knowledge about the pre-historic Neanderthals. For you readers who are interesting to learning and passing on your experience to your children, there is a Network of Heritance Sites which can be found: office@ice-age-europe.eu for pre-historic sites in Europe. For your convenience here is a brief list of them:

- *Prehistomuseum,* Flemalle, near Liege, Belgium
- *Krapina Neanderthal Museum*, Krapina, Croatia (recommended)
- *Prehistoric Museum of Solutre*, Solutre-Pouilly, France
- *International Centre of Prehistory*, Les Eyzies-de-Tayac, France
- *Isturitz, Oxocelaya and Erberua Caves*, Saint-Martin d' Arberoue, France
- *The Museum of Neanderthal Man*, La Chapelle-aux-Saints, France
- *Museum of Prehistory* Blaubeuren, Blaubeuren, Germany
- *Neanderthal Museum*, Mettmann, Germany (recommended)
- *Palaon – Research and Experience Centre Schrödinger Spears,* Schoningen, Germany
- *Archaeopark Vogelherd*, Nienderstotzingen, Germany
- *Fumane Cave*, Fumane Valpolicella, Italy
- *Museum of Human Evolution*, Burgos, Spain
- *Museum of Altamira*, Altamira, Spain
- *Caves of Santimamine and Bizkaila Museum of Archaeology*, Bizkaila, Spain
- *Tito Bustillo Cave and Rupestrian Art Centre*, Ribadesella, Spain
- *Ekainberri - The Replica of the Ekain Cave, Zestoa*, Basque Country,

Spain
- *The Gibraltar Museum*, Gibraltar, United Kingdom
- *Kents Cavern Prehistoric Caves*, Torquay, United Kingdome
- *Petralona Caves*, Greece, Petralona, Halkidiki, Greece (recommended)
- *Theopetra Caves*, Greece, Meteora, Kalambaka, Greece
- *Franchthi Caves,* near the Koilada village, Argolis, Greece

Whether our lost relatives the Neanderthals became extinct by natural selection, or they died out due to disease or warfare, their extinction from Europe and Asia was complete by about 35 thousand years ago. By 28 thousand years ago, the Cro-Magnon occupied much of southern Europe having out-competed the remaining Neanderthals. Slowly but surely Human were winning the game of survival. The question scientists are now asking is why humans succeeded? It seems that the Neanderthals went out with a 'whisper' rather than with a 'bang.' As for the humans, they had chosen the best territories, yet there are so many other causes which may have led to the extinction of the Neanderthals. Maybe it was the harsh climate, maybe it was the humans or some kind of disease, or they ran out of wild game, or a combination of a lot of different factors. Did humans have something to do with the demise of the Neanderthals? But the primary assumption for their demise may be that it was not modern man but Mother Nature. Without the competition from others, human population exploded in Europe with the striking progress in tool technology, craft and communication. Unlike our ancestors, modern humans are capable of altering their environment to meet their needs and, with such unprecedented ability, came unprecedented power.

Yet with all our entire natural advantages, it remains to be seen whether our human species will match the longevity of the Neanderthals. Just think for a moment; the Neanderthals lived in Europe for 250 thousand years, and that is what I will call, a successful adaptation. On the other hand, humans have been living in Europe for only 45 thousand years, and nature's jury is still out. If we cease to exist after 500 years or by tomorrow's 'Armageddon,' that will be a very rotten adaptation! Since their extinction, we are, sadly, the only remaining humans on Earth.

DIFFERENCES & SIMILARITIES NEANDERTHAL VS HOMO

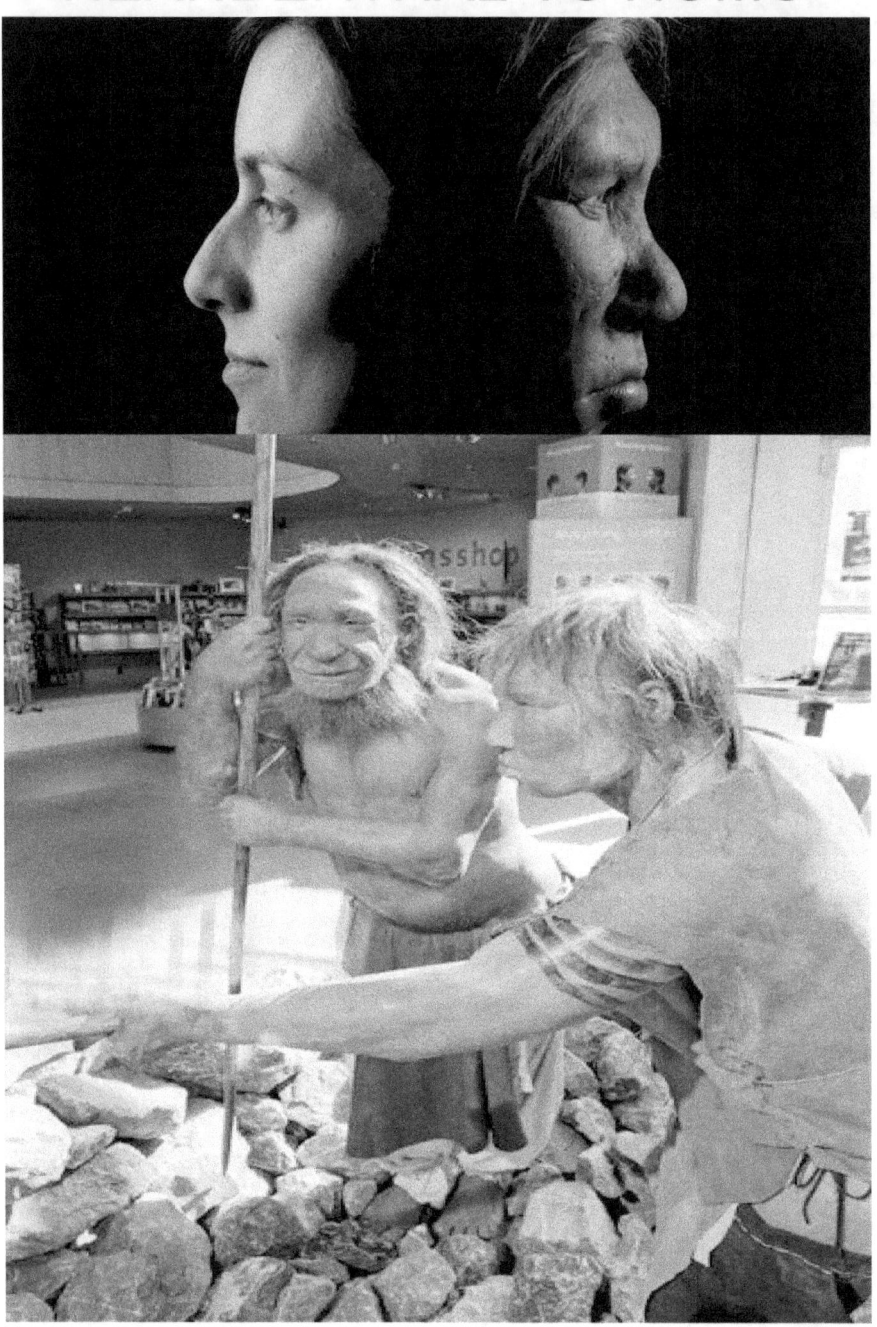

SCENES
NEANDERTHAL MUSEUM
METTMENN, GERMANY

SCENES
NEANDERTHAL MUSEUM
METTMENN, GERMANY

STONE TOOL-MAKING

CARVING PROCESS

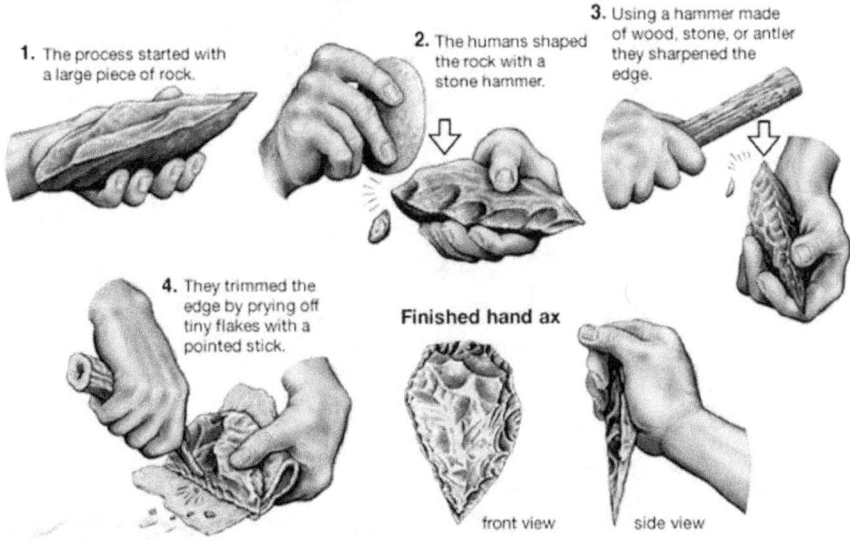

1. The process started with a large piece of rock.
2. The humans shaped the rock with a stone hammer.
3. Using a hammer made of wood, stone, or antler they sharpened the edge.
4. They trimmed the edge by prying off tiny flakes with a pointed stick.

Finished hand ax

front view　　side view

FIRE TO COOK & HEATING

PRE-HISTORIC HUMAN BURIAL CEREMONY

NEANDERTHAL CAVE FAMILY

BONE MADE TOOLS

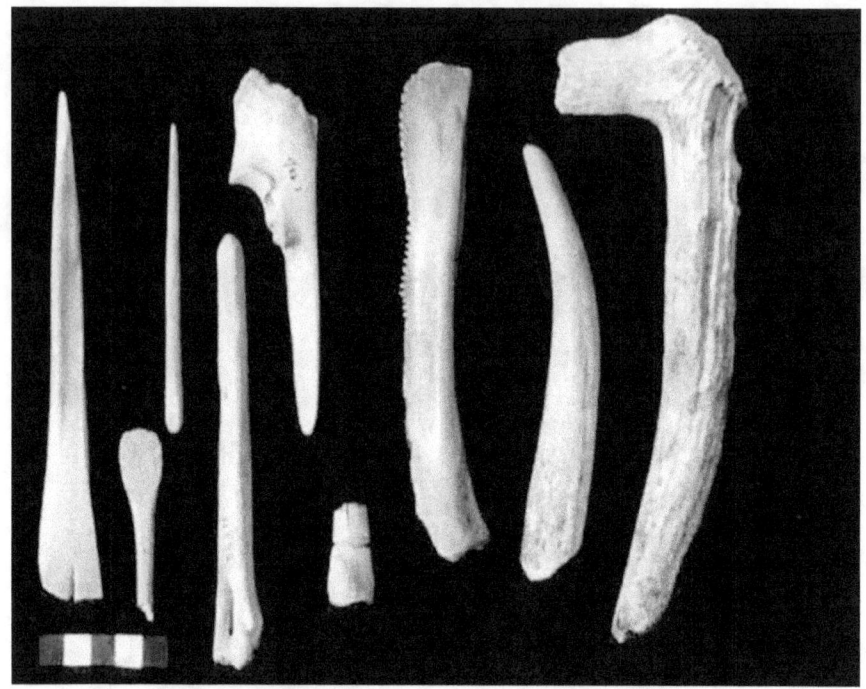

FINISHED HAND AX

PRE-HISTORIC MORALITY
CARING FOR THE SICK

PROVIDING FOOD FOR ALL

PRE-HISTORIC MORALITY CARING FOR INFANTS

PRE-HISTORIC SYMBOLISM & BEGINNING OF ANIMISM

CEREMONIAL DANCE

HAND-MADE TANNERY

FOR ALL SORTS OF USE

PRE-HISTORIC HABITAT 50.000 YEARS AGO

EARLY HUMAN HABITAT

EARLY HUMAN HABITAT MATALA CAVES, GREECE AT NIGHT

DAYTIME

EARLY HUMAN HABITAT MATALA CAVES, GREECE

A DAY IN THE LIFE OF PRE-HISTORIC MAN

A DAY IN THE LIFE OF PRE-HISTORIC MAN

THEY HUNTED & USED FIRE

A DAY IN THE LIFE OF PRE-HISTORIC MAN

TRANSFORMED REALITY INTO SYMBOLISM

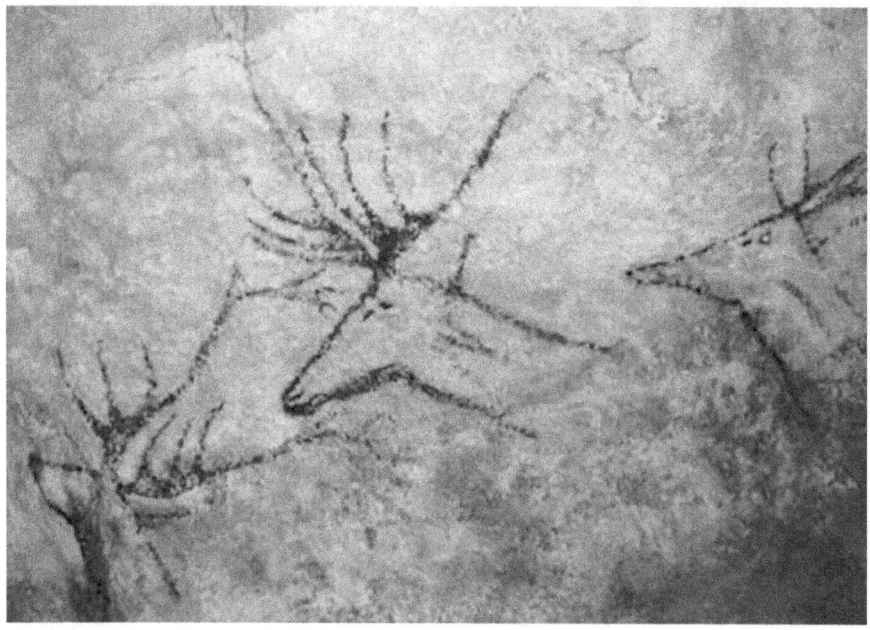

A DAY IN THE LIFE OF PRE-HISTORIC MAN

TRANSFORMED REALITY INTO SYMBOLISM

A DAY IN THE LIFE OF PRE-HISTORIC MAN

A CLOSE HUNTING CONTACT

EXTENDED FAMILY

NUCLEUS FAMILY

A DAY IN THE LIFE
OF PRE-HISTORIC MAN

A DAY IN THE LIFE OF PRE-HISTORIC MAN

SHALLOW RIVER FISHING

DIVISION OF LABOURING TASKS

GROUP SOCIALISING

INDEX I

Abuses, 10
Adaptation, 105
adaptation, 116
adaptation, 126
Adaptation, 161
Adaptation, 27
Adaptation, 44
aerodynamics, 86
Africa, 110, 119
African Continent, 15, 146
African DNA, 165
afterlife, 24, 25
Agasta humanoids, 146
Agasta, 149
Agricultural Revolution, 160
AIDS, 107
Alfred Russell Wallace, 13
Altamira, 157
altruism, 114, 116, 119
Amazon Rainforest, 15, 18, 42, 106
amphibians, 42
Andromeda Galaxy, 72
Animism, 33
animist, 13, 14, 18, 143, 148, 156
Animists' spirits, 159
anthropoid, 148, 149, 154
Antikythera mechanism, 73
Ape to Man, 50
Apes, 146
Aquinas, 77
Arabian Desert, 14
archaeological, 143
Archaeological, 15
Aristotle, 77
atheist, 10
atom, 36
Austerity, 113
austerity, 116
Bar Mathias, 10

Basilosaurus, 124
believe, 108
Bertrand Russell, 11
Big Bang, 12, 20, 35, 36, 40, 47, 51, 54, 70
bigotry, 10
biological life, 10, 14, 39, 111, 143
birth of the universe, 10
bitumen, 53
Books, 10
British Eugenics Society, 114
Bronze Age, 14, 38
burial grounds, 146, 147
burial, 148
Cambrian Explosion, 41
Canadian Arctic, 144
Catholicism, 13
cave artist, 156
caves, 147
Charles Darwin, 10, 13, 78, 85, 120
chemical elements, 38
chemical, 145
Christianity, 10, 16
chromosomes, 163
Copernicus, 85
Cro-Magnon, 34, 46, 72 143, 146, 160
Dalecarlia, 46
Darwin, , 32, 105
David Hume, 76
Descartes, 87
Dinosaurs, 43
DNA, 10, 39, 74, 108, 114, 118, 126, 152, 154, 161.
Dolphins, 123, 124
Düsseldorf, 145
Earth, 38
Ebola, 27
Eiffel Illustrated Exploration

Series Vol. 8, 86
European Continent, 151
embryology, 127
endosymbiosis, 40
energy, 36
engravings, 155
Eugenics program, 113
Eugenics, 119
eukaryotic organisms, 40
European Continent, 145, 154
evolution,13, 14, 23 , 105, 108, 122,
family tree, 161, 163
Fertile- Crescent, 11
Galileo Galilei, 85
Galileo, 35, 85
Genesis 1, 35
genomes, 163
geological, 143
geologist, 144
Gilbert, 87
God, 30
Golden Rule, 28
Golgi Apparatus, 125
grass, 44, 50
graves, 148
Gravity, 37
gravity, 39, 75, 80
Greek Orthodox Church, 29
healers, 29
helium, 37
historical, 10
HIV, 27, 107
Holocene, 52
Holy Books, 21
Holy, 10
Homeopathy, 19
Homo antecessor, 46
Homo Group, 46
Homo habilis, 46,151
Homo naledi, 48,168

Homo sapiens idaltu, 46
Homo sapiens, 34, 45, 144
human cranium, 145
human DNA, 165
human genome, 167
human origins, 11
humanist morality, 10
humanoids, 160
hunters and gatherers, 144
hydrogen atom, 37
hyoid, 148
Hyoid-bone, 47
Ice Age, 44, 49, 143, 145,152, 154,
Icelandic, 144
idealism, 159
immune system, 167
intelligent design, 10, 127, 128, 150, 164
intermixed, 154
Iran, 31
Iron Age, 38, 54
Jehovah Witness, 32
Jewish, 10
Jewish, 16
Joseph Priestley, 31
Josephus Bar Mathias, 33, 58
Josephus, 10
Kepler, 85
Law of Falling Bodies, 86
Laws of Chemistry, 55, 74, 75, 79, 90
Law of Motion, 88
Laws of Gravitation, 88
Laws of Nature, 167
Laws of Gravity, 74
Laws of Inertia, 86
Laws of Mathematics, 74
Laws of Motion, 87
Laws of Natural Selection, 74
Laws of Nature, 10, 15, 18,19, 20,

22, 25, 27, 33, 36, 37, 39, 45, 54, 69, 74, 76, 90, 118, 160
Laws of Physics, 74
Laws of Planetary Motion, 74, 85
Laws of Thermodynamics, 74
Leeuwenhoek, 87
Leonardo da Vinci, 91
life after death, 17, 160
Madrassas, 11
mammals, 123
material reality, 159
Material World, 160
materialism, 13
materialist, 34
Mediterranean, 10, 148
Mesopotamia, 11, 53, 55
metaphorical, 10
metaphors, 60
Meteora caves, 24
Mettmann valley, 147
Mettmann, 145
misogyny, 23
mitochondria, 40
Modern Man, 144
mononucleosis, 167
Moon, 39
moral, 15, 17, 117
morality, 14, 20, 81, 109, 111, 112, 115, 118, 128, 160
Moses Maimonides, 84
Mother Nature, 170
Mother Teresa, 23, 25
Muslims, 16
myths, 35, 58, 59, 143
Natural Selection, 119
Natural Evolution, 28, 124, 128 ,145
Natural Selection, 23, 44, 74, 79, 105, 111, 116, 118, 126, 161, 167
Nazca Lines, 84
Neanderthal DNA, 164

Neanderthal genome, 163
Neanderthal, 60, 153
Neanderthals, 14, 34, 45, 46, 48, 72, 143, 146
New Testament, 10
Newton, 87
Nile River, 148
Old Testament, 10
Origins of Species, 107, 108, 114, 118
Orthodox Church, 13
Pablo Picasso, 156
palaeontologist, 144
Pangaea, 43
pattern, 19, 149
pattern-meaning, 143
patterns, 59, 155
pattern-seeking, 17
Permian Extinction, 43
pedophiles, 24
Periodic Table, 75, 80
photosynthesis, 40
pirates, 57
Portugal, 154
Primates, 44
Prisoners of Our Ideals, 11, 16, 25, 33
proto-cultural, 11
protons, 36
proto-spiritualism, 11
quantum mechanics, 36
Qur'an, 10
religious industry, 11
Richard Dawkins, 117
ritual burial, 147
ritual, 149
Robert Boyle, 87
Roman Imperial Cult, 10, 33, 58
Sahara Desert. 123
Saudi Arabia, 31

Seek and you shall find, 17, 18
Shaman's, 24, 29, 159
Siberian Peninsula, 154
Slovenia, 168
Smithsonian Museum, 126
Social Darwinian, 112, 120
Socrates, 77
South East Asia, 146
Spain, 146
spirits, 159
spiritual-strength, 157
State of Nature, 109, 111, 117, 118, 119, 120
Stephen Hawking, 54
Stone Age, 13, 35, 47, 155, 160
stone-tool, 161
supernatural, 158
supernova, 37
symbolism, 19, 149, 155
South Africa, 158
state of nature, 111
Temple-Gods, 56
The Amazon Ilustrated Exploration Series, 13
Theory of Evolution, 125
Thomas Aquinas, 73
Thomas Hobbes, 52, 106
Thomas Paine, 28
Tigris-Euphrates Rivers, 53
Torcana Boy, 111
Tree of Life, 122, 129
Triceratops, 43
Uruk, 52
Valley of the Whales, 123
Venditive Cave, 163
voyage of the dead, 149
wall-arts, 149
Whales, 123
wishful-thinking, 34
Working man, 151
Zodiac Signs, 56, 73, 88
Zodiac, 19

CHAPTER II
HUMAN SOCIETIES: FROM PALEOLITHIC TO NEOLITHIC TIMES

It is the end of the last Ice Age and our close ancestors, the Neanderthals, have not survived Europe's freezing desolation. Yet, for the next 25 thousand years, the Humans learned to become successfully adaptable to both the European and Middle East environments by any means necessary. They were hunter-gatherers and traveled light along with their families. They survive one meal away from starvation and, because of their constant need for new food sources, they could never settle down. But these nomadic people were about to change the world, for their man-made Palaeolithic Revolution (Stone-Age in Greek) would make our contemporary civilisation possible. They would set humanity on a long biological, political, social, economic and technological journey to the modern world.

Around 20 thousand years ago, earth's climate began to change, the ice glaciers melted and with these geological changes, the world once again came to life. One of the best geographical places for humans to live now was in the Middle East's biologically diversified environment called the *Fertile Crescent* of Mesopotamia---from present day Palestine to Iraq. The Fertile Crescent soil is near important rivers including the Nile River, the Tigris and the Euphrates rivers and tributaries. It is a geographical region which curves, like a quarter-moon shape that stretches from the Persian Gulf, through modern-day southern Iraq, Syria, Lebanon, Jordan, the coast of Israel to northern Egypt along the Nile River. The hills were dotted with a variety of fruit trees which spread rapidly as nature's climate improved their growth rate. The hilly woodlands were like a garden supporting new species of edible plants, while animals flourished in the upland fertile lands. It was a hunter-gatherer's perfectly balanced environment. The region is important as the "bridge" between Africa and Eurasia, where climate changes during the Ice Age led to repeated extinction events when eco-systems became squeezed against it. It was here that nomadic groups found something new which would change humanity forever. They discover a huge variety of wild plants in the grasses. It was a vast supply of grain, and this was the core-beginning that made human social development possible. One may say that this region represents the *Cradle of Civilisation.*

The human presence is scattered across the valleys of the Fertile Crescent, but these ancient people left no man-made written language to tell their stories, and all the contemporary archaeologists could do, was to dig. For example, in the 1920's a great archaeologist, *Dorothy Garrot,* conducted excavations around *Mount Carmel* in Palestine. She was looking at a cave which she thought to be occupied by humans at least 50 thousand years earlier. Instead, she unearthed a human skeleton of a man buried around 15 thousand years ago. The man was curled up wearing an intricate headband made of seashells. This made her believe that she had discovered a new "people" and she named them, the *Natufians.* The Natufian culture was an Epipaleolithic culture that existed from about 12,500 to 9,000 BC in the Fertile Crescent region. This culture appeared in the region before the introduction of the Agricultural Revolution and carried on afterwards.

As Dorothy Garrot continued digging, she found something that archaeologists had never seen before. It was a hand-tool with a bone-handle holding a sharp curved edge that was coated with a natural residue of wild grass—an ancient form of wheat. The hand-tool was a sickle, a tool designed specially for cutting tall grass. This demonstrated that the Natufians were using a tool for harvesting large quantities of wheat. Every year, these ancient people would have found ripening wheat-grass in large fertile land areas. As time went by, many non-edible grasses were discarded by preserving edible grass-species for their own consumption: *barley and wheat.* These wild grasses were the forerunners of modern crops. As travellers, they had to carry everything they harvested, and this burden would ultimately change their way of life. These nomadic people, living in the Jordan valley, had everything they needed in one place, food and water.

Archaeologists estimated that there were no more than a few hundred families living in the Jordan and Palestine region at the time. There was enough wild wheat and barley to sustain them well; and one single harvester, when harvesting wild grain for 3 weeks, could sustain a family of 4 for a whole year. The kind of grains that were discovered by the Natufians still feed more than half of the world's population today. It should be noted that of all the foods the Natufians ate, grain was unique in one vital way; it did not decay. As they kept it dry, it lasted for many years. This meant that, for the first time, humans had food to consume for a long time. As they learned how to safely store their grain in large quantities, this became a core reason for staying in one place.

They also built shelters to last them from one year to the next. The landscape was chosen carefully and many of these shelters had stone walls. They remained in such shelters from generation to generation down through the centuries. These shared shelters were not large in size and the community itself was comprised of no more than 5 to 10 families or 25 to 50 people. Inside, each shelter had its own open fireplace where food was cooked.

Evidence left by early inhabitants; from pieces of flint, shavings of bones, burned seeds found in the ashes to complete stone-tools, has provided us with clues about their lives. For the archaeologists, these clues are a goldmine of information it showing the kind of wild game they were able to catch, which was vital to their daily diet. They were effective hunters and anything that flew, swam or ran was hunted and eaten.

While the Natufians were hunting anything, they were primarily aimed at catching large animals using the *slingshot* as a method of stone-killing. As such, they moved for many days at a time, with the rhythms of the seasons and animal migration, always staying close to their high protein food sources. Despite their hard life, they seemed physically fit, for they lived well and often stationed a lot to rest. Along with the hunter-gatherers' routine, as shown by well healed-bone fractures, their hunting was a dangerous way of life. Their weapons were fragile and thus prone to injuries from slightly wounded animals. Their well healed-bone fractures show that another member of the group took care of these injuries, fed and took care of the hunter back to health. Such moral obligation and value was mutually shared by all members of the group. This caring for each other demonstrates the *innate moral obligation* which was felt is still part of our natural biological instincts. These moral obligations; to take care of the needy, protect their women, the children and the old, were a part of the core-reality make up of the ancient communities. Since the members of the group were close kin, who were likely to meet each other again and again for the rest of their lives, this was a good prerequisite for altruism. Evolution and Natural Selection applied to all members of the group *"as a rule of thumb"* or the Golden Rule. This rule of thumb was ingrained in their brains—as well as in ours--and convinced people to be nice to everyone in the group because they were likely to meet those more often. Such innate moral instinct was not prescribed or inscribed upon the Natufians by a "theistic" power or authority, nor was it dictated to them by any other celestial form or an "intelligent designer" in the sky.

Their campsites show evidence of constant repairs of tools and, like all Stone-Age people, they relied on flint. By trimming flat stones in the right way, they were able to create a variety of cutting axes and piercing tools. These tools were precious for their survival as well as round-stones used in slingshots. Out of these tools stands out the bone-sickles laid with double blades for harvesting grass and plants more efficient. Those were all of the things that characterised the Natufian hunting-gathering lifestyle, the sickle for harvesting, the spear for hunting, and the sling stones for fighting and their colourful ornaments and decorations which were part of their culture.

As such, the Natufians had a unique artistic sense for carving decorations and carefully shaped their seashells as necklaces.

They also carefully shaped their mortars and pestles and produced those far greater than their needs. These mortar and pestle were made of a single stone, carved in a circular shape with smooth surfaces, with bevelled rims, with wide and balanced stance and with even thickness of the vessel. This item served the Natufians well for grinding seeds into powder to bake coarse biscuits made from a combination of different grains. They were baking a kind of pancake which was the ancestor of the Middle Eastern style of flat bread or *pita*. Skilful processing of the grains into fine powder meant that their teeth were preserved, since the coarseness of the grains was limited.

What is notable is the enormous size of the mortars and pestles, for they were far too large and heavy to be carried around while on hunting-gathering expeditions. Evidence suggests that the Natufians left them behind year after year. Eventually they began to settle down in the shelters where large grain-storage and a number of large mortars and pestles, were concentrated. In those settlements the Natufians understood how to tan leather and used the hollowness of gourds to store seeds, nuts and dried berries. They were, in fact, creating a balance diet; food with vegetable, meat and starch. Their daily activities and preservation techniques were celebrated and kept the clan together. It also meant that they could plan ahead and rely on the future. Inevitably they were directing the future biological evolution of plans by choosing the best, the biggest and the sweetest to carry home for eating and replanting. Unknown to the Natufians, it was the seeds from those plants which were thrown in their "garbage-pile," along with bones, that created a moist and organically rich growth garden. The seeds would sprout and cross pollinate to create better strains of plants out of these accidental gardens.

Evidence of hunter-gathering groups in Africa and Australia today shows that they have an intensive shared community structure; rather than the individualism of taking, they are sharing and giving. We know almost nothing of the Natufian's social structure, but in today's hunter-gathering communities, the social structure is complex, regulating members of small groups that depend on each other for support. We know that their concept of privacy was unknown and we know that groups met together periodically, as part of larger bands, to trade or share priced materials which helped maintain an extensive social structure of kin. This trade kept the wider Natufian culture together, it enabled them to introduce their tools to a wider region and they were also experimenting with the beginnings of trade commerce.

With the spread of trade commerce also initiated the spread of ideas, myths and legends, agricultural-tools, new styles of decorations and new foods. However, these meetings among clans had more fundamental purposes and objectives. Natural Selection, for their survival as a species demanded the injection of new genes into the clans. With permanent settlements now, the Natufian world was changing. Increasingly, they identified with the geographical areas in which these clusters of huts were located. Their burial rituals and beliefs are all but gone, but their burial decorations are preserved. Here people could make and keep ornaments and other symbolic possessions like beautiful necklaces made of shell, carved animal teeth and depictions of animal heads with long horns. Based on this evidence, we know that they held burial ceremonies for the deaths of prominent persons. They made their burial a sacred place, a tradition that humans still hold today. The grieving family added into the grave the kind of objects that were favoured by the deceased; knives, tools and wares which were used in daily life. These graves were found across the Natufian world. The dead were all under 55 years old and died from bone and skull injuries.

The Natufian way of life continued for 4 thousand years but, in less than 10 years, all came to an abrupt end. The ice glaciers returned to Europe some 12 thousand years ago, trapping the Earth's fresh water in a frozen state. The rest of the planet became colder and drier. Contemporary scientists called this short Ice Age the *"Younger Dryas."* In Mesopotamia and the Arabian Peninsula there were a vast drought and a great environmental catastrophe, resulting in a spread-out famine. It may have been a sustained series of the worst droughts so the wild grain-food that the Natufians relied upon for their survival just was not available anymore. This may have forced them back to a more nomadic life-style whereby they had to shift their effort and dismantle their groups into more manageable numbers during this drought period. Here it is important to notice that the natural world did not create natural resources to be suitable to the needs of the Natufians. In fact, the natural-world was not aware of the existence and consumption needs of the Natufians, for it simply went about its natural geological course based on the Laws of Nature. It was the Laws of Nature, where various natural conditions caused the creation of other causes; whether those causes affected the Natufians was immaterial. This means that Nature itself went about its "business" without being aware of the positive (fertile soils) or negative effects (Ice Age or drought) it had upon any living species—plants or animals--on earth, including the Natufians of the Middle East or the European Neanderthals of the Human race. In other words, there was not some mysterious force behind these environmental conditions which "gave" at first, and then "took-away," something that was valuable to the

Natufians or the Neanderthals.

The dry lands, which were as far as the Mediterranean Sea, the Jordan Valleys and up to the Carmel Mountain of Palestine, had negative effects on the village life of the Natufians. These villages were fragmented and their solid social structure became weaker. The only slim chance of survival was in the dry lake of Jordan which exposed a fertile plain. It was here, in the shores of today's Lake Galilee, that a few Natufian refugees attempted to survive. Fresh waters running down from the hills fed a handful of natural springs that kept this plain land moist and fertile. But there were new challenges to be faced, for this oasis was very different from the wetlands they once occupied. This new natural condition was met head-on through the process of *human adaptation,* which humans had practiced throughout their biological history.

Archaeologists concluded, from evidence found, that this new land had shorter grass; therefore the Natufians needed to create their own controlled landscape, by digging and planting seeds--from their own grain stock--which they had brought with them. This simple method of selective adaptation was the beginning of a new way of life which, ultimately, transformed the face of the earth. In fact, by adapting to this new method of producing their own food they became the world's first farmers. The drought lasted for over a thousand years and then in less than a generation, the Ice Age of the Younger Dryas ended. Earth's land became a lot more moist and warmer and, at last, the weather became regular and reliable. The new conditions were adequate for farming. These farmers invented a new way of life which contemporary farmers cannot deviate too far from.

Contemporary archaeologists are probing the land in the Fertile Crescent region for evidence of early farming. Among the extraordinary things they discovered was that the seeds of barley and wheat they found from the lands near the Dead Sea were much larger than the wild varieties. It told them that the early farmers were taking part in the *biological evolution of natural selection,* where the developed seeds had a new cultivate-strength and they were creating the first domesticated varieties: the new morphology of seeds. It took many generations for the wild grain to change their slim to bulging heads we recognise today. These changes had dramatic effects in the production of farming products. Farming became a time-consuming, labour intensive and very serious work production---from planting to harvesting to assorting to grinding. Storage capacity gradually increased as farming yield also increased dramatically and new granaries had to be built. Life for the villagers had become less care free as life became more intensive and practical. This new lifestyle came with a cultural cost, for they no longer had the time to create extensive varieties of ornamental decorations as Natufians.

Agricultural communities grew and developed by their practical tasks of grain production and distribution, along with trade and commerce among clans and tribes. Their subliminal focus was also concentrated on a sense of appreciation for the things they had achieved and the well-being they enjoyed. The direction of their emotional appreciation turned towards the Sun, which they viewed as the primary giver of all the things they had achieved. The Sun played an important role in the planting and the harvesting of crops and the focus of their beliefs was associated with it. The Sun became the object of veneration, a means to their daily schedule of early rising and resting after a long day's work, a time of thankful celebration with an emotional sense of protection and security. The need to be thankful and their fear of insecurity became a faith and a belief that the Sun was "up-there" for the sole purpose of meeting their exclusive personal and community needs. Conveniently, these beliefs clouded and by-passed their own human achievements, their own effort of hard work, their own ingenuity in the planting and harvesting; and instead of thanking each other, they turned their appreciation not on nature, but on the solar mythology of the "Sun." Thus they invented and created the pagan Sun-God with solar attributes in agricultural communities. The pagan Sun became personified as a male Sun-God which eventually developed into an intricate pagan mythology in many agricultural communities of the Fertile Crescent and beyond. There was no one present to suggest the need to control their thoughts. This means that whatever pattern-meaning their mind invented about the Sun, it was attractive and was believed to be true.

As such, for the ancient villagers of the Fertile Crescent, the glowing Sun-God gave them courage and a self-esteem, which they have never consciously had before; a stepping-stone to face the difficulties of their daily lives. The image of the Sun became their illusive self-consciousness; an abstraction of themselves as being encamped outside the world, but in a popular form. The pagan Sun became a universal source of consolation and justification and offered them a fantastic spiritual aroma. Through their worship they found an illusionary source of happiness, a perpetual state of affairs which needed more theistic illusions to support it, and a self-entrapment which humanity still faces today.

In the farming villages, the ancients treated their huts as permanent homes, and each year they burned their straw-roofs to get rid of the bugs and the floors were levelled and remade. Like their forebears, the Natufians, also carved stones with drawings, shapes or pictographs with scratch lines marking the signs of 'quantity' and these may be the first recorded numbers;

but not the first *grapto-keimeno* (stone-writing) found in *Kastoria*, Greece dated 7,250 BCE. The biggest changes in the farming villages were the birth of more children. A family could now feed more children which, after all, would also make farming work less burdensome. One must remember that for the hunter-gatherers it was the opposite, for they had to carry their small children on long trips, and could not have more than they could manage. Now farming families could support several generations, and thus give the communities a store-house of skills, talents and leadership wisdom.

Once the farmers began farming they had to maintain and repeat their work-schedule year after year and keep surplus seeds for the following season. They needed to continue growing food to support their own families and the rest of the community, which included the elders and tradesmen, the artisans and the young, the old and the sick. Inevitably populations grew with more communities, more people, more productive farming and more production of food. Humans were now living on a larger scale than before and this was a huge challenge. You see, communities had to be organised, division of labour had to be established, production and consumptions had to be recorded, large grain storehouses had to be built and the first bureaucracy and leadership had to be formulated. Out of this social structure, traditional leaders or chiefs had to step forward to arrange and control these socio-biological entities. This was the beginning of the creation of social institutions; having the elders or chiefs of clans, the shamans and healers, formulating the first bare-bones of a social support structure. Humans have now taken a giant leap forward into their future, their families and clans were united into larger communities: we were now living in *societies with leaders.*

The development of civilization in Fertile Crescent, including Egypt and Mesopotamia, was due to the Nile, the Tigris and the Euphrates rivers, which made agriculture easy and very productive. But the surrounding nations, at first, were pastoral. The civilization was founded upon the divined king with despotic powers who owned all the land. There was a polytheistic religion with a supreme god to whom the King and Temple-priests had a especially close relation. There was a military aristocratic hierarchy, and also an influential priestly class. The priestly class was often able to encroach on the loyal power if the king was weak or if he was involved in a difficult war. The farmers were serfs, belonging to the king, the military or the priestly aristocracy.

There was a considerable difference between various kingdom religious beliefs and organised theology. For instance, the Egyptians were preoccupied with death, and believed that the souls of the dead descend into the underworld, where they are judged by god *Osiris* according to the manner of their life on earth. Babylonia had more warlike development than Egypt. There was a period when the various cities fought each other, but in the end Babylon became supreme and an established empire. Unlike Egypt, the Babylonian religion was more concerned with prosperity in this world than happiness in the next. Magic, divination, and astrology, though not peculiar to Babylonia were more developed than elsewhere, and it was chiefly through Babylon that they acquired their hold on later stages of antiquity.

The religions of Egypt and Babylonia were like other ancient religions, were originally fertility cults. The Earth was female, the Sun male. The bull was normally regarded as an embodiment of male fertility, and bull-gods were a common site. In Babylon, the earth-goddess *Ishtar*, was supreme among female divinities. Throughout the Fertile Crescent, the Great Mother was worshipped under various names. When the Greek colonists arrived they found temples named after her, they named her Artemis and took over the existing cult. Notably this is the origins of *"Diana of the Ephesians."* Much later Christianity transformed her into the *Virgin Mary*, and it was a Council at Ephesus that legitimised the divined title *"Mother of God"* as applied to *"Our Lady."*

As it was the case, where a religion was bound up with the government of the Kingdome or of an empire, political motives did much to transform its archaic features. A god or goddess became associated with the State-power of the day, and had to give, not only an abundance of harvest, but victory in war. A wealthy priestly caste elaborated the ritual and the theology, and fitted together into the polytheism of several divinities of the socio-political components of the empire. Since religion was created to justify authority, we can be sure that it was totalitarian and strictly enforced by the priestly class from its very beginning. Under such circumstances there was no place for reason and common sense any longer and, whoever did not go along with worshiping and perhaps sacrificing to the new deities was killed in their names. In a short period of time, *humanity's 190 thousand years of atheist history* (from 200 hundred thousand of existence), was wiped out and the priestly class pretended that it had never existed in the first place. Being rational was not important anymore.

In the beginning the rulers declared themselves high priests or even deities of their cults. As time went by another cast would take over of the Gods and all their business. Literally the priests were deciding everything from the character of the deities to the rituals and sacrifices which of course benefited the priests. Many of them even managed to keep a tight control on the ruler himself or kill him if the priests considered him a heretic. Over time religions were refined to serve multiple purposes. For instance, the priests could explain natural phenomena such as earthquakes, thunderbolts and hurricanes, and the afterlife which was used to be the privilege of the chosen few. Through association with government, the gods also became associated with morality. The connection between religion and morality became continually closer throughout ancient times. By this time, some 3000 years ago, society had become completely religionised. It is most likely that religion was invented by humans during the Neolithic Era from about 10.000 to seven thousand years ago. The idea of religion spread like virus and within few thousand years the world was entirely affected by religion, that is, with the exception of the Tasmania Island which remained atheist because it was separated from the African mainland.

Primitive religion, near everywhere, was tribal rather than personal. Certain rituals were symbolically performed, which were intended, by complimentary magic, to further the interest of the tribe, especially in respect of fertility, vegetable, animal, and human. The gods were the gods of a conquering aristocracy, not the useful fertility gods of the peasants who tilted the soil. The gods of most elitist class claimed to have created the world, but the most they ever did was to conquer it. When the conquered their kingdoms, what did they do? Did they attend the government? Not a bit of it. Why should they do any day's honest work? Did they practice trade and industry? No they did not. Like the present day clergy, it appears that they fined it easier to live on the revenues and blast of theistic sense of guilt for the people who did not donate. The whole aristocratic caste was made of royal buccaneers. They fought and feasted, and play, and make music and danced; they drink deep and roared with laughter at the lame victims' who served on them. They were never afraid, except of the caste leader or the king.

The winter solstice was a time when the Sun had to be encouraged not to go on diminishing in strength; spring and harvest also called for appropriate ceremonies. These were often such as to generate a great collective excitement, in which individuals lost their sense of separateness and felt themselves at one with the whole tribal religion. All over the known world, at certain stage of religious evolution, sacred animals and human beings were ceremoniously killed and eaten. In different religions, this stage occurred in different dates. Human scarifies usually lasted longer and the sacrificial eating of human victims. Fertile rituals without such cruel aspects were common throughout the Fertile Crescent and Southern Greece, which were agricultural in their symbolism. The inhabitants had multitude cults to worship, in which often, a mere square stone-pillar did duty in the place of a statute of a god. The goat was a symbol of fertility, because the villagers were too poor to possess bulls. When the food was scarce, the stone-pillar was beaten for failing to provide them with fertile crops.

Far away to the north, another continent remained unchanged by its human inhabitants, and virtually unknown to the Middle East people of the Fertile Crescent of present day Syria, Iran and Iraq. Across the vast terrain of Europe 12,000 years ago a dense forest stretched from the coast of Brittany to the Black Sea. Here people still lived as they always had, hunting and gathering wild food while constantly moving from place to place. Eventually, the biological and social revolution that began in the Fertile Crescent would spread across the rest of the world. Nearly all of our ancestors would take on the task of farming but for others it would not happen for many thousand years. About that time Europeans lived a hard life; it was a way of life that lasted for more than 100,000 years. In Spain and Southern France our human-cousins, the Neanderthals, painted images of animals and they hunted for food. For hundreds of thousands of generations they followed and hunted the animal herds within 50 miles from their base-camps, depending on them for their survival that lasted until their extinction 35 thousand years ago.

Now, the Cro-Magnon that live in Europe were about to face a new challenge. They were confronted by newcomers of different people from a different world for the same food sources. This would change them and all human life. This challenge started in the Middle East. Unlike the European Continent, the Fertile Crescent produced an abundance of food from present day Palestine to Iraq. Here the hunter-gatherers lived well, and with the domestication of the dogs, they were able to track hunt much more successfully. Dogs have been our oldest companions in our human journey and death. Archaeologists found a 10,000 year old grave with a female skeleton, side by side with a puppy dog. Who ever buried her made sure to place the puppy next to her head and with her arm over the puppy's body. The assumption here is that, since they domesticated the once wild dogs, it must have set them thinking, why not other wild animals? It would supply them with meat, milk and leather, bones for the dogs and other domesticated usages, and reduce much of their burden of hunting.

Deep in the sand and suffering during the last dry season, the Middle East hunters were forced to change much of their way of life. While most hunters-gathers escaped to an oasis with soil, grass and water, others searched in their traditional hunting lands for what animals were left on them. But the drought eliminated many of the animals. To save themselves, some hunters began migrating further to the north, while others took possession of the smaller animals, such as goats, rather than killing them immediately. Those goats were the first domesticated farm animals and, in time, selected their breeding genes. Today in the Middle East, herders still herd goats the same way. Soon they added other animals to their domesticated list such as donkeys, sheep, pigs and cows. In fact, this small part of the Middle East supplied humanity with its entire domesticated species. From a Darwinian perspective these animals had a better chance of survival under domestication than living in the wild where, for carnivorous predators, they were an easy prey. For the inhabitants of the Fertile Crescent, these domesticated animals provided security of food and predictability.

The drought ended about 11,500 years ago and the world came back to life, and the herders and farmers came together and each owned half of the communities' life puzzle. The herders had the animals and the farmers had the grains to feed the stock and, for the first time in the lifetime of those communities, a ready supply of meat was brought together with cereals. This led people into a different way of life and, with herding and cultivating, they both had to adapt by staying out of each other's way. Not all people took after this new community lifestyle, for the people in the hills stay with herding animals and cultivating small gardens but left no evidence of large scale farming.

By comparing evidence, archaeologists have found remarkable differences herded animals made to farming life. In the lowlands communities were larger and more prosperous and this was because of the herded goats. These herded animals were truly the catalyst for the urban growth humanity known today. People came together in large communities because of the herded goats and extended families worked together and became accustomed to planning for the future. But there was also a downside; as people and animals lived crammed together, hygiene became a health problem and new diseases appeared. So the pressure was on to better organise and to keep everything apart; and to do that, they needed new towns built in new ways.

Small towns began to spread around the hills and valleys of Jordan as the population increased. There was an urban transformation taking place as more settlements were built to accommodate the expanding population. Completely depending on agriculture, they soon expanded into other major areas to begin the process of farming and herding once again. Archaeologists are investigating the evidence that remains of the development of housing structures in agricultural settlements; from a low, single room, round house to larger round houses with compact river-stone walls. These styles of town housing are separated by 9,000 years of history. Beneath these modern desert villages are the first examples of the building methods that are still used today. In these old, stone housing structures the archaeologists found that the rectangular walls and corners were well-built to stand the test of time. This was 4,000 years before the pyramids were built that the builders were using stone-chisels to shape doorways and windows with a sense of creativity and ingenuity. In Jeff Al-Ahma, in Syria, the first complex farming town community of the Middle East was discovered. Here archaeologists' mapped houses that were built more than 10,000 years ago and research revealed all the domestic architectural evolution, including circular to rectangular walls and houses with exterior rectangular style.

The rectangular shape house-style of Jeff Al-Ahma spread and new villages grow with new ideas which show how sophisticated the stone-age architects of these villages were. One can see a small plaza leading to shaped steps on central streets. Doorways open to family houses on each side of the streets. Houses contained mysterious tunnel-shafts inside the walls which turned out to be air conditioning, connecting the upper to the lower level interior of the walls, thus providing air circulation throughout the one or two story houses. Plaster was used to smooth the outer and interior walls and painted in bright colours. These new villages were bustling with life and commercial activities, they had plenty of food and things turned to much pleasanter times. They developed their talents into specialised jobs because they were now more free to devote time to leisure activities, such as knife-making, clay pottery for cooking pots and vases; straw-baskets and, most important, loom weaving cloth. Knife makers collected rose-coloured flint and made the finest blades. The first potters made containers of clay which were left to dry in the sun. Basket makers wove small and large utility baskets for trade with other villagers who used them to store or transport loads of dry-fruits or grain. The same skills were used to develop the first loom-woven fabrics. To do this the skilful artisans developed the earliest technology devised, the first looms which are still found in Middle East villages today. They developed a soft cloth from flax and made linen, which dyes coloured to customary desires.

Households grew to extended families, animal stables were separated from living space, front-rooms and bedrooms were separated from kitchens and storage-rooms and the need for privacy was brought. The architecture then went beyond what was needed for simple shelter. People were using architecture, just like today, to express ideas about the world, of how we should live in it, and how we should relate to our social environment. They paid much attention to the beauty of the domestication objects and possessions. For the first time in Middle East history we see people behaving just like we would behave had we been in their position with arts and crafts. This made life much more interesting, with deeper understanding of home-making. What we witness today is that the ancient people had turned the interior of their house into a living home.

About 9,000 years ago builders of the Middle East invented and developed the first man-made building materials which were smooth, clean and waterproof. These were instantly popular and in great demand, including *plaster* material, which was not entirely utilitarian or functional. Its uses make homes more attractive, more symbolic, more aesthetic value attached and with larger subliminal importance. Plaster material was very versatile and turned up in many sites. In 1975 the Jordanians, while constructing a main highway to Amman, discovered stone-age rooms of an ancient building where an archaeological recorded exposition shows the extended uses of plaster. This was a *Neolithic house* with a plaster floor, with a central groove for heating, cooking and for lighting. The plaster was of excellent quality and very sophisticated. This house was part of Al-Jazal, a large impressive town with hundreds of other similar houses. Plaster was part of its dazzle and every house had plaster flooring which is an expensive material. It is expensive because *lime-plaster* does not exist as a natural resource, for lime had to be processed. It was among the first labour-intensive, man-made material that was ever manufactured by humans. It came from mining and burning limestone in high temperatures and it is a process that requires a lot of labour time and consumption of fuel.

Pagan rituals, by this time, have not changed for the past 4,000 years. The body of a family ancestor has always been buried under the floor inside the house. This way, the family felt that the dead were still with them as a subliminal comfort. Some time later, they uncovered the body and removed the skull and plastered over it to preserve it and gave the image characteristics of the dead. In particular, the face of the dead ancestor was recreated over it with plaster, moulded to cover the orifices and painted it to resemble the face of the loved one. The painted characteristics, or portrait, on the plastered skull identified grandpa from uncle or from aunt. This practice was an ancestor-veneration and shared by many villages as a pagan cult. There was a sequence with these skulls that were selected in order to establish a connection and continuity with the past, connection with the land and perhaps with the household. A family, therefore, could trace its genealogy from one ancestor to the next, all the way back into the past.

Eventually the lineage went so far back that it was lost in the mist of time and the name of the ancestor became meaningless. It entered into a foggy mental-space where symbolism became reality and mythology obscured history and where no one knew for sure how the connections worked anymore. In particular revealed excavations archaeologists found a series of life-size plastered figures in their original state of about 8,000 years. They appeared to have a sense of simplicity which took these figures beyond known or identified ancestors. It is possible that these plastered figures that were buried under the house floor were symbolic or mythical cult figures rather than real ancestors who once lived in the house. The creation of mythical (typological) ancestors was a common practice, for they helped the hierarchical social status of families. These figures were tied together into the spiritual life of the early farmers. The evidence of the pagan cult spiritualism of ancestor veneration was scattered across the region and perhaps beyond.

The origins of pagan spiritualism were found in the middle of the Al-Jazal town where a completely unexpected structural style of a building was revealed. In the center of the town, archaeologists found this much larger round-shaped public building, for it was not a residential house. In its interior they found massive, large cattle horns, which once hung from the wall and were now lying on the floor. Upturned, headless human skeletons were placed side by side in a continuing bench. Watching over them were sculptured figure-heads of vultures. This is the earliest public building where a large number of town's people could gather together under one roof. After 700 hundred years of use something terrible must have happened to this structure causing its destruction.

Archaeologists found an unburied headless skeleton of a 15 to 18 year old young female with her fingers twisted in rigor mortis. Within hours of her death, the whole building went up in flames and her body was covered with burning timber. It was a violent end to this mysterious place. This was not a normal house, with no meeting rooms for political debate, but some kind of special building for some kind of special pagan activities going on. Those pagan activities were functioning under a pagan belief system operating on all sorts of different emotional levels. People were coming together to participate in worship ceremonies. These pagan cult worshipers left carved stone tokens with intricate designs on them; their meaning still remains unknown. There were animal figures associated with human figures and signs; for instance a fox, with a snake, with undulated lines, with a vulture. This combination of figures tells an *Animist* pagan story or a myth and it is associated with death and the vulture. The signs show birds of prey are lifting in the air, headless human bodies. These images of death occurred all across the region; vultures sweeping up bodies and taking off their heads. Centuries later, these images spread as far as 800 kilometres away into present day Turkey. Archaeologists are digging away an entire hill, where they find groups of standing stones or columns double the human height; they are beautifully carved with symbolic figures such as the bull and the lion, the snake and the fox.

Archaeologists now suggest that those columns were not there to hold the roof because their individual heights and sizes are different, but they were there for a pagan ritual platform, a platform where the dead bodies were exposed for the vultures to devour. It was believed that, as the vultures devour the flesh, the spirit would be set free. It is here that we witnessed, for the first time, an organised pagan religion of the dead being transformed from a family ritual to a huge public drama. These new rituals were played in the open air and in a special designated sanctuary. Since there was no settlement at the site, this must have been the place of performing rituals for a number of surrounding communities. This also suggests the communities were networking and that, whatever people were doing in their own community; they were coming together with all sorts of other communities to use one central site which they share. It appears that all the surrounding communities were sharing a common intrigue or fascination with ancestors' death and living creatures. The subliminal connection with the dead ancestor, his burial inside the home, the removal of the skull, the plastering of the skull and placement of it among the living relatives, projects an uninterrupted mythical continuation of the first *life after death* cult with the living world.

The journey from the first farming to cultist practices took about a thousand years and it was time to move on. As communities expanded they needed more fertile land for grain and herding. This is the beginning where extended groups began to colonize new lands and perhaps they needed to adapt to new ways in order to colonize those lands as new agricultural colonists. Between 8 and 7 thousand years ago, colonizing farmers spread out from the Middle East to Turkey and Greece. The journeys were pioneered by traders who made sea voyages in small boats. As such, farmers set out with seeds and a few animals with an aim of farming. These would-be European farmers found a vast continent and faced new challenges, in a new landscape with a new climate. The forest was dense so they moved up through the main rivers, such as, the Danube River, in small numbers and into a continent which was already inhabited. There were lot of people already living there and it was required by the new farmers to establish themselves around and within those powerful establishments and within the communities that were already present. The European hunter-gatherers, who have been living there since the last Ice Age, were in much greater numbers than the newcomers.

The European hunter-gatherers never found grains which could be used or found the right kind of animals which could be domesticated. Their shift to farming, therefore, could not have been possible. But these people were successful survivors of a harsh climate and a lot more skilful and ingenious "on their feet" than most of us are today. Slowly, the European hunter-gatherers were facing upcoming changes and, by 7.000 years ago, the new- comers were in full contact with the river fishing people of Eastern Europe, around present day Slovenia. Here, archaeologists discover how the hunter-gatherers and farmers confronted the new challenges. They would meet together to trade and hunter-gatherers offered horns and furs. As for the farmers, they offered grain-seeds and herded animals for the Europeans to develop and offered their ideas and skills for farming. This means that two ways of life were coming together, sharing new knowledge and forming bonds. Of course, the Middle East explorers pressed on, looking for good farming land to cultivate and survive. As such, the families became neighbours and hunter-gatherers soon will become farmers. When we refer to farming we need to understand that it was on a bare subsistence level of food production (nor a present day mass agro-production). This was the level of farming that was moving into Europe at this time. This was a peasant, simple farming, using a base range of tools and they were settling in small patches of land which was appropriate for farming and growing the grain-seeds that they had brought with them. They were constantly adapting to this new environment but also changing it because they were moving into a forester environment which needed the harvesting of its trees.

To the early farmers the forest must have been a fearful place, for it was easy to get lost, there were bears and wolves or perhaps the forest had its own sounds (made by unseen tiny animals moving around) which were interpreted as mysterious spirits. By now, the farmers did something that would change Europe forever, for they began to systematically clear-cut the forest and changed the face of Europe forever. They needed to let-in the sun by sawing-off southern Europe's forests with small stone axes similar to those they used in the Middle East. From there they moved towards the center of the European great forest and their simple technology changed to dominate larger standing forests. Some patches of forest could be burned, but large parts had to be cut down with stone axes, one tree at the time. The results were the appearance of scattered patches of human occupation, often quite a distance from one another, but forming a social connection with one another, that went across the European Continent. It was not a huge swath of clear-cut enterprise from coast to coast; it was rather individuals and small groups that set up their homes and expanded from the woodlands and beyond their homesteads.

As these pioneers were building their own way of life in Europe, they lost touch with the Middle East. Behind them, in the Fertile Crescent of Mesopotamia, the old way of life was in crisis. Over 2,000 years the villagers changed the land by their impact on the environment. Once upon a time, the people were moving around, they did not stay too long in one place and thus they did not have the opportunity to impact the environment. But now, as people were beginning to settle down in one place, the impacts they created built on each other, and they did continue affecting the environment generation after generation. In Al-Jazal archaeologists found evidence of that crisis, particularly in the wooden posts that held the roof of the main building. The posts that started being up to 60cm in diameter decreased gradually in size and this reflects the decrease of large trees in the close proximity to the town itself. Then the plaster began to deteriorate even though the builders cherished. You see, all the available wood which was growing in the near-by woodland hills was harder and harder to reach and, eventually, the supply could not keep up with the demand. There is evidence of clear-cut deforestation that spreads out from this ancient settlement; the forest that should be a renewable resource. In addition, there was now a problem with goats that love sweet brush, which when eaten away, causes irreversible deforestation. As long as there were goats around, those trees would never grow back. This means that, for the first time in history, human communities would be destroyed by the environment which they created. Large communities of several thousand inhabitants were beginning to be reduced to several hundred, even creating ghost towns. The town of like Al-Jazal was finally abandoned and its archaeological records almost disappeared after 2,500 years of settlement. As a result, many of the survivors were forced to become mobile or nomadic herders ranging across the open highlands. It would be more than 1,200 years before farmers found a new way to survive this environmental catastrophe landscape.

In the European Continent, farmers were still using methods brought out of the Middle East; except this world was quite different. A lot of the imported hand-tools had to be revised or modified and they had to work out means and ways to construct houses built out of timber (log-homes) instead of the adobe bricks they used previously. They needed to discover other ways of dealing with dense forest. As they moved towards the north, they encountered a European climate where the seasons were much shorter and the weather a lot more extreme. In this environment ambient farming seemed impossible and, for thousands of years, they had no answer to freezing winter and could go no further. This was nature's material reality which humans had to adapt to it; and they did.

Finally, they succeeded in breaking through their impasse by completely re-thinking and re-adapting their farming method. For the first time, they realised, that seasonal timing was very critical and worked out exactly when to replant, how to grow and how to harvest before winter set in. They also learned how to use porous soils and farming began spreading in all directions by continually clear-cutting more forest and planting higher yield crops. So the first wooden plough arrived for the solution to the problem. With the plough the farmers could now cultivate much larger areas and dug deeper to turn over these heavy northern soils. This was a unique European farming method and was adopted by other farmers with incredible speed. One of the reasons that such rapid expansion was so astonishingly fast was because farmers needed to cultivate more and more lands as communities and human populations were also rapidly expanding. They changed the environment so rapidly that they also created a new way of life. As such, they changed the material reality of the natural environment they lived-in.

Archaeologists call these new communities the "long house people," for they lived in these long log-houses together with their animals. These long houses were constructed with massive timbers and whole tree-trunks which held up the roof. The occupants' possessions revealed a new conformity; they all used one kind of axe and they had one kind of pottery in size as a new method of adaptation. It was also these long-house people who perfected the use of the most European farm animals: the dairy cattle. In only 300 years farmers spread out further north and into present day Russia and westwards to northern France. As such, the European Continent was dotted with cleared farming fields and the face of Europe has changed forever.

As the farmers moved north, they found additional hunter-gatherer groups who had plenty of food in a harsh climate that the indigenous farmers there struggled with. These northern people had studied their world for 5,000 years but they left little behind in their graves. But in Denmark, at Vedbaer, there is a cemetery with 24 bodies and they were buried and laid out on top of deer bones and swan's wings. These people however, show no influence from the Middle East and they had retained their own hunter-gatherer culture and were allowed to decay as they lay in their graves. Their skulls remained with the rest of their skeletons along with the decorated things they cherished. These hunter-gatherers were able to co-exist with the farmers because they were useful to each other and probably lived side by side for a much longer time than archaeologists previously thought and all sorts of sexual relations must have developed between them. The pool of newly introduced genealogical genes were widely spread which strengthened the biological make up of the European hunter-gatherer groups and vice versa. As the farmers became predominant, the hunter-gatherers must have melted away and joined the rest of the farming population. But the hunter-gatherers were creative and curious people, for they too adopted a kind of farming suited to their style of life.

There is little evidence to suggest that these two distinctive groups clashed violently with one another. Mostly they taught each other and there were plenty of opportunities to find land to farm. The advantages slowly went from being hunter-gatherers up on the hills, to going down on the plain with the rest of the farmers, exchanging things with them, interacting in human contact and being part of a larger group. However, ultimately the decisions that were made were about food, and the hunter-gatherers abandoned their life-style because of their fear of hunger and for the security of harvest in settled farming. Infusing farmer with hunter they created a culture which started out our western way of life.

The burial rituals included the traditional burial grounds in family caves in the belief that the new dead relative was now part of the whole and united in death. This was an illusionary attempt to create another world whose entrance was through a long underground passage or "passage-craves;" thus the myth of the underworld where the dead are located. Sometimes the entrance of the passage was aligned with a shaft where the rising of the sun would shine into the interior of the grave site at a particular time of the year. These were probably areas where ritual ceremonies took place at a critical time of the year. The final resting place was a separate chamber where the bones of the ancestors were kept. Relatives would go into the burial cave and mentally connect or 'communicate' with the dead in an active ritual worship. The rituals, in many cases, were set to communicate with the ancestors in particular difficult times. Perhaps with the help of hallucinatory herbs or devices, they altered their mental state in a wish to communicate directly with the dead. They formed a false pattern-meaning belief in the existence of spirits---in our spiritless world—and it was a very powerful emotional experience which was reinforced by mind-altering drugs that enticed them to mentally visualize another virtual world. In one grave, archaeologists found a particular clay cup with side perforations from where drug fumes were inhaled in those mind-altering rituals. To these people individuality in death did not matter and the ritual of shared burials, accompanied by drug-inhaled pagan ceremonies, continued for thousands of years.

Far away in the Middle East, a revolution was beginning to end this vision of harmonious community forever including the human identity. In southern

Jordan green *malachite* was exposed by the flash flooding of a riverbed. This earthly green material is a *copper carbonate hydroxide* mineral. The thing about malachite was that it was buried in very shallow pits, there was lots of it around and it could melt under low temperature. It did not take long for people to figure out how to repeatedly create a variety of items out of this melted material. The original miners were inspired by its bright green colour and ground it into bits for jewellery without melting it. But they had customers on the other side of the Dead Sea which increased the demand for extensive quantities of the material for use in metal production.
In southern Jordan, mining malachite became an exclusive production of the local people. The material would be loaded onto donkeys and carried about 150 kilometres to grinders and smelters for manufacturing. As the demand for the material increased, traders got involved who purchased the mined material directly from the miners and transported it to smelters. The smelters had a well-guarded secret of the exact way of smelting the material. By using blowpipes for super-heating the material, they created the first true manufactured metal which was then sold in crude bars to be re-smelted and re-cast into other specific copper items. Copper was used to make everything from ornaments to daggers, axes and chisels and people created various networks from making to selling copper products. In southern Palestine and around the Dead Sea, traders knew where the raw copper metal came from and the abundance of it and were ready to purchase any quantity. On the other hand, the people in southern Jordan were sitting on top of a huge metal resource, a perfect combination of supply and demand.
Smelted copper was the first metal and the most exotic one, and as such, it was a prime item and the prime traders were the *Rasulians* who loved to show their copper items. Copper could be re-cast into wonderful shapes and some items were re-cast into things that were not so popular with the Temple priests and leaders. Those pagan ceremonial copper items were hidden away from public eyes. They were high quality metal items which were extraordinary and not every day items. Archaeologists found a large quantity of these copper items carefully hidden away and have yet to figure out what their use were for. There were emblems, necklaces and other unexplainable symbolic things that were hidden away in a cave, and perhaps those were part of a secret ceremonial pagan cult. It appears that there was something despairing about this extraordinary horde. Those items were dumped in so deeply cave that it took almost 6.000 years before they were discovered.
Rasule region was in trouble because their powerful neighbours in Mesopotamia and Egypt had developed massive irrigation systems of their

own and they had their own olives, olive oil and salt to trade. For some unknown reason both ceased to trade with Rasule and this well-advanced culture declined and finally disappeared within one hundred years. Most of the brilliant aspects of the Rasulian culture died with it, along with their magnificent style of wall structures, their civic planning and their old pagan religious values. What seemed to have survived was the specialised productive agricultural economy. Newcomers in the area were more adapted to agricultural production surpluses. As the local copper-based economy came to a crisis and as the environment collapsed, those inhabitants who cleaved to the old ideas that the pagan gods can be made to provide them with a decent landscape must have suffered when that landscape did not respond to their demands. Rasule was the very first of trading societies and, after the economic decline, the survivors, still motivated by trade rather than farming, took their trade skills and moved outwards. This was a dazzling idea to move from the Middle East to Europe and begin to trade with salt from the salt mines of the Dead Sea.

Salt was then a white-gold in Europe and in Rasule there was the largest deposit of salt right on its door step. The wasteland around Rasule ran down to the shores of the Dead Sea where its beaches were already an ancient salt mine. Salt was then, as it is today, a product which preserves foods such as olives and fish and now it could be traded by boats hundreds of miles away into the new European markets. With donkey transportation, salt could also be traded in the near markets of Mesopotamia and Egypt. Now, once salt started to be produced on a large commercial scale there was a need to keep logistical track of it. This changes the market relations between producers and traders. This was no longer a case of a small homestead production of goods that was shared by their own household and local market.

The remarkable thing about trading with salt on such a massive scale was that it was done without the use of money and with no written numbers. Record-keeping and payment for goods were done through a system of token clay-balls where symbols of value were inserted between the two-halves of the clay-ball. For instance, for grain there was one kind of symbol and for a sheep there another kind and so on. These symbols could be small coloured stones shaped in different shapes or drawing-signs on one or both sides of the halves of the token clay that represented a given value. This exterior of this token clay-ball was then signed and sealed by a signing authority confirming the "monetary" value of it. Once the transaction was done, the token clay-ball was cracked open showing, in its interior, the symbols of the true value of payment for the goods. The invention and use of these tokens laid the first foundations of written language and arithmetic in later ages.

Perhaps the remarkable thing about this life-style was the location of the town and how people survived in the middle of the desert.

The point is that, as it is today, everything in the Middle East is about water. You see, all agriculture exists because of water. The key water problem in southern Jordan, where Rasule is located, was that there was very little fresh water. Therefore, to live and flourish in this part of the world, something had to be done in order to bring water into the area. The only method of bringing sufficient water was through multiple systems, of irrigation. The Rasulians were extraordinary pioneers and, when they were faced with a hostile environment, they neither died nor surrender. Instead, they studied, changed it and adapted it to their advantage. They built a whole network of irrigation channels, crafted to follow the slope of the hills, resulting in an enormous achievement. These canals are many kilometres long, not something 20 men with 2 donkeys can do. It probably took hundreds if not thousands of men to complete such an extensive irrigation project. This means that for the first time in their history, the Rasulians brought together a large number of people to complete a project. You see, it is a common assumption that the Egyptian pyramids were the first massive project that employed thousands of people in a complex society. But in Rasule, about thousand years before the construction of the pyramids, we have clear evidence of an organised society with a unique irrigation system.

This irrigation system must have been controlled by local leaders, an elite class of families who were enriched by trade. Thousands of workers had to be organised in a peaceful society, for there is no evidence of a mercenary army or slaves employed for public projects. It is peculiar however, how the leaders inspired the people to follow, and the answer lays in the pagan cultist symbols of the Rasulians: *the Star of Rasule*. This symbol was found in a family shrine and this motif appears nowhere else, a central star glowing in colour, containing figures with masked heads representing a Stone Age dream or an illusion. Using the Rasulian wall art, archaeologists formed a picture of the town's social order. It was held together by a pagan cult and this cult had a social purpose.

The priests set themselves off as something special, something elite, and these elites told people what the "gods" wanted of them. Of course, if the priests were part of the priestly elite families, or grand agricultural families; these were the people who organised and ran the society, in the way the power families dictated. There was, of course, nothing god-like or theistic about that, it was simply an invented social control method best employed to serve the interest of the powerful elite. Does this sound familiar? What we have seen since then, is the transition of a personal god to state-run gods;

from your god of your home, the god of your tribe or clan to the god or gods of your city's elite. In short, what we now think was going on was a new phenomena that demonstrates that people can be mobilised by their leaders because they believe that gods sanctioned it, that the gods willed or that the gods demanded. Water was the center of their lives and their cultist faith and perhaps the Star of Rasule was a vision order where worshipers came together as a society, forming cultist bonds under a delusional faith.

Far way in Europe the Stone Age farmers were part of the landscape. On the ocean shores the vast natural world was full of mystery and the people's cult reached out to the animals, creating the cult of *Animist*, including the Sun and the Stars that shone light on earth. People were governed by birth, death and the change of seasons, but there were no organised elites and people lived in simple small communities. Their primitive pagan beliefs sprang from a meeting combination of ex-migrant farmers and local hunter-gatherers. These people built grand projects such as erecting massive stone symbols across the clearings of Europe. Some symbolic monuments took generations to construct but, 2,000 years later another set of farmers brought with them another set of beliefs. These newcomers smashed the old symbolic monuments and turned them into underground burial chambers.

At that time Europeans were living very simply, farming collectively and only what they needed. The natural leaders in each small community were chosen for their hunting and farming skills and personal leadership characteristics. When someone died they were buried in communal burial chambers. In time, a new and mysterious culture appeared on the horizon and with a very distinct kind of grave: the round-hilly graves in places such as England, Scotland, Ireland and Scandinavia. The distinctive characteristics of their graves were that they were individual burials, where the body would be placed in it along with all the personal flavoured of the deceased. They were buried for instance with their favoured drinking cup and with their fighting equipment. These graves were named after their content, such as the *Pica* graves.

The Pica people were the traders of Stone Age Europe and by using carriage horses they brought new ideas and precious objects that turned Europe around. They were able to organise and trade supplies in small quantities; items like knives and daggers which were considered very precious and desirable. They traveled long distances and this gave them an entry into other societies. The numerous drinking cups which were found suggest the first use of fermentation of alcoholic drinks and new ways of getting drunk. The intricate decorative clay cups that were found were large enough hold a considerable quantity of liquor and the cups needed to be held by both hands and perhaps passed around between the participants. The drinking cups suggest that there were new things to get drunk on and using massed honey was part of their drinking rituals. Fermentation was one of the numerous ways of showing off an elitist status, along with having elite weaponry traded over long distances.

There were many different ways people off showing of the things they had that others did not nor could not have and being rich enough to have sources of sugar to provide for the fermenting of drinks. So the drinking cups were both a status and power symbol, a real symbol of wealth and the ability to mobilise these rare, sweet substances which could be fermented into something, was even more precious; the intoxicating substance of alcohol. These people brought the opportunity of change that shook the foundations of Stone Age life-style, for they believed much more in the value of the individual. They arrived as traders and stayed to farm and build their own characteristic houses and villages. In addition, they brought the art of smelting and they added a vital secret from their Middle East roots: mix tin with copper and you get bronze. This new metal process was so important that the metal-smiths had their own graves and they were probably clan chiefs.

In the beginning of the Bronze Age, much of the smelting was done by the chiefs themselves and we now see that this transformation was another way of showing off the chief's individual power, his status and securing his control over his subjects. It is; therefore, very characteristic to find the moulds in rich graves which were the graves of the chiefs. As such, the people who were in charge of the community were also in charge of the ongoing transformation of the community by creating knives, daggers and all sorts of metal tools and weaponry. The Bronze Age introduction consisted of technology that could not be made in the Stone Age such as daggers that became longer and used as swords or spearheads that were effectively secured at the end of a pole, and the whole nature of armament was transformed by the introduction of a real strong metal: Bronze. Needless to say these weapons exuded power, they were rare and dangerous.

We now see the rise of military elite with the power to achieve precisely what they demand, yet the discovered weapons show little signs of use. Perhaps those weapons were used for ceremonial purposes. The leaders built body-metal for battle protection and jewellery, again as symbols of their status and wealth. They also had another power-symbol, the mounted horse. The horse was once a pack-animal, now being ridden and the rider towered over everyone else, and they could move fast and cover long distances. Horses were expensive to keep, for a single horse eats more than a family and thus only the elite could maintain them. These accumulations of symbols suggest that the elite people were preoccupied with power and, as such, they were developing a new kind of society with leaders and followers. The leaders dominated the community life and the people who produced the necessities of life—the farmers—were the followers. Of course, these community dynamics created its own momentum for social change. With the accumulation of wealth, the elite could support new crafts and used natural material like wood in much more complex ways. They learned how to use it in a most imaginative way: the wooden wheel. Archaeologists have always wondered when the wheel was invented and now perhaps they can give a rather better estimation, about 5,500 to 6,000 years ago. The wheel invention came from the Middle East (like copper) and was used in a muddy landscape without roads. This new technology spread very rapidly because it fulfilled a greater necessity for transporting large and heavier loads.

Trade was now moving from Europe back to the Middle East and it started from the beaches of the Baltic Sea because it contained the one natural product that did not come from anywhere else and would go as far as Egypt: *the seaweed*. The seaweed was easy to collect, lightweight and nutritious in relation to its weight. Along with the nutritious seaweed, the beaches of the Baltic Sea brought to its shores: *the amber*. Traditional mythology tells us that, at the beginning of time, a river of tears flowed into the sea, turning the tears into amber, the clear tears of the innocent and the dark red were tinted by the evil and the corrupt. In real terms amber is the sap of fossilized pine forest and it grew among the seaweed when the sea was dry land and glaciers filled the valleys. As supplies of copper and tin were moving northwards; to balance the trade, first of all came the amber and then all other forest products.

The daily life of the community was bound by a network of sharing and obligation, so milk, grain and labour went back and forth. In a give-and-take situation the political elite offered social organisation and protection, and both safety and danger came from the armed warrior chiefs of clans. Communities expanded their farmlands and knowledge under the shallow shade of violence. These farmers were also able to breed sheep which offered a touch of luxury. The sheep fleece was different from the earliest open straight fibre; it was now curly and dense. This is the wool we know today. To use it, they developed the fine craft of spinning and weaving, and clothing now became more available to the farmers. Costumers wanted status and the wheel spinners and loom-weavers were also turned into dyers who extracted their natural dyes from plants in the forest. The same people were also healers. Their knowledge of natural plants provided them with remedies, and this was the beginning of medicine. The new spun wool was turned into luxury clothing and, beyond the immediate family those who could afford its price were the wealthy. The clothes were so loved that they also wore them into their graves. They were buried as individuals and they took with them their own identity, their clothes and ornaments. In these magnificent burial sites in Denmark the dead were buried in dugout tree-trunks and those are the most spectacular burials that we know which came from the Bronze Age.

We now have an open window to show us what life was like in Bronze Age Europe for a number of millennia. People were buried in their woollen clothing of brown colour wool, simple and rustic, but it was the height of sophistication and probably, as leaders, they could afford to be buried entirely in woollen clothes with their favoured metal weapons. The leader was buried with the appropriate weaponry. The coffin was laid above ground and the burial was an elaborate ceremony. Sometime later a great mountain would be built as a tomb in its place where the leader's name was expected to live on for eternity.

Across Europe archaeologists found ceremonial pools of water and many were guarded by pagan mother-figures which were important to the first farmers. From the beginning of human habitation people made offerings and now the warriors offered thousands more. Some wanted to believe in the existence of spirits and life after death and saw nature as an expression of that illusive belief. Yet, all around them, the lives of animals and plants continued to exist under the Laws of Nature: birth, growth, decay and death which they tended to ignore by the force of mythology and their wishful thinking. For them, the pagan Sun-God rose every day traveling across the sky powered by powerful horses. Across the Middle East the symbolised chariots of the Hittites and the Egyptians brought warriors and kings and the story of the first farmer ends with armies and the rising of the first cities. In Europe we see the first recorded images of violence. The farmers were running out of available land and evidence of property fences and stockade villages begin to appear. The last hunter-gatherers collided with the warriors and their way of life disappeared forever. At around 3,000 years ago there was an increase in the use of metals and the smiths discovered iron-metal which swept Europe. The Iron Age revolutionised farming with cheap, yet effective, tools and gave rise to a great iron civilisation. All of this was made possible by the first farmers of the Fertile Crescent of Mesopotamia some 12,000 years ago.

THE AGRICULTURAL! REVOLUTION AND THE DEVELOPMENT OF THE FIRST HUMAN SOCIETIES 10.000 TO 5.000 BC

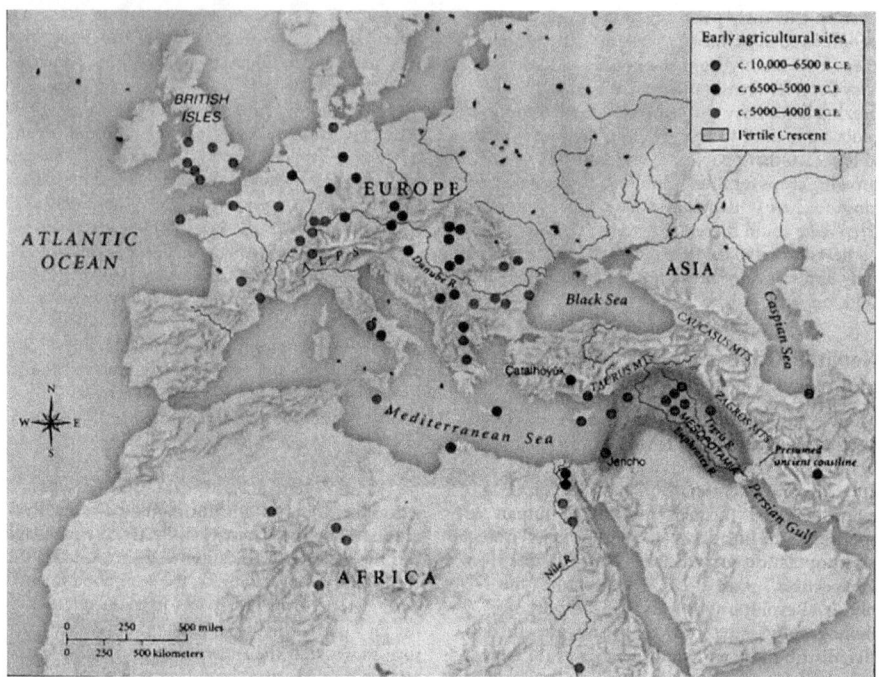

EUROPEAN STYLE TIMBER HOMES

BEGINNING OF MANUFACTURING

METALIC UTILITY ITEMS

A DAY IN THE LIFE OF FARMING COMMUNITIES

A DAY IN THE LIFE OF FARMING COMMUNITIES

A DAY IN THE LIFE OF FARMING COMMUNITIES

A DAY IN THE LIFE OF FARMING COMMUNITIES

"IRRIGATION SYSTEM"

A DAY IN THE LIFE OF FARMING COMMUNITIES

ADVANCED IRRIGATION SYSTEMS

A DAY IN THE LIFE OF FARMING COMMUNITIES

FIRST AGRICULTURAL SETTLEMENT OF THE FERTILE CRESCENT ESTIMATED AT 10.000 YEAR OLD

A DAY IN THE LIFE OF FARMING COMMUNITIES

A DAY IN THE LIFE OF FARMING COMMUNITIES "WEAT GRAINING"

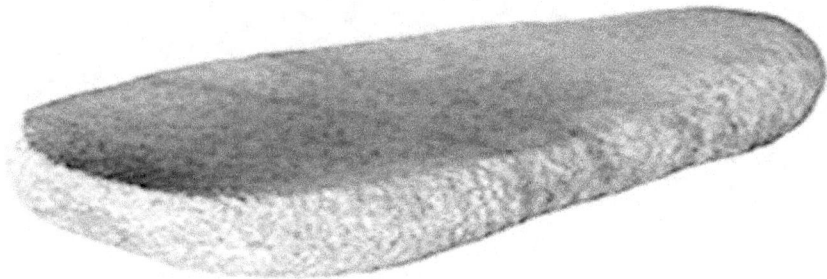

QUERN STONE FROM SYRIA 9500 BC

A DAY IN THE LIFE OF FARMING COMMUNITIES
"WEAT GRAINING"

MILL-STONE

A DAY IN THE LIFE
OF FARMING COMMUNITIES
"WEAT GRAINING"

GRAIN GRINDING IN EGYPT - 1352 BC

ADVANCED MILL-STONES

A DAY IN THE LIFE OF FARMING COMMUNITIES
WEAT-BREAD

BEER MAKING & ENJOYING

A DAY IN THE LIFE OF FARMING COMMUNITIES

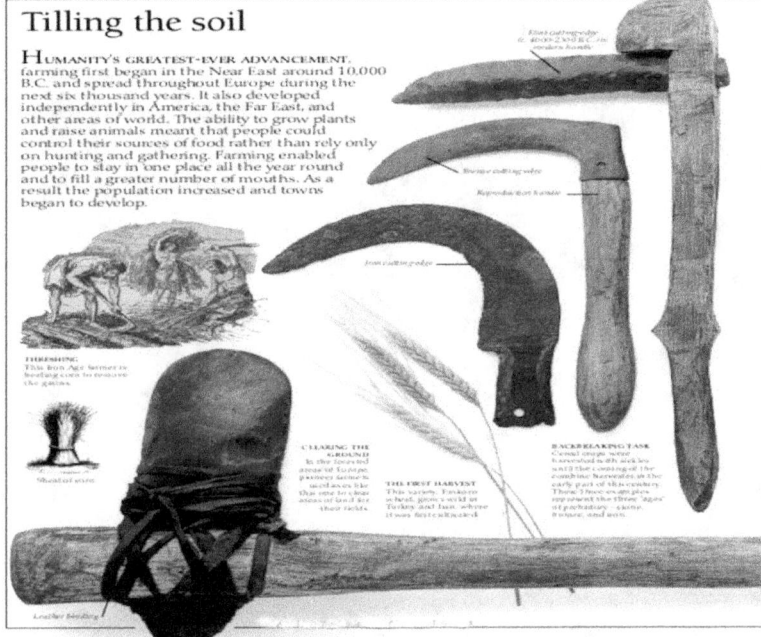

PRODUCTION OF OLIVE OIL

ILLUSTRATED:
NEOLITHIC SHAMANIC MOTHER FIGURES

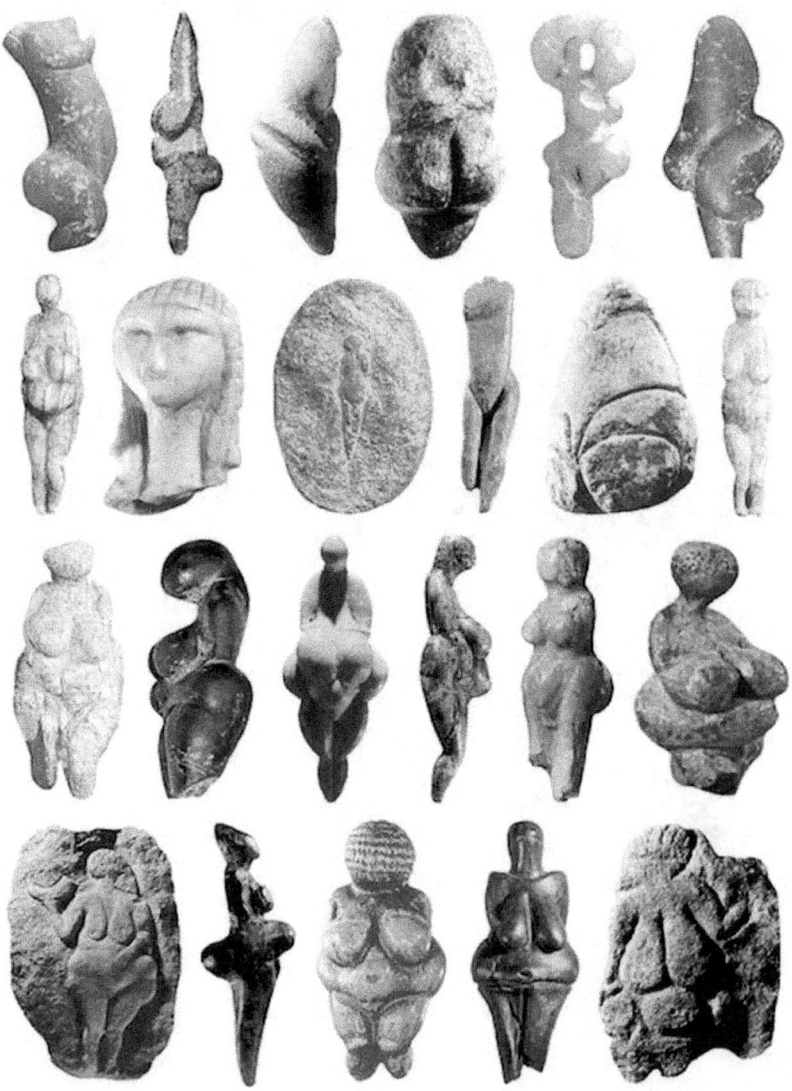

CEREMONIAL PRACTICES FROM ANIMISM TO PAGAN DEISM
"ANIMAL SACRIFICES"

CEREMONIAL PRACTICES
FROM ANIMISM TO PAGAN DEISM
" CELEBRATING FERTILITY"

FROM ANIMISM TO PAGAN DEISM

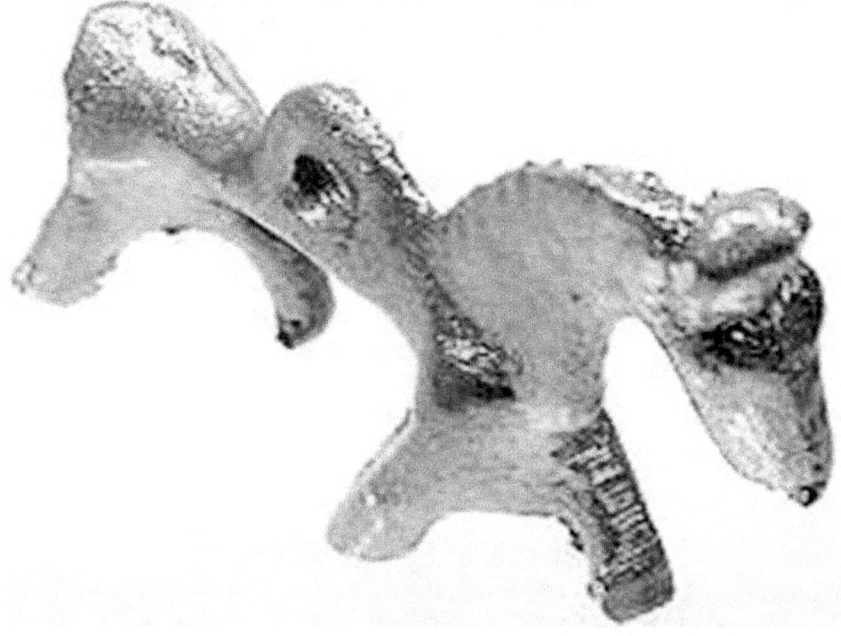

RASULIAN CEREMONIAL ITEMS

FROM ANIMISM TO PAGAN DEISM
CEREMONIAL COPPER ITEMS

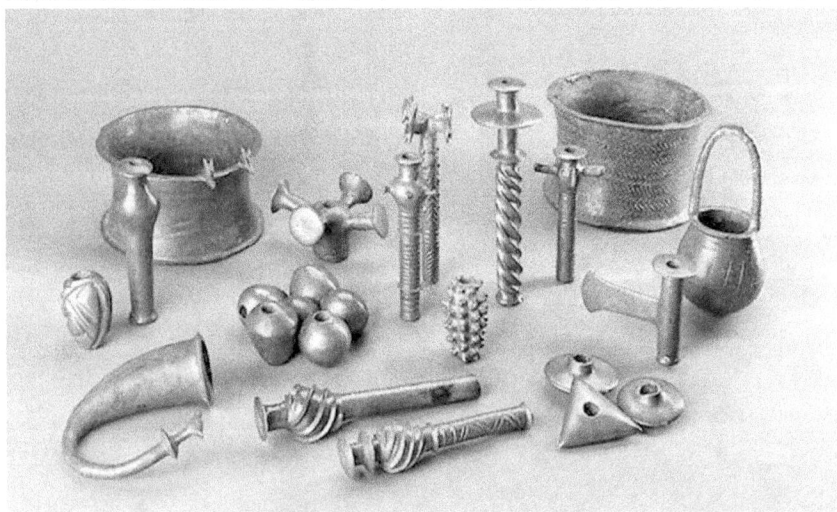

FROM ANIMISM TO PAGAN DEISM WRITTEN SCRPTCIRCA 7.000 BC, (CRIPTO-KEIMENO, IN GREEK)

Το πρώτο γραπτό κείμενο της Ευρώπης, αποτυπωμένο σε ξύλινη επιγραφή από προηγμένο άνθρωπο της νεολιθικής εποχής, που βρέθηκε στο λιμναίο προϊστορικό οικισμό του Δισπηλιού της Καστοριάς.

CEREMONY BEFORE A SMALL STATUTE OF A DEITY

PROTO-RELIGIOUS BELIEFS EXPRESSED IN STONE MONUMENTS

NEOLITHIC SHAMANIC OFFERINGS

NEOLITHIC PAGAN SUNCTUARY

ILLUSIONS AND SYMBOLISM IN EARLY SOCIETIES

Anatomically modern human groups begin to develop approximately 100,000 years ago. During these thousands of years there were famines, tribal wars, territorial wars, earthquakes, tsunamis and floods, deathly viruses, bacteria and ignorance of causes of events that caused epidemics which killed millions. Those natural conditions were not directed against or in favour of the human race's survival rates. In addition, there were constant scrimmages among small groups for food and shelters, and the abducting of women and girls for slaves from other tribes was a common affaire.

As mammal species, humans behave in solitary with other humans of the same group or tribe and provide food, protection and rudimental moral guidance to their offspring. Such rudimentary moral guidance included what was "good" or "bad" for the tribe, expressions of parental love and providing care for the sick or wounded. These were the origins of humanity's morality and they had no theistic base because the myth of God's involvement in human affairs had not been invented yet, not until much later. Questions about the structure and workings of the universe, of environmental causes and understanding or predicting natural causes or events were not answered by any means of scientific reason, for this was still humanity's infant state. Life in general was harsh and, because of our mammalian predatory nature, it was "brutal," "nasty" and "short" to quote the philosopher Hobbes.

During the first 90,000 of the last 100,000 years the concept of a monotheistic Sky-God was not yet invented. There was no Sky-God to intervene through "his" representatives in human affairs either morally, politically or physically. But around the Bronze Age—some 10,000 to 6,000 years ago—the Sky-God decided to intervene in human affairs through his Jewish representatives and other Middle Eastern religions. Through it the monotheistic Jewish God found a way to harness the power of people's pagan illusions, customs and polytheistic rituals for his political ends.

Ironically speaking, for hundreds of thousands of years, the Sky-God was idly watching the human race going through its trials and tribulations in order to survive. Another "cynical" view is that the Sky-God of the Jewish Religion decided to claim that the Universe, with its billions of stars, was created by him. The Genesis day of his choosing to intervene in the human race was some 6,000 years ago. During this time the Middle Eastern God dictated to the people that this was the correct celestial time-frame of his creation of the universe and his "chosen-people" were given the Old

Testament as the only written instructions they needed to obey. From then on the Sky-God intervened in the human affairs in Palestine, the Fertile Crescent and in the Arabian Peninsula by introducing human sacrifices, mass extermination of children, rape of women, tribal wars and genocides, incest, resurrection of the dead, the virgin-birth of His Son, the benefits of slavery, instructions on how to construct magnificent temples using slave labour, instructions about how a man should beat his wife such as, *"Don't beat her in the face and don't make her ugly"* and how the appointed Temple priests are God's representatives on earth.

In addition, the Sky-God offered the worst possible written explanation about the age of our species, of how we came about, the origins of our universe and our cosmos. To complete his totality over humans, God would not stop tormenting us even after death---either by everlasting praying and listening to harp music for eternity in Heaven or forever suffering in Hell. Most of its similarities have survived and raw absurdities continue to be followed to this day. The Jewish religion, for example, was the first which tried to explain these anomalies by offering fallacies, superstitions, junk theories of subsequent tribal cults, charlatan-magicians and mentally self- delusional prophets who heard voices in their schizophrenic brains about the callings of the Sky-God. There was literally no escape from the Jewish religious totalitarian dogma of continuing praise, fear and devotion to whatever little the people of faith were gaining out of it.

Religious totalitarian dogma begins as a minority group which tends not to dominate the county which flourishes at the moment. It does not want the people to compare its religious dogma with another. It will have a hostile tendency towards comparative religions. In time the Jewish religious cults became theocratic---the nature of theocracy which existed in the Bronze Age in Israel, or in early Christianity in the 340-450 AD, or in the Islamic theocracy which exists in Iran and Saudi Arabia today. Theocracies govern their people out of the theocratic-constitution of their holy book. The ancient Jewish, early Christian (and during the Catholic imposed Dark Ages) and the contemporary Islamic theocracies have equally matching tendencies and cannot be self-critical about the causes of their social oppression.

Pre-historic spiritual occults described humanity's place on earth in a distorted non-scientific process. Natural disasters such as tsunamis, earthquakes, hurricanes and other natural phenomena were viewed as spirits moving things because they were angry at people. Of course, there was no Charles Darwin around telling them about the *Origins of Species* or Isaac Newton to explain the mechanics of nature. Because of lack of reason and scientific explanation, ancient humanity deserves our understanding not our contempt. The intentions of the original occults' Animist spiritualism were an attempt to interpret the material functions of the world and man's inherited role in it. What was missing from their pre-scientific traditional explanations and thus could not gather in their cognition was the dialectical and empirical knowledge that was needed. Large and small communities simply followed and obeyed whatever dominant religious decrees were presented before them by whoever their present leaders were.

As new religious myths and symbols were invented there were new spirits and new gods to be praised all according to the agendas of the dominant classes. Thus we can see that, in many Mesopotamian regions, there were a number of different religious ideologies and gods and the establishment of various polytheist communities all competing for positions and wealth amongst each other. This competition aroused armed scrimmages and conflicts which set communities and people apart from one another. With the rise of religious totalitarianism, shamans and magicians, temple priests and tyrants, monarchs and despots, political and benevolent dictators (all intoxicated for more power), invented more mythical stories that were obeyed by the people. This was done without the benefit of reason and evidence and without the recognition of the differences between truth and delusion, fact and distortion.

Each hierarchical class had their own political and hierarchical symbols to propagate, and religion became a free enterprise product to be sold to whoever was willing to donate to, follow and obey the celestial spirits and their earthly representatives. Religion was a means of socio-political control, an imposed celestial theocracy interpreted and directed by those who claimed to have a direct access to the spiritual world of the Sky-God. As predatory beings, leaders were all self-appointed and kept their power over the people by any means necessary, including terrifying symbols of intimidating god-figures, physical intimidation and violence, coercion and manipulation, sense of fear and shame, human sacrificial offerings, paid forgiveness and absolution, illusive and delusive temple practices, stages of impressive religio-theatrics, harmonious music and elegant architectural structures. This is the foundation of the industry of religion which supported, and still supports, their own cliques of self-delusions, in their obedience to the symbolic images of the Sky-God. The religious theatrical props may have changed, but the show still is performed every Sunday morning across the nations' Christianised religious performances.

Spirituality predates organised religion and, as such, it gave rise to symbolic representation of superstition; a delusional belief in the existence of mysterious powers which humans' possessed, appeased, controlled and redirected at will. A Shaman witch-doctor in the Amazon Rainforest or the Animist-artists in pre-historic cave-symbols would paint a symbolic face on the woman's belly to encourage a healthy birth. In Greece, a rooster will be killed and blessed by an Orthodox priest and then hung from the building's tallest part to secure strong foundations. Other pagan symbolisms which have nothing to do with reality can be the following: a small eye-painted stone will be attached to a baby's clothes against *"mal ojo"* (a cursed or evil eye), beliefs that mediums and shamans have powers to communicate with the dead, that certain hallucinogenic drugs will help you connect with the spirit world, that the irrational healing system of Homeopathy is the only natural cure, that Tarot Cards would tell your future, that the Zodiac Astrology is equivalent to Astronomy, that Alchemy is equivalent to Chemistry, and the delusion of the Horoscope is your best daily guide. Without an exaggeration, this is the poverty of the human imagination, a mental world that does not exist, that creates nothing, a mere flow of images that come from nowhere and go nowhere, that produces nothing other than a meaningless and directionless imaginative world of spirits and symbolism.

Symbolism's long history can be traced back to the Stone Age some 10,000 years ago. Because our pre-historic ancients lacked a scientific explanation of the material world, they turned to the only possible avenue they had available to them, their pattern-meaning imaginary interpretation of their surroundings. For the next few thousands years, ancients symbolically saw the world filled with moving spirits; including their own bodily movements, which were the product of a spirit. The physical world was also reduced into a by-product of a superior spirit. From this singular spiritual belief the ancients went into multiple-spirit induced movements of all other earthly and cosmic bodies. For example, they saw the movements of tiny insects being the result of the spirits within them, those vegetable plants grew because of their spirit, the human-sperm contained a little person in it, and the sun, moon and stars floated on the air by the power of their individual spirits. In short, they saw the world filled with spirits each doing their specific task assigned to them by a superior spirit. Even their own bodily movements were attributed to spirits living within them.

Yet, nowhere can we find ancient records of spiritualism praising the physical world; the beauty of landscapes, the crops that earth produced or an overall appreciation for what sustained them. The physical world was taken for granted; it was there at their disposal, to take what they wanted and when they wanted. There is, of course, a double standard here; for, when it came to their own preservation, the ancients gathered empirical evidence from reality for their own survival and, through experience, they were able hunters, gatherers and adept to husbandry, building irrigation systems and transforming deserts to fertile lands, creating social structures and trading with other communities. But they had not developed, as yet, science or astronomy that described the workings of the universe; had no biology to analyse the origins of man and, no geology to explain tsunamis, earthquakes and climatic changes, and had no medical medicines or anatomical surgeries to cure their sickness.

They associated the entire living world with invisible symbolic spirits that moved about at will and caused things to happen and had dominion over peoples' bodies, family structures, stretches of forests and mountain tops. Unexplainable things, such as the eclipses of the moon, were attributed to magical powers of the superior spirit living somewhere in the sky. Birds that were hovering on an air draft or flying without failing did so because of magic. Magic which was able to suspend the Laws of Nature happened because an invisible spiritual being willed. Simultaneously, the Greeks, the Persians, the Syrians and the Egyptians regarded their Gods as being real living things rather than as imagined or non-existent spiritual entities clogged with mystery and temples' theatrical religious rituals.

The dimensional birth of delusional religious beliefs was eminent because humanity's infantile mental state had not sufficiently developed as yet. With no defining recognised differences between delusional beliefs and the physical world that existed independent of their minds' ideas and wishful thinking, humanity invented symbolic pattern-meaning and explanations of spiritual stories, magical invisible beings, and people were told to accept them or face the consequences. As mammalian predatory beings, we are also biologically programmed to assume deadly consequences. Simple people therefore believed what they were told to believe. Ignorance and fear promoted uncertainty and eventually—around 4,000 years ago---there was the first written account, the Holy Books, in order to maintain social consistency. This solidified the dominant position of the governing of the political hierarchy, priestly and military classes, and transformed into a semi-political system of benevolent tyranny.

Human beings, at whatever historical space and time, are still biologically programmed to look for patterns in life and assign symbolised meaning to them. Human beings cannot have patterns in life without assigning a meaning to them, for we cannot maintain in our brain a *"blank mental space"* between thoughts to be filled at a later day or time. Since the human mind's sole task is to produce and assign pattern-meaning it does not differentiate between *true and false* meaning for, if it does not have the first, it would invent the second. In other words, such a process does not differentiate between real and illusionary pattern-meaning, for our brain habitually provides us daily with patterns rather than no patterns at all. When our brain wants to have a direct access to reality; in order to produce a meaning, it stitches together past information from our memory storage. For any gap in our memory that still exists, our brain guesses as to what is out there in the world, which is related to our beliefs or expectations, and creates shortcut pattern-meaning. Most of us do not recognise those shortcuts unless we are confronted with visual misinterpretations or illusions which help us understand many of the shortcuts the brain takes. However, when those misinterpretations or illusions fulfil our "comfort-zone" we gladly preserve them, believe and live by them. When those 'comfort-zones' required the sacrifice of human beings, we acted upon them with the same zeal as a present day Christian prays to the Virgin Mary for a miracle.

Many religious illusions and delusions are founded on our expectations that have been wired into our brain. We assume that the world is stable, reliable and predictable based on what we were told and our past encounters and experience with it. Patterns are explanations (real or false) we seek to give meaning to past, present and future events (real or imaginary) based on correct or incorrect information that our brain stitches together. In fact, so strong are the religious delusions that, even when all reason and evidence point to things that are not what they seem, we still refuse to see other real alternatives. This is because we are biologically programmed to transform our wishful thinking into patterns, even when patterns do not exist. We still prefer patterns rather than no patterns at all. Our brain sees pattern-meaning in things in life, whether we want them or not, or where none exist. For instance, the cosmos that exists outside of our mind contains a universal reality, and this true pattern-meaning of *material reality* is all inclusive with our earth, but singular. Yet, we have invented false pattern-meanings of reality as 'comfort-zones' to mean "my-reality" and "your-reality" as if the earth's material reality is personal and transformative to choose at will. Can we say therefore that our universe contains 6,000,000,000 billion 'realities' as many as there are human beings on earth? Are we aware that earth's material reality does not exclusively belong to human beings; only the interpretation of it and that is where misinterpretations or illusions enter into them? False pattern-meaning become "beliefs," and beliefs are not material reality, rather they are comfort-zones created by our minds.

By the 1st century the Jewish Holy Books (the Torah and the Old Testament) presented a view of the world based on long-established primitive desert stories rather than on reason and the discipline of science of the time. These were myths from traditional Arabian tribal people who were steep in superstition, in predatory behaviour against other tribes, who believed and accepted these myths without recognition of the differences between verifiable evidence and delusion. People daily were bombarded with symbols prescribing primitive myths; from morning to night by the priestly class, self delusional pseudo-prophets, fortune tellers, street magicians, and all kinds of charlatans of the day. The result being that peoples' brains were creating shortcut pattern-meaning at will, depending on the attraction of the message the myths provided. For instance, pattern-meanings were created in peoples' brains in a dazzling irregularity for beliefs in "life after death," "heaven and hell," the "coming end of the world," "miracles" and "resurrections" among others. The most profound non-existent pattern-meaning was held for the contempt of the physical world, against material reality, against the Laws of Nature, which could not possibly be suspended, and in support of our false superiority over other forms of life.

In the entire diversified population of the Fertile Crescent and Arabian Peninsula, there were stages of permanent hostility. Fear and uncertainty created a dreadful, socio-religious culture based on despair and hatred of anything that was not described and approved by the holy-books and temple-priests. As oppressed, tribal, desert people many housed within themselves the "oppressor" who wanted to imitate the powerful who oppressed them. Myths and symbols were invented to describe the elegance of reality in a distorted way, and to show ignorant tribesmen how to imagine it, rather than learn how best to change it. It provided them with an authoritarian guidance of obedience to these myths, similar to those they were accustomed to living by, but within their own tribal social system. Intoxication for more power and wealth was the ultimate goal of both the tribal leaders and their holy men, who were ready to use any means necessary to preserve their privileged position. There were no civil legal institutions to oblige them to curb their mammalian predatory instincts and no natural philosophers (scientists) to point out their false pattern-explanations of a non-existent celestial power. Temple priests preached of God who gave Genesis (creation) to the universe, and who made a Man and a Woman out of clay; a familiar building material to tribesmen, used to build their desert clay huts. This God was good, they were told, with an occasional exception of evil temperament and acts committed against the personal or tribal social order including wars, famine and diseases. The irony was, and still is, as is the case of the Orthodox Jews, in believing that the social order of their tribes and its lands were given by God for their own exclusive benefit. This powerful Sky-God is having their best interest at heart, thus devotees praised God when things were good and prosperous and accepted "God's mysterious ways" when disasters struck their personal lives or their tribes' fortunes.

Generations upon generations of religious distortions had penetrated every aspect of Middle Eastern communities large or small, generating false patterns of life that did not exist. People were told to believe and have faith, but "believing" and "faith" are not investigative terms. They are terms utilised to entice submission, obedience and unquestionable devotion, and are against cognition. False pattern-meanings in religion and secular spiritualism are at the core of their functions, for without such false patterns, what else could they offer to humanity? The practicality of the industry of religion prescribes deceptional ways to priests, shamans or witch-doctors, encouraging them to believe that if God could perform magic so can they. They accepted donations to perform ecclesiastics (ceremonies) and made high sounding noises and used mechanical devices to fool people into believing in the magical powers of the "holy-water." In my book *Prisoners of our Ideals,* there are many examples given of ancient mechanical devices used by religious and spiritual temples to entice people to attend religious ceremonies, and many did! *Heron of Alexandria*, a Greek mechanical engineer, invented a number of mechanical devices which temple priests used to create "magic," awe and fear as a means of collecting donations. Religious ceremonies and performances became the core essence of theistic free enterprise practices which gradually turned to become the organised institutions of today's Catholic and Greek Orthodox Christianity with huge similarities and differences in style and successes.

Looking further back into human history we have discovered much verifiable evidence regarding the origins of symbolism and myth creation. Ground-breaking in palaeontology research and archaeology discovered more revelations about early (from 10,000 to 40,000 years of Human and Neanderthal) symbolic animist spiritualism and cave art. Archaeologists re-examine previous discounted evidence in favour of early ancestors' skills and abilities. Human DNA and Neanderthals DNA were genetically very close and are incorporated in the human race. A hallmark of our human species is our age-old striving for art and symbolism, ritual and adornment. We see the astonishing cave art and statuettes all across Europe and this is because humans were inhabiting new territories and displaying their presence. This diversified cave art displays a network of new arrivals and community bonding with other human groups. Communicating with others through symbolism and ritualistic art has long been considered a uniquely human trait. The intelligence of pre-historic man can be assessed by the kind of symbols they expressed and the extensive use of them. Evidence of Neanderthal symbolism has been elusive until recently. Statuettes made of *manganese dioxide,* a black mineral, found in a Neanderthal cave in France reveals that this mineral was used as crayons for cave art. Deep carving symbolism of different forms and shapes was discovered in animal bones. Evidence suggests also that the Neanderthals were cutting off the animal feathers from wing-bones and prey (with little value as food) to use in symbolic rituals, and as decorations for hair and bodies. Seashells with traces of red pigment extracted from iron ore, and with neatly drilled holes to be hung and worn as ornaments were found in Spain.

This evidence offers a gleam on the Neanderthals' mental capacity, skills and abilities. Anthropologists in France and Spain re-examine wrongly discarded Neanderthal artefacts found in the caves in the 1980's. Evidence found suggests that pointed slivers of horse bone were used with the red pigment *haematite* as a painting tool in decorative cave art. Although sulphated and difficult to see, the red pigment haematite was used as a predominant colouring mineral in these cave arts. Pencil-like slivers of bone contained red pigment on their tips, and seashells stained with the same red pigment were used as painter's brush and pallet. All these sea shells and pointed bone tips contain vast information about symbolic cave art and body painting kits. The stains on the interior of the sea shell reveals that it served as a cosmetic preparation kit, used to prepare a kind of facial make-up for both male and females of the group. This further explains the issue surrounding Neanderthal symbolism. It is now believed that Neanderthals used facial paint to distinguish members of the group as friends from tribal opponents, just as we do today.

Today, human habits and rituals of this kind remain practically the same. For instance, fans of particular soccer, hockey or football teams are painting their face and body with colours which distinguish their team from others. When people go to the stadium to see their team playing they know where to sit by the colours worn by identifiable supporters. In some European countries you won't dare go and seat with supporters of your opponent's team---especially if you wear the colours of your team. You will use an artefact which identifies you as a supporter of a particular team, and this kind of information tells something about yourself which is also transmitted to friends or opponents. Also, army uniforms with particular insignia attached to them serve to identify one national armed force from another.

The question that remains to be answered is, even if Neanderthals were painting and decorating themselves and behaving in symbolic manner, does this mean that they thought as humans did? We know that our human ancestors practiced symbolic ritualism and spiritualism, but similar evidence for Neanderthals' social behaviour has been elusive. However, a team of archaeologists in Southern Spain made an intriguing discovery of Neanderthal ritual. In this cave it was discovered to contain more than 300 bones from 10 Neanderthal skeletons. In a deep shaft, a female skeleton was placed in a foetal position, and this was not accidental. Some 20,000 years ago someone buried her in this position and covered her body with stones to protect it from falling rocks. The burial stones were laid in a symmetrical way, while the fallen rocks were not. In addition, near the female skeleton was found fossilised, cut-off, paw-bones of a panther, used for the ritual purpose of a funeral offering. Did the Neanderthal burial, contain complex rituals and beliefs? It can only be confirmed that Neanderthals were ritualistically much more advanced than they were thought to be.

Since of all mysterious of natural events the most prominent, puzzling and disturbing is that of death. The earliest traces of spiritual beliefs and practice have clustered around the burial of the dead, centred on what was to eventually become a highly developed cult. Various forms of burial in the early period of the Stone Age indicate a mode of cannibalistic spiritualism; of human parts eaten in order to obtain the vitality of the deceased. This was a common practice, with skulls been treated in a similar way in Spain and France---and much later in "head hunter" groups--before the arrival of the Homo sapiens some 40,000 years ago. The skulls found in France have been made into drinking cups, which indicates that they were used for sacramental rituals. Similar skull-cups have been found in southern Spain in caves full of wall paintings, as well as in Papua New Guinea.

For both the early Homo sapiens and the Neanderthals, a corpse was often laid in the grave containing quantities of sea shells and other objects in bone and ivory. The corpse was often covered with blood red dye representing the life giving agent and there were often cowries, shaped in the form of female genitals, as fertility charms and givers of life. Believing that if the dead were to live again in their own bodies, the colour red was an attempt to revivify them and make them serviceable to their occupants in the afterlife. The skulls were intentionally removed with flint knives after death and then dried and ceremoniously preserved with very great care, receiving a mortuary treatment. This skeleton preserving practice is still followed within the Greek Orthodox Church, in the Middle East, for preserving the skulls of notable monks and priests of past generations. It should be noted however, that the early people went through such ceremonial process in the disposal of their dead, which often involved reburial, in the belief that the life after death, was a means of their own temporal survival.

Some of the skeletons found had their limbs draw up in the sleep position of a fetus in the womb of its mother, indicating a rebirth after death. The practice may have been adopted sometimes as an attempt of the deceased return to molest the living by settling old scores or avenging any neglect in the ritual burial process. In other cases, skeletons preserved as trophies may have been more for the purpose of commemorating outstanding members of the clan or group. In this case, the skull was placed in a small chamber within a circle of stones, doubtless for sacramental purposes as it had been erected in a position suggestive of veneration, probably to preserve life. Throughout the ages, the deepest felt emotions, wants, hopes and fears of tribal societies have always arisen chiefly from the social life of the community and centred on propagation, nutrition and survival while living and after death. The pattern-meaning of interpretative reality of human life was formulated in the human brain. What was missing to complete this mental process were the non-existent patterns of life's continuation in the "life after death." They believed in what their human brain invented and, because they thought of them, they unrelentingly believed them to be true. Therefore, it was around these basic, biologically programmed, pattern-meanings that pre-historic, man-made religion grew and developed, concentrating upon the undiscovered mysteries of life. These pattern-meanings were passed-on to future generations with minor changes to their intended purpose and rituals processes.

The best way to make a first hand analysis of this very important aspect of the growth of the man-made, pre-historic religion is to examine a number of principle examples, such as the cave-paintings and engravings left behind by cave-artists. The best of them can be found in *Les Eyries* on the banks of *Vesere River* in the *Dordogne*, France, in the village known as *Font-de-Gaume*. In the same region a little further along the *Sarlat* road in the valley of the *Beune* is a very long, subterranean cave-tunnel called *Les Combarelles* with a number of impressive engravings. Not far way at *Laussel* a rock-cave shelter contained a design of a woman in an advanced stage of pregnancy engraved on a stone. The female is holding in her right-hand a horn of a bison and her figure is been covered with red ochre indicating the female's life-potency and life-giving properties. Other discoveries were recently revealed; more important cave designs in the regions of *Ange* in the *Pyrenees and Santander* regions in Spain. Some cave figures are high up on a narrow passage which would make it appear that the pre-historic artist could only have done these drawings while standing on the shoulders of his helper, having a flickering lamp burning animal fat with a wick of moss. Why were they done in such deep caves it is still a mystery, but it is inconceivable that they were painted for aesthetic purposes, "as art for art's sake," 3 meters (10 feet) above ground?

Then again, most of the notable cavern designs are symbols depicting and glorifying the art of hunting animals in the forest. In caves located south of *Toulouse,* France, skilfully included in the designs are animal wounds depicted in red ochre on the flank of a bison, by drawing round them its outline with its legs in the contracted position. In the front of the killed bison, club-shaped designs are placed to indicate spears which have frequently been located near the heart of the animal. Is that a sign of respect for the animal's bravery? In the longest cavern known, in *Montespan in Haute Garonne,* paintings are nearly inaccessible unless one is willing to go for a kilometre and a half stream before reaching the subterranean gallery. Deep in there, aside from the animal drawings, there are a number of clay animal figurines are depicting wounded bears and felines apparently in a position of Animist spiritual ceremony. In another cave in *Marsoulas,* also near Garonne, a series of multicolour drawings have spear designs painted and re-painted over and over which indicates that it was constantly renewed for Animist spiritual purposes to influence a kill in the chase.

Scenes of this kind could be multiplied to show the ritual aspects of the Stone Age which penetrated the inner depths of these pre-historic caverns. This however, was not the only intention practiced by the pre historic cults, for the groups' food supply had to be spiritually secured as well as procured. The hunting of specific animals for subsistence was made symbolic and fertility dances were performed to make the species increase and multiply and the depicting scenes are portraying such propagation. The material-reality of life was symbolically depicted but it was also genuinely believed to be real. A close attention to these drawings reveals a ritual symbolism and other scenes of killing an animal for food are rendered more realistic. These figurines are realistically displayed in the *Natural History Museum of Toulouse.*

Here we came to an important discovery of the symbolic origins of the propagators who were leading the animist rituals and were establishing themselves as the base for the future shamans, priests, clergy, imams, monks and holy-men of all past and present historical man-made religions. These propagators were depicted much later in the Iron and Bronze Age and were called the *Sorcerer,* with half human and animal figure characteristics. In the cave of *Enlene,* near the *Tuc d'Audoubert* was found a partly painted, partly engraved figure of a man known as the "Sorcerer" with human face and long waving beard, with the eyes of an owl, the claws of a lion and the tail of a horse. All these animal characteristics, which were revered by early humans, were projected onto a human connecting him to the legacy of animist power. This figure of the sorcerer was embodying the attributes and exercising the functions of a symbolically depicted anthropoid *Deity* which brought together man and animals in a mystic bonding and in a joint effort to conserve the well-being of the group and the abundance of food supply.

This motif occurs in various scenes of ritual dancing in rock-shelters where a group of narrow-waist women wearing skirts reaching to the knees but not depicting facial features are dancing around a naked man in a ritual with fertility purposes. It was this aspect of pre-historic spiritualism, in and after the Age of Palaeolithic times, which found expression in a number of female figures commonly known as *"Venuses."* They were introduced in the European Continent and from middle Russia to Siberia, where it appears the worship of man-made mother-goddess arose some 15,000 years ago. This was the earliest manifestation of the symbolism of deity, a prominent and persistent feature as is demonstrated by archaeological evidence. It was not however, until the Age of Agriculture, 5,000 years ago, and herding when was adopted in the Mesopotamia of the Fertile Crescent, that the female principle was personified as the Great Mother, with life-giving powers and functions which symbolised feminine characteristics endowed with pro-creative attributes. As the mother of the human race, she was regarded essentially as life-producer before her male partner was recognised as the power of the begetter. This deeply laid belief has been demonstrated in cave symbolism, in fertility scenes, dances and rituals which extended to the renewal of life in the here and in the belief in the existence of the after life.

For early humanity's existence, hunting, fishing and finding edible berries and fruits formed a staple diet which implied a sacred character and significance. This involved a variety of rites, rituals and motifs expressed in cavern sanctuaries and drawing techniques, ranging from magical hunting scenes to glorifying the hazards of the chase. In the great cave wall gallery of *Lascaux* must have been a cult-center for several thousand years as every form of the Palaeolithic art period is represented in it. In addition to the numerous expressions and representations of mythical animals, there is a sort of crypt with drawings portraying a hunter killed by a bison, with its flank transfixed by a spear exposing its intestines. This dramatic scene is dedicated to a deceased hunter who may also have been buried in the cave, as a great reminder of good and evil, by the artist who painted in this way. A masked sorcerer in a spotted skin stands by as some ancestral spirit believed to be the protector of all hunters.

While the cave artists' motifs underlining their art were many and various, there can be no doubt that primarily they were propagators of spiritual sanctuaries with an intensely inspired awe-ambient. Intentionally or unintentionally, those pre-historic sanctuaries housed rituals and dances which were held by shamans, who in turn controlled and maintained the ways of the peoples' deep emotions; because it was upon them that the collective hopes and fears were concentrated. The pre-historic caves and art functioned as the most outward expression of humanity's vital search for man-made animist religion. Having limited understanding of the natural processes and the Laws of Nature, the early man could not go beyond his own observations and the rites and rituals, cave paintings and engravings. Man was in need to establish friendly and beneficial relations with the unseen world of mysterious force that surrounded him. This unseen force controlled his destiny and this illusion was not very far removed from what, in our own idiom, could be described as the conception of divine pagan deity. Whether it involved any clear idea about the existence of a theistic entity is very difficult to support from the pictorial scenes found in the caves. It is true that from people living close to the state of nature, such as preliterate primitive peoples today living in the Amazon Rainforest of South America, there is a widespread belief in high dominant spirits (good or evil) associated with lesser spiritual beings such as shamans, totems, brave hunters, ancestors and local magical spirits. Within this symmetrical list of spiritual possibilities, no spirit stands above the rest as a shadowy powerful figure who might be concerned with man's daily affairs. This shadowy figure of supernatural God was invented much later, by men who used it to control and exploit the ignorant and fearful indigenous tribesmen.

It has to be noted however, that the primitive mind; whether in the pre-historic caves, in the Amazon Forest today or in the Arabian Peninsula tribal communities of the 1st century, has a very limited capacity and can hardly conceive of anything dictated beyond superstition. You see, natural processes could only be interpreted in pagan or animist terms. In evolutionary terms however, the minimum definition of religion was, and still is, the belief in the existence of a superior spiritual being. From this point on, pagan beliefs and animism appear to have developed into polytheism when, (as drawings of various pre-historic cave scenes suggest), the innumerable spirits in every tree and flower, every brook and river, every breeze that blew, every hunting effort, every child's birth, fertility and death were conceived as the works of separate spirits. When all these spirits were gradually personified by a further generalisation and abstraction, the instinctive biologically programmed pattern-cravings in the human mind were activated to simplify and were these ideas were unified into a non- existent life-pattern: a "comfort-zone" of illusions and delusions with religious flavour. In this way, simple personal spiritualism developed into dominant pagan animism, which in turn developed into wide-spread polytheism and finally to monotheism as

the final stage of delusional belief in a single "Lord of Heaven and Earth."
It would be pure speculation for us to assume that it was a process of the Natural Selection of evolutionary transitional thought of the pre-historic period, which accordingly led to the development of organised religion and the concept of a celestial God. It was not! The starting point of pre-historic religion was based on a creative assumption that some kind of mysterious power operates in the food quest, sex, fertility, birth, death and the sequence of the seasons. When the idea of each of these acquired an independent life of their own, in their various aspects and functions, then each found expression as spiritual beings or ghosts of the dead because the processes of the origin of life, biological evolution and natural selection had not yet been discovered. The recurrence of the conception of theism in all stages of religious development; from pre-historic times onwards; suggests that it arose by historical coincidence and human planning. This is evident in the rise of Judaism, Christianity and Islam, which were invented exclusively by *Man's design, not by God's*.

So far from polytheism passing into monotheism, speculations based on illusions and delusions about the cosmos led to the personifying process of the natural order of things. With a multitude of spirits and gods, and the making of a supernatural being, all being very vague and inoperative figures, obscured in the mist of animism and polytheism. It remains within the capacity of pre-historic mentality and speculative-animation of nature in relation to non-existent spiritual beings. They were organised on a personalised hierarchical base, to imaging one wholly exclusive God, Yahweh of Israel, Allah of Islam and the Trinity in Christendom.

Whether a mother-goddess of fertility or a powerful male deity was actually the earliest attempt to give expression to the concept of supernatural being in the symbolism of the decorated caves is not known. The sculptured Venus symbol, however, appeared later; the most prominent was about 2,500 BCE as the central features in Asia Minor, the Island of Crete, the goddess Athena in the Aegean or Isis of Egypt. As such, kings were identified with the Sun in the sky as a source of power and benevolence, the queen was equated with mother-earth as the core principle essential for the bounty of goodness. Therefore, as king he was re-born as god and his consort became the mother-goddess having been the dominant symbolic figure in the earliest pagan cults. Gradually, the mother-goddess became more clearly defined, with a distinctive awareness of the duality of man and woman in procreation; the latter personified the divine fertility associated with a young god. Yet, while the mother-goddess remained as the crucial symbolic figure, it was in the seasonal drama in where both partners created energy by their respective roles; the female as receptive and the male as active. From Neolithic times (about 7,000 years ago) and onwards, phallic emblems were incurably prevalent, though maternal imagery was predominant in the eastern Mediterranean region where the male god was subordinate to the goddess. Because the goddess was the source of life, and her male partner was secondary, the creative powers of both depended on forces over which man had but a limited measure of control. All life was born unto death and even the mother-goddess became a tragic figure as many myths portrayed her in pursuit for her lover-god. Within this view, early humans were linked to a new creation of myths and a strong link between women, food and ritual. Women controlled reproduction so lunar phases, seasonal renewals and harvest all reflected feminine power.

The natural order laid the early conception of the world, going back to the Stone Age, of the domination of the cosmic forces by a mysterious celestial entity which sustained the universe and its functions. As those were observed but misunderstood, they were felt to be responsive to human needs by means of spiritualism and magic, cult and religion; which involved animal or human sacrifices to appease the capricious God. It was however, only to secure the means of biological survival, to advance the confidence of life's harsh journey that supernatural aid was sound by pre-historic people living in the state of nature. These mysterious paths of life lead them to look forward to a continued existence beyond the grave, and to make preparations for the requirements of the afterlife. Death was not seen as a natural process of life itself, but something which needed to be conquered by means of magic or a miracle, which would suspend the Laws of Nature on behalf of the believer. For that, tribal communities needed an intermediary shaman, temple priest or magician who would go-in-between the unknown spiritual entity and the earthly occupants.

This role was given to the "medicine man," the shaman or medium man or woman who performed their curative magic over those who needed their spiritual guide. Spiritual guidance requires a story-telling and those with such talent became the shamans, priests, imams, rabbis or New Age gurus. Their story-telling was always very socially inclusive; in this way, religion and politics were never far apart. In the polytheistic societies of the Arabian Peninsula, the Fertile Crescent or the Amazon Rainforest, the spirits of importance varied with the circumstances of the tribe, though nearly all gave prominence to the sky above their heads. The sky is this vast space in nature with its ever changing moods, its sudden temper tantrums, its residents the Sun and Moon and the Zodiac Signs. It is clearly a force which can only be reckoned by the magical powers of the priests. In the story-telling, the polytheistic deities or a monotheistic Sky-God was always involved.

Pastoral societies, such as in the Middle Eastern, African or Arabian regions, will tend to have symbols and rituals linked to sheep or goats. This style of animism is described in the bible, in Genesis, where Abel offers the Sky-God the first born of his flock to be sacrificed. In the animist tradition of Christianity, people were reduced to Sheep and the priest became the Shepherd who guides those who neither can nor do guide themselves. This primitive animist ritual often involved the sacrifice of a pastoral animal or a human. The life destroyed is offered to the Sky-God and, as the animal's throat is sliced, the blood on the altar carries a symbolic appeasement to the blood-thirsty Sky-God. In other cases, priests or holy-men would release the tribes of its sins by loading them onto a goat, then releasing it into the desert to die along with the tribes' sins; thus we now have the term *"scape-goating."*

Within every religion on earth nothing is real and everything that is practiced is only symbolic in their essence. Lighting a candle to your favoured saint is a symbolic act, praying before the wooden statue of the Virgin Mary is symbolic unless you are praying to the idol itself, giving a hefty donation only helps the profiteers of the church. Religion is about story-telling, the more stories the better, for the odds are that one of these stories may apply to a believer. This symbolism is formulated in the minds of the believers and not beyond because it cannot go beyond the poverty of the illusive mind. As ideas in the mind, these beliefs have come from nowhere and they go nowhere, for beliefs in the mind contain no life, nor do they contain size, temperature or movement. For something to contain life it must have a given size, colour, temperature and energy. Religious ideas in the mind contain none of those and only represent the poverty of the human imagination. The superstitions of religious ideas were and still are, primitive instincts that many of us have fallen victim to by not professing to be ashamed of them.

Rituals and symbols need to be explained to people, for without guided explanations believers simply cannot guess the intentions of those who invented these rituals and symbolic practices. Inventing religious explanations and justifications—however absurd they may sound---is one of the most basic of human talents. This practice of story-telling, or re-telling the same stories with added variations, is rooted in the oral traditions of the tribal societies. The added variations are based on the socio-political agenda of the story-teller who wants to promote its successful conclusion. Biblical or messianic stories tend to promote the authors' view of the world and the socio-political objectives of the class or tribe he belongs to. The core root of religion premises is to provide myths or story-telling about why things happen as they do. This open-ended assumption gives leeway to any direction the story-teller may choose to take. The general intentions of rituals are lost in the mist of history but the practices continue regardless of whether people are still aware of them or not, their purpose is justified without reason and verifiable evidence.

In the Jewish religion there is a whole slue of explanations and justifications for imposing *kosher restrictions* on food and peoples' eating habits. Kosher food consumption is governed by strict rules and regulations, and in accordance with the Torah. For instance, the only types of meat that maybe eaten are cattle and game that have *"cloven hoofs"* and *"chew the cud."* This tribal animist tradition of the Torah proclaims that the kosher animal must be slaughtered by a ritual butcher, and the killing must be done instantaneously. In Islam, the *Hadiths* were written by people who claimed that Mohammad said "this" or "that" Hadith which Muslims follow and believe blindly. The Hadith are the symbolic reference of Islamic laws in both personal and social levels of obedience. There is great doubt about the authenticity of each Hadith, since only the author could verify the truth of each of them. In the **Qur'an 4:11** *"The male shall have the equal [social value] of the portion of two females,"* one can assume that the author of this Hadith had a very low opinion of women and thus he created a sexist Hadith to promote his own bias or agenda. The point is that rituals and story-telling of invented symbolic events can be found in tribal communities in the present day and evidence of them survive in more organised religions, in ancestor worship or the Christian Eucharist symbolising sacrifices. We have only traces of religious symbolisms of mankind of 5,000 years ago but it is safe to suggest that the rituals, rites and symbolisms were at least similar to those of tribal communities surviving today. But more mysterious evidence of spiritualism also survives in pre-historic caves and stone tooling.

Deductions about the spiritual symbolism, myths, story-telling and practiced rituals of our pre-historic ancestors rest largely on archaeological evidence. Grave decorations and burial customs, carved figures and cave paintings and designs on potsherds may be only mere traces left of a rich and intricate world of our ancestral brothers and sisters. Graves dating back more than 40,000 years indicate that burial symbolism included deliberate offerings which may suggest an illusive belief in the afterlife. Whether the intentions of our ancestors were to show respect to the dead or facilitate a symbolic travel to an illusive world is not known. Skeletons of our fellow-travelers and earth's second-human species, our cousins, the Neanderthals, buried in the *Zagros Mountains* of Iraq were positioned in a customary style and were surrounded with herbs and flowers. Shell ornaments were offered for use in the afterlife or as hierarchical status symbols. Other Neanderthal sites in Spain, France and northern Germany feature graves stacked with bones of cave bears and stone tools. Alignment of the buried body with the Sun might have had a symbolic importance.

Ethnographic studies of tribal people in the recent past could shed more light on man-made religious symbols of ancient humans and show parallels between shamanism and traces of 21st century tribal hunters-gatherers. The pastoralists' symbols are evident also in those of the Palaeolithic Age (which implied in their arts and artefacts). Other activities, such as dancing and feasting have given symbolic meaning for the purpose of ceremonies. Most of those rituals and symbolic practices may have been handed down orally, describing the hierarchy of deities and purpose of worship. Cult objects, particular figurines, provide clues to the types of symbolic rituals performed up to Neolithic period to about 2,000 BCE (based on radiocarbon dates). The latest evidence examined include temples, temple-models, altars and frescos, rock carvings and paintings, caves and tombs, figurines and masks and cult vessels including the symbols and signs engraved or painted on all of these. All these represent a slue of human inventions and activities; passed on from one generation to another for millennia, without God's participation in any of them. In some temples, animists' priests worshipped the characteristics of the snake. They made the snake's peculiar form and often its remarkable elegance was its exceedingly mysterious mode of progression. With its powerful gaze, its longevity, its habitual search for caves, ruins and lonely places and its ability to renew itself by shedding off its old skin for a new one, made it an object of pagan symbolism.

It is not surprising therefore those tribal societies in the Middle East and the Arabian Peninsula regarded the snake as a mysterious animal worth their story-telling and mythological qualities; associated with swift as disaster, deliberate retribution and incomprehensible destiny. The small size snake has often been regarded as a house-friendly animal even when it is poisonous; for according to ritualistic beliefs, poisonous snake's attacks only to avenge an insult or injury. The myth of Cleopatra's death by poisonous snakebite is attributed to the fact that the snake in the basket of figs was disturbed when the queen placed her hand in it to retrieve a fig.

Symbolism represents a metaphorical explanation which connects two things that are not related. For instance, the tribal Arabs looked at snakes as being *supernatural* and, in one case; Muhammad changed the name of man *called Hobad* (snake) because it was the name of a *devil that* is of an evil God*!* Now, the terms supernatural, man, devil and god are separate and unrelated subjects, yet the snake-symbol metaphorically "relates" these unrelated things in a story-telling of religion. Religion, whether primitive or organised, offers nothing real but it has a perpetual, enormous collection of stories and metaphors which, as they are told over and over again, take a life of their own. After awhile the believers do not bother to ask or question the legitimacy of these fabricated illusive stories and metaphors, and so they become real.

Spoken language is the primary means and guidance in the development and acceptance of things expressed in ritual, rites and symbols in pre-historic as well as in modern societies. Learning a "mother-tongue" is part of a natural evolutionary process which does not need formal teaching to acquire or to consider how it works. Great curiosity is expressed about the way words are formed and about the choices available in the construction of speech. Linguists estimate that, over the course of 20,000 years, the language spoken by early Neanderthals and Humans has ceased to exist in its original form and a new one has taken its place. Had the Neanderthals not become extinct, the progression of their spoken language would have followed an equal development. Cave art and engraved symbolism, for both the Neanderthals and Humans, must have biologically developed following the progression of limited linguistic abilities of both human species. Language and meaning of words must have progressed simultaneously with the act of hunting and protection of the group from predators. Warning sounds of impending danger would have become familiar to the ears of the old and the young, the women with children, and the hunters whose task was to protect the group. A sound-word for "danger" would eventually have been adopted by all members of the group. Language would have surrounded the bare activities of Neanderthals and of the early Homo sapiens, but language is one thing that archaeologists today cannot excavate for us to verify many aspects about the linguistic skills of our ancestors.

However, if we are to approach pre-historic life through material reality, it comes back to the question of our speech, the means by which humanity, from the mist of history, has always communicated. The meaning of "danger", "love" or "group solidarity" and other signs, only limits language based on the limitations of activities of social life. In pre-historic societies of Humans or Neanderthals, the use of language was restricted to the need of expressing certain activities such as hunting, dangers, retrieving a wounded hunter, lighting a fire, and so on. Intellect and science were not part of the early stage of life, but communication was and is part of the life process. It should be said that early human biological evolution had developed a natural language, for it was through that process they could differentiate right from wrong, true or false, or something pleasant from encountered unpleasant.

For every new event encountered a new linguistic phrase was discovered, as well as for the necessary interpretation and causes of such an event. By the time the Neanderthals and Homo sapiens had begun to organise their groups, choosing their leaders and develop the means of protection and hunting, language must have had to keep up with each step forward in the life of the group. As life circles were slowly advancing but still limited to daily survival activities, so was that speech also limited around those activities.

In cave symbolism, the limitations were based on the artists' abilities and skills and not on other factors. Freedom of expression was available for those artists' who could project their mental imagery in designs, colours and invented symbolic beings that did not exist. They were in control of their own life activities, for it was up to each artist to choose, at will, the mental-path of her mind's creation. Creations could take the shape of a horse with the design of a horn and create an image of an animal that did not exist, the unicorn. He could re-create the world's animals to his desire, adding or omitting parts of them and even distorting their basic realistic forms. For each of these changes, linguistic terms were discovered to accommodate these illusionary or real representations of artistic expression, while language still followed the slow, real progression of the social-biological development of the community. In other words, there must have been more terms discovered to accommodate the growth of the multitudes of cave art expressions, than to express and explain causes and events of real life itself. Imagine, if you could, for a moment, the cave artists' sense of power, to mentally create anything his imagination could invent.

Who, or what power, could now restrict the cave artists' from inventing a two-headed snake, or a being with many arms, or giant birds, or a dragon spilling fire from its nostrils' or spirits which controlled the weather or other terrestrial or celestial events? Fictional interpretations of animist art works produced the idea that animals and their representations are created objects to be acted upon. The bison, as a living symbol, embodied and was able to actively protect the hunter. It formed part of the interpretation of the existence of a superior spirit or itself as the symbol of that spirit. Burial of figurines may have been an effort to harness the animist spiritual powers of the engraved cave design of the bison. Another worshiped animal was the dog, given their tendency to behave protectively towards the group or tribe, and to sound alarms by barking.

The choices of the variety of animals to be symbolically created by cave artists were not at random, as its behavioural characteristics likely made it an especially appropriate symbol of worship. This explicitly addresses the issue of religion in its early formulation. Given that animals played such an important role in primitive and advanced religious beliefs and practices, as symbols or deities, as metaphors or as sacrifices, increased attention to pre-historic religion may offer us new insights in the emergence of the illusionary and delusionary behaviour of religious believers. The fact that animal sacrifices are such a prominent theme in the Old Testament may have contributed to the justification of human sacrifices in other instances, as proof of obedience to God's command. Some animals do appear as the symbolic representatives of deities---the golden calf of the *Exodus,* for instance---such animals are associated with idolatry and punishment. Those animals were not objects *associated with* persons; rather each animal was revered as the symbol of righteous religious behaviour by the biblical evangelists Mark, Luke and John. They promoted those animals as examples of purity, innocence and the embodiment of goodness or evil. These propagators were self-deluded by their own symbolic functions and set of assumptions.

I once knew a homeless person. I would stop once in a while by his "spot" and chit-chat with him on any subject he wanted to talk about. He was doing most of the talking and I was willingly listening to him. At one point the conversation turned on the subject about *"bull-shitting people"* of which the moral premise was, *"If you want to bullshit people go ahead, so long as you don't start believing your own bullshit."* The source and linguistic style of his may be termed questionable, but the meaning cannot be ignored; for self-delusion or self-deception is widely spread amongst those who still use negative symbolism as replacement for genuine reason and reality. Throughout history, artists have been inspired by altruistic motives, to transfer their surroundings into their work of art, to beautify a subject, or to demonstrate their artistic skills more than the object on their art. Poetic language and artistic expressions are all part of the great human inspired accomplishment called, positive symbolism. However, negative symbolism contains an ideological or political objective, a written dogma to be obeyed, and a delusion and distortion of what is real. It is not created for entertainment or aesthetic purposes but to fool people, for them to follow and obey a dogma written in metaphorical language and negative symbolism. In this process the perpetrators begin to believe and follow their own lies and delusions (by believing in their own bullshit").

The historical human tragedy is based upon the Judeo-Christian fundamentalism, in thinking, in social relations and in colonialism of native peoples in Africa or Latin America. The habitats were associated with animals and nature, and therefore untamed savages were awaiting the imposition of the Sky-God's order. The military expeditions, as part of a divine-hierarchy that gave them dominion over all animals---and animal like-humans---expanded the Judeo-Christian dominion to include new categories of animals and humans. The self-centered Judeo-Christian dogma stands in contrast to many indigenous symbolisms which regard animals and humans as existing along a continued process. In the Amazon Rainforest people of indigenous ancestry, the boundaries between them and the animals of the jungle are permeable and dynamic. Their relationship with the animals is co-operative rather than antagonistic, and animals are looked upon as living beings with agency, culture and society. Symbolisms of animal figures are highly contested symbols of conflicting religious and political values. Charismatic, exotic animals, such as big-cats, have a long symbolic history as decorative objects in Parisian Catholic cathedrals and the Tower of London which suggests that such practices date back to pre-historic tradition of cave arts from more than 40,000 years ago.

Finally, it was symbolism, which was imprinted in the Roman soldiers' shields, that projected a "God's protection" on soldiers willing to place it on their bodies. It was this powerful symbolism that give rise to the popularity of the underground Christianity within the soldiers of the Emperor Constantine the Great. It was the projected symbolic power of Christian symbol (not God) that Constantine the Great recognised and capitalised on behalf of the Roman Empire. This was the main reason that the Christian Dogma was accepted as the dominant religion of the Roman Empire in 325 AD. By historical coincidence the Islamic Empires' army was fortified and strengthened when it adopted the symbols and legacy of Muhammad and the Qur'an 65 years after the prophet's death in 632 AD. Until then the Muslim religion was little known outside the Arabian Diaspora of Jerusalem and the Arabian Peninsula. In both historical circumstances, the Christian and Islamic religions owe their rise and success, not on reality, but on the imaginary power of theistic symbolism. More about this in a later chapter.

PROTO-RELIGIOUS BELIEFS AND SYMBOLIC SPIRITUALISM

PROTO-SPIRITUALITY PRACTICED BY ANCIENTS

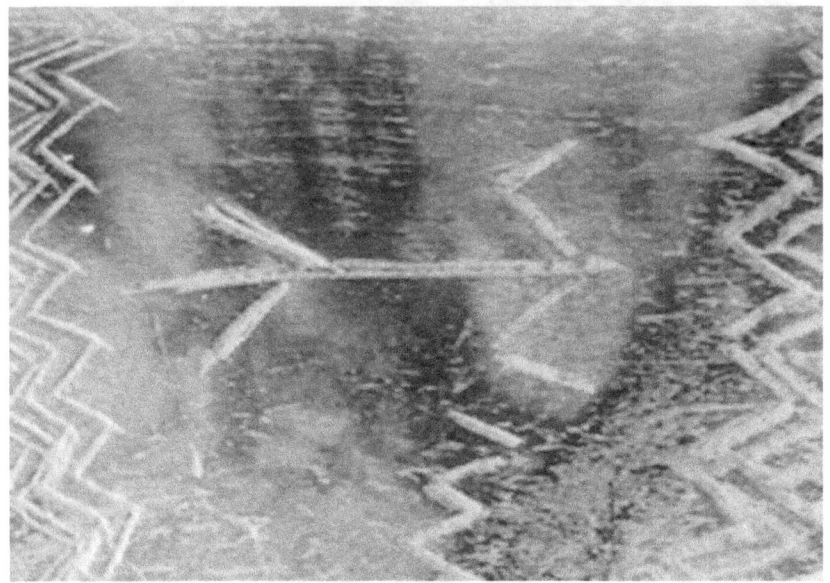

TOP: CELEBRATING FERTILITY

ACTIVITIES: PROTO-CULTURAL

PROTO-SPIRITUALITY OF WALL...

DESIGNS REACH THE STAGE WHERE...

THE SUBJECT AND OBJECT OR ILLUSION & REALITY ARE NO LONGER DISTINCT

PROTO-SPIRITUALITY OF WALL...

DESIGNS REACH THE STAGE WHERE...

THE SUBJECT AND OBJECT OR ILLUSION & REALITY ARE NO LONGER DISTINCT

PROTO-SPIRITUALITY OF WALL...

DESIGNS REACH THE STAGE WHERE...

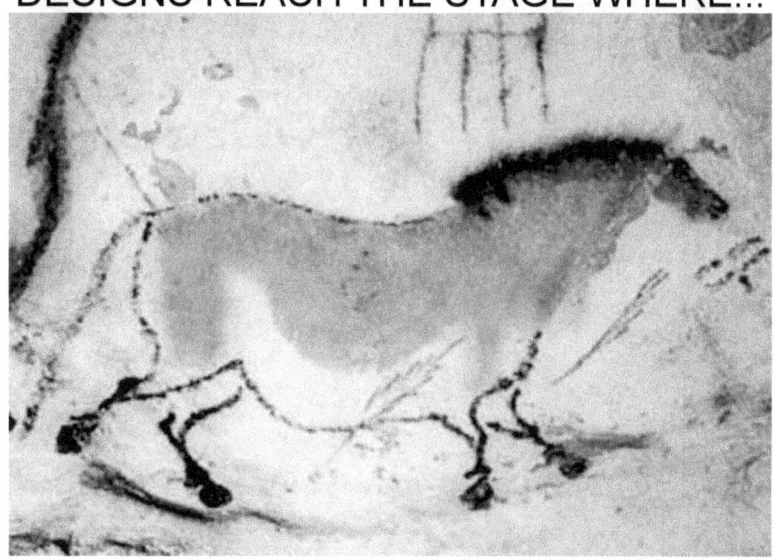

THE SUBJECT AND OBJECT OR ILLUSION & REALITY ARE NO LONGER DISTINCT

STONE TOOL-MAKING

CARVING PROCESS

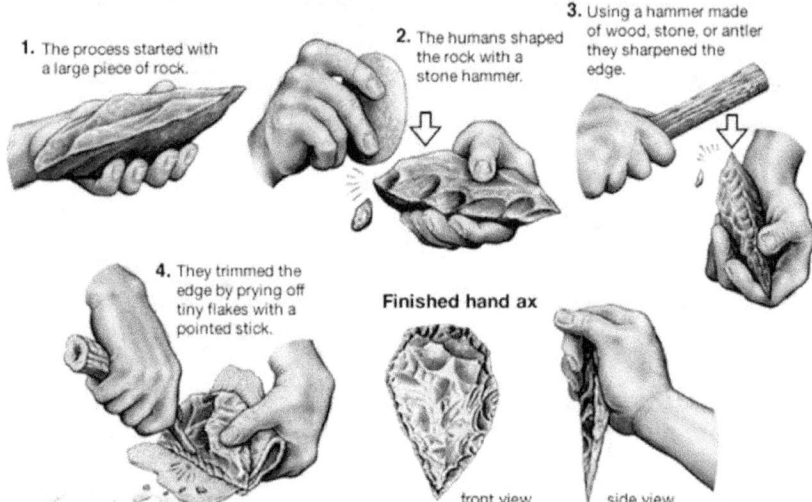

PROTO-SPIRITUALITY & RITUALS

SHAMANISM

RITUAL OF ANIMIST SPIRITUALITY

PROTO-RELIGIOUS BELIEFS

PRAISING THE ILLUSIVE ANIMAL POWER

AND CELEBRATING AN ILLUSION

PROTO-RELIGIOUS BELIEFS

PRAISING THE ILLUSIVE ANIMAL POWER

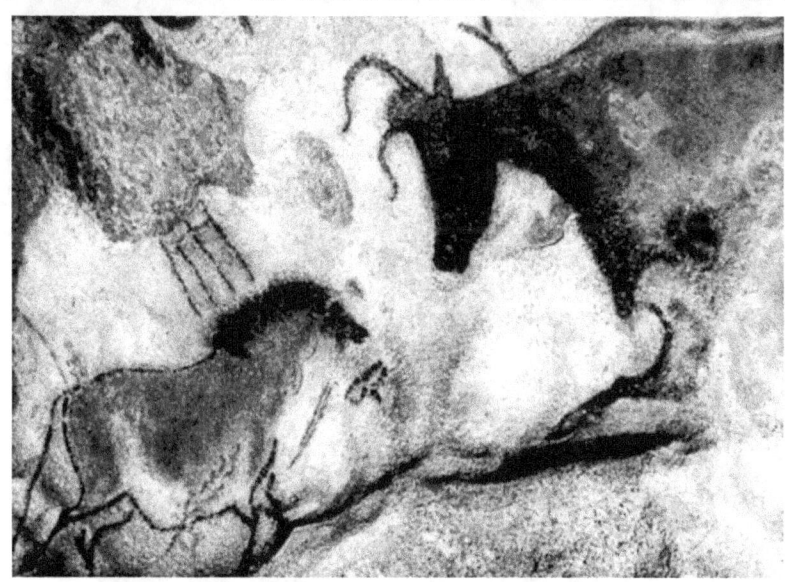

AND CELEBRATING AN ILLUSION

PROTO-RELIGIOUS BELIEFS
"THE DEATH OF A HUNTER"

PROTO-RELIGIOUS BELIEFS
"CEREMONIAL ITEMS"

PROTO-RELIGIOUS BELIEFS
"ANIMAL FERTILITY"

PROTO-RELIGIOUS BELIEFS
" SHAMANIC PRACTICES"

ROME'S IMPERIAL RELIGION OF CHISTIANITY

There are many stories in the cultist religious world; most are lost, scattered in the winds of time and beyond the memory of man. But this secular story, our story, of the man-made invention of Christianity should not be forgotten. Let us begin with the *premise* that Christianity was initially invented and propagated as Roman State pacifist philosophy of the 1st century (as Jewish "Christianity") and not as religion of Jewish origin.

This I will prove on the base of reason and historical written evidence. I claim that a fictional man, by the full *allegorical* name *Messiah Saviour* (*Kristos Issus, in Greek*) or Jesus Christ, was an allegorical creation not a historical one. The term Christ is now often used as if it was a person's name, one part of the name "Jesus Christ," but it is actually a religious title (the Messiah). The term "Jesus" is also a religious title (the Saviour) and both terms emphasizes the religious significance of "Jesus Christ" as a religious-title (not as a name of a man), the Saviour Messiah. You see, from the far historical distance Messiah Savour (alias Jesus Christ) appears in glorious image, an undisputed rainbow of magical power and glory. Every child in the Christian-world "knows" the Messiah's story; every devoted believer "recognizes" his slender frame, his flowing sandy hair, and his gentle blue eyes. But at close up of 20/20 the Messiah evaporates in the mist of mysterious ether, a phantom that leaves no imprint of historical trace. Long before the inventors of "Christ," the hero Nazarene, introduced something "new" into ethics and morality, Greek philosophers taught of morality, of brotherly love and the *Golden Rule*. Christianity had epithets of ethics and morality put into Messiah's mouth and then ignored them.

Messiah was not, and it is not, a normal name of a normal Jewish man; for if it was, other Jewish men would have shared a similar name; like David, Isaac, Joseph or Benjamin, etc. This fictional name is not shared by other Jewish men of the time. Although the title "Christ" or Messiah was shared by many street-orators of Jerusalem who claimed the power to "save" the world, to have healing power or that they were sent by God; all these characters were sharing a popular title, the Messiah. People were accustomed to expect the coming of the next grand-Messiah to deliver the wrath of God upon this unbearably painful life. This fictional figure of the Saviour Messiah or Jesus Christ was invented by the *Roman Imperial Cult*, the official religious scribes and propagators of the Roman State religion, past and present Emperors and, it applies only to this mythological figure, *the Saviour Messiah* or Jesus Christ. The term "Cult" was used by the Romans to mean "Worship," not in the modern sense.

In 27 BCE under Gaius Julius Caesar Augustus, the pagan theological body, the *Roman Imperial Cult*, lasted until the reign of the Emperor Constantine in 306 CE. It began as a form of official propagator of State Religion for the sole purpose of deifying a past or the current Emperor of the Roman Empire. This means that, as the Roman Empire grew, the Imperial Cult gradually developed more formally and constituted the worship of its Emperor as a deity. This phenomenon was not a spontaneous upwelling of devotion from the people of the Empire and its territories. This well financed bureaucratic body had its own Temples, Priests, customs and ceremonial rituals which it practiced in Rome and in the occupied territories like Palestine. In the occupied territories every Roman Emperor was set to be promoted and worshiped as the primary Roman God. An Emperor was held in a special religious significance, and also served both as head of state and as deity of Roman religion. Emperors took the ancient title of Pontifex Maximus (*a present title of Pope of Rome*), chief priest of the Roman State, a title that subsequent emperors would adopt.

It should be noted that this was a title-God who did not create life on earth, performed no miracles or special deeds, or being immortal. This mythology came later from the Jewish messianic claims. The title-God applied only to extraordinary men within the Roman Empire and its territories. The Roman Imperial Cult had the financial resources and the power to employ the services of Roman and ethnic scribes, specialists in typological allegorical "historical" works, historians and translators from around the Roman Empire.

During its long history, the Roman Imperial Cult was a well-functioning state bureaucracy with a solid experience of formulating a public image personality; such as in the case of a newly arisen Emperor and for his exclusive benefit. It must be noted, however, that in the Roman Empire there were multiple gods imported from abroad causing new cults to be established, and people could worship one or all of them. But by custom and legality the people were bound by Roman Senate Laws to recognize the current Emperor as the title-God and worship him. But just to enact a law was not enough for people to worship an Emperor, for they had to simultaneously be reminded of his political and military greatness by creating new traditions and customs on his behalf. This was an ongoing primary task of the powerful Roman Imperial Cult. Our focus here however, is to see how the Roman Imperial Cult was incorporated into the religious practices of Rome; and with the invention of the early *Roman State religion* *of Christianity,* it eventually became the foundation of *The Roman Catholic Church.*

The tradition of establishing and promoting the divine characteristics of rulers was started by the Roman Imperial Cult in the year 27 BC under the rule of Roman Emperor Augustus and lasted until the reign of Constantine in 306 AD. During this time, the Roman Imperial Cult placed emperors among the Roman state's multi-gods (pantheon of gods) and integrated them into the religious life of the Roman Empire. As a divine ruler, an Emperor received many honours, such as sacrifices, temples, priests, festivals and images that made him appear as god on earth. All festivals and celebrations were exclusively devoted to the military and political accomplishments of the Emperor as title-God. In order for the Roman society to be open to the idea of Emperor's worship of the Imperial Cult had to appear to be developed simultaneously as a unique Roman institution; by initiating the religious revival and civic restoration of the republic, from its numerous civil wars. This organization was able to create a culture of religiousness under whose influence people were born, grew and died.

Through the use of religion, politics and skilful propaganda the Roman Imperial Cult managed to establish an Emperor's recognition and celebration of his divinity even after his death. While alive, the worship of an Emperor resembled a living spirit that was present in all living things including people and lesser-gods. The adopted practices of his worship were an additional way for the public to expect his post-mortem potential divinity. The emphasis was a way of remembering the Emperor's greatness. Using images that depicted the Emperor as God, the people were reminded on a regular basis of his divinity by combining Roman religious worship with imperial worship.

As such, when people were worshiping him, they were simultaneously worshiping the Roman State. Most Emperors aligned their divine image with the Roman State in an attempt to amalgamate imperial and state with this religious practices that placed imperial worship within a set of religious traditions. This elaborate scheme of things relied upon the skilful talents of the members of the Roman Imperial Cult to be put in place and in a desired sequence. They truly believed that the Roman Empire did not really need military campaigns, soldiers and large financial budgets to conquer foreign lands; for the Empire could do all, by simply introducing the right-kind religious texts or philosophy with the right-kind direct messages to rule the people. This desirable sequence is called: *typology.*

Typology is a literary method of describing or mixing events, people, issues, military offences belonging to one era and then transferred to another; one myth replaced or combined with another; called writer's freedom among writers today; to rearrange fictional things in order to meet the objective of a narrative. In typology, writing a historical event can include a mythical narrative in it that alters the story to suit the writer's objective, and this kind of typology was expectable, acceptable, accessible and adaptable among Greek, Roman, Jewish and Egyptian writers. For instance, the allegorical creation of Hercules' exploration included fantastic journeys to the end of the world, battles with giant birds with steel-beaks—a mythology which is a mixture of typology and realism. The history of the War of Troy contains allegorical or mythical events such as the "Achilles' heel" and perhaps the Trojan-horse where Odysseus and his men were hiding. Odysseus's return trip to his home in the island of Ithaca took 10 years and the story is full of mythical events; such as when landing on the island of Lesbos the Queen transformed his men into pigs and Odysseus was able to re-transform them back into humans; and the typological story includes the mesmerising songs of the *Sirens* and so on.

In the Roman times of the 1st Century, historical narratives included typology of religious mythology and allegories of persons, events, times and locations. In short, written history was interpreted as allegorical works, with mysticism transferred from one religion to another and rearranged at will. This style of written typology was the exclusive prerogative and expertise of the scribes of the Roman Imperial Cult. This style of historiography, which included mythology or allegories, was acceptable and widely practiced, and no one rejected it for possible implications. An account of actual historical events always included some sort of typological narratives to "spice" the factual event. The influential role of typology has impacted humanity's historical accounts, so permit me to expand on its influence on writing religious events that never were.

It has been confirmed that the theist biblical narrative of the Genesis 1 creation myth of the first Jews (Adam and Eve) is not historical but typological. But what of the stories about Abraham; did the father of the Jewish religion ever exist? In according to the biblical scholar John Huddleston (professor of religious studies at the College of Charleston, Britain,) Abraham probably never existed. Yet, if you look at the Genesis narrative, it is presented as a family history; but if you investigate further in the book of Exodus, neither the events of Genesis nor the existence of Abraham ever took place. There was no captivity of the Jews in Egypt and there was no exodus from Egypt to Israel. In fact, the earliest mention of the name Israel, outside the biblical text, is by an Egyptian text that dates about 1200 BC and it mentions some scrimmages where the name of Israel appears for the first time. But the text does not explain what the term "Israel" means; whether it refers to a geographical region or a peoples' name. The point here is that the age of 1200 BC does not appear to be very ancient in terms of the claimed history of Abraham and Moses. So the whole Jewish tribal myth of being taken into captivity with Abraham first, then Isaac and Jacob and Joseph, and let out by the great hero Moses, who witnessed the "burning bush" and heard God's voice, then came down from the mountain with the Ten Commandments; there is no historical evidence at all because it is a typological narrative. Some circumstantial evidence may have appeared in the history of ancient Egypt, as a whole, going back long before the biblical text. There were tribal warriors who, for their own reasons, tended to raid Egypt from time to time and "liberated" or took away some Semites who left Egypt at some point, and such minor events have been typologically mixed with mythology to create the logical narrative of the Exodus. In 1948, the first prime minister of Israel, *David Ben-Gurion (1886 – 1973)* instructed Israel's field scientists and archaeologists to search the Sinai desert for archaeological evidence of the Moses' exodus but, to his great disappointment, none was found.

The Jewish religion is, of course, monotheistic and Christianity and Islam have inherited this monotheism. To understand how this monotheism started we must distinguish the ancient Israelite religion of polytheism to the monotheistic tribal god of Judaism. The concept of Judaist religious monotheism appears somewhat late, in 6 century BCE where we get the first reference to the *"One God and no other God"* i.e. monotheism. So, monotheism is not that old in the Jewish religion which it is contrary to the typological myth in the biblical Jewish history. Before the 6 century BCE they had One-God (Yahweh) which they worshiped, but simultaneously (and against the Biblical Law) were secretly worshiping other Gods. From archaeological evidence inscribed in clay jars from 8th century BCE refers to *Yahweh* and His wife *Asherat*, the *Canaanite Goddess*, and those inscriptions seem to indicate that the Israelites were introduced to other Gods by regional tribes with whom they were in contact. But this information was removed from the Jewish biblical texts. The Biblical text presents the official history of what "should have been" rather than what was taking place in family or private religious artefacts described as archaeological evidence.

Another story is the story of *King David*. Was King David a historical figure? We have no evidence for King David existing in the 10th century BCE. We have no evidence for Jerusalem in the 10th century under King David or *King Solomon* and of there being a mighty empire with international relations the way the biblical text presents. Honestly, one could not make the claim that David and Solomon did not exist, but they could have been very minor kings from tribal chiefdoms referred to as "the house of David," but this is a written text of a later 8th century BCE and not during the claimed times of the 10th century BCE. In terms of actual archaeological evidence about the existence of the King David Dynasty, we have nothing that puts David or Solomon in this period. The biblical texts were written to represent theological narratives which were much different from those outside of the biblical sources. So we have a real disconnect between how the biblical text presents this due to the theological agenda of the scribes and the information one gets from independent sources. Unless there is some authentication from outside authorities, I would say that none of these *Jewish, Egyptian, Mesopotamian or Hittite* texts should be read and taken at face value. Any serious historian who practices genuine historiography does not read biblical texts with the assumption that everything that he reads happened. The historian must have other ways to confirm what can be verified and what a writing technique of typology is, or if one can corroborate biblical narratives with other evidence which may point to other directions. One can not say that all things in the Bible are true or are lies, for one has to view each issue in the Bible with an objective eye. You see, theologian scribers who happened to have heard of an attractive "prophesy," would include this "event" in the biblical texts after the fact, and transfer prophesy to current times regardless of when the chronology of this "prophesy" took place. This kind of typology was not regarded as being dishonest for it was a normal literature technique or "a la cart" literature that served a desired objective.

To deal fairly with the origins of the Christian religion, we may ask whether it maybe have been a pagan religion by a different name, or if this was a Sun-God cult turned into a Jewish holy man (Jesus Christ?). Was this a belief of the Messianic Gnostics (of the Dead Sea Scrolls) who regarded the Bible as a religious allegorical rather than as a literal work? We must remember that, with all these, we are dealing with allegorical-literature and not dealing with literal-history as such. The answer therefore may be that there is no history to this "Jesus Christ" because it may be an entirely allegorical creation. We must therefore work outside the mainstream theology of religious institutions and *separate typology* and *historical facts*. This will give us the freedom to draw from startling evidence, if we are to arrive at verifiable conclusions about how Christianity was invented.

The key to enter the above lays in the *Dead Sea Scrolls*; the only Jewish historical literature that was ever discovered from the 1st Century AD or CE (Common Era), which was also the time when Jesus was preaching among the Jews. The historical Scrolls describe the Roman occupation of Israel as being quite oppressive, brutal in its implementation of Roman Laws and with zero tolerance of anyone opposing the Empire. In such a war-zone the rebel leaders and fighters described in the Dead Sea Scrolls (the *Zealots* and the *Sicarii*) were militaristic personalities leading an underground political-military armed struggle against the Roman Conquers. Their objectives were to push the Romans out of Israel and liberate its people by any means necessary, including violence. The Jewish *Zealots* and the *Sicarii* rebel fundamentalists were living and fighting predominantly in a war-zone called Galilee. This was a vicious war-zone with no particular rules of engagement between the Romans and the Jewish rebels. There were daily scrimmages and assassinations by each side, and torture and crucifixions on the part of the Imperial Roman forces. Violence was a daily affair and no one was immune from it including the old and sick, the women and children. This was the war situation in the Palestinian occupied territories that is described in the Dead Sea Scrolls; a war of liberation without romanticism, typology or half-truths.

The strange thing is that, amidst this violent turmoil, we have the Bible's pacifist characters, in the same historical period, who are preaching love, in **Luke 6:29 and 11:9** *"Turn the other cheek",* in **Mathew 5:44** *"Love thy Enemy;"* and **Mark 12:17** *"Give to Caesar what is Caesar's* (money from taxes)." Jesus said to the Jews *"Give to Caesar what is Caesar's"* at the time when the Jewish society, as a whole, was rebelling against Roman taxes! This was supposedly a Bible of Jewish origin, but its proclamations and pacifist behaviour were all in favour of the Roman's occupiers to pacify and control the people in Palestine, including the *Jewish fighting rebels*. This means that the New Testament is characteristically Hellenistic and Roman, rather than Judean. *'Love thy Enemy"* was no other than the Romans, who were torturing and crucifying anyone who dared to be against the occupiers' rule. The question is, how did a pacifist movement of *"turn the other cheek"* come to exist in a war-zone region that was occupied by Roman soldiers against Jewish Zealots who were determined to push the Romans out?

We need to understand that the traditional Jewish culture of the time was a warriors' culture; its coming prophets and messiahs were all warriors, not pacifists and submissive characters. How was it possible that amidst such a violently bloody environment there appears, out of nowhere, an active Biblical pacifist religious philosophy preaching civic obedience in favour of the Roman occupiers? How did this submissive theology come to exist in the middle of a war of independence? So, let us answer this question by taking things in parts from the beginning. Bear with me!

Our premise is based on two important works from the 1st Century, the

Gospels or the *New Testament* and *Josephus Bar Matthias's (alias Titus Flavius Josephus)* narrative, *"Wars of the Jews."* Josephus was a Jew and, a Roman Imperial Court scriber, who was employed by the Romans to describe the wars between the Romans and the Jews in the 1st Century. Prior to that, Josephus was a prominent *Jewish rebel leader* who was captured in 66 CE and became a "turncoat" (to save his life) working with the Roman Imperial Cult and as an official translator of the Roman Court. When we look at these two works, we notice amassing connective-similarities of facts and typology between them; for certain events from the Biblical ministry of Jesus are closely parallel to the military campaign of the Roman Caesar, *Titus Flavius (39 – 81 AD)*. This was a campaign that lasted 40 years *after* Jesus supposedly lived. Investigative efforts lead us to discover that the pacifist philosophy of "Christianity" was invented by the Roman Imperial Cult and propagated by a very powerful Roman family (the Flavians); General Vespasian and his son Titus, who have left us with number of clues in documents to prove it.

The Flavians rose to power through their extended family, military and political connections which, in turn reshaped the Roman Empire, starting with the construction of the famous *Coliseum* of the ancient Rome. The Coliseum, of course, was built as Flavian construction in the period 69 to 96 CE. It was under the Flavians that Rabbinic Judaism and the new pacifist philosophy of "Christianity" in Palestine that began to take shape. The question is; why were the Flavians interested in creating a new pacifist religion? You see, much like our world today, the world of the 1st Century was also marked by political power struggles, bankrupt economies, religious conflicts and endless regional wars. In the mist of all this turmoil, the Flavians took control of the Roman Empire and ushered an immense paradigm shift in order to pacify the people in the Empire and, most importantly, to defeat or pacify the Jewish rebellious Zealots and Sicarii of the occupied territories of Palestine.

Of course the Flavians' rise to power did not come from the void; it is necessary therefore to briefly look at the pre-Flavian period; and at the Julius-Claudia Dynasty. The beginning of the cult phenomenon was created by *Alexander the Great* in the Hellenistic East (Greece). The next cult arose in Rome as a unique state institution under Augustus. Beginning with *Julius Caesar* in the year 49 BCE, the *Julius-Claudian* family dynasty ruled Rome from 27 BCE until 68 CE (AD), or for 117 years, and transformed a republic into an empire. During these 117 years, this family produced all the famous Caesars: *Augustus* who was Caesar 27 BCE, *Julius Caesar* 44 BCE (which pre-dated Jesus), and *Tiberius* 14 CE who ruled during Jesus' death, followed by the infamous *Caligula* 37 CE, then Claudius 41 CE, and ending the *Julius – Claudian* dynasty with *Nero* whose reign began in 54 CE.

During their reign the Julius-Claudian family enjoyed a *God-like status* until the family began to degenerate and damage the Roman Empire. By the time of Nero, his infamous decadence was bankrupting the Empire, while simultaneously the Jews of Judea were staging a violent rebellion against the Roman Empire. Judea, which was also known as Palestine, was one of the conquered territories which made up part of the region of the Eastern Roman Empire which included Egypt, Syria, Palestine and parts of Turkey. Israel's tax collection was controlled by the Herod family, as Rome's tax collectors. This family were of a Greco-Arab descent that was put in power in Palestine to collect, manage and transfer tax money (in gold) to Rome. They managed to replace the previous tax-collecting Jewish family, the Macabian, who ruled and stole huge amounts of money.

The fact that the Jews were heavily taxed and were also ruled by a non-Jewish family did not sit well with the rebels. The Jews were further inflamed by Rome's legal requirement—as directed by the Roman Imperial Cult---which dictated that a statue of the Caesar should be placed in every Jewish Temple and be worshiped by the attendants throughout Judea. Remember that, in any territory of the Roman Empire, believers could worship any god or gods they wanted, but legally they had to submit to the Emperor as a God as well, or at least acknowledge that the Roman Caesar was also a divine figure. But the Jews of Judea absolutely refused and would have none of it. One of their key objections was, and still is, that their Jewish holy book clearly states that, *"you shall make no graven images,"* a religious commandment which was given to them by God in the Sinai desert. This meant that the Jews have never made or worshiped a statue or an icon which was a representation or an image of God. The Jews had a very different type of religion which was far more focused of their holy book and less focused on cultic statues.

In fact this presented real problem for the Romans who were trying to erect statues of Caesar in every Jewish Temple; but the Jewish population rejected that attempt because it aggravated them and enraged them. The Romans really did not understand that the Jewish rejection was about idol-statues not books; books that contained the Jewish Messianic Prophesies. The mood against Rome was based on an obscured prophesy from their writings that a Jewish "world ruler" would come out from Palestine. The Messianic Prophesies book inspired the Jews to expect a redeemer who would redeem Israel; rescue and restore Israel to power and leadership in the world. Now the coming of the Messiah that their biblical literature described was a Jewish indigenous warrior (just like mythical King David) was who could overcome any army because God gave him the power to do it. The assumption here was that if a Messiah had God's power then the Jews could easily defeat the Roman army. As such, the Jewish religions forbid the worship of a statue or an image of a Roman Caesar as their divine God.

The Jews had historically rebelled against Rome and were lead by a Messianic movement that had a series of Messiahs (or Christs) who had come forward to fight the Roman Empire. We must remember that the Hebrew word for "Messiah" is Kristos in Greek (or Christ); so the title of Messiah = Christ would apply to any of the numerous historical Messiahs appearing in this rebel Messianic Movement. Of course, the word Messiah or "Christ" could apply to any Messianic Movement in Palestine, but it is a later term or re-formulation of the Messianic Movement. This movement rebelled against Rome in 66 CE and it was a successful military victory because it was a huge and well organized movement of several thousand rebels. The victorious rebels set up a nation-state of Jerusalem within the Roman State Empire. There was a real danger imposed by this Messianic Movement, and at this point the Roman Senate and its military generals decided to do something against this rebellious threat before it could spread to other Jewish regions. It is a well known fact that Rome ruled its colonies with an iron fist and any resistance would be met with a brutal force, for it had zero tolerance to any sort of rebellious movement or resistance.

During Nero's reign, the most able military men of the Roman army were the Flavians; Vespasian and his son Titus. The Flavians, as you may recall, were a powerful and extended influential family that built the Coliseum in 69-96 CE. Vespasian and Titus were military men with long experience who spent most of their lives fighting rebel groups in Brittany and Palestine. By spending most of their lives outside of Rome they had accumulated great knowledge about the cultural nature of rebel groups. For over a decade they waged a war against the Druid rebel groups in Brittany and Gaul resulting in the complete defeat of the Druids and the destruction of any substantial evidence of their historical existence. It was Vespasian and his son Titus that the Emperor Nero called upon as his best generals to suppress the rebellious Jews in Palestine and recapture Jerusalem.

Both Vespasian and Titus went into Judea with a huge army of 80 thousand men plus an equal number of supporting staff in order to crush the rebellion. In the year 66 CE the Flavians began their military campaign against the Jews. They started the campaign in the north of Galilee with the first three key events taking place a) they destroyed the Jewish towns of Galilee;

b) they surrounded and captured the city-state of Jerusalem; and c) they capture the famous Jewish rebel leader Josephus Bar Mathias. Josephus later became a critical figure in the invention and formulation of the core aspects of the pacifist philosophy of "Christianity". Josephus presented himself to the Flavians as a sorcerer-prophet and because he was believed, and thus Josephus survived a Roman crucifixion. Josephus became an advisor and also predicted that Vespasian would one day become a Caesar and for this prediction alone, Josephus became a member of the Flavian household and later was given a Roman citizenship. When Vespasian became an Emperor, Josephus was adopted by the Flavian family and became: Titus Flavius Josephus. Emperor Vespasian used Josephus as a translator in his own court and as the main negotiator and mediator between the Roman army and the Judean rebels to surrender. As a Jewish "turncoat" Josephus advised Flavian Vespasian how to *theologically pacify* the Jewish population; a devised strategy against his Jewish rebel ex-comrades and against the rebellions in Palestine as a whole.

Meanwhile social and political chaos was increasing back in Rome where Nero's rule was threatened. In the year 68 CE the Roman Senate finally removed the decadent Nero who, in turn, committed suicide. As a result of Vespasian's military successes in Palestine, his family's political connections, and a vacuum in the Caesar's throne, Vespasian was the primary candidate to become Emperor, and he did. In the middle of the Zealots' rebellious war in Palestine, Flavian Vespasian returned to Rome and occupied the Emperor's throne in 69 CE. With the death of Nero, this marked the end of the 117 year rule of the Julius-Claudia Dynasty and the beginning of a new powerful dynasty under the Flavian family's extensively intricate rule; including the total control and direction of the Roman Imperial Cult.

The Flavians became the Imperial Family which included the Emperor Vespasian, his son Titus and sister or daughter Domitilla. With Vespasian becoming the new Emperor in Rome, Titus remained in the battlefields in Palestine and sets his military objective on conquering the city of Jerusalem which was still under the Messianic Zealots rebels' control. Titus encircled the walls of Jerusalem, eventually bringing a starvation on its occupants and finally destroyed the Temple leaving not one stone standing. The Jewish Temple within the walls of Jerusalem was razed in 70 CE. For the Jews this was the ultimate calamity because the Temple was the House of God and was completely destroyed by the Romans. Titus, of course, was the victor of this great siege and he carried the spoils of war back to Rome in triumph with all the gold treasures and most of the Holy Papyrus of the Jewish Temple, including their famous 7 branch candle holder. Today a visitor can see on the Arch of Titus, in Rome, the celebrated inscription of his tremendous triumphal capture of Jerusalem. The interesting thing is that all of the spoils of war from the Jewish Temple that were captured were put on public display in the Palace of Peace; except for one piece. This was a Holy Papyrus of the Jewish Scripture; as Josephus recorded that the Flavians took them and secretly placed them in their private palace where no one was allowed to see or read them.

Although Titus successfully ended the Jewish rebellion in Judea, another rebellion emerged in Alexandria, Egypt. The Flavians, by now, were convinced that their victory over Jerusalem did not mark the end of the Messianic Movement. They also realized that the Jewish messianic literature was fuelling the rebellions. When the Romans captured the Holy Papyrus of the Jewish Scripture, they had all other copies destroyed. In order to save any written material of the Messianic literature they had to be hidden (by the rebel leaders) and are now known as the Dead Sea Scrolls. This was the only way the Scrolls could be saved from Roman destruction. Beyond the Dead Sea Scrolls, there was not a single scrap of papyrus that had survived or been found of the Messianic Literature until the Scrolls themselves were discovered in 1946.

These Scrolls are real ancient treasures because they are the real voice from the past to tell us about the historical Jewish Messianic Movement. It tells us that the nature and acts of the Messianic Movement was violent and militaristic and not the pacifistic movement depicted in the Gospels. It means that the war against Rome was a Messianic War and the Scroll literature was not only a message of the Messianic Movement in Palestine but also a description and advocacy literature of a violent war against Rome. The Romans on the other hand were looking for a much needed way to subdue or pacify the Jew's religion by influencing it and by changing its course. But the Romans also knew that they could not destroy the Jewish religion all together and also because that was not their objective. What in fact was Flavians' objective was to create a new Jewish ideological-theology that was pacifist, (kind of "turn the other cheek," "Love one another," "Love thy enemy, "Give to Cesar [the taxes] that belongs to Cesar") and benign, instead of advocating militarism, rebellion against Roman taxes, against worshiping the Roman Emperor as a divine figure, and violence against the Roman occupiers.

At this historical point, there were appearing two (2) actively benign Jewish mixed ideologies; Christianized-theology and Rabbinic Judaism. Both were the new Jewish literatures which entered history. This mixture is described as a "peace-loving, turn the other cheek," Judaism, with a well-written Greek and Aramaic literature, and with an introduction of a new Christianised Jewish Messiah named, *Messiah Saviour*, or *Kristos Issus*, in Greek, or *Jesus Christ*. But, if the Flavians wrote the Gospels, how was it possible for a Roman family to know how to write Jewish literature that refers to the Jewish prophesies of the Gospels? The answer lays in the Flavians' collaboration: a) with a number of Jewish intellectuals b) the participation of the Roman Imperial Cult and with the philosophical evolvement of their own court scribes and historians, c) the theological writings of Josephus Bar Mathias and other prominent Greco-Jewish personalities. Josephus arrived back in Rome with Titus and became an adopted member of the Flavian family. This was an amazing turn of event for the Jewish "turn-coat," for he becomes a Roman citizen, has his own apartment within the Flavian family household and adopted the name *Titus Flavius Josephus* who, at this time, also began to write the *History of the War* between the Romans and the Messianic Movement. Josephus recorded that Titus gave him the captured secret Holy Papyrus of the Jewish Scriptures to read. It must be noted that Josephus' biography and recorded literature was always associated with the origins of "Christianity" as the new Jewish theological-philosophy that was friendly to Rome.

The interesting thing is that Josephus writes about events that are in parallel with what is written in the four original books in the Gospels by Mark, Matthew, Luke, and John. This is convincing evidence about the Roman origins of the Gospels. We know next to nothing about who these four people were; because the Gospels were written by other than these four people. It is known that the names Mark, Matthew, Luke and John were added later onto them as title-texts. You see, the original manuscripts of the antiquity did not have the titles, for instance, *"In according to Mathew"* or *"In according to Mark;"* and the Gospels were stories originally circulated without titles. Over time, these articles became associated with the present "authors" title-text in the 2nd to 4th centuries AD, past the age limitations of Jesus' followers. It is therefore clear that the names attached to the Gospels were not of the primary authors. In short, the Gospels are written as fulfilment-citations formula or as typology of events and periods of time that were connected with Jesus' long gone ministry.

In reading Josephus literal history of the period, side by side with the Gospels, historians have noticed parallels between these two literary works. It appears that Josephus' literary works quote events that typologically fulfills prophesies of the Old to the New Testaments, and the early Christians understood these connections. Because of this when the Bible was first printed in the Middle Ages, it included the history of Flavius Josephus (Bar

Mathias). He was employed to write the official literal biblical story that we still read today because all other histories of the period were collected and destroyed by the Romans. The Romans were ruthlessly searching homes and Jewish institutions to find historical copies that describe events in Judea contrary to Roman typological interpretations. This was the main reason that the Jewish Holy Papyruses (Dead Sea Scrolls) were removed from Jerusalem and were hidden in the desert caves. Josephus himself tells us this, in chilly terms, how the Romans exerted brutal control of independent literature of this period. The Romans arrested and executed any Jewish writer who wrote any alternative Jewish history of the war. The only officially approved copies of history were Josephus's, and his typological accounts were not a factual historical description of actual events, but a literal-prescriptive mix of partly-fictional and partly-factual events of Palestine.

Let us not forget who Josephus was; he was a chief propagandist of the Flavian Dynasty and the Roman Imperial Cult and, he was very successful and was well regarded by the Romans. He lived lavishly in Rome, was appointed as the Official Chronicler of the Roman-Jewish War, and he was using Jewish scribes under the Roman Imperial Cult influence and Vespasian's own diaries of the events. Also in the pages of his literary history, Josephus declared that the Jew's Messiah or Christ prophecy was wrong, and that the real messiah was none other than Flavius Vespasian and his dynastic family, Titus and Domitilla. They collectively twisted the Jewish prophesies to mean that the expected Jewish world-ruler—Messiah--would not come out of Palestine, as the Jews of Palestine for centuries expected and recorded. For the Jews, this prophesy applied to one of their own, but in according to Josephus, the Jews were simply wrong in their interpretation of this prophesy. Josephus used the most cynical interpretation by applying it to the rise of the Roman Emperor in Palestine. You see, Josephus recorded that the messianic prophesies were not predicted for a Jewish world-ruler but for the Roman Vespasian and his dynasty because he was, in fact, the world-ruler at the time. How convenient was Josephus's metaphorical and literal, but not historical, explanation? In fact all the historians of the Flavians recorded that the Flavian Caesar was in fact the Christ (Saviour) prophesy that was expected by the Jews.

It was very important for the Flavians' Imperial Family to be seen as the Messiah (Jesus) Saviour (Christ), as divine and Godlike. This was not a mere vanity on their part, for they were following the established Roman tradition set by the Julius-Claudia Dynasty before them, who presented themselves with the title-Gods for 117 years until 66 CE. The Roman Imperial Cult made sure that the tradition of Divine Caesar worship was now as strong as it was under the Claudia Dynasty; using their powerful tool of propaganda for controlling and pacifying their subjects' thoughts and beliefs i.e., a perfect Fascist State. When the Flavians inherited the throne they also inherited a vast and powerful Roman Imperial Cult bureaucracy. This bureaucracy was made of a body of scribes and propagandists that was already in place within the Roman Imperial Cult, with its 117 uninterrupted years of history, which was dedicated in promoting the idea of Caesar as the official Roman divine God—within a culture of multi-gods.

This was another part of the puzzle and it is important because it coincides with in the same period of time as the emergence of the Saviour-Christ Worship-Cult. This was a whole new social community of believers; a whole social theological structure based in Rome and in the conquered territories, which both were regulated by the Roman Imperial Cult organization. Anyone who wanted to succeed in trade, law, social status, in a key social area, or who wanted "to see and be seen" joined the Imperial Cult in Rome and in Palestine. In other words, these were the places where all the aristocracy, the influential movers and shakers of the Roman Empire, associated with each other. It was prevalent in all major centers, it had its own priesthood, its own ceremonies and celebrations and its own Coliseum Games. The idea of the Emperor becoming the focus of deity worship was well-established in the Roman political system, before Vespasian and Titus appeared. Above all, the Cult had many characteristics that would be later passed on and would colour the Christian Cult. It grew in the similar style; it made similar claims that were later transferred to Christ-Messiah. For 117 years the Julius-Claudia Emperors and important family members had made the claim that they were all of divine descent. They were therefore legitimate in according to the Roman Senate, the governing aristocracy. When Vespasian was declared Emperor by the vast Roman troops, his power base therefore was complete. With the change of dynasty, the Roman Imperial Cult had to create a new literary mythology to legitimize the new Emperor and counter the Jewish Messianic Prophesy, and somewhere along these lines things get mixed together.

When Vespasian died in 79 CE, his son Titus, as the new Emperor, began the political process of deifying his father and this was a somewhat complicated process because only the Roman Senate could bestow the title-God upon an individual. Titus came to the Senate and presented evidence that his father had been divine. Supporting evidence would have included Vespasian's military campaign throughout Judea, as well as background information, and political support would have arrived in Senate through leaders and members of the Roman Imperial Cult, from Flavian Josephus's court influence and

Jewish intellectual witness of the Judea events. It was during this period that the Gospels were written regarding---for the first time ever--the duality concept of the Son of God, and God as the Father, appeared in the history of Christianized religion.

This is because the theological structure of the Gospels, such as, the God (Vespasian the Father) and the Son of God (Titus) was in an equal structural formation that Titus presented to the Roman Senate. In turn the Roman Senate accepted Titus's evidence and Vespasian was deified, became "God," and Titus became, the "Son of God." In the *Triumph of Titus* monument that still stands prominently in contemporary Rome today; it is inscribed in dedication to the *Divine Titus the Son of the Divine Vespasian,* i.e. the Son-God (Titus) of the Father-God (Vespasian). The Roman Imperial Cult was set up to worship Caesar as God and it also provided the duality in the religious theological structure for the future Roman Catholic Church. This means that the symbols, wardrobe, paraphernalia and rituals of Roman paganism were transferred in their totality to the Roman Christian Church; including the worship duality of the "Father, the Son" (the Holy Spirit was added later). The most clear and obvious example was the title of the Roman pagan chief priest of the Roman Imperial Cult; the *Pontiff Maximums* (*PONTMAXAN MDCXII*) which became the current title of the Christian Pope of the Roman Catholic Church. When we look at who held the original Bishop positions in the early Roman Catholic Church, we see that they were members of the same pagan Roman aristocracy. They simply changed their wardrobe a bit; they were dressed in the same style of garments, but the ex-priests of a pagan cult now became the new Christianized religion priests of Rome.

It is important to know that there was a Pagan Temple which worshiped and celebrated the mysteries of the dying and resurrected God-man, and it was not Jesus (Saviour) but rather the pagan God-Mithras whose statues can still be found in the lower levels of ancient Rome's Catholic Churches. The Roman Imperial Cult's is theological plot to invent Christianity was very intricate, well thought out, and well-executed because it was done by people in the Cult who had vast religious experience; knowledge of foreign (Egyptian, Persian, Iranian and Iraqi) pagan mythology, and expertise in typology and twisting of events, backtracking the timing of events and historical facts in order to support their objectives. Now, through the Pontiff Maximmus Priest who was God's representative on earth, the Roman State counted on the scheme that it no longer needed a huge standing army to fight multiple wars and inflict punishment on the rebellious rebel peasants in Palestine and elsewhere. The Roman Christianity could; through its pacifist ideological religion, the "turn the other cheek", "give to Caesar what is Caesar's," impressive ritual celebrations, exquisite architecture, glorified music, including the reward of resurrection and eternal afterlife, miracles, personal feeling-good moments; influence, pacify and effectively rule the people in the entire occupied territories of Palestine. All this was assumed possible without the use of a costly army.

Over time Roman Christianized-movement was propagated throughout the Empire, but it evolved first as an underground movement because social changes do not come instantly or because of a written law. Followers of the new cult feared reprisals from the Roman polytheists whose ritual pagan practices were still very much imbedded in the hearts and minds of the average soldier and citizen within Rome and Romans citizens living in Palestine, Syria, Egypt and Turkey. Roman Christian theology was also propagated by the travellers and tradesmen who had an easy access to Roman-built roads which crisscrossed the Empire and its occupied territories. This was yet an ideological and a monotheistic theological movement, not an organized religion as we know it today.

One of the interesting points is to realize how extensive and influential the Roman Imperial Cult was in controlling and manipulating civic propaganda and theological literature. But when we suddenly see Romano-Christian monotheistic literature freely arising in this period we have to ask how did this ever happen? The assumption is that this could not have happened without some degree of complicity on the part of the Roman State controlling authorities and that, in one way or another, the Roman literati must have been involved in the production of this new religious monotheistic literature. Was there a conspiracy on the part of Roman ruling families to produce and disseminate this literature? This question is based on reason, because writing the allegorical literary works in the Gospels was a huge project to undertake; aside from translating the literature in Greek, Aramaic and Roman languages. The Flavian family, without a doubt, must have directed its outcome because it was in its own interest to do so. Other notable families mainly from Palestine were also involved in financing the research and general logistics in the scribing, production and propagation of the Gospel theological literature.

The production and dissemination of this literature was mainly financed by the wealthy Alexanders, a Jewish family who served as Rome's tax collectors in Egypt. Like the Herod family in Judea, the Alexanders also had a strong motivation of keeping under control the rebellious Jewish Messianic Movement in Palestine and Egypt and from threatening their position and wealth. One of the family members was *Philo of Alexandria*

(20 BCE-40 CE) a famous Hellenized Jewish theologian, who was already writing Jewish allegorical literature mixed with ideas from Greek philosophy, including customs and rituals of the Persian Zoroaster powerful religion (559 BC – 651 AC) and of Roman pagan beliefs of the 1st century. Many contemporary literary scholars are convinced that Philo's theological writings had formed the general philosophy of Christianity by producing a synthesis of both Greek and Messianic Jewish thought. Philo may have influenced St. Paul and the authors of the Gospel of John as well as the Hebrew *The Epistle*. In Philo's pages there is practically every concept that we can find with Christianity, including the *First-born Son of God*. His primary influence was in the development of the theological foundations of early Christianity. In his book *The Contemplative Life*, Philo combined Greek philosophy, older Stoic myths and legends from other religions existing at the time including; Krishna, Horus, Mithraism, Osirian, and Isis; and these he combined with Abrahamic Judaism. As such, the Roman Cult participants managed to historicize Philo's combined allegorical concepts such as; miracles, creation, divine mind of god, and others; and achieved writing the Gospels to suit the Roman Empire's Christian theological objectives.

In addition, Philo was from an extremely wealth family, and this is important, because here we have to "follow the money" when we are looking at major theological trends and their relation to the Flavians. Both the Alexandrians and the Herod Agrippa families were involved with the Flavians if we are to look closely for the origins of Christianity. This whole story has to do with body-politics of the period, and nothing to do with theism, deism, and magic, divine, celestial, spiritualism or supernatural involvement and influence. The concept of the Son-of-God and God was part of the theological setting of delusional props that served the political and financial interests of influential Jewish and Roman families: the Flavian Dynasty, the Herods of Judea, and the Alexanders of Egypt. Among these people there was another wealthy influential personality, *Princess Berenice* c. *28 AD* who was from the Herod Agrippa family of Judea. Berenice was the granddaughter of Herod the Great, and a product of Herod inter-marriage of a conquered Jewish messianic lineage. Princes Berenice appears in the New Testament and was an interesting character. Berenice is depicted with her brother Agrippa II during the trial of St. Paul, in a stained glass window in St. Paul's Cathedral in Melbourne, Australia.

Berenice had two or three husbands; among them her uncle *Herod of Chalcis*; and she lived in incest with her brother, *Herod Agrippa II c. 28 AD*, causing some scandal. She and her brother sided with Rome in its struggle with Judaea. The Emperor Titus apparently planned to marry her, but the Romans' great dislike of the Jews forced him to withdraw his proposal and eventually she became the mistress of Titus. The Herodian Dynasty ruled Judea Province between 39 BC and 92 BC. Those bonds of various relationships appeared to be the building blocks of a dynasty of powerful people; mixed-marriages "shaking-up" with the Roman conquerors, and the outcome was a whirlwind of ideas to create a benign ideology of Christianity. Berenice was a Herod related to the Alexanders and of course, the mistress of Titus. It is from this complex relationship of influential people that we get the first signs of the Christian ideology which led to the rise of the Flavian Dynasty.

The fact that Berenice was so close to the Flavians demonstrates that the three families were unified financially, romantically and in common theological and literal matters. This means that; under the guide and control of the three families (the Herods, the Alexanders, and the Flavians), Josephus and the Roman Imperial Cult; the Gospels were written as a synthesis of the dynamics of Judaism, Rome's and Middle East polytheist paganism, which eventually became Christianity. In fact, these three families had the motivation to invent Christianity; along with Josephus' expertise in Judaism, all had the literal ability to come up with these myths and fulfilment of prophesies. This means that the Flavians had the political motivation, the means and the collaboration of others which were able to begin constructing and disseminating the foundations of Christianity.

Adding to this background we have the supporting documentation of the Gospels themselves. The authors of the Gospels indicate to us their structure, how they were composed, who wrote them and why they were written. To begin with, these texts were not historically independent Jewish texts, but were written as literary allegorical works which followed classical literary models of the time. That is, a mixture of historicity with mythology in a typological style. Because, if we expected to get to know the historical witnesses to these texts, such as, Mark's, Matthew's, Luke's and John's, we would be faced with a problem: those are anonymous authors, creators of anonymous allegorical documents. You see, these texts were not written by the names attached to each text, for this is simply a typological Christian tradition of the named Gospels. Such tradition begins with a standard allegorical utterance, *"According to Mark or according to John."* Therefore, the idea that the Gospels are somehow a reliable testimony is simply not true. Even though the Gospels' stories themselves were elaborated in the New Testament, they started simple and, as time went on beyond the 2nd and 4th centuries, the Gospel's writers got little more fantastic. You see, fifteen years after Jesus' death, Mathew and Luke came along and their writings even get more amazing. By the time John appeared, sixty years later, we get an incredible legendary illusionary growth in the Gospels' stories. Future Gospel writers took the 'baton' of Christianity and took its attraction forward to their own field of religiousness.

The critical question we must ask now is why the Gospels are called Gospels—and in reference to what? Well, the term Gospels in Greek is *Evangelion* which, in translation means *"Good News of Military Victory."* In Greek military linguistic terms, *"to evangelize"* is to bring news of the favoured outcome of a military engagement, usually a victory. So, what was the good news of military victory for the Romans? Was this a cheerful message that would have also been celebrated by the Jews who were defeated in that period? Whose victory was celebrated in the Biblical-Evangelion? It appears clearly that "we" are celebrating Roman victories because these events (the Battle of Gadara, the Battle of the Galilee and the Battle of Jerusalem), are the battles that the Romans won and the Jews have lost during the Titus military legacy. In other words, why would the defeated Jews celebrate, in the Gospels, the battles that they have lost and that the Romans have won? Curiously, the term *Evangelion*, meaning *"good news of military victory,"* appears 77 times in the Christian New Testament and the verb *evangelizo,* meaning *"to announce good news,"* appears 55 times in the writings (Gospels), but it does not appear, even once, in the prior Jewish religious writings of the Old Testament.

The fact that the Gospels originally were written in Greek, and not in Aramaic or Hebrew language, is evidence of ownership; that they were not written by any followers of Jesus. The followers for sure would have spoken Aramaic, but being simple fishermen---not known for being educated---they would not have had the literary skills to write the Gospels in Greek or in Hebrew. If the Gospels were written by the Jews, why would they write and celebrate Roman victories? It just does not make sense! On the other hand, if we look closely, we can discover that there are actually clues as to who the real authors were. You see, lot of the Jewish literature advocated to turning away from the Jewish law and obeying Roman law. In fact, this fits perfectly into Roman propaganda for the purpose of obeying the Roman Senate laws, of worshiping a divine Caesar and pacifying the Jewish population in Judea.

In general, the portrait of Jesus as a peaceful rabbinic Jew who was wandering around as pacifist (preaching love and talking to simple folks like fishermen and farmers), was no more than an allegorical attempt to pacify the rebellious Jews. We must remember that the rebellious Jews followed and truly believed that the Jewish warrior God in the Old Testament was about God's wrath upon people oppressing Israel. Ideologically, such an attitude had its political and military consequences for the Roman occupiers. All this pacifism supposedly was happening in midst of a vicious war zone, a fight to the death, between the 80 thousand plus Roman soldiers and the hundreds of thousands of Judea rebels. Since Judea was, in reality, a vicious war-zone, why then was it not portrayed in the Gospels as a war-zone? The fact is, that the Roman propagandists of the new religion were very consistent in their message, had things under control, by advocating the peaceful social objectives that were in favour of the Romans, including Jesus saying "Render unto Caesar what is Caesar's," which was a reference about meeting tax money obligations towards the Roman Emperor. A significant theme in the Gospel writings is the numerous positive, obedient and accepted references towards paying taxes to Rome.

In **Mark 12:17**, it was about paying taxes to Caesar: *"Render to Caesar the things that are Caesar's and to God the things that are God's."*

In **Mathew 11:19** and **Luke 7:34**, Jesus is referred to as a *"friend of the tax collectors."*

The Apostle Paul in Romans 13, also states, *"Let everyone be subject to the [Roman] governing authorities, for there is no authority except....the authorities that exist [that] have been established by God."*
So why were the authors of the Gospels so concern about the Jews' money obligation towards the Romans? Why was St. Paul so forceful to convince the Jews to obey the Roman authorities? Meeting these social and financial objectives---for whose benefit would that be? Jesus' teachings and actions were well in line with Roman objectives to change the Jewish attitude of paying taxes to Rome. This was contrary to the Jewish people, who detested and rebelled against paying taxes to Rome, because, culturally and religiously, they considered tax collection as being sinful. Why then did Jesus, Mathew, Luke and Paul regard as lawful the paying taxes to Rome? Why were they teaching unpopular submissiveness to Roman oppression? This is also historically illogical but not completely unfounded. You see, history repeats itself; for as an analogy of submissiveness to Roman authority in the 1st century, a cult was established by Polish Jews during the WW II; with its headquarter in Nazi Berlin, encouraged its Jewish members to pay taxes to the Third Reich.
The perceptions of Roman characters in the Gospels were all portrayed in a

favoured way because they were pro-Roman and because they did not depict the Romans as the forces of evil. The authors of the Gospels have reversed that perception, for it was now the rebellious Jews who had become the forces of darkness. There are various very striking passages in the bible referring to the Jews with terms such as *"some people"* separated from the heroes of Jesus and his disciples, for *"those Jews"* who were objecting, or *"those Jews"* who were trying to walk the divine-plank. These allegorical passages give us clues that the authors of the Gospels were other than the Jews. These were works of literature, a story-telling, and created by authors who were talented in Jewish literature; such as Josephus, the Herods, the Alexanders, the Imperial Cult and Philo of Alexandria; but whose values were all pro Roman. You see, the Romans wanted to promote anti-Jewish propaganda, so they typologically rearranged the story of the beloved man-God, Jesus, to appear as though it was the Jews who brought about Jesus' death.

But in accordance to the legend, it was the Roman soldiers who arrested Jesus, it was the Roman judges who found Jesus guilty, it was the Roman governor, Pilate, who sentenced Jesus to crucifixion, it was the Roman soldiers who escorted Jesus to the mountain and put him on the cross, and all was done in accordance to the **Roman customs and laws.** But, because of the Romans' twisted arrangement of the story-telling, the Jews had to suffer throughout history. In fact, the Gospels were a piece of allegorical work that was not done independently by a well-established team of scribes, but by a literary team that was in Rome writing the book of Josephus' History of the War in Palestine. Josephus' books gave prominence to the Flavian Caesars which the **Gospels** also did, and as a form of epic, the Gospels were designed to allegorically magnify the divine status of the Roman Caesars. They were written in the court of Caesars.

But there is a twisted typological surprise in the mythical story of Jesus. You see, the story of Jesus takes place a number of decades (1 CE to 33 CE) before the Flavians came to power from 69 CE to 96 CE. Why had then the Flavians created a story about a Jewish Messiah that was not even from their own time era; (Jesus died in 33 CE)? The only legitimate explanation for this is that the Gospels were typologically backtracked or backdated 40 years; exactly 40 years from the time of the destruction of Jerusalem's Jewish Temple. Remember that the legend of Jesus started in 30 CE ending in 33 CE. Jesus' ministry ends at Pass Over in 33 CE which was 40 years before the Jewish Roman War; which occurred at Pass Over in 73 CE with the famous *Battle of Masada.* The Gospels were backdated to the period of 26 CE to 36 CE of Pontius Pilate; that is to say, before the first Jewish War and during the Julius-Claudia period. This is typical of Flavian literature---a mixture of historio-mythical-typological technique---and a Flavian objective to backdate the story 40 years and into the period of their skirmishes with their enemies; namely during the Julius-Claudia period from 14 CE to 37 CE, and during Jesus' lifetime from 1 CE to 33 CE in Palestine. Therefore generation after generation of Christians, including contemporary secular historians, are investigating the Julius-Claudia period for the origins of the Gospels but they do not really find any answers. This is because the Gospels were actually written 40 years later and during the Vespasian and Titus era (39 – 81 CE).

There are typological distortions in the Gospel regarding the capture and destruction of Jerusalem's Jewish Temple in 70 CE. These literary distortions were written after the destruction of the Temple, that is to say, during the Flavian and not during in the Julius-Claudia period. These prophesies for the destruction of the Jewish Temple were easily made because they were really prophesied 40 years after the fact and after the change of the Roman dynasty. This backdating of the Jesus legend, 40 years earlier from the time the Gospels were written, explains why many of these prophesies of Jesus came true.

The Gospels then were created as literary work of Roman propaganda, as some suggest, at the end of the Roman-Jewish War and under the reign of the Flavian Emperors, Vespasian and his son Titus. Could it be suggested then that the Jewish people, those who worshiped Jesus at that time, were in reality worshiping a metamorphosis of the Roman Caesar Titus? Did the Flavians' propaganda persuade the Christianized Jews to worship Caesar as their God---by giving them a *Saviour Messiah* or Jesus Christ, to the Emperor's likening? Is there a historical account for the existence of such a person with the first and last name, *Saviour Messiah*? Where did this man really come from? The strangeness and mystery begins with this man's title: Jesus=Saviour and Messiah=Christ (in Greek). Does this title strike you as a normal *first and surname* that a mother or a father would give to their boy child?

These two terms were fundamentally significant within Judaism and prior to the supposed existence of Jesus Christ. Let us not forget that most major biblical figures were called "Christ" (Messiah); such as David – the Christ; which, under the popular Greek or Jewish everyday language, would be called Kristos (Messiah). The usage of this term Kristos (Messiah) was acceptable as a title for a street-orator, for this was a common mythical name given to anyone whose religious fever enticed him into becoming a street-orator, predicting the end of the world or the coming of God's wrath for those who did not repent their sins. For example, *Judah,* a forgotten prophet who predated Jesus was a messianic figure or *Kristos* (or Christ) and has had a profound impact on the formulation of the allegorical creation of Jesus. However, we still have to ask the question: what is it that we know about Jesus Christ, the man? The general view among secular historians is that the existence of Jesus can not be defended because there is no historical evidence which can support that claim.

But if we are to "think outside the box" and set out on the path to investigate the "historical" Christ versus the literary and mythological faith-figure of Jesus, we suddenly enter into a void of a strange twilight zone. We may find impressive images that are part of the literary "Jesus" which is widely spread and accessible to the populous, but without any concrete evidence of the thing that is called Jesus. Concrete evidence would include archaeological evidence which was never discovered, or even Biblical descriptions of a **physical-Jesus** in the Gospels or in Paul's writings. In other words, a historian or an archaeologist can find no established physical or biographical narrative of an eye-witness to the existence of Jesus at all. It simply does not exist. Therefore, the religion of Christianity did not grow around an actual real man who had accomplished legendary things, but around a literary-figurate idea of a rabbinic man who never was. Again, there is no actual description to be found about what Jesus' physical appearance was anywhere in the Gospels.

The presentation of the Jesus character is somewhat of a collection of legends and personal attributes of many Palestine messianic leaders of the time. Most of the messianic leaders came to horrible deaths, such as from crucifixion, enslavement, stoning and torture. You may also recall that crucifixion was an exclusive Roman capital punishment for capital offences against the Roman State. In all these legends of Jesus we are dealing with, allegorical literature is not dealing with the history of this character. The evidence therefore is conclusive, that the Jesus-man never actually existed because the legend is entirely a literary creation of fiction.

It seems that the Roman literary hierarchy saw that the Jews in Judea were relying on prophesy, hoping that this prophesy would materialize, and anxiously waiting for their warrior Messiah (Kristos) to appear. For this reason the Romans provided the Jews with a benevolent Messiah, not a warrior as the original Jewish prophesy claimed. Thus, in the construction of the literary character of Jesus, the Roman authors borrowed religious concepts not only from Judaism, Persian Zoroastrians, and Egyptian Isis-Osiris but also from Greek Gods and cults that they knew. Secular authors today have noticed the similarities of the literary Jesus with pagan parallels such as the Solar Mythology where many Gods are taking the solar attributes in relation to the Zodiac Signs.

You see, as agricultural settlements grew into communities, the Sun-God became the focus of worship and veneration for the success of planting and harvesting of crops. The Sun became personified with various Gods such as Apollo – Sun of God, Krishna – Sun God of many cults and religions of the world. In Christianity we see a tremendous amount of worship of Son–God, which, it appears, was the original concept of the Sun-God. The concept did develop into a series of literary Gods; one of which had eventually turned from a Sun-God into a Jewish man, the Son of God in the Roman Christianity. This new Son-God shared his December 25th birthday which, in fact, was the pagan celebration of Winter Solstice as the birth of God of Light, when, at the end of a three day period, the Sun appears to be standing still (dead) and the Sun is once again reborn at that point.

You see, in the ancient world there was a development of interpreting the world in a mixture of *typology, historical facts, mythology, philosophy and pagan mysticism*. As such, scribes were writing or describing events in historical terms with a heavy dose of mythology and philosophical narratives which were supported—not by historical evidence---but by mysticism. On top of this mixture we have typology, a method of transferring or backtracking events from one time period to another. There was nothing cynical about this process, for the description or narrative was no more than a normal "academic" exercise among scholars, philosophers and wise men. For instance, in the case of Greek Hercules, there might have lived a real strong man who accomplished some historical deeds, but could not have travelled "to the end of the world" and witnessed a mythical man, "Atlas," who was carrying the "world's-globe" on his shoulders. This means that, across every nation-state of the known world, there was a form of experiential and philosophical spirituality and mystical cults or mystery schools which provided spectacular narratives to "spice" the historical accounts.

In the core center of these mystical cults there was their perpetual base of *Mythos*, a mixture of mysticism, pagan philosophy and creative mythology. These were symbolic myths with which the people went through an initiation process into a spiritual awakening: *Gnosis*. The common people, in fact, were accustomed to hearing such fantastic stories and probably paid more attention to them, because it generated in their minds spiritual illusions, wishful thinking, hope and all kinds from illusory phobias. The more they followed and believed in their illusions or delusions, the more they remained ignorant of the wonders of the physical world around them. It was the poverty of the mind's imagination which went no further than and not beyond the confines of their brain-cells. What we see in those myths however, are the elements of what would be some of the mythical and mystical base of the Jesus story and Christianity.

So, let us ask the question, were the characters in Christianity, including Jesus, created from pre-existing--non-historical--literary characters? You see, Jesus' character has some specific representation of episodes in his life that can be traced to other characters of the time. Within elements in the pagan mystery-schools we could

a) find a number of resurrected Gods who:
b) were born of a virgin mother,
c) had twelve disciples,
d) could turn water into wine,
e) bring a new religion of love,
f) were accused by the authorities of provocation of heresy and,
g) were put to death by crucifixion.

On a more personal level, if a follower or a believer wanted to symbolically communicate with this man-God, all the believer had to do was to take wine and bread to achieve an eternal life. All these, of course, are symbolic acts; a symbolism which replaced reality, which is the base of Christianity. Easter itself, which has a long pre-Christian tradition and celebration of the resurrection of Spring from Winter, is a pagan ritual of Death and Resurrection.

There are, of course, Old Testament parallels with Jewish, pagan and Christian mythology in the New Testament, such as the *Ascension*. There is a very dramatic ascension in the Old Testament with the two Jewish prophets *Elisha* and *Elijah*. The elements of their ascension story can be found in Jesus' ascension as well. Other Old Testament parallels are the food multiplications, rising of the dead miracle, walking on water miracle, do to others as you want them to do you, and the grant ascension to the Heavens miracle. The question is, is this fulfilment of some sort or is it a crudely plagiarized myth but useful theme? One can see where the scribes of the New Testament used characters and scriptures as a guide or blueprint to create the epics of Christianity. Jesus did or said none of the above, and there is little that is original with Jesus.

Many things that are notably useful in the Bible can be found in the Hellenic Stoic philosophy which was founded in Athens by Zeno of Citium in the 3rd century B.C., which predated Christianity. Stoicism in Rome, which was taught in the philosophical and ethical schools, was also promoted by the Flavian family as part of their grant scheme of things for the Jews of Judea. But, if we separate what Jesus said in favour of the Romans, all we have left is bits and pieces of truisms from prior Hebrew literature, pieces from Greek and Persian philosophies, and concepts from within Jewish theism. All we are left with is a speculation about who Jesus was but that does not stand proper close scrutiny.

We can also see that all of Jesus' mystic and motifs came from pagan mysteries. However, as time progressed, there were two religious-based distinctions which developed among the Flavian-Jewish religiousness: the *Roman Literalists* versus the *Messianic Gnostics*. These were the defining divisions within the Roman-Flavian Christianity which, until recently, had been largely unknown: *the inner-propagations*, which were represented by the Messianic Gnostics; and *the outer-propagations* of the new religion. The Roman Literalist scribes presented Jesus as a historical man, which later formed the religious base for the Roman Catholic Church. The Messianic Gnostics or inner-teachings were the most esoteric and mystical nature of Christianity. For the Roman Literalists, the outer was related to prescribe dogma, statues, icons, traditions, music, books and rituals that were extracted from other pagan mystical contents and experience. Many of the early followers of Christianity were Jews and Gnostics whose teaching of Christianity contained more mystical and esoteric Jewish and Gnostic elements, while the Literalist came to be concerned with faith, rituals and the literal interpretations of the approved, Roman-created, Gospel scriptures. The Gnostics claimed the mysticism of the Christian religion and the Literalist came to take the books, icons and teachings about Jesus as historical literal truth and the direct literal words of the duality of the Son of God and God. The Roman Empire came to propagate the literal viewpoint and tried to eradicate all of the Messianic Gnostic mysteries, teachings and beliefs that did not exactly line up to their approved, Imperial Cult written, scriptures. Part of their eradication process was the imprisonment, torture and executions of prominent Messianic Gnostics.

By the 2nd century the physical realm of Jesus was rejected by the Messianic Gnostics who saw "Jesus" as a metaphorical or as an allegory of religious purity, resulting in the cry that the Saviour (Christ) did not come in the flesh. Of course, we know that history has always been written by the victor; in this case the Roman Empire forces in Judea, and so we now have a "Jesus" who is presented as a real historical man by the Roman Catholic Church. All of the traditional legacies depicting the Roman's suppressing and torturing the Christians are correct. The Roman Empire had a particular hatred for the Messianic Gnostics who continued to rebel against Rome, mystics, magicians, fakirs, philosophers and non-Roman religious cults, which it saw as a threat to its stability in the occupied territories. The Romans in the occupied territories of Palestine persecuted the Messianic militaristic Jews, among them the independent Gnostic thinkers. With one exception; the pacifistic Christians who supported the Biblical decree "give to Caesar what is Caesar's" that group would have been promoted. The message to the pacifist Christians was simple; believe, have faith, follow the rituals and obey a submissive pacifism, which was vigorously promoted by the Roman Imperial Cult in Palestine.

The Roman Imperial Cult promoted the literal or practical side of this new religion which was propagated through their pagan style Temples, Priesthood, dress code, rituals and celebrations, all of which had already long been functional in Roman society by the Roman Imperial Cult. This new cult of Christianity offered the hope of a heavenly afterlife through believing in the historical and the literal authenticity of the written Gospels. This was completely opposite to the Messianic Gnostic's regard of their sacred books which had a more symbolic and mystical eye. But they were unaware that those mysticisms took place long before the birth of Jesus or the rise of Christianity. It was from such dividing concepts that the *Roman State Religion of Christianity* became widely propagated, and as the Roman Imperial Cult's Gospels spread from the Jews of Palestine to the "gentiles" and away from traditional Judaism, more and more of its followers were non-Jews.

Today most secular writers would agree that selective passages in the Gospels were directly written by the Flavians, with evidence showing that Vespasian and Titus were the original authors. For example, one of the most widely known prophesies that Jesus makes was about the coming of the Son of Man. In **Matthew 24:27,** *"For as the lightning cometh out of the East, and shineth event unto the West, so shall [sic] the coming of the Son of Man."* Many scholars believed that Jesus was talking in parables about the second coming of himself and that this "coming of the Son of Man" prophetical event would occur at some time in the future. Now, this event of the "coming of Jesus" had already occurred. You see, Jesus makes very specific prophesies of three important events that will occur when the Son of Man makes his reappearance:

a) the Galilee towns would be defeated,
b) Jerusalem would be encircled with a wall and
c) the Jewish Temple would be totally destroyed, not leaving one stone on top of another.

Jesus also said when this Son of Man will come He will come before the present generation which is still alive; and listening to Jesus' words, died away. For the Jews of the 1st century 40 years counted as a generation; and

thus the only person that could possibly be the Son of Man, which Jesus prophesied, was Titus Flavious. This is because it was Titus Flavious who
a) did destroy the Galilee towns,
b) did encircle the walls of Jerusalem and
c) did completely destroy the Jewish Temple.
All these three major events took place and were completed within a Jewish generation of 40 years. We must remember that the Roman – Jewish War took place because the Jews were extremely rebellious against Roman rule; they refused to recognize Caesar and call him their God and they refused to accept any worship of a statue of Roman Caesar. Regardless how much the Romans persecuted, jailed and tortured the Jews, the Zealots and the Sicarii rebellious resistance groups were always there and ready to fight the Roman occupation. To circumvent the Jewish stubborn resistance, the Flavians wrote the Gospels, where a Son of Man was predicted to come in the future. Titus fulfilled these three prophesies and became the Son of Man. Since then, the Christians have been worshiping Titus as the Son of Man without ever knowing it!

To further support the evidence that the Flavians invented Christianity let us look at the Roman Catholic Church's earliest Catholic Saints widely known as the Christian Flavians. The Flavian family were part of the early Roman Catholic Church in a variety of ways including being the first Roman Catholic Saints. These include Flavian Domitilla who was Titus' either sister or daughter, in which there is an inscription honouring Domitilla for donating the land which became the first Roman Catholic worship place.

There was a Christian Theologian in Alexandria, Egypt, named Titus Flavius Clemens or Clement of Alexandria who was the first that created and propagated the Christian symbols of Alfa and Omega, the Fish, the Star, the Boat and the Olive branch. It is not a coincidence that the Flavians used these symbols on their coins. The final conclusive evidence of the connection between the Flavians and Christianity is that in 325 CE the *Roman Emperor Flavius Constantine,* better known as Constantine the Great, declared Christianity as Rome's State official religion, only after receiving a boost from the Christian military mercenaries and their symbols. The successful military campaigns of the Caesars were important to all Romans.

It must be said that the Flavian Christians, who were the core group of the early Roman Catholic Church, and the first saints of the religion, must have known the real identity of the Son of Man that Jesus prophesied (who would crash Galilee, encircle Jerusalem with a wall and destroy the Jewish Temple), was no other than Titus Flavius. For anyone who is consistent and knows how to uncover the intricacies of the Flavians' involvement in the creation of the Roman Christianity, there are lot of clues pointing to the Flavians' creation of the Roman Catholic Religion. But the most intricate characteristic of the Flavians' involvement with their Scriptures' writings was their inclusion of a secret code within the Gospels' text. The Flavians used it in their documents, which enable future historians to uncover it.

Remember that Titus had the Jewish Scriptures which were captured in Jerusalem; now secretly locked in the Flavians' Palace in Rome. The literary team meticulously studied them and eventually discovered that there was a unique literary code hidden in the Jewish text. This Jewish code, which was a common ancient practice, was now used by the Flavians' and Josephus' literary team to place new passages into the Scriptures that had to be deciphered to be understood. This literary technique is known as *Typology* (in Greek Tipologia). I could not stress more the importance of typology, with forming the desired themes and the final outcome of an intended story.

The technique of typology was widely used throughout the ancient literary Hellenic and Hebraic world. Imagery occurs frequently in the prophets or prophesies contained in the literary texts of the Gospels. Typology in the ancient literary world was traditionally understood as the real meaning of a myth which was regarded to be as true as a historical record. Typology was using historical events or images from the past to provide form and context for future events that have yet to occur. In our contemporary language we tend to call this stereotyping; which typology provides as an idealized prototype with certain characteristics. For instance, ancient scribes would take an old story from sources unknown, from the Old Testament or the Zodiac Signs, and then re-tell it in a new form. As such, they superimposed a current history upon an old story by creating a multi-layered context. In Hebraic typology, texts were designed to be read in comparison to one another, or inter-textually. In doing so, a hidden meaning from one text would become apparent only to someone who understood the typological process and connection between the stories.

Hebraic typology connects prophets; events from the life of one prophet are placed into the life of a subsequent prophet. In doing so, it builds and shows a divine pattern (which was God's doing) connecting prophesies to one another. The Gospels show a method of deciphering this kind of typology that was used to create mythological stories. For instance, we have the Moses – Jesus parallels in the Gospels of Matthew. In the Gospels there is a prime evidence of this typology. What the scribe of Matthew did, was that he took events from the Old Testament and placed them into the life of Jesus. These events followed the same sequence in the story of Jesus as they occurred in the Old Testament.

Both the Moses and the Jesus stories have:
1) A Patriarch named Joseph,
2) Who traveled from Israel to Egypt,
3) Both returned from Egypt to Israel,
4) Had a ruler (Herod) who massacred innocent boys,
5) Had a divine character who stated that *"All the men are dead who sought your life,"*
6) Both had an event of passing through water, Moses separated the Red Sea; Jesus was given a Baptism which passed through water,
7) Both went into the desert's wilderness, Moses for 40 years, Jesus went into desert wilderness for 40 days,
8) These stories had three similar Temptations: a) Tempted by Bread, b) the statement which tells the Devil "Do not tempt God" and 3) the shared commandment to "Worship only God."

On the Way to Jerusalem:
9) Both Titus and Jesus paused outside Jerusalem's wall for a brief time before they entered into the city,
10) Both send messengers ahead before reaching Jerusalem,
11) Both stated "Do not bury your dead or look back",
12) Both Jesus and Titus were on the shores of Galilee, and
13) The Good Samaritan.

If you and I compare the life of Moses with the life of Jesus we could see a linkage that shows that the characters in the Gospels were religiously or divinely connected with those in the Old Testament. The life of the first Hebrew people's saviour Moses was used as the foundation to the life of Jesus, who claimed to be—for the Messianic Movement---the next Saviour of Israel. To comprehend the Jesus narrative in the Gospels, we must look at parallels of names, locations and concepts occurring in the same system which was used to connect Jesus to Josephus' literary works on Titus. This was Josephus typology which we must pay closer attention to if we are to understand the mythology in Christianity.

First, the concept in **Luke 5:1-11**, of *"The Fishers of Men"* is directly linked to Jesus ministry. While Jesus was on the shores of the Sea of Galilee he gathered his 12 followers around him and proclaimed to them; *"Do not be afraid, follow me and become fishers [or catchers] of men."* Now Flavius Titus comes to the very same Sea of Galilee shore location, he gathers his Roman generals and soldiers and declared to them "do not be afraid." He leads his naval-troops to attack the Jewish rebels' boats; and any of the Jewish survivors attempting to swim to shore, the Romans used their spears to "catch them," and thus the Romans became "the fishers of men." Both narratives are not exactly matched, but we should accept the similarities of both concepts in both stories. It is simply a type(ology) which is repeated across the New Testament.

The second concept is the *"Legion of Demons"* which was a customary concept in the Jewish traditions, and Jesus also was dealing with them. In **Luke 8:30**, Jesus performs an exorcism on a man because demons had entered his body. As a Jew, Josephus was also dealing constantly with devils or demons but he identified exactly who these devils were. For Josephus, the devils were the Jews of the Messianic Movement—the Zealots and the Sicarii--who were rebellious against Rome. In a Palestinian village of Gadara, Jesus encounters a man, whose spirit was possessed by demons; Jesus exorcised the man, and the demons escaped and rushed into the water. This is a parallel story to Titus' battle in Gadara where a single individual affects an entire legion of Jews (thus the Legion of Demons) with demonic spirit. It follows that this demonically affected group, in turn, affected another group, and these combined demonic groups are driven by the Romans into the sea. This appears to be of similar grim parable of hostile military events, done with a vicious sense of describing the literal suffering of men. This is also a morally evil description of how groups of Jewish rebels were viciously driven and drowned by the Romans into the sea.

The third is the next Gospel's concept of the Jesus crucifixion. In short, three men were crucified, two of them died and one survived. In Flavius Josephus' autobiography he vividly describes that when he was in Titus' entourage; during the ending siege of Jerusalem, he came across three ex-rebel comrades of his who were in the process of being crucified. Josephus pleaded with Titus for their release. After consideration, Titus gave his permission and the three men were removed from the cross alive. Due to injuries, two of them died soon after and one somehow managed to revive back to life. Now if we are looking for a type(ological) example of some idea that could be formulated into the mind of a famous scribe who was writing the Gospels out of this event, this would have been a very clear example. It appears to be quite a strange occurrence to find such an incident in Josephus' works, when it shows up in such dramatic form in the Gospels. **In** the Gospels, *Joseph of Arimathea* asks the Roman Commander to take Jesus down from the cross. According to all four Gospels, Joseph of Arimathea donates his own tomb for the burial of Jesus following his crucifixion. **Mark 15:43** confirms the literary story that Arimathea asked Pilate for permission to retrieve Jesus' body. In Flavius Josephus' literal history however, Josephus asks the Roman Commander to take someone down from the cross. Here is the linguistic trick used by Josephus in the

Gospels: remember that his complete Hebrew name is *Josephus Bar Mathias*, and *Joseph of Ari-Mathea* is a pun on Josephus' last name, because both are one and the same person. Can you identify the linguistic typological similarities? Clever devil! For the average person, with a busy daily life, the brief reading of the Gospels would not produce desirable results. You see, a lot of the Gospel literature is simply a very well-hidden and intricate Roman propaganda. Unless a person was willing to spend a lot of time and effort, such intricacies could not be revealed because the Romans were not writing an objective history based on historical facts.

We must also understand that, at the time when the Roman scribes; the Roman Imperial Cult, and Josephus were writing the Gospels, allegories, parables and metaphors were used as a science across the Roman, Greek and Jewish literary world. Educated readers of the time were expected to read a subliminal meaning "between the lines" in literal religious works. When we are dealing with Roman or Jewish literature we may say that both were much more sophisticated, multi-layered, allusive and much more illusive than they appeared on the surface. The significance of the Dead Sea Scrolls is that they are historical literature that has not been filtered through Roman sensors and therefore they could be classified as genuine Jewish account of historical events. The Roman Christian Gospels are not a simple literature; they are very complex, an allegorical literature that indulges in the literary showmanship that the Romans played. The more we understand about Roman writing styles of the time, the better we would also understand the Gospels and other Christian literature in that same timeframe.

True enough, all of the aforementioned parallels have also been briefly seen by other academics. However, little attention has been paid to noticing that these parallels were taking place within the same sequence; the kind that forms a typological pattern. Most of the contemporary religious academics tend to read the Roman literature of the Gospels on the traditional level, without thinking of challenging the contents. Only by carefully studying the multiple levels of these ancient texts, or perhaps in the original Greek language, could one discover a lot more than a handful of typological parallels between the Gospels and Josephus' literary works. In brief, the typology-theology of Jesus Christ followed an exact pattern sequence; with parallel names, locations, metaphors, linguistic techniques and concepts to Titus' military campaign in Galilee, Jerusalem and the entire Judea.

Once a reader of the Scriptures understands the system that the Romans had adopted to write the Gospels; the parallel pattern-sequence linkage between Titus and Jesus, they could discover a whole slue more of them. The readers must remember that metaphors usually connect two unrelated things or events. For instance, the metaphor stating that *"you are driving me crazy"* connects to unrelated terms and concepts, "driving" and "crazy," or the metaphorical image of *Unicorns* which connects *"wings"* and a *"horse"* as two unrelated bodily parts from two distinct species. By using these uncommon metaphorical parallels, the Flavians created their own metaphorical signature in the Gospels. It appears that the Flavians were identifying themselves to future readers as the authors of the Gospels. Again, these parallels in the Gospels are the Flavians' signature, a kind of literary vanity that some authors are still practicing today.

Remember, both Titus and Jesus started their parallel allegorical campaign at the shores of the Sea of Galilee, and from there they went into the interior territory of Galilee and followed that by sending messengers ahead before their journey into the city of Jerusalem. Both stayed in Jerusalem for awhile and, when both left the city, their campaigns came to an end. Both have similar episodes in the Gospels; the military story of Titus is set with parallels in the Jesus story. Now, Titus' messengers reported back to him that Jerusalem's Jews were fighting each other and, at this point, Jesus stated that "a house divided against itself cannot stand." As well, Josephus wrote that, in preparation for a military battle, Titus ordered that an entire line of fruit-trees had to be cut down along the walls of Jerusalem and in front of the Roman camp. Now, at this point in the Gospels, Jesus said that "if a fruit-tree does not bear good fruit, cut it down." During the military preparation, Titus pays close attention to the walls of Jerusalem, looking for the best location to build a tower from which the Roman army can launch an attack. Building tall towers against Jewish fortifications, such as at Masada, was a well regarded Roman military war strategy. At this point, and prior to the attack, Jesus in the Gospels **Luke 14:28** asks *"which of you would build a tower who does not first sit down to think about the cost?"*

At this point of history:

a) Titus sends Josephus in the encircled Jerusalem to ask the Jewish defenders about under what terms they were willing to surrender. In the Gospels Jesus describes a delegation that went to discuss a peace.

b) It must be noticed that at this point of the allegory, both Jesus and Titus entered Jerusalem in triumphal style; Jesus on a donkey and Titus on a horse, during which *"stones were set to cry out."* Each then was said to chase and drive out bunch of thieves, money-lenders and undesirables from the Temple.

c) This follows the historical fact that Titus surrounds Jerusalem with a wall, and the narrative includes Jesus' prediction that the city will be encircled with a wall.

d) Because Titus' wall created grave starvation in Jerusalem, Josephus wrote that a young woman named Mary, who called her son "a myth for the world," killed him and ate him and therefore turned him into a human Passover lamb. The Son of Mary was the human Passover Lamb. In the Gospels, Christians have the Last Supper served with lamb. Jesus tells his 12 disciples, "Take, eat for this is my body, drink for this is my blood," thus turning him into a Passover Lamb. One can see the typological involvement of myths and allegories in the early rise of Flavian Christianity.

The conclusion demonstrates that the Gospels were not the classical literary works of a group of uneducated Jewish fishermen of Galilee. Rather the Gospels are sophisticated literary works which combined religious and pagan myths of the times, Roman political perspective and desire for power. Reading the works of Josephus along side the New Testament conclusively shows that Jesus' life and events were not historical on their own, but rather were based on the military events and campaigns of Titus Flavius in Judea. Josephus' literary work of Jesus Christ was an allegory of the Roman Caesar Titus Flavian, the Messiah of the Roman Empire, the Roman Son of a God that the Christian religion was set up to worship. What is at stake here are the historical claims; the religious dogma that has forbidden the examination of historical discoveries or the exclusion of certain scientific discoveries and their teachings. Instead, Christianity is asking believers to faithfully and blindly believe what they were told and not the objectives they may show.

We humans today live in a time were some of us may be fed-up with many of the socio-political structures we live with today. We also recognize major frauds in corporate finances and in the heart of industry, and the plug of trust has been pulled from them. In addition, there is another looming fraud with part of Christianity and it is high time for "insiders" or conscientious "whistleblowers" of major religious institutions to "step up to the plate" to make this information available, not just to scholars and academics, but to the laymen as well. It is very helpful to hear a variety of voices in order for all of us to arrive at conclusive theories that are presented in this entire book. We need to have the courage to discourage or dismiss the invented religious myths of Jesus Christ; which are based on the delusions of people's personal relationship with the Son of God. The delusion that *"I have a personal relationship with Jesus"* is based on fear of *"losing it."* This, of course, is a very bad reason for being a believer—to take such as illusive image as literal reality. The Agnostics, as well as the early Gnostic sects, believed that the so-called, *"dying of Jesus"* and the *"resurrecting of God-man"* was an allegory or a metaphor, and were used as a symbolic personal growth: to die was to be in your lower nature and to rise was to be in your higher nature. The Roman literalists however took control of the original pagan allegory or myth and shaped it by taking the spiritual power away from the individual and placing it into a central religious authority.

In rediscovering the original allegory, people now have the freedom to choose between the two schools of thought. On a subliminal level, some Christian believers have developed their personal faith; that is that their faith in *"Christ"* is the Energy or the *"Force"* or the *"Power"* within them. This is how they interpret the ex-literal story now; the story has become once again an allegory of the *"Christ-within"* by rejecting the Church's central literal interpretation. You see, what threatens humanity is not the personal faith of an individual, but the organized, the regimentized religion on its globalised march. Such a globalised religious march; when it is taken far too seriously by the devoted faithful, would act out its worst precepts: the Crusades and the Islamic Imperial military conquests, the Islamic State of Iraq and the Levant, the Afghanistan's Taliban jihadists including the current global conflicts between Muslim sects of Sunnis and Shia, between Muslim and Hindu sects and between Buddhists and Hindus are just a few examples of organized religious extremism.

When we examined most religions of the world, we find that there exists between them a common thread which connects all faiths with all of their followers. It is upon this religious connection that we make the choices that now have become so critical to the future of our human civilization. True enough, the origins of religious thoughts are much unified underneath all of the behavioural devices; rituals, myths, literalisms, allegories and acts of symbolisms, taken for reality, which we witness on the surface. We have created a 'world divided' between symbolisms (taken for reality) and an undiscovered healthy naturalism. These origins are nature worshiping—as pagan Zodiac Signs---of the Sun, the Moon, the Stars and the Planets since the early days of agricultural development, beginning some 10.000 years ago. It would be most helpful for all humanity to realize that there is an underlying unity of nature worship. This is what humanity has historically been looking at, with great awe and reverence, for thousands of years. Perhaps it is extremely important for us to return to the origins of nature reverence and thus avoid the destruction of our planet. This can restore a balance between human activities and our planet in a significant way, for there is no Planet-B to count on. This is the only home we have!

You see, the very survival of humanity depends on viewing history from its natural or reality-perspective so we can be clearer on the historical facts, and still honour the myths, including their moral significance. In oral or written myths, it is what the scribe and the poet have said in them that is significant, and not what may or may not actually have happened. We may never know all of the details of what happened two thousand years ago, but the voices of each generation of academics are contributing to an ever growing dialogue on our behalf. We need to enlighten humanity in order to empower its conclusions.

It is very important for our culture to understand where Christianity has come from, that it is man-made, that this has direct evidence which we could actually walk through its path and come to this conclusion; that Christianity was an invention of the Romans; you can know now that it was an invented allegory to pacify their Roman subjects, including the Jewish Rebels in Palestine. How did humanity take a myth and turn it politically-organised religion? This remains an important subject to analyse. This point is very important, for it demonstrates; how past and current governments operate, the tools that governments used, the purpose that governments aimed for, in order to control the people. On the other hand, televangelists are getting away with distorting facts as mere theories. For instance, subjects such as Creation; they provide no evidence for their position other than recycling religious dogma. But when we look at the influence televangelists have in the mass media today we can easily see that it is increasing.

Atheists, secularists and humanists have the moral duty to challenge current religious dogma and consider the possibility that the factual-theory in this narrative is both relevant and correct. We also have to understand how right-wing politicians have used religion in order to control us. A typical method of controlling us is twofold: a) install fear in us of the "other," and b) then tell us who the "other" to be blamed, is. It is hoped that you, the reader, would be more sceptical when you hear an authority figure using religiousness or faith to interpret laws or believe in futuristic, apocalyptic, "terrorist" events to create militaristic governmental policies. In George Orwell's words, *"The war is not meant to be won. It is meant to be continuous."* Today it is in Syria, Afghanistan, Iraq, Libya, Yemen, Somalia, Nigeria, Kurdistan and central Africa, but tomorrow it might be closer to your home. The ethical message of this article, maybe drawn from the Roman allegorical character of *Messiah Saviour*, Kristos Issues, (in Greek) *"You shall know the truth, and the truth shall set you free."*

At this point, we should say something about this allegorical character named: Messiah Savour or Kristos Issues or Jesus Christ. There is no historical evidence that this Messiah Saviour ever existed, for the following reasons:
- There is no physical description of Jesus Christ anywhere in the

Bible.
- There is nothing written by Jesus himself to show what his thoughts were or about his prophesies.
- There is no archaeological evidence about Jesus in contemporary or archaeological sources.
- We have a Roman historian Josephus who lives in the same period, but we have no historical sources from Jesus who lived in the same historical period.
- Only in the 4 Biblical biographies called the Four Gospels are there Jesus-related events.
- We have little or no historical evidence as to who those 4 men were or if they were the invention of the Roman Imperial Cult and Josephus. If they were mere Jewish fishermen, then they were not educated enough to write classical works like the New Testament in the original foreign Greek language.
- Mathieu was written about the year 80 CE, Mark was written about the year 70 CE, Luke around 90 CE and John written about 100 CE.
- These so called biographies of Jesus were written in classical Greek language 40 to 70 years after Jesus died.
- Major events, such as the Crucifixion and Resurrection are not even mentioned in St. Paul's letters, who as Roman citizen, was considered a strong Roman supporter. He was a follower and propagator of Jesus mythology who operated in the Eastern Roman Empire: Jerusalem, Egypt, Syria, Greece and parts of Turkey.
- We know next to nothing about the historical Jesus, but, according to *Pope Leo X, (1513 – 1521)*, Jesus Christ was fable but Pope Leo was thankful for *"How well we know what a profitable this fable of Christ has been for us and our predecessors."*
- *Pope Paul III (1534 – 1549)*, expressed similar sentiments stating the there was no valid historical documents to demonstrate the existence of Christ. He admitted the *"Jesus never existed"* and the myth of Christ was a copycat of no other than the Sun adored by the cult of *Mithras, a Son of God, born of a Virgin on December 25th*.

We have now come to our final analysis of the mythology of Christianity by presenting St. Paul's involvement in its expansion. To begin with, *Saul of Tarsus* or *St. Paul (5 CE – 67 CE)* was a Hellenized Jew, a Roman citizen who was born in southern Turkey. As a Roman State tax-collector, Saul of Tarsus travelled extensively throughout the occupied Roman territories, and was a skilful logistical organizer with a forceful personality, which helped him to enforce the Roman rules of taxation. He was educated and spoke Greek,

Hebrew and Aramaic, and had a great knowledge in the cultural diversities of the occupied territories. During his tenure as a travelling tax collector, he became a fanatical anti-messianic because he was a devoted polytheist, like most Roman citizens were at that time. In time, Paul's intense hostility and persecution of Messianic Jews had a reverse psychological impact on him. That is, he began to identify with the plight of his victims. Eventually, Paul switched sides and became a devoted Messianic Jew and propagator of a new religion. What we know of St. Paul's knowledge of Messianic Christianized Jews is very limited, that is he never mentioned that:

- Jesus Christ was a historical figure, (St. Paul never acknowledged it),
- Paul never heard of Mary and Joseph,
- Never mentioned of Jesus visiting Bethlehem,
- Never heard of John the Baptist,
- Never heard of Jesus' miracles,
- Never quoted anything Jesus supposedly said,
- Never acknowledged that Jesus had a ministry of any kind,
- Never mentioned about Jesus' glorious entrance to Jerusalem,
- Never mentioned anything about the Roman Governor of Israel Pontius Pilate,
- Nothing about Jesus trial and the cheering Jewish mob,
- Does not appear to know anything about the "Jesus' story," or
- Even the "Idea" of Jesus existence.

It is up to the reader to further investigate the issues presented in this narrative. I have tried to present the invention of the Christian religion in a layman's language and away from the so called linguisisms of academia. I prefer to communicate with you; in a genuine layman's way, rather than present you with an arrogant whirlwind of ivory-tower nonsense.

In conclusion, this narrative's premise is to alert my readers of the need to know the truth about how and why ancient and contemporary governments create false histories and false gods. They often do it to obtain a social order that is against the best interest of the people. Christianity did not really begin as a religion, but as a sophisticated government of Rome project, a sort of propaganda exercise used to pacify the Jewish rebels of Palestine. Jewish religious sects, the Zealots and other rebel forces in Palestine, who were waiting for a prophesied warrior Messiah, were a constant source of violent insurrection during the 1st century. When the Romans had exhausted all conventional means of defeating the Jewish rebellion, they switched to psychological warfare.

As such, the Roman hierarchy surmised that the way to stop the spread of the zealous Jewish messianic activity was to create a competing belief system. That was when the "peaceful," "turn the other cheek," "give to Caesar what belongs to Caesar," Messiah myth was invented; for instead of inspiring rebellion against the Romans, this messianic message urged the Jewish rebels to pacifism and encouraged the Jewish population to "give unto Caesar" and pay their taxes to Rome. The focal point of this psychological warfare was the fictional character of the Saviour Messiah or Jesus Christ whose entire life story can be traced from other religious myths. The main author of the pacifist mythology was Josephus Bar Mathias who wrote the only surviving first person account of the *"Wars of the Jews"* alongside the New Testament. In those accounts, the prophesies of Jesus appear to be fulfilled by what Josephus wrote about, not only in the First Roman War, but also in sequent events and locations of the Titus Flavius military campaigns as described by Josephus. This is Josephus, signature, a deliberately constructed pattern of Jesus' mythological biography to fit the events, especially the biography of Titus Flavius against the rebels in the Jordan River (fishermen of men, the Fall of Jerusalem, the cutting of Trees around the Walls of Jerusalem and others). Other important participants of the promotion of the pacifist mythology in Palestine were the Roman Imperial Cult, the Alexanders and other Jewish theologians. The historical consequences of such pacifism were not the pacification of the Jewish rebels, but the emergence of an obscure cult into the status of the Christian religion that we know today.

The mythological structure of the later religion of Christianity may have given comfort to ill educated Christians throughout the centuries; it has also committed crimes against humanity, the Christian anti-science Dark Ages, damaging and repressive, an insidious and repressive mind control that has led the submissive faithful to serfdom, poverty, wars, and sickness throughout history. To this day, Christianity and Islam religions appear (allegorically) "in lamb's wool, but all of them smell like foxes." Once the Empire was administered by Christians, public libraries had their pagan books progressively replaced by Christian content books. Christian zealots closed pagan temples, public libraries and academies, destroying or scattering their libraries. Even as early 235 AD Christians such as Sextus Julius Africanus, were in powerful and influential positions in Rome. By 391 AD, an edit of Theodosius prohibited visiting pagan temples and even looking at their ruins. In Alexandria, pagans revolted, led by the philosopher Olymbius. They locked themselves inside the Temple of Serapes—and the Serapeium School of Astronomy--to protect its library and its contents. Vandals violently siege and captured the building and demolished, burnt its

astronomical and philosophical books and profaned its images.
This is the story of Christian crimes and vandalism which started the Dark Ages that almost wiped out human history:

- The New Testament itself in **Acts 19:19,** St. Paul in Athens offered 1 silver coin (talent) to pagans that surround their "magic" books of knowledge, and Christian converts burnt those books worth 50.000 pieces of silver.
- A few Church leaders founded libraries in the earlier days of Christianity and those included selective pagan works; mainly now called "the Classics," books like Homer's *Odyssey* which was regarded to be an allegorical account of the struggle for faith. Books by the Greek philosopher Plato were also spared because they were thought to be quite comparable with Christian ideals and particularly useful as a philosophy of its own; thus those books were housed in libraries that served the Christian purpose and survived to this day.
- Christian apologists like to justify (tit for tat) their own vandalism by citing the earlier persecutions of Christian by pagan Romans: under Nero (54-68), Domitian (81-96), Marcus Aerelius (161-180), Septimius Severus (193-211), Maximinius the Thracian (235-238) and under Diocletian (284-305). Apologists are eager to emphasise Diocletian's "Great Persecution" that only lasted from 303 until his abdication in 305 AD.
- The heretical Christian sect the Nestorians; once they were driven out of Syria in 485 AD, and fled to Persia, preserved some pagan literature and built a center of Greek culture including library of the classics. They attracted scholars from Greece; including some from pagan schools of Athens, and established a Hellenistic Diaspora. They preserved some Hellenistic culture and knowledge and eventually passed it on to Arabs who translated them into Arabic whence they eventually were recovered in the West at the Renaissance. Christian who hated the Nestorian as much as the pagans and sound to destroyed them both. To clam credit because their plans did not worked out as they expected is typical Christian trickery.
- Individual monks such as St. Benedict of Nursia (543 AD), who founded the Benedictine order, had some marginal effects in preserving ancient scholarship but mainly Benedictines were copyists of many pious forgeries. What they did tried to preserved them is because they trying to find nuggets of knowledge of learning and to find reasons for teaching them.

- When Christian could not suppress scientific books, they suppressed the information by declaring it heretical or blasphemous. A few examples will confirm it, and show what has been lost due to Christian bigotry. Anaximander and Thales thought that stars were suns with planets at immense distances from us. In 1600 the Roman Catholic Church executed Giordano Bruno, Italian philosopher and scientist, for a crime of heresy. He was taken from his prison cell in the early hours of the morning to the Piazza dei Fiori in Rome and burned alive at the stakes. His executioners were ordered to tie his tongue so that he would not be able to address those gathered. Bruno was bold and brilliant thinker but the Church was fearful of his secular ideas and for that, he had to die brutally. To this day, Bruno's writings are under secured lock in the Vatican. Lucretius implied the uniform acceleration of fallen bodies---not rediscovered until Galileo did---and that space was infinite and with infinite number of worlds in to.
- With that sort of background, it is hardly surprising that once the Church leaders got into power they went after and got control of the publication of any pagan literature they did not like. Naturally, the earliest Christian intellectuals were converts brought up in the pagan schools. Pagan books were the original stock of the Greek and Roman public and private libraries and made attempts to preserve them. These early Church intellectuals, having taken the step of joining the new Roman religion themselves were obligated to talk to their families and friends about the benefits of Christianity. But their arguments were intended to fool the gullible and the ill educated. In fact, pagans in general regarded Christianity as a superstition for the ignorant; because it lacked philosophical background, and appeared as a new version of the mystery religions.
- Were the pagan libraries in Greece, Rome and Alexandria were eventually destroyed? You see, Roman Emperors liked to commissioned public libraries; where education was available for everyone, not only for the siblings of the elite. Temples like the one belonging to the Roman Imperial Cult and others had libraries attached to them, and schools, collages and even public baths. The first known private library in the Roman Empire was composed of the captured library of Greek philosopher Aristotle and they were common by 50 BCE. According to Seneca, by 65 AD, almost all the upper-class homes in Rome, Greece and Alexandria had private libraries; a custom which was also common in beyond

the famous Library of Alexandria. Apologists Christians admit that the Serapeum Library of Alexandria was destroyed by early Christian fanatics; but it was a small temple library not worth a concern. This is a sophistry, for even if the library was a fraction of what it was, it was still a dominant source of ancient scholarship. According to the 4th century Bishop Epiphanius of Cyprus, (died 402 AD) in his biblical commentary commended that there were over 50.000 volumes in the "daughter" library; "mother" library was the Library of Alexandria founded by the Ptolemies, that he places in the Serapeum. Pagan private libraries were dispersed when the aristocracy were impoverished by the Christians.

ILLUSTRATED

ILLUSTRATED "CAESAR TITUS MESSIAH"

ILLUSTRATED
"CAESAR TITUS MESSIAH"

INSCRIPTION: DIVINE TITUS SON OF THE DIVINE VESPASIAN... FATHER AND SON GODS

ILLUSTRATED

TITUS MONUMENT & COINAGE

SECRET PAPYRUS & THE BASE OF THE NEW THEOLOGY OF CHRISTIANITY

Spoils of War

Spoils from the Temple of Solomon in Jerusalem, Arch of Titus, Rome, c. 81 CE.

THE ORIGINS OF THE ROMAN IMPERIAL OF JULIO CLAUDIAN'S DYNASTY

TEMPLE OF THE ROMAN IMPERIALCUILT

ILLUSTRATED
JEWISH THEOLOGIAN, PHILON OF ALEXANDRIA

ILLUSTRATED
JOSEPHUS, AUTHOR OF THE NEW RELIGION OF CHRISTIANITY

ILLUSTRATED

Spoils of War

Spoils from the Temple of Solomon in Jerusalem, Arch of Titus, Rome, c. 81 CE.

SECRET PAPYRUS & THE BASE OF THE NEW THEOLOGY OF CHRISTIANITY

ILLUSTRATED
JEWISH AUTHORITIES AND
SUPPORTERS OF ROMAN OCCUPATION

ILLUSTRATED SYMBOL OF JEWISH RESISTANCE

DAGGERS USED BY REBELS

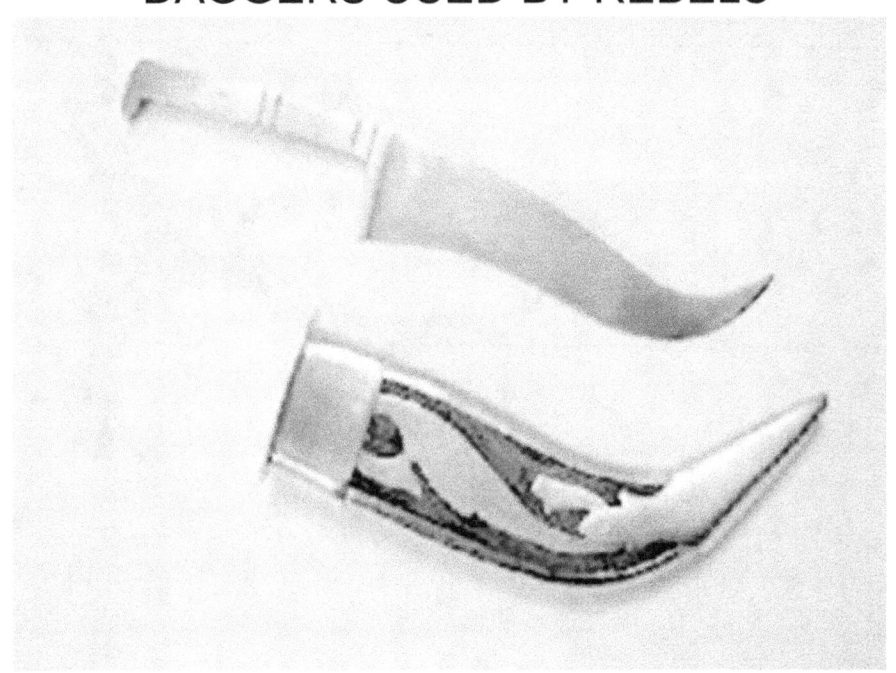

ILLUSTRATED SYMBOL OF JEWISH RESISTANCE

DAGGERS USED BY THE ZEALOTS

ILLUSTRATED COMMEMORATING COINS OF VICTORY OVER JUDEA AND ITS REBELS

CAESAR'S RESURRECTION AS GOD

ILLUSTRATED

ROMAN IMPERIAL COINS DOMITILA RECOGNISED AS THE FIRST CATHOLIC BENEFACTOR OF THE NEW RELIGION

ILLUSTRATED
FLAVIUS DOMITILLA, TITUS DAUGHTER OR NIECE, FIRST CATHOLIC SAINT

RELIGION OF THE DESERT

CHRISTIANITY

CHRISTIANITY

During the Neolithic Age, some 8,000 years ago, humanity in the Mesopotamian and Babylonian Region was advancing its Agricultural Revolution with the production and distribution of fruits, grains and honey. Farmers would build roads and irrigation systems which increased the agricultural production and transportation of grains, olives, oils and dates. The invention of the wheel and cart system of transportation advanced trade and the free flow of ideas among tribes and regions. There was an organized base of social activity around tribal and family identities and cultural ties within those boundaries. Artisans were fabricating all sort of mechanical tools and metal devices, such as, sickles and hammers, ploughs and nails, as well as spears and shield armaments of some kind. Men of letters and temple priests were employed by the upper classes to educate their sons and ex-fighting men to teach the military art of war. Street artisans, merchants, fakirs and street-orators were part of the daily scenery which included performing magicians, fortune tellers and holy men uttering predictions of futuristic events. Small scale textile workshops provided garments and wares made of loom-woven cloth for the local markets and the entire regional population. Open air markets were selling clay pots, metal tools, crafts, dyes, spices and everyday necessities.

In this vast desert countryside, numerous bands of local outlaws made up of nomadic Bedouin tribesmen, were robbing merchants of camel trade caravans or demanding toll extortion from travellers. Scrimmages amongst the hostile tribes were a common phenomenon; being predatory tribesmen, bandits were on the "look-out" for opportunities to exploit other weaker tribes. Tribalism and admirable warriors' heroic acts were part of the folkloric cultural tradition which was imbedded in the desert culture.

The rise of military classes and political elites that benefited from such scrimmages, were dominating people and tribes and formulating alliances with others whenever it was convenient and profitable. Eventually, they brought under their rule vast land territories which, in turn, increased their fighting power structure. The lower classes in large or small city dwellings were the producers of goods, the constructors of housing and constituted the fighting forces which were available for hire to local leaders as they deemed necessary. As such, under these conditions, life was "brutish, nasty and short."

For hundreds of years, this was a pattern of tribal conquest, consolidation of forces, territory expansion, degeneration and re-conquest once again. Invaders conquered, settled, expanded and then assimilated from tribal warriors to city folks. Every conquest left something behind. The city of

Babylon was constructed by the Amorites, and from this city emerged the first Babylonian Empire. The Babylonians were the pioneers of mathematics and astronomy. Others ethnic conquistadores erected libraries and paved roads and build great architectural monuments. The *iconography*, as a method of transmitting written ideas, was adopted by the Babylonians, the Sumerians, the Phoenicians and the other Mesopotamian cultures. Archaeological Carbon-4 evidence in 1998, conducted in *Kastoria Region*, Greece, however, suggests that *syllable-writing* text was introduced by the Greeks in Europe in the year 7270---a written alphabet with syllables as those we use today.

By the year 4,000 and beyond, the Mesopotamian Region, the Persian Empire and the Mediterranean coast---including Greece and Italy---were the most populous of the times. As the human population was growing so was the need to control the population and direct its energy to the political direction and objectives of the military and political elites. Empires were established and diminished as new military forces became stronger. Eventually, the Roman Empire emerged victorious in the region and spread itself from the east of Rome into present day Turkey as well as to the west into present day Britain including most of the Arabian-Mediterranean coast. The Egyptian city of Alexandria and the city of Jerusalem were the administrative and logistical centers of the Eastern Roman Empire in that region, including the Persian Empire. Conquering new lands was the main classical military objective of every upcoming imperial expedition. Size of the empire was of the utmost importance to military men; the more captured land the better. To achieve such a task required the hiring of a large number of fighting men, ex-slaves and mercenaries from every part of the Empire no matter their ethnicity, spoken language or polytheistic preferences.

Polytheistic religious activities were practically everywhere, propagated as a method of social control by the organized power structure of the dominant classes. In Egypt there were revered statues of Gods with human bodies and bull-heads resembling the pre-historical cave designs of the Homo sapiens and Neanderthals. Although the material and style were different, the illusionary subliminal message was similar to those in pre-historic caves. In Rome, Greece, Egypt and the Arabian Peninsula Gods and Goddesses each had their own Temples, and were in the forefront of the upward striving for political position and influence. However, legally, people living in the Roman Empire were obligated by Roman Senate Law to worship the Roman Emperor. Some religious temples were economically and socially successful, but most failed and were eventually replaced by other religious groups. In the vast Roman Empire and, in particular, the Arabian Peninsula, tribal Gods, vague spiritual entities, superstition and traditional magic practices formed a whirlpool of religiousness that people lived under and were obliged to follow out of custom, fear or insecurity.

The statues representing Gods and Spirits were the main "props" in the delusional theatre of the Temples' ceremonial activities. Mechanical devices invented by Greek engineers (Philo of Alexandria) of the time were creating impressionable theatrical special effects of celestial theistic intervention in order to fool the people. In my book, *Prisoners of Our Ideals*, there is verifiable evidence of such existing devices. Overall, in large or small societies, in nomadic groups and warrior tribes, religiousness was used as a method of social control, as a means of interpreting and explaining cosmic events, and a field where every self-proclaimed prophet or messiah could find an audience. There was a cultural environment niche where magicians and prophets from the desert, street-orators and self-delusional holy-men could all proclaim their own special relation to a God or Gods.

For instance, John the Baptist and prophet Ezekiel of the Old Testament were street-orators who achieved historical prominence, while many others did not. All of them share a common desire, that is, to entice people to listen and follow their own exclusive proclamations; whether it was about the coming of a Messiah or about the end of the world if people did not repent their sins. Metaphorically speaking, the "shopping-mall of religiousness" offered to its customers a "little of this and a little of that" of a limited variety of theistic goods; for most of the offerings were about "fear" and "punishment," "suffering" and "torment," "damnation" and more pain and suffering. The style and message of the prophets' proclamations was shared by all because they were simply following what was culturally and socially acceptable to the people at large. The general consent amongst the "prophets" was that people could only be enticed to obey and behave by inflicting them with a strong sense of fear, and guilt by magical spells and theistic customs, rituals and demands. No one was offering "love", "caring", "helping", "respecting", "freedom" and "humanist-based morality." These were not acceptable concepts, nor were they familiar, nor did they have any social value, nor were they ethically acceptable to the street-orators, prophets and educators under culturally acceptable norms. For them the world was an evil place, people were evil who could only be protected or saved from themselves by obeying under fear of a particular God or Gods.

This was the cultural environment, during the rule of the Roman Empire, that various polytheistic groups found themselves within, as well as the new Abrahamic monotheistic cult of Christianity. Therefore, I will present my reasons and evidence surrounding the rise of both the religions of Christianity and Islam, from a historical premise rather than theological. After all, it is evident that both the Christian Bible and Muslim Qur'an holy books are man-made and did not come from God.

CHRISTIANITY

The primary objective of any small or large secular or religious organization is to perpetuate itself; otherwise, a stagnated growth of an organization leads to its actual irreversible diminishing state. Members of such an organization, bound by that objective, combine their skilful abilities to drive a perpetual institutional growth and financial prosperity for their administrative hierarchy. For instance, in the initial state of Christianity, *Saul of Tarsus (St. Paul)*, 5 – 67 AD, travelled with one objective in mind; to organize, institutionalize, encourage and discipline the fledgling secretive Christian churches and communities. St. Paul was a Roman citizen of Greco-Jewish descent and a Roman tax collector who, in his early years, took part in the persecution of Christians, then an illegal cult. He later admitted that he also participated in the stoning-death of a Christian named Steven or Stefan. He was instrumental in putting his organizational expertise into and offering his logistical support to Christian groups around the Mediterranean regions. As an ex-tax collector for the Roman authorities, St. Paul was an experienced structural organizer of state enterprises who were responsible for collecting public taxes, discipline with the accounting of funds and depositing those in the regional coffers.

Looking further back, in the ancient world most popular religious temples were built in Greece, Egypt and Syria, Cyprus and Anatolia between the 6th century BCE and the 3rd century BCE. Some notable pagan temples; such as the Temple of Artemis, in Greece (589 BC); the Temple of Apollo (540-323 BC) in Delphi, Greece; or the Athenian Parthenon (447 BC) in Greece; The pagan Temple of Serapes in Alexandria was well organized and financed by their political or military supporters. The Oracle Temple of Delphi, begun as early as 1400 BCE, lasted under various oracles until the Temple was destroyed by an earthquake in 323 BCE. In most cases the temple's organization was based around their patron and not on their institutional structure. When the patron died or fell out of favour with the state powers, the inevitable diminishing of the temple's functions also became obvious. Lack of institutional structure weakened their base and inevitably it led to a path of deterioration of their existence. From that moment on it was a matter of time before they met their end.

St. Paul was aware of this! This is the reason he paid so much attention to the structural foundations of institutions and much less in the theism of Jesus' ministry. As an ex-tax collector for the Roman Empire, he was very familiar with the concept of institutionalized structure and power. This was the reason he demanded institutional discipline from group leaders. One must remember that those ancient pagan organizations were socio-political in their theistic core. Their existence, their economic base, their objectives, their expansion, their rituals and populism were clearly based on human socio-cultural affairs under the guise of a chosen theistic entity and not on institutional structure.

Hundreds of religious temples were part of the overall socio-cultural fabric of the societies they served. All were claiming to represent some kind of celestial God or Gods in their attempt to entice believers to their temples. They were all practiced in various rituals, traditional myths; magic, impressive ceremonies and fearful futuristic predictions of the kind that best suited their purpose. Wealthy temples were free enterprises, each competing with other temples in order to entice larger crowds of worshipers. They were also discriminating to who would be their worshipers, for most Temple priests wanted the richest and the affluent who were recognized citizens of their state-city.

Opposite to these prominent citizens, stood the new religion of Christianised Jews who were aimed to influence the slaves, the *proletariat* (non-property holders), the low social classes; who were not recognized as proper citizens, and those who were not invited to be part of the polytheists' temple's base. The temples' desired social prestige was based very much upon who's who among their patrons and within the attendance. Needless to say, that in every known human society--ancient or modern--the majority of the people are not the very rich and affluent but the middle, the modest or working class. Among other factors, these temples were facing constant threat from competition, lack of organizational structure, insecure financial support and exclusion of the majority of the people from their ranks. Upon the death of the main priest, the lesser ones could not maintain the populist support base of the temple. They were all man-made organizations, with man-made objectives, and whose religious leaders expected no celestial help from a supernatural sky-being.

The question still remains therefore to answer as to why a man-made religion like the Coptic Christianity succeeded at the time when hundreds of other religious temples of the ancient world failed miserably. There are some situations I call a 'historical coincidence; where a coincidental-person and chance events or a coincidental condition forms a complimentary bond with one another resulting in an ultimate favourable and mutually supportive outcome. Each side offers "something" that the "other" side needs; and as such, both are complimenting one another. In dialectical theorem it is called *"the complimentary unity of opposites."* To begin with, the *chance-event* or conditions that provided a favourable 'marketing' strategy for Coptic

Christian leaders was aimed at influencing the majority of the people of the times; the slaves, the poor and the lower classes. The primary *coincidental-person* in this case was Saul of Tarsus or St. Paul, a prominent supporter of the Christian faith among lesser others. This "historical coincidence" excluded the necessity for a celestial intervention over the upcoming relativity of historical events. St. Paul provided the organizational discipline, on one site, and the poor people provided the human base, as the complimentary opposite side, which formed the classical complimentary unity of the two mutually supportive opposites.

Ancient societies were marked by poverty, tyrannical laws, religious oppression, constant tribal wars, upper-class military and political corruption, and social injustices. There were no social safety-nets for any of the lower classes and life was "nasty, brutish and short" (Thomas Hobbs's words). One thing that most ancient societies shared was an imposing cultural religiousness which was imbedded in the social fabric of life itself. Under the delusional world of religiousness, lower classes, illiterates, superstitious, insecure and ignorant people found an escape route from the nasty reality of their miserable lives. In the delusional world of religiousness, life was perfect, full of harp music, elevated senses of relief, a comfortable sense of security, perpetual praises of God and rivers full of 'milk and honey.' These were the social conditions St. Paul found himself in---looking at it from the position of a comfortable upper-class son of a Roman family. He was well-educated, well-balanced, disciplined, with extremely good organizational skills. As a Roman citizen, he was once fanatically devoted to Rome's polytheistic Gods of Jupiter, Apollo and Bacus and a persistent enemy of the Christian faith. Living near the southern part of present day Turkey, St. Paul travelled to Damascus, Syria and Palestine. As such, he became acquainted with the workings of the Jewish hierarchy and the persecuted secretive religious societies of a new religion: the Coptic Christianity. As Christians of Hebrew roots they were persecuted but they managed to secretively identify one another with secretive signs, such as, the sign of a fish and other modes of communication. Their holy scriptures were written in Coptic language. "Coptic" simply means "Egyptian", a place in Egypt were most found refuge from Roman and Hebrew persecution. They are identified as Coptic-Christians because their denomination was organized in the Egyptian city of Alexandria. Their cohesiveness was based on the traditional tribal system of family ties and allied relations. There was no organizational support system nor was there a primary focus beyond their daily routine. When a head of the group died it had to elect another, amalgamate with a similar group, or face extinction.

Aside from his conversion to philosophy of Christianity, St. Paul brought a sort of technocratic skill, managerial experience and dominant personality. During his travels in the Middle East he encouraged the growing Christian groups to learn and pay attention to the organized side of their religion and to identify their main recruiting objective which were the slaves and the working poor. These groups were desperate for any given hope, even a delusional one, rather than having no hope at all. St. Paul was the coincidental-man for the coincidental-conditions that existed. No effort was spared, no excuses were justified and no leaderless and idle group was to be maintained. Managerial and skilful bureaucratic discipline was imposed and functioned as a well-oiled machine and group leadership began to show evidence of professionalism. The sentiment and religiousness of the secretive Christianity within the entire Roman Empire was for public consumption; the management of their enterprise was the exclusive political domain of the selected few. New Coptic religious groups were established with a rapid success throughout the Middle East, present day Turkey and beyond. Everywhere the groups had well-defined regional objectives of popular membership, of political influence and means of protection from hostile opponents. St. Paul had a tireless stamina and organizational conviction for the Coptic Christianity's success. He was right!

Along the way, St. Paul created many enemies within the Jewish society of Palestine and Roman authorities. As a well-bread Roman citizen with a degree of family political clout---not celestial influence---St. Paul was able to continue organizing secretive Coptic Christian organizations such as the *Brothers in Christ* which was quite popular among the slaves and the lower classes in the entire Eastern Roman Empire from Palestine to Italy, Spain and France. Well-constructed and hidden churches (Catacombs) provided security and ample space for members to meet, plan, solve tangible problems and provide material and emotional assistance to its members. Religious rituals and signs were invented and re-invented to create a magical culture for the ignorant and superstitious slaves, the poor and the emotionally destitute. Coptic Christianity was the only religious organization that took advantage of the vast underprivileged population that others failed to entice because their attention was geared towards the rich and the elite class citizens. It was the only religious group to pay attention to its organizational structure, and to replace the personality of the leaders with an institutionalized body function. A body of Coptic Bishops governed the regional functions of churches, organised and directed donations, and encouraged the young and energetic poor to join up.

One can see the organizational skill and effort it took to bring the original scattered Christian groups from their modest position in Palestine and Egypt to a well-functioning free enterprise entity, spread throughout the Roman Empire. Within three hundred years, the underground organization of Coptic Christianity had a perpetual goal of growth, a well-defined hierarchy, the right kind of social conditions and a vast 'clientele' to draw support from. There was no celestial assistance, no divine consultation, no supernatural intervention, and no godly voices coming from behind "burning bushes," no miracles of resurrection, no appearances and no blood crying Virgin Mary statues. These delusions were invented much, much later as new material to entice the new generations of faithful followers. By 60 AD St. Paul had constructed the base of Christianity as an organized religion, an organization that elected new Bishop leaders, new priests and had clear political goals during the next three centuries AD.

The stronghold base and secretive influence of the Coptic Christian faith was continuing to increase within the Roman Empire as the numbers of the Christian mercenary soldiers were multiplying. You see, since most of the paid soldiers of the Roman Empire were recruited from within the lower classes and slaves from the occupied territories, and since a large number of the populous poor and ex-slaves were Coptic Christians, their only open enemies to their faith was coming from the polytheist élites of the Roman Empire. The majority of the Roman governing elites, however, did not seem to be concerned with the growing secretive influence of the Coptic Christians within the Empire's army. These Christian soldiers promoted their faith to other non-Christian soldiers, which in turn promoted the monotheism of Christianity instead of Rome's polytheism. This was the essence of a classical perpetual goal, an aim which St. Paul installed in the minds of the Christian Bishops in the middle of the 1st century. This strategy bears the fruits of expansion of the organized power-base and influence of early Christianity. In other words, this expansion was a well organized and clearly defined political strategy, and the poor and the slaves in the occupied territories of the Roman Empire were used as the vehicle which carried forward the monotheistic ideological faith of Christianity.

At the beginning of the 4th century AD the Roman Empire faced its biggest challenge in its entire history. The Eastern Empire was so huge it stretched from present day Greece, Turkey down to Lebanon and Egypt, and the entire coast of North Africa up to present day Morocco. The Western Empire included Italy, Spain, France, the Netherlands and part of the Mid England. The Empire was carved up into four large parts, with two in the West and two in the East, each with its own Emperor. Through frequent wars with each other, all scrambled for power and control of Rome's Senate and its

Empire. One Emperor, however, was trying to keep the Roman Empire as a whole, including all its occupied territories of Palestine. This Emperor wanted a military and politically united Empire by any means necessary. This was the *Emperor Flavius Constantine* (272 – 337 AD), the descendant of the Roman Emperors Flavius Vespasian and his son Titus, the Biblical founders of Jewish Christianity.

The Emperor Constantine was seeking to form alliances with anyone who was willing and able to support him towards his ultimate goal. Above all, Constantine's army needed additional able-bodied men in large numbers in order to increase the size and military powers of his armed forces. The Emperor Constantine was an ambitious man looking forward to future glories against his enemies as a military man from his imperial throne as the Emperor of the Roman Empire. He lacked, however, a visually emotional powerful unifying symbol that would gather and bind together his soldiers; to provide them with an emotional fighting inner strength for him to use and thus achieve his political and military ambitions. What the Emperor Constantine needed was a volunteer fighting force that was an emotionally unified military army, motivated by its own collective ideology, and ready to serve Constantine's war ambitions. Such a symbolic image would have served Constantine well, rather than continuing to rely on the old, tired and over used imperial slogans which were becoming meaningless to his soldiers and the people of Rome. In terms of history, Constantine's decisions and political alliances would change the essence of the Empire and leave an impressive legacy of any of Rome's Emperors and would adopt a new religious order that would exclude all other polytheistic Gods for a monotheist God of Christianity. Constantine's slogan for his much desired ambitious unity would be that the army of Rome marches for *"One Emperor, for One Empire and for One God."*

In the autumn of 312 AD Constantine's army was camped 45 miles (100 Km) north of Rome. As one of the Emperors in the West, Constantine was preparing for a battle against his rival *Emperor Maxentius Augustus* from 306 – 312 AD who was occupying the city of Rome. But Constantine was short of military power, for his expected additional re-enforcements had not arrived as yet. As an Emperor, Constantine was very superstitious, seeking signs from Gods and taking advice from temple priests and mediums before any battle took place. Travelling with Constantine's army were members of a growing new religion called *Brothers in Christ*. Most of them were traditional slaves, down on their luck, and ex-war prisoners who were servicing the army's enlisted men and officers. Those slaves were the retched of the earth and a fertile ground for any religious cult who could offer them a salvation.

This was a slave's religion which could only find fertile ground within that class of people who were not allowed to worship the three Roman Gods. So, the Brothers in Christ provided them with a delusional hope of salvation from their dreadful condition when they saw no other, obeyed strict rules about pre-marital sex and observed the secrecy of their place of worship among others. The aim of this religious group was to replace the polytheistic traditional Gods of Rome; Jupiter, Apollo and Bacus and to establish itself as the monotheistic religion of the Roman Empire. Constantine's military weakness was a rare opportunity for one of his close advisers (the secret religious devotee, the Coptic Bishop of the Brothers of Christ, *Lactantius*) to approach Constantine and offer his advice. *Lactantius* (*Lucius Caecilius Firmianus Lactantius*), who was born in 240 AD and died in 320 AD, was regarded as a Sorcerer and was servicing Constantine in that capacity.

Like St. Paul, Lactantius was also a Roman citizen and not born into a Christian faith family. In 305 AD Lactantius, who became a secretive convert of the Christian faith, was appointed as teacher of Rhetoric at Nicomedia (present day Izmir, Turkey) by the Eastern Roman Emperor Diocletian. When the Emperor begun persecuting Christians, Lactantius resigned his post, about 305 AD and returned to the West. There he became a tutor to the Emperor's son Crispus and adviser to Emperor Constantine on a number of subjects including religion. His main personal goal was to repudiate polytheism and the superstition of pagan cults, proposing their replacement with the Christian religion as a true theism, or a rationalized belief in a single God. A well-educated and wide traveller, a Latin and Greek speaking scholar, an author of books, a disciplinarian, he was a much regarded tutor of the privileged sons of the Roman elite.

Being the first of the Roman Emperors, *Flavius Constantine* (272 – 337 AD) ---*full name, Flavius Valerius Aurelius Constantinus*--- is regarded by many historians of his time as the leading figure in the spread of Christianity as the official religion of the Roman Empire. Constantine, with Lactantiu's skilful guidance, was responsible for the reversal of much of the persecution of the Christian minority within the Roman Empire. However, the question we are trying to answer about Constantine's conversion to monotheist Christianity is, whether his conversion was due to a true shift of beliefs, a grab for power and stability, or both. One thing is for sure, I maintain that Christianity was initiated by Vespasian and Titus in the 1st century AD; it was man-made under favourable or opportunistic circumstances and not by a divine intervention. The reader should remember that it was the Roman Imperial Cult's conspiracy to invent Jesus Christ (named *Saviour Messiah*, or Kristos Issus in Greek) that it did not begin as pure religion but as a combination of an actual sophisticated governmental propaganda exercise and a competing belief system to pacify the rebel Jews in the occupied territories of Palestine. **Lactantius** propagated that the Christian God could intervene to correct human injustices. By most accounts he was a very poor theologian. But he was much skilled in the subliminal intricacies of influence peddling by positioning himself as an indispensable ally to Constantine. He maintained that the Roman Empire could be salvaged and better protected by rooting it in the Christian dogma, of a God as a divine fatherhood which would unite the Roman Empire in a universal fraternity mediated by Christ. He presented to Constantine the Christian faith as a popular morality by basing it in the Latin concept of *aequitas* or equity. If it be said that Constantine accurately converted to Christianity; why then he extended the use of pagan symbolism?

Simultaneously, both the Emperor Constantine and his opponent the Emperor Maxentius were preparing for the upcoming civil war. Because of persecutions, many Christian soldiers from Mauritania and Italy were encouraged by Lactantius to defect from Maxentiu's army to join Constantine's armed forces. Before the main battle, both sides briefly fought and Maxentius side prevailed. In the meeting between the two men, the Bishop-Sorcerer Lactantius convinced the Emperor Constantine that God would help him if only his soldiers' armoured vests could carry the painted sign of X with a P in the center. This X was marked on the soldiers' shields with a perpendicular line drawn through it and turned around at the top as P being the cipher of Khristos as a protective sign from God saying that *"Constantine cannot be overcome."* Legend has it that the Emperor Constantine, who was a very superstitious man, saw in his dream that the Sky-God visited him, just as it was predicted by Lactantius. In his dream, *"Constantine was advised in [his] dream to place the celestial sign of God on his shields ...having been armed with this sign, the army took up its weapons..."* written by (Lactantius, de Mortibus Persecutorum, Chap. XXXIV).

Here we have two complimentary pattern-objectives: one is Lactantiu's objective to re-enforce in the Emperor's mind the pattern-belief of the *"celestial power of the God's sign"* on Constantine's army; the other, Lactantius capitalizing on Emperor Constantine's superstitious pattern-belief of the subliminal suggestion of his dream. These two pattern-beliefs provided a core base for Constantine's acceptance of Lactantiu's induced suggestion, that the Christian God was powerful and on the side of the Roman Emperor. Constantine's acceptance of Lactantius powerful subliminal pattern-belief shows how deeply Constantine's dream and Lactantius influence had ingrained themselves into the superstitious mind of the Emperor. Of course,

Constantine still worshipped or praised the ancient Roman pagan Gods, while permitting the followers of the *"Brothers of Christ"* soldiers to openly praise Lactantiu's God. Arriving at this point was not an instantaneous thing, for around 312 AD Constantine began to create a positive view of the Christian people, as a result of Lactantiu's close relationship with and spiritual guidance of the Emperor. Still Constantine continued to use pagan symbolism as a "back-up" to his political ambition which was to preserve the unity of pagan and Christian forces under his command. For instance, while the Christian Symbol of X & P was painted on every soldiers' shield, the image of Sol Invictus, the ancient Roman Sun God, was clearly depicted on a bronze coin 312 AD with the text *"Soli Invicto Comiti"* or "to the Invisible Sun God, companion of the Emperor." Was Constantine's conversion to Christianity a political decision or was it religious belief? Was Constantine seeking the protection of both the pagan Sun God and the Christian God at a time when he needed help from real or imaginary sources?

Looking for a pattern, one explanation was as good as the next, when Constantine ordered his troops to paint the X & P sign on their armoured vests; "just in case" the new celestial God was more promising than the other three Roman Gods. In his desperation to find a solution to the shortage of troops, Constantine was willing to try anything in order to advance his chances of defeating his enemy Maxentius. Little did Constantine know that part of our evolution as humans was to look for patterns, and if he could not come up with a good pattern-explanation, Constantine's brain came up with a false-pattern rather than none at all. He simply did not know that Sorcery and the metaphorical letters of X and P were not "connected" to the upcoming deathly fighting battle; two unrelated things that are based on *metaphorical* belief rather than on reality.

On the 27th of October, 312 AD, to the relief of the Emperor Constantine, the long awaited allied troops finally arrived. Now his army increased its strength by many more thousands of additional men and slaves to service them---but still not enough to defeat the Emperor Maxentius. To the delight of the Coptic Bishop-Sorcerer--and in accordance with a historical legend--a meteorite was passing high in the sky and this was interpreted to Constantine as a sign from God to attack his enemy. No one knows for certain what Constantine's army witnessed that day, for whatever it was, it was less important than how it was interpreted.

In accordance to historical records, the Sorcerer-Bishop's interpretation of that day's event was that Constantine was God's "chosen-warrior" who was to be given the sign of X and P as a protective seal against the enemy's strong armaments. Fearful of offending the Sorcerer's God, Constantine was convinced and ordered his troops to paint that sign on the shields. After many of his troop's objections they obeyed the Emperor's decree that by that sign he will conquer Rome, and the order was given to paint that sign on all shields. The sign of X and P became widely popularized among the thousands of Christian and pagan believers, who openly saw it for the first time in more than two hundred and fifty years of Christianity's secrecy.

As the armed conflict progressed, advancing toward the city of Rome, Constantine became more and more inclined to believe the Sorcerer-Bishop's insistence that the Emperor believe in the Sky-God, and this belief had become a powerful motivational force for Lactantius over Constantine. By the time Constantine's army reached the Milvian Bridge at the River Taurus just outside Rome, the Emperor was under the superstitious spell of the Sorcerer-Bishop. The Emperor was told over and over again that the all powerful Sky-God was on the side of Constantine's army, and the only thing that was demanded of the Emperor was for him to believe!

Constantine's decision to fight under *the Brothers in Christ* symbol of X & P was shocking to his polytheistic troops who initially refused to obey the Emperor's order, but after the order was given again the troops complied. For generations upon generations the Roman soldiers went to their battles under the protection of their traditional polytheist Gods, but as the X and P symbol spread among the troops, the sign became popular, or not as rejectable as before.

The armies of both sides were now ready to fight to the death, and the bridge over the river Taurus was the only means of crossing towards Rome. A trap that was set at the Milvian Bridge against Constantine's army backfired and the bridge collapsed resulting in the death of many, including the Emperor Maxentius himself. Their heavy metal armour prevented them from swimming and this contributed to their drowning. This was a remarkably easy battle and victory over the enemies of Rome, and the Sorcerer-Bishop made sure to convince Constantine that it was God's all powerful hand that had something to do with his easy victory. But there were still Roman generals who were obedient to the memory of their Emperor Maxentius and were willing to stand and fight against Constantine.

On October 28th, 312 AD, just after daybreak, Constantine's army took their position a few miles north of Rome. As they positioned, the Emperor gave a command that the troops must place their shields with the X and P letters high up in front of them. Constantine truly believed by now these symbolic letters were God's protection of his soldiers. His spies told him that the enemy had amassed 75,000 heavy armoured men, and based on that information, Constantine despaired finding a real or an imaginary ally he could muster.

The battle was intense, bloody, brutal and decisive. Thousands of soldiers died or were wounded from both sides in that single battle. Why did the Sky-God protect some of Constantine's soldiers who painted the Christian sign on their shields, but not others who also had the Christian sign on them, allowing them to die? Were they too overly confidant that God would protect them and decided not to be more careful? The next day, on October 29, 312 AD, Constantine triumphed over the enemies of Rome. The Coptic Sorcerer-Bishop saw an opportunity to go for a "kill" or a "pay-back time" and took a gamble over Constantine's conviction on recognising the powers of the new Sky-God over the traditional polytheistic Gods of Rome. Overwhelmed by the speed of events, and not being sure which Gods to trust, Constantine asked the advice of the Sorcerer-Bishop. Lactantius put his best arguments forward to convince the Emperor that the monotheistic God was far more powerful, who blessed his arms and who was forever on the side of the Emperor. These man-made delusions are in the core of every traditional religion that claims God is exclusively on their side.

Arriving in the city of Rome and parading triumphal before hundreds of thousands of people, this exposed further the Christian symbolic sign on the troops' shields and raised questions of its significance. In fact, the political leaders in the Senate of Rome wondered about this symbolic sign and the additional carried pole-banners with the X and P instead of the traditional Roman Eagle. By now the Senators realized some important changes, in that, the X and P was a Christian sign and that the Sorcerer-Bishop held a prominent parade position next to the Emperor Constantine. Did Constantine believe in the celestial powers of the Sorcerer-Bishop, who claimed that, he spoke on behalf of a monotheistic God? Did God give Constantine his victory over the enemy, as the Sorcerer-Bishop claimed, and not his enemy's military mistakes and the Emperor's taking advantage of them?

Lactantiu's power of suggestion led Constantine to believe in God's intervention over the internal affairs of Roman politics and hostilities. His delusional obedience to the Sky-God, and his belief in celestial intervention had robbed his soldiers and generals of the reality of their military bravery and heroism. It neither was the thousands that fought and die nor was it the planning of military manoeuvres that brought about a decisive victory, but a single delusional thought of God's intervention. The hold of delusional power on a single person or on many must never be underestimated. Emperor Constantine became the future stepping-stone of the monotheistic Christian religion in the Roman Empire. He now holds the political and military powers of a benevolent tyrant whose decisions were totally obeyed, as they were the laws of the land. Now that Constantine felt obligated towards the Christian cult, Lactantius saw this sentiment as a huge opportunity to capitalize on the Emperor's weakness. For after all, he believed in the existence of the supernatural and he was an Emperor who was accustomed to following the traditional practice of asking the unseeing Roman Gods for help. He wanted to give something back to please Lactantius for his Sorcerist powers.

Lactantius skilfully claimed that the Emperor was under no obligation and none was expected of him. However, because Constantine was God's "chosen" he should service the Lord by letting his own sister Constantia be baptized as a Christian. This act set the establishment of the prominent Christian ritual of baptism for others to follow. Constantine moved to his palace in Milan where he was contemplating a solution to the Christian issue, and where he now was occupied with uniting the Eastern with his Western part of the Roman Empire. Wars were fought to that effect. Lactantius kept reminding the Emperor of his obligation to God; to uphold a decree of tolerance for all religions, and allow Christians to openly practice their religion by allowing them to build their churches above ground instead of the underground *catacombs*.

The Emperor's decree of recognizing the new religion of Christianity was strongly objected to by the Roman Senators who were determined to hold onto the traditional Gods. It appeared that the man-made polytheistic Roman religion was now facing the political dilemma of a monotheistic God which was to be worshiped in the Roman Empire. Lactantius reminded Constantine that his fighting armies in the East were still wearing their shields with the Christian sign of X and P and, if he wished God's help to victories, the Emperor must choose Christianity as the official religion of the Empire, and that while each Roman citizen could worship as he chooses, the Christian God was the primary and only true God of the Empire.

In his meetings with his generals, Constantine took a pragmatic political stand and was quoted as saying, *"I believe in whichever God looks kindly after our enterprise, the one who can bring peace, security and stability."* He supported the Christian God because that God served Constantine's political and military objectives, that his soldiers were confident about the Christian sign on their shields, and that he could finally repay his obligation to Lactantius's God. To Constantine this was not about God or Gods; this was about cementing the various necessary political alliances for a stronger Roman Empire. He feared that if Rome continued persecuting the Christians it would make the Christians stronger and may cause splinters amongst the population and in the army. If the Empire tolerated them, it would win their support.

In his writing the Sorcerer-Bishop Lactantius regarded the so called Milan Decree---to establish a legal recognition of his religion---as a landmark in Christian history. The *Edict of Milan* of 313 AD was an agreement to treat Christians benevolently within the Roman Empire. The document known as the Edict of Milan (*Edictium Mediolanense*) is found in Lactantiu's *De Mortibus Persecutorium*. After years of underground hidden activities of the Brothers in Christ, Lactantius had achieved, in short time, a century's old desire of the Christians to gain a legal recognition. This of course was by no means Constantine's altruistic negotiation, for both of them were gaining what each wanted in return. The Emperor was gaining hundreds of thousands of ready-to-fight soldiers for the Roman Empire and Lactantius's expectation of having Christianity integrated into the socio-cultural fabric of the Roman society. Nothing celestial about that, is there?

These were pure and simple political negotiations between the two politically skilful leaders playing their 'best-hands' to gain the maximum benefits from their friendly opponent, and God's hands and help were nowhere to be found. It was with the help of the Christian soldiers that Constantine's allies defeated the Eastern enemies of the Roman Empire and this brought about a much desired peace. Lactantius, however, was not satisfied with the new developments for he wanted much more; the complete destruction of the old polytheistic religion, and the founding of a new Roman Empire with a monotheistic religion of Christianity. Lactantius strength was two fold; the hundreds of thousands of Christian soldiers in the Roman army and the powerful influence of the X and P sign, which by now all Roman soldiers, Christian or pagan, were wearing. In fact, the Emperor was completely mesmerized by this sign and its powerful influence over his soldiers. As luck would have it, this was an extraordinary historical coincidence for Lactantius to live in; the physical conditions (the Christian soldiers) and the complimentary aspect of the spiritual, the delusional belief in the power of the Christian sign, shared by the Emperor and his armed forces.

By now Constantine was turning more and more to Christianity and looking for God's sign to achieve his goals and appease the Christians. Constantine now began visiting the Christian districts where the secretive societies of the *Brothers in Christ* were located in order to learn more about Christian Church. What Constantine witnessed was a corporate organized hierarchical religion that was well-function, with their efficient structured managerial style and obedient followers who were mainly war-captured, ill-educated, ex-soldiers turned into slaves, poverty-stricken peasants and artisans. This was a man-made secretive religious organization that was under skilfully hierarchical discipline with total control over its members; the kind of social structure that Constantine wanted to impose upon the Roman Senators and society as a whole.

Constantine gathered some valuable information about the expansion of this secretive society; that for 300 years it secretly continued spreading from Palestine to Armenia in the East, and to Spain and Britain and the European Atlantic shores to the West. He saw monotheism as a means to social bonding, a cohesive political ideology of the working poor, the ex-slaves and the able and willing fighting men under his command. This was Constantine's ultimate military vanity; the desire to assume total power over a large Empire; for *One Emperor, for One God and for One God to Worship*, and the world would be his and his alone. By now Constantine wishfully believed that the Christian God gave him the power and the authority to achieve his imperial goals, a belief that Lactantius so convincingly and conveniently had formulated and projected for him.

In Rome on July 25th, 315 AD, Constantine's army paraded the streets in full gear with Christian signs and pole-banners of the same, with the vivid sign emblazoned on the Emperor's chalice. In his speech to the massive crowd he declared that the Roman Empire was *One Empire, had One Emperor and had One God*. As part of the ongoing ceremonies, Constantine was expected to make a traditional animal sacrifice to the Gods. When Constantine entered the Gods' Temple, he told the priest that his rituals were meaningless and that his Gods were dead. This was raw politics, and Lactantiu's politically ambitious mission was accomplished! Constantine's assault on Roman tradition went even further, for he began diverting public funds intended for the construction of polytheistic temples to new Christian Churches and buildings, including the now famous St. Peters in Rome. He promised to build churches throughout the Empire, and for this, the world will forever know the name of Emperor Constantine. All political and religious opposition from the Senate regarding Constantine's insult to them was met with arrogant dismissal from him.

In the city of Nicomedia (present day Turkey) of the Eastern Roman Empire, the news of Christianity's influence in the Western Roman Empire was not received well and the Senate's opposition to it was emphatically noted. The Christian Bishops were now exempted from paying taxes and were free to accumulate as much wealth as they desired with no fear from the tax authorities. The *Brothers in Christ* organization was perpetuating itself and now had also the absolute power of its enormous wealth at its disposal. All Christian ex-slave soldiers, the working poor, the artisans and men of letters were obligated now to contribute donations to the organization's wealth chaste. In addition to the growth of its prominent position, Constantine ended all persecutions against the Christians by issuing the *Edict of Milan*, also known as the *Edict of Toleration*. Constantine's legalistic desire was to achieve some form of peace within the entire Roman Empire, and this was described,

"...was a decisive step from hostile neutrality to friendly neutrality and protection... [the Edict] ordered the full restoration of all confiscated church property to the Corpus Christianorum, at the expense of the imperial treasury, directed the provincial magistrates to execute this order at once with all energy, so that peace may be fully established and the continuance of the Divine favour secured to the emperors and their subjects."

For many Roman citizens Christianity was still regarded as a spreading disease, and the ultimate goal of the Eastern leadership was the death of Constantine. Assassination plans were plotted from all sides. On the Temple of Jupiter in Rome, ceremonies were conducted in the presence of Constantine who still could not shake off the old traditional Roman Gods. The attempt to kill Constantine was in this temple but the attempt failed and the assassins were killed. Not trusting anyone anymore but the Christian God, Constantine went into a killing spree throughout the Roman Empire of everyone who opposed him. In the year 315 AD, Constantine declared that the Western Roman Empire was the Christian God's holy-war against the polytheistic Gods of the Eastern Roman Empire.

This must be noted by the reader, for this was the first religious war to be recorded in human history; not to defend but to establish or enforce the Christian faith as an official organized religion. It was a phenomenon that was to be repeated many times over since its conception; against other splinter groups of Christians, and much later against the Jews and Muslims of Palestine. The conflict between the opposing forces of Rome was long and bloody, but Constantine insisted that he was at war, a holy war, in order to bring peace to the Roman Empire. At stake was nothing more than the political survival of the Empire. It was a war which pitted the traditional Roman polytheist Gods against a dynamic new monotheistic Christian faith, and Constantine's army was marching in the name of a "true monotheistic God."

The first recorded holy war of 315 AD proved to be an indecisive battle where neither side could deliver a final killer blow. An uneasy peace lasted until 323 AD when the Eastern Roman forces attacked Christian communities killed their priests and bishops, confiscated their accumulated gold and properties, smashed their Churches, and a new holy war became inevitable.

The decisive battle took place in Chrisopolis (present day Turkey) on the 18th of September, 324 AD. In the midst of the bloody battle, Constantine raised his Christian banners depicting the X & P insignia. Historians at the time described how these Christian banners struck terror on the superstitious Eastern Roman armed forces. They feared the magical powers of the banners causing them to abandon their arms in a hasty retreat. This was a military opportunity for Constantine to deliver the final blow to his enemy's soldiers. The slaughter of the remaining opponent's forces was merciless. The Christian faith marked its birth with the blood of thousands of polytheistic "others", and the Christian God was present to decide who lives and who dies.

On the 9th of June, 325 AD, at the Council of Nicaea, Constantine forged ahead with his vision of a Christian Empire by bringing hundreds of bishops from every corner of the Roman Empire to work on building a hierarchical governing body of this new religion. This is the year that a man-made religion, socked in terror and blood, was established as an organization whose future acts were as bloody as its past. Torture, burning heretics alive, burning witches alive, the torture chambers of the Inquisition, the repeated Crusade holy wars against Muslims, branding the Jews as Christ's killers, the expulsion of the Jews and Muslims from Spain, as anti-scientist against Galileo, the rape of children and women, the lying to the poor to accept their poverty, that suffering is God's gift to humanity (in according to Mother Teresa), its crimes against Canadian and Australian indigenous children in Catholic Residential Schools, against the use of condoms, the deception of miracles, the delusion of its propaganda in Ireland, its God delusion of life after death, its false pattern explanation of Hell and Heaven, its support and harbouring of the Nazi war criminals, its undeniable support of benevolent dictators (practiced by Mother Teresa), its accumulated extravagant exhibition of wealth; and many more, are all part of its anti-human legacy. This terrible legacy, whose root lies in a historically proven product of deception, was created out of a culturally hostile civic environment of Jewish society, of Bedouin tribesmen, of delusional street-orators, future tellers, self-proclaimed prophets, cultist mystic Temples, and ignorant warrior tribesmen from Palestine and the Arabian Peninsula.

Taking briefly a leap forward to our time, one must remember that religion is like an old country general store, it has little bit of "this" and little bit of "that" selection of "goods" for everyone's desire; as in according to, Matthew 7:7 *"Seek and you shall find."* The business of religion has followed Adam Smith's assessment as to why the established clergy are more successful but do less good, than the clergy who go out to collect their own keep. It follows the market principles of supply and demand, and religion is now a gigantic industry; you have the mega churches and the pastorpreneurs. This is a business that knows how to segment and re-segment and there is something for everyone; services for bikers, gays and drop-outs; you have the "Scum of the Earth" Church in Colorado; Bibles for cowboys, brides, soldiers and rap artists; you have theme parks for every faith; faith-based schools; and scare-of-purgatory churches. This business model is now spreading overseas, with South Korea leading with its 5 mega churches, and other evangelical faiths are expanding to China, Africa and South America. Only in Russia, where the Russian Orthodox Church has a monopoly in religious establishments, competition from other faiths is not permitted. The Hindus and Muslims are looking closely to the American model and methods used in order to adopt them. Islam has its own version of televangelists, some of them spectacular successful by following the American-Christian model. Their followers are more determined to obey their religious dogma and take their convictions to their workplace, in their personal and social interactions, health care, business practices, in the voting booth and in the armed forces. Times and places and even faiths may have changed, but religion as industry, still functions similarly from time immemorial.

The religious entrepreneurial structure was in full force by the time the Council of Nicaea took place in 325 AD. Its aim was to eliminate all possible opposition to its establishment as the official religion of the Roman Empire. The Emperor Constantine wanted a unified empire and looked forward to achieving this solution through the Council of Nicaea. However, up to this point there was no unified body or "Christianity" amongst the many competing Christian sects functioning in whatever region the Roman Empire was established. The much desired unity that was to be established by the Council of Nicaea was in regards to the character of the Christian dogma which prevails to this day. A period of political uncertainty for the monotheistic religious supporters of the Roman Empire preceded the Council. Legend has it that Constantine legalized Christianity and allowed its practice but Christianity was not yet the official religion of the Roman Empire. Other polytheistic groups stood in its way simply because Constantine still needed their political and military support. Therefore, Christianity was officially tolerated in the Empire. It was not until February 27, 380 AD that Christianity was left as the unopposed official religion under the rule of Emperor Theodosius I.

By the early 320's AD, a new splinter religious force appeared in Palestine and Alexandria lead by the *Bishop Arius* (250 – 336 AD) who claimed that Jesus Christ was not God but God's messenger i.e. a prophet. This claim led to further religious divisions with Bishop Alexander, of Alexandria, Egypt, who declared Bishop Arius a heretic. The tension between these predominant factions was very intense and was brought to the attention of the Emperor Constantine who did not want to have the threat of new division. Constantine saw this dispute between Christians and Arians (supporters of Bishop Arius) as a divisive threat to the Empire and invited both religious groups to Nicaea in 325 AD to find a solution. No other groups were invited to participate. This meeting was not about recognizing Christianity as the official religion of the Roman Empire. The meeting was a preventive measure against divisions of any sort within the Empire. A solution was found that the Church of the Eastern Roman Empire would stay under the label of Orthodox and the Western Church under the label of "Christianity." Both opposite sides were not prepared to compromise their long road of climbing to political power, wealth and influence. With less than 5% of his subjects professing to be Christians, Constantine endorsed Christianity as the most favoured religion. Though his Council of Nicaea was ever after hailed as the loadstone of Catholicism, he died an Arian supported at the age of 65.

The religious industry was eventually divided in 1053 AD into two camps ever since, the Greek Orthodox Church in the East, and the Catholic Church of Vatican in the West. The essential causes of such division had little to do with particular religious beliefs, and more to do with competition and power seeking among powerful religious corporations. Both sides used religious differences as pretexts as to the fundamental causes of their division. In previous centuries other religious groups such as the Sibelius had dealt with religious issues of the 3 in 1 = God, the Father, the Son and the Holy-spirit, (*Homoousios*) and opposite groups like the Arians who believed in the Divine Three and that each of these were separate entities (*Heteroousios*). Emperor Constantine used his power to force Trinitarian (Homoousios) views on the Christians. As such, Constantine pushed his own particular view, although he was not yet a fully converted Christian. Other issues that had to be dealt with by the Council were the declaration of the day of Resurrection, confirming 20 canon laws and other minor religious issues. It should be noted that the celestial God had played no direct or indirect role in the official recognition of Christianity by the Roman Empire. Human affairs such as politics, military alliances, imperial ambitions, ignorant superstitious beliefs and Christians capitalizing on an opportune chance within the Roman army were what led to the establishment of Christianity in the Roman Empire. Like all religions, cults and spiritual entities this was, and still is, a religion not by God's but by Man's Design.

In the 4th century AD, however, the role of the Christians in the Roman occupational army of the Middle East was far more extensive. The Roman occupiers were well aware of the numerous religious cults that were part of the cultural religiousness of the Middle East. One of those was the Christian cult of Jewish citizens. Their existence did not interfere with the army's functions. Their religious beliefs were no stranger than any other cults in the region. There was nothing unique in seeing a cultist trying to convert a Roman soldier to their cults' beliefs. Some were converted and some were not. The organized effort of the Christian cults, however, was far more organized and focused and thus more effective than most others. Cultists were tolerated in general and there were others who openly practiced their cultist beliefs without any objection from the Roman military authority. Its aim was to recruit as many able men as mercenary-soldiers willing to fight against the Zealots and other rebel groups. The religion of the recruiters was a minor affair so long as they kept it discrete. Many did, including the Christian cults. In fact, most villages that were recruited to the Roman army were from nearby villagers no more than a few hundred yards away from the military base. Food, mending of soldiers' clothing and sexual contacts between soldiers and local women were part of normal social affairs. Christian women marrying Roman soldiers would tend to try converting their husbands into their faith and most of them did!

After all, the Roman army's task was not to defend their Rome's polytheistic Gods against any other, but to maintain law and order within the occupied territories of Palestine. Christian Jews were persecuted by the Judea religious authorities who viewed them as outcasts from the norms of their faith and society. As a result, many of them joined the Roman forces as a means of escaping persecution from the official Judaist governing bodies of the day. Archaeological evidence discovered near Tel Megiddo, Israel, show compelling connections between the Roman army and its secretive Christian soldiers.

Here the sixth *Ferata Legion* camped permanently and controlled the north part of Palestine. A few yards away from the army base was the full functioning village of *Tel Megiddo* which was a major servicing centre of the Roman occupier. The Emperor Constantine was well-aware of the Christian influence in his army, the inter-marriages between his soldiers and local Palestinian women, the potential recruitment of more able bodies of fighting men, and the frequent conversion of his soldiers to Christianity. Under those circumstances, Constantine had little choice but to recognize Christianity, thus ensuring its political and military support to maintain law and order within the Eastern Roman Empire. Constantine's decision was not based on some celestial revelation from the Sky-God, but it was based on the practicality of solving real life's problems that the Roman Empire was facing at the time. The theistic concept of "God" was just that, a mental-concept, a false pattern-belief, a mental prop with no external power to control and redirect external political events. As Constantine started to eliminate any internal opponents within the occupied territories of Palestine, and much later, of the Western Roman Empire, he also declared the legal status of the cannon laws of the Christian religion that became universal today. His declaration was as follows:

a)   We believe in one God,
b)   The Father the All Mighty
c)   We believe in one Lord, Jesus Christ,
d)   We believe in one Catholic and Apostolic Church,
e)   We acknowledge one Baptism for the remission of Sins,
f)   We look for the Resurrection of the Dead,
g)   The Light of the World to Come (second coming of Christ)
h)   Amen

With these declarations, the Emperor Constantine created a man-made religion without God's help or guidance but with another man's help and political guidance, Lactantius. These two leaders, one as the head of the Roman Empire and the other as the spiritual leader of the Christian soldiers within that Empire, bonded out of political and military necessity for their mutual benefit. This is the art of pure politics based on priorities, First on the laws of necessity, Second, the laws of "want," and Third, on wishing to achieve a desire. Lactantiu's writings constituted the main source of guidance to Constantine's rules, keeping united the Christian soldiers, and using them against Jewish rebellious uprisings and tribal scrimmages. Constantine, Rome's first Christian Emperor, has left a legacy which more far reaching and long lasting than any other Emperor of his time. Clearly the religion made by a few selected men of the ancient world has placed humanity onto a path of spiritual destruction of those who still believe in its dogma. One should not forget the organizational skills of the *Roman Imperial Cult, Joseph of Arimathea skilful typological propaganda, Philo of Alexandria* theology, *St. Paul* administrative efficiency; which converted tribal leaders into corporate-leaders by disciplining them, and positioning them into powerful influential and financial positions that they could not afford to loose. Such hierarchical power structure still dominates small and large religious cults and even primitive spiritual groups. Under such hierarchical structures they maintain their dominance; not because of some celestial force, but because of their ignorant and ill-educated followers. All the reader has to do is to ask an average Sunday praying Christian believer if he or she knows the historiography of the religion called Christianity? Do they know that most written biblical materials were formulated centuries after Christ's, written by people who never met or talked to Jesus? In short, Christianity, with its dogma, gradually evolved over a number of centuries and out of the crashing rubble of the Roman Empire.

Before we go to our next topic about the historical origins of Islam, I must confess that the core of my analysis of the rise of Christianity and Islam is presented from a *historical, dialectical and scientific premise* rather than from a theological or philosophical point of view. I have tried to stay "on course" from the pre-historical analysis of how proto-religious rituals were conducted in pre-historic caves and how symbolic images took on a life of their own to be treated as reality. I have tried to explain all these from a geological, *biological, scientific and historical base, from the "Big Bang" to Stone Age*, to Iron and Bronze Age.

Christian Vandalism:
In the 1st century and beyond.

Architecture

Existing public buildings such as forums, libraries, odeon, theatres, museums, stadiums, hippodromes, circuses, gymnasia, pagan-temples, public-baths and amphitheatres, were often vandalized or destroyed. The charitable endowment of public buildings ceased almost completely when the Church imposed total control. Almost every European village has a medieval church or monastery near by; generally build with better materials than any other local building. A vanishing small numbers have comparative public service of church build schools, hospitals and other useful public service.

Public Education

Many architectural techniques were destroyed. Educating the poor; had been taught to read and write in pagan time and the wealthy were expected to build schools for them. However, education became a Christian monopoly and made available to the priests and the sons of the wealthy. Students' reading was restricted to Christian indoctrination. All literature was banned, including the Bible. The few who were allowed to learn to read were restricted to books and Christian legends presented as facts. Other secular pagan books were generally burned or hidden away on remote monasteries.

Democracy

Greek political system of Democracy was condemned as un-Christian, since the Bible presupposed Kingdoms and Empires.

History
Factual historical accounts were replaced by legends, typology, fabrication and propaganda. Sympathetic chronicles on the Church were permitted and objective histories were "lost."

Civic Laws
Laws were converted from a partially independent instrument of justice to a system of principles of natural law. Instead, there was a trial by order, exclusively serving the interest of the Church. This led to the inequality which was fundamental principle of ecclesiastical law.

Study of Nature and the Planetary System
The study of the Universe, popular in the ancient world, stagnated during the Roman Catholic imposed Dark Ages, in the 4th century until the Enlightenment in 1500's. Research of Nature and Universe was suppressed until then because the Church insisted on the Biblical interpretation of Creation and, its infallibility as a handbook of all world knowledge.

Sculptures
Polytheistic sculptures of the ancient Greek and Roman world ceased to be produced. The best statutes of the antiquity were destroyed or defaced. Inferior material was produced for the church, generally for propaganda purposes. Nothing compatible in classical workmanship was produced until the Renaissance in 1500's.

Medicine
All medical process was halted and surgery was prohibited because a body-part amputation and public health was considered unchristian and, illness was viewed as God's punishment for a sin.

Philosophy
Existing philosophical works and manuscripts were destroyed; genuine Greek and Roman philosophers were censored, prosecuted, imprisoned and sometimes killed. The only significant philosophical progress was "heretic" such as in Hypatia's who made such attainments in literature and science.

Hypatia (370-415) female philosopher and astronomer was killed by a Christian mob, driven into a range by claims that she was interfering in a religious dispute between the Christian Church of Alexandria and the pagan governor of the city Orestes. Book burning was first promoted by St. Paul in the 1st century and continued in the Middle Ages. The idea of encouraging the masses to read was traditionally seen as undesirable. Ancient philosophy was finally revived by Cosimo de Medici in his Platonic Academy in Flores.

Michael Servetus (1511- 1553) was burned alive at the age of 42. Michael Servetus had wide ranging interest in science, medicine, theology, law and the humanities. He made important contributions in medicine and anatomy; correctly describe blood circulation between the heart and lungs, independently of the Egyptian Ibn al-Nafis.

Antoine Lavoisier (1743-1794) was guillotine at the age of 50. He advanced chemistry on a rigorous scientific footing by emphasising the importance of accurate measurements. He also wrote the first list of the chemical elements---a forerunner of the periodic table.

Giordano Bruno (1548-1600) burned alive at the age of 52. Giordano supported the view that the Earth orbits the Sun and, that the Earth is not the center of the universe. He held the view that distant stars are orbited by their own axis, possibly inhabited, planets. He insisted that the universe is infinite in size and has no center. Bruno was imprisoned for seven years and, eventually the Catholic Church decided that Bruno was heretic and he was burned at stake in Rome. He was also declared heretic for his religious views about the Catholic Mass and the Trinity.

The Christian Church vandalism continued for centuries at the end of the 4th century. Christian mobs were free to vandalise, attack and destroy synagogues and temples, statutes and frescos with impunity. The Christian leaders dissuaded the Roman and Byzantine Emperors from paying compensation for the destruction of synagogues and temples. For example, the canopy under the dome of the Vatican Church (St. Peters) is made of 200 tons of bronze stripped from the Athenian Parthenon in the 16th century and, part of it went to make a papal-canon. The construction of St. Peters had been started by Bramante who destroyed much that could not been preserved from the old basilica. He also pillaged various old buildings for stone, marble and other materials. Rafael, who took over the project after Bramante's death, calls him Ruinante (Ruinner).

Book burning, an example set by St. Paul in the 1st century in Athens, was the favoured vandalism activity of the Christians during the Dark Ages and Middle Ages. Medieval Christians insisted of throwing all books into the fire and, Holy Books could easily be identified because they would not burn. This supposed method enables Churchmen like St. Dominic to destroy any book they wanted and, acclaim their book burning as proof of heretical content. These acts of vandalism were not restricted to Greek and Roman "heretical" books. In Palestine, in 1242 under the command of Pope Innocent IV and, the head-churchman Albertus Magnus, Jewish Talmudic books were banned and destroyed and, centers of Jewish scholarship were set on fire. Wagonloads of Jewish books, including rare manuscripts, were burned in Rome by the Inquisition. Jewish and Arab classical books, if discovered, were hidden or burned, heretical books were burned, books exposing the

Church of forgery and corruption were burned, books containing original ideas were burned and, books or items of innocent fun, amusement, interest or beauty were burned. In 1497, Christians of Florence, Italy, were enticed by Friar Savonarola and his armed guards to burn in the "bonfire of vanities" countless works of art, pictures, musical instruments, songs, poems, including books of Ovid, Cicero, Boccaccio, Petrarch, and Poliziano all were consigned to the flames. This bonfire, lit on Shrove Tuesday 1497, was 100 feet wide and sixty feet high. The hysterical crowd sang T*e Deum laudanum* as it burned.

Numerous keen Christians have occupied their time cheeping away the genitals of male statues or installed metal fig leaves on the nude statues or painted over in the Vatican, museums and art galleries throughout Christendom. Michelangelo's *Last Judgement* in the Sistine Chapel was sanitized in this way. Moreover, in the 20th century, Australian authorities had impounded a copy of Michelangelo's David on the grounds that it was indecent. In 2005, officials in Bartholomew County, Indiana, require copies of classical nude art to be removed out of public view because they would be considered obscene under Indiana's law. The statues included Michelangelo's David and the Venus de Milo.

ILLUSTRATED
THE BATTLE OF MALVIA BRIDGE

WITH CHRISTIAN SYMBOLS IN SHIELDS

ILLUSTRATED
THE BATTLE OF MALVIA BRIDGE
BANNER OF THE NEW RELIGION

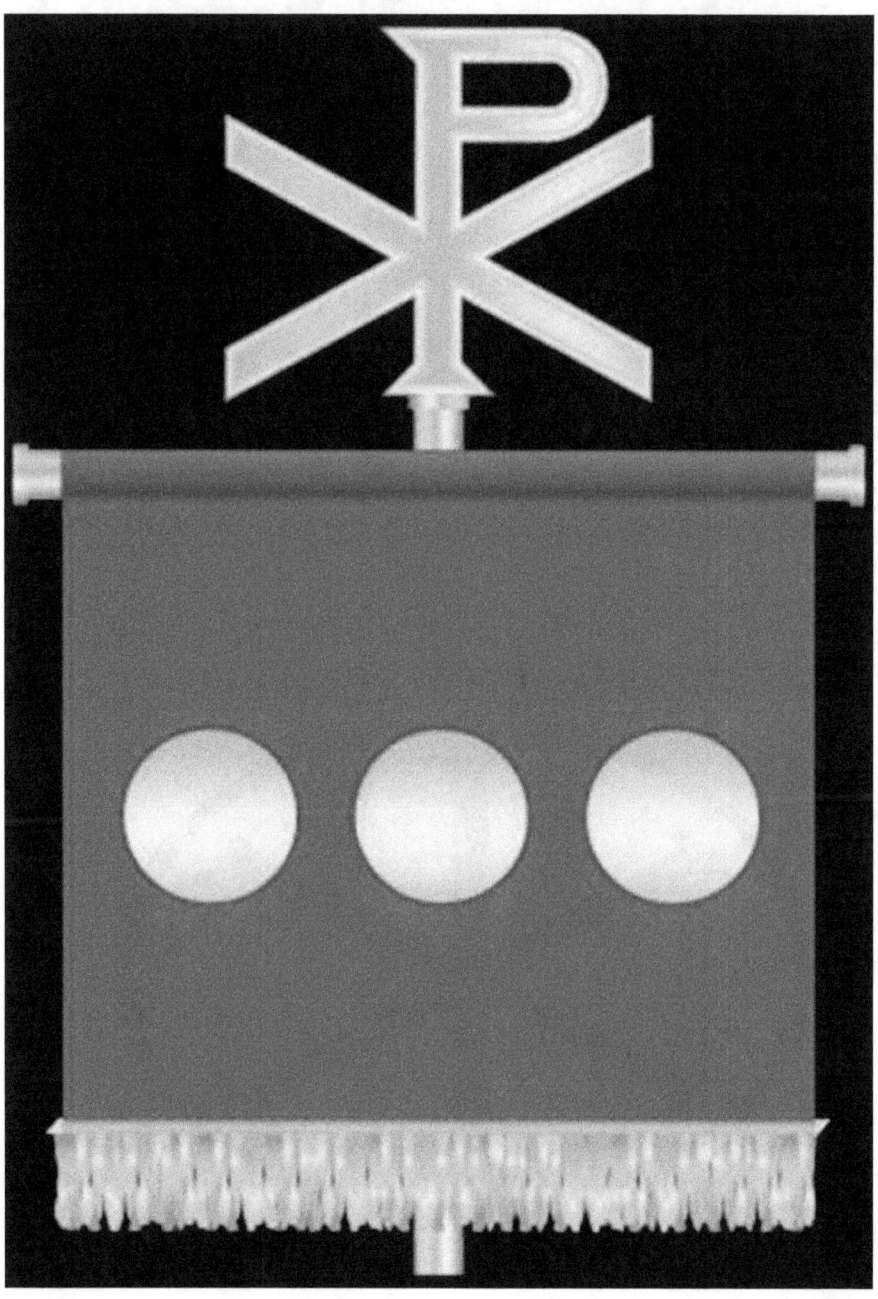

ILLUSTRATED
THE EMPEROR'S SORCERER, THE CHRISTIAN PROPAGATOR: LACTANTIUS

THE MAGICAL PROTECTIVE SHIELD

WHICH POWER CONSTANTINE BELIEVED

ILLUSTRATED
THE MAGICAL PROTECTIVE SHIELD
SUPERSTITIOUS SUGGESTION & BELIEF

ILLUSTRATED
THE MAGICAL PROTECTIVE SHIELD
SUPERSTITIOUS SUGGESTION & BELIEF
OF THE ROMAN SOLDIERS

ILLUSTRATED MAGICAL POWER OF THE CHRISTIAN SYMBOL SPREAD IN THE ROMAN EMPIRE

ILLUSTRATED
CONSTANTINE DECLARED CHRISTIANITY THE OFFICIAL RELIGION OF ROME

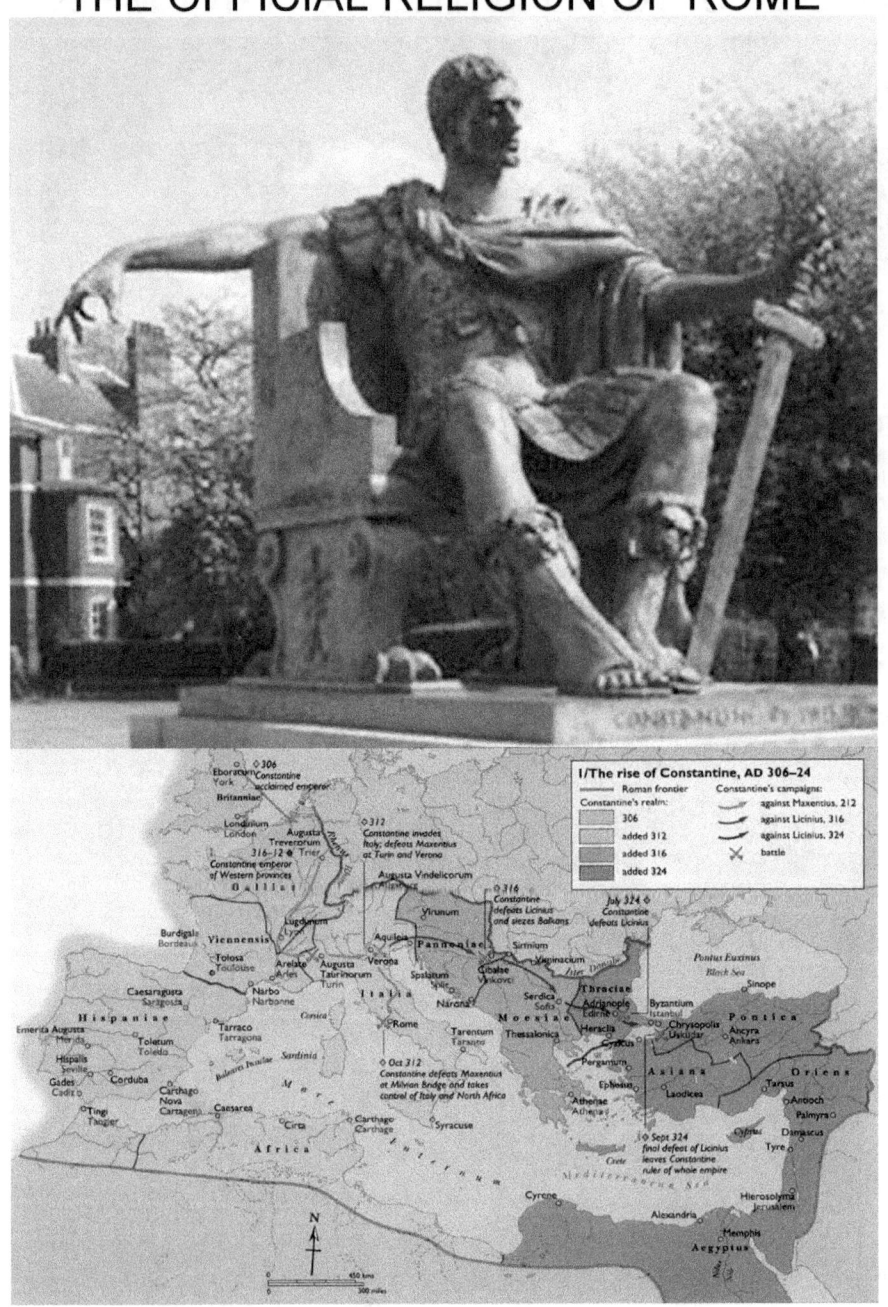

ILLUSTRATED CHRISTIAN CULTURAL VANDALISM AGAINST THE GREEK CIVILISATION

ILLUSTRATED CHRISTIAN CULTURAL VANDALISM AGAINST THE GREEK CIVILISATION

ILLUSTRATED CHRISTIAN CULTURAL VANDALISM AGAINST THE GREEK CIVILISATION

ILLUSTRATED CHRISTIAN CULTURAL VANDALISM AGAINST THE GREEK CIVILISATION

DEFORMITY OF STATUTES

ILLUSTRATED
CHRISTIAN CULTURAL VANDALISM
AGAINST THE GREEK CIVILISATION

DEFORMITY OF STATUTES

ILLUSTRATED CHRISTIAN CULTURAL VANDALISM AGAINST THE GREEK CIVILISATION

DEFORMITY OF STATUTES

ILLUSTRATED CHRISTIAN CULTURAL VANDALISM AGAINST THE GREEK CIVILISATION

DEFORMITY OF STATUTES

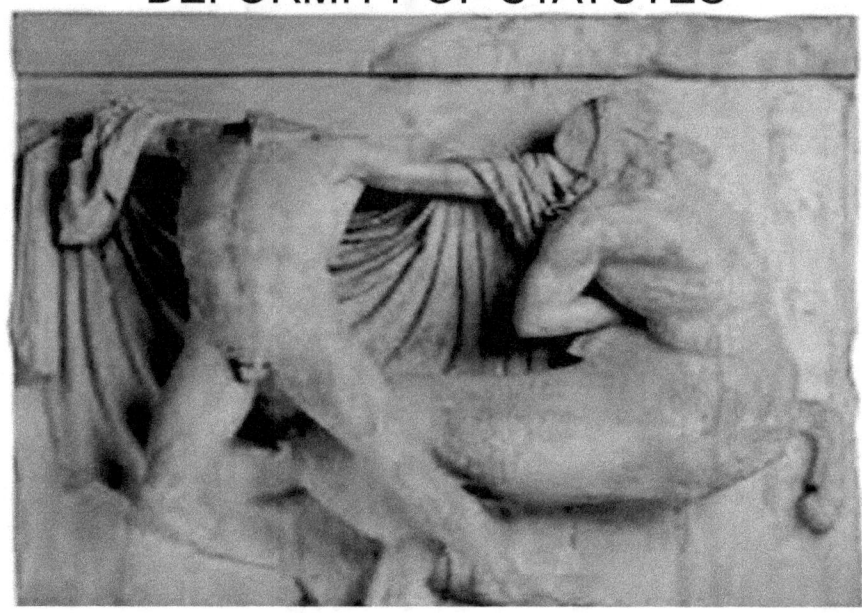

CHRISTIAN CULTURAL VANDALISM AGAINST THE GREEK CIVILISATION

DESTRUCTION OF PARTHENON'S
PRICELESS MARBLES

CHRISTIAN CULTURAL VANDALISM AGAINST THE GREEK CIVILISATION

DESTRUCTION OF PARTHENON'S
PRICELESS MARBLES

CHRISTIAN CULTURAL VANDALISM AGAINST THE GREEK CIVILISATION

JUSTIFYING HUMAN SLAVERY

CHRISTIAN CULTURAL VANDALISM AGAINST THE GREEK CIVILISATION

JUSTIFYING HUMAN SLAVERY

CHRISTIAN CULTURAL VANDALISM AND CRIMES AGAINST HUMANITY

ILLUSTRATED CHRISTIAN VANDALISM : ST. PAUL'S BOOK BURNING

CRONOLOGY OF CHRISTIAN CRIMES AND VANDALISM

To help counter Christian apologists, a Greek correspondent, Florin Achaios, has submitted the following chronology of Christian persecutions especially of the Greeks in the Eastern Empire, with Constantinople as its capital, beginning at 314 AD.

- 314, Immediate after its full legislation, the Christian Church attacks the gentiles (Pagans). The Council of Ancyra denounces the worship of *Goddess Artemis*.
- 324, The Emperor Constantine declares Christianity as the only official religion of the Roman Empire. In Dydima, Asia Minor, he sacks the *Oracle of the god Apollo* and tortures the pagan priests to death. He also evicts all the pagans from the *Mount Athos* and destroys all the local *Hellenic Temples*.
- 326, Constantine, following the instructions of his mother Helen, destroys the *Temple of Asclepius* in Aigeai of Celicia and many *Temples of the goddess* Aphrodite in Jerusalem, Alpaca, Mambre, Phoenicia and Baalbek.
- 330, Constantine steals many Pagan Temples of Greece to decorate the Nova Roma (Constantinople), the new capital of his Eastern Empire.
- 335, Constantine sacks many Pagan Temples on Asia Minor and Palestine and orders the execution by crucifixion of "all magicians and soothsayers." Martyrdom of the Neo-Platonist philosopher *Sopatrus*.
- 341, Flavius Julius Constantius persecutes "all soothsayers and Hellenists." Many gentiles (pagan) Hellenes are either imprisoned or executed.
- 346, new large scale persecutions against pagans in Constantinople. Banishment of the famous orator *Libanius* accused as a "magician."
- 353, an edict of Constantius orders the death penalty of all kinds of worship through sacrifices and "idols."
- 354, a new edict orders all the closing of all the Pagan Temples. Some of them are profaned and turned into brothels or gambling houses. Executions of Pagan priests.
- 354, a new edict of Constantius orders the demolition of Pagan Temples and the execution of all "idolaters." First burning of libraries in various cities of the Empire. The first lime-factories are being organised next to the closed Pagan Temples. A major part of the holy architecture of the Pagan turns into lime.
- 359, In the Greek city of Skythopolis, Syria, the Christians organise the first death camps for the torture and executions of the arrested non-Christians from around the Empire.
- 361-363, Religious tolerance and restoration of the pagan cults declared

in Constantinople (11 December 361) by the Pagan Emperor Flavius Claudius Julianus.
- 363, Assassination of Julianus (26 of June).
- 364, Emperor Flavius Jovianus orders the burning of the Library of Antioch.
- 364, An Imperial edict (11 September) orders the death penalty of all those that worship their ancestral gods or practice divination "sileat omnibus perpetuo curiocitas." Three different edicts (February 4th, September 9th and December 23rd) order the confiscation of all properties of the Pagan Temples and the death penalty for participation in pagan rituals, even private ones.
- 355, An Imperial edict (17th of November) forbids the gentile-pagan officers of the army to command Christian soldiers.
- 370, Valens orders a tremendous persecution of non-Christians in all the Eastern Empire. In Antioch, among many other non-Christians, the *ex-governador Fiductius* and the priests *Hilarius and Patricius* are executed. Thousands of books are burnt in the squares of the cities in the Eastern Empire. All the friends of Julianus are persecuted *(Odebasius, Sallustius and Pegasius etc)*, the philosopher Simonides is burned alive and the philosopher Maximus is decapitated.
- 372, Valens orders the governor of Asia Minor to exterminate all the Hellenes and all documents of their wisdom.
- 373, new prohibition of all divination methods. The term pagan (pagani or peasants) is introduced by the Christians to demean non-believers.
- 375, the *Temple of god Asclepius* in Epidaurus, Greece, is closed down by the Christians.
- 380, on February 27th, Christianity becomes the exclusive religion of the Roman Empire by an edit of Emperor Flavius Theodosius the Great (379-375 AD), requiring that: *"All the Various nations which are subject to our clemency and moderation should continue in the profession of that religion which was delivered to the Roman by the divine Apostle Peter."*
- The non-Christian are called "loathsome, stupid, heretics and blind." In another edict, Theodosius calls "insane" those who refuse to believe in the Christian God and outlaws all disagreements with the Church dogmas. Ambrosius, Bishop of Milan, starts destroying the entire pagan Temples of his area. The Christian priests lead the angry mob against the Temple of the *Goddess Demeter* in Eleusis and try to lynch the *hierophants Nestorius and Priskus*. The 95 year old hierophant Nestorius ends the Eleusinian Mysteries and announces the predominance of *"Mental Darkness over the Human Race"* (the coming of the Roman Catholic imposed Dark Ages).
- 381, on May 2nd Theodosius deprives of all the rights of their Christians that returned back to the Pagan religion. In all of the Eastern Empire the Pagan Temples and Libraries are looted or burned down. On December

- 21st Theodosius outlaws even simple visits to the Temples of the Hellenes. In Constantinople, the Temple of the Goddess Aphrodite is turned into bordello and the *Temples of the Sun and Artemis* into staples.
- 382, "Hallelujah" (Glory to Jewish god Yahweh) is imposed in the Christian Mass.
- 384, Theodosius orders the Praetorian Prefect Maternus Cynegius, a dedicated Christian to co-operate with the local bishops and destroy the Temples of the Pagan in Northern Greece and Asia Minor.
- 385-388, Maternus Cynegius, encourage by his fanatic wife and, Bishop St. Marcellus with his gangs scours the countryside and sack and destroys hundreds of Hellenic Temples, shrines and altars. Among others they destroy the Temple of Edessa, the Caereinon of Imbros, the *Temple of Zeus in Apamea, the Temple of Apollo in Dydima* and, all the notorious death camps of Skythopolis, Syria. Temples of Palmira. Thousands of innocent pagans from all sides of the Empire suffer martyrdom.
- 388, Theodosius ordered to be burnt *Porphyry's (322-300 AD) Treatise against Christians.*
- 388, Public talks on religious subjects are outlawed by Theodosius. The old orator *Libanius* sends his famous epistle *"Pro Templin"* to Theodosius with the hope that the few remaining Hellenic Temples will be respected and spared.
- 389-390, all non-Christian date-methods are outlawed. Hordes of fanatic hermits from the desert flood the cities in the Middle East and Egypt and destroyed statues, altars, libraries and pagan temples and, lynch the pagans. Theophilus, Patriarch of Alexandria, starts heavy persecutions against non-Christians and turns the *Temple of Dionysus* into a Christian church, burns down the Mirthraeum of the city, destroys the *Temple of Zeus* and burlesques the pagan priests before they are killed by stoning. The Christian mob profanes the cult's images.
- 391, on February 27th a new edict of Theodosius prohibit not only visits to pagan temples but also looking at the vandalised statues. New heavy persecutions all around the empire. In Alexandria, Egypt, the pagans lead by the philosopher *Olympius*, revolt and after some street fights they lock themselves in the *Temple of Serapes (the Serapeium)*. After a violent siege, the Christians take over the building, demolished, demolished its famous library and profaned the cult images.
- 392, on November 8th, Theodosius outlaws all the non-Christian rituals and names them "superstitions of the gentiles" (gentilicia superstitio). New full scale persecutions against pagan. The *Mysteries of Samothrace* are ended and the priests slaughtered. In Cyprus, the local bishop "saint" Epiphanius and "saint" Tychon destroy almost all the temples of the island and exterminate thousands of non-Christians. The local Mysteries of the Goddess Aphrodite are ended. Theodosius' edict declares: "the one

that won't obey pater-Epiphanius have no right living in the island. The pagans revolt against the Emperor and the Church in Petra, Aeropolis, Raffia, Gaza, Baalbek and other cities in the Middle East.
- 393, the *Pythian Games, Aktia Games and the Olympic Games* are outlawed as part of the Hellenic "idolatry." The Christians are sack the Temples of Olympia.
- 395, two new edicts (July 22nd and August 7th) cause new persecutions against pagans. Rufinus, the eunuch Prime Minister of Emperor Flavius Arcadius directs the hordes of the baptised Goths (led by Alaric) to the country of the Hellenes. Encouraged by the Christian monks the barbarians sack and burned many cities *(Dion, Delphi, Megara, Corinth, Pheneos, Argos, Nemea, Lycosoura, Sparta, Messene, Phigalea, Olympia etc)*, slaughter enslave numerous gentile Hellenes and burned down all Hellenes Temples. Among others, they burned down the Eleusinian Sanctuary and burned alive all its priests (including the *hierophant Mithras Hilarius).*
- 397, *"Demolish them!"* Flavius Arcadius orders all the still standing pagan temples to be demolished.
- 398, The Fourth Council of Carthage prohibits to anyone, including the Christian Bishops to study of the books of pagans. Porphyrius, Bishop of Gaza, demolishes almost all the pagan temples of his city, (except 9 of them that still remain active).
- 399, with a new edict (July 13th) Flavius Arcadius orders all of the still standing pagan temples, mainly in the countryside, to be immediately demolished.
- 400, Bishop Necetas destroys the *Oracle of the God Dionysus* in *Vesai* and baptises all the non-Christians of this are.
- 401, The Christian mob of Carthage lynches non-Christians and destroys temples and "idols." In Gaza too, the local bishop "saint" Porphyrius sends his followers to lynch pagans and demolish the remaining 9 still active temples of the city. The 15th Council of Chalcedon orders all the Christians that still keep good relations with their gentile relatives to be excommunicated (even after their death).
- 405, John Chrysostom sends hordes of grey dressed monks armed with clubs and iron bars to destroy the "idols" in all the cities of Palestine.
- 406, John Chrysostom collects funds from rich Christian women to financially support the demolition of the Hellenic Temples. In Ephesus he orders the destruction of the famous temples of the Goddess Artemis. In Salamis, Cyprus, "saints" *Epiphanius and Eutychius* continue the persecutions of the pagans and the total destruction of their temples and sanctuaries.
- 408, The Emperor of the Western Empire, Honorius, and the Emperor of the Eastern Empire, Arcadius, order together all the sculptures of the

pagan temples to be either destroyed or be taken away. Private ownership of pagan sculptures is also outlawed. The Judges that have pity on the pagans are also persecuted. "Saint" Augustine massacres hundreds of protesting pagans in *Calama*, Algeria.
- 415, in Alexandria, Egypt, the Christian mob, urged by the bishop Cyrillus, attacks few days before Pascha (Easter) and cuts to pieces the famous *female philosopher Hypatia*. The pieces of her body, carried around by the Christian mob through the streets of Alexandria, are finally burned together with her books in town of *Cynaron*.
- 416, the inquisitor Hypatius, alias "the Sword of God," exterminate the last pagan *of Bithynia*. In Constantinople, (December 7th) all non-Christian army officers, public employs and judges are dismissed.
- 423, Emperor Theodosius II declares (June 8th) that the religion of the pagans is nothing more than "demon worship" and orders all those who practicing it to be punished by imprisonment and torture.
- 429, the Temple of the *Goddess Athena (Goddess of Wisdom) of Parthenon on the Acropolis of Athens* is sacked. The Athenian Pagans were persecuted.
- 438, Theodosius II issues a new edit (January 31st) against the pagans, incriminating their "idolatry" as the reason for the recent plague!
- 448, Theodosius II orders all non-Christian books to be burned. All copies of *Julian's* work which could be found were destroyed, and they would have been lost entirely if bishop Cyril of Alexandria (376-444 AD), had not cited extracts from the first three of the seven of Julian's books in his refutation of him, while admitting that he would not cite some of his arguments.
- 450, all the *Temples of the Aphrodisias* (city of the Goddess Aphrodite) are demolished and all of its libraries burned down. The city is renamed Stavroupolis (city of the cross).
- 457 to 491, sporadic persecutions against the pagans of the Eastern Empire. Among others, the physician Jacobus and the philosopher *Gessius* are executed. *Severianus, Herestios, Zosimus, Isidorus,* and others are tortured and imprisoned. The proselytiser Conon and his followers exterminate the last non-Christian of Imbros Island, Northern Aegean Sea. The last worshipers of *Lavranius Zeus* are exterminated in Cyprus.
- 482-488, the majority of the pagans in Asia Minor are exterminated after a desperate revolt against the Emperor and the Church.
- 486, more "underground" pagan priests are discovered, arrested, burlesqued, tortured and executed in Alexandria, Egypt.
- 516, Baptism becomes obligatory even for those that already declared that they are Christians. The Emperor of Constantinople, Anastasius, orders the massacre of the pagans in the Arabian city *Zoara* and the demolition of the *Temple of the local God Theandrites*.
- 528, Emperor Jutprada (Justinianus) outlaws the *"alternative"* Olympian

Games in Antioch. He also orders the execution; by fire, crucifixion, tearing to pieces by wild beasts or cut to pieces by iron nails, all those who practiced "sorcery, divination, magic or idolatry" and prohibits all teachings by the pagans *("the ones suffering from the blasphemous insanity of the Hellenes").*
- 529, Justinianus outlaws the *Athenian Philosophical Academy* and has its property confiscated.
- 532, the inquisitor Ioannis Asiacus, a fanatic monk, lead a crusade against the pagans in Asia Minor.
- 542, Justisianus allows the inquisitors Ioannis Asiacus to convert the pagans of *Phrygia, Caria, Lydia and Asia Minor.* Within 35 years of this crusade, 99 churches and 12 monasteries are built on the sites of demolished Pagan Temples.
- 546, hundreds of pagans are put to death in Constantinople by the inquisitor Ioannis Asiacus.
- 556, Justisianus orders the notorious Amantius to go to Antioch, to find, arrest, torture and exterminate the lost non-Christians of the city and burn all the private libraries down.
- 562, mass arrests, burlesquing, torture, imprisonment and executions of gentile Hellenes in *Athens, Antioch, Palmyra and Constantinople.*
- 578-582, the Christians torture and crucify gentile Hellenes all around the Eastern Empire and, exterminated the last non-Christians of *Heliopolis (Baalbek).*
- 580, the Christian inquisitors attack the secret temple of Zeus in Antioch. The priest commits suicide, but the rest of the Pagans are arrested. All the prisoners, the *Vice-Governor Anatolius* included, are tortured and send to Constantinople to face trial. Sentenced to death they are thrown to the lions. The wild animals being unwilling to tear them to pieces, they are end up killed. Their dead bodies are dragged in the streets by the Christian mob and afterwards unburied in the dump.
- 583, new persecutions against the gentile Hellenes by Maurisius.
- 590, in all the Easter Empire the Christian accusers "discover" pagan conspiracies. New storm of torture and executions.
- 692, the "Panthekto" Council of Constantinople, prohibit the remains of *Galends, Brumalia, Antesteria, and other Pagan/Dionysian celebrations.*
- 804, the gentile Hellenes of Mesa Mani (Cape Taimaron, Lakonia, Greece) resist successfully the attempt of Tarasius, Patriarch of Constantinople, to convert them to Christianity.
- 950-988, violent conversions of the last gentiles Hellenes *of Lakonia* by the Armenian "Saint" Nikon.

For readers wishing to learn more about Christian crimes and vandalism see: Vlasis Rassias, *Demolish Them!* Published in Greek, Athens 1994, Diipetes Editions, ISBN 960-85311-3-6

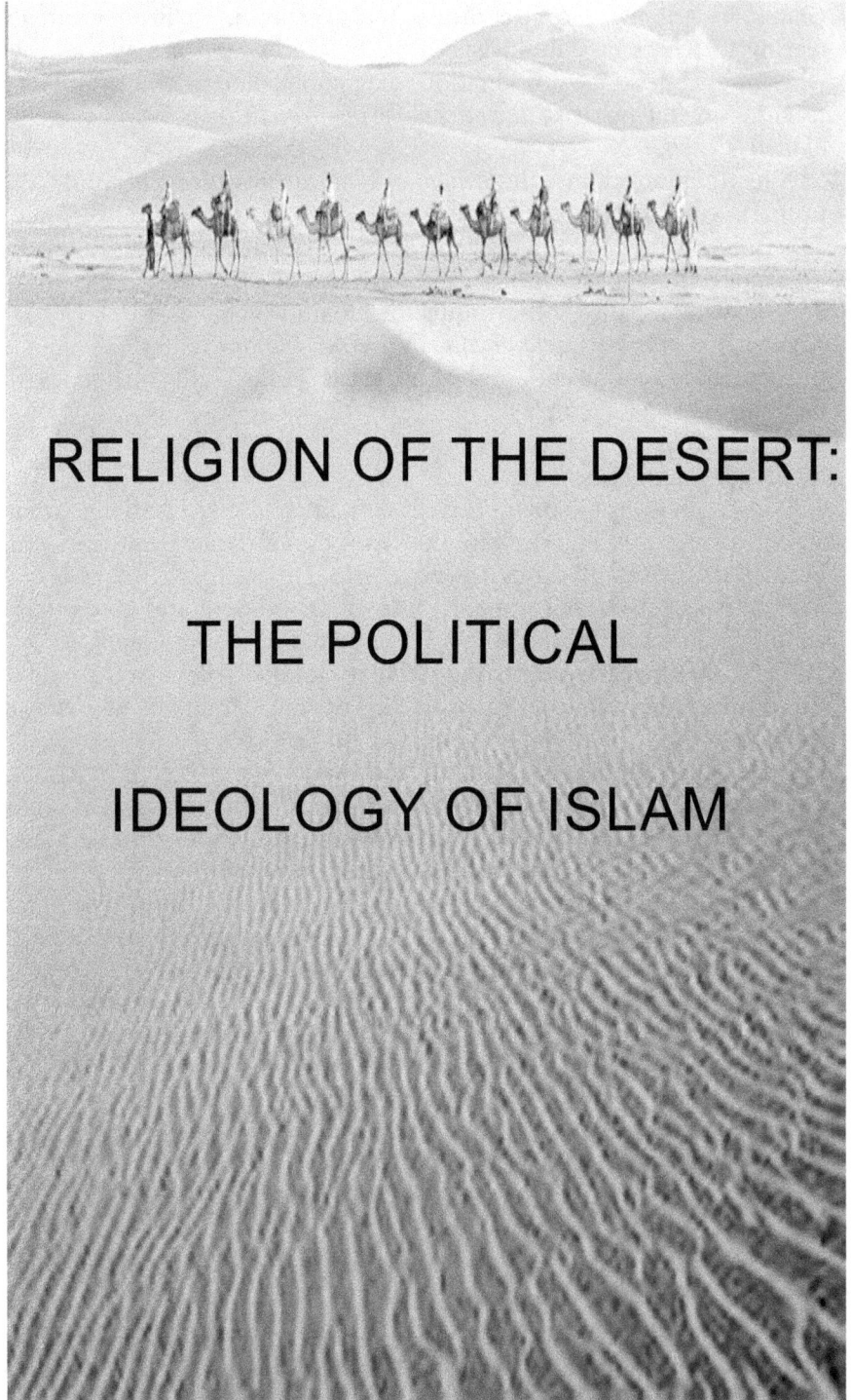

RELIGION OF THE DESERT: THE POLITICAL IDEOLOGY OF ISLAM

THE RELIGION OF ISLAM

I am making my position clearly, it is because, I'm a non- believer of any of the Abrahamic religions of Judaism, Christianity and Islam or any other theistic or spiritual entity. I'm looking at the rise of religions as an academic rather than as a person of faith, and with out prejudice Islam. As a historian, I'm looking for verification of historical evidence about claims that Muslim faithful have made about the historical legitimacy of their religion. For instance, what the Qur'an has given to Muslims and what they believe, about some fundamentals, what has historically happened and when it happened. To begin with, some of the Qur'an's claims may have never happened and therefore are pure myth. A Muslim believer may say that the Qur'an comes from God, as a non-believer I have to question the Qur'an's stories about the Virgin Mary, the Coptic Christians, and of miracles; even about reference to Alexander the Great. What are these Christian and other pagan stories doing in the Qur'an?

The problem, as a historian, is in the very things that a believer theologically believes that the Qur'an came from God. It is truly very difficult to know where to start. Wading through Mohammad's legend and interpretations, rather than evidence, is a tiresome venture. But, as a historian, I must investigate the literal evidence to such claims. The key for investigating Islam is, of course, the Holy Book of Qur'an because it is the bedrock of Islam. The problem came when I started looking at the earliest comments about Muhammad, the earliest life of Muhammad; the earliest historical evidence of the Arab invasions; for all such recorded events came about 150 – 200 years after the lifetime of Muhammad. For a historian, this is a big problem because then, I was required to decide whether these sources could be trusted as a source for events which may or may not have happened two centuries previously.

The core premise of my analysis is based on the distinction between what were the "Arab" invasions and what were the "Muslim" invasions which is now called: the Muslim Empire. In other words, we must distinguish between what constitutes Arab conquests and Islamic conquests for the former were not related to the Islamic faith. I suspect that throughout the years apologists of the Islamic religion are conveniently inter-mixing these two in order to create something greater than it was. But one name keeps cropping up in the beginning of forging the legend of Muhammad the Prophet: *Abd al Malik ibn Marwan* (646 – 705 AD). The significance of the name will be clear by the end of the article about Muhammad and Islam.

The core of my dilemma about the validity and legitimacy of the Qur'an is

in the belief that it was instructed by God to a man, Muhammad, who was:
a) entirely illiterate,
b) who had to translated biblical stories that were written in Aramaic and Greek into Arabic language,
c) who lived his entire life in the desolated Arabian desert,
d) but he is able to describe valleys with orange and fig trees, grains, honey, water falls and architectural structures which
e) he could not possibly have witnessed because he was describing things that were not part of his exclusive Arabian Peninsula geographical region.

These fertile lands that are described in detail in the Qur'an existed in the *Fertile Crescent* region 1,459 kilometres north of Medina and Mecca, in the northwest of the Arabian Peninsula; where Muhammad never lived or visited this far north.

Mohammad lived in the desolate Arabian Desert and in the settlements and villages near the cities of Medina and Mecca; where none of these kinds of agricultural products could be produced and waterfall landscapes could ever have existed, or architectural structures could have been built by the unskilful and ill-educated tribal men. The Arabian Peninsula is far south of the Fertile Crescent, a geographical area of harsh barren desert, a place very few nomadic tribesmen travelled through, with no farming, no pasture, no food except some dates and no natural or man-built water wells. The authors of the Qur'an therefore used a *typology* to re-range the geographical characteristics of the Fertile Crescent and inserted this written typology into the desolated Arabian Desert to present an ideal picture of a productive, fertile geographical area that never was!

Some things we know for sure, that Muhammad was a historical figure, that there were Arab historical conquests, but the chronological sequences of those events need to be placed in order. Understanding the religion of Islam requires us to have a peripheral knowledge of the appearance of pre-Islamic Arab cultures that emerged in the Fertile Crescent Region. *The Nile River* and the Tigris-Euphrates Rivers in Syria allowed easy access to trade and commerce leading to the growth of cities and civilizations. Farmers in the region would build irrigation systems supporting settlements, villages and towns. The geographical positions of those settlements, villages and towns were frequently attacked, as tribal warriors were the Bedouins who conquered and forced populations to relocate in order to provide them with sustenance support. Warring and scrimmages were part of the cultural norm of the numerous southern nomadic desert tribes, such as, attacking to steal food and livestock, and capture men, women and children for the slave market.

Each Arabian Peninsula desert warrior identified himself with the tribe he and his family belonged to and was related to other families through kinship and marriages. On a much larger scale, a dominant warrior from the Fertile Crescent outposts near the Arabian Desert would bring conquered towns and villages under his rule and form larger united political entities like cities, a kingdom and even an empire. The citizens will become city dwellers made up of merchants, shopkeepers and artisans, soldier-mercenaries and farmers. This repeated process was a pattern of conquest, consolidation, expansion, decline and again conquest. This process resulted in the first historically recorded civilization which was located in the lands between the Tigris-Euphrates Rivers, later known as Mesopotamia and Babylon. The Sumerians were the first who started the whole process of unification of tribal settlements, villages and cities into a single political unity called the Sumer. Some of their achievements during their dominance were the introduction of Arabic writing, the wheel-cart and other things. Later the Sumerians were conquered by the Academia's who were conquered by the Amorite nomadic tribes. In turn they were later conquered by other nomad tribes who were also conquered by others and so on. Most grand cities like Jerusalem and cultural, agricultural and other civic activities, however, were not located in the desolate Arabian Peninsula but rather in the Fertile Crescent. When the archaeologists were searching for ancient towns in present day Saudi Arabia they found some evidence of ancient Arabian towns, but Mecca is absent from that evidence. This is because evidence suggests that Mecca never existed prior to the 4th century AD when Yemeni pagan tribesmen began to migrate to the area. Without pasture and capacity to produce food, the area was settled late when the overland travel along the Red Sea became sufficient to support Mecca, through trade, as a resting place.

Every conquest in the Fertile Crescent left something behind. The Amorites founded the city of Babylon in 1894 BC which developed into the Babylonian Empire. Babylonia was an ancient Akkadian-speaking Semitic state and cultural region based in central-southern Mesopotamia. The Babylonians were the pioneers of Astronomy and Mathematics, and when the Assyrians conquered the Babylonians they established the Assyrian Empire and preserved and adopted everything the Babylonians had achieved during their time. Assyria was a Semitic Kingdom and Empire and existed as an independent state from about the 25th century BCE until 612 BCE. The Assyrians developed new innovations, used paved roads, developed the first administration where subjects of the Assyrian Empire reported and asked for caravan trade permits. They contributed to the Arts and Letters by building the first known public library; available to the ruling upper classes, their families and their offspring. These ruling classes were the typical tyrants but not worse than the previous rulers of the time. They also followed the previous public control methods by moving whole populations into new areas for new agricultural schemes, and divided members of various tribes to reduce their strength and influence.

Eventually the Assyrians lost their power and were conquered by other tribes such as from remaining members of old tribes of Babylon and Assyrians who also fought each other for about two centuries, until the Assyrians returned to power once again and re-established the Assyrian Empire and their divide and rule strategy. Eventually members of the old Babylonian ruling classes re-established the *Second Babylonian Empire* reaching from present day Lebanon and Syria to Sinai and Saudi Arabia. They also introduced to the previous adherents of other tribes expanding knowledge in *astronomy, medicine, architecture and mathematics* and the beautiful hanging gardens of Babylon. Regardless of who was in control of the region, the rulers followed the same pattern of divide and rule by uprooting and resettling large populations.

The Babylonians were the first to capture the city of Jerusalem and drive the Jews into exile. Then came the Persians from the East, and the Babylonians were defeated but their infrastructure and socio-political system was preserved and adopted by the new conquerors. The Persian Emperor, *Cyrus the Great* (580 – 529 BC), conquered vast lands from present day Turkey to India and from the Nile to the Indus River. The Persian political objective was fundamentally different than all previous empires, in that, they did not uproot the populations of the lands they conquered. Instead, they freed the Jews and allowed them to return to Jerusalem and pursued a policy of multi-culturalism. People were permitted to live their lives as they saw fit so long they paid their taxes to the central authority and they could worship at whatever Gods they wanted. The Persian Empire built its own roads throughout the empire and had their own currency. Perhaps these roads helped *Alexander the Great* (356 – 324 BCE) to speed up his own conquest of the Persian Empire, bringing new ideas to be implemented in the lands. For instance, Alexander insisted that soldiers and his generals take Persian wives as part of a wider vision in which all men, regardless of their ethnicity, would be bound by a common culture. When Alexander died at the age of 33 his generals divided the empire among themselves with many wars fought against one another. War was part of the socio-political scenery of the ancient world from localized tribal scrimmages to imperial objectives. What the lower classes and tribes lacked in culture they made up for in warfare. They invented the steel-tip on their poles and the armoured vests which the

Roman Emperors adopted later for their soldiers and horses of their armies. The Persian Empire had its own monotheist religion the *Zoroastrianism* which was founded on the belief in the existence of *Hell and Heaven, Good and Evil*. It was one of the earliest recorded monotheistic religions--600 BC to 650 BCE. It became the official religion of Persia at the time when the Roman Empire was falling apart and Christianity was embedded in its ruins. The Roman Empire was then divided into East and West with west falling into Germanic tribes and the east becoming the Byzantine Empire which included Greece, present day Turkey and a large part of the Middle East. All of the above took place before Muhammad was born to become the Prophet of Islam.

It was in the Arabian Peninsula that the Bedouin tribes were the most warlike people, who were organized in clans and clans into tribes and who had their unique "honour-system" of traditional unwritten rules. The term Bedouin, derived from the Arabic badawi, a generic name for a desert-dweller found throughout most of the desert belt extending from the Atlantic coast of the Sahara Desert via the Sinai Desert and Negev to the Eastern coast of Arabia. The Arab population consisted of many tribes who spoke the Arabic language but had polytheist religions based on nature, animist or pure-spirits. This was the pre-Islamic cultural demography of Arabs in the Arabian Peninsula. Conquerors had come and gone, who had their own administrative structures and rules but as far as the Arabs were concerned, those were strangers who temporarily possessed the land. There were the Romans, the Persians, the Greeks, the Assyrians, the Babylonians and later the Ottomans. The Bedouins were no different than any other nomad warlike tribal clan or tribe of the Arabian Peninsula. Because of the roads built by the Persian Empire, Arab merchants, as well as the Bedouins, travelled long distances within the Arabian Peninsula to trade their goods, and such trade practices would often lead them to the cities main trade centers of Mecca or Medina.

As tradesmen gathered in Mecca, tradition dictated that leaders of clans make offerings and prayers on the spiritualistic-cube *The Kaaba* (the cube in Arabic). This was a mud brick cubical structure about 3 ft. (one meter) tall with no roof, where believers of different gods would reach inside and place a small statue of an image of a god. In total there were about 360 little statues that resembled each clan's choice of gods. There were no disputes between tribes as to whose god was better than another's. Sometimes desert storms would cover the Kaaba with sand and tribesmen would dig out the statutes and place them back after removing the desert sand. The clearing of desert sand was a regular exercise since the Kaaba's mud brick walls were no more than 3 feet high. It was a primitive structure but had a religious significant to all Arab nomadic tribesmen passing through Mecca. Above all, the black *Meteorite-Stone* which was located in the center of the Kaaba increased the spiritual significance of the cubical structure. Prayers were offered to spirits and gods on health for his extended family, wealth and profitable trade by each merchant.

The Kaaba in Mecca was one of a number of sanctuaries in the Arabian Peninsula, and all of them served a man-made desire for spiritual protection against nature, sickness, enemy attacks and whatever specific agenda each clan or tribe had in mind. Disputes among clans or tribes were settled by killing one another, by *superstitious premonitions* and by the clan's power. The Kaaba was a cluster of deities whose meaning and purpose has been lost in the nebulas of history. Prophets and future tellers in the Arabian Peninsula were a common phenomenon as much as it was in streets of Palestine before and during the Roman Empire. Each Arab prophet was inspired by his own beliefs and expressed doubts about the power of all other gods but his own.

This was a predominant culture of oppressive religiousness; where everything that was going on in the world of the Arabian Peninsula was explained in illusive terms to the ignorant clans and tribesmen. Such socially embedded hostile culture was further manipulated by the upper classes and pagan priests whose agenda could be served at will. Political power and greed, uncontrolled desire for increased influence, possession of more irrigation lands and personal capriciousness were the flavours of the day. Every aspect of daily life was manipulated and governed by a spiritual expectation, honour and victory over the clans' enemies. War and killing was the only desirable solution to tribal problems.

Legend has it that the first Kaaba was built by the Jewish Patriarch Abraham who placed the Black Stone in it. No written evidence was found in the Old Testament or in the Qur'an confirming such a claim, but this mattered little to the desert tribesmen of the time. Because of this myth, which the Bedouins and other Arab tribes believed, they all came to worship in Kaaba unarmed and in truce. This truce lasted only until they departed and returned back to their old perpetual warfare. The truce facilitated trade, renewals of old bonds with other tribes, and arranged marriages with strong allies and family ties. Feuds were not permitted while all tribesmen were within the compounds of the Kaaba. The spiritual and economic activity was very hard to separate but it did serve its purpose in this pre-Islamic time. In fact, the Kaaba made Mecca an important place to re-establish old bonds, trade and a spiritual renewal of those tribesmen who had placed within Kaaba their small sacred clay idols. Here a merchant also could find a variety of spices, silks from

India, perfume from China and Egyptian linens. Mecca therefore was a city built by people from past generations, who built the Kaaba to house their clay idols, who created a robust economic activity based on trade of goods, a city which served human relations of bonding together with friends and family, bonding and a secure place where no hostilities were permitted. Mecca was a sanctuary where tribesmen were protected from any form of violence. In Mecca there was a rich mix of foreign cultures, for there were Christians and Jews and the Arabs of the desert who followed an animist religion.

Social Darwinism, of the survival of the fittest, in a primitive state of nature, was very active in this brutal state of social affairs, and a full violent force was activated as soon the tribesmen left the Kaaba sanctuary of Mecca behind. Merchants and their helpers, who travelled long distances, were heavily armed against bands of armed Bedouin thieves and bandits who roamed the desert of the Arabian Peninsula seeking their next victim. In this Peninsula armies of nomadic Arab tribesmen swept the coast of Africa. Their contemporaries tell an extraordinary story; that God sent them a prophet and then gave them an empire. But is this the historical truth? I am not convinced! True enough; the Arabian Empire was one of the most decisive events in history; but it was not the initiator, but the later comer built on previous Arab *Umayyad Caliphate* conquests.

But we still need to answer the question whether the conquering Arabs of the 7th century were Muslim at all? This is a fundamental question to answer about the Arabs of the 7th century who built an Arabian Empire that gave the world the religion of Islam. It has been said that Islam was born in the full light of history for all academics to study and admire its awesomeness. But this is not the case, for when it comes to the beginnings of Islam there is no historical evidence, only a kind of shade of a nebula-mist that does not easily reveal its secrets. The problem with investigating the rise of Islam is that there is a total *lack of historical evidence* to tell the story, that is, through Muslim historical testimonies of the 7th century. But there is none, none at all! No material sources can be found to support a historical evidence of Muslim beliefs! But there is a metaphor which states that the Muslims' beliefs and the understanding or verifying of historical facts cannot be squared. But is this my historical choice of writing or not writing the Arab history? I suggest that humanists and atheist historians must write history, even if the truth may offend most religious believers. We must have the courage to say things that believers do not say; and things that may shock believers or may even offend them! After all, isn't *"the truth shall set them free"* from religion?

It is a common knowledge that all historical Empires such as the Persian, the Babylonian, the Assyrian, the Greek, the Empire of Alexander the Great or the Ottoman Empire have left material evidence of their existence; their victories and defeats and their accomplishments. They left written records, statues and art and, of course, numismatics (coins) depicting the Emperors' or Caliphates' heads on them. Prominent citizens' testimonies describing historical events of the time are available (within limited degree) to present today's historians to make sense of those who were here before us. When the Romans conquered the Middle East they left behind all kinds of evidence where today's visitors can observe and admire the archaeological remains of the Roman Empire. The Persians left evidence of their military expeditions against the Greeks and pictorial evidence of their Zoroastrian religion. There are Greek coins depicting the head of Alexander the Great as a symbol of their brief but impressive accomplishments.

But with the Arab conquest, there is silence about the origins of Islam. Let us investigate the issue by starting in the 7th century where the ancient world was about to change forever. In Constantinople, the year 632 AD, marked the 3rd century as the capital of the eastern Roman empire of the Byzantine Empire. This was a Christian universal autocracy of a dying Roman Empire where, almost 10 centuries later, the Ottomans conquered the city and turned the *Cathedral of Agia Sophi*a into a Mosque. There is historical evidence which explains how historical events happened and when were happened. The Romans had by now forsaken their polytheism and became monotheist Christians in 325 AD, thanks to Constantine the Great.

But what we do not know, is how and when the Arabs became Muslims. Any journey into the past may or may not reveal or lead us to absolute historical evidence. Would this be enough for an atheist, like myself, to discover the origins of Islam? Was the religion of Islam made by men and historical circumstances or was it created by a powerful celestial entity which delivered the Qur'an to Muhammad? By the year 630 AD the Roman Empire had overcome the worst crisis in its history. Its old archenemy, the Persian Empire, had overrun the Roman armies from its most productive Fertile Crescent provinces, resulting in the Persian army eventually reaching the outskirts of Constantinople. After 24 years of war, the Persian armies were defeated and the Byzantine theocratic Empire was once again masters of the eastern Roman lands.

In Wadi Rum, Jordanian, the Arab Bedouin nomad tribes are passing through and have also travelled the deserts of the entire Arabian Peninsula for thousands of years. They identify themselves as Bedouin Arabs and they are the face of the Arab Conquest in the 7th century. They also claim that Mohammad (full name: *Abu al Qasim Muhammad 'Abd Allah ibn 'Abd al Mutalib ibn Hasim* 570 – 632 AD) was an Arab born in Mecca. The powerful

Bedouins were the shock troops who swept out of the Arabian Peninsula and, in a short time, they, with other Arabian tribes forged a colossus empire spanning from the Arab Peninsula to the entire coast of North Africa and into Spain, Persia and Anatolia. In the Peninsula desert no one doubts that it was the Bedouin Arabs who conquered half of the world. They did so against all odds, by not seeking worldly rewards, by having left behind their families and children, by being killed, starved or loose their directional way. They claim that their conquests were for the success of Islam. Everything they had accomplished, the victories, the conquests and the empire was for Islam. They did all their conquering because Mohammad started everything and that is why their conquests were successful. Was the religion of Islam the main motivator behind such splendid military campaigns?

But how do the Bedouin descendants know for sure that Islam even existed during the times of their ancient conquering expeditions? To the Western world, the Arab Bedouins were notorious savages, the scum of the earth, the most feared and despised of all the other barbarians who tried to conquer the European Continent. Yet, in a mere 100 years, into the first half of the 7th century, the Arab Bedouins deprived the Eastern Roman Empire of much of its richest agricultural and mineral producing provinces, crashed the powerful Persian Empire (Iran) and took possession of most of the Middle East. This is a staggering Arab Bedouin military achievement!

But for the most fundamentalist Muslims ---even today---this was a miracle which only God could have made possible. This absurd belief robs the Arab Bedouins of their own dignity, their own courage and their sacrifices, and gives credit for their achievements to an illusive and non-existent entity. Only through such people as the Arab Bedouins was the whole of North Africa transformed in just a few decades, and the Arab scholars and architects who followed afterwards built a new civilization throughout the Middle East, North Africa and Spain. This is a historical fact! What is not a historical fact is the characterization of such achievements as having been "Muslim." Just because an author, artist, scientist or a military man achieves something extraordinary it does not make it a "Muslim" or Christian," "atheist," "deist" or "Jewish" invention or accomplishment. In other words, the religion of a person has nothing to do with that person's scientific inventions or historical achievements. Was Einstein's scientific work "Jewish" just because he was Jew or were Newton's and Charles Darwin's biological discoveries "Christian"? Is naming accomplishments as being "Muslim" or "Islamic" an intentional characterization to *inflate the status of the religion of Islam*? My suggestion is yes, for it was done deliberately by *Caliph Abd al Malik Marwan (646 – 705 AD)*, the real creator of the Mohammad' legend.

The legend or myth now has it that all these extraordinary events began when an illiterate merchant called Mohammad heard the voice in his mind of the Jewish-Christian Angel Gabriel telling him *"Oh Mohammad obey the Apostle of God."* Through this message, according to the myth, the Christian God has spoken to the Arabs, and the message was clear as it was elemental; there is but one God and Mohammad is the Prophet of God and Islam is "submission to God." The myth starts when Mohammad hears a voice telling him to ascend his magical *Winged-Horse of Fire* called Al-Buraq (meaning "White Horse" but seen as "Thunder-Lightning") and fly from Mecca to Jerusalem and back during the *Isra and Mir'raj or* "Night Journey" which is the title of one of the Sura (chapters), Al-Isra, in the Qur'an. In Jerusalem Mohammad ascends to the Heavens and meets Allah (God) who tells Mohammad to pray 50 times a day. Returning down from the Heavens Mohammad reaches the 5th Heaven and meets Moses who asks Muhammad "How many times Allah tell you to pray"? Mohammad replies, "50 times per day," but Moses sends him back to the heavens to ask Allah to reduce the number of praying. After a number of repeated negotiations and trips between God, Moses and Mohammad the numbers were reduced from 45 to 30, then 20, 10 and finally there is a negotiated solution between God, Moses and Mohammad of 5 prayers per day. If you think this myth is silly, ask the opinion of any Muslim, even an educated one, for Muslims believe this story to be true! This story was told that it happen in the year 621 AD. The following year, Mohammad moved from Mecca to Medina with about two hundred tribal followers. Ten years later, in 632 AD, Mohammad was dead, after conquering and controlling the primitive towns of Mecca and Medina. Was this legend that gave the Arab Bedouins an Empire or was it not? By 632 to 644 AD the Arabs Abu Bakr and the Caliph Umbar take over Mecca and Medina and begin to spread out to conquer the great cities of the Levant, Damascus, Syria, and Cairo in Egypt, Jerusalem, in Judea, Basra and Bagdad, in Iraq. No sane historian would doubt that the Arab conquests took place, but the core question still remains; was it because of Islam? These conquests were not religious, (the term "Muslim" was not invented yet), for these expeditions were typical of the times; the more Arab land was conquered the more resources were captured. There was nothing "Islamic" about it! In fact, the terms "Qur'an" and "Muslim" was introduced in 650 AD when the confused message of the old Qur'an was re-compiled by four of Mohammad's companions into the new Qur'an that Muslims use today. That, of course, was 18 years after Mohammad's death.

Everything that we know about Mohammad's biography is from various records collected by *Ibn Ishaq* 765 AD *(Siratul Rasu'allah).* This means that

Mohammad's first written down biography was not recorded until the year 765 AD or 133 years after Mohammad's death, in 632 AD! But we do not know on what recorded base Ibn Ishaq wrote Mohammad's biography! The question now rises: what were the records about Mohammad's life, how, and from what base, were they chosen?

The *Haddith* are the compiled recorded sayings (myths or rumours) of Mohammad, which tells us something about Mohammad's life and his sayings. Each page or pages on a Haddith tells an oral story of someone who claimed what he heard Mohammad say about something or someone. The original numbers of the Haddith are claimed to be around 6,000 to 500,000 recorded individual sayings which were given to the first non-Arab, Persian Haddith compiler, and *Muhammad ibn Ismail al-Bukharin in* 870 AD to investigate the legitimacy of some of those. The concerns were that most of the Haddith may not have been from Mohammad's original recorded sayings; but were from people with a particular agenda, looking to advance it into the mainstream of Haddith. For instance, any *imam* (Muslim clergy) who was in favour of underage arranged marriages would tend to record this as having been Mohammad's saying (a Haddith); thus it would be included in the recorded Haddith. Others may describe matters of respect and propriety while others may go all the way back to Mohammad's time pertaining to his practices and his time.

Of the original list of Haddith works compiled by the non-Arab Bukharin included the final 7,275 validly Haddith. Next, appears the non-Arab, Persian Islamic imam *Muslim bin al-Hajjaj* (815 – 875 AD) who compiled 9,200 additional legitimate Haddith. Next in line appeared a noted non-Arab, Persian collector of Haddith *Abu DA'ud* (817 – 888 AD) who chose 4,800 legitimate Haddith out of the 500,000 he read. The next, non-Arab, Persian Islamic compiler of Haddith was *Muhammad ibn Isa a-Tirmidhi* (824 – 892 AD) who wrote one (1) of the six (6) canonical Haddith compilations in Sunni Islam. Next a non-Arab, the Persian Ibn Majah 824 – 887; a noted Haddith collector, wrote one (1) of the six (6) canonical collections dealing with science. Next in line was the non-Arab, Persian Al Nasai 829 - 915 CE who compiled the last of the six (6) books of medieval Haddith. As you can see, the Haddith were compiled by educated scholars of non-Arab Persian descent, by nationality and language. These scholars were amongst the educated classes of Persia (Iran) which was part of the great civilizations of the Fertile Crescent of the Levant; which included Damascus, Jerusalem and Cairo, Basra and Bagdad but none of the Arabian Peninsula. It took them from 870 AD to 915 AD to compile the six (6) canonical books of selected Haddith out of the original amount of 500,000. These Haddith were compiled, analyzed, selected and written into six books some 283 years after Mohammad's dead, in 632 AD. Why then had the Arabs of the Arabian Peninsula contributed nothing in the written Haddith? Was it because there were no Arab scholars and no proper classical civilization in the desolate desert of the Arabian Peninsula?

A Jewish or Christian believer would tend to make the same "jump" as the Muslims do today, for they all believe in their own myths without any historical evidence. Believers believe in things they are told to believe, and their ignorance of the historical roots of their religion, or lack of evidence to a religious claim is simply swept "under the carpet." This is called blind faith! Of course taking that jump into the leap of faith is not as easy as it sounds. Scepticism or doubt is not about a leap of faith, but it is about penetrating and distorting the facts, legends, myths or interpretations of historical claims. In this case, the life of Mohammad and the Arab Bedouin conquests all need to be investigated to verify the roots of Islam. We need to verify whether the religion of Islam "piggy-backed" on the shoulders of the Arab Bedouins' military expeditions as much as Christianity "piggy-backed" on the shoulders of Emperor's Constantine military dire needs and expeditions. Was this also the case for opportunistic religious-parasites, which needed to survive by leeching-on to gain life from life and spread their roots? This is a radical view and research on the roots of Islam could sharply divide the world from the earlier Islamic interpretations; for, on one hand, not to reject the Muslim stories, and, on the other, we simply not to accept them as true and verifiable either. This is a historical dilemma, for the only possible solution is to sidestep outside the Muslim traditions and start all over again from the beginning.

There is a metaphorical wall about what we know of Mohammad's life, which we simply can not bypass. We know that Mohammad existed and that he was active somewhere within the Arabian Peninsula, and we know that he was associated with the Muslim scattered leaflets of the original Qur'an and that his associates contributed to its revised making in 650 AD, 18 years after Mohammad's death. But it does not tell us anything more about what really happened, which any serious historian or believer would like very much to know. We have absence of evidence that does not allow us to tell a story on the basis of the canonical sayings of the Qur'an. We have bits and pieces of sayings but they do not add up to a verifiable story, for the Qur'an is a holy book that was written as a theology and not as a historical account. But we have no historical eye-witness accounts; we have nothing to steer us in the right direction of writing a historiography of Mohammad's life and Islam, much less of God's involvement. From current evidence:

- First Arab reference to Mohammad, as a Prophet, is from about 691 AD, in an inscription on the *Dome of the Rock*, in Jerusalem, that is, 59 years after Mohammad's death in 632,
- First reference to "Muslim" from non-Arabs is from 690 AD, that is, 58 years after Mohammad's death,
- First Arab reference to "*Muslim*" is from about 749 AD, that is, 117 years after Mohammad's death,
- People of the Arabian Peninsula were not referred to as "*Arabs*" but by the name of their tribes: *Saracen, Hagarene, Ishmaelite, Maghraye, Muriajirous, Banu Hashi, Quireish and Bedou* (Bedouin is a misnomer). Each member was only loyal to his family and his tribe,
- The first reference to "Mecca" as a "Holy" place was not until 741 AD, that is, 109 years after Mohammad's death.
- The first confirmed Mohammad biography, within Islamic sources, was not written until Ibn Hisham in 833 AD, that is, 201 years after Mohammad's death. Hisham selected the most favourable material to write Mohammad's biography.

Of course, contemporary Muslim narratives claim to know everything about Mohammad's history, his 9 wives, his character and even his favoured food. This is a whole world of storytelling which it is founded on myths and legends about Mohammad; that camels were his favoured animals, about enduring lack of water and food and about his strength of crossing the deserts in order to spread the message of Islam and finally was there a travelling merchant called Mohammad? The evidence is near non-existent. The dilemma is how do we know what was he like and what really happened, and separate myths and legends from historical facts. The earliest biographies available to us were written some 133 years after Mohammad's lifetime. Traditional religious academics claim that religions begin by "positive history" which means oral narratives of the history of a particular religion. Oral traditions however, are based on memory and memory can be selective based on what the oral traditionalists' agenda is, and what is selected to be remembered and how they want to explain it. Some parts of an oral traditional narrative must be historical, but most of it is not history, for it is a legend or a myth. It is because oral traditional narratives are re-shaped, re-thought or have been taken out of their original context, cleaned up for new functions, and manipulated by personal agendas to emphasize one's chosen preference of certain memories.

Because Islam arose in a remote and desolate part of the world we do not have any mode of written cross reference, nor do we have the key to unlock the mystery of a claimed event that supposedly took place. An entire Islamic moral universe has been built and told around the myths and legends of Mohammad's legends and brief history. The mythological intricacies surrounding the origins of Christianity and Islam were oral traditions narrated by human beings for other human beings, where they injected God and miracles, magic and prophecies into those in order to 'spice' and give them a believable importance.

Contemporary Muslim academics claim that before Mohammad there was the *Age of Ignorance* in the Arabian Peninsula, where a Bedouin father could slaughter his own daughter in "honour-killing" or bury her alive if she offended the family's honour. Legend has it that it was Mohammad who put an end to many terrible practices rooted in the Arab Bedouin culture. Yet, a visitor in the Middle East (even today) can witness these terrible practices that are still surviving in Palestine, Pakistan and many Arabian countries today. While the stories and legends may be moving narratives, where do they come from? Are they really true? Is the emphasis placed on the "sacred" nature of these myths and legends rather than on their negative effects on humanist rights and morality? The so called "sacred" is the ultimate path to blind faith and it is against all human reason, truth and intellect. Muslims' sacred message today is that the Great Arab Bedouin Conquests of the 7th century were all about the spreading of the word of Islam. This is not true, because the conquests were about land and food resources, the traditional looting and trading of slaves. But in the mid 7th century no evidence exists of finding a religion called "Islam" anywhere in the historical records of the Bedouin conquests.

The city of Jerusalem is a place where, over time, a number of historical walls have been built in order to keep its citizens safe. However, no one has ever built a tall enough or strong enough wall to keep its citizens safe forever. This is because the capital city of the 3 organized faiths has historically invited the wrath of a number of competitive religious conquistadors'. Even today, the memories of the one-time world of the Roman Empire 6th and 7th centuries live on; in the street names, in the city's architecture, in the general sense of anxiety and insecurity of its people. Yet, for thousands of years the city of Jerusalem was re-shaped and re-mapped in accordance with the religion of its rulers. When the Jews were the masters of the city, they built a grand building: the Temple Mariah which dominated all other buildings. In 70 AD the Jerusalem Temple was completely destroyed by the Roman Emperor Titus in order to eliminate the Jewish rebels, the Zealots and the Sicarii. In the 3rd century, when Emperor Constantine the Great became Christian, Jerusalem was by then, transformed into the focal point of Christian pilgrims. There were new building structures dominating the city's sky, and Christian influence is still evident today noted by the street names of religious reference. As inventors of Christianity, the Roman Empire officially believed in the Christian God, and the Christian God believed in the Roman Empire and both have left evidence for us to investigate. The power of religiousness, of Roman architecture, of myths and legends are inter-twined and it is deeply felt as a visitor strolls from street to street and from one monument to the next.

In the year 636 AD, the Christian God could no longer protect the citizens of Jerusalem from the Bedouin warriors who appeared outside its walls. As the Bedouins were getting closer, the Christians could do nothing about it other than watch from their walls and wait for the Arab warriors to enter the city. Out of the desert the Arab forces came and they were powerfully irresistible, and, in the same year, the Arabs beat the Romans in the region of Yarmouk. Following their victory, the Arab armies defeated the Persians in the region of Qadisiya, and eventually conquered the great cities of the Levant. Both defeated Empires were far too weak to defend their territories and thus could not resist the invasion of Arab hordes. The invaders captured the richest provinces of both empires which provided the Arabs with much needed resources. Next the Arabs set their eyes on the biblical promised land of milk and honey that God also promised to the Jews. The Arabs came to the Promised Land to claim that right for themselves. By 670 AD, just a few years following Mohammad's death, the Arabs captured that promised land of the Jews through peaceful negotiations.

The Romans had made the *Promised Land* a Christian land, and the Jewish religion and political elite had flourished under Roman rule. Each religion left behind their culturally hereditary mark with written records, coins, monuments and places of worship. In Persia, their citizens went about practicing the Zoroastrian ceremonies of their religion in places that were built and designated in accordance with their cultist rituals. Those were regions clearly identified as being Christian, Jewish or others; places set by custom and tradition. If the conquering Arabs arrived with a new religion, evidence of this should be found confirming its foundation. What is known is that the Arabs were a relatively small group of desert warriors who were peacefully ruling a much larger population that had established religions and religious ideas. Neither the Christians nor the Jews reacted against the Arab rulers who did not impose upon them any hostile ideology of a foreign religion. They called themselves "Believers" without specifying their religions; whether they followed a guide of traditional polytheistic religions, as they were believers of the Kaaba of Mecca in the Arabian Peninsula. In general, the evidence suggests it is not clear what the Arabs' religious beliefs were some 60 years after Mohammad's death. Some historians maintain that a number of the Arabs occupying Judea began to follow the Christians while others followed the Jewish dogma. Both followers of the Christian and Jewish religions viewed the Arabs as people of the desert who were strangers with unrecognizable beliefs, customs and traditions.

In time, the Arabs became closer to the Jews; than to the Christians, by praying in the Jewish Temple Moriah, which the Christians viewed these practices with suspicion. But the Jerusalem Jews viewed and hoped that the Syrian Arabs from the desert came as liberators, because they were permitted to return to the Temple Mount and pray there once again. There was also a wide-spread belief that the Arab Bedouin perhaps were a kind of messianic people whose leader perhaps was the long awaited Messiah who would permit the Jews to re-build the Temple. Both the Christian and Jewish leaders and scholars of the time were wondering about the Arabs; about their beliefs and if what they were doing, they were doing in the name of a new religion. Less understanding was, what the Arabs were doing, was in the name of an unknown religion called Islam.

You see, the conquests under and by Muhammad were from 622 – 632 AD and were conducted within the Arab Peninsula, Yemen and Ethiopia only; but never too far north towards Jerusalem or anywhere in the Levant. If there were any "religious" tribal scrimmages those could only be within the Arabian Peninsula, which does not constitute imperial conquests. In fact, these scrimmages can be identified as localized wars among various Arabian Bedouin tribes and the minor Muhammad's Muslim affiliated tribe: the Banu Hashim. The question is; did the religion of Islam even exist in the early years following Mohammad's death in 632 AD? Because, in Jerusalem, 30 years following Mohammad's death (in 662 AD), the city continued without any new outside interferences. There were the usual Christian and Jewish pilgrims in the streets, and the believers were attending their Churches and Synagogues and both religions were practicing their customary rituals. But where was Mohammad's monotheistic Islamic religion of Muslims, in all this?

In 662 AD, 30 years after Mohammad's death, the Arab ruler of Jerusalem, the *Umayyad Caliphate* (661 – 750 AD) *of Damascus, Syria,* was celebrated as the new leader of the newly established Arab Empire. Umayyad exhibited little or no signs at all that he was Islamist; not in his detailed kept records; not on his newly minted coins and not even in others' written accounts of the period. In short, there is not even a single mention of the Prophet Mohammad. The entire notorious myth; that the religion of Islam conquered the whole coast of the Holy Lands and the Fertile Crescent's five grand cities, plus the entire Mediterranean coast up to Spain because of Mohammad's teachings, is shattered to pieces.

Tracing the original sources of Islam is more than challenging because of the mystery, its myth or legend, plagiarism, and its typology of other religions' myths and legends. The lack of historical evidence suggests that the 'origins' have never existed. The Qur'an was composed somewhere in the Arab Peninsula and it tells of Mohammad seeking the path that Abraham followed. That path or place is perhaps where one may find the roots of Islam. In the city of Hebron, the occupied city of the West Bank, in Palestine, there is the Tomb of Abraham, the father of the Jewish religion. In accordance with the legend, Abraham was praying to a monotheistic God, while others were following pagan traditions of polytheistic Gods. Abraham convinced the people that if they believed in one God, that God would give them the Promised Land and they would become God's Chosen People. These beliefs were reinforced by Abraham's son Isaac who continued claiming the rights to the Promised Lands such as Israel. Abraham's second son, Ishmael, is revered as the father of the Islamist. One must remember that this Abrahamic messianic association is much older than Islam itself. However, this remains central to Islam today, for in accordance with the Muslim believers, Abraham is their prophet and that the religion he founded was Islam, not Judaism. Chronologically this claim was not possible!

The premise of this delusion is clear, for Abraham's legend or existence took place more than 2,000 years before the first appearance of Islam in the mid of the 7th century. In the myths uttered in the Qur'an, Ishmael helped his father Abraham build the House of God in the place called Bakka or Mecca, the birth place of Mohammad. The settlement of Mecca was the place where everything began; the cross-roads of faith, myths, legends, and the pagan and historical events of Islam. In such a Holy place we can assume that we could find solid archaeological evidence of the beginnings and origins of Islam. But there is none, because all the initial descriptions and prescriptions written in the Qur'an originated in and around the Palestine region including Jerusalem and not in Mecca or Medina as it is claim by Islamists today.

Any early appearance of Islam in Mecca or Medina cannot be confirmed from any independent source outside the Qur'an, but there is a major problem. Aside from a single ambiguous mention in the Qur'an, there is no other mention of a holy place called Mecca or Medina; not even once for over 100 years, following Mohammad's death. Historians can not even confirm that Mohammad was born or came from Mecca. There is no evidence of this or any other known alternative birthplace nearby Mecca. When we look at Mecca we see additional problems, for in accordance with the Qur'an's

typological geographical description, the settlement was;
a) It is located in a valley,
b) Has a stream going through,
c) There had a pillar of salt resembling Lot's wife from *Sodom and Gomorrah* legend,
d) Surrounding the settlement of Mecca, there are fields, grass, and grain, fruit and olive-trees and,
e) There are mountains overlooking the Kaaba.

This was a typological description of a "Mecca" that never existed, for
f) Mecca then and today is located in a desolate desert, it has no valleys, or olive trees, it has no stream (except a dugout well called Zamzam),
g) It has no mountains overlooking the Kaaba and
h) The legend of the pillar of Lot's wife salt's location is 700 miles to the north.

In fact, even today, there are no olive-trees or fruit trees in the entire of Saudi Arabia, but only in the land near the Mediterranean Sea, i.e., Israel and Palestine. Mecca therefore is not in these fertile valleys, and Islamic sources tell us that Mecca was located in "mother of all settlements" but does not tell us where these settlements were located. Islamic Traditions tells us that the typological "location" is where Adam and Eve were cast out from (Sura 7:24) and that is the reference location for Mecca. This is not in the Qur'an but it is written in the Traditions of the 9th and 10th centuries. If this is the case, Mecca must be the oldest city in history because Adam and Eve were sent there. In the same Mecca, Traditions' typology tells us that Abraham lived in Mecca and built the Kaaba. Has any Muslim propagator or apologists ever noticed that Abraham lived and died in (West Bank) Judea 2,000 years before Mohammad?

In the Qur'an the believers are directed to pray facing the direction of the Holy Sanctuary but it does not say that the Holy Sanctuary was located in the direction of Mecca. Early Mosques and contemporary archaeologists in search of Islamic evidence suggest something different. In accordance with Dr. *Tali Erickson*-Gini, from the *Israeli Antiquities Authority*, the remains of an early Mosque in the *Negev desert* was not facing south towards Mecca, but towards the sun rising of the east i.e., the city of Petra (present day Jordan) the city between Basra and Avdad of the Negev highlands. Why were the Mosques built before 750 AD facing Petra instead of Mecca? This ancient Negev Mosque was built about 120 years after the death of Mohammad and before the direction facing towards the Mecca was preferable. Mecca of the 7th century was in fact a secondary or of a minor importance as a settlement; it was even off the main trade routes of Arabia. In fact the earliest maps of the Arabian Peninsula trade routes do not show Mecca until 900 AD! Early Greek trading documents called Crone refers to the towns of Ta-if (southeast of Mecca), Yathrib (later Medina) and Kaybar, but never Medina.

This indicates that there was no reason to pray towards Mecca because it had not actually been fixed yet or that it was not a well-established town or that the builders of Mosques were perhaps directed otherwise. Perhaps this finding of the remains of an early Mosque is not as convincing, but early Christian writers are describing the praying habits of Arab Bedouin invaders as praying facing north towards the *"Station of Abraham"* in Hebron and not south towards Mecca. The Qur'an does not state that Mohammad lived in Mecca (Bakka) or that Mecca was the place where God made his first revelation to him. In fact nowhere in the Qur'an does it clearly say where God made his first revelation other than in the Sanctuary, but no one clearly knows where this *Sanctuary* is located. It is therefore difficult to "read between the lines" in the Qur'an's text itself and discover the location of the Sanctuary.

Mecca, as a mud-hut settlement was always a worship place for pagans, and worshippers of idols and polytheistic gods of all sorts whose statues could be found in the early mud structure of the Kaaba. The strange and ironic thing is that the Qur'an tells Biblical typological stories of Jewish and Christian origins, typological events, and claims the patriarchs of other religions, as its own. For instance, the Qur'an says that *"Abraham was not a Jew nor was he a Christian; but he was Upright, and bowed his will to Allah's, (which is Islam), and he joined not gods [but] Allah."*

The authors of the Qur'an were well versed in Biblical mythological stories and names of biblical persons such as, Abraham, Moses, Jesus, Virgin Mary and others such as Alexander the Great. In these Qur'an inscribes in biblical traditions and post-biblical stories and alludes to biblical developments and offered them to the readers. Post-biblical developments were described of negotiations or theological debates and questions between Christians, and Jews in Jerusalem of the time whose roots were the Hebrew Old Testament and the Christian Bible New Testament. The authors of the Qur'an wanted to engage in these theological discussions and present their own views. Stories told in the Qur'an were about the people in the Arabian Peninsula who supposedly were farmers and large scale agriculturalists. The strange thing is that, at the time, the Qur'an's description of such people and of their occupation was not real but typological. There was not a single farmland, no were there farmers or agriculturalists that produced olives, oranges and grapes in the desolate deserts of the Arabian Peninsula.

For obvious geological and climatic reasons, the desert is not a fertile land

and can not support such agricultural enterprises. There was no agricultural base in Mecca nor were there valleys, and the authors of the Qur'an simply re-arranged (typology) the geography of land and people in order to give a "seat" to Islam in the great theological debates of the time. The farmers who were keeping cattle and producing olives and oil, vines, fruits and vegetables or grains were from Syria, Lebanon, Judea, Palestine, and along the riverbanks of the Nile (the Fertile Crescent region) and not from the barren desert lands of Mecca. This is the reason why successive Arabian horde invasions were directed towards fertile lands, but not once had they ever invaded the infertile desert of the Arab Peninsula, except for religious reasons. In such desert, there were no olive trees, no orange trees and no grain farms to such a degree that could entice an Arab invader to invade such non-productive land.

The question is, if the city of Mecca in the Arabian Peninsula was not the starting point of Islam, where was it? If we could accept certain Qur'an clues about the location of the Arab farmers and agriculturalists, which were living in fertile lands with plenty of water for raising cattle, goats, sheep, vines and vegetables, and who were knowledgeable of the biblical traditions, then we must look for the right kind of landscape and for the growth of civic societies. These clues may lead us north of the Arabian Peninsula, to the area of the town of Avdat, in the Negev, where the 7th century Arab farmers were a mix of idol, monotheistic and polytheistic worshippers, living on the fringes of the Roman Empire. Much of the town's pagan animist past was flavoured with early Coptic Christian theology.

This area was a rich agricultural land; green as far as the eyes can see with a sophisticated irrigation system that transformed desert to bloom; was in the Fertile Crescent of Palestine and Judea. The northern region as a whole seems to fit the description in the Qur'an much better than further to the south in the desolate Arab region of Mecca. Was the region and town of Avdat the place where the Qur'an was composed? When you read through the Qur'an what is really striking is its extended verbalism which is full of illusions and typology of landscapes and events. But with one exception, as in the case of Avdat, the description of the people is exact, as well as the description of the irrigable lands, paganism, and the Christian and Jewish mix of religiousness. In fact, not far from the town of Avdat, a strange hint in the Qur'an may actually indicate where it was originally composed; in the south side of the *Dead Sea* near the borders of Palestine and Jordan.

The Qur'an describes the event of Sodom and its destruction. In it, there is a narrative of how people would pass by the deadly site of the destroyed town by day and by night and how others could also see the remains of its destruction. One wonders, if Mohammad addresses the people in the area as saying *"we can see them"* passing by day and by night; what is Mohammad doing in South Dead Sea area more than 1.000 km from Mecca? If we are looking for clues where the Qur'an was composed, it is like a prospector searching for a mineral, and the narrative is just a small sign of where the mineral maybe discovered. If this single narrative originates from the remains of Sodom where do the Qur'an's remaining narratives come from? Can this narrative be attributed to a single person living in a particular area at a particular time and did the rest of the Qur'an components come from others and from elsewhere?

True enough, trying to discover the origins of the Qur'an and of Islam is like chasing a desert mirage, for the illusions and typology are there, but historical reality is eluding us. The Arab Umayyad Caliphate of Damascus, Syria, conquered vast areas of the world; in the East, Syria in *634 AD, India was invaded in 665 AD, Byzantium of Constantinople was besieged in 669 AD and in 715-17 AD, and, westward, Egypt was conquered in 642 AD, Carthage in 697AD, and Spain in 711-12AD*. During this whole historical time, the Arab Umayyad Caliphs of Syria did not talk about Mohammad, nor about Islam and neither did they mention Mecca. For nearly 60 years following Mohammad's death, no inscriptions of any sort described a leader like Mohammad in documents, monuments or coins as was customary of the time. At some point in history the Arabs did just that, by placing Mohammad's face in a coin. This was done 60 years after Mohammad's death. Why did it take such a long time to figure out Mohammad's importance? Let us see!

This explanation may suffice, in that, in 693 AD the Byzantine Empire of Constantinople (a major competitor of Islam's religious prominence), for the very first time, issued coins depicting Jesus' head as a divine image. This was a change from the traditional practice of issuing coins with the emperor's image, his heirs or his favoured general. The very image of Jesus on the Byzantine coinage, however, caused a serious problem for *Abd al Malik*, (646 – 705 AD) the builder of the *Dome of the Rock*, the creator of the world religion of Islam and of the *typological legacy* of the Prophet Mohammad. You see, in the world of commercial trade, the Byzantine coinage was traditionally used as a means of exchange and payment between the Byzantine and other countries including the Umayyad Empire merchants. Now the new coinage, with Jesus' image was also the official coinage used by the Caliphate merchants, store keepers and average Arabian household in the Fertile Crescent. The Byzantine coinage, with a miraculous image of Jesus as Lord, could not be used by Muslims because they were offended and because they were commanded by their religion not to believe but destroy all idols and idolatrous images. You see, the legend on the reverse side of the coin explicitly said, *"Jesus Christ Lord Saviour King of those who rule."*

For obvious reasons, this coinage created an immediate reactionary need for the Caliphate of Umayyad of Syria to issue a coin suitable for Arabs to handle, and at the same time, to counter-balance the Byzantium's religious message on its coin. The new Umayyad coin; depicted the clear image of the Mohammad as a "Messenger of God," showing him surrounded by his closest companions, his brother-in-law and his wife. The legend on the reverse observes the very creed of Islam, *"Muhammad the Apostle of God"* a direct paraphrased message of the Byzantines' coin: *"Lord Jesus Christ."*

Every inscription and every ancient coin tells a story and conveys an idea of power, but sometimes what is not inscribed on a coin tells more of its significance than what is on it. For instance, why is Mohammad's name not mentioned on the coins of the 7th century Arabian Empire? The rulers of the Arabian Empire had on their coins the heads of military leaders, perhaps to commemorate a famous battle victory, or the head of a distinguished military hero. Every empire needed to have a unifying symbol to consolidate its power and to spearhead its armies under the power of that symbol. Yet, up to this historical point, the Arab rulers seemed to ignore Mohammad's potential significance! Coincidently, the very first Arab coin with Mohammad's image unintentionally generated the religious curiosity of his importance; and the Arab Umayyad rulers opportunistically capitalized on the significance of its popularity, among the Arab-Bedouin tribesmen of the Arabian Peninsula. Maybe the rulers needed 60 years to figure out what Mohammad's significance was and what the story was all about or maybe the issue was not why Mohammad was not on the coin at the beginning but how it got there at the end.

By the mid 7th century, the Arab Umayyad Empire was rich beyond imagining and it stretched from the Middle East to Iran, the entire Arabian Peninsula and Yemen, the coast of Egypt and Libya, Georgia, Turkey, Greece and part of Southern Italy. But who had the power and the right to rule the Arab Empire? This was a vital issue which the Arab tribesmen could not agree on amongst themselves. By the 680's AD there were scrimmages amongst the Arab Bedouins, tribes against tribes and allies, against other allies of different persuasions, sporadic rebellions and civil wars. Among the localized fighting tribesmen was a little known fighting force with religious character affiliated with the supporters of the dead warlord, Muhammad. The so called Prophet Muhammad was a *little known figure* beyond his limited supporters within the desert regions of Mecca and Medina. Something was missing from the Umayyad Arab Empire; something like common uniting power. That "something" was a central ideology; a political and military power which could unite the people in order to keep together the Arab Empire under a common ideology and cause. What was needed was a dominant political ideology as a means to the final complete reunification of all the fighting forces under the Umayyad's Caliphate of Damascus, of Syria.

Political unrest threatened the Arab Empire, and from the depths of the Arabian Desert a new dominant claimant to the Empire emerges: his name is *Abdulla Ibn Al Zubayr* (624 – 692 AD). Al Zubayr was about to change the Arab Umayyad Empire's misfortunes, for he realized, like the Roman Emperor Constantine the Great in 325 AD, the influence of an ideology of a celestial symbol on the simple-minded and superstitious tribal people. Ibn Al Zubayr needed a cast-iron symbol which would serve him as a unifying base of the Arab peoples, and that symbol was found in Mohammad. After all, Muhammad was still a relatively well known warlord, who had been a religious believer, with armed forces capable of imposing his beliefs on tribesmen. In 686 the new claimant of the Empire stamped coins with an ingenious inscription *"In the name of God, Mohammad is the Prophet of God."* This coin was distributed throughout the empire and into the hands of every tribesman leader and layman, to merchants for every sales transaction, as ransom payment for kidnapped persons, for every dowry received or paid out, as payment of taxes, and, above all, as a means of transmitting the new powerfully direct symbol of unity and a message from God to the Arab people.

One must remember that the Christians of 325AD were organized in clandestine groups within the Roman Empire, and that the leaders of the organizations could demand the submission of its believers to the new order of things. As the religion, Christianity was maturing and these organizational structures became a large part of Rome's military force, but, above all, they served as a wide-spread bonding power of the Roman Empire on the day Christianity became its official religion. The Christian monotheistic God (as ideology) became the powerful force; which dismissed as of Rome's other gods as false gods, and became the dominant proponents of the Emperor's military goals. Constantine adopted the kind of symbols that were widely spread among Christian and polytheistic believers like wild fire. The power of suggestion or symbolism was a perfect example of influencing and modifying mass behaviour, as it is evident even today by the influence of mass media. Both the secular military objectives and the Christian leaders and soldiers in the Roman armies served their purpose towards their desired goals.

In the case of the Arab Empire, attempts were made to unify itself under one powerful image and message, but Mohammad's religion was not mature enough to fill the much needed social gap that was missing. Islam was not an overnight success in spreading across the Arab Empire, but as war waged on, and battles were fought, the once symbolic legend of Mohammad was transformed into a reality and became more and more influential and stronger. Arab-Bedouin tribalism remained strongly bound to the desert culture and those tribal leaders began to recognize that Mohammad, since he also was a tribal leader, was one of them by birth, language and by culture. By the beginning of the 8th century, the religion of Islam was recognizable by large numbers of the Arabian population and had begun to spread beyond localized regions, desert tribes and conquered cultures of other peoples.

Here we come to a crucial point. What if it was not Islam which gave rise to the Arab Umayyad Caliphate, but it was the Arab Umayyad Empire which gave rise to Islam? What if the religions of Islam "piggy-backed" on the shoulders of the Umayyad's military successes and leeched on it like a parasite? After all, Christianity did just that under Constantine the Great. As the Roman armies became stronger and stronger, spreading from one culture to the next, so did the new unified force of Christianity. As for the Arab Emperor Abdulla Ibin al Zubayr, he also realized that as the Caliph of a tribal empire he must interject the support of the Almighty, in the image of Mohammad; and that he could demonstrate upon what basis he was making that claim. Constantine, who made the same claim, turned for support on the Christian groups who laid the ground-work for both the success of the Roman Emperor and for the celestial God. The legend of the Prophet Mohammad, printed in every document and stamped on every coin, propagated the unity-factor amongst hundreds of thousands of Arab-Bedouin tribesmen and their dependent. During the times of conquest and military expeditions, a number of self-proclaimed emperors had come and gone, but the discovery that the name of Mohammad was used by all as a bonding power of national character, was not forgotten by any of the subsequent military rulers of the Arab Empires.

The continued civil war between many factions was a very close-run thing but another victorious warlord the *Umayyad Caliph Abd-al-Malik* (646-705AD), was determined that the subliminal power of the image and legacy of Mohammad would not fall under the control of another dangerous military rival. You see, by the 680's CE the Romans knew a thing or two about religion and political power, and when they became a Christian nation they had re-drawn the map of Jerusalem. But Abd-al-Malik had also his own ambitious plans, to set out and build a holy city in the name of the new religion, Islam.

But he needed a face and a religious and political ideology to cement the unity of his Umayyad Empire: al-Malik found his solution in Prophet Mohammad imagery and the Qur'an. Abd al-Malik accomplished his objective 60 years after Mohammad's death. As the conqueror of Jerusalem, al-Malik ordered the construction of the *Dome of the Rock in 691* AD which is the oldest Islamic worship building in existence. The Rock of the Dome is a design mixture of Roman and Byzantium styles with its pillars and mosaics, and Abd-al-Malik plugged his Islamic legend and dominion into the power-base of the Jewish and Christian world religions: Jerusalem. The building of the Dome of the Rock was a profound statement to the world; that the religion of the Umayyad Arab Empire of Syria, in the eyes of Allah, is Islam.

Up to this historical point, Islam was relatively obscure until it was officially adopted by Caliph Malik as a unified religious-political ideology of his warlike empire. Before this time, no mention of Muhammad, Islam or the Qur'an can be found in any of the Caliph's coins, inscriptions or documents. In other words, there was no mention of Muhammad during his actual lifetime, anywhere in oral popular storytelling, papyrus scripts, monuments, in the Qur'an or in any other sources outside Mohammad's own followers of the mud-settlements of Mecca and Medina. In fact, while in the Christian Bible the name of Jerusalem is mentioned 668 times in the Qur'an, the names of Kaaba, Medina and Mecca or Muhammad are nowhere mentioned in the Holy Book of Qur'an.

In 1972 during the restoration of the Mosque of Sarna, capital of Yemen, workers discovered a mash of old parchments circa 705 – 715 AD with Qur'an verses. These Qur'an verses are fundamentally different than the *Uthmanic Script* version, and Sarna verses are the world's oldest Qur'an verses which were written in 702 CE about 70 years after Muhammad's death. Al-Malik compiled his Qur'an from fragmented plagiarisms taken from ancient Christianity (Byzantium), Judaism (Jerusalem) and Zoroastrian (Persia)—the common religions of the region during his raids and looting spree and those verses have their words changed, have been washed off and rewritten, reformulated with entire chapters rearranged. In fact, there are 7 different versions of the Qur'an which makes it near impossible to know which one is the official version from original sources: *a) Ibn Amir (Bazra) 736AD b) Ibn Kathir (Mecca) 73AD, c) Abu Amir al-Ala' (Damascus) 770AD, d) Hamzah (Kufah) 772AD, e) al-Qisai (Kufah), 804AD and f) Nafi (Medina) 785AD.*

The absence of such important names suggest that Caliph al-Malik's intention was to build the legacy of the religion of Islam, with the Qur'an and Muhammad away from the desert of the Arabia Peninsula and much closer to Jerusalem, home base of the world's other dominant monotheisms. Malik wanted to build legitimacy and a cosmopolitan importance to a religion which none of these had achieved so far in the uncivilized and tribal world of the Arabian Desert. Under pressure to produce a suitable written document; which Malik's Imperial armed forces would believe, submit to and follow; he forced men of letters and scribes to collect from scattered Qur'an verses, borrow, plagiarise, plundered and pirated and copy other religions' biblical verses, in order to build the text of the Qur'an. For instance, it is known that Islam does not permit the reproduction of a person's or animal's image because no one could give life to that image. This Qur'anic verse was taken from .

EXODUS 20:4 which states that *"You shalt not make unto thee any graven image, or any likeness of any thing that is in heaven above or that is in the earth beneath, or that is in the water under the earth."* Also, from the.

Ten Commandments, *"thou shalt not make unto thee any graven image"* which is an abbreviation from the *Book of Deuteronomy*.

Malik's very first coinage used in his Empire had Mohammad's image, or what Malik thought Mohammad looked like, because he never met Mohammad. It is beyond the scope of this narrative to go into the numerous Qur'an plagiarized verses and typology from other religions, but it was important to establish the fact that the Qur'an was written by many who had no original material to insert into the Qur'an, no theistic intervention and therefore were obligated to thieving, lie and hide the originality of these plagiarized verses. You see, the authors of the 7th century Qur'an could not predict that one day in the future ordinary people (like you and I) would discover such bland intellectual theft. This has created an enormous problem for contemporary Islamic apologists trying to explain such discrepancies. There are well-financed western apologists by theocratic states of Saudi Arabia, Iran and Turkey; yet the truth can not be hidden from independent investigation.

Most Muslims, like most Christians and Jews, are ignorant of the facts as recorded in the legends or traditions surrounding their religion. It is because what has eluded the understanding of most believers, is that there is not a single letter, a word, a sentence, a paragraph or a chapter in the Torah, the Bible or the Qur'an that could have been revealed by any *"Intelligent Designer,"* a celestial divinity, God or Allah. There is not a shred of verified evidence of miracles and resurrections, the existence of personal or religious spirits and God's or Allah's direct or indirect interference in human affairs. Without exaggerating, the best supporters of these religions are;
a) Peoples' delusion and ignorance,
b) Obedience to blind faith,

c) Using the term *"I believe"* as substitution for verifiable evidence (or I think); and

d) Their willingness to accept the dogma they are taught.

On the exterior walls of the Dome of the Rock in 691 AD, the Caliph Malik did not even insert quotations from the Qur'an about Mohammad or a message that tells the world of the coming of a new religion. Messages were inserted on the exterior and the interior of the Dome much later by the Iraqi *Caliph al-Ma'mum* (786 – 833 AD) who inserted also his name as is evident from the inscriptions. This is a profound grand statement; which the Ma'mum Muslims have superseded all other religions including Judaism and Christianity, and that Islam has arrived and it is here to stay. In other words, there can be no other religion in the making after Islam. Abd-al-Malik and later Ma'mum began to rule the empire as self appointed deputies of Allah, just as the 'Christianized' Roman Emperors *Flavius Titus* (31 – 81 AD) and *Flavius Constantine the Great* (272 – 337 AD) have done before them. But unlike the Roman Emperor Flavius Titus, who destroyed God's only symbolism of the Temple of Jerusalem in 70 AD, the Arab Emperors built Allah's symbol: the Dome of the Rock (the House of Allah) in Jerusalem, and focused, directed and gave meaning to peoples' attention.

Why was Jerusalem a city of no importance to Muslim chosen to begin the religion of Islam a city of no traditional importance to Muslims, instead of Medina or Mecca which supposedly were the original holy cities of Islamists? For the Arab Emperor Malik the choice was simple: Jerusalem was the center of the religious world, while the Bedouin-Muslim desert settlements of Medina and Mecca were still insignificant as a power base for the new religion. In addition, both desert places were located more than one thousand kilometres from Jerusalem, and from that distance it could not influence Islam's prominence over Judaism and Christianity. The Roman Emperor Constantine in 324 AD cared little about the spread of the religion of Christianity in Jerusalem or Palestine, and cared much more about receiving the fighters needed from it to fight its foreign enemies. As for, Abd-al-Malik, "being the "new kid in town," needed to pronounce his fighters' faith and give them the reason to live, to kill and die; first for the glory of the Syrian Umayyad Empire and second for the celestial Allah. The building of the Dome of the Rock gave prominence to the faithful; a desire to kill and die for the Caliph and Allah (or God and Country). Although Abd-al-Malik was the dominant ruler of Jerusalem, he was also an Arab by ethnicity, tribe, culture and language, and the religious influence of Judaism and Christianity was a bit intolerable. He was familiar with the Muslim religion because he was born in Mecca (but raised in Medina and Damascus) and because of these reasons Malik promoted his birth-place as a means of strength and as ideological unity for the Arabs. So much so that today the term "Islam" has become a false synonymous term to the *national identity* of "Arab." Mixing these two terms has given *Islam a political-religious ideology* of distorted national character. As such, the political ideology of Islam is a theocracy; with its own legal framework of Shari'a Laws, which it is a legal system based on religion that is predominant as the political system of Iran, Saudi Arabia and the core political ideology of Islamic radical groups.

A scribe in the court of Abd-al-Malik announced that the Arab Emperor was the custodian of two holy places; one was the Dome of the Rock and the other was the "Sanctuary" which location still remains a mystery to this day. All we have is that this second mysterious holy place or Sanctuary is located in the desert of the Arabian Peninsula. Was this mystery place located within the city of Mecca? The Sanctuary of Kaaba, in Mecca, was the only known pre-Islamic traditional pagan worship structure, the only prominent holy structure in the Arab Peninsula. Making the Caliph Malik the custodian of the Dome of the Rock, in Jerusalem, and the Sanctuary of the pagan Kaaba, in the Arab Peninsula formed a "bridge-of-faiths" (between two historical locations) and united the faithful to the pagan-religion of Islam. But why was the Sanctuary such a grant mystery? Why was it built there and not in another place, like Jerusalem? Is it because we still do not know the actual religion of the Arabs in the 7th and 8th centuries? Can we presume that this was Malik's secretive Sanctuary for the benefit of the Arabs who lived in the Arabian Peninsula desert? Was it because Allah's Qur'an was speaking to them directly but did not want the Christians and the Jews to discover it and impose an undue influence over their religion of Islam? Was this mysterious Sanctuary the pagan Sanctuary of Kaaba?

Without offending the religious sensitivities of Muslims, I maintain the Qur'an is a source of the most illogical, confusing, obscure, vulgar and contradictory mixture of fragmented plagiarisms taken from early Christianity, Judaism and Zoroastrian; outright lies, deceptions, anti-female, anti-science, cultism and paganism. This was the compiled ideological work of the Syrian Umayyad Empire, Caliph Abd al Malik, which was written in Syro-Aramaic language which roots include Hebrew, Ethiopic and Akkadian, ancient Babylonian, Assyrian and some Arabic. The Qur'an therefore was not written in Arabic but in Syro-Aramaic, a language spoken in Syria but not by the Arabs in the Arabian Peninsula. It is full of Christian and Jewish characters, invented stories and parables, metaphors and typology. The question is, if the Qur'an originally came from the Arabian Desert, then how did these foreign Syrian parables and characters get into the book? Were they simply plagiarized stories that were written in Syro-Aramaic? Was this their familiar language? Was it because everything that needed to be said; about God, angels, resurrection, miracles, heaven and hell, the destruction of Gomorrah, Lot's wife and Abraham, Moses and Gabriel, Adam and Eve, the Garden of Eden and Noah's Flood; in the Torah and in the Old Testament, had already been said and written in Hebrew and Aramaic?

Was it because the authors of the Qur'an were not able to invent new biblical stories, new parables and new mythical characters or did they not have the time and the inclination? Did they instead choose the most lazy and easy way to create a new religion; by means of plagiarism from other traditional non-Arabic sources? Could perhaps only the ignorant Arabian Peninsula tribes of the desert be persuaded of the originality and legitimacy of the Qur'an's stories and characters, and of it being God's final world? We have one book that was created out of nothing and we do not have the means to unlock its delusional origins, or maybe that is the core point with the Qur'an, for we are not supposed to unlock Allah's magical mysteries. Its simplicity to its believers is that Allah's message comes to the Prophet Mohammad and the Prophet lives in the desert amongst his people and traditional tribes. But can we rule out that the uneducated warlord and merchant Muhammad got his ideas about a religion in the barren desert? Was the barren desert populated by scholars, theologians, philosophers, men of letters, "people of book," or other religious propagators who could create the holy book of the Qur'an?

Evidence shows there were no Christian or Jewish, Syrian, Persian or Iraqi scholars living in the desolate desert of Mecca and Medina, nor were there places of worship other than the idolatry of the 3 foot tall mud-cubical of the Kaaba in Mecca. All the records reveal emptiness of the desert; and to make sure that Mecca gave Muslims a "Tabula Rasa" (a blank slate) to put their prophet beyond the reach of history.

Here, with all honesty, we can look to Islam and the Qur'an from a non-bias way and analyze the pettiness of its claims without malice, without offering philosophical or theological "medicine" to cure its delusions and illusions. The militaristic origins of Islam and its continuing path of externalised Jihad is a concern of the civilized world. We must live in an environment that questions everything because humanity has saw and continues to see, with ISIS in Iraq and Syria, the effects of blind faith from religious ideologies. Studying the problem of Islam is a peel-stripping process and at the end we may have something to show or nothing convincing of its legitimacy.

There are biblical stories that we could believe, but there is no evidence to support those beliefs about Moses and the "burning-bush" and about the 10

Commandments. The only evidence that we have when looking at the old Christian Churches and Monasteries, the Jewish Synagogues in Jerusalem and the Mosques in Iran, is the history of religion, empire and militarism as an old partnership which, between them has turned mere desert places into holy lands. As such, the world of God was built by the *militaristic World of Man!*

What I have hoped to show, even briefly, is that out of the ancient world came the subsequent rise of the Arab Empire in the 7th and 8th centuries. Questions have been raised about the origins of the Arab Empire, the Qur'an and whether the religion of Islam evolved from 60 to 200 years after Mohammad's death or was the sudden gift from God, as the blind faithful believed. I looked at the issues of Christianity and Islam from a historical perspective rather than from theology or philosophy. True enough, this was written from a non-believer's historical perspective rather than from a believer's faith. Together the three main organized religions constitute a historical movement which has greatly impacted (without exaggeration) every aspect of our ancient and contemporary lives. Together they have transformed the way humanity contacts its thinking process and sets its moral and ethical issues. For instance, looking at the historical evidence of the appearance of the Qur'an, there are things about it that may not be true for a historian non-believer, but true to a follower of the Muslim faith. As a Muslim you may believe that the Qur'an comes from God, but if you are not a Muslim then you are obliged---as much as a Jew or a Christian---to explain what all these miracles, hell and fire, and claims of resurrection are doing in these holy books. For a believer, the contents of the holy books are simply easy to except and believe in its traditions---like the Qur'an came from God. But to a non-believer it is a problem which needs to be solved by historically verifiable evidence not by theology or the linguistic trickery of metaphors or typology.

In accordance to the Muslim tradition, God's revelations descended upon Muhammad, an illiterate Bedouin-tribesman, in the middle of the barren Arabian Desert, hundreds of miles from any traces of civilization, with no Jewish, Persian, Syrian or Christian scholars to learn from, who was surrounded by pagans and pagan traditions, and with the mud structure of Kaaba filled with pagan worshiped idols. If a non-believer does not have evidence that those revelations came from God, then who are the authors and where do they come from? What this confirms is that the origins of the Qur'an can not be true and could not have been created as a Holy Book that originated from the depth of a barren desert. The primitive Arabian Bedouin settlements and villages were in the middle of nowhere, had no access to the world of knowledge and scholarship and nothing to do with the monotheistic world of Judaism and Christianity. Some Qur'anic verses and *Hadiths* (rumour-stories) were originally created, but they were created out of that primitive tribal culture, which it is evident by the un-intelligent style of their narrative content.

These are stories told about Mohammad's life, about him seeing the injustices around him, the savagery of tribal wars and the treatment of females within the family, but not a single evidence exists that tells us where these stories come from! The oldest Mohammad biography known today is from about 800 AD and almost 200 years after his death. Within that period of time the Arab Umayyad of Syria conquered and carved out a huge empire from Persia to the Mediterranean coastline. It appears that the religion of Islam "piggy-backed" on the shoulders of the Arab-Bedouin armies, and evolved over the centuries, in the form that we now recognized. So the question we are confronted with is to what extent these stories told in 7th and 8th centuries AD about Mohammad's life are true?

The myth of the rise of Islam follows a tradition which claims that the Arabs of the desert mounted their camels and horses with the Qur'an in one hand and the sword in the other, and conquered the world and founded a Muslim Empire. But if this is the case, there is a peculiar silence about the existence of a prophet called Mohammad in any Arabic document at the time of military conquests until almost 60 years after his death, and then only in a single series of coins and in a single sign on the Dome of the Rock which were both designed for political and military reasons by the Caliph of Umayyad Empire Abd al Malik Marwan. There were no prime references or biographies of Mohammad until several decades into the 8th century AD. The problem lies with the false claim that the Arab Empire established by Abd al- Malik in (646 – 705 AD) was, in fact, a Muslim empire and that Islam was fully formed before the Bedouin hordes started their conquests. This is an utterly false claim because Islam was gradually created some 60 years after Mohammad's death. With no exaggeration, it is very peculiar that there is such absence of evidence; whether in written records, in architectural records or in evidence of coins. This concludes that the Qur'an did not come from God and that Islam did not suddenly become a dominant religion that conquered the world as it is widely believed and propagated by those who want to give a false prominence to a tribal religion.

In fact, the Arab armies of Syria had, long before the appearance of the religion of Islam, conquered the Persian Empire, the Fertile Crescent and was already into a long war against the Western Roman Empire, the Byzantium Empire, and Jerusalem which was lost again to the Arab conquistadores of the Umayyad Empire. Thanks to the military ambitions Caliph Malik and his construction of the Dome of the Rock—which practices the pagan idol worship of a black meteorite---Islam went beyond its obscurity of the Arab Peninsula and onto the world's central stage of established religions in Jerusalem of 691 AD. The Syrian Caliph Malik's paid "men of letters" created the religion of Islam out of the Arabian pagan tribal traditions of the Bedouins warlords.

The historical evolution of cultism follows a gradual process of expansion until a certain point in time and space, when an outside power forcefully impacts it and gives it a boost forward to become an eventful religious institution. This is what the evidence suggests that happened, and this also corresponds with the way Judaism, Christianity and Islam have evolved in a relative historical period. The forceful impact of the Roman Empire on the Coptic Christianity; with its official recognition of it, give it a means for its expansion, after 325 years of relative obscurity. The rise of Islam is part of that recognizable historical evolution, not as part of Judaism or Christianity, but as part of the evolving trilogy of Abrahamic religion. The Arab Empire was conquering other lands and civilizations for its own military and political reasons and the religion of Islam gradually became the galvanizing, bonding force of the undisciplined tribal Bedouin fighters, which gave them a sense of historical identity. There is no convincing evidence to support the claim that the Arab fighters who conquered the whole entire Persian Empire; who conquered provinces of the Roman Empire; were in fact of Muslim religious faith the way we understand it today. The Roman Empire soldiers, as well as the Bedouin fighters of the Arab Empire were pagans, and polytheistic by long established traditions, although in both armies there were later elements of monotheistic followers. It does not appear that a religion that we recognized today as Islam really begins to become coherent until 150 - 200 years after Mohammad's death.

If we have learned anything from Natural Evolution and social development, nothing is instantly created, but there is a gradual process of growth. The same appears to be the case with a religion, for it takes time for it to become a coherent organized entity with strong conviction and with a strong foundation to spearhead into the future. It first appears as a pagan-cult and then, when historical circumstance favours it, it may gradually evolve to become an organized religion with its rituals and beliefs, and solidify its dogma within the community to last for many centuries into the future. This happened with Christianity which first appeared as a local Coptic cult and later was adopted by the Roman Empire to become the religion we see today. It took 200 years before we started getting commentaries on the Qur'an and collections of Mohammad's life and sayings through the Haddith which is a natural growth time for social development, based on convincing historical evidence. This is the Natural Evolution process which contains no sudden theistic boost to forward it or to counterbalance it or re-direct it into the future.

The Qur'an could not have been written by the Bedouins living in the desert, for it must have been written further north and within the productive region of Palestine. The Qur'an contains references to large scale agricultural lands of "milk and honey" with products such as olives, oranges, grapes, vineyards and grains (and juicy fruits) that could only have been produced in irrigable and fertile lands, thousands of miles away from the inhospitable, hot and dry desert of the Mecca area. The Qur'an therefore could not have been given by Allah to Mohammad in the dry-lands of Mecca, as Muslims claim. It had to be written by people living in the north of the Arabian Peninsula, who lived and were familiar with irrigable lands, agricultural products and their seasonal cultivation and harvesting, and domestication of dairy animals.

The written myth of Paradise is referred to in the Qur'an as a place close to Mecca; where Adam and Eve were originally rejected from, and has been relocated into the void of the sky, full of lakes and rivers, a land of milk and honey, vineyards and juicy fruits along with the Allah's gift of 72 virgins for each martyr. This imagined and idealized place was typologically re-created from real existing fertile lands with an abundance of fruits and goods. The desolate places of Mecca and Medina were not one of those lands that are described in the Qur'an.

This brief narrative is about a human past in human terms, to map out the historical facts even as these "maps" wrongly lead us into "heavenly places" and sacred lands, a trilogy of religions humans have built in God's land; which He promise the same real-estate to two different peoples (Israelis and Muslims) who now claimed it as their own. Both are ready to kill each other, one in the name of "Israel" and the other in the name of "Palestine." A land where the Jews, Christians and Muslims still fight over the assumed promise God made to mythological Abraham thousands of years ago. Was there really a promise or is it that believers re-write history as they want to believe and are willing to kill and die for their visions of heaven and of the stories that still generate powerful illusions for believers? We can certainly say that the current monotheistic religions were not originally created by God's design, but were raised from a set of historical circumstances. They began from the humble origins of paganism and evolved into organised religions via the Roman Empire, and out of the birth convulsions we witnessed the appearance of the religion of Islam which was born out of the Arab Empire.

There is a general misnamed identity of the people of Arabia by lumping together their national, linguistic, ethnicity' cultural definitions of birth with their religion and faith into one "big pot." For instance, there is a misnamed, or change of identity of, Arab nationality associated with the identity of the religion of Islam, as having been a nationality of Muslims. Let's us clear some general definitions which may help us to undo the deliberate distortion of the Arab nationality with Islamizing the Arab national identity, and thus diminishing any distinction between them. The Arabian people are now identified as Muslims and Arabian historical achievements---before and after Mohammad---are now called Muslim or Islamic civilization instead of Arabian, Persian (Iranian) or Yemeni. This is far from the truth, and the Muslim deception of the Arab civilization follows its long established practice of distortion, linguistic twisting, plagiarism, lies, half-truths and spread of total deception from its beginning to the present. This distortion began about 691 AD in order to give a prominence to the religion of Muslims and place Islam on par with Judaism and Christianity. Greek and Persian philosophies, which were copied and adopted by Islam, have been hijacked to mean "Muslim" philosophy, morality and law. True enough, some of these philosophical, scientific and technological texts were interpreted into Arabic, but do these translations make them Muslim? The claim that Muslims invented this or that is plainly false unless it can be proven that it was the religion of Islam itself that invented them. For instance, an architectural structure, a scientific invention, a biological discovery or a medical cure are just that; human discoveries from Hellenic, Hellenistic from Alexandria, Arab from the House of Wisdom of Bagdad, not Jewish, Christian, Muslim or atheist. Is there a Christian medicine, or a Muslim or Jewish biological discovery? It appears that there is an inherited and perpetual inferiority complex due to the poor historical legitimacy in the claims of superior "Muslim" accomplishments.

Let us begin:

a) An Arab is the nationality—not the religion--of a person born in Arabia, who speaks Arabic and is culturally Arabic-oriented by custom, rituals and cultural tradition;

b) Islam is a religion---not a nationality--which was established in the 7th and 8th centuries and it was eventually adopted by Arabs and non-Arab nationals, such as, the Persians, Turks, Africans or Indonesians. The head of the religion of Islam is the Prophet Muhammad;

c) A Muslim is the follower of the Islam faith who obeys the rules set in the Qur'an, who may speak or may not speak Arabic or share with other Muslims a common cultural identity or a "Muslim" is a religious identity---like a "Christian" or a "Jewish" a "Buddhist" or a "Mormon." If someone believes in the dogma of Islam, or Christianity, or Buddhism; such religious choice does not contain a national identity or an ethnicity of a person; and

d) The Qur'an is Islam's holy book which contains verses and instructions which Muslims around the world may read or obey its instructions.

Historically, the Arab population in the vast Middle Eastern Arabia and Arabian Peninsula were divided (like any other nationality) into the people living mainly in the villages or towns of the Fertile Crescent and those who lived in the barren desert. They may or may not have shared tribal roots or family ties but they share some pagan spiritual beliefs and of course the Arabic language or a mixture of Aramaic with Arabic. The Arab Bedouins were nomadic and lived in the desert which was absolutely their only means of survival and source of subsistence. Major tribes such as the *Qehtaniyan, and the Adnaniyans* were sub-divided into many smaller tribes and those into family clans within each one of them. Due to proper education and civil guidance they were open to superstition, idololatry (like the Kaaba idols or the black stone), local customs and rituals. Attacks on each others' family and tribal merchant caravans resulted in frequent killings and extortion demands. This state of anarchy, lack of law and control, was due to the absence of a central governing power, (a Leviathan) and this became the reason for the desert Arabs to be divided into numerous tribes leading to a nomadic life style. In addition, their reason for their frequent migration, along with their camels and goats, to oasis places in the deserts, was because this was where water and fodder could be found. Where they found water and oasis greenery the Bedouins pitched their tents for awhile and, as soon they found a better place, they assumed their migration once again across the desert.

These wanderings and state of homelessness were occasionally interrupted by indulging in excessive bloodshed with other tribes and obliged them to undertake constant travelling and migration. Their bravery was proverbial! They possessed great skills in horsemanship and archery and seldom committed a breech of honour or trust, which was considered an unpardonable sin. They were devoted to their polytheistic idol-worship, a faith which limited their use of language to their faith only, and this *limitation* applied to their degree of civilization and culture. It is possible that their ways were very ancient and took shape gradually and over a long period of time. It is not possible that their limitations in the Arabic language could be related to the advancement of any literature or scientific discoveries which, otherwise, would have always been a means of progression for arts and letters. That is, most of the nomadic desert tribesmen could neither read nor write and prayers for a specific deity were passed on by oral traditions. Their language limitation, their constant migration, the threat of wars and famine, their geographical isolation from centers of civilization and other reasons prevented them from establishing relations with advanced nations. Their lives can be simply described as having been *"nasty, brutish and short"* (using Thomas Hobbes' words).

There is no doubt about the fact that the Arab desert nomadic tribesmen possessed extraordinary fighting spirit in the art of warfare. This fighting spirit was certainly noticeable by Arab leaders whose tribes were engaging in religious warfare; so much so, that even the leaders of the new religious cult of Islam in the 7th century made wide use of this skill after it was organized. Injecting them with the religious virus of blind faith, this Arab-Bedouin tribal force was ready for killing and martyrdom. Conquering others' land, wealth and resources; as it was a traditional practice for their own survival; these tribesmen were ready to do now, exactly what they have been doing since the dawn of their history. They continued with their habit of bloodshed and pillaging by destroying the life of other tribes, and this did not produce any advancing results on their own cultural development. Self-glorification of their plunder was one of their family's clan or tribal honourable status.

The social conditions of the faithful Arab desert tribesmen, with all the chaos and savagery, could not possibly produce a culture of intellectual powers that the religion of Islam claims to have produced. The tribesmen were sent to conquer the world under the old traditional warfare of pillaging, killing, raping and stealing, but under a new and well organized military imperialist power: the Umayyad Empire of Syria. They were blindly armed with the religious justification that their barbarity was approved and encouraged by the Prophet Mohammad and the religion of Islam. It has also become evident that Islam was the natural outcome of that barbaric tribalism, since from its beginning; it was based on the perpetual dominance of warfare and subjection (Jihad) rather than on its intellectual powers and invention.

Muhammad and his top leaders reflected the tribal realities of murder and of plunder in the Arabian Peninsula in mid 7th century. They represented their groundless beliefs, their illiteracy and tribal superstitions which restrained them from any growth of intellect and advancement. For the next 100 years following Mohammad's death, the religion of Islam had a single objective; to use the tribal mode of warfare to capture as much territory as possible, convert people to Islam or collect taxes for those who wouldn't and build a religious empire based on faith and the rule of religious Shari'a Laws. In each city or nation the Muslim tribesmen conquered, they followed their old established tradition of killing, stealing and destroying what was not in favour of the Muslim dogma, and plagiarized; and claimed as their own, any cultural literary body of medicine and science. In each case the Muslim leaders attempted to alter the world's history in order to belittle non-Islamic Arab civilizations and their historical heritage. Plagiarizing any cultural and scientific knowledge, it remains obvious that scientific and literary progress under Islam remained stagnant due to Islamic faith and its restriction on scientific investigation, for their mode was to conquer, to steal and to plagiarize. Plagiarizing can be seen in the Islamic literature of myths, events and religious characters stolen from the Torah, the Old and New Testaments and Zoroastrian faiths; and from Greek, Hebrew and Persian parables and philosophical narratives. We must therefore do justice and separate the Arab and Middle Eastern accomplishments and scientific and technological inventions, literature and styles of architecture and remove those from *"Muslim"* or *"Islamic"* tribal labels.

Let us begin with a final basic question: were there civilized and cultured non-nomadic Arabs living in the cities of Arabia? Historical evidence has concluded that the Arabs of Syria, Egypt, Persia and Iraq have been civilized for ages; long before the people living in the Arabia Peninsula in the mid 7th and 8th centuries in the largest settlements of Mecca and Medina. The literature of the civilized Arabs was expressed in correct Arabic and Aramaic language and it is evident that they were part of a deep-rooted civilization. Their language was rooted with Hebrew, Syriac, Assyrian and Chaldean, and those languages were inter-connected at one time and had branched out from one language. A relatively peaceful civilization existed in the regions of Saba and Ma'arib of present day Yemen.

Praises of those civilized societies of the Fertile Crescent region were mentioned in the Old Testament by Herodote, and the renowned historian Mas'udi who writes that the cities *"were surrounded by beautiful buildings, shady trees and running brooks."* The main roads in Syria, Persia and Bagdad were covered on both sides by shady trees, the land was developed and prosperous, water was abundant, and its government was stable. Having trade relations with advanced civilizations in many cities of Persia (Iran), Syria, Alexandria and in Bagdad (Iraq) is sufficient to demonstrate that civilization and culture were present in most Arabian cities. External safety factors were in favour of the Arabian cities because the dominant empires of Persia, Rome and Greece ransacked the entire world, including the Middle East, but did not pay any attention to the desolate Arabian Peninsula.

Muslim propagators and apologists have always maintained and declared that Islam is a religion of peace and gives equality to women. But why is there a need for apologists to keep emphasising that Islam is a religion of peace? Britain was the only colonial power with close involvement with Arabia and the social functions of Islam. The late British Prime Minister Winston Churchill (1874 – 1965) is quoted here in reference to the Islamic religious culture under close scrutiny:

"How dreadful are the curses which Mohammedanism lays on its votaries! Besides the fanatical frenzy, which is as dangerous in a man as hydrophobia in a dog, there is this fearful fatalistic apathy. The effects are apparent in many countries. Improvident habits, slovenly systems of agriculture, sluggish methods of commerce, and insecurity of property exist wherever the followers of the Prophet rule or live."

This is the point I was making; that the tribesmen of the desolate desert of the Arabian Peninsula live in a geographical region that they could not possibly experienced cultivation of crops or trade with other tribes from the Fertile Crescent. Under their living conditions, the Bedouin could not appreciate the value of trade and property, much less intellectual and cultural progress. Furthermore on the above quote:

"A degraded sensualism deprives this life of its grace and refinement; the next of its dignity and sanctity. The fact in Mohammedan law every woman must belong to some man as his absolute property—either as a child, a wife or as concubine—must delay the final extinction of slavery until the faith of Islam has ceased as great power among men. Individual Muslims may show splendid qualities. Thousands become brave and loyal soldiers of the Qur'an; all know how to die. But the influence of the religion paralyses the social development of those who followed."

It should be noted the Paul Weston, chairman of the Liberty GB was quoting the above; and for that alone, he was arrested for quoting the famous British Prime Minister: according to the Washington Times.

ILLUSTRATED

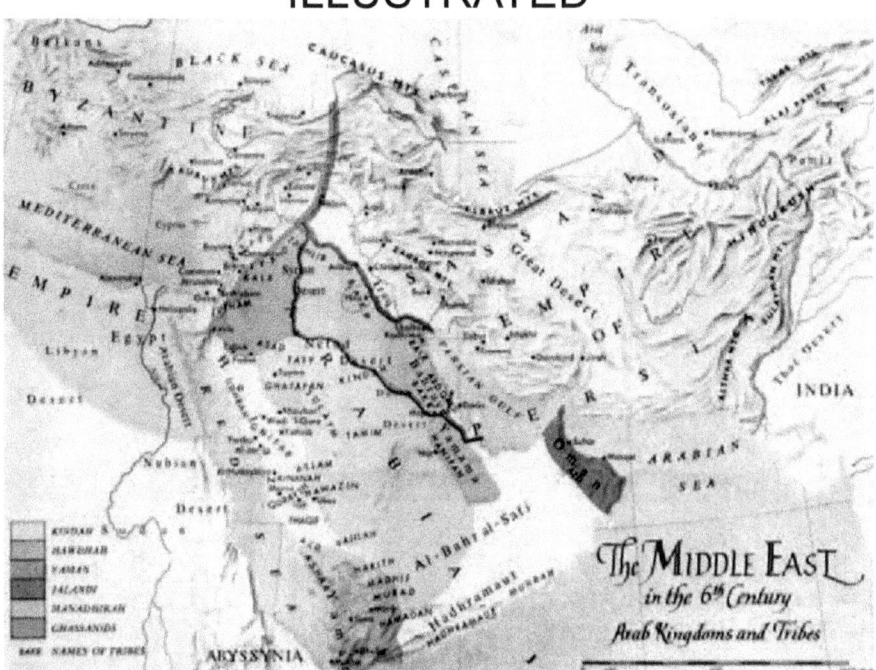

ARABIAN EMPIRE IN THE 6th CENTURY

ILLUSTRATED
DOME OF THE ROCK : MONUMENT OF UMAYYAD CALIPH ABD-AL-MALIK

SYMBOL OF ISLAM

ILLUSTRATED BY ITS OWN CONVICTION : ISLAM IS NOT A RELIGION OF PEACE

TRADITIONAL BEHEADINGS WHICH ARE STILL ENFORCED TODAY

ILLUSTRATED

MALIK'S INTRODUCTION OF MOHAMMAD TO ARABIANS & THE WORLD

ILLUSTRATED ISLAMIC VANDALISM & CRIMES AGAINST HUMANITY

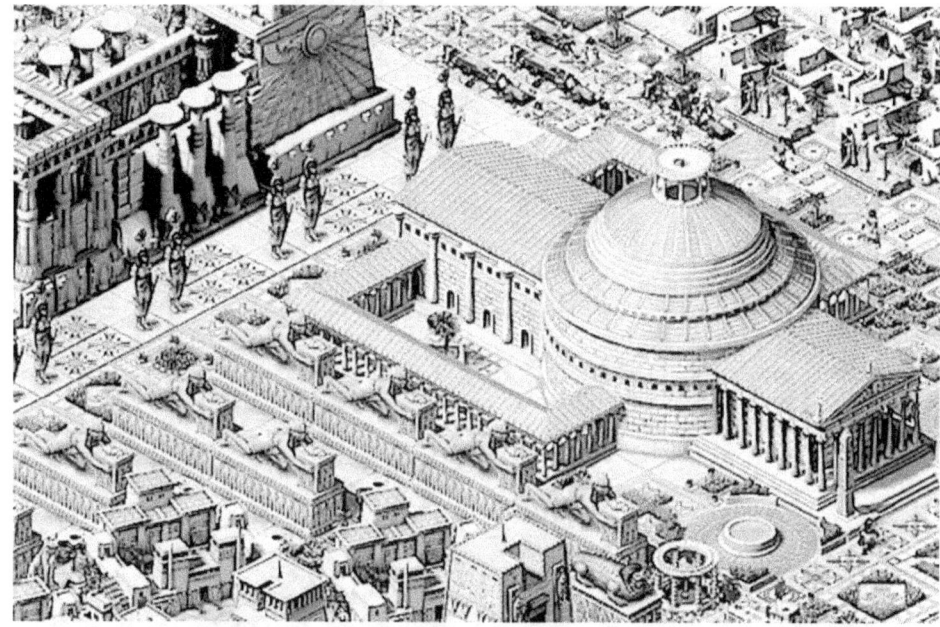

CALIPH OMAR BURNS THE GREAT LIBRARY OF ALEXANDRIA IN 642 AD

ILLUSTRATED
AISHA MOHAMMAD'S 9 YEAR OLD WIFE

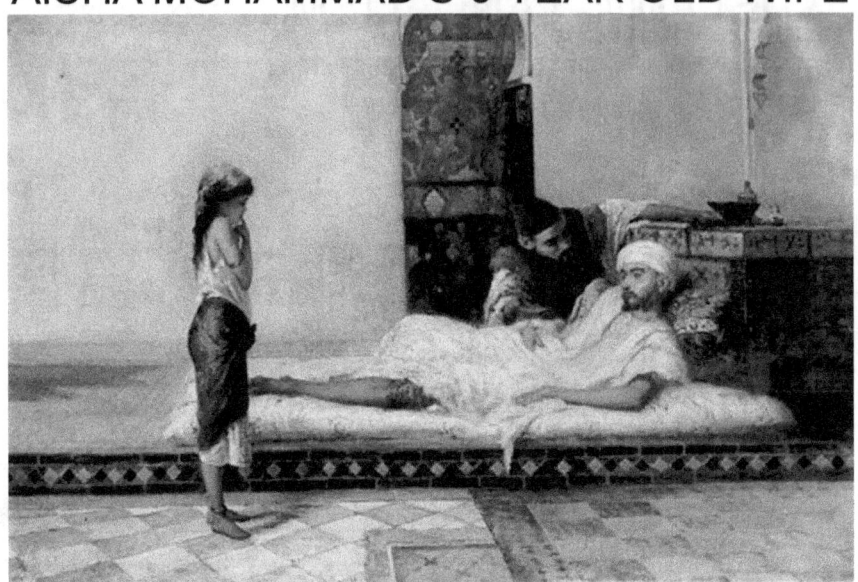

FEMALE SEX SLAVERY

ILLUSTRATED
BOY SLAVERY & PEDOPHILIA

وێنەیەکی زۆر دەگمەنی ساڵی ١٩١٠ کە کوێلەیەکی کچ بە بێ جلو بەرگ ئاو دەکات بەدەستی گەورەکەیدا بۆ دەست نوێژ و نوێژ کردن!!!

ILLUSTRATED
ARABIAN SLAVE MARKET OF AFRICANS

WESTERNER'S SLAVE MARKET

ILLUSTRATED
YEMENI SLAVES PURCHASED IN GOLD

ILLUSTRATED
PLAGIARISING OTHER CULTURES' FINDINGS AS "ISLAMIC" DISCOVERIES

DESTRUCTION OF OTHER CULTURES

ILLUSTRATED
ISLAM COPIED THE JEWISH TRADITION
"DO NOT REPRODUCE LIVING IMAGES"

YET, IN THE FIRST 100 YEARS OF ITS EXISTENCE ISLAM PERMITTED THE REPRODUCTION OF IMAGES OF LIFE

ILLUSTRATED

THE DESOLATION OF THE ARABIAN PENINSULA WHERE MECCA IS LOCATED

REFERENCE OF FIRTILE LANDS IN THE QUR'AN ARE NOWHERE TO BE FOUND IN THE MECCA REGION

INDEX II

Abd al malik, 419
Abraham, 204, 290
Abrahamic monotheistic cult, 347
Abrahamic religions, 399
Abrahamic, 303
Abu bakr, 408
Adaptation, 205, 218
Adornment, 257
Aequitas, 355
Africa, 203
After death, 363
Afterlife, 209, 259, 265, 267, 302, 313
Age of agriculture, 262
Agnostics, 321
Agricultural revolution, 201
Agricultural, 345
Agricultural-tools, 204
Air circulation, 212
Alchemy, 253
Alcoholic drinks, 223
Alexander the great, 402
Alexandria, 346
Al-jazal, 217
Allegorical character, 322
Allegorical creation, 286, 291
Allegorical-literature, 291
Altruistic, 271
Amazon rainforest, 263, 272
Amber, 225
Ancestor-veneration, 213
Ancient pagan, 349
Angel gabriel, 408
Animism, 266
Animist, 214, 223, 252, 253, 261, 263, 267, 270
Anthropoid deity, 262
Antoine lavoisier, 369
Arab bedouin, 407
Arabian peninsula, 204, 251, 256, 400
Arabian-mediterranean, 346
Arch of titus, 297
Art of smelting, 224
Art of war, 345
Art, 257
Artemis, 208, 345
Arts and crafts, 213
As art for art's sake, 260
Ascension, 311
Asherat, 290
Atheist history, 208
Australia, 203
Babylonia, 208
Babylonian empire, 346
Babylonian, 345
Baptism, 396
Barley and wheat, 201
Bedouin tribes, 403
Bedouins, 407
Beliefs, 259
Biblical founders, 353
Biological evolution, 205
Biological, 265
Black sea, 210
Black stone, 404
Bronze age, 261, 226, 251, 224
Bukharin, 409
Burial cave, 219
Burial ceremonies, 204
Burial rituals, 219
Burial, 259
Byzantine coinage, 419
Byzantine empire, 403
Canaanite goddess, 290
Canonical, 410
Carmel mountain, 205
Cave art, 257
Cave artists, 270
Cave arts, 272
Cave symbolism, 262
Caves, 267
Celestial god, 422
Celestial symbol, 421

449

Celestial theistic, 347
Charles darwin, 251
Christian apologists, 326
Christian god, 356
Christianity, 251
Christ-messiah, 300
Civic obedience, 292
Clay pottery, 212
Clement of alexandria, 314
Clergy, 261
Council of nicaea, 363
Constantinople, 406
Cooking pots, 212
Copper carbonate hydroxide, 220
Copper, 220
Coptic christianity, 349
Council of nicaea, 365
Crucifixion, 309, 323
Cult, 265
Cyrus the great, 402
Dark ages, 369
David ben-gurion, 290
Dead sea scrolls, 291, 297, 299, 318
Dead sea, 220, 418
December 25th, 310
Deforestation, 217
Delusional belief, 264
Delusions, 255
Denmark, 218
Desert stories, 255
Dialectical theorem, 349
Dialectical, 252
Dict of milan, 360
Divination, 208
Dna, 257
Dogma, 251
Domitilla, 296, 314
Dorothy garrot, 201
Druid rebel, 295
Eastern europe, 216
Eastern roman empire, 294, 323, 346
Egypt, 207

Egyptians, 254
Emperor flavius arcadius, 395
Emperor maxentius, 355
England, 223
Epipaleolithic, 201
Ethics and morality, 286
Europe, 210
Evangelion, 305
Evolution, 202, 269
Fallacies, 251
Farmers, 207, 211
Fertile crescent, 200, 206, 209, 210, 217, 226, 251, 256, 262, 400, 401, 418
First farmers, 205
Forest, 216
Gadara, 317
Gaius julius caesar augustus, 287
Galilee, 295
Giordano bruno, 327, 369
Gnosis, 310, 321
God as the father, 301
God of light, 310
God's chosen people, 415
God-like status, 294
God-mithras, 301
Golden calf, 271
Golden rule, 202, 286
Gospels, 304, 307, 318
Grapto-keimeno, 207
Graves, 204
Great mother, 262
Greco-arab, 294
Greek colonists, 208
Greeks, 254
Haddith, 409
Hallucinatory herbs, 219
Head hunter, 259
Healers, 225
Heating, 213
Hebrew old testament, 417
Hellenic temples, 392
Hellenistic culture, 326

Hercules, 289
Herders, 211
Herod agrippa ii, 303
Herod agrippa, 303
Herod of chalcis, 303
Historical event, 289
Historiography, 289, 368
History of the war, 298
Hittites, 226
Holy lands, 415
Holy papyrus, 296
Holy sanctuary, 416
Holy-men, 261
Horoscope, 253
Hunter-gatherer, 218, 200, 202, 207, 210, 215, 226, 203, 202
Hypatia, 369
Ibn ishaq, 408
Ice age, 200, 20, 215
Ice glaciers, 204
Iconography, 346
Ideological faith, 352
Illusions, 255
Imams, 261
Incest, 303
Innate moral obligation, 202
Inner-propagations, 312
Intelligent designer, 424
Ireland, 223
Iron age, 226
Irrigation channels, 222
Isaac newton, 251
Isaac, 290
Isis-osiris, 310
Islam, 290
Islamic theocracy, 251
Jacob, 290
Jeff al-ahma, 212
Jerusalem, 296
Jerusalem, 401
Jesus christ, 286, 320
Jesus-man, 309
Jewish temple, 307, 313

Jewish zealots, 292
Jihad, 427
Jordan valleys, 205
Jordan, 211
Joseph of arimathea, 317
Joseph, 290
Josephus bar mathias, 296
Kaaba of mecca, 413
Kaaba, 416
Kastoria region, 346
King david, 290
King solomon, 290
Knife-making, 212
Lactantius, 367
Lake galilee, 205
Laws of nature, 204, 226, 254, 256, 263, 265
Les combarelles, 260
Libraries, 346
Library of alexandria, 328
Life after death, 215, 226, 256, 260
Lime-plaster, 213
Literal evidence, 399
Literal reality, 321
Literal-history, 291
Loom weaving, 212
Magic, 208, 254
Magic, 265
Magicians, 251, 252, 220
Man-god, 311
Material-reality, 261
Mecca, 401
Mechanical tools, 345
Medicine man, 265
Medicine, 226
Mercenary-soldiers, 366
Mesopotamia, 204, 207, 221, 262, 401, 252, 345
Messenger of god, 420
Messiah saviour (kristos issus, in greek), 286
Messiah savour, 286
Messiah, 320

Messiah, 347
Messianic gnostics, 291, 312
Messianic prophesy, 300
Messianic, 295, 297, 414
Metal devices, 345
Metaphorical language, 271
Meteorite-stone, 404
Michael servetus, 369
Military elite, 224
Milvian bridge, 357
Miracles, 302
Monks, 261
Monotheism, 263
Monotheistic sky-god, 266
Monotheistic tribal god, 290
Monotheistic, 290, 358, 414
Moon, 265
Moral instinct, 202
Morality, 209, 250
Morphology of seeds, 205
Moses, 290
Mother-tongue, 269
Mount athos, 392
Mount carmel, 201
Mounted horse, 224
Mystery schools, 310
Mysticism, 289
Myth, 250, 257
Mythical cult, 214
Mythical events, 289
Mythical narrative, 289
Mythology, 213
Mythos, 310
Myths, 203, 256, 265
Natufian's, 203, 201
Natural dyes, 225
Natural selection, 202, 204, 264
Neanderthals, 204
Negative symbolism, 271
Neolithic era, 209
Neolithic house, 213
Neolithic, 265, 268
New age gurus, 265

New testamen, 305
Nomadic herders, 217
North afric, 407
Numismatics, 406
Of christianity, 288
Olympic games, 395
Oral traditions, 266
Osiris, 208
Outer-propagations, 312
Pagan ceremonies, 219
Pagan cult, 214, 222
Pagan deity, 263
Pagan kaaba, 426
Pagan libraries, 327
Pagan mythology, 301
Pagan myths, 320
Pagan spiritualism, 214
Pagan sun, 206
Pagan traditions, 415
Pagan, 250
Painting tool, 258
Palaeolithic age, 268
Palaeolithic revolution, 200
Palaeolithic, 262
Palestine, 251
Parallels, 315
Passage-craves, 219
Passover lamb, 320
Pastorpreneurs, 364
Pattern-meaning, 206, 219, 253, 254
Persian empire, 346
Persians, 254
Personal faith, 321
Philo of alexandria, 303
Physical-jesus, 309
Pica graves, 223
Pioneers, 217
Plagiarism, 415
Plagiarized verses, 424
Plaster floor, 213
Plaster material, 213
Polytheism, 208, 263, 290
Polytheist religions, 403

Polytheist, 252, 323
Polytheistic deities, 266
Polytheistic gods, 358
Polytheistic religion, 207
Polytheists, 302
Pontifex maximus, 287, 301
Pontius pilate, 323
Pope of rome, 287
Positive symbolism, 271
Priestly caste, 208
Priests, 261
Princess berenice, 303
Rabbinic judaism, 293, 297
Rasulians, 220
Rebels, 292
Red ochre, 260
Red pigment, 258
Redeemer, 294
Religion, 265
Religious cult, 353
Religious extremism, 321
Religious title (the messiah), 286
Religious title (the saviour), 286
Religious virus, 434
Religiousness, 288, 349
Religious-title, 286
Resurrection, 323
Resurrection, 311
Ritual, 257, 250, 266, 349
Roman capital punishment, 309
Roman customs and laws, 307
Roman empire, 287, 346
Roman god, 287
Roman imperial cult, 286, 293, 294, 296, 323, 324
Roman imperial cult's, 354
Roman laws, 291
Roman literalists, 312
Roman propaganda, 308
Roman senate law, 346, 287
Roman senate, 301
Roman state pacifist philosophy of the 1st century, 286
Roman state religion, 287
Salt mine, 221
Saul of tarsus, 348
Saviour messiah, 286, 324
Saviour of israel, 316
Saviour-christ, 300
Scandinavia, 223
Scotland, 223
Seaweed, 225
Secular story, 286
Self- delusional prophets, 251
Senate laws, 305
Settled farming, 219
Shamans, 207, 252, 257, 261
Shari'a laws, 435
Sheep fleece, 225
Shelters, 201
Sicarii, 292, 314
Sickle, 201
Sirens, 289
Sky-god, 251
Slaves, 250
Slaves, 349
Slingshot, 202
Socio-biological, 207
Solar mythology
Solar mythology, 206
Son of god, 301, 320
Son of man, 313
Sorcerer, 261
Sorcerer-prophet, 296
Southern greece, 209
Spirits, 251, 252, 253
Spiritualism, 257, 265
St. Pau, 303
Star of rasule, 222
Stars, 223
State of nature, 263, 265
State religion, 287
Statuettes, 257
Stoic myths, 303
Stone age, 253, 261, 265
Stone housing, 212

Stone tooling, 267
Stone-chisels, 212
Stone-killing, 202
Stone-tools, 202
Story-telling, 265, 266
Straw-baskets, 212
Street-orators, 347
Sun god, 356
Sun, 206, 209, 223, 265
Sun-god cult, 291
Sun-god, 206, 226
Superstition, 252, 256, 263, 251, 266, 421
Symbolic image, 353
Symbolic ritualism, 258
Symbolic, 220, 252, 266
Symbolism, 213, 253, 257, 264, 268, 272, 311
Tel megiddo, 366
Temple of asclepius, 392
Temple of serapes, 348
Temple priest, 265, 252
The alexanders, 324
Theist, 289
The contemplative life, 303
The epistle, 303
The polytheist élites, 352
The roman catholic church, 288
Theism, 264, 354, 250, 257
Title-god, 287, 300, 299
Titus flavious, 314, 293
Token clay-balls, 221
Towns, 211
Tribal cults, 251
Tribal myth, 290

Tribal societies, 260
Tribalism, 345
Triumph of titus, 301
Tunnel-shafts, 212
Typological allegorical, 287
Typological distortions, 308
Typology, 288, 298, 301, 310, 315, 318
Umayyad caliphate, 405
Umayyad coin, 420
Unknown religion, 414
Vases, 212
Virgin-birth, 251
Wall art, 222
Wars of the jews, 293
Wild grain, 205
Winter solstice, 310
Wooden plough, 218
Wooden wheel, 225
Wool, 225
Working poor, 349
World divided, 321
Yahweh, 290
Younger dryas, 204
Younger dryas, 205
Zealots and sicarii, 293
Zealots, 292
Zealots, 314
Zodiac astrology, 253
Zodiac signs, 265
Zodiac signs, 310
Zodiac signs, 321
Zoroaster, 303
Zoroastrian, 413

BOOK II

CHAPTER III
THE NATURAL EVOLUTION OF ATHEISM

This is a narrative about what is often referred to as, the natural evolution of atheism. This is the history of the growing conviction of disbeliever that God does not exist. This is not a mere shadow of doubt in God's existence or "walking with atheists" in order to convince the reader about the moral legitimacy of atheism. This would be inappropriate and vulgar. My own life's experience is dotted with the penalties, dangers and risks of exposing me as an atheist in primitive indigenous communities in the Andean Sierras of South America, when visiting the Shamans in the Amazon Rainforest, and when I was living incognito within a fundamentalist Christian community in Peru. Those are briefly described in my book *Prisoners of Our Ideals* and in the children's book, *"The Call of the Shamans."*

In my travelling around the world's religious sites and schools of thought, talking to historians and scientists, I inevitably discovered that the history of religious faith and atheism seemed to be far more complicated than I originally thought. In the world's mass media we read about people's leap of faith or about religious dogmas that have been questioned and this require me to expose what has been implanted in our thoughts for a number of centuries. My brief conclusion is that most people, who believe in God, believe in the belief of God. Others call themselves "atheists" simply because they are angry at God for not preventing the death of their sick child or a friend's or for not delivering on their wishful thinking. My atheism was not from a point of rejection of anything and my religious upbringing was scarcely something that I needed to rebel from. Perhaps my childhood rebellion was directed towards me being in the Greek Orthodox Church and listening to hums and language that I did not understand instead of playing soccer with my friends or looking at the pretty girls.

I grew up in a European city with a large surviving Jewish population. Along with my neighbourhood Jewish friends, I hardly remember any of us ever thinking or talking about God of any kind. I had no religious motives for being in the church nor did I ever understand that I was made a "Christian." I can now recall that most people who had attended church services, including my parents and my grandparents were "Sunday-Christians" because they knew little or absolutely nothing about the original roots of their religion. For them it was enough to attend Sunday services and light candles, follow traditions and customs, cross themselves a few times, give a hefty donation, and all was now well between them and God. My socialist father was expressing his scepticism about God's existence, and my mother was pleading with him that, if and when the socialists ever took control of the country, could they please leave God alone!

Before me, of course, there were prominent atheist scholars and philosophers who were asking the pertinent questions about the natural history of atheism since classical times such as the Syrian poet *Abu al-Alaa al-Maarri (973-1058) or* the ancient Greek philosopher *Epicurus (BCE)*. It may come as a surprise, but atheism is the world's oldest view of humanity and predates any religion of the last two hundred thousand years. Atheism was present in Africa where human beings were living in small groups and later in larger settlements. The first groups of Homo sapiens (wise men) living in the Palaeolithic Stone Age had acquired stone tools and were aware that they had to depend on themselves to survive in the natural world. They learned from their ancestors how to survive and how to use their stone tools for hunting and to defend their own. None of them had asked where they came from. This was because Homo sapiens needed more complex language to answer such dialectical-material or biological questions. Once they developed and articulated the ability of language they had other important issues to discuss, such as co-ordinating hunting and gathering activities and agreeing about the kind of moral rules they needed to live by to insure the well-being of others, such as the women, children, the old and sick. They know of no God, know nothing of eternity, had no shrines to deposit their emotions and sorrows, and they had no conception of an "intelligent designer."

As the millennia went by, Homo sapiens may have become curious about their physicality or their origins, but we are not aware if they started asking where they came from, as if the "from" was a place beyond this world. But we know, from their cave designs and figurines that they did not come up with meaningless answers, at least not just yet! Humans began leaving Africa and started to populate the rest of the world. Many groups were burying their dead but their burials were not ritual, they were a way of removing decomposed bodies from the community for hygienic reasons. Other groups practiced cremation of their dead which served the same purpose. Pre-historic cave artists painted animals in various states and others painted just their palms because they enjoyed painting. Some depicted animals were painted in a magnified way because each artist had his own taste and ability.

During the Palaeolithic and Mesolithic centuries, humanity lived by its own wits, skills, strength and tool-invention, that is, of its own intelligent creation. It seems ironic, but if God existed during this period of thousands of years, he did not show himself to any one of us on earth. As if, for nearly two hundred thousand years, God was looking down at humanity's progress and perhaps was wondering why (for the last 190,000 years) no one had ever asked him for help. It seems that about six thousand years ago, God decided, on his own accord and for the first time, to get involved and interfere with the affairs of the human race.

The first hard evidence of the existence of political or man-made theism appears about six thousand years ago which confirms that the Egyptian society was becoming religionised by Temple priests and militarists. Although the Egyptian elite created fantastic animal scenes and statues and paid certain pious attention to familiar animals, such as crocodiles, monkeys and snakes, there is no proof that these animals in turn worshiped any celestial body. One may say that dogs worship their owners, but they worship something material. Dogs have no Temples, Churches, Synagogues or Mosques nor Bibles or Talmud nor the Qur'an and no descriptive dogmas to follow; the "God" whom they worship is nothing more than an ordinary living man who feeds them and pets them.

It appears that religion was invented by man sometime during the Neolithic Agricultural Revolution, from seven to five thousand years ago. During this agricultural revolution human groups began to develop into communities and from communities into societies. As time went by, individuals in large communities no longer knew one another anymore, and the desire to dominate and control such large segments of population must have been strong with the elite classes in societies. Man is the only designer of his social affairs and in the process man made them a bit complicated. But to claim that it was God who designed man's social affairs does not make any sense. The theistic opinion is that religion is general and universal and this is promoted from the ancient times by high functionaries of the industry of religion. Yet it is opposed by social philosophers, biologists, writers and archaeologists, tradesmen, travellers and social workers, even rebel Catholic priests and Protestant missionaries in almost every part of the globe, stating that there are societies devoid of organised religion. In some cases philosophers denied the existence of religion because the tenets were unlike the conventional or maybe have, to some extent, something to do with the general definition of religion. Within this scope of definition the mere sensation of fear or the belief that there are probably other invisible beings more powerful than a human is sufficient alone to constitute a religion; then I submit that religion is general to the human race. In some tribes in the Amazon Rainforest there is no existence of God; and everything that cannot be accounted for by common causes is not ascribed to a Sky-God or creation; the sudden death of a family member was caused by a hunting accident or disease, not killed by God. On the whole, therefore, some sort of religion seems to belong to man as man, one type of religion may differ from another as far as lust differs from love, opinion from knowledge, or cartoon from art.

In a historical context, it is important to articulate the natural history of atheism because, in current times, the intense commitments to different forms of monotheist religions have acquired such a strong and dangerous political connotation, especially between fundamentalist Christianity and orthodox Islam. The widespread suspicion cast on atheists or disbelievers is becoming a real threat to free thought. For the politically motivated religious propagators, atheism is not a small and irrelevant group of free thinkers, but a growing social, intellectual and scientific force. They believe that atheism, science and free-thought would be corrosive to their religious dogma and they are worrying about it. I must admit that they are correct! Atheism is corrosive to religious dogma, whose God states that, *"If you do not believe in me, you'll burn in Hell forever."* Contemporary atheists have preserved the long tradition of scepticism, for men and women have been sceptical in God's existence. For instance, *Epicurus 341 – 270 BCE "Is God willing to prevent evil, but not able? Then he is not omnipotent. Is he able but not willing? Then he is malevolent.... Is he neither able nor willing, then why call him God?"*

Is there really no God? If there is really no celestial dimension to our cosmos, then why have people dismissed natural history in so many different cultures around the world? The great majority of human beings recognise the term "God" and the practical form which this term takes is called religion. But the definition of this term is very wide and vague and requires a brief explanation. Its variation follows two paths; either it is a simple recognition of an existing Sky-God in the universal order of both material and moral; or it contains further religious speculation with regards to the hollow claim of the creation of the universe. This is because there are so many different forms of scepticism and free thought? Of course, being an atheist is very complex and questionable; to mean a-theist which begs the question, what is a theist? As for me, I do not believe in any form of religion. I will have nothing to do with the delusion of life-after-death. In according to the heroic figure, the British poet *Lord Byron (1786 – 1824)*, *"there are hundreds of million of people who are miserable enough in this life without speculating upon another."* Strangely enough, it is quite difficult to find a straight- forward book on atheism; including my own, on the shells of religious bookstores. In the case of Islam for example, after 1500 years of establishment, we would hardly recognise any openly sceptical message of its supernatural claim; that the Prophet Mohammad descended on his horse towards the Moon and split it with his sword. One can be sympathetic towards any centuries-old author of atheism; because of the cruel penalties which could be inflicted upon him, who dared question the legitimacy of monotheistic religion? Books on atheism were regarded as "subversive disbelief" and such arguments paradoxically could only be found among believers.

This was because Christianity; since the time of the Emperor *Flavius Titus (39 – 81 AD)*, has continuously been redesigning itself and theologians often formulated the most dangerously sceptical arguments in an effort to test the strength of their faith. As such, these theologians unknowingly furnished future atheists with ready-made intellectual weapons against their religious dogma. Their arguments of beliefs—as mere religious thoughts---would be meaningless unless they were accompanied by certain expression of feelings and participation in rituals, prayers, candle-lighting and religious services. It was the physical expression of such rituals that reinforced the theologians' beliefs, rather than their religious ideology. All of this dramatises the believers' attitude towards this life and the delusional hope in the existence of life-after-death. Their fear of death was but illusionary and meaningless. In the words of the atheist who also influenced Thomas Jefferson, the Greek atheist philosopher Epicurus: *"Death does not concern us, because as long as we exist, death is not here. And when it does come, we no longer exist....Why should I fear death, if I am [existing], then death is not, if death is, I am not. Why should I fear that [which] does not exist, when I do [exist]."* He clearly did not believe in life-after-death.

In one way or another pagan or religious rituals imply the existence of celestial entities, which no one can possibly know; an existence which must be believed instead. Believing, however, implies that one could be wrong about his beliefs, but knowledge implies solid verification towards the existence of someone or something. In religion and politics the notion of believing is a fundamental premise for debating; such as *"I believe in God"* or *"I believe we should not go to war in Iraq."* In political debates, beliefs are about what ought-to-be; referring to moral or ethical premises, human rights, equality or democracy. In the case of religion, however, there is no legitimate moral or ethical debate because issues of morality and ethics were part of humanity long before the invention of religion.

One of the problems we have in telling the story of atheism is that, even in the most primitive form of human community, religious beliefs were almost always eventually associated with authority and power. As those powers became more complex, so were their association with tribalism, clannish or patriotism. Centuries later, nowhere is this association more obvious in the western world today than in Israel and the USA. The religious overlay of patriotism is ingrained in their cultural psyche, which is in a permanent state. More people go to their place of worship than anywhere else. Since 9/11 the religious fever has become more intense in the US. In the case of Israel, the intensity of religious-patriotism is propagated by the claim that *"we are the chosen people"* and because God created a religious overlay of patriotism when he promised the Palestinian real estate to both the Jews and the Muslim Palestinians. The irony is that people in the US have forgotten, or are no longer taught, that their country was founded by secularists and atheists who were escaping from political oppression and religious persecution. Leaders of the American Revolution, Thomas Paine and Thomas Jefferson, were both secularist (deists) but not religious. In fact, the second President of the United State John Adams was an atheist; so were Abraham Lincoln, George Washington, Benjamin Franklin, James Buchannan and James Madison, among others.

US President John Adams (*1797 – 1801) stated that,

"God is in essence nothing that we know off, and until this offal blasphemy is got rid off there never will be any liberal science in the world."

US President Thomas Jefferson (1801 – 1809) declared that,

"The clergy believe that any power confided in me will be exerted in opposition to their schemes, and they believe rightly."

The atheist *US President James Buchanan (1857 – 1861)* states his views on religion as such,

"I have seldom met an intelligent person whose views were not narrowed and distorted by religion."

The views of *US President Abraham Lincoln (1861 – 1865)* on religion were well known in close quarters,

"My only views on the unsoundness of the Christian scheme of salvation have become clearer and stronger with advancing years."

The war in Iraq had a faith-based patriotism, and religion was used as a means of public persuasion, a sort of pagan origin, to call on God with religious verbalisms, and made it seem though that, if one opposed the US militarism, he or she, in fact, opposed the Lord. Right wing fundamentalists are eager for the appearance of a Christian "Ayatollah" and what the disillusioned citizens want, the American Congressional leaders and Presidents tend to provide. You may recall that, in 1987, President George Bush Sr openly declared that American atheists may have questionable rights to American citizenship by stating, *"I do not know that atheists should be considered as* *patriots, nor should be considered as citizens."* It is a well-known fact that no American leader who wishes to enjoy a political popularity could risk being exposed as an atheist. Yet there are a substantial minority of political leaders who hold no religious beliefs but are reluctant to advertise their atheism. This is because the Christian religious ideology is very influential in American public life today, although the Constitution does separate Church and State. This overshadows the non-religious significance of the originators of the American political life.

If we are to judge the standards set by the right-wing George Bush Sr (or even by George W. Bush Jr.), it would appear doubtful that any of the greatest American presidents of the past would have been elected to office today if they were known for being atheists. Of course, it would be wrong to even suggest that the USA is an uncomfortable place for an atheist to live and prosper, and no comparison can be made with Saudi Arabia, Iran or with certain Andean Sierras communities of South America. In Europe, I will feel quite at home as an atheist, especially among those people I meet in the small restaurants and outdoor cafés who have no faith and do not subscribe to any official sanctioned religious-patriotism of their forefathers. It gives me a real sense of ground level perspective of how the average man and woman were affected by religious dogma in their lives. For them and me, some tenets of monotheistic faiths, although most frightening, their bloodstained theological and ideological differences seemed ridiculous.

For instance, the difference between Jews and Christians, who both espouse from the same non-sense of their Abrahamic faith, have historically been shackled together. This created anti-Semitism which has derived from this loony relationship, starting even before the appearance of the misanthropic Protestant demagogue *Martin Luther (1483 – 1546)*, the theological anti-Semitist forefather of Nazism. Once you shackle together two loony theologies such as Judaism and Christianity in the Holy Land's territory, you see the formation of the largest outdoor lunatic asylum of alienated people in the world. They pray day after day to a geriatric and senile celestial God in the sky, pleading for him to send another messiah to apocalyptically save the world. Their religious climax is, of course, the crucifixion. The atheist British physician, writer and social reformer, *Havelock Ellis (1859 – 1939)* stated that, *"The whole religious complexion of the modern world is due to the absence, from Jerusalem, of a lunatic asylum."*

We are surrounded by Christian architectural heritage evident in impressive churches and cathedral sites. History has given religions gravitas, buildings and music; but this is the history of humankind and should not be confused with the buildings, the priests' robes and music belonging to God. This is because these are laboured outcomes of humankind. This is from where the theological myth, depicted in statues and stained glass, was mimetically spread in our minds in a rather misleading way. All the same, when you visit the ancient monasteries and places of worship in Greece, Italy, France and Russia, the images of Christianity are inescapably and undeniably beautiful. Images in religious icons, hand-bound bibles, costumes and ritual celebrations tell a story of Christianity that was never there. This includes the Cambridge stained glass images of the *Heroine of Hell*—the *Anastasis* (in Greek "resurrection") where Jesus goes down to Purgatory and smashes down its doors to free Adam and Eve! This of course is not mentioned in the Gospels but it is part of the ongoing sequence of the re-invention of the Christian myth. These are stories of mythical or allegorical events that are deeply ingrained in the minds of the literalist Christian believers. But to deny the artistic depicted beauty in these icons would be no more than the result of the visitors' impoverished imagination. But I do not think these images and worship of God represent the truth! In *Aristophanes (446 – 386 BCE),* own words, *"Surely you don't believe in the Gods, What's your argument? What's your proof?"*

What we discover, when we are looking for the names and origins of the first historical atheists, who began to question the origins of our cosmos, is that the Greek philosophers were asking materialist questions when they had no scientific reason to do so. Yet they correctly believed that all cosmic matter was made of atoms and began to question the nature of reality itself. It was with the questions raised by the ancient Greek philosophers that we were allowed to enter the core essence of the history of atheism. In our quest to unravel the literal wisdom of atheism we discovered the role of early Christianity's "heavy-handed" or malevolent attitude towards the ancient Greek culture and civilisation. The end result was that it simply achieved the physical destruction of the ancient civilisation of Hellenism.

There is well documented history of St. Paul's personal fanatical extremism against anything or anyone who was on the opposite side of Paul's theistic objectives. As a Roman polytheist Paul was against the Jews' monotheism and the Christian-Jews in Judea and Palestine. By his own training as a Roman tax collector, Paul was accustomed to persecuting anyone who did not pay taxes—mainly the Messianic Jews. Paul had a "legalistic" mind and was able to formulate legal tax-offences against able tax-payers. Organised and logistically astute, Paul used his personal practical skills successfully. This means that when he became Christianised, Paul used his personal traits against the polytheists who he so devoutly once supported. Everywhere Paul travelled, he organised scattered Christianised groups by having them choose able leaders, collecting donations, and thus propagating the spread of Christianity without ever referring to Jesus Christ since he never existed. His promotional activities were with zeal and were more technical rather than theological. In other words, theology was a secondary objective rather than his main goal, which was to organise, train and create the hierarchical leadership and structure within Christianised groups.

In the year 51 of the 1st century, Paul went to Athens, Greece by boat. What Paul saw was that the Greeks were worshiping multiple Gods and had Gods for every reason and season, pagan rituals, agora of street philosophers and notable philosophical schools of thought of every stripe. Books on *Periergos* (*Curious* in Greek) were books of knowledge and ancient technology. Such books included pagan magical arts which were promoted by ancient Greek writers. Periergos books were publicly burned and their writers were persecuted by Paul and Roman authorities. It should be noted that the study of pagan arts by Athenians was prohibited and persecuted under Paul's zeal in Judea, Palestine and Greece. Sculpture-artists, poets and writers of mythology, private tutors, music and theatrical performances, well-paid street-consorts and builders, temple-priests and future-tellers were all present and part of the cultural center of Athens. Some gentile Athenian groups had already been Christianised to Paul's surprise. But the power-base of those who were opposite to Paul's theological ideology was far greater than those of Judea and Palestine. He immediately began to organise mass rallies against anything that was opposite to Christianity. However, Paul soon noticed that spreading ideology was not enough, for a major event was needed to generate massive public interest. Paul knew from past experience the power of money, that "money sells", that money was a powerful incentive for the average Athenian person. In massive rallies Paul offered silver coins---drachmas or shekels to anyone who brought books of knowledge---magic books as he called them-- to be burned in bonfires. In **Acts 19:18, 19,** *"Many of those who practiced magic brought their books together and began burning them in the sight of everyone, and they counted up the price of them and found it 50.000 pieces of silver."* There are multiple references of payments made to individuals who brought their pagan books for burning; one silver coin per book, totalling 50,000 silver coins for an equal amount of books. A labourer earned one silver coin per day's work. The question is where Paul did come up with such a tremendous amount of money to disperse for book burning? Was this an act of religious barbarism and the beginning of the destruction of Hellenic civilisation? Were there other zealous barbaric acts against those Middle East cultures which stood in the way of Christianity? Did Flavius Titus and the Roman Imperial Cult use their wealth of silver coins and invent the new religious-philosophy (later, Christianity) as means of pacifying any rebellious Jewish Messianic hostile opposition?

Ephesus was a coastal city of the Roman Empire in Asia (present day Turkey) and was the most easily accessible city, connected by land and sea with the chief cities of the province. Its location therefore favoured its religious, political and commercial trade; it had an exceptionally fine climate, an unusual fertile soil, all of which presented a most advantageous field for St. Paul's religious adventures. Under the rule of the Greek civilisation, ancient pagan rituals gradually supplanted those of the Orientals, and the Greek language was spoken in place of the Asiatic. St. Paul came to the city of Ephesus and became known to all the Greeks and the Jews spreading his rhetoric of Hell and Fire, and fear fell upon all the superstitious people who turned over their pagan sculptures and their books of knowledge for burning. Christianised groups possessed valuable lands, they controlled fisheries, and its priests were the bankers of their enormous revenues. Because of their power and influence, the common people stored their money for safe-keeping and the early Christians became the bankers of the new religion. God had nothing to do with such a novice commercial development.

In the British Museum, the Acropolis Marbles are on display for international visitors to view the sculptured marvels of the ancient Greeks. They were removed from the Acropolis in 1801 by Lord Elgin who discovered them buried in mud. In the process of cleaning them, strong chemicals were used to "white" those more for aesthetic and commercial reasons; and in the process they were further damaged due to the chemical reaction with the marble. They were removed from a civilisation with which we no longer have any contact at all. What visitors see today are the ruined fragments of statues which were defaced some years following the adoption of Christianity by the Roman Emperor Constantine in 325 CE. From this point on, Christian power grew and their first aim was to smash pagan temples and rampage through the streets, while cultured pagans were appalled by their vandalism.

The Eastern Christians attacked the Parthenon sculptures, scratched and defaced Greek history and, in this way, they wrote their own. They hacked its statues to pieces, mutilated and the sculptures of a number of metopes in other parts of the Acropolis' Temple. These statues were seen as an idolatrous threat to the new religion in the Eastern Roman Empire. Although idolatry was seen as the principal threat to Eastern Christianity, the culture represented by these sculptures contained un-illustrated themes which later were recognised to be much greater threat, that is, the Greek pagan thinkers and atheist philosophers. These sculptures were seen as expressing subversive doubts of the role of the celestial or supernatural being in the natural world.

When we are looking for the atheists of the ancient world, we identify men who began to make extraordinary claims about the material nature and origins of the cosmos. Philosophers such as *Democritus,* who lived 400 years before Christ, felt that happiness and contentment was humanity's ultimate objective, and that all matter was made of atoms or individual particles. Democritus materialist *"Theory of Atoms"* held that everything is composed of "atoms" in infinite numbers, in motion, and the "atoms" are indestructible; have always been and always will be. This included the soul; if the soul or *pnevma* ever existed, and that everything that exists today, existed forever, therefore the earth was never created. If we can see through the mist of history, can we ask, is this the beginning of atheism? Of course, atheism means something different in polytheistic versus monotheistic societies with religious institutions. In polytheistic societies, individual theism or atheism was not a threat because there were no organised religions per se. In monotheistic societies, we have to ask, who is threatened by atheism? This question is normally associated with the organised religion of Christianity and how it reacted to put the deviance back in line. You see, if there is no church as it was in polytheistic societies, then things might look different. To be an atheist in the ancient polytheistic world was much easier because of the originality of new ideas and new questions posed by philosophers, which were impressive and quite alive.

The first Greek philosopher who addressed the question of the existence of God or Gods was Epicurus. His arguments against the existence of God or Gods are as vivid and powerful today as when they were first expressed in 300 BCE. In addition to his doubts about the existence of God, Epicurus clearly did not believe in the life-after-death. This notion was celebrated 400 hundred years later by the atheist Roman poet *Lucretius (99 – 55 BCE)*, *"Long time men lay impressed with slavish fear. Religious tyranny did domineer at length the mighty one of Greece began to assert the liberty of men."* Was this an atheist warning against the domineering tyranny of upcoming religion of Christianity? Lucretius spent a considerable amount of time and arguments showing people that a God or Gods have no role in our lives, that our *"Fear is the Mother of all Gods. Nature does things spontaneously and by herself without their meddling."* It is encouraging knowing that in the ancient world there were thoughtful people who were beginning to express doubts about the existence of deities or about those who said they did believe in them. Another prominent Greek philosopher,

Aristotle (384 – 322 BCE) said *"A tyrant must put the appearance of uncommon devotion to religion. Subjects are less apprehensive of an illegal treatment from a ruler whom they consider god-fearing and pious. On the other hand, they do less easily against him, believing that he has the Gods on his side."* On the subject of religious tyranny and peoples' apprehension, the Roman philosopher, orator and political theorist, *Tullius Cicero (106 – 43 BCE)* tented to agree on peoples' apprehension or fear, *"On the subject of the nature of the Gods, the question is do the Gods exist or do they not, for it is difficult to deny that they exist. I will agree, if we were arguing the matter in a public assembly. But in a private discussion of this kind, it is perfectly easy to do so."* The Roman statesman Lucius Annaeus Seneca (4 – 65 CE), *"Religion is regarded by the common people as true, by the wise men as false and by the rulers as useful."*

Once the Roman Emperor Constantine adopted Christianity as the official religion of the Empire, pagan philosophy as a whole became somewhat suspiciously subversive. In fact the ancient Parthenon Temple of the Goddess of Wisdom, Athena, partly demolished in the 6th century, and what remained became one of the earliest Christian churches devoted to the Virgin Mary. At the same time, on the orders of Emperor Justinian, the Greek schools (the Philosophical Academies) were abolished. Occupying the religious establishments of others was a common occurrence amongst theocratic rulers, such as, the Orthodox Christian Church of *Agia Sofia* in Constantinople (present day Istanbul); Turkey was converted into a Mosque after it was captured in 1453 by the Ottomans. The Muslim *Dome of the Rock* was built in 691 CE on the foundations of the Jewish *Temple Mount* which is located in the Old City of Jerusalem. The thousand years that followed the abolition of the Greek philosophical schools has come to be known as the Catholic Church's Dark Ages, a somewhat cliché label, but nevertheless true enough because it is near impossible to eradicate clichés. Nevertheless, it was the Arabs and the Persians who re-emerged the long-lost radical materialism of the Roman and the Greek philosophy. The Arabs also concluded that all phenomena, including human consciousness are the result of material interactions. These materialist ideas in the 6th and 7th centuries were, of course, inconsistent with both of the tyrannical religions of Christianity and Islam; thus the ideas of materialism became dangerous to expresses them openly.

In the historical evolution of atheism or sceptical thinking that emerged out of Greece and Rome, we are discovering that by the 5th century they were facing serious challenges. Christianity had taken over as the official religion of the Roman Imperial Cult; becoming the Roman Catholic Church and closing down those Greek philosophy schools that encouraged a rational materialistic view of the cosmos. As a result, Christianity dominated and controlled all rational thought for more than a thousand years without having to justify to anyone its irrational theology. During this time, Christianity was so successful that it appears there was no room for sceptical thinking, much less openly declared atheism. Despite Christianity being so successfully powerful in Europe, we now witness that many of its grand churches remained unused or un-occupied. It still remains historically hidden as to why this is so. Of course, it is very difficult for someone, like you and I in the 21st century, to know peoples' past general mentality, especially attitudes towards religion. Widespread ignorance due to lack of education in reading and writing was a common phenomenon. Since ancient times, only the priests, wealthy and influential people were privileged to various levels of education. Education, therefore, was the privilege of the few and the books which were written by the privileged few were responses to others' of the elites and educated lot. The common people were not regarded as part of the common-denomination. They were simply living *"from hand to mouth"* as John Locke stated much later. For instance, in 13th and 14th century England or France, many a common people attended mass in churches, but the thoughts and inspirations of these blameless illiterate men and women left no marks on records. But, given the fact that now-a-days nearly everyone of us can read and write, future historians could uncover records of opinions and beliefs of today's ordinary people.

But, to understand the insights of the religious mentality of the past, we need to look at the way religious ideology was communicated to the ordinary people, and for what purpose. The church leaders knew that the ordinary people were illiterate, so they needed to find an effective way to spread their religious ideology by looking at pictures, where each picture was worth a thousand words. Relating messages through pictures was a common practice of the time. Shop keepers had signs of "Bread" painted over their bakeries, seamstresses had signs of "Needle and thread;" and blacksmiths had signs of "Hammer and Tongs," and so on. The signs' message was unavoidably direct, leaving no room for mistake. But the churches' wall pictures and icons contained subliminal messages which were simplistic and easy to accept. In the Roman Catholic and Greek Orthodox Churches, pictorial stories in the form of frescoes and icons are still used as a means of communication with their followers. Of course, the original intentions of pictures were to communicate religious messages, but they gradually became objects of theistic worship. Some14th century Catholic frescoes, such as, in Padua, Italy, describe the entire biblical myth of Christ from birth to crucifixion and to resurrection. With the astonishingly rapid spread of Christianity, religious beliefs in Europe were far reaching and change its character irreversibly. Although it took some time for the meaning, the creed and sacrament to develop out of these frescoes, soon these pictures followed an organised and centralised dogmatic authority. And instead of the free thinking and unauthorised version style of themes, these pictures soon became an organised sacred text, maintained by central ecclesiastic authority, supervised and willingly well-financed. They were strictly interpreted by a dogmatic authority, and as such, the pictorial meaning of the once loose folkloric pagan antiquity, these Christian images of Saints and God began to emerge as articles or objects of idolatric faith by giving them honour and worship.

The central message of religious icons, which was inherited from the Jewish religion, was that there was one and only one God, who had created the cosmos with the specific purpose of giving his most favoured creature a home and to exercise the moral principle of choice. The next distinctive feature of the story is that it stands in contrast to the undated episodes of pagan mythology and symbolism. However, the mythological events depicted and described in the New Testament appeared to have taken place in a recent past. The story of Jesus is presented from the beginning (birth) to the end (resurrection), in an extraordinary documentary form which leaves no room for a believer to doubt the credibility of the story. Even though the frescoes' subliminal message swings from the extreme-mundane to the extreme-miraculous, doubting the story would have been almost inconceivable. Such pictorial sequence of mythological events must have dominated the mentality of the city poor, the country peasants and merchant classes in the 14th century.

In contrast to Judaism and Islam, which prohibited pictorial representation of living things, the Roman Catholic and Greek Orthodox Church were thriving on it. The result was that the Christian imagination was almost surrounded by an impenetrable psycho-drama of religious imagery. During the Middle Ages, even secular buildings such as government ministries were surrounded by religious images of the town's or tradesman's protector. By the 15th century there appears to have been a secular trend of expressing religious scepticism in a modest form. This was due to the rising influence of people who travelled in other parts of the world and encountered oriental faiths that worshiped no God. They discovered diversified beliefs that they did not share. Buddhists did not believe in a personal God or life after death, resulting in the rise of comparative philosophical scepticism or atheism. Does this classify Buddhism as being an atheist or a secular faith? It also became clear to Europeans that there were other worlds, in previously undiscovered parts of Asia and the Orients, where the inhabitants were not aware of Christianity. In the early 17th century, Jesuits who had just returned from China had to reconcile themselves with the fact that there were other civilisations in which the concept of monotheism, or monotheistic Christianity, played no role. These Oriental faiths sustained morality and ethics to millions of people for millennia without injecting fear and insult into its followers.

But there was another emerging secular trend that had its roots in the past Greek, Roman and Middle Eastern paganism. Those were ideas from the past whose roots lay in various forms of popular pagan scepticism and materialism. The appearance of this trend of popular materialism had its roots in pre-Christian ideas from Epicurus, Lucretius, Democritus and others. Remember that; from Lucretius came the materialist idea *that, "Fear is the Mother of all Gods. Nature does all things spontaneously, by herself, without the meddling of Gods."* The newly converted Christian Roman Empire commenced its strenuous efforts to "Christianise" some of the earlier pagan philosophies by reviving ideas from Aristotle's and Plato's known surviving works. These ideas were valued because they conveniently supported elements of Christian theology. As for the materialist philosophers such as Lucretius, Epicurus and Democritus; they were simply ignored and dismissed as having been "atheist" villains. However, the emerging Arabs philosophers of the Middle East, and later in Spain, had managed to preserve the entire body of Aristotle's work from Christian destruction and vandalism. As such, Spain's scholars of Cordoba, such as *Averroes (1126 – 1198)*, and the *12th and 13th century Schools of Translators* in Toledo, Spain, began to recognise in the works of Aristotle, aspects of his philosophical thoughts that were not so conveniently consistent with Christian religious beliefs at all. For instance, Aristotle's ideas that the world always existed and that there might not be an immortal soul, were obviously in contrast to the Jewish, Christian and Muslim beliefs in: a) the immortality of the soul, and b) God's creation of the cosmos.

Averroes's version of Aristotle's work were soon to be translated into Latin and spread throughout Europe, especially in Italy. The re-translating of most of Aristotle's 42 books from ancient Greek to Arabic text then into Latin occurred over the span of 100 years, from the middle of the 12th into the 13th century. Thus the preservation of ancient Greek ideas was a major contribution by Arabian civilization. In Padua, the ecclesiastic authorities reacted to the author's description of the pervasiveness of the Christian faith. For the next five centuries, intellectual and thoughtful Europeans would

gradually transform Aristotle's ancient ideas into what eventually would emerge; a confident modern atheism. In fact, it is quite difficult to imagine the intervening thought which linked the religious frescoes with the profane secularism of the new schools of science and technology. It was the starting point of the gradual erosion of the monolithic confidence of the Christian religion. Of course the conventional view was that geological, biological science and the mechanical technology during the Industrial Revolution were the most significant factors in undermining the monolithic religious faith. The world's first orbital flier, the Russian cosmonaut Yuri Gagarin, speaking from orbit on April 12, 1961, said *"I do not see any God up here."*
It is true that early Christianity had inherited the Ptolemaic concept which claimed that the Earth stood at the center of universe and that the Sun, the Moon and planets were revolving around it. *Claudius Ptolemy (90 – 168 AD)* was a Greco-Egyptian writer, an astrologer and interpreter of *Zodiac Signs*. The Zodiac (in Greek, the *Circle of Animals*) was invented by ancient Egyptian astrologers. It took 12 lunar cycles (i.e. months) for the Sun to return to its original position. For Ptolemy, all the planetary bodies and their movements were God's creation. Of course it was not difficult for people in the Middle Ages to believe that the Earth was the center of the universe because they could "see" it happening all around them: the Sun went around the Earth every day, there was a daily "sunset" and "sunrise," the Moon also went around the Earth every night and so did the stars. According to God, man was His supreme creature, the special creation of one God. If that creature was the epicentre of everything God created, then why shouldn't man believe it to be true? Of course, due to much later geological and biological discoveries of the origins of life, man's delusion was about to be modified.

Beginning with the discoveries of the Polish *Nicolaus Copernicus (1473 – 1543), Galileo Galilei (1564 – 1642), and Johannes Kepler (1571 – 1630)*, it soon became apparent that the Earth and all the planets revolved around the Sun, of which the latter was one single star among millions of other stars. It must be quite difficult for current man today to imagine how unsettling Copernicus's ideas must have been to Christians when they were first published, *"On the Revolutions of the Heavenly Spheres" (De Revolutionibus Orbium Coelestium)* in 1543. Copernicus identified the concept of a heliocentric solar system in which the Sun, rather than the Earth, is the center of our solar system. It is hard to underestimate the importance of Copernicus's work, for it challenged the age-long views of the way the universe worked. The realisation that our planet Earth, our solar system and even our galaxy are quite common phenomena in the heavens provided a sobering view of the universe. The false reassurance of God's Genesis was gone, and the new cosmological reality of the world, as less secure and comfortable, came into being. As such, Copernicus's work was not completely divorced from the ancient Aristotelian views: that the planets were assumed to move in circles around the sun.

In the biological sphere of medical science, new ideas began to change man's perception of his own body. Belgian anatomist *Andreas Vesalius (1514 – 1564)*, published research compiled from dissecting human bodies and illustrations accurate human anatomy. The book *"De humani corporis fabrica libri septem" (1543)* is a set of illustrated books on human anatomy. This publication was presented to the medical researchers and students for their own studies. By coincidence, 1543 was also the year that Copernicus published his own work on the heliocentric structure of the universe. His book, *"On the Revolutions of the Heavenly Spheres" (1543)* was based on the alternative model of the Ptolemy's universe. This was a year of these two remarkable scientific discoveries, and the fall of Eastern Christianity of Byzantium into the hands of the Ottoman Muslim in 1543.

Although the Christian ecclesiastical authorities of the day were suspicious, it is, nevertheless, quite difficult to identify any religious scepticism on the part either of the two scientists: the anatomist Vesalius and the astronomer Copernicus. Since the human body was believed to be God's finest handywork, the book's illustrated anatomical details of the human body simply reaffirmed the ingenuity of God's design, and also because the same principle was held for the structural design of the universe. Without a doubt, both scientific works must have caused a dent in the rigid crust of the Christian dogma, although not yet on the authority of the biblical scriptures. Most of the students and scientists of both pioneers were devoted Christians; and despite the fact that their scientific research was somewhat mechanical and obeying the Laws of Nature, it was still an undeniable confirmation that this was God's creation. For a long period of time, the description of the mechanisation of the world co-existed, relatively, quite comfortably with the belief in God.

The French atheist, rebel and writer, Victor Hugo (1802 – 1885) author of *Les Miserables,* was in favour of science and of the masses' secular education, and for both to be out of the Churches' grip. He stated, *"There is in every village a torch, a school teacher, and an extinguisher, the priest."* If we consider the profound achievements of Copernicus, Vesalius and Galileo simultaneously, we also find the Church's indifference or anti-scientific ignorance towards these achievements. Was that because there might have been Popes and Cardinals, Bishops and Priests that were far too stupid, apathetic or plain ignorant to see that science and scientific education could help the general population, including their believers? But the clergy were actually not acquainted with the new advances of medical, biological and geological science; they perhaps presumed that there was a thriving conspiracy, by people of science who were sceptics. The leaders of the faithful, or of the status quo, assumed that the scientists were far too dominated by their own secular curiosity.

It was known then that the religious authorities were very much connected with the social, political and economic powers of the day. Mildly put, science of the day was far too curious for its own good, and that intense scientific-curiosity breathed from the elites a religious contempt. Without a doubt, however, the scientists' curiosity and observation were far more credible than religion's revelation about God's creation. This was so elegantly put by Galileo Galilei against the Church's anti-science stand, *"In question of science, the authority of a thousand is not worth the humble reasoning of a single individual...To command the professors of astronomy to refute their own observations, is to command them not to see what they see and not to understand what they understand."* Did Galileo understand that if you could reason with religious people, there would be no religion? It is commonly known that Galileo was arrested by the Church's inquisition and was pressured to recant his scientific observations. But Galileo refused to recant his views about the universe and was subsequently confined to house arrest for the rest of his life. It took 342 years (1984) for the Roman Catholic Church to apologise to Galileo for its stupidity and the injustices imposed on him during his lifetime. Galileo reasoned that, in the field of science and scientific observations, the delusional concept of religion was irrelevant. It is also true that scientists in the Middle Ages had no difficulty reconciling their science with religion. It was the Church's anti-science dogmatism that lead to the arrest of the Dominican friar and cosmological theorist *Giordano Bruno (1548 – 1600)*. Bruno was a devoted follower of Galileo's universal theories. Bruno was imprisoned and tortured for eight years before he was burned alive in Rome's public market. This barbaric act shows that it was the Church that behaved with vicious brutality, as if there was an inevitable conflict between science and faith.

This was a time when scientists were redrawing the universe and for that they were prosecuted by the powerful Roman Catholic Church. However, simultaneously, something dramatic was happening within Christianity that was paving the path towards atheism. This, of course, was the Reformation in which radical clergy, which were once the fabric of the Christian dogma, now paved the way for a permanent ecclesiastical schism. This caused further schisms in the monolithic Roman Church which continued to this day. You see for the first time in its history, Roman Christianity was falling apart and was no longer this monolithic Roman State Religion, as it was during its invention under the guidance of the *Roman Imperial Cult,* the Jewish turncoat *Joseph Ben Matityahu* (alias *Titus Flavius Josephus)* (31 – 100 AD) and Emperor *Flavius Titus (39 – 81)* era of the 1st century. As for potential atheists, these schisms was seen as solid indications that perhaps they had human causes rather than God's preferences for one sect over another or that, perhaps, none of the dogma was true.

The new religious sects, the *Anabaptists* and the *Unitarians* for instance, were regarded as being radical agnostics or little short of atheists and were persecuted by both the Protestant and the Catholic Church. The Anabaptists are the direct descendants of the *Amish, Hutterites* and *Mennonites religious sects*. Many of these sects were forced to flee the Russian Orthodox Church persecutions, ending up around the world, including in North and South America. Many sects regardless of their protestations to the contrary, were still widely regarded as being atheist. The Unitarian believers who insisted on their Unitarian faith of normative ethics and moral actions, were accused of heresy and burned alive at the stake. The prominent Unitarian *Matthew Hammond,* who, in May 1579, was accused of heresy and burned at the stake by the Church of England, was one of them. Hammond was accused of denying Christ as the Saviour and for that his ears were cut-off and he was then burned alive in Norwich Castle. Hammond proclaimed that *"Christ is not God, not the saviour of the world but a mere man, a sinful man and an abominable idol. All who worship him are abominable idolaters and Christ did not rise again from death to life nor did he ascent into heaven."* The denial of Christ as a supernatural being was enough to cause Hammond's tragic death although he was not prepared to call himself an atheist. This is a contradictory period of denials and accusations of heresy which lasted over two centuries. During this time of ambiguity the Unitarians were denying the existence of the supernatural and simultaneously also denying being atheists.

Intellectual opinions on atheism at that time ranged around the speculative proclamations about whether atheism itself existed or not. The confusion or contradiction arises from the same ecclesiastical authorities who ferociously hunted down atheists and atheism, yet were the same authorities that were denying that atheism existed in the first place. As for the atheists then, as it is today, the denial of God's existence is simply impossible to prove, and therefore the logic of the theists' argument follows, that atheism does not exist. The general premise of the theists' was that many people were pretending to be atheist or that any serious person would not adopt such vile position. Those pretend atheists simply needed more time to come to reason and their senses. The atheists' arguments, of course, had their limitations by the fact that they could not argue for the non-existence of non-existent entities, such as, "flying-witches," "unicorns," "monsters," "miracles," or delusional beliefs in the human mind. This much they knew, but they did not know of the necessity for man to control his mind's thoughts.

Atheism therefore, was regarded as a derogatory social label which a number of prominent people tried to escape and some are still trying to avoid. Prominent atheists such as Sam Harris and Jonathan Miller, the late Christopher Hitches and Richard Dawkins and others are reluctant to use the term "atheist" and would prefer to coin themselves as "disbelievers." But, if we are to look back into the history of atheism, we need to name the identity by which many brave men and women stood proudly by that name. The issue of atheism is a very serious one and trivialising its term-identity is disrespectful to the memory of those who lost their lives refuting the existence of theism. So were there any prominent or laymen atheists in the 18th century? There must have been because so many sermons were preached against atheism and so many pamphlets and books were written combating atheism, that it seems quite evident that some short of atheism was present. Even for the less educated masses that were not equipped with reason, nevertheless they too had sensed that something opposite to religious dogma was beginning to emerge. All the same fear of the derogatory nature of the term "atheism" was equally present along with openly declared atheists. The people, who were very much involved in the development of atheism, while hiding under clever linguistic censorship, were still committed atheists, except they were afraid for their lives. The term atheist was a label which was avoided as much as possible either for reason of family ties to church, personal safety, business relationships, academic status or plain fear of unknown consequences. This hide and pretend situation lasted right up to the end of the 18th century when the "boogie" word of atheism was no longer so derogatory. However, the theists still use the term in religious gatherings and in "hell and fire" sermons against those who deny God because the atheists are still on the side of the devil.

Atheism, of course, is not a fad of some neo-cultural trend because it has a long historical tradition. The first recorded atheist was *Diagoras of Melos* or better known as the *Atheist of Melos* (born in Milos), Greece. He was a 5th century BCE ancient Greek poet and sophist who openly declared that there were no Gods. Throughout the antiquity Diagoras was regarded as an atheist and he willingly gave offence concerning the worshiping of the

Greek Gods. When he spoke against the Greek religion, the authorities accused him of impiety and forced him to flee Athens. Legend has it that Diagoras was on a ship during severe storm weather and the crew thought that they had brought it on themselves by taking an ungodly man on board. Diagoras wondered aloud if the other boats out in the same storm also had an ungodly "Diagoras" on board. Even within the Catholic establishment there were notable theologians who appeared to have strong doubts about the validity of the religion which they were preaching. For instance, the popular French Catholic Theologian *Pierre Charron (1541 – 1603)*, in his book *"Of Wisdom"* wrote that, *"All religions have this in common, that they are an outrage to common sense, for they are pieced together out of a variety of elements, some of which seem so unworthy sordid, and at odds with man's reason, that any strong and vigorous intelligence laughs at them....For the strong intellect laughs at religion, while the weak and superstitious mind marvels at it but is easily scandalized by it."*

The period of Reformation was a time of "work in process" and a new beginning of restructuring the Christian religion. This task was at the hands of other Christians which appeared to function under a linguist's metaphor of "same old wine in a new bottle." Those "other" Christians called themselves, *Deists*. They were simply protesters of the religious dogma and authorities of the time. While they still believed in the existence of a supreme-being and the dawn of creation, they did so based on reason and nature, but were indifferent to supernatural revelation such as miracles. Of course, their rejection of religious dogma was not based on science but on a revised caution, if not scepticism, in the established Christian theology. They were dissatisfied with the state of Christianity, especially with the violent behaviour of the ecclesiastical authorities of the time. In Protestant England there was a tolerant atmosphere where certain factors favoured deism; so long as those deists were of a certain privileged class, they were tolerated when they speculated on the nature of Christianity. Their naturalism included human beings, which deists believed shared an undeniable sense of the sacred and that under the superficial rituals and superstitious behaviour, humans could identify a universal monotheism that was common to all human societies. You see, the initial desire of the deists was to redesign a more humane Christianity, one that did not put so much gravity on miracles, rituals and supernatural dictations, but rather to maintain a benign theological reasoning, including the divinity of Christ and the presence of a celestial entity namely, an *Intelligent Being*.

Although the deist movement grew quite rapidly in the 17th and 18th century it was still near impossible to identify any prominent personality who was explicitly an atheist. Yet, in the middle of the 17th century we find some one who was close to it: *Thomas Hobbes (1588 – 1679)*. Thomas Hobbes was an English materialist philosopher, academic and political scientist. He studied the ancient Greek materialists and atheists, Epicurus, Democritus and Lucretius. As a materialist he applied a material explanation to things like spirits and miracles and about claims that God has reveals his will to people with visions or dreams. As such, Hobbes denied the existence of the spirit or immaterial and was against conventional religion. Hobbes lays the grounds for atheism by the fact that he concentrated his arguments into a singular path of materialism. Nothing else exists but matter and material relations. It is matter we see, sense, touch and feel, and there is nothing else. For Hobbes, *"The Universe, the whole mass of things is corporeal, that is to say, a body that has the dimensions and magnitude, length, breath and death. Every part of the Universe is a body and that which is not body, is not part of the universe and because the universe is all, and that which not part of it, is nothing."* You can see that, with this statement, Hobbes provided most of the core material and dialectical arguments for atheism. The question still is whether we found our first outright atheist. But we can see that Hobbes had no room for immaterialism such as spirit, the immortality of the soul, miracles, God, illusions, and ghost-in-our-minds, and perhaps the grand delusion of the suspension of the material Laws of Nature. On the contrary, for Hobbes, the speculation of immaterialism was a self-contradictory, as in meaningless, "rounded-square" or "circular-rectangle." Yet in his thesis *Leviathan,* Hobbes saw humanity living in a primitive *"state of nature,"* with greed, impulses and violence; and this was the reason why humans needed *"a common power,"* such as the social structure of governmental and religious authority, to keep humanity in an orderly manner. His socially inclined arguments were based on the material necessity of government; and this material necessity also applied to church, rather than for pure theistic reasons.

Throughout the last part of the 17th century, atheism was regarded as a menace to the social order of things. Members of the British Parliament for instance, vigorously debated a bill designed to combat what they called, the blasphemy of atheism. When the first reading of the 1697 Blasphemy Act was proposed, there was no specific mention of atheism. However, within the wording of the Blasphemy Law a document that is located in the Achieves of the House of Lords, atheists would have been open to judicial charges, under the accusation of *"denying Christianity to be true."* When the final reading of the Blasphemy Law was passed, the Act included atheism as an illegal offence which carried the penalty of death, without forgiveness or reprieve.

This shows how serious the subject of atheism was regarded. As early as 1677, there were documented Parliamentary debates about establishing a blasphemy law in order to combat the religious beliefs of British ethic groups--under the belief of "polytheism"-- and against atheism. This was happening while the deists were addressing and reconstructing Christianity while opposing atheist forces which were also entering the arena of social reform. We are now in the 21st century and the question is; which US states legally ban atheists from holding public office? Let us turn our attention to a rather peculiar set of 7 US state laws relating to prohibiting atheist from holding public office:

- *Arkansas*, *Article 19, Section 1*: "No person who denies the being of a God shall hold any office in the civil departments of the state nor be competent to testify as a witness in any Court."
- *Maryland*, *Article 37*: "…for any office …in this state, other than a declaration of belief in the existence of God…"
- *Mississippi*, *Article 14, Section 265*: "No person who denies the existence of a Supreme Being shall hold any office in this state.
- *North Carolina*, *Article 17, Section 8*: "The following persons shall be disqualified for office: Any person who shall deny the being of Almighty God"
- *South Carolina*, *Article 17, Section 4*: "No person who denies the existence of a Supreme Being shall hold any office under this Constitution."
- *Tennessee*, *Article 9, Section 21:* "No person who denies the being of God,…shall hold any office in the civil departments of this state"
- **Texas**, Article 1, Section 4: "… [No one person] shall be excluded from holding office on account of his religious sentiments, provided he acknowledges the existence of a supreme being."

At the time of writing, none of the above laws are enforceable because the US Supreme Court, in 1961, affirmed that no religious test shall be held for a public office. Yet these laws, in all 7 states, are still in their legal books although are not enforceable. The Maryland law is especially interesting because it says that no religious test is required to hold an office as long as you believe in God. The hypocrisy is that if these laws were written against gays, African-Americans or Jews, the politicians would be in an uproar to remove the idiotic laws from the books. Yet, the laws against atheists still remain intact in the seven (7) states nearly five (5) decades after they were dismissed by the US Supreme Court.

Militant atheism rose within the intelligencia class of the French radicals such as the novelist, playwright and journalist *Emile Zola (1840 – 1902)*, who said, *"Civilisation would not attain [to its] perfection until the last stone, from the last church, falls on the last priest."* Simultaneously the world of science was steadily progressing; with the recognition about the all powerful Laws of Nature, science began to influence our knowledge of the material world around us. According to *Isaac Newton's (1643 – 1727)* theories about gravity and the Laws of Motion, it certainly made it impossible for an intelligent person to adhere to the Earth being the center of the universe, which the Catholic Church was still preaching to its ill- educated and ignorant followers. Therefore, it seems that out of this science-theology relationship, two distinct branches were developing. The first we have seen with Copernicus and Galileo. The second were people who were not scientists but were social theorists who cleverly used scientific terminology to establish a theological premise of God's existence-- which was, in itself, self-contradictory. Their attempt was to present an objective evidence of occurring celestial-mechanical processes and invoking biology as conclusive evidence for an *Intelligent Designer* (the re-invented name for God). Accordance to Anglican clergyman *Samuel Clarke (1675 – 1729)* a lecturer on the existence and role of the Intelligent Designer, *"The late discoveries in anatomy and physics, the circulation of blood and the exact structure of the heart and the brain, they are insensible marks of conscious [Intelligent] contrivance."* Trying, of course, to insert biology into theology does not necessarily follow the mechanical process of Natural Selection. Clarke simply visualised the nature of the "Intelligent Designer" as a pre-determined conclusion, which could only lead him to a theological interpretation of biology and biological process. The fact that the Anglican clergyman was trying to reconcile the Newtonian mechanics with the role of an Intelligent Designer shows an increased and unavoidable contradiction between science in the natural world and religion. My favoured atheist philosopher, writer and social activist *Bertrand Russell (1872 – 1970)* said, *"So far as I can remember, [there is] not one word in the Gospels in praise of intelligence."*

As we have seen since the days of Reformation, the intellectual path to atheism was structured not by scientific or by biological conclusions, but rather by deists, gentlemen of the upper English class who attempted to re-invent a more reasonable and benign Christianity. Unknowingly, men of Hobbes's deist intentions paved the way to forging the atheists' path that would eventually be turned against the whole idea of religion. All of the deists had noble intentions and were trying to identify what was common to all religions and the primeval origins of their commonality. Among the most elegant and significant writers who were able to clearly express the deists' notions, was *David Hume (1711 – 1776)*. It is quite true that David Hume never clearly expressed his atheist ideas and inclination; he was most sceptic of them all. The Scottish moral philosopher and pioneer of political economy, *Adam Smith (1723 – 1790),* paid an eloquent tribute to Hume, *"I have always considered David Hume as approaching to the ideal and perfectly wise and virtuous man as perhaps the nature of human frailty will allow."* Contrary to Hobbes's view of man as being a dangerous creature, Hume held a less pessimistic view of humanity. His own views on religion stood in the way of his academic advancement, because his scepticism about religion was regarded by the clerics as being too atheistic. Hume however, stood by his conviction, *"Generally speaking errors in religion are dangerous; those in philosophy are only ridiculous."* One must remember that all high level educational institutions were religious foundations and were administrated by clerics. Hume eventually delivered a devastating blow to religious beliefs, in his book, *"Concerning Natural Religion"* which was only permitted to be published after his death, *"God's power is infinite, whatever He wills is executed, but neither man nor any other animal is happy. Therefore He does not will happiness. Epicurus' old questions are yet unanswered, Is He both able and willing to prevent evil? Then when [He will end] evil?"* Nonetheless, up to this historical point there is no one who could whole heartedly deny the existence of God.

When we are looking back at the history of scepticism, deism and particularly of atheism, we can see, without a doubt, that the religious dominance of humanity has prohibited the advancement of atheism in the populous or at the average men's level. Academic personalities and elites, who touched on the subject of scepticism in God's existence, understandably did so with prudence and self-protection. Subliminally, of course, there was this lingering conviction among the sceptical academics that there must be "something" else with a divine purpose in this universe of ours. By the end of the 18th century, European core scepticism was shifted from Britain to France. The French philosopher, historian and writer of scientific works *Voltaire (1694 – 1778)* became famous for his attack on the Catholic Church. Voltaire popularised his militant atheism by directing it towards the populous, *"Those who can make you believe in absurdities, can make you commit atrocities."* Legend has it Voltaire's last words on his deathbed were, *"Now is not the time to make new enemies"* in his response to a priest asking Voltaire to renounce Satan. Voltaire transferred David Hume's ideas to France and, despite the strong Catholicism, philosophers and social activists were reaching atheist conclusions with mild to no reaction from authorities.

By the end of the 18th century, atheism in France was a hot topic of discussion among the populous and self-taught intellectuals, and an ongoing debate between laymen supporters and opponents of atheism. At this stage the subject of atheism was no longer an academic pursuit of the social elite or renowned philosophers. It reached the "street-level" of the popular sentiment of supporters and opponents of atheism. In 1770 Paris there was a reaction by those who condemned atheistic ideas when they saw that a number of popular books were published that year in favour of atheism. Needless to say, copies of these 'subversive' books on atheism were collected and publicly burned by the official executioner of the day. At the same time French social thinkers were reaching conclusions about the legitimacy of atheism that their English counterparts still remained reluctant to conclude. However, as brave the French authors were there were still signs of reluctance among them, for three of the seven books on atheism were published under an assumed name, people who being dead long ago.

We now know that one of the anonymous author's of these three, unarguably atheist books *"The System of Nature"* were written by the German-French intellectual *Paul-Henri Thiry, Baron d'Holbach (1723 – 1789).* D' Holbach did not agreed with Hume's assumption the there might be "a supernatural first cause" or with Hobbes' deism of the "immortality of the soul." Instead, he argued that,

"If we go back at the beginning we should find ignorance and fear created the Gods, a fancy, enthusiasm or deceit adorned them, weakness worships them, credulity preserves them, and custom, respect and tyranny support them, in order to make the blindness of men served their own interest. If the ignorance of nature gave birth to Gods, the knowledge of nature is calculated to destroy them; It is only by dispelling the clouds of the fandoms of religion that we shall discover truth, reason and morality."

The fact is that D' Holbach was the first intellectual since the ancient Epicurean times to declare, without any reservation or hesitation, that there was no God and no supernatural dimension to the universe. His book *"The System of Nature"* was erroneously known as 'the atheists' bible' but nevertheless, he was an enormously important figure in the history and development of contemporary atheism. His home in Paris is in *rue Royale, Butte Saint-Roch* (number unknown) which is still regarded as the birth-place of modern atheism; and perhaps it was here where D' Holbach wrote of the necessities of atheism. The French Revolution came a few years after D' Holbach's, and France became a secular state and D' Holbach's ideas played a significant role in constructing the foundations of French progressive free thought. Strangely, neither his numbered-address on rue

Royale, nor his grave in the Church of Saint-Roch can be found in Paris.

Perhaps D' Holbach's ideas were too much to stomach even for the Republican revolutionaries of 1789-1799. Well, since that time, life has moved on; the streets in Paris have changed with full mechanised mobility, traffic going in all directions, rue Saint-Roch is now full of elegant shops where ladies still stroll, window shopping as in the old days. The one thing that definitely has changed, however, for the better is that neither the Catholic Church nor its denials are significant any more. Sadly, when the burning of the seven atheist books once became a controversial moment in the history of atheistic thought, it is now apparently being forgotten. On the other hand, what seems to be apparent is that the subject of militant atheism became closely integrated with the ideology of armed revolutionary movements; in the Americas with the American Revolution, in Europe with the Bolshevik Revolution of 1917, and in Asia with the Chinese Revolution which ended in 1949.

By the time of 18th century, atheism had emerged from the French and British salons of the intellectuals to the popular radical associations, bookshops and sidewalk cafés, gatherings of university students and self-educated men and women in controversial thoughts. Still, atheism was socially confined to the educated and the privileged, for the wage-earner of the working classes still remained ignorant about the absurdities of religion. Yet, over the next two hundred years, atheism would begin to influence the lives of ordinary people and the once submissive behaviour of the working class would undergo a radical transformation. How was that possible? Let me remind the reader that, in 1770, Baron D' Holbach wrote a militant atheist book, "The System of Nature," which the French authorities not only banned this provocative book, but publicly burned it as well. In his time, D' Holbach was regarded as the 'Newton of the atheists' and his book was regarded as the first ever openly and devoutly atheist literary work. However, D' Holbach was not as brave as some academics believed, for after all, his book was published under a pseudonymous identity to protect him from government reprisals. But his statements, such as this, were regarded as far too radical, *"It is only by dispelling the clouds and phantoms of religion that we shall discovered truth, reason and morality."* Still, it appears that, even when atheism finally emerged from the fine salons of the intellectuals it was still not a safe idea to promote. In England, the intellectual elite did not dare to go as far as the French intellectuals went. This was because the English intellectuals were fence-sitting between *atheism and deism.* They could not deny the existence of God and were quite eager to reconstruct their deity to resemble some distant cousin of Christianity. They had a real choice to make a stand on behalf of humanity but they chose to sit out of the controversy and let future generations face the burden. To be on the safe side; of spreading controversial ideas to the populous, they also refrained from talking about atheism in the presence of the house and social club servants. They feared and shared a thought that attempted to undermine the religious faith of the populous and this was politically dangerous to their privileged status. Atheism, therefore, was also seen as an inseparable part of a populist social ideology that could undermine the present political establishment.

By the end of the 18th and beginning of the 19th century, a more popular and perhaps more socially subversive scepticism began to appear. Although this scepticism was not the expression of an explicit atheism, it was, nevertheless, of a lower to middle class radical form of religious deism. One of which, in England at least, was to find itself in enormous conflict with the legal and political establishment. The radical sceptic *Thomas Paine (1737 – 1809),* for instance, introduced a more popular and more argumentative subversive form of atheism that included political reform for the lower and middle classes. An Anglo-American political philosopher, Thomas Paine influenced with his writings the American Revolution (1775 – 1783), and the French Revolution (1789 – 1799) and positive atheism ever since. Sadly, Thomas Paine could not awaken the American people's faithful devotion to the biblical justification of human slavery until a young man called *Abraham Lincoln (1809 – 1865),* had read Paine's writings which duly inspired him to struggle for change and the abolition of slavery. Being truthful towards his positive atheism was valuable for its own sake,

"Of all the tyrannies that inflicted mankind, tyranny in religion is the worst. Every other species of tyranny is limited to the world we lived in, but this attempts to subscribe beyond the grave and seeks to pursue us into eternity....It is from the Bible that man has learned of cruelty, rape and murder, for the believe in a cruel God makes a cruel man and the Bible is a history of wickedness and serve to corrupt and brutalise mankind."

Thomas Paine represented the lower and middle classes and, as a self-educated author with a radical scepticism, he was expressing ideas in a style of language which was typical of the laymen of the day. This means that Paine's books, *"The Age of Reason"* and *"Common Sense,"* were written by a self-educated man for the public at large, and not written as purely scholastic works. Without an exaggeration, Thomas Paine was the most popular self-educated thinker and orator that England has ever produced. For the first time in history, there was a self-educated man who was regarded, as the political philosopher of the lower and middle classes. He was a natural leader of the common people, who wanted to liberate the masses from colonial and religious tyranny. This was because Thomas Paine's atheism and populist struggle represented a single front. So you see, his sceptical attitude was supported by a profound mixture of atheism and deism; which was quite different from that of the privileged classes, from which deism was originally born. He did not *benefit* from university education because he had *no money* and he was not a member of the established *privileged class*. But his readings and self-education in political philosophy and activism had a profound impact in both the American and French Revolution.

What appears so striking is that the elite's intellectual conclusions about populist atheism were that these ideas were, in fact, very dangerous ideas. These populist atheist ideas, published in cheap print, were not regarded as being false arguments, but were dangerous because the elite regarded them as being true materialist ideas. Spreading knowledge of materialism was a means of possessing and giving the power of materialism and naturalism to larger sectors of lower and middle classes. By the 1820s there were natural leaders among the British and French lower classes who, as atheists, were arguing that there is no rational material evidence for the existence of God. They had to overcome tall social obstacles they saw in the distant future, and they took chances that were worth taking. They stood by their position and it became popular to say that a person should not ground his faith and morality on God's existence. As such, they did not choose the path of least resistance for their own convenience.

The social elite, on the other hand, acknowledged that it was socially dangerous for the lower and middle classes to even be aware of materialism. It seems that the debate on atheism contained within itself a kind of social importance. For the deist social elite, it was acceptable to contemplate with thoughts about atheism, but not to propagate, publish or make it widely available to the general public. They feared Thomas Paine's public announcements such as,

"All national institutions of churches whether Jewish, Christian or Muslim appeared to me no other than human inventions set up to terrify and enslave humankind, and to monopolise power and profit."

In *"The Common Sense"* and *"The Age of Reason"* Thomas Paine identifies social problems in the USA with his atheist principles which stimulated him to criticise the power and authority of the Church. He encourages people to create their own moral rationality and sensibilities including their natural ability to interact morally with their fellow human beings. This was contrary to what the religious authorities were advocating; that without the Church and government to guide the people they would eventually regress man to the "state of nature" in Hobbes' words. His new book *"The Rights of*

Men" (1791)* tore apart monarchies and traditional institutions and, when it appeared in the spring of that year in London, it sold more that three million copies. According to the publishers the book *"eagerly read by reformers, Protestant dissenters, democrats, London craftsmen, and the skilled-factory hands of the new-industrial north."* For a short time, Thomas Paine remained in the American colonies and helped to write the American Constitution and coined the name The United States of America. In appreciation for helping in writing a secularist constitution that saw the separation of Church and State, the government gave Paine his own resident estate in N.Y to continue his work.

Reading from the pages of "The Age of Reason," it is near impossible not to reflect on the mental and moral delusions that religion has produced in human societies around the world. It has twisted and prostituted the inherited moral kindness of the human being, causing them to believe in things created by the minds of professional liars or self-delusional rabbis, clergy or imams. Fundamentalist religious believers have mentally prepared themselves for a final martyrdom and every other faith-inspired crime. The Right-wing fundamentalist zealots take the trade of the rabbi, the priest or imam, Buddhist or Hindu for the sake of profit and social position. In order to qualify for the job, they begin to refine the art of deception. Can the reader conceive anything more self-dehumanising and more destructive to one's own morality than this?

My intention in this book is by no means to condemn those who believe; and in the process of writing this book, I also maintain the right to declare the things that I do not believe and offer the reasons and evidence for not believing them. I follow no church of any kind, no New Age neo-spiritualism, because spirits do not exist in this spiritless world. As an openly declared positive atheist, I have the same rights to my beliefs as the individual deists have theirs. I can only hope that soon, the deists will get-off their fence-sitting and make their brave journey to reach the side of *materialism and naturalism*. For the Right-wing theist of America, it is hardly surprising that they regard that atheism and radical deism have gained a dangerously popular reputation. For such idiotic claims, they only have the support of America's religious establishment.

Let the theists answer the author *Percy Bysshe Shelley (1792 – 1822) on "The Necessity of Atheism"* that

"If [God] is infinite good, what reasons we have to fear Him? If He is infinite wise, why shall we have doubt concerning our future? If He knows all why warned Him of our needs, and fetid Him with our prayers? If He is everywhere, why raise [churches] to Him?"

Nevertheless, humanity has realised that, to achieve the material base of morality some secular alternative utilitarian approach was needed to guarantee the social stability of society: the greatest good for the greatest number of people. Within the concept of centuries old Utilitarianism there was a practical need for revolutionary, social and scientific action; as we have witnessed in Europe after *1848's Age of Revolution era* and for the next one hundred years. When philosophical atheist principles re-surfaced, they took a much more revolutionary character in their political agenda around the world.

During this time there were a large number of so called "common people" who did not follow any particular religious denomination. Biological science was also progressing and debates between theologians and academics, about the origins of life itself, were still fluctuating between religious mythology and biological evidence. The planetary structure of the universe was, by now, an established fact, as was originally declared by Copernicus and Galileo. The rapid development of science however, was about to embarrass the theologians of Jewish and Christian faith in their belief that life on Earth in accordance with Genesis 1, was created by God in six days. The science of Geology, for instance, was about to subvert the theological idea that the Earth was created as recently as about six thousand years ago. Contrary to this absurd claim, geological evidence confirmed that the Earth has existed for millions of years (approximate time was still undiscovered at this time). It was upon this geological evidence that the naturalist *Charles R. Darwin (1809 – 1882)* would base his theory about Natural Evolution.

This theory of evolution was inevitably contrasted with the ideas of the religious establishment, as well as an unexpected thread to the core foundations of their two thousand year old biblical beliefs. Charles Darwin's biological book the *"Origins of Species" (1859)* was published twenty years after it was first written. Darwin's theory was based on the notion of variation, and the numerous traits and adaptations that species different from each other also evolved over time and gradually diverged. Thus variations in organisms are apparent within species throughout the natural world. Such variations are evident in colours, structures, organs, and physical traits which differentiate a multitude of species from one another. Heredity is the mechanism that perpetuates such variations. The paradox is that the *Origin of Species* was written by a wealthy, upper middle class individual whose book would shake the intellectual foundations of his and of the European establishment in which its religious life was based.

The Origin of Species was an all inclusive work of Darwin's dangerous ideas about evolution of life as we know it today. Without an exaggeration, if we were to give a Nobel Prize to a single best idea anybody ever had, we would be giving it to Darwin for his idea of Natural Selection. His ideas united the two most distinct features of our universe: the world of purposeless and meaningless matter in perpetual motion on one side, and the world on meaningful, purposeful matter on the other. We know now that the ideas Darwin was proposing were truly revolutionary ideas; a) that biological science could accelerate from it, and b) that no religious dogma could ever replace it. Darwin's revolutionary idea is about who we are, what we are made off and what life means; so far as science can answer that question. In many ways, Darwin's ideas were the single most profound discovery that science has ever made. But you see, in Darwin's days, the idea of evolution was regarded as highly unorthodox because it went against all of assumed natural history. Natural Evolution jeopardised the standards of the day's science and it also jeopardised the standards of a stable society which was under the Churches' Biblical authority and guidance. Fearing ecclesiastical reaction to his work, and because his wife was also a devoted Christian, Darwin kept his work secret for twenty years before publication. After all, Darwin was a respectable member of the elitist upper classes, yet also a scientist with dangerous ideas.

Darwin's work began with the observation that individuals differ from each other, and these differences might be advantageous and give individuals an edge for food or finding a shelter to survive. He realised that, in nature, individuals compete for resources and those with some kind of advantage are more likely to adapt and survive. He said, *"It is not the strongest of the species that survive, not the most intelligent, but the one most responsive to change [adaptation]."* This Darwin called, *Natural Selection* because the forces of nature select which organisms will survive based on their adaptability. You see, Darwin's work will call into question God's role as the creator of nature and this will ultimately undermine the European religious, social and political establishment. By 1859 his book on the Origin of Species had turned the theological and social establishment on its head. You see, by forming a theory of the origins of species, Darwin advanced the challenging of the assumption that God himself was the origin of everything. It was a devastating challenge and a dangerous idea. But this scientific theory was different, for up until this historical time, theologians and ecclesiastical philosophers could present clever logical arguments against the sceptics, deists and atheists of the world. But it was not possible to argue against scientific evidence that could not be classified as being "atheist" when it was only presenting geological and biological evidence for the sake of science--- not against anyone or anything theological. There was not an exchange of *verbalisms* of mythology, customs and traditions, logical twists and clever counter arguments, as theologians and philosophers were accustomed to do. Darwin's Origin of Species was not directed in support of or against any establishment because verified science, per se, cannot be classified other than what it really is, scientific discovery.

The Church, once again, followed its long anti-scientific tradition attempting to defeat Darwin's scientific theory and evidence, and when it could not, it simply tried to merge with it. This follows the old saying, *"if you cannot beat them joint them."* Starting with the skeleton similarities of hands and feet in the mammal kingdom, this was regarded as the first blueprint of creation in the Creator's mind. But for Darwin, the skeleton similarities in the mammal kingdom indicated one thing and one thing only, that mammals shared an ancient common ancestor. Religionist scientists regarded some organs as being far too complex to have being accounted for by gradual, natural selection; such as the eye for instance. Rather, such a perfectly complex design, as the eye is, required the divine skills of an Intelligent Designer i.e., God. Is not the eye a God's given gift? Yet, once again, there absolutely no any biblical reference to kind of intelligence!

Christians saw that Darwin's theory of the origins of species, and of humanity, would jeopardise the Christian theology of salvation, for God now has been made remote of all the things that were happening in nature and in the universe. For the materialist, if natural selection by itself and unaided by God could make an eye, then what else could nature not do? Could it not do anything and everything in perfection? For the religious people in Darwin's time, the very existence of a perfect organ like the heart or the eye was taken as proof of God, as proof of the existence of a celestial designer. How else could all the intricate organs and sub-structures of the eye come together, in just the right way, to make vision possible and so perfect? Today, of course, medical science has confirmed that the eye is not exactly perfect at all. In short, the eye contains profound optical imperfections, and such imperfections prove the yet incomplete evolutionary process of the eye. Nature does not create things the way an artist or a designer does with his art work. Natural Selection simply favours random changes that make organs more fit or adaptable to survive. Imperfections in their design often result from evolution's constant adjustments or *tweaking*. One such imperfection is retinal-damage, not an uncommon problem due to the way human eyes evolved from light sensing brain tissue in our ancient ancestors. This is just one example of imperfection in the human eyes. You see, evolution starts with what is already present and can modify an organ, but it can never do a grand redesign. Therefore, the human eye, with all its optical perfection, has clues to the fact that its origin is of the blind process of natural selection and evolution.

The newly discovered billions of years of Earth's history gave ample time for Darwin's slow evolution process to work. As for the believers in God's creation, they eventually realised that they might have a problem. You see, Darwin's scientific discovery of Natural Selection and Evolution was the first of its kind to subvert one of the primary arguments in favour of God; because it does away with the idea of creation by an Intelligent Designer, for there was no mind, mentality or conscious objective view at work here. Natural Selection and Evolution is an unintended consequence of unsolicited variation, for evolution is not very inventive or an ingenious novelty nor is it driven forward because it foresaw some benefits in the future. Natural Selection is simply a random selection process---with many bad mutations which do not survive---but it produces things with an illusion of designing, but they are really not novelty. The details in the structural organisms hardly support the idea of a benevolent designer. In Darwin's words,

"I cannot persuade myself that a beneficent and omnipotent God would have created the ignominy dye with the expressed intention of feeding within the living bodies of caterpillars or that God would have created and designed that a cat should play with mice."

The theological reaction to Darwin's theory of Origin of Life was vicious and dramatic. The Bishop of Oxford, *Samuel Wilberforce (1805 – 1873)* who upon reading Darwin's book declared *"Is it on his grandmother's or his grandfather's side that he claims dissentience from a monkey?"* I once witnessed, in a South American village, a peddler of religious icons using the derogatory tone, "are you descended from a monkey or are you God's creation?" However, I am not sure whether his stupidity helped him to sell more icons. The response of the intellectuals and philosophers who rejected Darwin's discovery by claiming that there is a metaphysical side to nature, and a man who denies this may sing the human race into the lowest grade of degradation which may have fallen ever since historical records were kept. For obvious reasons, the monotheistic church was upset by Darwin's Theory of Evolution because it denied the core idea of a celestial creation, from which all natural forms of life have been explained and established in the last few hundred years. As for the fundamentalists of the religious establishment, it was most shocking to learn that man was included in this Theory of Evolution. The idea of man being a mere descendant from apes; man had lost his special spiritual priority. Man was no longer the core reason or star of God's earthly creation. What would they have thought if they knew of that man is not the descendant from apes, but rather that, *man* *is an ape himself?* For the stupid and ignorant fundamentalists, Darwin's theory of man being an ape was, and still is, a pure blasphemy.

With time, educated Christians had to reconcile their beliefs with the undeniable Darwinian biological discoveries. The point is that the religious had to visualise the make-up of living things in a completely new way, one in which God could no longer be regarded as the only intricate or intelligent designer. On the other hand, those who were still sceptical towards religion were also beginning to feel more confident about their scepticism, which now included science in addition to their reason, i.e., secularists. By the middle of the 19th century there were numerous secular societies with titles such as "secular" or "ethical" or "humanist" in their printed pamphlets. Some newly elected secularist MPs to the British and in the Greek Parliament (2015), were brave enough to refuse pledging their oath to the Bible; rather they affirmed their allegiance to their obligations. Eventually, the secularists' affirmation was reluctantly accepted.

By the end of the 19th century, European atheists appeared to be overconfident that atheism would soon triumph; that religion would soon decline or simply die out. So why does faith survive when all evidence suggest according to the atheist German philosopher Friedrich Nietzsche (1844 -1900), that *"God is dead"?* The statement that "God is dead" has become his best known remark. On the basis of it, most social thinkers regard Nietzsche an atheist. The famous German atheist psychologist *Sigmund Freud (1856 – 1939,)* believed that religious beliefs, regardless of the religion, are an expression of psychological neurosis and distress, wish fulfilment, an infantile delusion and an attempt by the person to control the outside world. In his earliest writings about religion, *"Obsessive Actions and Religious Practices"* (1907), Freud stated that religion and the mental illness of neurosis are similar products of the human mind; that an individual's compulsive behaviour is a personal religiosity; that religion's repetitive illusionary rituals, is universal neurosis; and that some believers are attracted by the sense of the belief, but not believe in religion. Above all, Freud claimed to understand the core nature of all religions. Freud saw religion as an illusion; although he describes it as a wish-fulfilment. It is quite difficult to see it entirely as such since this illusion has punitive thoughts (Hell and Fire) as well as benevolent characteristic thoughts (that God is all good). However, Freud explained such obvious contradiction, it is quite clear that he saw religion as false and profoundly unhelpful. Religious teachings, after all, are neurotic relics and the time has come to replace them by controlling our thoughts, because they are the result of irrational manifestations of our mind. For obvious reasons, Freud's theory was unsettling the conventional religious beliefs.

But the social implications of Freud's psychoanalytical theory of religion were trivial in comparison to the politization and radicalization of atheism by German social theorists like *Karl Marx (1818 – 1883), Friedrich Nietzsche (1844 – 1900)* and others. Nietzsche, in his book *"Thus Spoke Zarathustra"* replaced the idea of God with his mythological super-human *Wotan* and thus declared that *"God is dead."* Karl Marx stated, *"Die Religion…ist das Opium des Volkes,"* that,

"Religious distress is at the same time the expression of real distress, religion is the sign of an oppressed creature, the heart of a heartless world, the spirit of a spiritless world, it is the opium of the people. The demand to give up the illusions is the demand to give up the [material or social] conditions which needs illusions."

For Marx, religion give, the low classes an acceptance of their plight in life and gives them false comfort in their circumstances by pointing out that Jesus (or a given saint) had suffered and was also poor. You see, whatever Freud's idea was about the origins of the "infantile illusion" in the beginning of the 20th century, atheism of the European left-wing radicals was a declaration of faith in Karl Marx's philosophy for social and economic changes. These political radicals "highjacked" atheism and were determined to establish an illusion-free-zone, and in turn, they became the new propagators of an oppressive utopia in Russia and much later in China. The scheme resembled the textual script of the *"Animal Farm: A fairy Story" (1945) by George Orwell (1903 – 1950)*, where the once oppressed farm animals became the oppressors following their liberation. In the *"Pedagogy of the Oppressed"* (1970) the Brazilian educator *Paulo Freire (1921 – 1997)* quotes the German humanist philosopher, *Erich Fromm (1900 – 1980)* declaration *"that every oppressed person houses within itself the oppressor."* This is exactly what has happened with the radical atheists of the late 19th and early 20th century. With the Russian Bolshevik Revolution of 1917, they were transformed from being religiously oppressed to becoming atheist oppressors.

After centuries of persecution, torture and imprisonment by the religious fanatics of the Roman Catholic and the Russian Orthodox Church, atheism became the rebels' ideology and misguided political goal and turned them into oppressors of the oppressors. For the radical atheists, Karl Marx's "opium of the people" was an anathema that would have no place in the coming political millennium. In short, the radical atheists were determined to establish an unadulterated illusion free zone. In Russia of 1917, the rebellious atheists established the first atheist state in the world. The paradox was that the fundamentalist atheist state envisioned a new golden era for humanity, but it tormented, tortured, imprisoned and killed far more victims than Christianity in its most excessive brutality. Inevitably atheism was unjustly associated with political violence, without it ever having expressed an atheist political strategy, a social design or an atheistic system of organised beliefs. Still, it was found guilty by association to the political strategy of communalism.

By the end of the 20th century, atheism has become accepted and much wider spread than ever. Without exaggerating, the world's dreadful social and economic conditions, the Catholic relation with Colonialism, Fascism, the Nazi war criminals, cruelty and child molestation, the criminal residential schools, religious dogmatism and violence, anti-gay and anti-abortion, HIV and Ebola diseases, extremism between Muslim factions armed with religious fanatics, extreme televangelism, have all undermined the belief in the existence of a benevolent God. Although this is not the whole story, without a doubt peoples' higher civic education, the positive role of science, new space discoveries, open scepticism and advocacy have advanced the status of atheism as being an non-ideological descriptive or prescriptive mode of realism. Thanks to the mass media that is revealing the world's economic and political discrepancies, this inescapable exposure represents an unprecedented problem for the devoted fundamentalist Jewish, Christian and Muslim. You see, as we have enter into the second decade of the 21st century, the questions of religious beliefs and atheism are brought out in the open, and more questions are asked about the role of religious influence and conflict around the world. Opposition to theism is brought about because it is based on the religious values it advocates, it is regarded as being harmful. Contemporary atheists want to put behind the harmful effects of religion and concentrate of humanist values, where the question of religion is simply minimised. They want to treat religion as an ancient mythology to be used in a brief academic time as reference among students and teachers. Darwin's time is of essence, *"A man who dares to waste one hour of time has not discovered the value of life."* Darwin, of course, is in good company with the TV character, Homer Simpson who said, *"Why should I spend half of my Sunday hearing about how I'm going to Hell?"*

Of course I have wondered many times what it would be like to live in a society without religion, without religious conflicts, beheadings and live burning executions, religious brainwashing of children in faith-based schools and female genital mutilation. Can you?

ILLUSTRATED
"THE NATURAL HISTORY OF ATHEISM"

MYTHOLOGY

HORUS

- HE WAS BORN OF A VIRGIN ON DECEMBER 25TH

- HIS BIRTH WAS ANNOUNCED BY A STAR IN THE EAST AND WAS ATTENDED BY THREE WISE MEN.

- HE WAS A CHILD TEACHER IN THE TEMPLE AND WAS BAPTIZED WHEN HE WAS 30 BY 'ANUP THE BAPTIZER'

- HE HAD 12 DISCIPLES, HE PERFORMED MIRACLES, HE WALKED ON WATER, AND TRANSFIGURED ON THE MOUNT.

- HE WAS CRUCIFIED, BURIED IN A TOMB AND RESURRECTED.

- HE WAS CALLED THE 'WAY, THE TRUTH, THE LIGHT, THE MESSIAH, GOD'S ANOINTED SON, THE SON OF MAN, THE GOOD SHEPHERD, THE LAMB OF GOD, THE WORD'

- HE WAS 'THE FISHER,' AND WAS ASSOCIATED WITH THE LAMB, LION AND FISH ('ICHTHYS').

MITHRAS

- HE WAS BORN OF A VIRGIN ON DECEMBER 25TH.

- HE WAS CONSIDERED A GREAT TRAVELING TEACHER AND MASTER.

- HE HAD 12 DISCIPLES AND HE PERFORMED MIRACLES.

- HE WAS BURIED IN A TOMB. AFTER 3 DAYS HE ROSE AGAIN. HIS RESURRECTION WAS CELEBRATED EVERY YEAR DURING HIS PRINCIPAL FESTIVAL, HELD ON WHAT WOULD BECOME EASTER.

- HE WAS CALLED 'THE GOOD SHEPHERD, THE WAY, THE TRUTH AND THE LIGHT, THE REDEEMER, THE SAVIOR, THE MESSIAH.'

- HE WAS IDENTIFIED WITH BOTH THE LION AND THE LAMB. HIS SACRED DAY WAS SUNDAY.

FROM VIRGIN BIRTH TO RESURRECTION THE STORY OF JESUS CHRIST IS MERELY A RETELLING OF THE STORIES OF GODS WHO PREDATED HIM BY HUNDREDS OF YEARS.

ILLUSTRATED

ILLUSTRATED
"THE NATURAL HISTORY OF ATHEISM"

ANDREAS VESALIUS

ADVANCED MEDICAL RESEARCH AGAINST THE CHURCH'S ANTI-SCIENTIFIC DOGMA

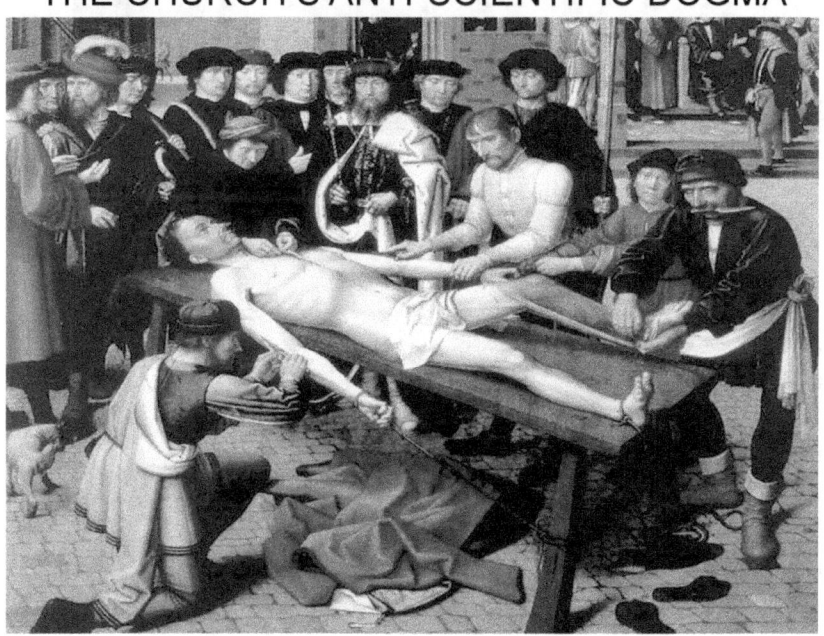

ILLUSTRATED
"THE NATURAL HISTORY OF ATHEISM"

ILLUSTRATED
"THE NATURAL HISTORY OF ATHEISM"

"It is proof of a base and low mind for one to wish to think with the masses or majority, merely because the majority is the majority.

Truth does not change because it is, or is not, believed by a majority of the people."

Giordano Bruno (1548-1600), Italian scientist and philosopher

THOSE WHO CAME BEFORE US

DEATH DOES NOT CONCERN US, BECAUSE AS LONG AS WE EXIST, DEATH IS NOT HERE. AND ONCE IT DOES COME, WE NO LONGER EXIST.
-Epicurus

ILLUSTRATED
"THE NATURAL HISTORY OF ATHEISM"

Fables should be taught as fables, myths as myths, and miracles as poetic fantasies. To teach superstitions as truths is a most terrible thing. The child mind accepts and believes them, and only through great pain and perhaps tragedy can he be in after years relieved of them.

Hypatia of Alexandria

THOSE WHO CAME BEFORE US

"THE NATURAL HISTORY OF ATHEISM"

THOSE WHO CAME BEFORE US

VICTOR HUGO

"THE NATURAL HISTORY OF ATHEISM"
CHRISTOPHER HITCHENS

THOSE WHO DARED

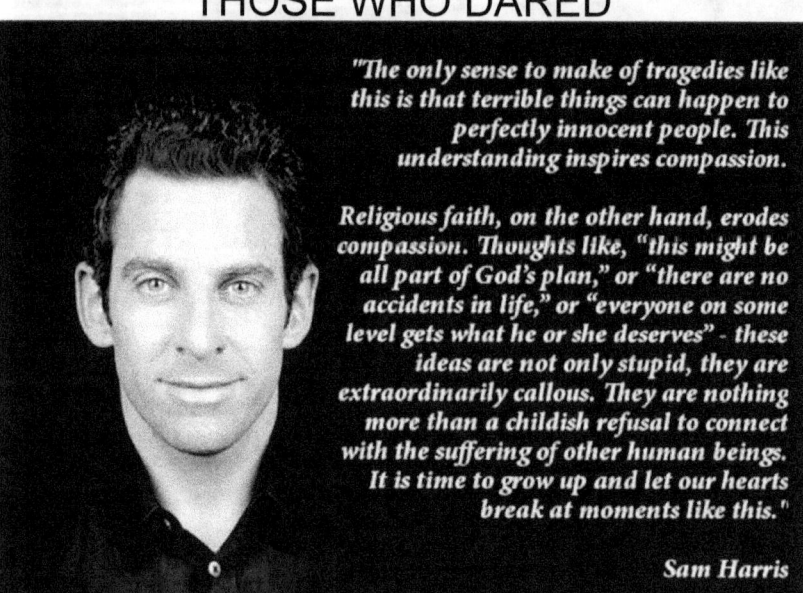

"The only sense to make of tragedies like this is that terrible things can happen to perfectly innocent people. This understanding inspires compassion.

Religious faith, on the other hand, erodes compassion. Thoughts like, "this might be all part of God's plan," or "there are no accidents in life," or "everyone on some level gets what he or she deserves" - these ideas are not only stupid, they are extraordinarily callous. They are nothing more than a childish refusal to connect with the suffering of other human beings. It is time to grow up and let our hearts break at moments like this."

Sam Harris

ILLUSTRATED
SIGMOND FREUD
"RELIGION IS COMPATABLE TO A
CHILDHOOD NEUROSIS"

ILLUSTRATIONS
AUTHOR OF "GOD DELUSION"

"We are all atheists about most of the gods that humanity has ever believed in.

Some of us just go one god further."

Richard Dawkins

ILLUSTRATIONS
ATHEISTS' ON MORALITY

IF THERE IS NO GOD, WHY BE GOOD?

"As Einstein said, 'If people are good only because they fear punishment, and hope for reward, then we are a sorry lot indeed.' Michael Shermer, in *The Science of Good and Evil*, calls it a debate stopper. If you agree that, in the absence of God, you would 'commit robbery, rape, and murder,' you reveal yourself as an immoral person, 'and we would be well advised to steer a wide course around you.' If, on the other hand, you admit that you would continue to be a good person even when not under divine surveillance, you have fatally undermined your claim that God is necessary for us to be good. I suspect that quite a lot of religious people do think religion is what motivates them to be good, especially if they belong to one of those faiths that systematically exploits personal guilt.

It seems to me to require quite a low self-regard to think that, should belief in God suddenly vanish from the world, we would all become callous and selfish hedonists, with no kindness, no charity, no generosity, nothing that would deserve the name of goodness."

-Richard Dawkins
The God Delusion

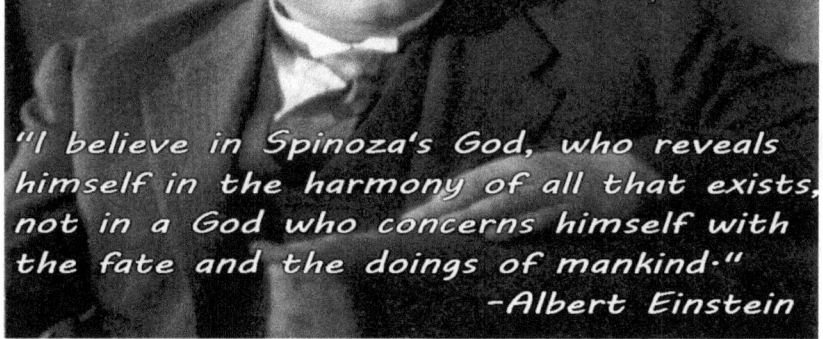

"I believe in Spinoza's God, who reveals himself in the harmony of all that exists, not in a God who concerns himself with the fate and the doings of mankind."
-Albert Einstein

PAGAN MYTHOLOGY IN ORGANISED RELIGION

From as far back as 10,000 years, human history has inherited an abundance of cultural symbols inviting ancient peoples' respect and wonder of the one magnificent object in the sky: the Sun. It is not difficult to understand the ancient peoples' fascination with the Sun. Each morning the Sun would rise, bringing joy and security, heating the earth's habitats from the cold winter days, and land cultivators understood that without the Sun, crops will not grow and humans would not be fed. Humans were also aware of the stars in the sky. Over many centuries of studying and speculating about them, ancients learned to track their movements such as eclipses and full moons, and to anticipate celestial events such as the passing of meteorites. Not having a fully scientific understanding in meteorology or astronomy, celestial objects, events and constellations were described and prescribed in metaphorical symbols, such as the astrology of the Zodiac Signs. The Zodiac (a Greek word meaning "circle of animals") was first developed in ancient Egypt and was later adopted by the Babylonians within the context of divination. By 600 BCE the Babylonians had devised the twelve-sign zodiac markers in the sky along the ecliptic path which the Sun followed. Thus astrological and other pagan myths have dominated stars and constellation meanings for millennia.

Traditionally, the Zodiac Signs, and the names of certain stars, once carried a cultist meaning to the Hebrew patriarchs and ancient Israel. They were given a theistic meaning which was conveyed in the Hebrew story of the Messiah-redeemer which was re-adopted by the Christians of the 3rd century and known as the Gospel of Jesus Christ. It must be said that, in this article, I shall not theologize or "Christianise" the Zodiac Signs or astrology but will merely uncover the relation between religion and ancient cultures which has distorted the meaning of astronomy through astrology. This distortion does not need my help, for their pagan meaning in Hebrew and Christianity has given to gospel-meaning for those signs and stars through a persistent and systematic biblical exegesis surrounding a number of verses. Books by *Frances Rolleston* (1781-1864) the *Mazzaroth, the Constellations;* by the theological author *Joseph A. Seiss (1823-1904), The Gospel in the Star; the Companion Bible* and *Witness of the Stars,* by the *Anglican Minister E.W. Bullinger (1837-1913)* were some of the proponents of Christianising the Zodiac Signs. Those books were read widely because, after all, religion and the zodiac signs were based on popularity, not on scientific evidence and dialectical reason.

Different cultures invented and re-invented unverified, symbolic descriptions of given stars associated with their chosen animist spiritual beings or planting seasons, such as, in the *Neolithic Agricultural Revolution*. Of course, no culture had an exclusive interpretation over objects in the sky. Various cultures inter-changed or copied interpretations of stars and some modified them to suit their own cultural objectives. In metaphorical terms, any star's Zodiac Sign was just as important as the next, for all prescriptions and descriptions of its structure and purpose was logically explained in delusive-terms but with a believable linguistic harmony. There are several variations of a legend attached to the zodiac's twelve animals; each culture relied heavily on legends and myths for the explanation of events, and gave human meaning to things in the sky. Of course, the weakest link of the Zodiac Signs is that the actual and all-inclusive Universe did not comply in according to the human mind's mythology, for the Cosmos has its own governing Planetary Laws, not necessarily on par with primitive astrology. I say "primitive astrology" because there is evidence that the early caveman, the Neanderthals and Homo sapiens, developed markings on bones and cave walls showing that the lunar cycles were being noted as early as 45 to 35,000 years ago.

Egyptian pagans, who invented the circular Zodiac Signs, conceptualised the Sun in the center and divided the circle into 12 equal constellations and 4 seasons that reflected the 12 months of the year. Some Zodiac Signs reflected human figures while others were of animals. Regardless of which culture adopted the original Zodiac Signs, the identity of the constellations remained similar; they were surrounding with elaborated god-myths involving their movements and human relationships with them in the sky. This made it easier for the elites and the ill-educated and ignorant to accept the Temple priests' and professional future tellers' assumptions of the workings of the Universe.

This elaborate Zodiac Sign system lacked scientific reasoning, investigation and evidence because those methods were in their infant state, and continued to be, for many a centuries. Its invention may have been for cultural reasons but, soon enough, it was used as a means and base of political and theistic power and control. The rulers and Temple priests' hierarchy saw and used the Zodiac constellations as a means of promoting their agenda and their own privileged positions of power and wealth. People were basically ignorant, not too keen on challenging anything that could not be contradicted, and saw their Temple priests' explanations as a good-will guideline to stability. As for those individuals who did not follow what was dictated to them; perhaps because they believed in another God, they were seen as a rebellious threat to the dominant hierarchy, and were accused of *Apostasy* and were simply killed or driven into exile.

In the Zodiac myth, the Sun was promoted not only as the light of the world, but also as the Sun-God who was all powerful and a saviour of humankind. The 12 constellations were seen as places where the Sun-God had travelled and were personified into celestial events that were happening at the time. The 12 Zodiac personified events were adopted by the Christian mythology which also has its 12 Apostles. Each constellation was named: Capricorn, Aquarius, Pisces, Aries, Taurus, Cancer, Leo, Virgo, Libra, Scorpio, Gemini, and Sagittarius. They all had a different role assigned to them over the lives of humankind.

In this article, I claim that the Egyptian mythology of Son-God Horus is the root of the Christian typological mythology re-adapted around the Son of God, Jesus. This was a part of the typological work of the Roman Imperial Cult, Josephus Bar Mathias, Vespasian and Titus Flavius, the Alexandrians of Egypt and of the pagan theologian Heron of Alexandria of the 1st century AD. About 3,000 B.C. the Egyptian God *Horus* (Sun-Light) was the personified Son of the Sun-God who was in eternal struggle with *God-Set* (Darkness). Both represented humanity's moral struggle between Good and Evil. This ancient mythological struggle between Good and Evil is, by far, the biggest and the longest "battle-ground" humanity has ever endured and which it still endures to this day. The interesting part of this invented typology is that the Son-Horus of the Sun-God was born on December 25th a day which many others shared as their birthday, including the Son of the Christian God, Jesus Christ.

The entire traditional myth of Jesus' life appears to be a direct plagiaristic story of Horu's life background, from childhood to his ending as Son of Sun-God. For instance:
- the Son-Horus of the Sun-God was born of a Virgin Mother *Isis*—like the myth of the Virgin Mary—and was accompanied by a bright star in the East---similar to the night Jesus was born.
- Upon his birth, Horus was visited and adorned by 3 Kings---similar to the myth of the 3 Wise Men who visited baby-Jesus the night he was born.
- At the age of 12, Horus became a renowned child teacher---a similar typological myth was passed on to the child Jesus.
- At the age of 30, Horus was baptized in the river, similar in age to Jesus, by a prophet Adapt, and from that moment on Horus began his ministry as the Son-God of the Sun-God.

- In Jesus case, he was also baptised by the prophet John the Baptist and thus he also soon began his ministry as the Son of God.
- Horus had 12 Disciples who travelled with him while performing miracles, curing the sick and walking on water.
- In the Jesus myth, he also had 12 Disciples (Apostles) who also travelled with him while performing a variety of miracles, curing the sick, making the disable walk and resurrecting the dead.
- Horus was eventually betrayed to the authorities by one of his Disciples *Typhon* and after he was tried, Horus was crucified.
- Some 3,000 years later, this myth was plagiarised and repeated by having Jesus' Disciple Judas betray him leading to Jesus trial and crucifixion.
- On the 3rd day following his crucifixion, the Son-God Horus was resurrected from death and ascended to a celestial place next to the Sun-God.
- Such unlikely mythological event was also repeated for Jesus who was also resurrected after 3 days and ascended to celestial heaven.
- Finally, Horus was known by a variety of symbolic names such as "the Truth," "the Light," "the Good Shepherd," and "the Lamb of God." Christians today are called "the Flock" of sheep, and the priests are called the "Shepherd," who leads the "flock" of people who do not mind this demeaning description of them. Peoples' ignorance of the mythological roots of their religion permits the priesthood-charlatans and fanatical televangelists to exploit peoples' insecurities in the name of power and profit.
- Horus was born Annu, the place of bread – Jesus was born in Bethlehem, the House of Bread.
- Horus is the Morning Star – Jesus is the Morning Star.
  Here is a list of other similarities between the Egyptian Son-God Horus and the Son of God, Jesus:
- Horus and the Father are one.
- Jesus says, "I and my Father are one. He that seethes Him seethes Him that sends Me."
- Horus is the Father that is seen in the Son.
- Jesus claims to be the Son to whom the Father is revealed.
- Horus was the way, the truth, the life by name and person.
- Jesus is made to assert that he is the way, the truth, and the life.
- Horus was the plant, the shoot, the nectar.
- Jesus is made to say" I am the true vine."
- Horus says, "I open the Tuat that I may drive the way the darkness."

- Jesus says, "I am come a light onto the world."

Whoever wrote the Old Testament and later the Christian Bible (some suspect it was the historian Josephus Bat Mathias and his company) must have known the immense Middle Eastern collection of cultic religious myths circulating from present day Iraq and Iran to Mesopotamia, Egypt, Greece and down to Ethiopia and beyond. Self-proclaimed scholars, philosophers and prophets of the day were available to serve any important Pharaoh, Temple priest, Polytheistic or Monotheistic Cults with religious or deist agendas to promote. Putting pen-to-paper by plagiarising or borrowing parts of another cult's mythology of non-existent Gods was an easy typological task and fooling the uneducated, ignorant populous was much easier. Religious plagiarism was by no means a unique trade-craft of the Christian or the Muslim Qur'anic dogmas alone. All the proponents of plagiarised myths were comfortable in presenting these myths as their own. You see, they never expected that one day, in the distant future, the ill-educated and ignorant would become highly educated to the point of challenging the "originality" of the stories they claimed as their own. For instance, Muhammad's myths and unverified accomplishments and Qur'an's "scientific" explanations have been discovered to be false and, are now an embarrassment to religion of Islam and to its apologists.

Whether the Horus myth or legend, it is true or not is immaterial. Legends and myths of imaginable, supernatural men and women were circulating in plain social levels and were paramount to those who promoted them. Myths of "Life after death," "Resurrection" and "Miracles," and Mohammed's "Flying horse over the Moon" were propagated to such a degree that they became believable to the ignorant who remained ignorant because of their lack of reason and scientific evidence; for if they had reason, there would be no Muslim religion. Private beliefs and feelings became the predominant prerequisite over investigation, knowledge and proof. It was therefore reasonable to accept the "Unexplainable," the "Unseeing," the "Mysterious Ways," the "Esoteric," and the "Subliminal;" all metaphorical prescriptions of whatever the rulers and priestly classes were propagating. Reading, writing and speaking other languages was the educational prerogative of the ruling classes who used them, by any means necessary, to control and exploit the uneducated, ignorant and obedient; including lying, plagiarising, deceiving and implanting fear of God into them. Due to self-deception, even the well- educated believed in these myths, for they were attracted by the sense of the belief itself, even more-so than the object of their belief.

The deception in the Jesus myth adopted by the Christian dogma was rooted in polytheistic believes and cults of previous centuries. Numerous examples exist confirming the deceptive myth on the "originality" of the Christian religion, for another myth confirms the legend of the *Attis,* a goddess who lived in ancient Greece about 1200 BC, who was born of a virgin mother on December 25th, crucified, her body was placed in a tomb and after 3 days, *Attis* was resurrected. Was this some kind of astronomical historical coincidence? In historical context; Persia, Mesopotamia, Egypt and North Africa were crossroad between Greece (with its easily accessible 1400 islands), Arabia and India. Communication, trade, arts and letters between cultures—by land and sea—were definitely very active. The appearance and disappearance of religious cults, prophetic chiliastic declarations of the coming of the "end of the world" and humanity's doom and gloom was at an obscenely depressive level but also an essential part of religiousness in this vast cultural region.

Greek, Aramaic, Egyptian, Persian languages (and much later Arab) were spoken, written and used to translate or mistranslate philosophical, medical and astrological texts. Ritual habits and oral story-telling were interpreted and re-interpreted and then travelled to far regions and back. Religious temples in these countries and regions were operating as free enterprises, each competing with other temples to entice more of the public with spectacular theatrics of fire and sounds. This ancient Bronze and Iron Age industry of religiousness operated on the assumption that the public would believe any reasonable sounding claim but who had not the faintest idea of the kind of Gods that were represented in each temple. This *modus operandi* enticed each temple or cult to borrow, plagiarise whole, or parts of, established rituals, myths and superstitions and promote those as their own original-text, delivered by God, to his representatives on earth.

- *Mithras of Persia* (present day Iran) 1,200 BC was born on December 25th of a virgin mother had 12 Disciples, who performed miracles and who, upon his death, was buried for 3 days and was resurrected. Mithras was also known as "The Light," "The Truth" and many other titles. The Christian litany to Jesus could easily be an allegorical litany to the Sun-God Mithras. The Sun-God Mithras is regarded as the pagan Jesus Christ or Messiah Saviour (named in Greek) who was often represented as carrying a lamb on his shoulders, just as Jesus is. Midnight services were found in both religions, the Virgin mother was easily merged with the virgin-mother Mary. Petra, the sacred rock of Mithraism, became Peter, the foundation of the Christian Church.
- In India, 3 centuries after goddess Attis, or about 900 BC a new man-made God was invented by the name *Krishna of Hindustan,*

who was born of a virgin mother of *Akee*. A star in the East signalled his coming, he performed miracles; he had disciples and, upon his death, was also resurrected. It appears that the religious industry of the time had a poor record of selection of religious claims for, throughout the cultural region, there was repeated or slightly modified speculations used by the religious entrepreneurs.

- Both Krishna and Jesus were held to really be god incarnated.
- Both were incarnated and born of a virgin mother.
- The Father of each was a Carpenter.
- Both were of royal descent.
- Each had the title of "Saviour."
- Both were "without a sin."
- Both were crucified.
- Both were crucified between two thieves.
- In Greece, the same old myth was repeated but slightly modified as in the case of *Dionysus* who, in 500 BCE, was born of a virgin mother on December 25th, who was a travelling teacher and who also performed miracles such as turning water into wine. Dionysus was referred to as the "King of Kings," the "Alpha and Omega;" titles with subliminal religious connotations. Needless to say, Dionysus, upon his death, was also claimed to be resurrected!

Now, Christmas is one of the most important celebrations in Christianity that has deep roots in mythological traditions. In Greek tradition we find similarities in the myths of the birth of Christ and Dionysus. In December the ancient Greeks celebrated the birth of Dionysus, calling him the "Saviour" (or Christ in Greek) and "divine infant" whose father was Zeus, the God of all Gods. On December 30th, ancient Greeks commemorated his rebirth. The most well-known Greek tradition is the singing of Christmas Carols. In ancient Greece there were specific carols for the rebirth of Dionysus which were sung by children symbolising joy, wealth and peace but sung only in the homes of the rich. These Carols were sung on the island of Samos where Dionysus was born.

The world, which was known then as the Bronze Age, had its share of polytheistic cults whose main goal was to established themselves as the "One and Only" true religion—representing whoever was "God" at the moment. Peoples' anticipation of religious promises was at its highest point; cults and temple priests were under enormous pressures to public expectations or face the consequences of diminishing returns in their power and profits. The question still remains to be answered as to why did most ancient cults and temples and religions invent myths and up coming prophets of the time share the same attributes with one another, such as: the day of birth December 25th, the virgin birth, death by crucifixion, the inevitable resurrection, and the same number of 12 Disciples? To answer these questions we must investigate the latest of the Roman Imperial Cult's self appointed prophets: Jesus Christ. Not wishing to appear redundant, I must repeat the Jesus myth as my premise.

Jesus was born on December 25th in Nazareth, not in Bethlehem, in the present day Palestine region, of a virgin mother who had given an immaculate birth to baby Jesus---before marrying her husband Joseph. Jesus' birth was announced by a star in the East which the 3 Magi (wise men) followed to lead them to the "Saviour." At the age of 12, Jesus was a renowned teacher, and was baptised at the age of 30 by John the Baptist and, like the Son-God Horus, Jesus began his preaching thereafter. He also had 12 Disciples who were travelling with him while he was performing miracles such as walking on water and raising the dead. Jesus was betrayed by one of his disciples, Judas of Iscariot, was put to trial and found guilty, was then crucified and buried in a cave. After 3 days of burial, Jesus was resurrected and went to heaven.

Here, it is where one may have a historical problem believing such a fabrication of such an unlikely event, that the statistical chance of Jesus birthday and resurrection coinciding with the others mentioned above, is totally and completely astronomical. Unless, of course, the whole existence of Jesus is a symbolic, metaphorical myth copied or plagiarised from other sources---due to a lack of imagination on the part of the proponents of such a nonsense-story. Language permits humans to invent symbolic, metaphorical terms and myths by using delusional-based linguistic terms in order to "connect" unrelated events, concepts or bodies. Using only reality-based linguistic terms would not support metaphorical concepts, but a mix of both would do the task. The Zodiac Signs are all metaphorical entities "connecting" unrelated bodies like animals to stars, stars to human figures and planetary positions to human conditions. Metaphors do not tell lies or truths or distort of them; they simply provide a means to prescribe-connectors to unrelated concepts. Humans use metaphors to describe "unexplainable," "magical," "esoteric" or "mysterious" concepts. Using symbolic-based terms and metaphors to describe or prescribe something eliminates the necessary need for a priest, rabbi or imam to provide evidence, proof, reason or scientific confirmation for a claim. For example, the metaphorical term "miracle" is used as a means of suspending the Laws of Nature, thus connecting two unrelated events: the non-existing "miracle" to the reality of the Laws of Nature.

The originators who invented the Zodiac Signs used theism which was used as the metaphorical concept of the Sun-God, which is located in the centre of the circle of the Zodiac Calendar. The cross that divides the Zodiac circle is of a practical nature---it is the 4 equal dividing parts of the 12 constellations. All other 12 Signs of constellations are based on metaphorical myths symbolically connecting the unrelated stars to animal or human figures. This made it possible for the originators to give a logical meaning to the whole concept of the Zodiac Signs. We find no other Gods and no theistic claims or supernatural entities governing the manifestations of the Zodiac Signs. It simply represents the manifestations of the human imagination to create a mythological entity that offers a sense of a natural order in the sky. It offers no legal and moral guidance, no religious dogma, no suspension of the Natural Laws, no theistic fabrications and not an everlasting obedience to a celestial entity. It is simply an astrological myth---with a foundation the reality of the stars--and nothing more! What then is so important with the December 25th day for Christians and other theistic cults for whom so many regard as a day of holy significance? Let us see!

On December 24th the Eastern star *"Sirius"* is the brightest star in the sky and it aligns itself with the 3 of the brightest group of stars in our *Orion's Belt*. This group of 3 stars are called "The Three Kings," a name which still stands after 3,000 years. The pagan myth of "The Three Kings" was widely known throughout the ancient world. This explains its popularity with the general public and with any religious cult's agenda which included the use of the December 25th day. All "The Three Kings" and the star "Sirius" are pointing to the East on December 25th which coincides with the birth of the Sun-God in the Zodiac Calendar at Winter Solstice. This is why "The Three Kings" follow the Eastern star "Sirius," in order to locate the sunrise (the birth of the first day of witter Solstice), thus the birth of the Son-God of the Sun-God.

The *Virgo* Sign is the constellation of a series of stars which are called *Virgo the Virgin (*Virgo is Virgin in Latin) and its pictorial representation is of a young girl holding a stem of wheat—the sign of harvest time which is around the month of September. The name of the ancient city of Bethlehem is literally translated as *"The House of Bread"* with the symbol of the wheat and it is also the constellation of *Virgo the Virgin,* a metaphorical symbolic celestial sign in the Zodiac calendar, not on earth.

Here is the symbolic metaphorical root of the *"Resurrection"* which theist-temples around the ancient world adopted to support religious fabrications. The reality of the stars is that on the days of December 22nd 23rd and 24^{th,} the Sun is at its lowest point in the daytime horizon, which metaphorically it represents the perceivable death of the Sun---and the resurrection of the Son-God on December 25th. During the December 22nd, 23, and 24th the Sun appears to reside in the vicinity of the Zodiac Southern Cross or Crux constellation, thus the Sun was metaphorically "dead" for 3 days and then was symbolically resurrected or born again. On December 25th the Sun appears to begin, once again its familiar angular movement of one-degree upwards in the sky and this completes the metaphorical and symbolic "resurrection" or the birth of the "Son-God."

Of all the astrological symbols surrounding the mythical Jesus, the symbol of the Cross is the most prominent one, next to the virgin-birth. The Zodiac arch symbol is divided by a vertical and a horizontal line. These 2 lines form a visible cross in the center of the Zodiac Signs and over the yellow symbol of the Sun-God. This forms the *Cross of the Zodiac* and the Arc of it is part of the sign of holiness of the Sun-God. The Cross of the Arc was adopted by many religious cults as far back as 3,500 BCE. It symbolised the "holiness" of a prophet, a temple-priest, a magician, a notable travelling teacher or a spiritual man or a woman--by placing the yellow-coloured Arc at the back of the head. It was later adopted as a Christian symbol of Jesus and his 12 Disciples, as a sign of their holiness, and since then it has been brilliantly introduced into the enterprise of religious deception. The scale of metaphorical symbolism in theistic circles is vast and unquestionably attractive, well-placed and extensively promoted. It captured and transformed the pagan symbolism of the Zodiac Signs, and built around them unfounded religious suppositions for supporting their aims.

True enough, the Zodiac Signs carry an unlimited symbolism within the role of Sun-God, a focal point of realism in the interpretation of its theorem. The Sun-God controls the daylight of the world and the darkness of the night, which is the center of this phenomenon. The Sun-God appears every morning and would appear once again in the next and the morning after, which represents the glory of the Sun-God who supports life on earth. This man-made theorem provided humanity with answers of a kind that did not enslave it to any religious dogma, tyranny or lies for thousands of years and long before the appearance of Zoroastrianism, Judaism, Christianity and Islam. From the early period of Bronze and Iron Age history, a heavy dose of religiousness was intersected into the interpretation of nature and the universe. Those were explained by ignoramus lack of knowledge, and by the cunning political and religious schemes of deceitful rulers and cultists' priests. Readopting and manipulating the pagan meaning of the myth of the Zodiac Signs was a task for the unintelligent and lazy schemers; the ready-made theorem of the Zodiac Signs provided them with ample information to build their distortions of their religious enterprise upon. Priests and rulers were not knowledgeable scholars or innovative enough to invent an original theistic theorem. This is why they all adopted the metaphorical mythology of any revelation from any part of the world and from any pagan theism that suited their lust for power, profit and theocratic dictatorial control over their subjects.

In a normal course of events, the promotion of the latest prophet or messiah---in a long list of them—falls within groups of individuals who were functioning independent of the messiah himself. In most cases, the promotion of a given prophet or messiah would depend on the invented popularity and the believability of the myth they were attempting to solidify. Most of the prophets or messiahs had long been dead---by the time legends or myths were invented about that "holy man"--as is the case with Moses, Jesus (Josephus's fabrications) and Mohammad (plagiarisms in the Qur'an's Haddith).

The premise of their theistic mythology was the Zodiac constellation system which gave them the foundation of structural, logical explanation and presentation of the internal structure of their religion. The *Sun-God* became "God", the *Son-God* became Jesus as the "Son of God", the 12 Constellations became the 12 "Apostles," and the Constellation the *Virgo the Virgin* became the Virgin Mary and the Resurrection is the logical interpretation of the appearance of the daily or "reborn" sunlight; a sequential metaphorical connection to forming the story of Jesus and God; with one exception, the mythical story of Moses, Jesus, Mohammad's and God, is entirely false.

The poverty of the Biblical narrative---among other things---is demonstrated by the repetitive use of the number 12 which appears on numerous occasions. For instance, there are the 12 tribes of Israel, the 12 Sons of Jacob, the 12 Judges of Israel, the 12 Great Patriarchs, the 12 Princes of Israel, the 12 Old Testament Prophets, the 12 Kings of Israel and the 12 Disciples of Jesus. The number 12 appears to be a repetitive customary copying, which may have something to do with the initial number 12 in the myth of the 12 Zodiac Constellations of the cosmos. Equal, logical, repetitive sequencing of the metaphorical and subliminal core of the Zodiac structures, is evident in the shared similarities of the following: the God-Attis, the God-Krishna, the God-Horus, the Holyman-Dionysus, the God-Mithras the Son of God-Jesus, and many others. It is not surprising that this is not the final list of mythological holy figures or Sons of Gods who shared similar backgrounds and characteristics.

Born on December 25[th,] for instance, and of a virgin mother, or crucified and

resurrected are the following figures:
* *Osiris and Horus of Egypt, 31st century B.CE.*
* *Zoroaster of Persia, 3rd century B.CE.*
* *The Viking God Odin of the Scandinavia, circa 1st century B.CE.*
* *Thammuz of Syria, circa 410 B.CE.*
* *Baal and Taut "the Only Begotten God" of Phoenicia,*
* *Adad of Assyria, 820 B.CE.*
* *Aclides of Thebes, 1200 BCE*
* *Hamolxis of Thrace, circa 6th century AC*
* *Thorn, Son of Odin of the Gaul's, Roman Era*
* *Cadmus of Greece, King of Thebes, 2000 BC*
* *Ixion and Quirinus of Rome, Greek mythology*
* *Prometheus of Caucasus, Greek Mythology*
* *Genghis Khan of Mongolia, (1162 – 1227), Mongolia*
* *Gautama Siddhartha—Buddha--of Nepal, between the 6th and 4th BCE*
* *Romulus of the settlement of Rome 753 BC,*
* *Huitzilopochtli (god of war) of the Aztec.*
* *Hercules of Greece, Greek Mythology*

By the 1st century, regardless of their religion, ethnicity or where people grew up; they were bombarded daily with a heavy dose of cultural religiosity, the likes of which can still be found today in most Latin American, North Arabia and African countries, Italy, Greece and Russia. Today a heavy religiousness all over the world is made of street preachers, catholic priests, fundamentalist of evangelical leanings the likes of the corporate *Seventh Day Adventists, Jehovah's Witnesses*, religious schools, theological seminaries, Mega Churches etc., all competing for the attention of the confused, the helpless, the ill-educated and the poverty-stricken population. The acts of praying and repentance are instilled within them as the only solution offered to the wretched, perpetual-sinful and ignorant Christians or Muslims. They are crossing themselves or praying for more than 5 times a day, convinced that God or their favoured saint will save them from their misery. Often, one hears (I have witnessed it) of someone who is saving his little money to pay for a private seminar on "theology" hoping that he can then find solutions to his life's problems.

During the Bronze Age---some 2 thousand years ago--the cultural religiosity was at its peak propagating the "end of the world," the discovering of the "unknown God," fearing the "wrath of God," and the coming "of one true God." Temples were competing with one another to entice worshipers with deceitful magic tricks and spectacular showmanship the likes of the Mega-churches' Evangelical rallies in Brazil and the USA today. Self-appointed prophets, future tellers and fakirs were the frequent street spectacles peddling their own self-deluding oracles—the kind one finds in Indian, Pakistani or Thailandian streets today.

The Fertile Crescent, Mesopotamia and the Arabian Peninsula have always been a historically intensive tribal region and desert tribal ties were extremely important. Each tribal society was governed by its own inherited traditional customs and passed them on those to the next generation. Ignorance was not only an individual trait but a cultural phenomenon that embraced each tribal ethnic society as a whole. Education, in general, was the exclusive prerogative of the ruling classes as also was any inherited wealth. Because people were not literate, they depended on the words and decisions of their pagan religious leaders, whose views were very narrow and confined within the ancient customs, traditions and personal feelings. Various tribal societies formed a multipot of pagan worship of traditional celestial protectors and newly invented idol Gods, the likes which were housed in the Kaaba Cube of the Arabian Peninsula. Educators were elders who were teaching pupils the metaphorical events of the metaphysical cosmos, but failed to teach the material reality of the universe simply because the natural world was not as intricate as the mythological invention of their oral story-telling was. Illusions and delusions gave them the freedom of speculation without the need of prove their assumptions, and metaphorical terms were used as 'connectors,' to conclude or seal their speculations, between unrelated events or things.

In Mesopotamia, Greece and most of the Arabian Peninsula there were Gods for every occasion and temples for every believer who was seeking an entity to belong to and a sense of security and solidarity (phenomena we still witness today with members of mega-churches). Escaping from freedom (to use Erich Fromm's words) was a psychological comfort-zone and religious submission brought about a sense of protection from the unknown, evils, gods, fairies, saints, illnesses and demons. Typical of religiousness, the entire diversified cultural regions were propagating a sense of strong negativism of the material world that people were living in. That sense of social doom and gloom was constantly reinforced by temple priests and paganists, who were in the business of providing a "salvation" for those who were willing to submit to their temples' persuasions, make donations and participate in ritual ceremonies. For example, at certain ceremonies, naked worshipers will present gold offerings to a Sumerian *Goddess Inanna* at her temple in the city of Uruk. Uruk was literally an independent city-state. Another Goddess-Ishtar was a Goddess and Shepherd of Uruk and doorkeeper of the *Na* (heaven) who also briefly lived in the Underworld, to be resurrected at Midwinter (Winter Solstice) on December 25th.

So, how does all of the above relate to today's organised religion? Today's monotheistic religions of Judaism, Christianity and Islam have their ancient roots in polytheistic traditional tribal ties and superstitions in the Arabian Peninsula and Greece. Although Christianity has overtly forsaken its polytheistic tribal roots, covertly it simply has replaced "gods" for all reasons with "saints" for all seasons. The Catholic Church alone has more than 6,000 saints in its registry. Amongst the 6,000 Catholic patrons and saints, for example, if you *"seek you shall find"* you will find one or another for nearly everyone's delusional needs; from curing the sick, as in Santa Rosa de Lima, Peru, to St. Nicolas--of the Greek Orthodox Church in Greece--protector of fishermen.

Sainthood is a mythical relic of the past and manmade through our imagination, such as, *Saint Dominic* who falsely stargazes through state of the art astronomical instruments, and *Saint Margaret of Clitherow* who is today's patron of businesswomen who holds a cell phone in one hand while she is holding a modern briefcase in the other. Personal feelings of a Saint are symbolic, not evidence of truth or reality. This is not harmless religious symbolism, for believing in them---and treating them as if they are real--creates an internal acceptance of delusions in other spheres of life in the existence of UFO's, green Martians or Sasquatch. Without realising it, we are constructing metaphorical prison-walls of "comfort zones" around us. Those are based on subliminal faith in all sorts of delusions which are mostly and deliberately propagated by deceitful or self-deceptive institutionalised religious bodies.

Through historical deceptions, humanity has been confronted by well-organised groups which have divided us and scattered within the endless void of religious fanatism, fatalism, war mongering, anti-women, anti-science, genital mutilation of both boys and girls, superstition, tribalism, the biblical blessing of slavery, child sexual abuse, torture chambers of the Inquisition, the burning of people alive, anti-Semitic, anti-abortion, anti-contraception, anti-gay, the biblical mass extermination of children, submission to a religious totalitarian system, eternal damnation, born in sin, all done in the name of a biblical, self-declared, "I am a jealous God", a "Capricious God," a "Vengeful God" of purgatory, a God who will never leave you alone even after death, a God who can read your thoughts, a God who demands an eternal praise from you and who eternally listens to harp music in heaven. A leftover from its polytheistic roots that still remains and forms the core of Christianity's delusions is the 3-in-one-god fallacy: the Son of God, the Holy Spirit and Sky-God, all in one Troika of Gods!

This is the short list of frightful actions and superstitions that humanity has suffered in the last 50 centuries. Religion must be declared a crime against humanity! It is time to put an end to it and, escape from religion and emancipate ourselves from it!

In the normal course of human relationships, when one commits an act of evil against another person, the victim will tend to sever any attachment with the offender. There will be no sense of respect, no sense of care or love for the offender. This is a moral decision we all take based on our survival instinct, self-preservation and protection of our family members. We also condemn acts of violence against innocent persons whether young, old or helpless. It is one and the same moral decision we take to protect our family members or our neighbours against anyone who intends to harm another. Yet we who have witnessed an evil act, who will take a moral and lawful position against any offender; why do we continue permitting religious acts of violence against humanity, against our children, instead of taking a stand against members of organised religions who are dedicated to deception and abuse?

What will it take for you and me to avoid and overcome such a double moral standard? Why do we have such an un-natural obedience to organised religions which blind us so deceitfully? Have we not read the latest news about religious crimes against children? Why do we remain ignorant about the history of our religious institutions? Do we prefer to remain blindly faithful against truth, reason and evidence? Are we afraid of losing our freedom from religion, and do we willingly surrender our self-respect, our intelligence and our dignity? Religious ceremonies sound peaceful, lovely and up-lifting, but this is the beginning of deception that leads us to experience archaic rituals of medieval faith, candlelight and utterings of dead languages, and no one does it better than the Jewish, the Greek Orthodox and the Roman Catholic. The assault on the senses appeal to us not to think, not to question, not to doubt, not to analyse, but to retain our blind faith by assuming we become more virtuous.

True enough, mega-church ceremonies that gather huge crowds are very seductive because they create in us a sense of belonging with something that it is bigger than us. But is this a viable position for us, to relinquish our sense of freedom and our sense of wonder about how humanity began on earth? How can we then explain the mysteries of life, the elegance of the universe, the beauty of reality and the essence of our humanity without becoming victims of religious superstition and of a celestial dictator called the Sky-God? Biological science, in the last 180 years or so, has steadily overturned religious fallacies about how life began on earth. Strangely, the followers of Judaism, Christianity and Islam prefer the dogma of their religion over biological scientific of the origins of life, the age of our planetary system and the humanist moral base of our behaviour. Fundamentalist and polemical faith around the world is on the rise. It shows how dogmatically religious explanations undermine our educational system, our choice of life-style, our choice of medical and reproductive methods; and in general, instead of verified scientific evidence.

Atheists and humanists must not become overconfident that reason and scientific evidence will overcome or at least rollback religious dogmatism. The enemy of reason, truth and science is the irrational religious faith which is feeding criminal intolerance to its believers throughout the world. We should increasingly be concerned about warped and twisted religious morality which is fed to our children in faith-based schools which can last a lifetime. These children are socially segregated by the closed culture of fundamentalist propaganda described as an educational system, which is financially supported by public money. It prevents them from looking at life's reality, the origin of life and the humanist morality of our species.

The danger is that children in religious schools are indoctrinated with much more than crossing themselves, lighting candles, singing hymns and saying prayers; and parents paying are for it. Education passes through a religious filter in sex education and alternative lifestyle choices, but is limited in curriculum science. Each faith-based school teaches their own version of truth and that there is the one and only true faith which the children must follow in accordance to their holy-book, rather than learn through reason, evidence and science. There is no encouragement to think critically to understand the world in an analytical fashion. They prescribe faith-based lessons that are not supervised by outside educational authorities. To be within the legal requirements, faith based schools teach evolution vs. creation with faith-based curriculums which briefly present the evolution side but also affirm what their particular faith believes about creation. Do the teachers know the truth between evolution vs. creation? I assume they do! Then why do they insist of teaching faith based creation? Is it because they make their living out of lying to children, and therefore do not care, so long they continue getting paid?

Students may express their personal opinions about human evolution or creation, but those are based on personal beliefs and assumptions, not on scientific evidence about the origin of our species. This is because students are not taught the science of human biology, the Darwinian *Theory of Evolution, the Origin of Species*, from ape to man and the astronomical origins of the universe. In elementary "science" classes, every one of the students affirms their own beliefs that humans were not evolved but were created by a mythological God. The truth is that the Neanderthals, the Cro-Magnon and the Homo sapiens were not evolved from apes---*we are apes*---nor were humans evolved from monkeys or chimpanzees but rather from a shared ancestor which was neither human, monkey nor chimpanzee. The faith-based schools claim that they want their students to be open-minded but, through faith-guidance, teachers reject the factual and scientific core evidence of the origins of man. Where does this lead? Do students need to choose between what they 'believe' and what the factual and scientific evidence demonstrates? Since when has the term *personal-belief* become an investigative term? Is the notion of subjective personal belief the equivalent to truth and scientific evidence? The industry of religion encourages the notion that it is enough for us to *believe,* for this is all that God requires from every student of traditional faith-based schools.

Faith based schools create social barriers among young people of different communities and religions, where there are none. Based on their political rights to preserve their traditions and their beliefs, faith based schools create a divisive force of an "Us" and "Them" mentality. This is a social segregation which it is conveniently called "self-identity," but this sense of identity sets them apart from other members of the community. The young students become strangers in their own land where they were born or raised. We have been warned by recent tragic events created by religious divisions, tribal discriminations in the Arabian Peninsula and Africa and the continuing undeclared social divisions between Catholics and Protestants in Northern Ireland. The equally religious fanatical Irish Protestant, the late Oliver Cromwell once said that he makes no bones about it by stating,

"Catholism is more than a religion. It is a political power therefore implied to believer there will be no peace in Ireland until the Catholic Church is crushed."

This is a tribal style of vengeance that has been carried on throughout many centuries and it is generated by labelling people as belonging to a certain religion rather than seeing them as individuals. The Russian Orthodox Church has forced the government of Russia not to allow any other religious faith to build their worship places within the national boundaries of the country. Atheist and Humanist do not need to shout and be dogmatic anti-god but rather explain the god-fallacy through dialectical evidence in today's age of scientific reason. We need to understand the extent of obscurities and irrational behaviour of some of the believers, regardless of their ethnic origins. For instance, this article appeared on Al Jazeera news on December 15, 2014 which states,

"Devotees of a dead guru who has been in the freezer in North India since January [2014] won a court battle delaying his cremation for at least another seven weeks. Supporters had approached the court in Punjab state seeking a delay on an earlier order for the cremation of Hindu "god-man" Astutost Warryana whom authorities declared dead on January 29 [2014] ...Followers have insisted their spiritual leader is not dead but in a state of deep meditation and will eventually return to lead them. ...Ahead of [the court's] decision thousands of followers massed at guru's ashram in Nurmahal at the weekend in a show of support for the guru whom they said should be allowed to continue his "Sadhana," the highest level of meditation."

WHAT IF ISLAM IS TRUE?

In the last 50 years there have been many claims against or in support of the religion of Islam. Most of these claims are based on philosophical and theological arguments presented by moderate or fundamentalist supporters of other religions such as Jewish, Christian or secularists of every sort. It has become common place on both sides of the argument to debate whether Islam is a religion of peace or not or whether Islam is even a religion or a political ideology, or a combination of all. Above these arguments, we now have the apologists of each religion who are trying to justify the practices of their respective religions in all levels of social life. This is a common and acceptable discussion taking place among friends and co-workers, neighbours and family members as well as among academics, whose apologetic agenda should be treated with a conscious approach. In addition, skilful language is used for or against the religion of Islam, such as the term "phobic" to apply to any disagreement you may have with your opponent. In this case if you show evidence of religious deception you become "Islamo-phobic." The Israeli right-wing politicians have followed the same linguistic trick by claiming that any arguments against Israel's governing policies towards the Palestinian people are termed "anti-Semitic," a claim which is completely false.

Let us therefore begin with the social definition of what a political ideology is; it is a power that controls every facet of the citizens' life, of its followers by organising them in according to its political agenda. The Nazi Party of Germany, for example, was a political ideology which immersed itself into every aspect of its institutional or private citizens' lives. Every economic and social group was organised under the guidance of the Nazi ideology, which stood on the top of the socio-political pyramid, controlling the underling community sectors. This control is total, and is given the term "totalitarian" or "Fascism." This is a factual, not a philosophical argument, for factual evidence exist to prove it.

In our discussion we need to ask; is the Islamic religion a totalitarian system that controls the socio-political lives of its followers? Remember that all organised religions have their Holy Books which represent the guiding power of each religion. In the case of Islam, there is a term---*din*---which is translated to mean "a way of life." This term refers to more than just a few beliefs and rituals to follow in Muslim Friday prayers, for "a way of life" means something for every Muslim to follow under Islam every day, in war, in economics, in marriage, in women and children, and in any issues deemed against the religion of Islam. In short, Islam, by its own written and traditional tribal guidance, is more than just worship and beliefs, for it embraces every part of their social living: it is therefore totalitarian.

In western societies, politicians, Muslim religious leaders and others, portray Islam as a religion of peace (but why this call is necessary?), modesty, self-control and decency, a pure and uncorrupted "way of life." Have you ever noticed that no other religion starts with the term "religion of peace" other than Islam? Why do apologists of Islam feel obligated to stress the peaceful nature of their religion? Is it because; in the history of the Islamist Jihad's religion there was never a search for peace? However, criticising Islam as a religion, or as a political ideology does not make one anti-Islamic, just as criticising the British government does not make one an anti-British.

Here, I propose to present factual Islamic evidence and written deceptions, and I will leave my readers to make their own conclusions. Muslims throughout their history believed that the Qur'an was written by Allah and not by men. Atheists and humanists do not think that there is any evidence that the Qur'an comes from God. In fact, it is recognizable that the Qur'an is a non-Arab product of the antiquity or tribal culture of the Near Eastern historical background that embraces Persian, Roman Christian and Jewish civilisations. Evidence of this claim lies within the Qur'an itself, which contains all kinds of echoes from other cultures about Abraham and Moses, the Virgin Mary and even Alexander the Great. The idea of the Prophet took centuries to be formed by the invention of tradition. This is the period of antiquity where extraordinary military and religious savagery, violence and sanctity were fused together to create new empires and destroy old ones. The religion of Islam was in the center of such violent conflict because it was, and is, the product of a much broader monotheistic religion which tried to transform the pagan ethical and moral presumptions of the Jewish and Christian faiths, and much of the world as it existed in the 7th and 8th centuries.

Monotheism gave the newly established empires a form of legitimacy with the claim that the "One and all powerful God" was on their side. When the Roman Emperor Constantine the Great converted to Christianity in 325 AD, he authenticated God's power with his own colossal of imperial expansion. Monotheistic religion became a very useful tool for the Persian Kings, for the Caesars and ultimately for the Arab military pre-Islamic Caliphs. Conquering and pillaging provided a much needed dignity and food to people who were poor and weak, the ignorant and oppressed who, to that point in history, were not recognised as a valuable part of society. Up to this point, the tendency of the people in the Arabian Peninsula was to construct pagan idols of faith which ultimately served as the base for participating in monotheism.

As monotheistic religions, Judaism, Christianity and Islam are considered to be very distinct from one another but, in reality they are not. In fact the historical antiquity demonstrates that they are not distinct entities, but that they were always a mixture of gradual and sudden changes of swirling beliefs. As they advanced and developed they created myths claiming that the way they are distinctive now, they always have been.

Mohammad came from the pagan settlement of Mecca which did not have any Jewish or Christian elements, a settlement which is located in the middle of the desolate desert and thousands of kilometres from the nearest Roman frontier of Palestine and the Mediterranean coast. Due to its geographical isolation; this is the reason why the origins of the Qur'an's must have come from outside this desert. This is precisely why the Muslims make the case that the Qur'an comes from God, for it could not have come from other religious human sources. But the human sources of the Qur'an appear to be very clear, based on its own written biblical stories from the Old Testament and Judaeo-Christian traditions. Besides, it is proven that the Qur'an was written centuries after Mohammad's death.

There is no doubt that, for Muslim believers, the Qur'an is believed to have been written by God, for it is a fundamental belief requirement before one can call himself a Muslim. But if you are atheist or humanist, not a Muslim; you have no obligation to follow what is demanded of you, you can now analyse or criticise the Qur'an objectively. You need to look at the Qur'an as you would look at any ancient book, including the Bible, Homer's Iliad or the Old Testament and search for their human origins, in order to have a base for further investigation. If you are not willing to do an objective investigation on the origins of the Qur'an textual messages then you are effectively becoming a Muslim, dealing with faith and theology rather than with the history of Islam. Because the myth of the origins of the Qur'an, as it is told by Muslims, omits the historical evidence of the Roman, Persian and Christian influence upon Islam in the 7th and 8th centuries. This was a historical period in the Middle East where it was believed that anything that was happening in that savage tribal world was because of God willed it. The Arabs of the period, just like everyone else, were looking to the heavens for answers to tribal wars, sicknesses, plagues, the suffering and the poverty, and were wondering about solutions to these problems on earth.

As the Arab-Bedouins began to conquer the Persian Empire and others, they also began to believe that it was God's will that they play a special role in formulating a new empire. It is true that Mohammad's so called Revelations from God had a huge role in these conquests and, for Muslims of the period, these Qur'an passages were not mere words but messages that came directly from God to the Arab fighting forces. However, the process by which these Qur'anic verses were shaped into a religion was a vastly more complicated process than Muslim tradition will have us believed. Academics and scholars, in the last 50 years, have begun to look at the religion of Islam as part of the western socio-cultural setting, and as part of the new trilogy of western religions. They began scrutinising, in depth, the religion of Islam in the same manner they had scrutinised Judaism and Christianity in the past.

In the past, these historians have recognised that Judaism and Christianity are products of human cultural civilisation as much as they are of prophetic religious instigation. The myths that are told about the origins of their faith---in their holy books---may or may not have a spiritual or theological significance, other than what their believers believe them to be. The Qur'an is believed, by Muslims, to be much more literally the word of God than Christians believed of their Bible. This kind of absolutism prevents Muslims from questioning the base of their faith or any part of the Qur'an. This means that the martyr's reward of 72 virgins, the strong belief in the actual existence of a place in the sky called Paradise, the importance of virginity and the sexualising rewards of believers, and other, are fundamental to all Muslims. It has become the task of the apologists of Islam to de-emphasise with half-truths such fundamental messages of the Qur'an.

What the Qur'an says about:
SEX AND VIRGINITY AS REWARD
For the sex-starved tribal Arab men, the Qur'an offered them a delusional means to satisfy their sexual fantasies and cravings. Many attempts have been made by apologists to de-sexualise Islam from its core emphasis on the sexual satisfaction of its male followers. For instance, Islam allows sex with pre-puberty girls, for a man having sex with up to 4 wives and sex

with slave girls. Mohammad had sex with 9 wives—breaking his own 4 wives rule---and had sex with *Ishia* his 9 year old wife; he had sex with his female war captives and his servant girls. Islam proclaims that "virginity" is the ultimate reward a martyr will receive upon entering Paradise, where 72 virgins will be awaiting those who fought and died for God. But, in according to *Hadith,* the 72 virgins will be the minimum a martyr will receive, and God will give the martyr the miraculous extra sexual strength and an eternal erection to daily copulate with at least 100 virgins.

In the standard consumerist slogan that "sex-sells," then the Qur'an's emphasis on the martyr's sexualised life-style is far more prominent than in any other cultures that Muslims condemned as being sexually immoral. The current problem lies with the apologists of Islam who try to re-interpret the scriptures and make the sexualised religion more palatable to the followers in the West and to the critics of Islam. However, any linguistic tricks, half-truths and outright distortions cannot obscure what is written in the Qur'an. The sexualised tone of Islam is based on Mohammad's own attitude and behaviour which all Muslims were obliged to follow:

Qur'an 33:21 *"indeed in the Messenger of Allah [Mohammad] you have a good example to follow."*

So, here are some brief sexualised examples for Muslims to follow,

Qur'an 44-51-54---*"As for the righteous [martyrs] they shall be lodged in peace together [in Paradise] amid gardens and fountains, arrayed in rich silks and fine brocade. Even thus; and we shall wed them to dark-eyed Houris [light-skinned young virgin females]."*

The emphasis on Houris fair-skinned females is used as a "hook" to entice the sexual desires of the tribal men. The term *Houris i*s subliminally related to young virgins which combines the totality of sex with 72 virgins. The term *"wed or wed-them"* means having sex with the Houris.

Qur'an 52:20---*"They [martyrs] will recline [with comfort] on thrones arranged in ranks. And we shall marry them to houris, with wide lovely eyes."* The term "marry" to Houris is used as metaphor for "sexual relation" to light-skinned girls.

Qur'an 55:54-56---*"They [martyrs] shall recline on couches lined with thick brocade, and within reach will hang the fruits of both gardens [one being of the female's-garden, the other of Paradise]. Which of [the two of] your Lord's blessings would you deny? Therein are bashful virgins whom neither man nor jinnee will have touched before."* The *"Bashful virgins never touched before"* offers the martyr a gift of sexual purity; for once a girl is "touched" she becomes impure and unclean and therefore undesirable.

Qur'an 55:70-74---*"In each [of the gardens] there shall be virgins chaste*

and fair. Which of your Lord's blessings would you deny? Dark-eyed virgins, sheltered in their tents, [which would you deny?] whom neither man nor jinnee will have touched before"? This is a clear message to the martyrs that the dark-eyed virgins will be chaste as part of the Lord's blessings. Not much demonstration of love and emotional affections there, for what counts is the "chaste" and the sex.

Qur'an 56:22-24---*"And [there will be Houris] companions with beautiful, big, lustrous eyes---like unto Pearls well-guarded. A reward for their [martyred] deeds of their past [life]." H*ere again is the emphasis on the beauty of female characteristics that tribal men find attractive; which is also the overall delusionary appeal of fair-skinned *Houris* sexual enticement.

Qur'an 56:35-38---*"Verily, We have created them [Houris] of special creation, and made them virgins, loving [their spouses only], equal in age, for those [martyrs who are] on the Right Hand [of Allah]." T*he emphasis here is twofold, the miracle of special creation and making the *Houris* virgins. Both were made for the exclusive use of the martyrs' sexual needs, especially for those who have proven their beliefs can now sit on the right-hand side of Allah.

Qur'an 78:31-34--- *"Surely for the god-fearing awaits a place of security, gardens and vineyards and maidens [houris] with swelling breasts, like of age, and [just as] a cup overflowing [juice]."* Indeed, Paradise, in these verses, is described in favourable terms as an actual place which is full of pleasure for martyrs of Islam. These passages are literally believed by all Muslims, suicide bombers, including Muslims who have been culturally educated in the West.

Apologists of Islam are not very happy with the way westerners are viewing and criticising the Qur'an and are determined to "dress up" its verses and justify its focus that appears to be against the norms of a civilised culture. A special attention has been paid by the Saudi family of Saudi Arabia, aimed to "clean up" Islam's global negative image, especially regarding the term "virgin," which has become an all inclusive, sexualised image of Muslim social environment. How far, those apologists are willing to go in order to twist and distort the Qur'anic verses to silence their critics? For instance, in 2000, the apologist of Islam, secretive author Christoph Luxemburg, (a pseudonym) wrote that there are many miss-interpretations in the translation of the Qur'an including the term *"Virgin"* which should have instead been written as *"Raising"* and that the *houris* with *"swelling breasts"* refer to nothing more than "white raisings" and "juicy fruits."

This claim has become the focus of much satirical ridicule (by the late actor Robin Williams) and others. However, this claim of "Raisings" instead of "Virgins" gave other apologists of Islam an avenue to pursue the same idiotic path. So much for academic credibility! For instance, the Canadian author, gay-feminist, sometimes a proponent and other times an opponent of Islam, *Irshad Manji*, in an Oxford interview claimed that there is, in fact, an miss-interpretation of the term *"Virgin,"* which, instead, should have been written as *"Raising."* The question which was put to her was; *what is your view of the 72 virgins a martyr would receive in Paradise?* Manji answered that the term "Virgin" is a miss-interpretation of the term "Raising." The martyr will receive *72 Raisings* instead of *72 Virgins*. Imagine for a moment a hijacker or a suicide-bomber willingly going to his death, in order to receive Allah's *blessed-box of 72 raisings*. Needless to say, in a written note of encouragement to his fellow suicide-hijackers, the 9/11 ringleader, Mohammad Atta, cheered their impending "marriage in Paradise" to the wide-eyed 72 virgins that the Qur'an promises to the departed martyrs. This is the Islam's life-after-death! Allow me to---deliberately-distort---a Qur'an verse reading the term "Raising" instead of the correct term "Virgin." Let's hear how this verse sounds, in an example of the apologist's achievement in idiocy and absurdity:

Qur'an 55:54-56 (from above) ...Which of [the two of] your Lord's blessings would you deny? Therein are **bashful Raisings** which neither man nor jinnee will have touched before.

Qur'an 78:31-34... (again from above) Surely for the god-fearing awaits a place of security, gardens and vineyards and **maidens-Raisings** with swelling breasts, like of age and [just as] a cup overflowing [fruit-juice].

It is curious to observe how the three monotheist religions sprang out of the end of pagan Zodiac Signs mythology. All three religions incorporated their reputed founders to be celestially chosen: for the Jews was Abraham, for the Christians it was Jesus Christ and for Islam was Mohammad. This trinity of the chosen man-gods was no other than a substantial reduction from hundreds of pagan man-gods. The icon and statues of the Christian Virgin Mary succeeded the statues of the pagan Greek Goddess Dianna of Ephesus, the glorification and deification of pagan heroes changed into canonization of Catholic and Greek Orthodox Saints. As pagans had their numerous Gods and Goddesses for every reason and season, Christian mythology invented Saints for everything! The Christian churches drew a full crowd of believers, as the ancient Roman, the Greek Temples and Parthenon were also as crowded. Rome, of course, was the birth-place of both Churches. All Christian monotheist religious theology is a substitute of the idolatry of the ancient pagan mythology and propagated for the purpose of power and wealth of the Roman Emperors Vespasian and Titus Flavius.

It is still our core purpose to abolish this wide-spread fraud.

MEDIA DISTORTION

There many claims by professional commentators who are projecting the Qur'an's teaching as being "original" in nature because of the originality of the messages of the Qur'an. Claims are declared that "Islam is a religion of peace," or how Man was created, which differs from Jewish or Christian mythology. For instance, apologists of Islam, such as ABC's Diane Sawyer, claims that Allah created Man and Woman out of Dust, while others claim that Allah created them out of his Breath. There is a core design to hide the Islamic plagiarism due to the lack of originality of its message. Why will an American corporate network so blandly try to present the Islamic Qur'an anti-science verse-distortions other than the way it describes its own biblical events? Is it because ABC must cater to the financial influence of the Saudi Arabia investment in the corporate media and educational institutes of America?

AGE OF MYTHOLOGY

ILLUSTRATED SIMILARIES
ISIS-THE EGYPTIAN VIRGIN GODDESS

GREEK GOD DIONYSUS & SANTA CLAUS

ILLUSTRATED SIMILARIES
PAGAN ZODIAN SIGNS

VIRGO- EGYPTIAN ZODIAC SIGNS

ILLUSTRATED SIMILARIES

ILLUSTRATED SIMILARIES
VIRGIN MOTHER ISIS NURSING HORUS

ILLUSTRATED SIMILARIES

The template for Jesus (right) was copied almost event for event from that for Mithra (left).

ILLUSTRATED SIMILARIES

THE PAGAN SUN-GOD NAMED FOR THE THE CHRISTIAN GOD

ILLUSTRATED SIMILARIES

GOD MITHRA & HIS 2 DISCIPLES

ILLUSTRATED SIMILARIES
THE RESURRECTION OF LAZARUS

Horus

Egyptian god worshipped since 2200B.C.

Born of a virgin
Had 12 disciples
Healed the sick and injured
Raised Asar from the dead ("Asar" translates to "Lazarus")
Crucified, then resurrected after 3 days
Known as "the lamb", "the way", "the light"

GOD MITHRAS WITH HIS SKY ENGELS

ILLUSTRATED
FATHER OF THE MEDICAL DELUSION
OF HOMEOPATHY
SAMUEL HAHNERHANN 1755 - 1843

HOMEOPATHY'S BASIC INGREDIENT

THE ENTRAPMENT OF BELIEFS

There two points I wish to bring forward in association with the term *belief*. The first is that the term *"belief" is not an investigative term."* An investigative term includes terms such as, reason, evidence, verified-truth, scientific, archaeology, astronomy, and etcetera. The second is that *"just because you "believe" in something does not make it true."* This means that personal feelings and beliefs are subjective and do not constitute objective, verifiable evidence, unless *beliefs are associated with reality*. For a believer to claim *"this is how I feel or this is how I believe"* it is meaningless because the material reality of our surroundings does not function on the basis of one's feelings or beliefs. A belief occurs as a mental act which habitually places a sense of trust in another person, in a futuristic occurrence of a possible event or in blindly following a certain faith. A child places trust in its parent and, in turn, accepts what the parent does in confidence or trust. The process of trust require for a person to believe in two things: an emotion and logical sequence. A "belief" requires a blind feeling of "truth" and some form of logical structural-reality is required to communicate that "truth" in a written or spoken language. A "belief" is an emotion which is "attached" to an idea, a person or a real-thing which also represents a mechanical thinking state.

The belief in a *"life after death"* refers to an imaginary world beyond the grave, which has a strong correlation with primitive pre-historic human thought for at least 40,000 years. Archaeological evidence of (early-man) Homo sapiens and (fellow-travelers) our cousins Homo-Neanderthal remains indicate that both human-species buried their dead with stone-tools and shells, bones and weapons, ornaments and clothing, as provisions for the journey to the new life ahead. Both Humans and Neanderthals, appear to have developed *proto [early]-spiritual beliefs* in the process of creating a more advanced artistic expressions in their cave, involving supernatural animals and superior hunting skills.

Proto-spiritual beliefs are sentiments which begin to guide spirituality towards the preliminary stages of an image or an illusion. At this stage, proto-spiritual beliefs are non-religious in the classical sense because they do not form part of a dogma, they do not clearly identify the object of their worshiping, and thus do not transcend beyond the confines of their sentiments. For instance, primitive indigenous groups still living in the Amazon Rainforest of South America follow *proto-spiritual beliefs* in their burial practices by painting their faces with Jaguar-spots, as a sentiment of unity of strength with the dead. The "Jaguar People," as they are known, do not carry on with elaborate burial ceremonies, they do not follow any sort of religious dogma nor do they have a clear image of the life beyond. They live in a condition close to the State of Nature, and within this physical environment the Jaguar People still live in a so-called "Stone Age" cultural setting. These are similar to the *proto-cultural* settings the Homo sapiens and the Homo-Neanderthals lived in some 35,000 years ago.

As time went on, *proto-religious* ideas began to be formulated in the minds of the Homo sapiens, but the basis of their *proto-spiritual beliefs* were assisted by the Neanderthal input during their 10,000 years of co-habiting with the Homo sapiens in the European Continent. The extent of the interrelation between proto-spiritual and proto-religious beliefs have not, as yet, been established, but the impregnation of these two styles of sentiments is evident. The beliefs of a "world-beyond" or "life after death" and the existence of the "supernatural" still persist to this day. Neanderthals may have become extinct approximately 40,000 to 30,000 years ago but Humans survived and expanded. The Neanderthals' *proto-spiritual beliefs* (as they were once upon the time) have also been extinct, but the core essences of their proto-spiritual beliefs still continue to survive with similar paths of non-religious beliefs *under: Homeopathy, Lexicology, Numerology, the Zodiac Signs, Tarot Cards and Horoscope, asto-traveling, out of body experiences, and* in a number of other secular New Age absurdities.

Neanderthals were different in bodily structure (they were shorter but a lot stronger than humans) and may have lacked advanced biological evolutionary development, but that was due to a matter of evolutionary progression and not to a lack of biological attributes. They are confirmed anthropoid-ape-species, as humans are apes. They lived in organised groups, they had development defences against hostile groups or wild animals, they took care of their wounded and their dead, they cooked their food in the fire and they had a speech pattern to communicate among themselves and with the Cro-Magnon (early humans). They had developed a cave-art with proto-spiritual and illusionary harmonious designs, they decorated their bodies and their hair, they had crafts to wear or to hang and they were sociable when they were not threatened. In fact, due to sexual encounters between Humans and Neanderthals, we share 2% to 4% of our DNA with the Neanderthals, especially with the northern parts of the Mediterranean region.

Following the extinction of the Neanderthal some 40.000 to 30,000 years ago, it was the Homo sapiens who gradually transformed their shared proto-spiritual beliefs into their own proto-religious beliefs, which eventually developed into the first signs of organised religious beliefs, within the Fertile Crescent and Mesopotamian regional hierarchical societies, during the last 12,000 years. Throughout the ancient myths and historical accounts described in the Old Testament and the oral traditions of the Middle East and Mesopotamian population, reverence has been paid to beliefs of mystical symbolism. The use of symbolism involved the creation of images and symbols to represent supernatural beings and concepts. Because supernatural beings and concepts violate or suspend the Laws of Nature, there is a fundamental difficulty in transmitting and sharing them with others. To overcome this fundamental weakness, religious propagators throughout history anchored them in physical forms such as customs and rituals, special diets and moral-codes, books, music and ceremonial theatrics. When translated into physical forms, supernatural concepts become easier to propagate and for believers to believe and accept them as being true. War symbolism constructs religious beliefs and concepts enabling one group to identify another as evil that must be eliminated. Without their physicality, the meaning of those mental images is incomprehensible. Of course, good people would do good things and bad people would do bad things regardless of their religion or lack of it. But only under religious influence would good people do bad things to others.

In our times, Christian army-clergy in the war-zones of Afghanistan, Iraq or Syria, for instance, would tend to "bless" armoured vehicles, guns and soldiers as if this ceremonial blessing would form an actual protective shield against incoming strikes. Believers also slaughtered each other in religious wars, genocides and tribal scrimmages over beliefs in religious ideologies and combinations of belief-systems. Historically, different types of beliefs have propagated more hostilities among tribes and groups and have created more potential dangers that could threaten the lives of villagers and nomadic people. Semi-organised monotheistic tribal tradition included the idolatry of polytheistic religion's *Kaaba* structure in the Arab Peninsula region and still plays a significant role in the support and propagation of Abrahamic and Muslim beliefs and faiths. This has resulted in the easy acceptance of the convenience-route provided by beliefs, rather than conduct human affairs on the basis of deciding to difficult investigative processes. Faith-based beliefs, in support of non-existent "supernatural" events, gave credence to multiple superstitions, mysticism and miracles, (beliefs without credible evidence). Over many a millennia, many forms of beliefs substituted philosophical of theological "truths" without containing the slightest backing of reason and verifiable evidence.

Cultural generations of Middle East parents taught their children the accumulative beliefs and superstitions of their tribes and each generation, and were able to build upon those, new beliefs to cope with the uncertainties of their surrounding social conditions. Of course they suffered great enmity and felt helpless, insignificant and insecure in the face of natural forces and their own finite life span. This was because of lack of knowledge in the workings of the natural world, of the Natural Evolution, the Laws of Nature and the natural processes of life. Some coping mechanism, such as illusive beliefs, had to be developed in order to reduce peoples' level of anxiety.

As hunters-gatherers, our human ancestors developed primitive, instinctual beliefs of God, based on personal preferences, in order to lessen whatever they felt was the cause of their personal uncertainty. Beliefs became a convenient short-route to arrive at a favourable and beneficial outcome of their wishful instincts. Beliefs were not used as a method of investigating the subject of the truth or false nature of their beliefs. How could they? It was much easier to believe in the vital-powers of the rocks, mountains, rivers, the Sun and the Moon, unseen forces, each animated by a spirit capable of responding to the wishes of the believer. In turn, tribal chiefs, Shamans, native-healers, temple-priests, mediums and charlatan-magicians and military leaders offered people what they needed, an illusive control over the suspension of the Laws of Nature (miracles or resurrections), false assurances, false confidence and false peace of mind, in the whirlpool of an illusive comfort zone. The obvious fact is that humans invented Animist beliefs to respond to a social need and the illusion of God was created by humans along with the concept of spirits; God did not revealed himself or the spirits to the tribes.

To this day, there is very little indication about how the concept of belief was adopted by humans in the mist of our history. One possibility is that, as children, we learned what and how to believe from our parents, as an expressed mimetic inheritance from one generation to the next. As children, we do not have the mental capacity to investigate what we are told and we accept, without question, the religion of our youth. We simply believe what we are told to believe and have imprinted these learned beliefs in our memory. The ability to control our beliefs, on the basis of "true" or "false," remains an open question depending on whether we have developed the intellect or whether the cultural settings we live-in will permit us or encourage us to question those beliefs. During adolescence our brain may begin to understand the consequences and may lead us to modify the early learned religious beliefs so as to avoid their debilitating effects.

In an altruistic parent-child relationship, more than any other species, we survive by the accumulated experience of previous generations and we have the need to pass it on to our children for their protection and well-being. The behaviour of the children to obey and believe their parents' authority is probably a good thing. When the parent tells the child about the world, it is because the child does not yet have the capacity to know, and if the child ignores its parent's advice, some injury will likely result. A good parental advice to a child will be, *"don't touch this hot iron"* but the child's brain does not distinguish between what good advice is from an idiotic advice such as, *"pray to God for rain."* Under false beliefs, a child may develop an excessive sense of "entitlement," to be granted his beliefs or wishes and be given what he asks. As an adult, he might expect life's entitlements *("life owes me a living")* instead of earning that himself.

Religious beliefs are mimetically widespread but, having said that, we must be careful not to ask the wrong question about their prevalence or pervasiveness. Religious beliefs may be a by-product of something else, such as; a mental escape from dreadful social conditions, such as poverty or ignorance, lack of education or theocratic domination, fear from not believing or an illusive sense of personal belonging, and so on. Concentrating on the by-product does not provide us with any advantage because it is the consequence of something else. We need to look how the causes arose in the first place. As a by-product, religious beliefs do not provide us with historical evidence, because they are psychological predispositions which, in themselves, have been part of our primitive survival mechanism for thousands of years. In real-material life, they have consequences which probably do not have beneficial value, because traditional religious believers, or New Age theists, do not know if these beliefs have any real value or not. Their brain possesses a rule of thumb that states: believe, without question, whatever your priest, your imam, your tribal elders or your latest New Age guru tells you, without any reservation.

Following adolescence most children no longer need to listen to and obey their parents because their brain now is fully developed and they now can think for themselves. Growing up however, is not sufficient for evolution to clean up these ingrained belief traits, so the religious beliefs they have inherited from their parent remain in the way they communicate through spoken or symbolic language. Utilising religious beliefs while young may also lead to bad consequences later in adult life, for learning about God's punishment if you are sinful, of Hell and Fire for eternity, all those and others surely contain acceptable and justifiable beliefs in violence.

The earliest evidence of modern human culture, from ancient Mesopotamia and accounts from the Old Testament, reveal that humans practiced some form of violence against fellow humans. These violent actions appear similar to the violence engaged in warfare, against other tribes believed to have hostile intentions. But God was always on one side of the conflict, with priests blessing weapons, along with beliefs to justify genocides, massacres, executions and even sacrifices. Those societies believed in spirits and Animism, the belief that some animals possessed a spirit. They constructed false pattern-explanations about things in their world, based on their ignorance of natural phenomena such as the wind, the movement of animals and even the human breath which was associated with "spirit," "pnevma" or *anima*. Everything around them was viewed with a pattern-seeking method and, as such, they could not possibly explain the difference between beliefs, reason and evidence. The ordinary people in these societies hardly had anything that would be called "knowledge," and this alone, would isolate their tribal belief system further. For instance, if you lived in a tribal society that held strong beliefs and you came across another tribe with entirely different pattern-set of beliefs; also without an understanding of the difference between beliefs and evidence how could you not feel threatened by those beliefs which conflicted with yours? In this case, conflict between tribes was inevitable and contradictory religious beliefs fuelled those conflicts.

With language came the contemplation of belief systems and the introduction of religious terms and concepts that became the necessary tools of communicating those beliefs to the tribesmen. They introduced religious concepts and terms such as spirit, souls, God and Heaven to justify matters of ghostly concepts, not only in religion, but in language as well. In our daily affairs we express terms and beliefs without thinking about them because they exist in the linguistic structure of common communication derived from ancient tribal belief-systems. Since no one can see these "beliefs," people still accept them as "real," based on nothing more than faith, without ever investigating whether they exist or not, or if they are based on reason and evidence. Therefore, *believing is equal to evidence, believing replaces reality*, and *believing is the driving imperative in one's life*. For instance, the influence of religious terms in our society and in our secular legal system is quite evident. An accused person, standing before a justice, can legally claim that the reason he shot *"the man who was approaching me"* was a legitimate self-defence because he *believed* his life was in danger. We use terms such as "believe in yourself," as if the only obstacle between failure and success is your lack of belief. What about the necessary material conditions, such as training or the right circumstances that would be the primary foundation for your success? The good intentions of convincing a child to "believe in you" may be a noble suggestion on the part of the parent, but does not hold any true value beyond its subliminal level and, can also create an *"over-inflated self-esteem"* believing that you are worthy of anything you desire.

The concept of "belief" is so fundamental to religion that without it, religion could not have existed, for the whole propagation of religion is based first on the act of "believing" and second, on belief-concepts. In religious language, the term "believe" predominates over all other terms and concepts, for without "belief" all other religious concepts would fall off the clouds. These religious terms are integrated in our ordinary communication, not just in Sunday's prayers. We now believe—as being real---in inmate objects, spirits, gods, angels, ghosts, aliens, UFO's, Homeopathy, Tarot Cards, miracles, resurrections, faith-healing, life after death, Hell and Heaven, shamans and future-tellers, knocking on wood, prayers for every season; without ever questioning the reliability of their sources.

The advertising industry, as a whole, is *marketing "beliefs"* rather *than products*; in order to induce beliefs in our minds, for the industry knows that when the person "believes" in something then that person can also enticed or be controlled. In my book, *"Prisoners of Our Ideals,"* I have extensively written how the advertising industry sells "ideals," not "products" and that in western societies, the concept of "believing" in the "ideal" and a noble way of thinking. Idealism, beliefs and faith can overpower the mind of a person to such an extent that what is a "virtual" becomes "real" even if it is contrary to evidence. This person will continue to mimetically believe in it for no other reason than that others around him are also mimetically believe in it; as it has been the case for millennia, ever since tribal spiritualism was introduced and practiced in ancient societies.

The ending of religious influence in our lives, our children's lives and in our communities, requires more that just rejecting the God delusion from our brains. One area of concern is the use of language in our daily affairs. The induction of religious terminology, such as "belief," into our daily communication can cause confusion between the speaker and the listener; from the mildest form of "belief" to the absolute forms of "belief" in religious theology. In religious settings, the term "belief" is a mental act that is an absolute requirement demanded of the believer and which is unmistakably clear. However, in our daily lives, the act of believing is not required from a speaker or a writer, for he or she could simply substitute the term "belief" with a more descriptive term such as "think" in order to avoid confusion. For instance, a better way of saying, *"I believe it will rain tomorrow"* would be said, "I *think* it will rain tomorrow." The thinking process is determined by our physical surroundings, not the other way around. Therefore, based our external experiences of dark-clouds which can produce rain, we attempt to predict tomorrow's weather by forecasting it from past external experiences, but out prediction-thoughts cannot be absolute because our prediction of rain may not happen. To make predictions on issues or events that may or may not happen does not require "believing" in the future events, but rather a lucky guess will do as well. Believing represents a type of mental thought that is a sub-class of other kinds of mental activities. On the other hand, thinking may or may not include believing, therefore, when thinking takes place it could represent a single idea or a sequence of ideas absent of emotionally misguided beliefs.

Because a belief contains a grammatical sequence, you should consider whether reason and evidence have anything to do with that belief. A variable of beliefs used in language does nothing towards structuring reason to discover evidence because beliefs do not equal reason and evidence. Belief terms add to the confusion because they may contain many meanings. They may range from a harmless guess, *"I believe that it will rain tomorrow,"* to an absolute certainty, *"I believe in God or the Qur'an is God's perfect book,"* where the reader or listener, may understand a totally different meaning than what was intended. It would mean that you must eliminate your freedom of speech, for you cannot criticise the verses of the Qur'an because it is *"God's perfect book."* Many Muslims violently have reacted to western criticisms of the Qur'an because they believe that it is Allah's perfect book. It is not!

Further, if you say to a religious person, *"I believe in reason and science,"* he might believe that you mean it as an absolute in the way he believes in God or the Bible. The confusion may go further by the miss-interpretation that can lead a Christian or a Muslim to believe that science represents religious faith. Religious opportunists can twist the miss-interpretation just to "prove" that some scientists believe or have faith in God. A number of prominent intellectuals and atheists' scientists have used the term "belief" out of habit in their presentation about reason, logic and science. My question is, why use the term "belief" at all? Why not avoid the confusion, simply by not using the term "belief," and substitute it with a stronger and more descriptive term, so that these scientists do not have to keep repeating and re-explaining the meaning of the "belief" terms they used? One can clearly see that a religious person, who held beliefs in the absolute of God and supernatural events, would use the term belief because he has a faith. Throughout history, however, humans have invented and have developed intelligent concepts without the need of belief.

In the last two thousand years, we have invented rules and regulations, local and global maps, infield and outfield games, economic and social laws, architectural and logical models without requiring a mere or absolute belief. For instance, an architectural model may show all the pertinent parts of the project, but to believe that the model equals the actual architectural structure, would produce false belief. Also, we have invented, soccer, hockey and baseball rules, but we neither are nor obligated to believe in any of these rules or to attach some kind of supernatural "truth" to them. Fans simply enjoy these games, simply for the games themselves. In every major town and city, we have invented "traffic rules" for bicyclists, motor-vehicles and pedestrians with signs and preventive warnings of all sorts. Sometimes we break these rules simply because we do not believe that these rules are absolute, but we realised that they are a system of behaviour to permit human activity and mass transit to function. Our behaviour towards social rules, and our experience in predicting social conditions of all sorts, is based on these and these rules alone and not on emotions connected to beliefs.

Secular or non-theistic use of beliefs still constitutes part of the ex-religious beliefs the meaning of which was originally introduced into the grammatical structure of language in pre-historic through Neolithic times. Terms differ not only in their spelling but in their meaning as well. There are people who cannot distinguish between what constitutes and what does not constitute a belief. For these people, belief has infiltrated their minds and their linguistic mode of speaking and writing, and everything that is perceived and is interpreted incorporates a belief including all their past experiences. Such people live entirely within a world of subjective reasoning, because their thoughts prescribe a belief which is in the mind and thus every belief refers to the self. They cannot obtain knowledge without owing a belief and their accumulated accepted knowledge required beliefs. However, one can accumulate knowledge without owing a belief, if and when the term belief becomes meaningless to him and with no need to believe it, and when he realises that not all things accepted by him require belief. In this case, his knowledge and experience would not fall subject to belief.

Religious Beliefs and Violence

As a rule, in every armed conflict resides a prime reason as to why the brutality of war occurs. Most attention has been paid on politics, territorial boundaries, nationalism and terrorism. Although these constitute unreliable reasons, we rarely investigate the deepest roots for the justification of violence. However, posing the question, *"Does any solution exist for solving the war conflict?"* This question draws a slue of solutions and on the top of the list rests belief in religion. How many times have we heard the standard slogan that *"Islam is a religion of peace"* or that *"Christianity is about love and peace"* and *"Judaism stands for peace, equality and tolerance?"* Throughout the centuries, time and time again, the belief that these religions offer real solutions for peace and happiness has proven tragically wrong.

In every century, in the history of these religions there is a clear inclination towards violence and war. Historical evidence also demonstrates that for a short period of time Christians got along with Muslims, Jews got along with Muslims and Muslims lived in peace with Christians, but for how long? It matters little that each religion has peaceful factions, which avoid direct conflict with their citizenry and their own beliefs, when each religion also has violence-oriented extremists who represent their religious commitment. To claim that ISIL, the Taliban or the religious-fanatics of Boko Haram does not represent the "real" Islam, then who has the absolute authority over this claim or, is it the Qur'an?

Qur'an 65:4, *"You can rape, marry and divorce pre-pubescent girls"*
Qur'an 4:3, 4:24, 5:89, 33:50, 58:3, 70:30, *"You can enslave for sex and work"*
Qur'an 4:34, *"You can beat sex slaves, work slaves, and wives"*
Qur'an 24:4, *"You will need 4 Muslim male witnesses to prove a rape"*
Qur'an 9:29, *"Kill Jews and Christians if they do not convert or pay Jizya tax"*
Qur'an 8:12, 47:4, *"Crucify and amputate non-Muslims"*
Qur'an 9:111, *"You will kill non-Muslims to receive 72 virgins in heaven"*
Qur'an 2:217, 4:89, *"You will kill anyone who leaves Islam"*
Qur'an 8:12, 47:4, *"You will behead non-Muslims"*
Qur'an 9:5, *"You will kill and be killed for Allah"* (verse of the sword)
Qur'an 8:12, 8:60, *"You will terrorize non-Muslims"*
Qur'an 3:26, 3:54, 9:3, 16:106, 40:28, *"Lie to strengthen Islam"* (Taqiyya deception)

The Christian genocide against the polytheistic Latin American natives during the expedition of the Conquistadores is well-documented, and extremists' priests were the parasites living off the armed conflicts, in their quest to convert the natives to Catholicism. Beliefs and, in particular, very dangerous beliefs; which stemmed from religious beliefs and tribal superstitions evolved into dominant religions which began out of armed conflict of wars. Their holy-books condone the armed conflicts of war and all three religions justify the slaughtering of civilians in order to get at their enemies (God's collateral damage?) All three holy books contain apocalyptic prophecies of the end of the world. Are there religious advocates who truly believe in those lethal prophecies? Yes they exist and these religious beliefs provide a justification to their proponents with the power of self-fulfilling prophecies in destruction, war and the end of the world.

This poses a question; respecting one's freedom of expression of belief, even if these beliefs are absurd, does not necessarily means that we should respect the beliefs themselves or the violent actions that result from them. We must confront and question religious beliefs and traditions that trigger or cause the oppression of others, who may or may not follow these beliefs. There is no doubt that people have the right to exist in their own land and culture, but since when do beliefs in-themselves have the same right? In Muslim countries, where daily confrontation stems from the right of certain beliefs to exist; instead of believing in the right of these beliefs over the lives of people, leaders must respect and protect people, not their religious beliefs. Many naïve and over-polite atheists and humanist instead of being arrogantly against those dangerous beliefs, simply hope that, one day, those beliefs will diminish. If we are ever going to terminate the dangers of religious beliefs, we must first get rid of the dogma of faith. The dangers of allowing the intrusion of religious faith into governments, public and private schools, world politics and everyday life has proven too high to further ignore.

Theocratic governments such as Iran and Saudi Arabia, Hamas and Hezbollah base themselves on religious concepts; the members of the top brass of their militaries believe that Allah stands absolutely on their side. Their politico-military apparatus continually prays five times a day to this unproven deity to intervene on their behalf. The question is, have prayers and beliefs ever been able to stop war and violence? This has never been the case; on the contrary, religious inspired violence ends because secularist political or social bodies intervene to offer peaceful alternatives to violence.

Pre-historic artists' created cave animist-symbols which inspired proto-spiritualistic emotions, which in turn, created beliefs in the groups' collective mind. In time, those beliefs were accommodated with a well-formed dogma to create polytheist cults and religions, with monotheism as the more advanced dogma of beliefs. From the pre-historic cave artistic expressions of the killing of an animal, to the symbols used by warriors throughout history to inspire violence against their enemies, to today's religious symbols used by autocratic governments, the underlying message is based on the belief and justification of killing something "other." This has not changed much from the primitive to modern times, for beliefs and symbols are still used by warring governments, and the military-clergy personnel who pray to their God that allows and justifies the killing of their opponent indiscriminately.

Religious oriented factions, such as those in the African Continent, the Middle East and Asia, as well as, the fundamental Christian rightwing evangelist of the USA (G.W. Bush) and Britain's (the late Margaret Thatcher and ex-Prime Minister Tony Blair) have triggered numerous military conflicts in many underdeveloped countries such as Iraq, Syria, Afghanistan and Libya. For centuries, a brave few humanist and atheist, scientists and philosophers have encountered violence against them by the Jewish, Christian or Muslim ignorant and fanatic masses. The core of such conflict was, and still is, between Biological Science and Faith. Faith simply means that the ignorant do not want to know about reason and evidence. Let us pay honour to the scientists like Richard Dawkins, Sam Harris and the late Christopher Hitchings who are appealing to reason and knowledge, proven evidence and atheist morality. The faithful are devoted to prejudice, to fear, to the magic of miracles, to the delusion of the hereafter and to the mega-churches that promote them. Their promoted beliefs are false and their superstition is degrading, especially when it is embedded in common language, for instead of saying "Think" they say "Believe."

Terms that we speak and structure are the only link between them, and linguistic structure becomes the only content of knowledge. When we formulate verbal structures that contain no observable empirical evidence, such as "believing" they can never provide us with any structural information about the material world we live in. Therefore, such verbal structures that are absolute induce delusions, if we believe in their semantic arguments. A religious person acts as if he lives in a virtual world, for he is consistent with his beliefs, but has problems adjusting them to his social conditions, and also, he is confronted by unavoidable linguistic difficulties. A rational non-believer person does not abide by beliefs, and in the event that beliefs are creeping into his mind, and building a delusional world, he saves his mental-health by controlling or rejecting them. A religious person acts upon his beliefs but cannot adjust himself to a world which stands contrary to his religious delusions. When this moment arrives, he chooses his beliefs and all the arguments for them, but becomes faith-blind towards any arguments opposite to them. In such a case, it is not the disbelieving arguments that endanger our educational and social integrity, it is the religious beliefs.

The point is, we are all capable of believing in things that are not true, such as the Tooth-fairy, Santa Claus, UFO's, Homeopathy and future-telling Tarot-cards, but we take a defensive stand when we are proven wrong, by twisting the facts to show that we were right in the first place. But, sooner or later, all illusions and delusional beliefs are confronted by solid material reality. There is an old Arab saying, *"A camel can only see another camel's hump,"* referring to a believer who can only see another believer's faults but cannot see his own. It is reasonable for a believer to believe that if a belief is being widely accepted, there must be something reasonable about it. I do not think this can hold true when we study the history of widespread delusional beliefs about the end of the world (by chiliastic cults) or about the appearance of the Virgin Mary in some cave in Spain or France and such other absurd massive delusions as the earth being flat.

In pre-historic societies and early civilisations there were no massive hysterical beliefs amongst the people. Today we know that there are far more absurd religious beliefs in the so-called civilised societies than in the past two thousand years. If you are Evangelist you believe that there are absurd beliefs among Mormons, if you are Christian you believe that there are idiotic beliefs amongst Muslims, and if you are Muslim you believe that all other religions are wrong because Islam is God's last confirmed religion on earth. If you are a Liberal you believe that Marxists must be wrong in their "superstitions" about Capitalism, if you are Conservative you are aghast at the Greens, who you believe that are totally irrational in their beliefs about the environment and equal distribution of income. These beliefs in question are, of course, theological in their essence, because there is no reason to think that any traditional beliefs of "others" are wrong but yours are correct. A person, so far as he is not under theocratic restraints, is free to establish his own identity, his own responsibilities and his own destiny. I am sure that believers who believe in the belief of faith are wrong, for they are preserving the myth of God, as a path to truth, when that faith has backed them into a "mental-prison" of believing. Here is a brave step forward towards embracing a dangerous idea! Before you appeal to reason and evidence, when faith has backed you into a mental corner, think about whether you really want to abandon scientific reason when it is on your side.

What blinds us, and makes our progress very difficult, is our unawareness that our religious beliefs have become absolute and should be dismissed. Verifiable material reality, instead, has been dismissed and, in its place, all kinds of religious beliefs have been erected; to the degree that our human intellect has been forfeited by the act of committing ourselves to a belief. Such slue of beliefs are re-enforced by religious propagators such as Churches, Mosques, and Synagogues in order to fit myths and delusions into their pseudo-realities. These religious houses are the foundations for spreading fear, while trying to explain to the ignorant and ill-educated the nature of the unknowable.

THINKING WITHOUT BELIEVING

Many people do not miscomprehend what is a belief and what is not a belief, but for many the vocabularies of beliefs have so infiltrated their linguistic structure that everything perceived, factually explained or theorised incorporates a belief which includes personal experiences. Information our intelligence receives from the external world does not require belief, because beliefs do not have bilateral symmetry requirements. For instance, information received from the Internet, books, non-fiction stories, science and theories all represent and express mimetic ideas, but you and I do not need to believe in any in order to think, analyse or criticize them. This process does not apply to religious people who must believe what their holy-books say, but are not permitted to analyse or criticise their content.

Biological Evolution through Natural Selection requires the external information received to be stored in our brain's chemical structures of pattern-meaning without differentiating between what is a belief or what is thinking. Both represent a form of mental activity where simple beliefs and thoughts co-exist with pattern-meaning and, at this stage, the only difference amounts to their semantic designation, where "thinking" can be substituted to "believing" and vice versa. They eventually diverge, the path of "belief" advances towards intransigence and the path of "thinking" leads to factual knowledge. Thus, beliefs do not require external factual evidence (beliefs in miracles, astrology or Hell and Fire) while knowledge does not require reliance on beliefs; knowledge of Natural Selection, the Earth orbits the Sun and airplanes flying are confirmed, regardless of whether we believe in them or not. Therefore, the *mental path to knowledge requires external verification* by observation or experimentation by reliable means, whereas the intransigence of beliefs does not.

We need to be on our guard in our brain's thinking process not to evolve a combination of beliefs with factual knowledge, even if we are scientists, philosophers or story tellers. Factual knowledge must coincide with the natural state of affairs if we want to utilise it, religious beliefs require no external confirmation (other than it might coincide with it). Inflexible "religious-like thinking" can affect us all, regardless of our education, knowledge, background and cultural level. This is because we are biologically programmed to look for pattern-meaning, and when a real pattern does not exist, our brain invents a false-pattern because it cannot leave a "blank-space" in our thinking process. The so-called "blank-space" is filled with opinions, assumptions, religious beliefs, personal-beliefs, rumours, wishful-thinking, ignorance, superstitions or dogmas.

Fortunately, scientific beliefs do not appear as prevalent as they were once, with scientists attaching their own beliefs to theories of people such as, Newton, Darwin, Freud, Jung or Einstein. These early scientists stubbornly held to their beliefs; resembling inflexible religious-dogmatism, even when presented with verifiable evidence that contradicted their beliefs. The much reduced scientists' stubbornness in the scientific community today has generated better communication and a broader understanding of solving ecological, medical and economic on a global scale. On a human scale, a humble acceptance of another scientist's scientific theory which contradicts one's own may be a welcome sign. The process we call knowledge occurs when scientific facts can stand as evidence, and we do not need beliefs to understand them, because the theories that explain those facts are adequate. There simply exists no apparent reason to attach beliefs to knowledge.

BELIEVERS AND BELIEFS

It is interesting to observe believers who are viewing other peoples' fundamental beliefs. Like the Arab proverb about the "camel's hump" they most always see the problems of other believers' high-level fanatical beliefs, but they never accept those who practice lesser beliefs than them. Believers tend to position themselves with enough reserved beliefs to be self-centered in their subjective dogma. Like the stand-up comedian *George Carlin 1937 – 2008* said, a self-centered believer is like the driver who notices that *"Anyone going slower than you is an idiot, and anyone going faster than you is a maniac."* Most people do not own beliefs of every kind, for we disbelieve more that we believe. In other cases some religious believers have fewer beliefs than others, but non-believers are at the bottom of the scale. If you are a religious believer you may tend to dismiss the beliefs of other faiths, while perhaps you are dismayed when non-believers dismiss yours.

On the scientific level, regardless of how a religious scientist has attached solid faith to his scientific theory or evidence, no matter how convinced he is over his religious convictions, there has never been a case of scientific evidence or theory that required the concept of God, miracle or any sort of religious superstitions. In addition, not a single mathematical equation includes a theistic symbol, nor is there the slightest evidence of magic, ghosts or inner-spirit appearing to occupy our computers, machines or our bodies. An atheist or humanist can live his life in accordance with the Laws of Nature and live as long as the most fundamental believer. The beliefs carried during the life of a scientist or a lay person has no bearing, whatsoever, on the skills of the lay person or the usefulness and inventiveness the scientist brought into the world. In spite of the temporary mental comfort-zone that a belief might bring (as do opiate drugs) what purpose can a belief serve in providing useful knowledge about the social and natural world?

When a scientist dies, his beliefs die with him. His work may be remembered if the scientist had invented proven scientific knowledge in his field of expertise or about the world, yet only the scientific knowledge remains useful. Whether the scientist believed in Christianity or Islam during his lifetime has no usefulness to the knowledge he discovered and brought to this world. The scientific knowledge brought by the scientist, who is no longer living with us, does not require us to believe in it, but to look at what grounds and to what degree the evidence supports his theories.

Verifiable knowledge does not require support from belief. No degree of praying, or strengthening your beliefs through sheer will-power, will improve your knowledge. Nor is it necessary for knowledge to rest in a situation between an extreme belief and non-belief to correctly understand the knowledge. Most religious advocates speculate that all knowledge derives from beliefs, that knowledge describes true-beliefs, and that knowledge cannot exist at all without beliefs. Humans beings grow up surrounded by countless beliefs, the need may even be ingrained in our genes, but there is no basis for religious advocates to maintain that an intelligent human cannot understand knowledge without beliefs. The human brain has the capacity of understanding abstract concepts, and even the ability to invent abstractions about abstractions (mathematics); at least some humans have that capacity. True enough, a belief may have an adverse effect on knowledge and persons learn to act on knowledge without inserting their beliefs for, after all, people do have the ability to disown a belief. As for religious people they do not have that ability; perhaps because their cultural upbringing prevents them from doing so. In short, most of us have learned to accumulate knowledge without owing a single belief and perhaps this is an advantage for the perpetuation of knowledge rather than a disadvantage.

There are no benign forms of beliefs that are supported by scientific evidence, because beliefs act as barriers towards further understanding and prevent scientists and social philosophers from seeing beyond their current faith position. For instance, the Greek philosopher Aristotle while observing the celestial wanders (the Sun, the Moon and the Stars), believed in the existence of a prime mover (God) who moved them in the space. The scientist Isaac Newton thought of the theory of relativity and established predictions of gravitational events; but a single belief in the absolute time, prevented him from formulating a workable theory. Opposite to that, Albert Einstein saw through the terms of relative time and formulated his now famous General Theory of Relativity. But even Einstein's also famous belief, that *"God does not throw dice,"* prevented him from understanding the pure randomness in sub-atomic physics and barred him from accepting the consequences of quantum mechanics. Contemporary objective scientists have now provided evidence that, for quantum mechanics to work, Mother Nature not only plays with dice, but randomness is also a requirement for a statistical accuracy.

In short, perhaps humans are biologically programmed to acquire cognition in stages; beginning from ignorance, graduating to beliefs and finally advancing to knowledge (with shades in between each stage). Thinking, instead of believing, simply removes unnecessary mental obstructions, because even a benign belief can form problematic mental barriers. In the ancient world, spiritualism progressed towards faith and dogma in both religion and ideologies (Bible, political ideology of Islam) which honour war and encourages superstition, slavery and intolerance. We see intolerance in the Catholic religious Inquisitions, "holy wars", "jihad" and religious discriminations in Islam. During the Black Plague of 1628 millions of people died out of ignorance of the disease, but the Catholic Church promoted the superstition that this was God's punishment for their sins. Meanwhile, the same religious leaders did little to encourage experimental hygienic or medical investigation as a preventive measure. In the late part of the 20th century, the world has witnessed the rise of the fanatical ideology of political Islam as it has destroyed the lives of millions of people who belonged to various Islamic sects. We have witnessed the Catholic Spain and Italy produce Fascism, and Christianised Germany create Nazism and the Holocaust with the blessing of the Catholic Church and the Calvinist Manifesto for destroying the Jewish race, confiscating their property and drive them out of their homes for "killing" Jesus Christ. To this day we can witness religious intolerance in Northern Ireland, Bosnia, Sri Lanka, in Israel, Saudi Arabia and religious wars in most Muslim Arabian and African countries. The tragic event of 9/11 could not have occurred without the belief in life after death and Allah's reward of the 72 virgins for each one of the 19 suicide Muslim believers. Without exaggeration, only religion can produce a moralising concept for war against another faith, and only an autocracy like Iran and Saudi Arabia still propagate faith-based science programs.

There are a number of questions about religion that do not have answers based on reason and evidence. For instance, why does religion create so many atrocities against innocent humans? An attack by a 57 year old Christian fundamentalist in Colorado Springs in 2015 killed three and injured nine innocent victims outside a Planned Parenthood abortion clinic, because he was "pro-life." Being pro-life he had no problem killing people but how can he be "pro-life" and kill someone? It was an absurd belief that enticed him to go outside the abortion clinic shouting, *"stop killing or else I'll kill you"!* Is it because religion expresses everything living in terms of belief, faith and absolutes without presenting reason and understanding? Is it because religion places reality, human affection, happiness, morality and solidarity in a non-existent supernatural realm inaccessible by the mind of man?

555

How can human beings ever achieve the peace professed by their religious books (Old Testament, Bible, and Qur'an) yet have their God condoning armed conflicts and violence against women and children? Why must believers accept primitive tribal superstitions and mysterious beliefs from an unknowable God who inflicts crimes against humanity for mysterious reasons beyond the comprehension of man? How can we ever understand Natural Selection and Human Evolution, the physics of the cosmos when 42% of American's still believe that a celestial fandom created everything just a few thousand years ago (in fact during the Neolithic time of the Agricultural Revolution?). How can we be happy and lead a full life when religion denies the nature of sex, dictates who you are supposed to love, and that Catholic, Protestant and Muslim religious-pedophilia, Muslim-bestiality and Muslim child-bride marriages as acceptable?

Parents who follow the Christmas tradition teach their children to believe in images and concepts of Santa Claus, the Tooth-fairy, and letters to Santa address North Pole, supernatural Saints and God, and that a miracle (resurrection) can suspend the Laws of Nature on behalf of the believer. These parents do not understand the dangers that their beliefs can cause. There are claims that some "children's stories" are harmless and that eventually children overcome their naïve stage of childhood; this is a naïve assumption itself. The question is, however, do parents tell their children that these "children-stories" are not true and that they are imaginative? Because, if children accept them as being true, then adults are preparing their mental-stage; not only to accept beliefs (as being true), but to honour and fight for them. One should remember that, for a religious believer, an expression of an *"idea-in-and-of-itself"* represents belief. Thus, daily images in mass media represent distortive opportunities for the unaware to believe in them.
The advertising industry of imagery, which includes image-churches and political parties, is an enormous influential entity whose core goal is to sell the "image" rather than the product. If, instead, we taught our youngsters about beliefs and how they infect the mind and the misguidance they can produce, society would have little need for psychologists "to redirect these ideas" in their minds later in adulthood. Children should learn the differences between fiction and tech-virtual, reason and factual evidence from an early stage. Without believers, there would be no one to believe them, and the distortion of reality portrayed in those fictions and tech-virtual could only represent just that: fictions and tech-virtual. The rule of thumb is: do not believe in everything that goes in your mind, but regard things along the scale of probabilities, things that appear absurd, place them in the low-probability level, things the appear reasonable place them in the

high-probability level, and regard everything as probabilities, not as beliefs. **Most** people, who are functioning on reason and evidence, including writers, maintain that *reason* must be accompanied by *evidence*, for mutual support. Of course, it is more prudent to attach evidence to reason than to maintain a belief without evidence, but why must we be compelled to attach beliefs to evidence at all? Why not stand on the evidence without attaching beliefs at all? Why people tend to follow certain religious belief-systems remains unclear, perhaps because of family dynamics and birth, social influence or personal survival strategy. In this case, reason and external evidence such as, family ethical structure or social conditions would convince a person to follow a given faith as the means of a personal and social survival measure. In fundamentalist Muslim families not believing in Mohammad and Allah can be an utter embarrassment against their family's honour, or face imposition of death for *apostasy,* the changing of one set of religious beliefs (in their minds) for another set of beliefs (also in their minds) from different religion. In the most dangerous form, benign beliefs can take their most intransient property as faith, a reliance on false-hope and ignorance. As beliefs inside their heads begin to take over the evidence from outside their heads; the process causes a "split-mind" or self-induced religious schizophrenia found in most believers of organised religions.

Instead of "housing" beliefs in our heads, we can establish theoretical evidence, a predictive and productive way of understanding our natural world and the consequences derived from it. Most religious propagators who tend to challenge the science of biology and human development attempt to make their case equivalent to faith. Their argument of *"Intelligent Design"* (a modern God) is built around linguistic terms used by science and scientists rather than on terms used by belief, faith and religion, in their attempt to "update" the Biblical Creation of life and the Universe. This may give the faithful comfort, but reducing scientific theory to the level of faith falsely places both on an equal level. However, verifiable biological and scientific evidence do not rely on faith, nor does it require beliefs or absurdities of an "Intelligent Designer" who set out to biologically design millions of extinct, and those still surviving species on earth. It does not make any difference how believable a belief is, and who created that belief; if it is against reason and evidence, it is false. Beliefs of any kind are pre-conceived forms of ideas which, in effect pre-determines what is real. Coupled with a lack of information, a pre-conceived belief of what is real and what it is not, can lead to false conclusions. For instance, if we see a painter painting a person in an abstract form (a metaphorical image) and ask him why he does not paint a "real" person by showing him another painting of a "real" person (also a metaphorical image); the correct response would be, that comparing two metaphors (forms of beliefs) would lead us to false conclusions about what is, in fact, real. Without resorting to belief, we can look at an image and see that it only resembles some aspects of a particular person and that an image or belief represents only an abstraction (form of belief). Without a belief we can question the proposition before arriving at a conclusion.

If a belief system teach you that "sex is bad" and that only "godly belief will guide" you, or suppresses freedom of speech, a believer may become deprived and depresses, or turn angry and violent. To counter-balance such conditions, a believer will turn to a specific hope, a form of wishful thinking, and a faith which hinges on ignorance. Our desires are natural feelings; we simply cannot avoid them because of our biological make-up. Most of us use our minds as a tool to satisfy the desires within us. With reflection we learn the limits of our desires, but beliefs mixed with desires (wishful thinking) can cause debilitating disappointments and regrets.

Religious beliefs and faiths are a limited mental activity which produces an unnecessary, confusing and, at times a dangerous false sense of trust and misleading information; a mental activity coupled with a feeling of "truth." Faith and beliefs rarely agree with the natural world around us. History throughout the centuries has demonstrated that beliefs and faith, of the most intransient kind, have served as the trigger for tragic violence and destruction and sustained the socially illiterate, ignorant and superstitious people. Replacing beliefs with predictive reason, experience and evidence provides a means to eliminate the dreadful consequences of superstitious mental activity.

Beliefs and faith, preaching and elaborate ceremonies do not establish "truths," facts or means to verify an investigation. It does not matter how many millions of people still believe, or how many centuries they are still misguided by their beliefs and faith, or how important they believe their beliefs are to them or how good these beliefs make them feel when those beliefs do not agree with evidence, they simply cannot have any validity to the outside world. To this day, all things we know about the world, all scientific theories, all the biological evidence provided by Charles Darwin's *Natural Evolution* and *Natural Selection*, we can express without referring to a single belief. Without an exaggeration, even at its most benign socio-cultural level, a belief can act as barrier to further understanding. When we do not know something, our brain would naturally create a *non-existent pattern-meaning* to fill the mental-gap and it would most likely prove false. If we do not know about something then our brain would seek a false-pattern, in a form of a belief, because we know that. Most of us have uncertainties about the world, and the best way of handling those involves thinking in terms of probabilities, so what use does a belief have, other than being a mental disruption? If abstracting is part of your mental-activity, you may begin by replacing believing with thinking!

Instead of adopting a *"false comfort-zone"* in belief, we can utilise a hypothesis or preliminary-theory to make intelligent predictions based on probabilities about the world. In linguistic form we can replace the term "belief" with "thinking" which better describes what we really think about the subject, and the foundation on which our argument is based, for or against it. We can use our imagination to create new concepts towards a desired goal; knowing that mental "concepts" are not evidence, but a mental-activity which needs to be modified in according to external evidence. The wonders of our cosmos give us powerful incentives to further investigate its origins without submitting our ideas to centuries of traditional and primitive desert religious superstitions and time-consuming barriers. Scientific theory with healthy imagination can yield inventive prospects and points of view. By expanding our knowledge of language and eliminating unworkable essence terms, we can communicate without resorting to metaphors and algorithms and pre-conceived conclusions based on past beliefs. Our sense of wonder about our physical surroundings and our universe provide us with energy for exploration. How much more magnificent the results may be from useful thinking than one based on belief or faith!

The expression of beliefs comes as an emergent ability of our spoken and written language and from our understanding of the mechanisms of beliefs. This capacity has allowed us to project abstract symbols from the mind to symbols outside our body and mind. We have created unique vocal patterns and artful cave scratching designs on stone, bone and wood and much later on papyrus. In time, we developed biological abilities to learn how to compare the sounds and designs to beliefs in the brain. We learned and taught ourselves how to remember and how to associate and communicate external symbols through a common adaptation, the alphabet, through time and space. With these linguistic tools emerges the spoken and written language. The invention of language produced a constructive and exciting result, an innovation to "house" our thoughts in our brains and to *mimetically transfer* our ideas to another human being who lives near or at a long far distance or at some future time. The invention of writing must have appeared as supernatural, to those who used it in the dawn of human history. The first known forms of writing that appeared as *grapto-keimeno* (written-text) in *Kastoria,* Greece (about 7,250 years ago) consisted of pictorial characters and drawings representing actual things.

Unfortunately, our linguistic capacity developed more rapidly than our brain's ability to observe, interpret and store all global information gathered from the outside world. This flaw stemmed also from not understanding the difference between the symbols cave artists' created and the real-things and, the beliefs they aimed to represent. We are biologically programmed to look for patterns and sometimes we confuse the two by believing in them, even when their pattern-representations no longer exist. Our brains can also attach emotions to the symbols we believe to be of some importance. Religious symbols can evoke different emotions depending how you felt the first time you saw them. Our brain not only has the capacity to believe in things that do not exist but also can create false pattern-symbols that point to nowhere but themselves and take those as facts. We can intelligently predict doing all sort of things in the future before we actually do them. This mode of thinking produces all sorts of desirable results, such as, planning a vacation, purchasing a new car, or methods of hunting-gathering of foods which allowed us to survive and a desire for living.

However, our brains have not yet evolved to accurately interpret or represent the world around us; it evolved only to enhance the survival of our genes, so our brain creates false-patterns of belief to fill the gap between knowing and not-knowing, real or non-existent. You see, the brain cannot maintain a "gap," or a neutral-spot between thoughts, so it fills it by creating all sorts of beliefs, a near-matching to your wishful thinking. Wishful thinking is a belief that creates a short-cut pattern, which expects that the Laws of Nature will be suspended when you ask for a miracle, including the afterlife. The problem with beliefs, however, gets a bit more complicated. We can imagine of images of unique animals, people, and places in the universe that do not exist. For instance, a unicorn, superman flying, Jesus walking on water, the mysterious Paradise, monsters, dragons and Gods are just a few examples. We can even believe in them as all powerful entities. We can imagine and believe in all sorts of characters: the little people like the 7 Dwarfs, giants like the Biblical Goliath, and distorted scary people like the Archangel Gabriel with his giant wings and sword. Our beliefs of what they represent cannot be ignored, because millions of people around the world get fooled into believing in the existence of non-existing things. Muslims believe that the Prophet Mohammad flew to the Moon on his Winged-horse and split it in half with his sword.

If, because of ignorance, we fail to understand the differences between our brains mental-images and what occurs in the all inclusive material reality outside our brains, a belief system can result that includes superstitions and illusions taken as facts and mimetically passed on from generation to generation. Religion is a hotbed of voluntary ignorance which all three monotheisms each make their contribution to. As such, they enforce repressive behaviour, groupthink, and cult-like behaviours, for people who are unable to contextualise the collective forms of delusion. It is visible in their claims that they are not aware of the distinction between beliefs and material reality. This coupled with a lack of critical thinking results in a sort of self-referential groupspeak, blind faith and ignorance. In fact, religious belief, by its very nature, is extremely problematic and presents problems of reason or logical problems that do not withstand rational thought. It is a self-deception of religious belief formation process, for religious beliefs are primarily prescriptive, serving as an antidote to a perceived ill. The choice is to be critical, curious and creative in the exploration of all knowledge without the filter of religious belief which counters the flexibility needed to increase knowledge and independence of thought.

IN THE NAME OF POLITICS, RELIGION AND MILITARISM

RELIGIOUS FUNDAMENTALISTS

DEAD CHRISTIAN & MUSLIM SOLDIERS:

THE DELUSION OF BELIEF: WHOSE SIDE IS GOD?

A SAD STATE OF AFFAIRS

ILLUSTRATED
WAR IS THE POLITICIAN'S GAME, THE PRIEST'S DELIGHT AND PROFESSIONAL SOLDIERS TRADE

ILLUSTRATED
IS LIKE TALKING TO THE WALL····

OR TO ONESELF

ILLUSTRATED

GOD'S PERMISSION TO KILL AND DIE

ILLUSTRATED

ISRAELIS BLESS THEIR KILLING MACHINE

ILLUSTRATED
PRAYERS DID NOT HELP THE JEWISH SOLDIERS AND VICTIMES OF WAR

COULD MUSLIM PRAYERS PROTECT ?

ILLUSTRATED
COULD FEW BUCKETS OF WATER HELP?

THE RESULTS OF RELIGIOUS FANATISM

ILLUSTRATED

MASSIVE GOD DELUSION

Indicrinating children for violance

HUMANIST vs. BIBLICAL MORALITY

Human beings are social creatures, therefore we are curious about how things began to be adopted in the society we live in, or in other far away cultures, especially about the origins of things we deem important. This is not all about justifying our individual curiosity but, in a broader sense, of theoretical and practical interest to all of us. For instance, evolutionary adaptation may explain how and why a simple or complex adaptation developed over time, in terms of selection and by hereditary variation. In such cases the early Greek thinkers called the evolutionary accounts as *archi*, or *origin* an understanding of the initial formation of any given concept or principle such as morality or ethics.

If there was ever an evolutionary account of the origins of morality, it has unfortunately been lost in the mist of the pre-historic human evolution. As a result, we should not expect to find a single, unified or written dogma of morality outside the existing theocratic verses or narratives. Humanist morality however, is the result of the gradual adaptation of our social life. As such, morality varies between groups of hunters-gatherers; in historical times and geographic environments, and degree of contributions into our social lives from one generation to the next, up to and including the present times. The great Charles Darwin, in 1859, divided the issue of humanist morality between Natural Selection, culture, the collective process of learning from parent to child, and from within some innate human faculty. Morality, therefore, is not the product of one specific or a few adapted human traits, for it may be the product of natural selection, but not specifically selected as a functional entity. Social learning may organise human behaviour. From this point on, through adaptation to a given human environment, it is shaped by cultural evolution, family and social structure, geographical space and time and other social factors.

Aspects of human social behaviour may have been inherited from apes most closely related to us biologically (since we are Apes), where we find shared characteristics from a common ancestor for our evolution of humanist based morality. This means that, in order to adjust to his social environment, man shared an interest in the social life with others, this leading to the natural adaptation of morality. From a sense of social cohesiveness, implicit in the social interaction of group-living apes, a limited social and moral system arose out of co-operation, shared social obligations and emotions. These emotions and social capacities laid the "building blocks" of social behaviour among themselves which provided the raw material for the evolution of humanist morality.

Contemporary investigation into understanding morality leads us to paths by which humanist morality evolved, from the social behaviour about right and wrong and behaviour in every day life. Morality is definitely associated with the social behaviour of humans with each other, rather than a system of ideals or religious fallacies. Even though humanist social morality is complex, there are enough traces to the behaviour of many other social animals behaving morally, including our long extinct human ancestors, the Neanderthals and Cro-Magnons. Typical moral behaviour can also be found in animal groups of apes or elephants which, as highly social mammals, they are known to exhibit traits of empathy and altruism. Social animals exhibit a willingness to defend their young, even under difficult circumstances where the chance of their own death or injury is evident. As social animals, their chances of survival and reproduction are better in groups than living alone.

Human reproduction is intricately linked to virtue and morality (modesty), in particular with females who tend to be under greater intense scrutiny regarding sexual behaviour. The differential application of male to female sexual morality may be evolutionary adaptation because females dedicate more resources and energy into bearing and rearing children, so they need to select a male who is willing to assist them with financial support and protection, in the rearing of children. Women, because of their physiology, have evolved with stronger preferences for long-term partners, whereas men have evolved with mixed preferences for both long-and-short-term partners. In developed societies, feminists, with a strong sense of *entitlement*, are seeking the dismissal of female physiology and the biological need of "long-term partner," and replacing both with *"group-seek"* identity and *state economic support.*

Society's standards of virtue and modesty assume that men are more flexible in dropping this standard for short-term partners because, in such relations, there is no parental obligation. In this regard, female promiscuous behaviour would be maladaptive, as they would have to raise their children with no, or only temporary, parental support. In most developing, conservative or traditional societies, female adultery is regarded as a greater moral-offence than is male adultery. In traditional cultural societies the female moral virtue of fidelity is related to the family-identity, property and community status, all of which are transmitted through a patriarchal hereditary line. In such societies it is vitally important to the structural order that females be monogamous. As such, their male partners are assured that their hereditary line, property and family legacy would be left to offspring that are biologically theirs. The offspring's paternity must be known in relation to other members of the extended family, in order to assure a continuity of the family's homogeneity. Sexual morality and female parental preferences are also linked to the evolution of female-choice which is linked to their direct gene benefit (good genes vs. weak genes) correlated with male fitness, sexual selection and visual attraction.

Humanist morality has been based on sympathy and community ties, and there is no need to obey religious fallacies, for this would be based on fear of punishment and the delusion of a reward in the afterlife. Religion cannot be the answer to the moral truth. All of the biblical scriptures of the Jewish Torah, the Christian Old and New Testaments and Islam's Qur'an were written by people who, because of their historical time, had less knowledge about science and biology than today's average person. Their world view was very narrow as much as it was Abraham's, Moses', Mohammad's or Jesus' which limited their knowledge of social issues such as ethics, values and morality. The people who wrote the holy books knew nothing, or next to nothing, of the facts that are relevant to us in the 21st century. They were all part of Middle Eastern desert culture based on traditional superstition, internal wars and idolatry of conflicting beliefs. They knew nothing about the origins of life, the relation between mind and brain; they did not know that mental illness is a medical suffering, they knew nothing about DNA and viruses, nor did they know about Human Evolution, Natural Selection, the Origins of Species or computation, electricity and the Laws of Nature because none of these are in the scriptures. None of them were philosophers on issues of morality, ethics, justice and civic law. They had no idea why people got sick and died, other than deaths in tribal wars. Most of the people of the scriptures were no wiser than the average Afghanistan, Taliban or Boko Haram tribal warlords today. They had absolutely no notion that slavery was a crime against humanity or that owning people and treating them as tools or commodities was ethically and morally wrong. Jesus and his Apostles, Mohammad and his companions could not see that slavery was wrong and condemn it for the human suffering it caused.

Today we do not have Jewish, Christian or Muslim morality since we do not have Jewish, Christian or Muslim scientific discoveries or inventions. The religions of the inventors have no relation to their discoveries, inventions or morality, for their religious rules of behaviour, traditions and rituals do not constitute a scientific base or a humanist moral or ethical fibre. Devoted Christians believe that the Bible is the moral guidance; for it is the work of God, and Jesus is the Son of God. Followers of the Christian religion truly believe that they will find salvation after death. They repeatedly have been told that those beliefs hold true because the Bible contains the word of God. While these devotees go about their daily affairs, they feel free to criticise any public policy they do not agree with, any difference of opinion amongst scholars and printed themes about the philosophy of life. Yet, for some unknown reason, their intellectual forwardness stops in its tracks when it comes to reason with the primitive Biblical themes. It appears that they have imposed upon themselves a voluntary ignorance, censorship or a gag on the subject of religious beliefs which they tend to follow. Little do they know that we need knowledge that frees our human intelligence from the scriptures that were written long ago by socially and morally ignorant men! **Atheists**, secularists and humanists reject the notion that religion has the exclusive prerogative over morality, since morality was inherited by humanity long before the concept of God was invented by man. In prehistoric hunter-gathering communities, man found that cooperative hunting worked better and, genetically, clans who followed the *Golden Rule* to promote sharing of food and protection had better chances of survival. For instance, the humanist moral principle of the Golden Rule (and variations of it) surfaced in larger human communities as early as 5 thousand years ago during the Babylonian rule. The reciprocal moral-ethic of the Golden Rule means that people should aim to treat each other as they would like to be treated themselves, with tolerance, consideration and compassion. This humanist Golden Rule was transmitted from generation to generation by social consent and it has never been regarded as a dogma of an absolute or perfect celestial command. It is imperfect because it derived from human sources, emotions and experience. It simply requires strangers to think about others and neighbours to think about their neighbours and try to give consideration. As such, the Golden Rule is a general moral rule of humanist behaviour which might or might not apply to every detail of life. Nor does it mean to make the assumption that others who share the same emotions are to be afforded respect and consideration. Let us take it humanly. No one is ever going to love his neighbour like he loves himself or his family, but a mutual respect can be realised.

As it can be seen, the Golden Rule cannot be claimed by any philosopher, political ideology or religion. It only indicates that the Golden Rule could be adopted as a standard behaviour through which disputes could be resolved. Here are some moral code variations of the Golden Rule, as it has been expressed in different historical times.

Pittacus, 650 BCE, *"Do not do to your neighbour what you take ill from him."*

Confucius, 500 BCE, *"Do not unto another that would not have him unto* you. Thou needest this [moral] law alone. It is the foundation of all the rest."

Thales, 464 BCE, *"Avoid doing what you would blame others for doing."*

Sextus the Pythagorean, 406 BCE, *"What you wish your neighbours to be to you, such be also to them."*

Aristotle, 384 BCE, *"We should conduct ourselves toward others as we would have them act toward us."*

Aristippus of Cyrene, 365 BCE, *"Cherish reciprocal benevolence, which will make you as anxious for another's welfare as your own."*

Isocrates, 338 BCE, *"Act toward others as you desire them to act toward you."*

Mahabharata, 300 BCE, *"This is the sum of duty: Do naught unto others which would cause you pain if done to you."*

In Homer's Odyssey 700 BCE Greek mythology Goddess Calypso tells Odysseus of Ithaca *"I'd be as careful for you as I'd be for myself in like need. I know what is fair and right."*

Maeandrius of Samos (Greece) 522 BCE, *"What I condemn in another I will, if I may, avoid myself."*

Isocrates (Greece) 436 BCE, *"Don't do to others what isn't good for you."*

This Golden Rule moral guidance simply means trying to empathise with other persons, including with those whom you view as being different from the rest. It is empathy that is the core essence of kindness, compassion, understanding and reciprocal respect. These are the social and moral qualities we all tend to appreciate being shown, from wherever we are, from whatever ethnic background, and from wherever we come from. We may not know what it is to be different from others, it may not always be possible to avoid causing suffering to others, but it is not difficult for most of us to imagine what will cause us to be inflicted with pain.

This is what *atheism* describes as a world view or life stance that focuses on the natural and humanist ethics and rejects the theistic, autocratic or "supernatural" moral dogma. It is not a faith position that implies a belief without verifiable evidence. This absence of religious belief does not eliminate the capacity of human beings to behave responsibly and morally. To solve our problems and recognise our knowledge of what humankind has already achieved, we must continue to behave positively in order to reach our human potential and to celebrate our humanist creativity. Atheism and humanism are based on reason and science rather than theology, superstition and appeals to a celestial Sky-God. However, atheism and humanism are not *scientism*, for we value science only as a means of achieving knowledge without any superficial claim that science holds the answer to everything.

As we become more knowledgeable we also become more intelligent and care less for preachers and more for the riches of humanity.

There a number of moral issues that were once part of a religious and ideological dogma, but they were, and still are, opposed by atheism and humanism's view of the world. We think these issues are morally wrong, such as, racist and sexist behaviour or a local or the global economic system that destroys the environment and peoples' lives. These immoral issues are regarded in and of themselves wrong, because they contribute to the suffering of human beings. This conclusion has been formulated by humans in their long historical struggle against the devastating effects of such practices, and not because such moral rules have a divine source that is imposed on human society by a celestial entity.

Religious dogmatic morality is absolute, which propagates the stoning of people to death for adultery and apostasy, cutting some hands for stealing and punishment for breaking the Sabah (day of rest). Humanity does not need absolute morality but rather a morality that is well thought-out with reason, that is arguably intelligent and that creates the kind of society we all would want to live-in. If we look at morality of civilised societies we see that we support equality between men and women, being gentle and kind to our fellow human beings and being kind to animals and the environment. All of these are entirely recent adaptations, the roots of which have developed over historical times through consciences and reasoning; sober discussion and argument, and legal, political and moral theory. Those have no, or very little, basis in Biblical or Qur'anic scriptures, although you can "cherry-pick" occasional moral verses. However, we should not forget and leave-out all the horrible verses---just because we have "grown out of them"--- but be thankful to secular morality and common consent.

Religion works for most believers because people horribly want religion to be true; that they are supervised, that God looks after them and that they might be rewarded or punished in the afterlife. It has this terrible servile effect and this why it is claimed to be morally superior to being an atheist. An atheist would maintain that he would rather live without that gushy master-slave mentality and to be condemned in this and the afterlife. Empathy inspires morality: defending a helpless person, helping an injured child, a soldier who dives on top of a grenade and sacrifices himself to save his comrades. These acts do not require divine sanctions or permission to act with bravery. It is innate in our species and we can all be inspired. We do not get this valorous courage from God for, if we did, that would degrade our moral values and rob ourselves of our integrity by giving it to some unknown entity. This gives me a chance to illustrate this question of example of moral action via a real event.

This is a personal story that I witnessed in a Toronto supermarket's cash-register line. There was a person in front of me and another who was ahead paying her grocery bill. As the woman was searching her handbag for money, a $ 50 bill fell out of her purse onto the floor. She failed to notice it, but the man behind her reaches down, picks up the $50 and passes it on to her. What happened next shocked me, for the woman loudly praised and thanked the "Lord" for recovering her money but not once did she turn around to thank the man for his act of kindness. That woman, in fact, robbed that man of his moral integrity, dignity, honesty and empathy and gave her gratitude to a non-existent Sky-God instead. For this woman, the man's act was not kind, was not honest, it had no moral standing, he was irrelevant, she simply had abolished human morality---however insignificant or significant his act of kindness was. This means that the individual's example of morality was nothing but dust.

On a more philosophical plane, how do we hold the sentiment by which we view our own moral behaviour and thought? Is religion the answer to human problems? Religion provides delusions as cure-all proposition for our problems, what is good and how we should achieve it, how we should know it, and how to explain suffering. All these pertinent questions deserve answers, if only we could simply project them upwards to a celestial judge and an absolutist dictator. This is a horrible idea, that there is a "big-brother" in the sky, who owns us, who knows what is best for us, who supervises us during the day and even while we are asleep, who knows what we think, who can punished us for our thoughts and who dictates our moral and ethical values. For the religious to wish this to be true is to live as an abject slave. There are no absolute solutions to the human problems, and the sooner we confirm that, the sooner we could become determine to finding the causes and earthly solutions to our human problems. Humanity has survived slavery, feudalism and imperialistic wars. We have educated ourselves and now we have arrived at an intellectual position of knowing what is morally correct. What may be required of us is to acquire the moral and intellectual courage to state publicly, that the anti-humanist, political ideologies of religions must be stopped; that this gusty religious proposition is based on lies and enough is enough of the historical religious crimes against humanity.

We are not leaderless. The late *Christopher Hitchens (1949 – 2011)* laid the ground work and the example for us to be outspoken and be arrogant towards religious demagogues, and Richard Dawkins has given us the inside narrative of Darwin's Natural Selection and Natural Evolution, as has

Sam Harris who identified the enemies of reason and science and, read the *Brief History of Time,* by the physicist-cosmologist Steven Hawking who, openly declared *"There is no God"* and others. Let us celebrate the ancient scholars of morality who stood by their humanist moral convictions against the tyrants of the day.

The Greek philosopher Socrates, when he was on trial for his life, accused of blasphemy, answered this age-old question by referring to an internal *"Daemon"* (not demon) that he had, an *inner-critic,* a consciousness; that was telling him when, in fact, he was wrong, even when he was uttering his best rhetorical arguments. His inner-critic would warn him that his arguments, although clever, were nevertheless, dishonest. Any human being with an average moral standing has an inner-critic. *Adam Smith (1723 – 1790),* the Scottish moral philosopher, called our "internal-witness" our means of being self-critical of our behaviour and moral sentiments.

The moral question may also apply to people behaving morally well when no one is around to watching them. There is no one (I think) that has difficulty understanding what has been said. For instance, we pay our taxes by declaring our correct income; we do not steal someone's purse just because no one is looking at us, but we tend to behave morally. Of course, there are people who do not behave morally well, who do not think about anyone else, who only think of themselves. In either case, there is no evidence that God has ordered people to behave morally nor is there a Devil who makes them think only about themselves. Those are human choices based on personal circumstances, family upbringing and cultural and civic education. We see them around inflicting pain and insulting others, for among us there are sociopathic and psychopathic people who care about no one else, not even for themselves. Nastiness is in nature as well as in the civil societies, but can the Christians claim that even those "nasties" were created in God's image?

Now let us come to the moral dilemma of "miracles" which cure the sick, raise the dead and the Virgin birth, amongst others. *David Hume (1711 – 1776),* Scottish philosopher, radical empiricist and religious sceptic, stated that miracles are not part of the natural order; rather miracles suspend the Laws of Nature, such as Jesus resurrection, the Virgin birth, the raising of the dead and the instant curing of the sick. Religious leaders see morality as a necessary method of employed to control human desires and impulses. The underlying assumption is that humans (because they were born in sin) are sinful; they will seek to engage in crimes against society, if they are left to their own devices. Such distorted assumptions supports punishment for "moral offences" because they assume that human beings are naturally violent, selfish, greedy and xenophobic, and women are wicked and who must be kept in a inferior social status than men.

Under such religious assumptions humanity must live under constant threat from above, and punishment would be delivered by God's chosen few. God made himself known to few men---why to so few and so late we do not know---and ordered them to purify the world. In other words, men were born in sin and now are ordered to get pure under threat of punishment. This assumption is false as are the beliefs that God created man and watched over him, created man sick and then ordered him to get well on the pain of hell and fire; that man cannot do anything without God; and concur that there is no moral restraint on us if we do not concur with the idea that we are the property of a super being. It is very disturbing to know that the most vale and the most callus, the cruellest and the most brutal crimes against innocent people in the Middle East and Africa are committed by those who believe that they have a divine right and permission to commit them.

In the mass media; from Internet to social-media to printing press, used by the industry of religion, it is propagated that, and without God there can be no morality. They claim the moral superiority of their religion, pointing to the charities they support and the moral acts they promote. This is a problematic claim, and a fallacy, because atheists support equal charities and support and promote humanist morality. Can the religious demagogues name a charitable act that is of their exclusive divine providence that could not possibly be supported by atheists? Could the same demagogues make a moral or ethical statement that atheists could not possibly make because of their rejection of religion? If we could reverse these points, could the reader imagine an evil act that only a devoted believer would be likely to commit? Could I named the Taliban who threw acid on a little girl's face because she wanted to go to school, or the suicide bomber who kills others because they are of a different religious sect (or entirely other religion), or those who mutilate the genitals of boys and girls is entirely religious, or that the Catholic and Muslim clergy and the Afghan war lords who engage in pedophilia? No one could claim that child abuse is entirely religious, but it is close to be an entirely religious. I challenge any religious demagogue who claims that it is the atheists and secularists who are the immoral ones. It is a nasty thing to say that it is the divine who prompts them to commit any atrocity in the name of their religion yet they are those who are the most fanatical, the most violent and the leading opponents of humanist values, morals and civilisation.

To ask, therefore, a humanist or an atheist where we get our morality from is both hypocritical and insulting to us. We reject the accusation that we will not know right from wrong if we are not guided by a "supernatural" Sky-God. This is a degrading accusation against the human race, and an insulting assumption, that if there is no objective ground of right and wrong without God, then everything is permitted. This belief may be useful to a religious sociopath or psychopath who restrains himself from committing a horrendous crime because he truly believes that God will punish him for such cruelty.

Our notion of right and wrong is innate to us, that is, it comes from humans. We know that to get along with others we must exhibit a sense of moral behaviour towards them, that committing a crime against another is both illegal and immoral. As independent human beings, with our own biological and evolutionary internal compass and sense of decency, we can tell right from wrong. Otherwise, we could not have survived as the human race nor could we have developed as rational human beings. When we do something good for another, it is the human-in us that is shinning, not a religious obligation towards others. Why are some religious believers degrading this shinning humanist morality by claiming that it is a heavenly gift given to us by a delusive entity in the sky? By their delusion they are robbing themselves of their human dignity, the quality of their humanness, and all for a false belief.

Most of us have a materialist view of the world, with the metaphorical "mind" (brain's energy) being part of the material substance called the brain.

- We are half of a DNA chromosome away from a chimp, a plant or other animals.
- Natural Selection and Evolution are not aware that our species is still here or that most planetary events have not occurred with us in mind.
- Therefore, we cannot be self-centered as some religious people believe that we are the center of the earth.
- The world around us is material, and we are a matter that thinks and feels, that our brain's mind is material (energy), that natural evolution and adaptation's material-process has created us the way this process has developed.
- In other words, it is not our mind that determines the existence of the material world, it is the other way around; it is the existence of the material world, including our brains, that determines the existence of our minds. Therefore the mind is the activity of the brain-matter.

The lesson taken from this short narrative is that:

"The mind is the brain, and this is a material world before it is anything

else. That, there is nothing outside the material world, that everything that has occurred in this universe is natural to this universe. That, there is nothing outside of this universe, and therefore there is no such thing as "beyond-natural" or "super-natural" or outside the natural universe. We do not know of another "outside-world" beyond our universe to call it super-natural. Anything that has occurred within the infinity of our material-world was necessary, normal and natural. If it is necessary, normal and natural, then it has materially occurred. If it did not materially occur then it does not exist." (Quote from my book, *Prisoners of Our Ideals*).

In the history of the 20th century humanity has witnessed and endured World War I and II, Fascism, Nazism and Stalinism, all morally reprehensible happenings. It is beyond the scope of this book to interpret those events. However, there is a need to describe some of the historic premises of those events in the hope that the reader will decide to independently expand on his knowledge of them. The premise is the claim made by religious people that atheists and atheistic regimes have committed equally reprehensible immoral acts against humanity, in some cases, more than the religious fanatics, even during the Crusades. Let us look at these regimes that officially were declared to be "atheistic" while causing the deaths of millions of people.

In Russia, during the three centuries of absolute monarchy of successive Czarism, the people of Russia were never introduced to democratic reforms, human rights or the rights to own their labour as their property. The Russian people were property under a feudal-fiefdom, whose owner had ownership of the land, the animals and the peasants who lived on and worked the land. The owner was the absolute power of the fief with absolute power over the life and death of everything that lived in his large estate. The peasants were culturally subservient, domicile, docile, superstitious and living in constant fear, uncertainty and perpetual ignorance.

On the political level, the Czar was the monarch with the absolute power over every aspect of the social, political, and economic life of millions of people. The Czar's decree was absolute and any opposition to it was dealt by the secret police and internal spy system. The Czar was also the Head of the Russian Orthodox Church and, as such, he had the power to declare any religious decree of his choosing. The peoples' choice was obedience or death at the hand of the regimes forces. Most choose obedience as a balance of well-being, with the exception of the revolutionaries, the Spartacus-anarchists and rebel conspirators. These political conditions lasted for a few centuries, while the people of Russia were transformed into sheep-like flocks.

In the religious environment, the Russian Orthodox Church had developed into a powerful dominant force and owner of wealth and fiefdom lands. In its Sermons to devoted religious peasants, the Church reinforced the delusion that God has created the lives of the peasants, in the way and manner as it was at that moment, and that it was their obligation to accept and obey God's laws. The ruling elite, the Russian Church with its hundreds of thousands of well fed clergy, the business class were all benefited by the setting of such absolute system of political-religious affairs; that is, with the exception of the subservient and domicile people. The culture of servility was ingrained in the social fabric. Therefore, Stalin did not create the peoples' subservient mentality or the oppressive conditions before 1924, when he took over political power following the death of *Vladimir Lenin's (1870 -1924).*

Stalin was a political animal whose objectives were the enforcement of the political ideology of his own particular style of Communism. True that he was an atheist and that he went after the hierarchy of the Russian Orthodox Church who opposed him (in favour of the Czar) and this is the reason most of its leaders migrated to Greek monasteries of *Agios Oros* and Europe. As for the lower clergy, who lived among the peasants, were an inseparable part of the peasants social environment because they were peasants of the same social stock. They were not discriminated against due to their beliefs so long as they maintained control over their flocks and obeyed the laws of the land; something that they were accustomed to doing for centuries. Stalin went after the Church's leadership, not because of his atheism, but because he wanted to destroy the political power and influence of the Russian Orthodox Church.

The forced migration of tens of millions of peasants took place because of his political ideology of collectivism of farms vs. the private ownership by his opposing forces. Stalin caused the deaths of millions of people he cared nothing about the value of the human life because he followed his particular brand of Communist ideology, not because of his rejection of God. As for the people, they were accustomed to political oppression for centuries and did now what the new-Czar was enforcing upon them. Stalin became a god-like figure for the peasants just as the Czars were god-like to be praised and obeyed. Stalin was the untimed supreme authority, a spiritual entity, which carried with it the long feudal traditions where people praised the Supreme Leader, as they did over centuries with each succession of Czars, and as people still do today in North Korea since 1952.

The political ideology of Fascism grew in the 1920s and 1930s first in Italy under the Fascist dictator *Mussolini (1883 – 1945)* and then in Spain under the Dictator *Francisco Franco (1882 – 1975)* following the defeat of the

Republican forces in 1936. Both Fascist leaders were devoted Catholics and both the Italian and Spanish Catholic Church provided financial and moral support to both dictators. The murderous bombing of the innocents in the Spanish town of *Guernica* in April 26, 1937, by the German Nazi air force, was never condemned by the Catholic Church In fact, religiousness was so ingrained into the cultural fabric of society that many normal moral aspects of ordinary life were condemned by the Church and were re-enforced through the Fascist dictatorial laws of Franco's and Mussolini's. The heavy religious atmosphere was felt in birth-control, in common-law unions, in religious indoctrination of school children and other areas. Homosexuality was not only openly condemned by the Church but it was legally and viciously pursued by the militarised police of both Italy and Spain. In fact, the famous Spanish poet and playwright *Federico Garcia Lorca (1898 – 1936)* was sentenced to death for being politically active against Franco's dictatorship and for being a homosexual. In short, the political oppression of the people of Italy and Spain was done with the moral blessing of the Italian and Spanish Catholic Church.

Nazism is a degrading form of German paganism. Based on its messianic aspects, some historians, political scientists and philosophers who have focused on the esoteric aspects of Nazism, would regard it as a *political religion*. Outside the academic circles, public interest was focused on the relationship between Nazism and Christianity. The debate was focused on whether Hitler was a Christian or not. Historians looked at the Germanic Neo-paganism and Nazi occultism and have generally agreed about the Nazi policy towards religion. The objective of this Nazi policy was to remove any reference of Jewish content from the Bible---the Old Testament, the Gospel of Matthew—thus transforming it into so called, *Positive Christianity*. The Nazi Party's program of 1920, in point 24, endorses Positive Christianity; because it does not oppose the customs and pagan moral traditions of the Germanic race. The religious beliefs of the Nazi leadership, including Hitler's, diverged strongly towards Evangelism and support of the occult of *Ariosophic Welttanschauung* philosophy.

During the Nazi period of terror, the Catholic Church stood idle towards the atrocities committed against humanity. However, the Church made sure to celebrate Hitler's birthday by giving church mass to thank God for preserving Hitler's health. The political support of the Catholic Church towards the Nazi leadership is well-documented by historians; the U.S Office for Strategic Services (pre-CIA) and German, Austrian and French analysts of WWII. In fact, one of the most prominent moral and ethical supporters of Nazism and Nazi leaders before and during the Nazi era was

Eugenio Pacelli (1876 – 1958) who became *Pope Pius XII* the so called *Hitler's Pope*. The Pope's desire was to centralise the power of the Papacy in Germany and had subordinated opposition to the Nazis to that goal. His anti-Semitism prevented him from carrying about the European Jews. In fact, Pope Pius XII was a "fellow traveler" of the Nazis and he never spoke against the Nazi policies even after the end of the WWII. He was more open to collaboration with totalitarian right-wing regimes such as Spain and Italy who were hostile to left-wing ideas and groups. He facilitated the rise of Hitler through his passive inaction and silence which ultimately condoned and enabled the Holocaust. Subsequent research revealed that, in the post-war the Vatican provided travel documents to Nazi war criminals of the likes of Adolf Eichmann, Josef Mengele, Klaus Barbie and thousands of war criminals en route to South America. This offers a significant insight into Vatican moral standing, particularly in the case of such Nazi brutality.

So, let us take the opportunity to view some of the Biblical non-allegorical and non-metaphorical guidelines set by God to Christian believers. These passages were chosen at random.

- **John 14:6** *"I am the way and the truth and the life"*
- **Mathew 25:21** *"His Lord said unto him. Well done, thou good and faithful servant"*

   You are praised for being an obedient servant, and not as a free man, to a Christian dogma. Slaves were once praised as being obedient to their master in inhuman conditions. As followers of the Christian dogma, their lives were all-inclusive in a faithful obedience, for it was more valuable to them than Sunday's prayers. The sad thing is that these good people believed that the Bible was redeemed by God and not by people with religious and political agendas who were spreading their collective delusions for public consumption. The Afro-Americans today are the most devoted followers of the same religious system that once morally promoted and biblically justified their enslavement.

- **Exodus 20:5** *" I the lord thy God am a jealous God"*

The Christian Church still has to credit religion as a source of ethics and morality; and from where would we get these, if it was not from faith in God? As an atheist, I do not regard religion as being our moral or ethical source. I do not regard as being legitimate; the religious explanations of the origins of our species, our universe or of our destiny, for those have long been discredited. I maintain that religion is neither moral nor ethical. Religion cannot set moral standards by declaring that one person's punishment for another person's sins is legitimate. You see, the Bible claims that God sent

Jesus to be crucified for our sins. This is a preposterous and cruel immoral act. What kind moral standard is set as an example when a father sends his own son to die, in a most cruel way, for the sins of others? Is it ethical to believe and follow this claim? The doctrine of *vicarious redemption* by human sacrifice is utterly immoral and unethical, and a demonstration of a sickly and compulsive love of Christianity. The name of the practice of sacrificing one for the sins of another, in primitive Middle Eastern Bedouin tribal communities, was called "scape-goading." The tribe's people would ceremoniously pile-up the villagers' "collective sins" on top of a goat and then drive it away into the desert to die from thirst and hunger. They believed that this would drive the tribe's sins away and die with the goat which is an immoral and cruel belief. The underlying connotation is that a person, who has committed a crime, can pass the sin of his crime onto another, which diminishes one's responsibility for his own anti-social behaviour.

Christians have been told that they must share the guilt of Jesus' sacrifice although no one was there at the time to object or to stop the public torture and execution of a delusional and eccentric street orator-preacher. The whole doctrine of collective guilt is a continuation of the dogma that humans were born in filthy sin from the time of Adam and Eve in Genesis. But if you commit the right religious action and pray you can evade God's punishment, not just in this life but in the afterlife as well. That is in accordance with the New Testament because in the Old Testament, as gruesome as it is, (recommending genocide, racism, slavery and tribalism), and as cruel and immoral as God is, he does not promise to punish the sinful in the afterlife. In our basic integrity and knowing the differences between right from wrong and choosing the right action from a wrong one, we must repudiate the notion that we do not have an innate moral discrimination unless it comes from a loving and fearful celestial entity. My question to the religious priests and clergy is; is it not an immoral act on your part to rob peoples' integrity for the sake of making a comfortable living by doing so? Is it not a falsity and insulting to us for the clergy to claim that we get our morality from religion?

Atheists maintain that objective morality does not require an external theistic or non-theistic foundation of any kind. How do we know that there is goodness in the world without the guidance from a "supernatural" entity? This question alone attacks humanity in its deepest integrity in that, without religion, we will be nothing, that we will have no principles, no humour, no irony, no happiness, and no sorrow if we are not the property of a celestial dictator and yarning for his rewards and fearing his punishments. This question attacks our humanist essence to its core, including our sexuality, in that, it projects in us a sense of shame, guilt and fear and yes; even when these religious claims are fallacies, they are still the source of immorality, misery and unhappiness. Religion claims a monopoly on morality by claiming that there are moral actions and statements that an atheist cannot make, such as, "love your enemy." I do not think that this claim is a moral one, for should we love suicide murderers, or the village-council who orders the rape of a family's female as vindication for someone else's crime? Should we love the "martyr" who kills anyone who is not of his religious sect? No, of course not. It is positively immoral, cowardly and distressful to say that one loves a suicide martyr. Remember, the "love your enemy" propagation was invented by the *Roman Imperial Cult* to influence and pacify the Jewish rebels who were rebelling against their Roman enemies.

Let us assume for a moment that the Qur'an's verses and the entire Islam teachings are true. In this case, if you are a believing Middle Eastern fundamentalist Muslim, you may feel safe! What if you are not a devout Muslim? What if you are Hindu or Buddhist, Jewish, Christian or an atheist? Then what are the dreadful consequences for us and our children? You must remember, that Islam claims to be the last religion among the Abrahamic religions and that the Qur'an is God's perfect book given to a perfect man called Mohammad. If you reject this claim you are—as well as I—going to Hell for eternity, where your skin will burn and peel off your body, to be grown again in order to burn off again in an endless cycle of suffering. Your children who are not Muslims will suffer the same consequences for eternity because of you. If you are a Christian or a Jew you were misled by your religion, or if you are an atheist you were misled by reason and science; for all of us to appreciate the true word of Allah. Therefore we all are going to hell for eternity.

So, if everything the religion of Islam has said is true, how should we view God in moral terms? If you are not a devout Muslim, then you were born in a wrong religion, in a wrong culture, to the wrong parents and in the wrong geographical place and time. Therefore, you must appreciate how bad a position you are now in. If you are not about to receive Allah's compassion and forgiveness for your helpless position, then Hell is awaiting for you and your family. Do you think that you are about to receive God's forgiveness for being born in a Catholic or in a Jewish family? As well, Hell is waiting for our children because we mislead them by giving them the wrong religion or taught them reason and science.

The question that should be placed upon you now is how must do you worry, what level of insomnia have you suffer from it, or have you lost your appetite over this? Can you appreciate how little you suffer from it or how little sleep you lose over these delusions? Just think and feel for a moment how free you are and will continue to be in the face of this possibility. What are the chances that the rest of humanity (some 4 billion non Christians or non Muslims), who do not believe in the Bible and the Qur'an, are going to Hell for eternity? Why not oppose such theocracy and its depredations world-wide? Let us advance the humanist cause of those in Afghanistan and Israel, in Iraq and Somalia, Syria and Pakistan, in UK and France, and help them to resist those Islamic religious fanatics whose desire is to encompass the destruction of civilisation. These religious fanatics sincerely believe that they have God on their side in wanting to achieve the ultimate Armageddon of the world. We should boycott the Israeli fanatic settlers' land grab, settlement-building and other violation of Palestinians' human-rights. These fanatics believe that when they fulfil the ancient prophecy of the return of the Jews, the final Armageddon will take place and the fanatics will all ascend to heaven.

You see, Jewish and Christian religious fanatics in the USA and UK believe in the Armageddon prophecy and are helping to achieve this prophecy. The Jewish fanatic Sheldon Adelson, (the Las Vegas casino magnate, with property interests in East Jerusalem) and Mega-Church pastor John Hagee are accused in court of financing the construction of settlements on Palestinian soil. It is repulsive to see, in monotheistic religions, that a large part of their doctrine wants us all to die; they want this world to come to a vile end. Whenever you read the Biblical scriptures or listen to the proponents of these predictions, you will find that their destructive desires are inseparable from their Jewish, Christian and Islamic religion. In a cynical way, these religious fanatics do not want heaven to be crammed with everyone (Christians, Jews, Muslims or non-devoted believers), just the chosen few, and the rest can go to hell. As such, the "boycott Israel" movement continues to gain support.

Yes, this is what the Jewish, Christian and Islamic dogmas claim would happen on the Day of Judgment. The Day of Judgment would come with the End of the World. On that particular day each man, woman and child would be judged in according to their religious devotion and circumstances. For instance, a primitive native in the Amazon Rainforest who has never heard of Jesus or Mohammad would not be judged too harshly because of his ignorance of Christianity or Islam. Anyone else, whether non-devoted Muslim, Christian, Hindu or Buddhist, Animist or cultists, agnostics or atheist would all be judged in according to the degree of their sinfulness. Some will go to Hell for a short time, others for a longer time of suffering, and most will go to Hell and Fire for eternity. None of us would escape

God's Day of Judgment.

Of course, the propagators of this religious absurdity did not account for the huge logistical problem God will face. There will be a line-up of 4 (out of 6) billion young and old men, women and children each telling God his circumstances, each pleading for clemency and forgiveness. If it takes one (1) minute per person, (which includes his testimony, asking for clemency or forgiveness), plus God's time to make his decision, it will take 60 persons per hour, times 24 hours = 1, 1440 (per-day), times 30 per month = 43,200, times 12 months = 518,400 per year with no rest. How long will it take for God to judge the rest of the 4 billion of sinners before passing his judgment?

On a more serious note, the *moral necessity of atheism* must affirm its anti-theism by not taking a favoured position towards any religious pluralism of faith or schisms over another. A number of churches, synagogues and mosques are all claiming to hold their faith based on their particular kind of truth and they compete with one another. This phenomenon of pluralism and schisms within existing faiths is susceptible to a very simple explanation. The long history of religious pluralism of various temples, churches and faiths is attributable to the fact that Man created God and not the other way around. If this premise is true, by verifiable evidence, then God's religion is not a mystery at all, but it is schismatic if not schizophrenic. The only confirmed affirmation of someone being wrong, or being self-deceptive or delusional, is the person who claims that he possesses the knowledge that God created an immoral, sinful and degenerate mammal called Human, in his own image, and that he (the believer) knows what God thinks or what his intentions are. Even for religious or spiritual persons it must be a profanity, a blasphemy and very deeply offensive to tell the rest of the mammals that he (the clergy) is the only mammal who knows how God's mind works, for his arrogance and the impossibility.

The moral imperative of atheism or anti-theism is to assert that if it was actually true that we are part of God's divine design, what that would actually mean? Would it mean that we would be living under a permanent supervision and surveillance over our lives and those of others? That this supervision began before we were born, that it continued over every moment of our lives and even after our death, because this godly surveillance is inescapable? It would be like living in a celestial "Islamic" Iran, Saudi Arabian or under a Taliban religious theocracy. Your only right would be to praise the autocratic Ayatollah or Supreme Leader or the quasi-religious leaders of Saudi Arabia.

This brings us to compare them to the officially declared "atheist-state" of North Korea, which is, in fact, a quasi-religious and totalitarian state. The first *Supreme Commander Kim ll-sung (1948 – 1994)* period established his supremacy as a semi-god that people had to praise constantly. The enforced political culture of complete obedience to the "Dear Leader" impregnated every sector of social structure and family morals. His son, *Supreme Commander Kim Jong-Il (1994 – 2011)* period inherited his father's oppressive system and furthered the quasi-religious character of the North Korean society. By supreme decree it maintained a "re-incarnation" worship style of the dead "Dear Leader" and a moral obligation by everyone to keep praising Kim ll-sung for all he had done for them, to repeatedly praise and thank him all the time, even when they were alone and before and after going to sleep. In schools, children were obliged to remain in a state of worship and daily praise the dead "dear leader" and bow before his picture. This state of affairs is the manifestation of the creation of a quasi-celestial earthly "promised land"---which resembles the Christian delusion of "God's Kingdom" on earth and a promise of Paradise. This permanent system of praise still continues at present under the new "Dear Leader" the *Supreme Commander Kim Jong-un* who since 2011 has become the reincarnation of the father and grandfather, quasi-religious idols, which the people of North Korea did not choose to have.

Between the two autocratic and theocratic systems; one under the Taliban or ISIL rules the other under the North Korean quasi-religious social structure, there are fundamental differences. In North Korea a person can escape the oppressed system he lived under all his life, when he dies. All his earthly problems are over and done with. Another choice, but with limited possibility of success, is to physically escape over the militarised borders, and into South Korea. More and more people continue taking this brave option. But in celestial Islamic Paradise, where your only right is to praise (the right to thank and give thanks and more praise), where you have no power (to refuse what is imposed upon you), there will be no escape for all eternity. The puzzling question to religious believers is why do they want to live under such a system? What is their moral obligation towards such a system of delusional beliefs? What will it take for them to escape this intolerable, hideous, permanent realm of oppression? How lucky most of us are for living under liberal democratic systems.

The struggle to overthrow the shackles from such an oppressive system and free ourselves from a religious mental-prison is a pre-condition for our material freedom. For freedom-cherishing atheists, religious subjection (an infinite and inescapable subjection) is revolting and against all morality and reasons. Above all, it is dreadful to be preached to by fellow mammalian apes that have no special knowledge or wisdom, but want to exert power over other mammalian apes like the rest of us. Do the Popes, the rabbis or the mullahs operate in another dimension than the rest of us? Is this dimension of this life or of the next? By the dominant and influential positions, they now hold, it appears that these religious leaders want to exert power in the here and now. If these religious propagators were to declare that our religious kingdom is not of this world, then they have to relinquish and surrender their secular power. They claim that they hold the secret knowledge of God's intentions, and such claim gives them right now and right here, a secular power over the morally deceptive followers.

Why should matter to them any issue of this world, when their kingdom is not of this world and they are only preparing people for the afterlife? Why are they against the legal right to an abortion, divorce or the use of condoms when, in the kingdom of the afterlife, all these religious "moral" issues would continue to be meaningless? Why should a Catholic woman who is married to an abuser or a child molester, a drunk or a bully, remain with that man? What if this woman wanted to live with another man? This woman should not accept an absolution from the church in this life or in the afterlife for leaving an abuser and deciding to marry a better man. Why should a woman in Uganda, Africa, be forced by the US religious, right-wing elite class, to remain sexually unprotected in order to meet some absurd religious dogma opposed to the use of condoms? What would happen when her partner comes in the middle of the night drunk, demanding to have "his thing" with a chance of her getting an unwanted pregnancy or Aids?

The Church's immorality is evidently clear by its forgiveness of the religious discrepancies of its rich donors and Hollywood famous that marry and re-marry many times over. Yet they are overlooked---such being the case for the justifiable comments made by the deceptive Catholic Mother Teresa concerning the "unhappy marriage" as Princes, Diana's decision for divorcing Prince Charles. This was, and still is, the case of indulging the rich and famous, while preaching abstinence and misery, shame, guilt and afterlife revenge to the rest of us. This is a false and medieval claim of power in the secular world, based on the medieval deception of the Catholic Church's sale certificates of "forgiveness and absolution" to the rich and famous of the time. Speaking metaphorically, atheists, humanists and secularists should not be *sitting silently on the fence*, with a blanket of "moral-neutrality" over our heads. We should not stand still while our intellectual and mental freedom is threatened by the false claims that the church holds the knowledge of the comings and goings in the celestial "world-beyond."

Are we accused by the weakling minded that if religion declines to its lowest level, what then of us? Would we be left with nothing but ourselves, with nothing to inspire us, with no awe to fulfil our daily lives and no wondering about anything beyond ourselves? What about our senses? Are we to live without transcendence and the feeling of awe? In my book, *"Prisoners of Our Ideals,"* I have devoted a whole chapter on the beauty, inheritance and vastness to our material world. Replacing the poverty of religion and its theological and philosophical deformities can only free us.

Adopting inspirational living modes, cultural diversities and geographical awesomeness would take many volumes to describe. Let me however; offer you few a brief examples of how you may wish to fulfil your life as part of this material world:

- Get out of your religious nightmares and get in to your humanist dreams!
- If you live in your past you get depressed!
- If you live in the future you get anxious!
- When you live in the present you are at peace!
- Make peace with those who are no longer with you!
- Get out of your anger and get into your passion!
- Find your silence!
- Put an order into your inconsistencies!
- Subdue your fears!
- Remember a moment's wish that was worth a lifetime experience!
- Catch a fish with your bare hands!
- Run with the bulls in Spain!
- Witness a volcano erupting!
- Ride the world's highest and longer roller coaster!
- Visit the Acropolis!
- Laugh until your cheeks hurt!
- Skinny dip at noon!
- Do nothing!
- Run a marathon!
- Visit the Greek Islands!
- Travel far, far away in a hot air balloon!
- See the Aurora Borealis!
- Learn another language!
- Learn to play a musical instrument!
- Give a homeless person $100!
- Get a sexy tattoo on your_____!
- Take a chance and leave a job you hate!
- Spend your holidays volunteering in a soup kitchen!

- Reach 100 years of age!
- Plant a tree!
- Spend a few moments with the book *"A Brief History of Time"* by physicist and cosmologist Stephen Hawking.
- Discover the extraordinary majesty of our Universe!
- Have a look at what pictures the Hubble Telescope has been sending back to us about the Universe!
- Look at the wonderful reflection of the stars at night!
- Spend some time looking at the extraordinary discoveries that have been made about the unwavering spiral of our own DNA!
- Do all of the above as a starting point!

As atheists we know, of course, that we have innate in us an appreciation for beauty, an appreciation for literature, and appreciation for irony and splendour which is our great saving element in our human discourse. We do not follow Astrology and believe that the stars' position has some influence in our lives or believe in Alchemy. For the first time in written human history we know how lucky and privileged we have become to possibly and closely discover the origins of our cosmos as well as what the nature of our human species really is. We can realise and contemplate the majesty of our universe (without a need for an argument about celestial Intelligent Design or Original Cause). Is it not more awe inspiring and more transcendent to read and contemplate about our Universe than reading the Bible's non-sense about the "burning bush?" It is more intellectually rewarding to study our cosmos, the similarities in the DNA we share with our other extinct human species, such as, our cousins the Neanderthals.

I maintain that this study it is far more rewarding than to rely on unfounded and unsupported words of Stone Age biblical tribesmen who were ill educated and no more civilised than the Taliban warlords today. As for our DNA, we discover that we are part of the animal species with which we share traces of DNA make-up and that there is no doubt that we are Ape mammals. We now have discovered that there is no legitimate argument about racism, for biological science confirms that there is no race-gene in our physical make up. The barbaric and stupid arguments about race in Nazism which humanity paid a high price for in the WWII should be thrashed away. Racism is a primitive and idiotic construct made of literally nothing, but it leads towards creationism. Once you study Darwin's on the *Origins of Species* you will able to do away with all the delusional biblical arguments about any creation myth of "God's chosen people."

The industry of religion in the USA has continued to deceive people to believe that the world is a mere 6,000 years old and that we were living once in a kind of "Jurassic Park" where Dinosaurs, Stegosaurs and Allosaurus shared the earth with humans. They ignore the fact that about 60 million years ago a meteorite collided with earth in the Yucatan Peninsula nearly destroying and killing most life species on earth. Our species survived the doom and gloom of Ice Age, continuous darkness and horrendous environmental disasters. We survived those but many species did not and thus they went extinct. Biological science has established that human beings were not around fishing, hunting or gathering at the time. It is pure and outright religious deception, presented in a US Creation Museum claiming, against all scientific evidence that these pre-historic species lived along side humans some 6,000 years ago. Without exaggeration, there is a strong sense of unscrupulous immorality on the part of those pseudo-intellectuals and liars who follow an established historical trail of religious deception and diminish human dignity. Teaching children in religious based schools such lies should be considered child abuse!

Facing such extraordinary and wondrous cosmology, there are still semi-educated or ill-educated and unfortunate people who do not challenge themselves intellectually, conveniently dismissing reason and evidence, science and space discoveries. All they wish is to follow more Astrology and Horoscope or Cultism of various kinds, as a sanction of faith in their daily lives. Do they ever wonder what they are throwing away by their intellectual laziness, sinking them into shallow superstition? Does it matter to the rest of us what these obnoxious and ignorant people believe? I say yes it does, because they are spreading their delusions to their children and our society backed by faith and fanaticism, for it is utterly cruel and utter reactionary opposition to scientific evidence.

Charles Darwin outlined his ideas about competitive anthropology from his extensive knowledge of different religions and religious beliefs from around the world, as well as at various times in history. He studied the Old and New Testament and the Hindu scriptures and came to the conclusion that scriptures were unreliable and contradictory. Such conclusions were formulated by him before and during his famous voyage onboard the *Beagle (*from Dec. 1831 to Oct. 1836) in search of biological evidence presented in his on the *Origin of Species* in 1859. While seeking to explain his observations, Darwin continued reading during his South America expedition:

"...and read a good deal on many subjects: though much upon religion... During these two years I was led to think much about religion. Whilst on board the Beagle I was quite orthodox [with strong beliefs] & I remember

being heartily laughed at by several of the officers (though themselves orthodox) by quoting the Bible as an unanswerable authority on some points of morality....But I had gradually come, by this time, to see that the Old Testament from its manifestly false history of the world...and from its attributing to God the feeling of a revengeful tyrant, was no more to be trusted than the sacred books of the Hindoos [sic] or the beliefs of any barbarian."

Charles Darwin was in the process of becoming a confirmed *materialist*, concluding that religion and morality is not synonymous, that morality does not depend upon religion, although this is an automatic speculation on the part of the ill-educated and ignorant. Materialism holds that *matter* is the fundamental substance in nature, and that all human phenomena, including feelings and emotions, illusions and delusions, wishful thinking and spirits and all sorts of mental manifestations are the results of material interactions.

Finally, according to *The Webster Dictionary of Christian Ethics*, religion and morality *"are to be defined differently and have no definitional connections with each other. Conceptually and in principle, morality and religious value systems are two distinct kinds of value systems or action guides."*

Albert Einstein's
"God letter" wrote to Jewish philosopher Erik Gutkind.

"The word God is for me nothing more tan the expression and product of human weakness, the
Bible a collection of honourable, but still primitive
legends which are nevertheless pretty childish. No
interpretation, no matter how subtle, can [for me]
change this.
For me the Jewish religion like all other religions is an incarnation of the most childish superstations.

ILLUSTRATED

RELIGIOUS CRIMES AGAINST HUMANITY

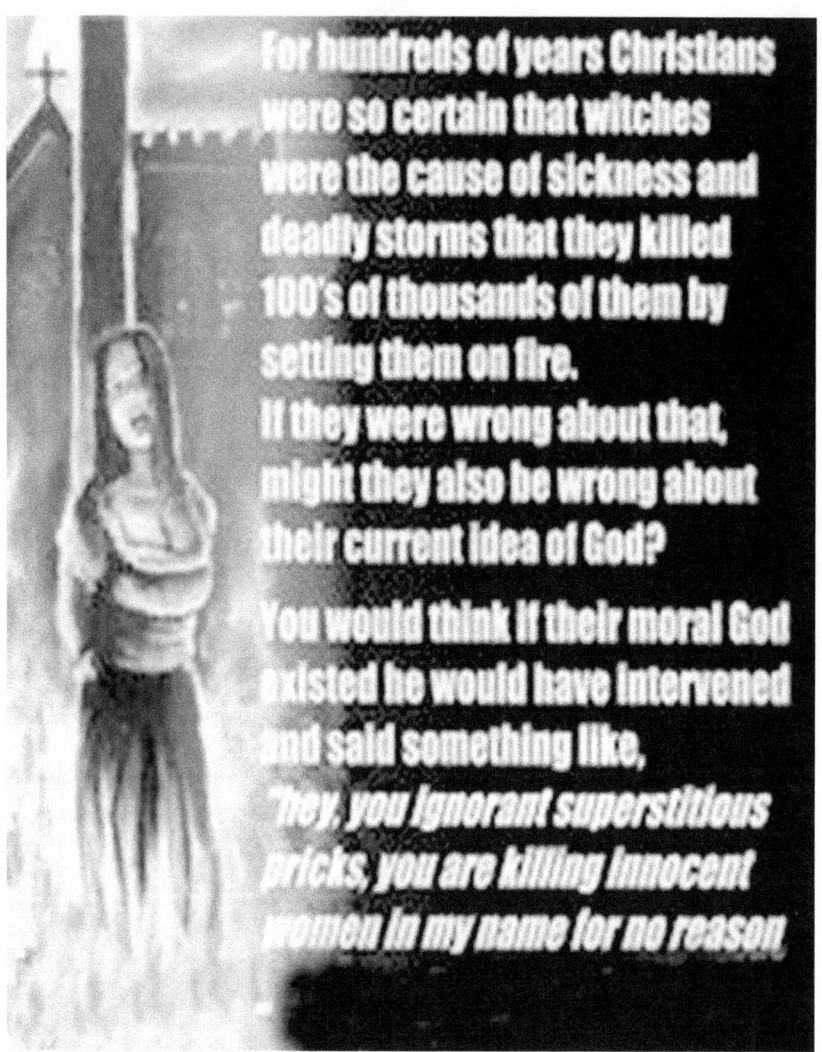

It is an insult to humanity, to say our morality is completely dependent on someone else giving us a list of dos and don'ts, an insult to say we have no innate sense of right and wrong, that we have no independent ability to see what is good and what is just.

ILLUSTRATED
NATURAL MORALITY

ILLUSTRATED

Humanism rejects religion. It attributes nothing to the so called "supernatural." In this there is an awakened liberty that releases us from the shackles and servitude mentality of old superstitions so that we may realize our full potential.

A system of morality which is based on relative emotional values is a mere illusion, a thoroughly vulgar conception which has nothing sound in it and nothing true.

(Socrates)

ILLUSTRATED

BIBLICAL JUSTIFICATION OF SLAVERY

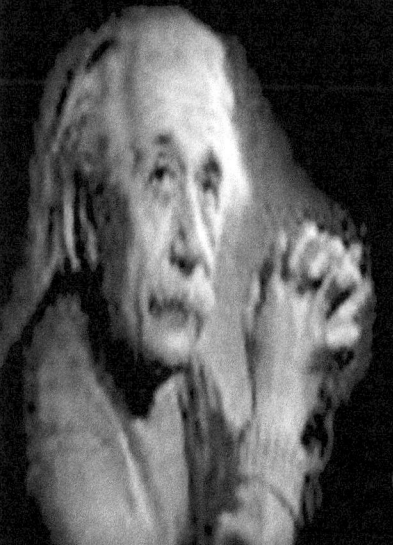

DEATH & THE AFTERLIFE

Pattern-meaning is an interpretation of our experience of past events which are stored in our brain for future use. Our brain does not differentiate between what is a true and what is a false pattern. Any thought or assumption that is based on "intuition" or a belief without verifiable evidence is a false pattern-meaning. Therefore, there is always a balance between true and false patterns that our brain must produce daily in order to meet the demand. When the demand is overwhelmed our brain is forced to take "short-cuts" and produce false pattern-meaning.

As human beings, we are biologically programmed to look for patterns in our lives and surroundings in order to explain what we feel, our own fate and to have command over our lives. Such pattern-explanations are mostly based on our past experiences, other peoples' views and our own sense of realism. Our brain does not contain "blank" spots where no pattern exists or to be filled in later. When we do not see patterns, we are at loss; therefore our brain tends to invent one where none exist. This is a delusional pattern perception so we do not feel helpless. We give meaning to prescribe something where there is no meaning or where the pattern interpretation is particularly meaningless. For instance, when you see the road in front of your house is wet, our brain would invent two pattern-thoughts; either it rained or a water-truck washed the road. Which is it then? Details of "wetness" can lead us to one or another pattern to explain the wetness of the road. Based on our past experience, there can be one of the two explanations; therefore, one of the pattern explanations is wrong. In our everyday life, our brain has to provide pattern explanations of everything that it is going on in our life and at certain point—because of the demand—our brain takes "shortcuts" and invents patterns where there are none.

Metaphors and symbolisms are pattern-meaning which provide us with connectivity---a convenient pattern-meaning--where there is no relation between two or more metaphorical or symbolic concepts. For example, if I say to you, *"You are driving me crazy"* it is a metaphorical statement of *"driving"* and *"crazy,"* which are two unrelated concepts that we know for sure, but we still use them. Some of us knock on wood or step over cracks on sidewalks or use an old garment to change our luck. We know that those patterns are delusional, yet we still prefer not to think of them as such, and continue to carry on using them and, in fact, believe on the superstition.

Let us look at the delusional pattern-meaning of *"life after death"* where we have two distinct metaphorical patterns of *"life"* and *"death,"* that are not related, for when you are alive you are not dead, and when you are dead you are not alive.

We have invented a pattern-meaning where none exist, in order to allay our insecurity and fear about death. The concept of afterlife may make you feel OK but it is definitely a delusional pattern where no reality pattern-meaning exists. In reality, if there is life after death, then why do we die? Here is the problem with the life after death delusion and its religious root. To hold onto this none existent pattern is a detrimental position for your overall physical and emotional preservation. Do you realise that religion and the afterlife are man-made concepts which share a commonality of being a meaningless fantasy created long ago by deceptive humans who claimed to have a direct access to the divine, and thus gave themselves power by doing so? Those self-deceptive people believed in the lie of life after death pattern by claiming to know its existence, and who have tyrannized us for centuries by claiming to hold the keys to the mystery of life-after-death.

Religion through its delusions and rituals claim to know something that the rest of us do not know, and to have celestial powers that it does not have. But, if you make the right donations and utter the right kind of prayer, the Laws of Nature will be suspended on your behalf so you can enter heaven. Otherwise, you may get the severity of eternal torture in Hell and Fire which includes any anabaptised children around the world, those who are homosexual, or those who do not participate in the fraud of donation giving. To support this fraudulent pattern of life after death, the Catholic Church and its minions promise the remission of your sins, and the gates of heaven will be open to you for a price. This is how the ground was broken for the Vatican and St. Peter's church in 333 AD, and was finished in 1450, from the backs of the Roman slaves and donations extracted from Christians under the celestial thread of the all powerful Sky-God.

Growing up as Greek Orthodox, it was explained to me that death comes to us in this way: the *Archangel Thanatos* (Death) appears before you, at an unexpected moment, perhaps when you read your favoured book, and tells you that your life's "party is over" and you must drop your book and follow him. Although the life's party is not over and it still going strong, you must leave because the Archangel Thanatos orders you to do so. How helpless, disappointed and diminished you must feel! But this is nothing yet, in comparison to what it is waiting for you once you arrive in the afterlife place (heaven). You are arriving in heaven, where the party is going on for an eternity, and now you know that you can never leave, for you have to stay, tired or not, while the Sky-God insists that you have a good time. It is like the *Eagles 1977* song, *"Hotel California"* lyrics that *"you can check* *out anytime you like, but you can never leave."* The musicians at the party are replaced from time to time, and at one point the harp musicians arrive and will play their harp day-in and day-out, while you recollect that, in real life, you could not stand listening to *harp music* for longer than five minutes. I mean really, how torturous that would be! We are all going to die, none of us will ever get out alive, and that is a real pattern, which explains life's biological process: birth, growth, decay and death. Will you really feel blessed if I say to you that the Sky-God *"will refuse to let you die,"* who reassures you that He *"will never leave you,"* that *"for eternity you'll see me by your side"* because *"I'll always be there"* and because *"you are my absolute best friend, I'll never let you feel sorry,"* but, in return, *"you will not be allowed to object to any of my decisions?"* Do you still feel blessed?

The Islam religion has made the idea of life after death as being a place that contains rivers of milk and honey, mountains, valleys and lakes, with 72 virgins waiting to be taken by the faithful "chosen martyrs" which makes the delusions of heaven and afterlife sound even more ridiculous. As Mark Twain said in his book, *Letters from the Earth,* that a delusional believer believes he will go to heaven and lay in an imaginable valley where he will listen to praying and harp music, and collect flowers all day long and for eternity. Furthermore, here is some food for thought! Let us imagine that you are visiting the Amazon Rainforest today, with its attractive giant trees, which is called, the "canopy of the world." On top of the canopy, hundreds if not thousand of species, such as monkeys, spiders, birds and plants live there never to set foot or root on the ground. You return the next month and you find fewer giant trees than before. Will it seem to be a different rainforest? The Amazon Rainforest is continuing with its ways as ever, whether the species that live in it realised it or not even when humans are not around to witness the elegance and beauty of its reality.

The same applies to our universe. Such a dominant physical space is all inclusive, without any part of it in favour of one species over another, in near or far distance. This means that, for millions of years, humans have been born, grew and died by the millions, without the Universe noticing any changes occurring in our planetary cosmos. Humanity, as a whole, is part of that Universe, but in an insignificant measure. Understanding this reality, we can see that the Laws of Nature cannot be suspended in humanity's favour nor can we have a "heaven" and an "afterlife" in the sky. I often wonder why religious people are devastated when a loved one dies; when they believe that they and their love ones will meet in heaven and live happily forever in the afterlife.

On the other hand, atheist and humanist understand that humanity does not need a validation from the Universe to have a sense of significance in our participation and existence on Earth. I ask you then, why must we be willing to sacrifice our sense of humanity, our sense of dignity, to sacrifice our collective human experience, our collective human knowledge of science, medicine and culture and all that we have accomplished, on the altar of antiquated myths, magical delusions and false pattern explanations about "life after death?" If so, we are not living our lives today, but living for dying for "the afterlife."

On a lighter note, because of their fear of dying, people wrote their own end-story, a religious fallacy of a celestial heaven where they will be reunited with their loved ones, their enemies, their ex-bosses, their ex-girlfriends, their ex-wives and their ex-mother-in-laws. As such, since nearly everyone goes to heaven, they will experience eternal joy, constant sadness and embarrassment for all times of angriness, depending on who they'll meet and how often! Living for the life after death and obediently following "what to do" and "what not to question" basically devalues your life before you die! It diminishes the value that you place on your life and the here-and-now. In the plural sense, religion attempts to destroy our humanist sense of morality in the here and now by claiming that it does not matter how evil you were in life, for you will be safe in the life after death; but only if you believe, because God said in ***Hebrews 8:13*** that *"I will forgive [your] wickedness and will remember [your] sins no more"*

Most of us value our lives on the basis of what we have achieved or our failures and the goals and dreams we have yet to accomplish. We have a good reason to get up out of our bed each morning and we are looking forward to the day's challenges, planning our next projects or whatever we wish to do. At the end of the day, we can look back and assess the value that we have created, the family members we encountered and the projections we have fully met. We have alternatives to live for and loved ones to reassure of our intentions. If some things remain incomplete today, there is tomorrow or the next day to look forward to. The only alternative limits we have are of our choice, time-wise or circumstances.

The afterlife alternatives however, can be worrisome, troublesome, idledsome and can also be scary. Imagine heaven's eternity, for a moment. In eternity everything that can be accomplished has been accomplished. Beyond all our actual achievements, everything else will be limitless and pointless to an existence. The beginning of each new day will be identical to the ending of that day, a limitless and pointless repetition of a fruitless existence.

The truth of the matter is that we have the here-and-now to achieve, enjoy, laugh and cry, love and feel sorry, take a walk in the park, do volunteer work, write a poem and teach our children the truth about our Universe. When the "*final curtain*" comes down (using Frank Sinatra's 1969 song "*I did it my way*") none of us will ever get out alive. It is pointless to worry about death for, when it comes, none of us will know the truth at that point, and we will not know, wish, think, remember or dream anything. Let us take courage from the knowledge of what a human being is; we are a physical being with an active brain that "houses" our identity, our collection of lifetime memories, our hopes, dreams, desires and our consciousness, all of which exist as the material product of our brain but ends at death. This is it!

Knowing this indisputable evidence, let us celebrate the gift of life in the here-and-now as best we know for both ourselves, our loved ones, our environment and the rest of humanity. How lucky we are to have been born! Death is part of the natural world which is devoid of sadness, tragedy or fear of the end. Our here-and-now life is genetically related to past generations of our DNA ancestors and we will be the next DNA ancestors of our future offspring who are yet to be born. We are prescriptively entangled with those who came before us, for our lives are somewhere, at best, affected by the scientific discoveries of Charles Darwin, Isaac Newton, Albert Einstein and Louis Pasteur. These entanglements of course go beyond the scientific minds, for our lives are also entangled with those persons who bake our bread and your daughter's birthday cake, the taxi driver who gets you to work on time and the lady who takes care of your elderly mother.

As such, we are intertwined with lesser and greater things without needing to invent grand-schemes and delusional patterns which inevitably can lead us into a dead-end path. Poetically speaking, 5.4 billion years in the future, our material body will still continue being immortal as stardust and, after the planets' nebulae fade away, every atom of us will be recycled back into the cosmos and we will once again remain part of the elegance of our universe.

For hundreds of years humanity was not able to criticise the lies told by religion on pain of death. These days, religion comes to us in its civilised manner or gratuitous way, but it is still the same *wolf in its new fur coat*. This is because it had to abandon so many of its groundless claims, and because atheists and humanists know so much more about religious delusional patterns regarding life after death. Do you think that we have the right to forget how vicious and murderous Christianity and Islam behaved when they were strong?

There is a real asymmetry between scientific reason and religion which has departed, unobserved, from peoples' attention. There is a persistent effort by religious advocates not to own the original Biblical claims repeated over millennia. The claims, about how the universe is structured, its predictions about the future, what has occurred in the past and life after death; are not comparable. For example, Buddhism, like all religions, makes certain claims for millennia, about how the cosmos is structured, offers predictions of about the future events, explains what has happened in the past and life after death (re-incarnation) that are, in fact comparable. In its doctrine, Buddhism claims to be true, believes in the life after death, and has Karma and a doctrine that believes in re-incarnation. The form of your re-incarnation will depend on your good deeds in the here and now and you might be reborn in various realms. This means, if Buddhism is true, then Judaism, Christianity and Islam are absolutely false, including their claims about life after death and matters of other things.

The real difference between scientific reason and organised religion is that the latter does not hold to its literary claims for millennia. For the most part believers believe that the written Old Testament and the New Bible are not man-made and they do not believe that these are no more than just books. In fact, the false pattern explanation is that, by reading the Old Testament and the New Bible, believers become knowledgeable about the universe, the suspension of the Laws of Nature, life after death and the virgin birth of certain people. Such literature is profoundly anti-scientific---and remains so because religious advocators cannot edit the holy books nor can they edit these false pattern explanations found in them. It is profoundly wrong to claim that anything that cannot yet be explained by scientific reason, that it is still mysterious to us, must therefore be attributed to a "supernatural" being. This absurdity would lead us to believe that nothing remains to be scientifically explained or is potentially explainable.

Anyone who stood over the grave of a loved one could have asked the question, "now what?" Is there life after death? Apologists claim that people should not take the belief of "life after death" too literally, that believers should not make up the idea of the existence of an imaginary world and reduce the belief into non-sense. Religious dogma believes human beings are not entirely material, that there is something non-physical, something eternal about humans, some mystery at the core of our material existence. They claim that there is some mystery surrounding our material existence, therefore the afterlife is not a physical place that believers literally go to but a *metaphorical voyage*. While alive, this metaphorical trip is in the false consciousness of the believers and the belief in the afterlife is the distorted continuation of that consciousness.

Atheists, humanists and materialists maintain that, when death ends life all thoughts, ideas and memories die with our body. This goes against the traditional belief of the afterlife and some---with justification---claim that neither believers nor atheists really know what happens after death because we simply cannot know. But I think that we should consider what this concept of the afterlife does in terms of the dying. There are millions of people in improvised countries around the world, where people dying due to malnutrition, deceases and environmental disasters. Most of these people believed in God while praying that their innocent children would be safe. In their children's death, their prayers were not answered. Now the belief of the afterlife comes, in the middle of this death reality, with the celestial promise that, at the end, all these deaths would make sense, that somehow the end of these children's existence would be comforting before God. There is no evidence for this, and the belief of the afterlife becomes a substitute for wisdom about how to experience the uncertainties in our lives. We know that everyone will die at the end, that there are tragic circumstances, that evil and injustice sometime get the upper hand, and that the only justice we make is of our own doing. As such, we have the moral and ethical responsibility to absorb this down to the core of our essence. The notion of the afterlife is plain "happy-talk" on how everything is going to work out and that all this is part of God's plan. This is also another way of circumventing our moral and ethical responsibility towards ourselves, our family, our own children and others.

Theologians claim to know about the "beyond" when they cannot possibly know, but what they are emphasising, instead of knowledge, is intuition such as hope, wishful thinking, trust and loyalty. They are trying to ground intuition as a substitute for "knowing" about the afterlife. But, they also admit that there are people who use the afterlife to avoid their responsibility. But at the same time, they are claiming that, for a person who is dying, this belief inspires them to live their last moments with dignity and connection with it. They used the afterlife as a metaphor for the "oneness" of this life with the afterlife. They introduce intuition, trust and wishful thinking as a "bridge" to reach the afterlife. Simultaneously, they are skilfully avoiding the fact that symbolism and metaphors and "happy talk" are not our universal material reality. Is the belief of the afterlife, for a person who is dying, a "good thing"? However, to believe in anything that religion makes you feel good or better about is a contemptuous belief, a contemptuous position and a contemptuous religious point to promote. Religious fundamentalists are employed in hospitals for the terminally ill to comfort the dying with the "happy-talk" of the afterlife. The question is: will the hospital hire an atheist to tell the dying that the Christian afterlife is *"bull-shit"* and no more?

Here are two additional points about the afterlife delusion that are the same in the religious delusion in general. Karl Marx did not say that religion is "the opium of the people," for religion and the afterlife also have also this in common. First, they are man-made, which is very important to acknowledge; and secondly, they are claims made by humans who interpret the divine in order to give themselves power by doing so. We all must admit that we do not know about the afterlife, because we simply cannot possibly know! Those religious demagogues, who for centuries have tyrannised humanity, and still do, by claiming that they are God's chosen people who hold the key to Heaven and Hell, are simply exploiting the ill-educated and the superstitious. Religion claims to know things that it cannot know and claims to have power that it cannot have. As for believers, for the right appreciation and the right donation, you too may get to Paradise, but if you do not, you may get pain for eternity. There is also the element of fraud which is at the core of religious claims; for instance, Saint Peter's Basilica, in Rome, was built from the sale of indulgences and donations of the rich in exchange to certificates for forgiveness for all their sins. So, if you were a rapist, a child molester, a murderer or simply an evil person, for the right donation all your crimes were forgiven. Even today, all over Europe, Catholic Church prayers are performed for the remission of souls. There are continued attempts to revive the idea of remission of souls for cash or in kind. Lies and exploitation of the ill-educated or naïve people are still part of the industry of religion.

The worst concept, beyond the life after death idea is the more dramatic, is the concept of eternity of life. Imagine, for instance, that you were told by *Archangel Thanatos* that he has great news for you! God has spared you from death and, from now on you will live for eternity! This is a celebration forever, but you can never leave it! You must stay at the party because Archangel's Boss said so, and the Boss insists that you must have a good time, or else! Here is the problem; it is of the eternal image of the monotheistic Father who never dies, who is around you for eternity, who keeps reinsuring you that He will never leave you, you'll never see the end of Him, and you will never have the chance to feel the human emotion of being sad for the death of a loved one! This Sky-God will always be present with you because He is the absolute and powerful benevolent dictator. On the other hand, you cannot appeal His decision! Do you really believe this irony will cheer you up? No, the dreadfulness of such desire is the absolutism of it and the lack of appeal. This situation will be a lot worse than living under the dictatorship in North Korea or the theocracy of Iran, the Taliban, the ISIS and Saudi Arabia. At least in those countries you could free yourself by escaping or by dying. Is it fair to speak about God in the same terms as a human dictator? I think yes, they are equivalent because the characteristics of imposed supervision and oppression are the same.

The religious traditional vision of what God could be is very limited and partial, but assuming what it would be like to have a God for eternity and to "enjoy" a perpetual "happiness" in the afterlife is not difficult to envision. In death you loose everything in this world but the afterlife "gives" you back everything that you lost. But the notion of the afterlife tends to lead you to neglect of what is important in this world, for if the afterlife is perfect why do we need to better our lives here? So is death a final state of life? Is there not "something" that continues it's "living" after our death? The survival of consciousness independent of the brain is still a debatable subject today by neuroscientists and philosophers. This question however, is quite different than the religious belief that is mandated by following the path of reward or punishment in the afterlife. Believing in the afterlife can be just as totalitarian and terrible as believing in a secular utopia (North Korea) or a religious utopia (Iran, Saudi Arabia) on earth.

Spiritualism of the late 19th century had a subliminal relationship with the afterlife; as a strong fraudulent movement of "crossing-over," which flourished after WW1, with the promise of putting people in touch with their dead relatives. However, not a single or interesting message was sent from the "other-side," at least not scientifically verified! There was, of course, babbling from the "beyond" uttered by professional charlatans. Pitifully, millions of people paid attention to it, and also paid cash for their delusions. The interesting thing is that the concept of the afterlife does not apply to other animals or the *Neanderthals* and *Cro-Magnon* human tribes who were extinct about 30,000 years ago. Why then were those human species never mentioned in any of the monotheistic holy books? Who then has the afterlife of Heaven and Hell for them? Are then (among us) only the religious *Homo sapiens* of certain tribes or beliefs, God's chosen people?

The afterlife entails the resurrection of the dead; which is more than peoples' belief that only your soul flows to the afterlife through a tunnel of light, while your body remains on earth. The Canonical Law describes the resurrection of the dead---not just the soul-- for the afterlife and God's work begins at that moment of death by reassembling all the body parts. This is the vision offered by the three monotheistic religions. This also shows the improbability of it all. In the simulated or virtual world of the afterlife everything is possible, but any "activity" is only simulated, not real. Simulation of reality is not reality! For the human consciousness to survive the brain's death could only be achieved if a man created and lived in a simulated world, just as in the simulated computer games. But simulated-worlds and simulated computer games are artificial and man-made. Both can be dismissed or deleted by either a click in the computer-terminal or by dismissing the idea of afterlife simulation in our mind. With the destruction of the computer-terminal (its death) all simulated games within it are terminated as well (their death). So it is with the death of the human brain which, while alive, "housed" hundreds if not thousands of ideas, memories, emotions and simulations which we identify and define the as: consciousness.

Religion is monolithic and the worst of religion is that it is not fluent, not evolving, not self-reflecting and does not have the capacity to change convictions. The wreckage of religion is very extensive and its errors are so deep that self-reflective is not permitted. The diversity of its ideas is just that, a diversity created to ensure the survival of its dogma. The more diversified its ideas are, the more "goods" the believers could find and select from to support their delusions. It is like walking into an old style village general-store where you could find a *"little of this"* or a *"little of that"* to fulfil your immediate needs and desires, for there is something for everyone!

It includes the idea that believers must believe in the resurrection because we do not experience eternity in this life-time; although eternity exists in the present moment, if you attain the right consciousness, you can be in eternity now. This absurd kind of uttering of a slue of ideas is like the old style carousel where everything flows round and round with no ending and no arrival destination. Behind the religious idea of judgment and the afterlife reward of heaven and hell is somehow an equalisation in the struggle of life. Imagine a poor African woman, who is suffering from lack of food or medical attention and, at some point, she loses her baby. When her tears dried up, imagine how she must have prayed to God, as compensation for her suffering, to be told, by religion, that this was part of God's plan, and that her life will get better in the afterlife. This makes her suffering meaningless and rather obscene; that God makes you suffer now (while you are alive) but He would make your life better later on (after you are dead). That kind of religious belief tends to perpetuate the idea that a human is being used as an experimental object, an idea which is obscured by God's randomness in the reward or punishment in the afterlife. This kind of religious belief maximises chaos and maximises the acceptance of God's tyranny, deliberate cruelty and injustice over us. Reason and our material reality have to repudiate this repulsive away of thinking.

It is quite difficult for religious advocates to argue in support of God in the 21st century when they pronounce proclamations of the 2nd century, even though they use much of the written material of the time to explain their beliefs. Their dilemma is the same. The dilemmas they now are faced with is the extraordinary difficulty of explaining the afterlife to people who are educated and are accustomed to questioning everything about their own lives and about their surroundings. Those believers are now admitting that, for a fact, when a person dies he loses everything, and that has always been the case, and religion in one sense, has always realised it. This eventual loss has been used by the Jewish faith as the foundation to make this world a better place through charities and providing services to the needy. This was practiced in small Jewish communities in Europe. However, because their Jewish religion is monolithic, these Rabbis cannot deviate too far away from the original dogma and assert the assumption that, as it is possible that there are *other universes* aside from ours, it is not possible that there are also *other lives.* They omitted, of course, admitting that there is only one, all inclusive, material Universe with many galaxies, stars, planets and moons. This assertion of many "other" lives includes the afterlife; but this is a mental assumption, for our Universe does not function in according to our mental assumptions. The problem with this belief is that, the existence or non-existence of other universes does not depend on believing whether they exist or not, for their possible material existence has nothing to do with our beliefs. On the other hand, the notion of the afterlife is strictly based on religious belief for its existence. To believe in the afterlife, without knowing what it is or how it works, and that this world is not the only one we have, is pure invention of the imagination.

The Laws of Nature cannot be suspended on behalf of the monotheistic religions even if they claim to be agnostic on the subject of the afterlife. The only thing a religion can offer you on the subject of the afterlife are images, symbolisms and metaphors of it, for it offers you an imaginary Garden of Eden, which there is no description of in the Bible, and a place where a believer would study the Talmud with God along with billions of other souls. This non-descriptive approach used to explain the afterlife, is like a common-wisdom. You see, the reason that there are multiple kinds of diet-pills is because none of them work, for if it worked, you would get only one diet-pill. In turn, the reason the religious leaders are offering multiple images of the afterlife is because none of them know what the afterlife is.

It is very tragic, and simultaneously very clever, the way religious leaders try to introduce, in their arguments about the afterlife that the problem lies with the atheists who doubt because of the failure of their imagination. Clever arguments accept that as an atheist, I can also imaging an afterlife without God, or a God without an afterlife, or multiple Gods without an afterlife. Why not? One atheist's imagination is as good as the next! Like the late Christopher Hitchens said, *"There could also be a God with a sense of humour where good people went to Hell and evil people carried on as in his initial creation, ruling the roost."* We can all image a lot of ways, but those who claim to know in advance the descriptive or prescriptive details of the afterlife, who continue to rule the mental-lives of millions of believers, they just invent multiple pseudo-explanations about the afterlife. Some 2,000 years ago, a mythological and sadistic indigenous pseudo-intellectual in the Roman Province of Palestine started this tragic delusion of the afterlife. It has, ever since, mentally-tortured millions of lives. It is not a failure of the atheists' imagination, but the perversity of the religious imagination, for the afterlife is not possibly knowable; that much we do know. These demagogues have much to explain about their dogma of resurrection and the afterlife.

Religious apologists suggest that religion is like science; putting out a claim, having a debate over it and, if the claim is valid we believe it and if it is not we should discard it. This logical conclusion just proves the atheists' point that religion is man-made, as is science, music, biology or astronomy. Except that the core of religion is made up of *linguistic-metaphors*; *subliminal-symbolism* and *multiple-imaginations, wishful-illusions* and *crude-delusions, deliberate-lies* and *outright-deceptions*, that none of which represent reason and evidence. There is confusion between science and religion which needs to be clarified because religious apologists refuse to own their very clear propositional claims that have been made by every religion since time immemorial.

For instance, claims about how the Universe is structured, claims about what would take place in the future, what has happened in the past, about the afterlife's Heaven and Hell, and all these claims are incompatible. For instance, Buddhism has *Karma,* has re-incarnation, a re-birth in a different forms (as bird or an animal) or different realms and so on. This religion has its doctrine, its structural beliefs and it claims to be true. It does not have God, Saints, delusional Mother-Teresa, miracles and the physical resurrection of the dead. Every religion has made these claims about the afterlife and all manner of other things. However, the fundamental differences between religion and science are that every religion is beholden to its literature and the majority of believers do not think those are man-made and they do not think that these "holy-books" are just books. You see, if you read the bible like a theatrical or movie script there would be no need to debate religion and science.

Religious people however read the bible like it is written by God and thus it cannot be edited, or criticised, dismissed in parts or treated as a metaphorical script of religious stories. Everyone then has this idea that they have knowledge about the afterlife, the end of the world, the virgin birth of certain people, and those are claims to be held as being true. Those claims are profoundly anti-scientific and, within their core texts there are life-destroying lies and non-sense that people believe and follow. The so called "near-death" experience is the closest afterlife support-claim that has been made by spiritual or religious people who have encountered that experience. A number of studies have been done, on a variety of "near-death" experiences based on personal testimonies. To begin with, the definition of "near-death" experience cannot be related to death and the afterlife, because the person in the "near-death" experience did not die. On the other hand, if you're heard that your best friend "Bob" died on Monday was buried on Wednesday and you then see him shopping in the local Wal Mart on Friday, you may conclude that Bob's announcement of his death was premature (not resurrected).

The author *Carlos Castaneda (1925 – 1998)* wrote a number of books about shamanism and "out of body" experiences, which are identical to "near-death" experiences. Castaneda told good stories and gave enigmatic advice to people who desperately were looking for answers about their spiritual or true nature. Whatever the case might have been, Castaneda sold millions of books about "astro-travelling" and "out of body experiences." These books bring certain rationality to the arguments of near-death and out of body experiences. However, the Laws of Nature run on their own structural functionality which is not always based on man's linguistic, logical or rational arguments. One of the most frequent stories told ---and the most persuasive--about an out of body experience was reported by a hospitalised woman. That particular night she flew out of her bed and flew around the outside perimeter of the hospital. While she was doing her flying (like Mary Poppins) she saw a shoe on the ledge of a window. When she woke up she reported the location of the shoe as evidence of her out of body (or near death) experience. The location of the shoe was confirmed! Now we all hope that the single shoe was reunited with its missing pair!

In other cases, surgeons reported placing a placard with random numbers high above the patient's head. They hoped that in the event of an out of body experience, the patient would identify these random numbers. There was a sign that someone placed high above on the ceiling of the operation room for those with an out of body experience which read: *if you can read this, you are already dead*. I assume that the surgeons are still waiting and hoping for some kind of confirmed results. On a more serious note, a near death experience does not count for anything or the coming back experience from the near-death, nor did the account of what you believe happen to you while you were gone. What you can image happening to you, is what can happen to you with the help of medical science, while you are still alive, is all of the above. This idea of consciousness rising or dis-associating from the body is common enough for people to assume a near-death experience is testable. It is as common as of people who believe in the notion of past lives having been a Prince or Princess or something noble, and so on. This belief is real to them, for it is subjective and wishful thinking like Heaven and Hell. I can understand the desire and wishful thinking for Heaven and the eternal life of the afterlife, but having a wishful thinking for Hell it is not easily explained, other than as a wishful thinking for other people to go to Hell. For those people who wish Hell for others, their reward is watching their enemies' eternal suffering. This is the very unpleasant part of our primate species to which we belong; with all our fantasies and wishful thinking, which religious fathers of the 2nd century exploited. As for the benefits of Heaven and the afterlife that Muslim men; each get 72 virgins but the women only get their ex-husbands back (is this reward or a punishment?). Is this not a man-made wishful thinking?

People believe in the afterlife because it gives them a false hope or they find the idea very consoling, but science is not committed to the idea that there is no afterlife or that consciousness is identical to the brain or that materialism is true. Science is completely open to wherever in fact is true. If it is true that consciousness is running like software in the brain, and that the consciousness leaves the brain after its death, then science would accept any findings if we discovered it to be true. There are ways which we could discover the association between brain and consciousness. For instance, when some part of the brain is damaged and then it is found that part of the consciousness associated with the damaged part of the brain is also lost. Brain damage due to a car or work related accident is a common phenomenon. You may begin to lose part of your memory faculties but still be able to function. Any additional damage to the same brain would also cause additional lost of consciousness, where you may remember the names of your neighbours, but not the name of your favoured pet. Does this mean that everyone with brain damage has lost a partial consciousness or ability to pronounce certain words but not others? When the same brain is now completely destroyed by death, there is very good reason to think that consciousness (or soul or pneuma?) does not survive intact or in part. It simply ceases to exist along with the brain's faculties. Neurological scientists in the last 160 years have accumulated enough reasons and evidence to confirm that, when you are damaging the brain, you are damaging the mind as well. If and when scientists discover new evidence confirming the existence of the "soul" then science is open to further investigation. There are ways to discover new evidence of the mind-brain relation if the argument of the existence of the "soul" was true. But there are very good reasons, and additional scientific evidence, to confirm that it is not true. There are no spirits in this spiritless world!

If everything that religion propagates about the mysteries of the "soul" is believed by millions of believers, it is because religion uses pseudo-scientific terminology to explain the brain-soul relationship, and what happens after death, but do not present convincing evidence to support such claims. The usefulness in holding to these religious traditions of the 2nd century books is therefore completely non-existent. If a religious person says that he holds the belief in the afterlife because it makes him feel good, well that is his prerogative. But we must be careful here, because humanity's oldest fear is that of death and oldest wish is to survive death, and this is at the root, in the belief of an, afterlife. It is not a coincidence therefore, that this fear of death propagates the belief in the afterlife. This belief may make people feel better (so do drugs) but religious leaders ought not to be actively marketing this delusion by exploiting peoples' fear.

The fact that people have reported that they had a feeling of "near death" and that afterwards they no longer feared death, does not confirm the existence of the afterlife. People have reported all kinds of delusional feelings they had about being kidnapped by UFO's or that they had a vision that the statue of the Virgin Mary moved or that her eyes were bleeding or that they saw Jesus face in a piece of toast. In my book *"Prisoners of Our Ideals,"* I explained how the statue's "bleeding" trick is done and other inventions religion has used to fool people in the last 2,000 or more years. There is no doubt that, to believers, these experiences are real, but trying to convince the world that their delusion must be believed as being true, is both idiotic and plainly deceptive. This religious propaganda has been going on ever since the first divine promise of the afterlife was given to ill-educated and superstitious tribesmen in the past millennia. Religion does what it has always done, that is, assimilates people's delusional "experiences" in order to shape their faith. Analysing human consciousness and how medical treatment affects it, I think deserves a scientific evaluation, but the way religion explains "soul" as consciousness is like serving an old wine in a new bottle just to make it look better.

Some people's serious health conditions sometimes affects or reinforces a faith that otherwise would not have been adopted. Capitalising on peoples' fear is a contemptuous religious act, as one may witness by visiting hospitals with terminally ill people. There you may see a priest, an imam or a rabbi offering false consolation and outright lies during an ill person's last days on earth. To suggest that their favoured pet or their loved one will be waiting for them in the "beyond" or in the "afterlife" should be regarded a fraudulent act. As for the ill person, if he believes in the afterlife, he is told that he should not feel a fear of dying because he is departing a temporal life for an eternal one which lasts much longer than the time he spent on earth. I have also heard that there are fundamentalist believers who approach a dying person that they do not know saying that, *"I'm saying this as a friend, this is your last chance to believe, aren't going to take it"?* The behaviour of trying to convert a complete stranger or non-believer is considered, by religious believers, to be normal, polite and even a humanitarian gesture. But I would maintain that this is very depressive and alarming to be spoken of this way. This is nothing new, for there are a number of fraudulent and nasty stories that are circulating of famous people like, Thomas Paine or Charles Darwin and others, who supposedly became believers on their deathbeds. This is not true! To a less educated person, a very ill person, or to an advanced-aged person or in a moment of weakness, this religious venom can be very dramatic and depressive.

On the other hand, let's assume the opposite and have a bunch of atheists going from hospital to hospital visiting the terminally ill patients in pain or weak from chemotherapy treatment and saying to them: *"Look you only have a few days to live, do not live your last days as a serf. Your priest and your religion have been lying to you. You can achieve your freedom by recognising and rejecting all religious bullshit!"* This will be unethical on the part of the atheists but if it is done in the name of religion it has social licenses to abuse the ill or dying and that should not be acceptable. Another story goes as such; in his deathbed the Italian political philosopher *Niccolo Machiavelli* was visited by a Roman Catholic priest who asked Machiavelli; *"do you denounce Satan and all his works",* but Machiavelli refused to answer and the priest repeated, *"do you renounce Satan and all his works,"* at which point Machiavelli finally responded," *father at this stage of my life it is not wise to make enemies."* Now, from a moral stand this would constitute an unethical act, a mean, cruel and anti-humanist behaviour the worst kind by a priest. This kind of militant empiricism is equally offensive and problematic on both sides.

A belief in the afterlife gives the religious visitors of the terminally ill something to say, in the most difficult moment of someone's life, and to those who are loosing or have lost someone. It gives the believer something to say to a patient that an atheist does not have. If the belief of the afterlife is believed by someone who just lost a loved one this is really consoling. There is nothing better in terms of consolation than to believe that the child you have just lost is now in a perfect place, protected and cared for, and you will be re-united. Except this consolation is not based on truth but it is based on a long held fear of the process of dying, the process of being ill with pain and the promise of the afterlife.

We are, or most of us are, going to sleep every night. At some point during our sleeping time, we are entering a deep state of unconsciousness. This deep state of sleep is a time of complete disengagement from the environment. During this sleepy stage the world just disappears, we lose everything, and we are not aware of anything that it is going on around us. For most of us, a deep sleep state is synonymous with oblivion, for we lose our sensory experience, we forget our life, our overdue mortgages, and if we do not ever wake up we would not notice the difference. If death is synonymous with non-existence or oblivion, then in reality there is nothing to fear, and sleeping into it may feel just as comfortable as going to deep sleep. Like Mark Twain (1835-1910) said, *"I've been [in a non-existent state] for billions of years before I was born and this did not caused me the slightest inconvenience."* A living person cannot more suffer the eternity of the after-death than the time past before he was born. What makes people fear death is that their loved one's dying and there is nothing they can do to help. These people look at the loved one and think that because he is a good person he deserves an afterlife. This emotional subjectivism--philosophically speaking---may have grounds of validity within the afterlife concept, if there was no God to spoil it with his autocratic presence. If there is a celestial dictator who distributes reward or punishment in the afterlife, your loved one can never be sure what he is going to receive from God!

Some religious apologists maintain than more that any other belief, the belief in the afterlife has undermined religion because the St. Peters Cathedral was built by the donations of believers who were promised an afterlife for a hefty amount of money. Other Jewish leaders, although they believe in the traditional transcendence of the afterlife, they also maintain that the real afterlife is here on earth. This is because a dead father's children would follow his good deeds and therefore he lives as an "afterlife" through them. Take your pick, for one or the other idiocy, for both choices are man-made to serve God for an exchange value and as a price for the afterlife. A number of serious atheist educators are motivated by the desire to educate people to dispel their illusions of the supernatural, which many of the promoters and practitioners of faith do not believe either.

Take the idea of a martyr, who dies and kills others in a cause for his faith, is it not a delusion of Mohammad's? It is however written in the holy book of Qur'an and it is believed by a huge number of Muslims. But, if there was a brave Muslim scholar, who was willing to challenge the authenticity of the "martyrdom" we would be living in a much safer world. The problem of denouncing "martyrdom" has further implications, in that it would also have to renounce also the idea of resurrection, because martyrdom follows the martyr's resurrection in the afterlife. The Christian faithful buried their dead in the slight hope of resurrection. As a faith, it does not have the arrogance that it once had of its notion of resurrection. This is the base from which monotheism continues to exert its extraordinary and lethal power over its followers. If religion promises that there is nothing after death that would be the end of it.

The atheists' arguments with religion, over a number of centuries, are that religion has a flimsy relation with evidence; that it makes very large claims for itself in terms of salvation, redemption and eternity in the afterlife. Its false claims about the amount of evidence it can muster for its unfounded dogma, constitutes its original sin. It deals in absolutes and wants us to think of a God who is somewhere in sky but who functions as a dictator in this world. Living on earth is like an under-room, a rehearsal for the afterlife, for once you pass through the narrow passage of death there is another whole world which is waiting for you. There, in the afterlife, every tear would dry and every injustice would be compensated which, if it was true, it would be a terrible exercise in self-torture having God see how you would behave. You could be accused that if you do not believe in this afterlife, then you do not believe in God, you do not believe in the biblical redemption and salvation and certainly you don't believe in the resurrection. The fear of excommunication would be with you for the rest of your earthly life, and your punishment would come in the afterlife. Yet, what is the most powerful wishful thinking in the human species is the conquest of death and the achievement of immortality.

Long before the man-made invention of Christianity, the ancient Egypt rulers believed in and strived for immortality a lifelong quest. Upon death, the proceedings of the ritual ceremony were a kind of preparation for the final journey into the other world and the everlasting of the afterlife. The Egyptian High Priest, who was also the innkeeper of the afterlife mysteries, would attend the traditional ceremony to ensure that the dead ruler would be well-received by the God of the Underworld. Burial decorations were part of the send-off which symbolically would accompany the dead ruler to his final destination with immortality. The belief of immortality in the afterlife was the foundation of the Egyptian life and splinter polytheistic groups shared and practiced the same religious and culturally symbolic rituals. The Egyptian civilisation lasted for more than 3,500 years before Christianity. Their wish to live forever spread to the entire region of neighbouring groups and Empires, each with its own variation of traditional ceremonies for achieving immortality. The belief in the afterlife was ingrained in the social fibre and cultural life of their people. It was inconceivable to believe that this life was the only one and that there was no other.

No citizens craved more for immortality than the elites and rulers of the Middle East and rulers of Egypt, Persia, Syria, Iraq neighbouring empires, for they had more to lose in this life than anyone else in the lower classes. They built Temples and Monuments, Pyramids and secret burial chambers in order to protect and preserve the dominant position and their exclusiveness to the journey in the afterlife. All the "others" who did not follow or could not afford the cost of proper burial, their souls were condemned to a state of limbo, that is, to a state somewhere between this life and the afterlife. This limbo-state was believed in, and perhaps is still propagated in the Catholic religion, where only the baptised children get to heaven and the afterlife. The unbaptised millions of other children in Africa or in the Amazon Rainforest; who died of deceases or starvation before they were baptised, will remain in limbo; their souls will be floating in the unknown. Think for a moment about the mother's suffering who, in addition to her pain on her child's death, has to suffer a religious cruelty, torture and psychological torment for her dead child's limbo state.

From early human history, we are the only species on earth that is aware of death and the only species that is irreconcilable with death. We know our biological composition and we know that we are made of, the same as biological elements as other species. This includes stardust from the Big Bang, because other stars had to die in order for the earth to be formulated. Therefore, it is probable that, when we die our human elements will return to the natural biological and chemical cycle of our world. One can assume that there may be animals that fear death, but the notion of denying death is unique to humans. This notion of the afterlife is carried even further to include our favoured pets. There are cases where animals are buried in their own cemetery plot and are given religious ceremonies. This way their owners are secured of reuniting with their pets in the afterlife. This is enough to show how wishful thinking can reach the ultimate state of ridicule.

Wishful or delusional thinking for the afterlife is a hope and a hedonistic desire to conquer death, because we have not come to terms with our own extinction. The question now is why will people with wishful thinking want help? Is it because not all our wishful thinking is transparent to us? Of course, not all our wishful thinking is hedonistic, especially in regards to other people. For instance, some fundamentalists in the US have a wishful thinking regarding *"Muslims are bad, Christians are good"* which is a hateful wishful thinking and criminality. But call yourself, a priest, imam, rabbi and there is nothing that you can say and not get away with! We should all be prepared to encounter the stupidities and nastiness of religious people's wishful expressions. These kinds of people, who openly declare that they are the people of faith, should not get respect for it nor should their statements produce respect. For hundreds of years we have listened to priests about how wonderful the afterlife is; a place with endless praying, endless worship, endless subjection and endless tedium. One may think that after thousands of years of religion, God would have had enough of the song and dance of the dead souls in heaven. The tormenting of the dead souls increases, as there are instructions written by a prominent Christian father, *Tuterian,* who writes that the dead souls could go to the edge of heaven and look down on those damned that are tormented in hell.

This is a foundational building block of Christianity that cannot be retracted or edited, and it is too late to dismiss it as a metaphorical statement. The belief in the afterlife is a fundamental tenet of most religions, not all monotheistic, including *Hinduism, Buddhism, Sikhism, Christianity, Zoroastrianism, Islam, Judaism and the Baha'i* faith. But the belief in the immortal soul is not shared by all. Take the belief of the "soul" itself, for instance; in different religions, and even in different denominations within a given religion, it has various meanings and is used in different ways. Various branches of Christianity have disagreeing views on the soul's immortality and its relation to the body. The soul, according to the Abrahamic religions, belongs only to human beings and becomes immortal in the afterlife. Other religions such as *Jainism and Hinduism* believe that even non-biological entities such as rivers and mountains possess souls, a belief that is called *animism.* Animism (from the Latin *animus*) is a pre-historic belief that was practiced by the now extinct human species of the *Neanderthals* and *Cro-Magnon* where a proto-supernatural spirit was attributed to animals in their cave artworks some 30,000 years ago in Spain, Southern France, Germany, Croatia, Greece and beyond. This belief system developed to become the foundation of organised monotheistic religions and to include human souls in heaven and hell of the afterlife. This pre-historic and primitive belief in the afterlife is an extreme oppressive belief, because the Christian Churches, the Mosques and Synagogues would not be here if it was not for this delusional belief, nor there would be religious Madras promising afterlife with 72 virgins to martyrs and would not be incubating suicide bombers. There would not have been fanatical Jewish settlers in the occupied territories of West Bank, Palestine, believing that if they could only steal enough Palestinian land, this alone would bring on the Messiah for humanity's final Armageddon, and all the misery the settlers have caused would be justified. I would say, without exaggeration, that religion is a crime against humanity! I would never apologise for this militant statement.

A fundamental mistake occurs the moment heavenly religion speaks for God and Man. In religion, Man has found only a reflection of himself in the fantastic delusion of heaven, where he sought the "other" of himself, who no longer felt that this "other" was a mere appearance of him. In this non-man of the "other" he desperately seeks to find the real Man he already lost. As a physical Man, he makes religion, for religion does not make him. Religious faith is practiced by a man who has lost himself or a man who has not yet found his true self. Man knows that he is not an abstract entity squatting outside of the natural world. In fact, Man is the world of human community, which, in turn, makes religion, with a false consciousness of the world, an imaginary world. Religion is the general illusion of such world; its logic is of a delusional world of moral sanctions and a justification for false consolation of the sinful. It is a fantastic and a magical realisation of a man who has not acquired any true essence of a real Man. The rejection of religion is, therefore, the directly or indirect rejection of that delusional world, whose spiritual opiate aroma is religion.

Religious suffering of the ill-educated, the ignorant and the extreme poor is, at the same time, an overwhelming evidence of real human suffering and peoples' subliminal-protest against real suffering. It is a suffering of a real Man who is under God's dictatorial oppression, a Man who lives in the core of a heartless world and who is an oppressive spirit of a spiritless world. The rejection of "religious-happiness" restores real happiness. To call on you to give up the "religious-happiness" is, at the same time, a prerequisite of giving up the social conditions that generate delusions of that sort. The rejection of religion, therefore, is the core prerequisite argument of that veil of tears and pain, mental-torture and confusion of which religion is the cause.

Atheists, humanists and secularists should endlessly support the end of the world of religious deceptions and establish the world of Man. It is the immediate task of all of us, including biological scientists and secular educators to unmask the theology of self-entrapment of religious believers. It is imperative to continue criticising the anachronism, the nothingness of the afterlife; exhibited only to believers whose wishful thinking is that the rest of us should believe in the same delusions. Are they not trying to hide their delusions and seek refuge in hypocrisy and verbalism?

As the Stone Age and Bronze Age people went through their pre-historic development with *proto-imagination* and *proto-mythology* we also have to go through our post-historical development in secular ideas, in philosophy and in reason and science. It is wrong not to demand the end of the religious indoctrination of children in religion based schools, and not just stop at the demand without seriously implementing the termination of the brainwashing of school children. We cannot implement by turning our backs to religious industry by muttering a few trite and angry phrases about it. We cannot abolish religious indoctrination without making it a reality.

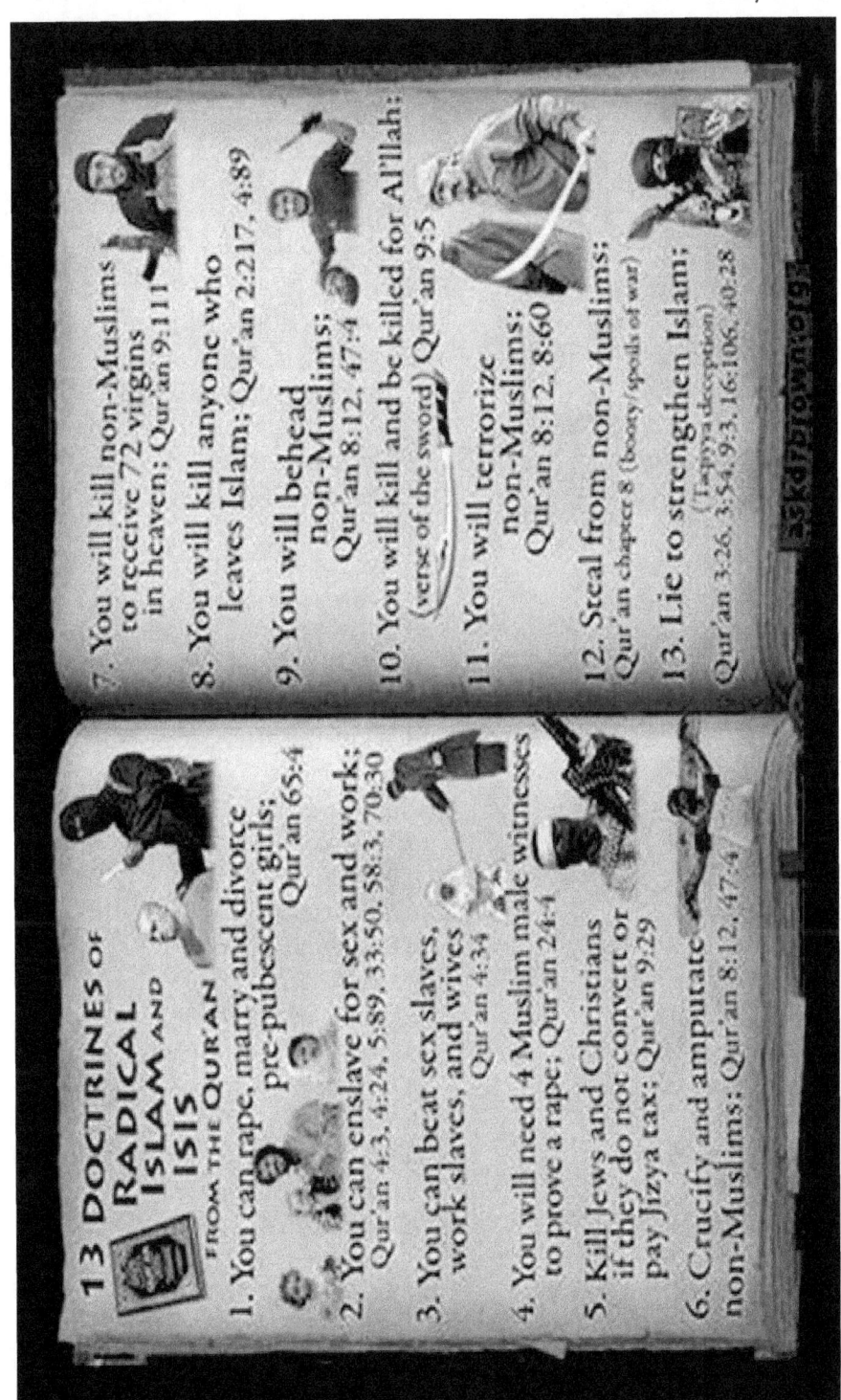

INDEX III

A cave-art, 540
Carlos castaneda, 621
Charles darwin, 575
Christoph luxemburg, 526
Cross of the zodiac, 513
Francisco franco, 587
Hubble telescope, 596
A brief history of time, 596
A common power, 477
A false-pattern, 552
Abraham lincoln, 461, 483
Abrahamic faith, 462
Abrahamic, 590
Absolutism, 524
Acts 19:18, 19, 464
Adam smith, 480, 582
Adaptation, 575
Adultery, 576
Afro-americans, 588
Afterlife, 577, 589, 594, 610, 615, 626
Albert einstein, 613
Amazon rainforest, 456, 458, 539, 591, 611, 627
Anabaptists, 474
Andean sierras, 456
Andreas vesalius, 472
Animism, 628, 542
Animist-symbols, 549
Apostasy, 506, 557
Arab-bedouins, 524
Aristophanes, 463
Aristotle, 467
Armageddon, 591, 629
Astrology, 504, 597
Astro-travelling, 621
Atheism, 456, 459
Atheist of melos, 475
Atheist, 475, 553

Averroes, 470
Behaviour, 575
Belief of faith, 551
Belief of god, 456
Belief, 539
Benjamin franklin, 461
Bertrand russell, 479
Bethlehem, 507, 512
Big bang, 627
Biological science, 550
Blasphemy law, 477
Bronze age, 630
Byzantium, 472
Canonical law, 617
Cave artists, 457
Cave artworks, 628
Celestial, 460
Charles darwin, 575, 613, 486
Christopher hitchens, 620, 550
Conquistadores, 548
Cro-magnon, 520, 617, 628, 576
Cultist, 504
Cultural, 461
Czarism, 585
D' holbach, 482
Dark ages, 467
Darwin, 552
David hume, 480, 582
December 25th, 509, 511, 515
Deep sleep, 625
Deists, 476
Democritus, 466
Diagoras of melos, 475
Dialectical, 477, 505
Dionysus, 510
Disciple judas, 507
Dna, 596
Dna, 613
E.W. Bullinger, 504

Einstein, 552
Emile zola, 478
Empathy, 576
Entitlement, 576
Ephesus, 465, 459, 466, 480
Erich fromm, 491
Ethical fibre, 577
Ethical, 460
Ethics, 470, 575
False belief, 584
False-pattern, 559
Federico garcia lorca, 587
Final curtain, 613
Flavius titus, 464
Frances rolleston, 504
Friedrich nietzsche, 490
Galilei, 471
Garden of eden, 619
George orwell, 491
George washington, 461
German paganism, 587
Giordano bruno, 473
Goddess inanna, 516
Golden rule, 578
Greek atheist, 460
Hadith, 525
Happy talk, 615
Harp music, 611, 611
Harris, 550
Havelock ellis, 463
Heliocentric, 471
Heresy, 474
Hitler's pope, 588
Homer simpson, 492
Homo sapiens, 457, 505, 520
Homogeneity, 577
Houris, 526
Human evolution, 556, 577
Humanist, 575, 611
Hunting-gathering, 560

Hysterical, 551
Ice age, 597
Icons, 468
Idolatric faith, 469
Industry of religion, 458
Inspirational, 595
Intelligent being, 476
Intelligent design, 557
Intelligent designer 488, 457, 479
Isaac newton, 613, 479
Ishia, 525
James buchannan, 461
James madison, 461
Johannes kepler, 471
John adams, 461
Joseph a. Seiss, 504
Karl marx, 491
Knowledge, 554
Laws of motion, 479
Laws of nature, 472, 477, 479, 511, 542, 553, 560, 610, 611, 614
Life after death, 539, 555, 609, 459, 460, 466, 527
Lord byron, 459
Lucius annaeus seneca, 467
Lucretius, 466
Magical arts, 464
Mark twain, 611, 625
Martin luther, 462
Martyrdom, 626
Material nature, 466
Materialism, 467, 470, 484
Matthew hammond, 474
Mega-church, 518
Mental act, 539
Mental-prison, 551
Mesolithic, 457
Mesopotamian, 540
Messiah, 629
Messiah-redeemer, 504

Messianic jews, 463
Metaphors, 609, 615, 619
Meteorites, 504
Militant atheism, 482
Mimetic ideas, 552
Mimetically, 463, 545
Mithras of persia, 509
Monotheism, 470, 549
Monotheist, 459
Monotheistic, 462, 466
Moral code, 578
Moral legitimacy, 456
Moral necessity of atheism, 592
Moral rules, 457
Moral, 459, 460
Morality, 470, 575
Mormons, 551
Mother Nature, 555
Mother Teresa, 594, 620
Muslims, 551
Mussolini, 587
Natural Evolution, 486
Natural Selection, 479, 552, 556, 577
Nature cannot, 619
Nazi brutality, 588
Nazism, 462
Neanderthals, 505, 576, 617, 628
near death, 623
Neolithic, 458, 505
New Age, 540, 543
Newton, 552
Nicolaus Copernicus, 471
odiac Signs, 471
Old Testament, 543
Origin of Species, 486, 577, 596
out of body experiences, 621
pagan mythology, 469
Palaeolithic, 457
Palestinian land, 629

pattern-explanations, 544
Pattern-meaning, 609
Paul-Henri Thiry, 481
Paulo Freire, 491
penalty of death, 477
Percy Bysshe Shelley, 485
Periergos, 464
Pierre Charron, 476
Planetary Laws, 505
polytheist, 463
polytheistic, 466, 509
Prisoners of Our Ideals, 456, 545
proto-cultural, 540
proto-spiritual, 540
proto-spiritualistic, 549
Purgatory, 463
Raising, 526
redemption, 626
Reformation, 473
Relativity, 554
Religion, 629
religious-happiness, 629
religiousness, 509, 515
resurrection, 626
Richard Dawkins, 550, 582
ritual, 457
Roman Imperial Cult, 464, 467, 590
Roman State Religion, 474
Russian Orthodox Church, 586
Saint Dominic, 517
salvation, 626
Sam Harris, 582
sceptical thinking, 468
scepticism, 469
schizophrenia, 557
Schools of Translators, 470
scientists, 546, 549, 461, 490
sexual fantasies, 524
Shamans, 542
Sigmund Freud, 490

Son-God Horus, 507
Stalin, 586
stardust, 613
state of nature, 477, 484, 540
Stone Age, 540, 596, 630
Sun, 504
Sun-God, 506
superstition, 577
swelling breasts, 526
symbolic, 513
symbolism, 469, 615, 609, 619
symbols, 504
theism, 458
theist morality, 550
theistic worship, 468
theistic, 504
Thomas Hobbes, 477
Thomas Jefferson, 461
Thomas Paine, 461, 483

Tullius Cicero, 467
Tuterian, 628
twelve-sign, 504
typological, 506, 508
Underworld, 626
Unitarians, 474
Utilitarianism, 486
verbalisms, 488
Victor Hugo, 472
Virgin Mary, 527, 551
virgin mother, 510
Virgin, 526
Vladimir Lenin's, 586
Voltaire, 480
white raisings, 527
Yuri Gagarin, 471
Zodiac myth, 506
Zodiac Signs, 504, 511, 527

CHAPTER IV
FAITH VS REASON

Hundreds of millions of devotees around the world literally believe in that their Torah, the Bible and the Qur'an are not written by bookish men but rather were written by God himself. Most of them also believe that the world is little more than 6,000 years old, that our original ancestors are Adam and Eve, and that humans were not evolved from prior life forms. This is an extreme blind faith and in every respect it is irrational, idiotic and against all available scientific evidence. These extreme views are not rare, for the majority of Americans believe in these religious distortions of the natural world which include half-truths, outright lies, myths and superstitions. Implanting in our human brains these non-existent pattern-explanations of life makes it nearly impossible for the believer to differentiate between real dialectical reasoning, knowledge and primitive mythology. This also represents a vast number of misinterpretations in polytheistic religions; for so many millions in their daily lives, such as in India, Thailand and Myanmar among other countries. The resulting consequences are terrifying and even lethal.

Such misinterpretations of our natural world are hostile against everything reasonable we learned through scientific evidence, humanist morality and strived for happiness. In this case, faith is a strategic blueprint for the devotees to follow which leaves them with little or no free choice. This is an extraordinary faith based dogma which is built on lies and deception; and which sets it apart, from our secular cultural humanist context. The terrifying and lethal descriptions of barbarism that is advocated in the Holy Books of the three monotheistic religions leave little room for a sense of joy and appreciation of life's richness when the devotees read them. It should be noted that these biblical descriptions are written not as metaphorical allegories but as prescriptions for how to live, directions for how to keep slaves and how to rape young girls. This is a fatal embarrassment for preachers and religious advocates who claim the Torah, the Bible and the Qur'an are the best books written on moral wisdom that humanity has ever had. Are we still slaves to primitive traditions and superstitions?

The instructions on slavery and raping of young girls have had fatal consequences for human civilisation. In the Christian tradition, St. Paul confirms slavery and instructs slaves that they must serve their masters well and especially their Christian masters. The Qur'an explains the *Curse of Ham* which confirms the justification of the 30 million slaves and the slave trade in Christian and Muslim African and Arabian countries. Most people in the western world believe that slavery no longer exists. But the slave trade is held on traditional grounds set by these primitive holy books. Remember that their reference to God is not something mysterious, something that exists in the human consciousness, or that God is a pure mystery or a pure energy. The God that is referenced in the Biblical Books is a personal God, one who answers your wishes, a creator God who created the cosmos with one mammalian-primate in his mind; who instead of visiting galaxies upon galaxies, he is instead especially concerned with us and what we do in our lives, with whom we intend to sleep and what kind food we intend to eat. This God will never leave you alone and will even be with you after your death. This God created the cosmos as a giant experimental playground to test our beliefs based on faith and not on reason and evidence.

Moreover, the religious claim that the holy books are the perfect magical books and that their contents are so superior, precious and irreplaceable that it is impossible that they were written by men rather than by God. This God must have been multilingual, for the holy books were partly written in Persian, Greek, Jewish and Arabic with detailed authoritarian cultural instructions which would put to shame any serial killer. In our human history there are other books such as Darwin's 1859 *The Origins of Species* or Isaac Newton's *Calculus, Optics, Gravitation and the Laws of Motion written in 1665*. Most of us, who read them, and scientists in any field, agree that these books are the most extraordinary examples of human intelligence. The point is that no one is tempted to claim that those books which display an extraordinary human intelligence are magical books, that they were not written by God nor that God helped Darwin and Newton to write them under any celestial dictation. It took a number of centuries for biologists and scientists to improve the scientific theories presented in those books, yet an effort to improve the deceptions written in the Torah, Bible and Qur'an will be a waste of time and a futile exercise. Faith and Reason, Humanist Morality and Science may co-exist today but it is a co-existence in a divided world and not a co-existence of mutual support and unification.

The justification of many despicable acts described in the Old, and New Testaments and the Qur'an does not hold a moral record. To be told to love someone, to be told that we were all born in sin, which we need to repent, that we will always be guilty about some unknown sin, that we will always live with the pain of sinfulness, is the most despicable religious demand placed upon us. It is long pass time to bring ourselves into the 21st century and stand side by side with scientific knowledge that we have acquired and with the brilliant insights we have discovered, which capture our intuition of what it is to be ethical and reasonable.

In fact, the "Golden Rule" of *"Do to others as you want them to do to you,"* is a popular wisdom that we find it ourselves through our intuition from tens of thousands of years of humanist morality, solidarity and social bonding, and long before the Torah, the Bible and the Qur'an faith books were written. We are our own guarantors of reason and ethical behaviour. We have chosen to abide by humanist ethics; and not by those prescribed to us by Jewish, Christian and Muslim primitive traditions, which have collided over hundreds of years with civil and secular ethics. Religious traditions are the enemy of reason.

When you read the Old Testament and Qur'an you can find scores of theological justifications to inflict terrifying and lethal punishment on many who have not committed a capital offence. For instance, changing one's religion (apostasy), or a woman's absence of virginity on her wedding night or being a witch, are offences punished by stoning to death. Such atrocities have happen throughout the history by organized religions and still continue to this day under fundamentalist Muslim rule in many parts of the world. The Taliban in Afghanistan, the Iranian theocracy and the fanatics of the ISIL in Syria and Iraq are terrifying leftovers of primitive religious traditions. The Christian villain St. Paul stated that such atrocities should not be taken seriously because the End of the World is coming soon and thereafter all such violent acts will be corrected and all slaves and masters will be equal. Such idiotic explanations were used to justified crimes against humanity.

Islam was established by a tradition of tribal warrior clans. The Prophet Muhammad was a leader of a warrior clan which defeated or consolidated other clans in the Arabian Peninsula. A schizophrenic and epileptic Muhammad heard voices in his mind and attributed them to God who ordered him to commit the atrocities he inflicted. It was a war (Jihad) situation which left Muhammad a choice of war, negotiations or with the partial destruction of others' or Muhammad's clan. He ordered the killings of 800 Jews who refused to help him in his war effort. One of his 9 wives was named Aisha who, at 9 years old her marriage to Muhammad was consummated and she entered his household with her toys.

After Muhammad's death on June 8, 632 AD, the spreading of Islam was conducted in 661 AD, by means of constant and bloody religious wars (Jihad) under the direction of the Syrian Empire of Umayyad. This Holy War (Jihad) against the infidels of the world and other faith groups within Arabia has been built into the core of the Islamist political ideology as can be witnessed in some Arabian countries. The apologists of Islam in the West are trying to portray it as a peaceful religion; they are hiding behind people's ignorance of the spreading ideology of Islam, from the desert of the Arabian

Peninsula to Spain. The peaceful spreading of Islamist ideology in the West is still part of the fundamentals of Jihad with the desire of converting Europe and North America to Islamist faith. Treating Islam as an academic subject and not as a real threat to humanity would have terrifying and unavoidable pan-Islamic consequences.

Apologists of religion present an old and tired argument that Christianity had its Reformation leading to the creation of many sects around the world; and that it is assumed that the Muslims have not had their own as yet. This is true for Christianity whereby of their main Catholic and Orthodox bodies there were divided into different sects which settled their own differences over time. But this sub-protestation phenomenon is not absent from the Islamic religion. The religious Islamic Reformation is very much present with its total of seventy-three (73) distinct sects within Islam from the moderate sects in the West to the fundamentalists in other parts of the world. All such seventy-three sects within it are actively interpreting Islam according to their own convictions---just like Christians---and changing religious agenda. It is not the lack of reformation which makes Islam a violent religion; it is because such a path is the core of its existence. They collectively brooding their support over agreeable religious passages but also providing the shape of future theocratic states like Iran and Saudi Arabia. It must be understood that these theocratic countries are the product off and not against Jihadists militant puritans. There can be no compromise or religious reform between fundamentalists, newly established splinter groups and up coming re-interpretations of Islam by its seventy-three sects. This sets a conception of a religion with infinite swings in all directions to be used by militant Muslims as they see fit.

So what best reflects the reality of our cosmos and humanity is it faith or reason? Both have the burden of truth with one side or the other claiming to hold the correct view and proof of evidence. Faith on one side represents organised religion or a spiritualism of sorts that does not involve theism. Organised religious faith claims that God is space less, immaterial, powerful, moral, and a personal intelligent creator. For religion, cosmology signifies that the cosmos had a beginning and therefore it needed a beginner. The cosmological fact of the Big Bang was the beginning of the cosmos, but that beginning does not provide evidence of the existence of a beginner, (God) the creator of the cosmos. In this case the science of cosmology has been hijacked by religion to give a pseudo-scientific legitimacy to that claim, instead of maintaining the tired old Biblical myth of the anthropomorphic Sky-God who lives in a celestial heaven. This is religious reverse engineering; or in layman's terms, the "old wine in a new bottle," to be more convincing to new and much more educated generations. You see, in the 21st century the Greek Orthodox and the Roman Catholic organised religions could not possibly been sold to us; this as a new invention of their delusion, superstitions and outright lies of their dogmas. Messianic religions were invented in a geographical area where the Humanist-Reason as a way of thinking did not exist. The average men's' and women's' thoughts did not pass "from hand to mouth" as John Locke said in his political agenda. In the deserts of the Middle East, countless gods and lesser-gods were believed on the basis of existing delusional traditional faiths which excluded reason as a way of presenting reality to the desert people.

Our humanity has been Balkanized by different beliefs; with Christians against Muslims, Muslims against Jews, Buddhists against Hindus and different militant sects of Muslims against each other. The millions of people living under these theistic communities organize their daily affairs around the verses of their holy books. These faith-based books hold incomparable views of the world and of God's exclusive real-estate in the Middle East. These Bronze Age written religious passages have been adopted by people who hold 21st century destructive technology as their exclusive guide-line to their beliefs and behaviour.

The term "Belief" has the most infested mimetic influence in human communication. Beliefs do not represent the real world; but they do represent a reflection of it, in our own image, as we wish it to be. This is the difference between beliefs and "reason to hope," where the latter represents human aspirations. When a person hopes that something is true, it has to do with the real world; but when a person believes that something is true then that person imposes upon reality his beliefs. This person also becomes prisoner of his own beliefs. This is why beliefs take our emotions into a fixed pattern of "no going forward" into any alternative; thus beliefs are generating irrational expectations of the world around us. For instance, if a friend comes to you saying that your house is about to collapse, and you believe this to be true, your whole mental process changes instantly, until it is confirmed otherwise. When you believed that what you were told it was true, your whole behaviour changed based on the significance you placed upon such belief. Religious beliefs change our behaviour because we place a significant irrational importance upon those beliefs. Since those irrational beliefs do not exist in a vacuum, believing in them could cause us to adopt an irrational behaviour towards pending issues.

For instance, the Jews believe that God gave the Jews an exclusive real-estate in the Middle East as their exclusive property. Since the construction of the Dome of the Rock in 691 AD, Muslims also believe that Allah gave them an equally exclusive real-estate which happened to be the same property that was given to the Jews. Both people believe in God's double brokering of the same real-estate. How many people on both sides must die defending their beliefs of their theistic rights to the real-estate that God brokered for them? These beliefs of both the Jews and Muslims, mixed together with hundreds of other hostile prejudices, has lead to genocide, the Palestine occupation, settlers, Israeli apartheid and apocalyptic prophecy of geopolitical consequences.

Let us take the Biblical prophecy of the Second Coming of Jesus Christ. For instance, if a mushroom cloud suddenly appeared over the bible-belt of Salt Lake City, in the State of Utah, 57% of the people would see a silver-lining in it. They would be convinced that the end of the world finally came; and that any moment now, they would be embraced in God's bosom and be on the way to heaven. This assumed "end of the world" is the timeless desired goal of the Jewish, Christians and Muslim fundamentalists. Yet it is taboo to criticize their religion or criticize that some religions are propagating violence in a way that is getting people killed. Fundamentalists really believe that certain books were written by God with a message that death in pursuit of Jihad (Holy Wars) is the highest good; that the death of the unbelievers' families and their children cannot come soon enough. Devotees are motivated by their beliefs and, because of the existing taboos, the rest of us feel powerless to openly criticize those beliefs and show them to be destructive, terrifying and even lethal.

In fact, because of these taboos, we have made concessions to the religious fundamentalists and allowed them to make a reality with their beliefs and expectations about the world. Their beliefs have contents that are representational of the world they see through the lenses of their blind faith. As such, the propagators of religious faith are extremely deceptive and interject their primitive beliefs into scientific utterance. For instance, the myth that God created Adam and Eve out of mud has now changed to suggest that human species were created by God's "intelligent design." Because the complexities of life forms are now well-known to have evolved through Natural Selection and Adaptation, a biblical claim that God created life out of mud sounds very idiotic. Yet this is the very same pseudo-science that your children and mine may be taught in school someday. Because of their pseudo-science these liars and plagiarists are really eroding the prestige of science in its pursuit of discoveries in biology, medical and environmental culture. They would encourage the distortion of linguistic terminology, in academic presentation of science, by the insertion of primitive theism dressed up in modern terms of scientific-meaning. This would even spread a profound confusion between genuine scientific meanings and bastardized terms of theistic origins.

Believers of creationism, of course, do not care much about the religiousness of the neo-scientology of "intelligent-design" (ID). Their claim is that living organisms on earth are far too complex for evolution to have taken place; therefore an "Intelligent Designer" must have created them. This concept was first introduced by ancient Greek philosophers and now it is revived by the creationists. As for the average devotees, their simplistic minds are more attracted to the easy-to-understand patterns of the original biblical myth of the mud creation of Adam and Eve, the talking snake and a bunch of apples. It is the professionals of the industry of religious demagogues, the ones who make their thinly veiled printed lies and exploit the simpletons of religious faith, that we should hold it in contempt and expose in mass media.

When you hear about "intelligent design" (ID), it is another word for creation, and it is a tactical attempt by the demagogues to hide the unintelligent and primitive roots of religion. Their arguments in support of ID are the same old ones which have been refuted since Darwin's *Theory of Evolution*. Since their arguments lack any coherency, creationists fall back to their old "Bogey Man" scare tactics against atheists who also are evolutionists. Fundamentalists are using popular phobias which claim that if you *"teach your children evolution they'll soon get into drugs, Hard Rock Music, sexual perversion and become atheists."* It should be noted that many prominent members of the Catholic hierarchy are evolutionists (evolution is God's doing?). It is ironic, but I have to ask: do creationists know that profound knowledge of Darwin's *Theory of Evolution* is extremely corrosive to religious faith? If they know this, then they are deluding themselves by believing in creationism or are simply confused. Otherwise, what logical reason do they have for continuing with their religious demagogy of faith and creationism? Are they afraid of the positive power of Natural Evolution which is, in its essence, atheistic?

Humanist ethics and morality is the core, profound and necessary building blocks of our civilized society. There is nothing we need to believe based on insufficient evidence in order for us to have deeply ethical lives, to build sanctuaries or help the disadvantaged and to come together as communities. We have rights but also responsibilities towards each other. Our next door neighbours have the right to believe in religious myths about life after death, resurrection and the coming of Jesus Christ; and because they believe them, we are told to respect their beliefs. Where else do we submissively play by these rules? We criticize our leaders, political ideologies, government policies, business practices, abusers of human rights, environment policies and our education system. Nowhere in our constitution does it declare that we must respect policies that we do not agree with or deceptions about biology or cosmology just because someone believes in these outright deceptive beliefs. Why are we so polite to religious deceptions, human rights abuses of children by priests, listening to sermons about Hell and Fire or that we were born sinful and now we are ordered to repent or else? In all other fields of life, we do not instantly respect someone's beliefs, but we tend to evaluate peoples' supporting reasons, the way a person articulates his beliefs and, in turn, we accept them, question them, or reject them. Except on matters of religious faith!

For thousands of years, humanity's ill educated population was under the total control of the industry of religious culture where we were told what to believe, what to think, whom to sleep with, what to eat and to obey rituals we did not understand, temple sermons and languages we could not comprehend. For thousands of years 98% of the people living under such theocratic cultures could not read or write and simply lived under fear, slavery and obedience. Adaptation to such psychological terror entered our psyche and passed on from one generation to the next until 500 years ago where the brave few began to question the religious elite. Then the reign of terror began against those who dared to question the powerful religious cliques. The Vatican Inquisition mob spread terror and torture, ordered the live burning of women, the mass deportation of Jews from Spain, the crusade wars against Islam, and its anti-science which, Dark Age subdued progress for 10 centuries. Jews, Christians and Muslims need to remember that human adaptation is not only biological, it is also psychological. They have feared the rabbis, priests and mullahs of religious institutions and its power for centuries and today they are still the meek *"who did not conquered the world"* but have evolved following a centuries old path of mixture of submissive faith, obedience and fear.

Humanity has lived in an uncertain world for a number of centuries. We have been biologically developed with the capacity of protecting ourselves and our families against domestic and foreign threats and environmental uncertainties. Each morning we get up to do our daily tasks; with no guarantees that our day will unfold peacefully. Uncertainty is the complimentary and positive companion of freedom. Escaping from your freedom; because of fear or lack of confidence in yourself can only lead you into submission to a real or imaginary celestial autocracy. Having faith in ourselves is not the same as having a religious faith. Religious faith is a belief, based on insufficient evidence, that, if you submit to the authority of the holy book, your life will unfold correctly. If it does not, it is because you are sinful, or you have not prayed enough, or your beliefs are weak. One way or another, it is your fault, for God cannot be held responsible for your failures. Religious faith expects you to believe that some mythological figures were divine, that presumptuously knowledge God will take care of us in this life and in the life after death. We must rely on faith that something is true, with no sufficient investigation or dialectical evidence of proof. In any other case not involving religious faith, you will not relying on faith just because someone tells you something is true.

On the other hand, if a dear person develops cancer and the doctor tells you that there is nothing it can be done to cure the disease, and now you praying to God for a cure and that person is finally cured, you probably spend the rest of your life believing that your payers were answered by God. However, this is not a religious faith and there is not a divinely sent cure. It is a practical scientific reason for such medical success. There are powerful drugs for curing a certain types of cancer. In this case, mathematical statistics can convince you that in this life, there is still room for good science; as well as, a pure coincidence of making a mistake in the original medical prognoses. No one should rely on faith because faith alone keeps the wheels of cognition spinning around endlessly looking for a pattern-meaning where no pattern really exists.

Human beings were not biologically evolved to believe in God or born to seek religion or mysticism. We were born with a biologically programmed safety mechanism to look for patterns in life. Through cognitive experience, our ancestors were able to recognize patterns of danger where really danger existed or patterns of safety where safe-harbours really existed. This triggered their survival instincts that now had a choice of confronting or retreating from such dangerous situations or seeking safety. In other cases, a sound in the forest, for instance, could trigger a false-alarm or a false pattern-danger which did not exist. Throughout the millenniums the human brain biologically developed to create patterns in life for every reason and occasion. Our brains still function based on the same principles, from the moment we get up in the morning to the time we go to bed. Patterns are generated at the speed of travel that electrons take from one anatomy of the brain to the next. Our brain does meet the demand for shortcut pattern-meaning as frequently as it can, but at times, it invents pattern-meaning where there is none. This is the biological obligation of our brain and this is how humanity has survived earthquakes, tsunamis, diseases, and by guessing unforeseeable events. Sometimes our brain gets things right, other times it does not.

Patterns do not contain senses of good or bad, moral or immoral, and truth or false qualities. That is not the brain's function, for the brain generates thousands of patterns per day; some true and some false, and in order to meet the demand, it creates shortcuts. It generates shortcuts of patterns based on our past memories of experience some of which maybe true or false. Like the sound in the forest or the wrongful medical diagnosis of the cancer patient, a false pattern was generated where no pattern existed. In both cases, the human brain is programmed to generate patterns, rather than no patterns at all. It cannot help but to generate patterns because blank-pattern-space does not exist in our brain. This is how our thinking brain works and it is our own responsibility based on verifiable evidence to manage our mental illusions, delusions, wishful thinking, desires, religious fallacies and authoritative comfort zones for our insecurities.

Our ancestors faced tremendous challenges against all odds from other hostile species and environmental causes for you and I to have the quality of life we and our children now have. We have survived religious wars, ignorance of our cosmos and we now have the undisputed evidence that as a species we are capable, determined and strong in developing the kind of civilization we did. Don't you think it is ---metaphorically speaking-- about time for our ancestors be proud of us? Let us shake off the shackles of the celestial dictator who only exists because of our false pattern in our brain, a pattern of a celestial God that does not exist! So let us grow up and face the world's uncertainties as our human ancestors did! Let us not continue with our meekness and respect or fear the liars of religion, even if those liars are self-deceptive and victims of their own delusions. Let us also not forget nor forgive what the "holy-men" of Judaism and Christianity and Islam have done and their crimes against humanity when these religions were strong. No, do not live the life of a *"meek"*, nor *"turn the other cheek"* and continue with the abuse!

The industry of religious faith oppresses every aspect of human life on this earth; from the faith based schools to blood transfusions, abortions to use of condoms, to genital mutilation of both male and female, to love of poverty but not of poor people, to the extravagant exhibitions of wealth by clergy working in underprivileged societies, to the construction of magnificent temples to provide impressive ceremonies, to feeding and supporting a slue of non productive servile nuns around the world, to running a multibillion funding enterprise for an army of digitally insane televangelists; all intoxicated by the wealth and power they have accumulated over the meek of the earth. In laymen's terms this is called Social Darwinism, (the survival of the fittest) where the strong survived over the week. While our secular civilized societies, over the last two centuries, have built social-cushions to lessen the terrible consequences of Social-Darwinism, the industry of religion is still fixed in its primitive ways---the strong over the week---as they were once practiced by tribesmen in the deserts of the Middle East in the 1st century and in the Arabian Peninsula.

We are facing a problem of overpopulation where resources are scarce at best. Yet the Catholic Church believes that birth control and condom use is somehow immoral. This is genuinely an idiotic idea, for the power of the human brain is insufficient to provide a reasonably good argument in support of this idea. Place for a moment your thoughts in mid Sahara desert, in Africa, where 3 million people die each year from AIDS. In the middle of this human tragedy, you have the well-fed Catholic priests or a US Evangelical preacher who literally are preaching in a language of intimidation to the ignorant inhabitants on the immorality of birth control and the use of condoms. These Sub-Sahara desert villagers have no other means of information apart from what the priests tell them to follow. Before their eyes, millions of men, women and innocent children are dying each year from this terribly painful contaminant of faith. This amounts to genocidal idiocy supporting an apocalyptic prophecy of the end of the human race, and where faith interrupts ethical arguments about the use of condoms. Their Sky-God must feel very proud of them for placing their irrational moral teachings in superior place than the deaths of millions. Some kind of all-loving God!

Why is the Catholic Church as fanatically against stem-cell research? Briefly, stem-cell research involves human cells which help scientists to prevent diseases that kill cells within organs or impair a person from living a normal life. For instance, insulin producing cells are dead in a pancreatic organ, and dead cells could be replaced with healthy cells to help the patient. Millions upon millions of people are dying from otherwise curable diseases such as from heart failures, or diabetes in adult or juvenile patients. In the process of creating healthy stem cells, scientists need to destroy about 150 human cells for every one healthy cell. Is 150 cells a high number? If we look at the brain-cell number of a fly or a mosquito we could count about 100,000 cells for each of those. Scientists could develop 666 healthy human cells at the cost of destroying cells that fit in a space of a fly's brain. Stem cell research holds enormous potential for healing a broad spectrum of diseases. The Catholic Church argues that life begins upon conception and scientists' research on embryonic cells commits murder. The destruction of an embryo that occurs when embryonic stem cell are removed has upset the religious right in the USA and elsewhere, just as blood transfusion into a sick person has upset the Jehovah Witness religious sect.

The late Christopher Hitchens (1949 – 2011), was correct when he declared that *"religion poisons everything."* Without an exaggeration, when you look around you, you find that every single progress in humanist themes, every improvement in civil or criminal law, every better treatment of medical prevention, every attempt to abolish slavery, every moral progress that has been made by humanity, has been consistently opposed by organized religion; which is the number one enemy of human moral principles. Religion has attempted to retard human progress (Dark Age) throughout the centuries. Do not let this happen to the people in your neighbourhood.

Is there a space for co-existence between faith and reason? The time for respecting someone else's religious faith is past overdue. We assume that we do not have the right to criticize someone's irrational beliefs. Yet this is exactly what we often do in our lives, for we criticize people who believe in horoscopes, and future tellers, in the irrational medical service of homeopathy, in believing that Elvis Presley is still alive and that holy water has the power to cure sickness and so on. We apply reason with our criticism in everything that it is irrational, unproven and mystical. We generally respect other peoples' reasons but not their beliefs. This we do as rational human beings and in our intellectual honesty. There is really a conflict between faith and reason. Religious twenty-first century claims about God have exactly the same primitive status as the polytheistic Gods had in the first century Arabian deserts, even though those claims are dressed up in pseudo-scientific patterns such as "intelligent design" (ID).

This argument defeats itself because any designer who designed such complex living organisms must also be far more complex itself. What else does this designer is capable of, that in a war situation our side will win, that is capable of seeing our climatic disasters and be indifferent, but hears our prayers as a candle is lit? What kind moral standard is this? The elegance of humanist morality is so corrosive to religion because it simply sees humanity's necessities without involving external agents. The God delusion and mythology is simply a bad one and incapable of meeting the high standard requirements of humanist morality. There can be no genuine co-existence between faith and reason because faith stops any further conversation due to its fixation on its primitive myths. No one can advance a rational argument between faith and reason because faith blocks every ethical conversation that involves morality, science, war and peace, sex education and human health, evolution and biology, and between beliefs and their physicality. If your beliefs are genuine part of the physical world that could be proven, then your beliefs contain reasons which make them believable. No one could deny their legitimacy, the honesty of the evidence of your presentation and your effort of expressing them. Religious faith is the only area of our lives where one can submit to it by having no reason or vague reasons. For the devotee it is considered a noble stand; as to show God that nothing will ever separate him from his blind faith.

Having noticed that faith and reason can only co-exist in separate realms, many of us have decided to let religious faith alone, because after all, if we continue ignoring it, it will simply go away. This "fence-sitting" stand is a mistake. Reason and faith are in conflict because faith has nothing to say about how the world works. Religious faith is not something resembling a fuzzy feeling or warmth and or about the "other reality." There is no other alternative reality because reality is not a concept or a choice of personal perception. Rather reality is the physical embodiment of the cosmos we live in it, and which exists independently of our correct or incorrect mental process of it. False concept-reality is accepted and acted upon by blind faith. But that is not the religious faith we know and see practiced in faith strong countries. Religious faith makes claims about the existence of the afterlife, non-existent biblical historically-typological events, and how reality works--which only science can confirm. This is where the conflict between reason and faith lies.

Science works on the basis of various presented hypotheses which scientists test and observe to see which of these hypotheses co-relates with evidence. The evidence which is available at this time and space is strongly against believing about the alternative theistic world that religious claims make. Science, which includes biology, investigates natural phenomena with evidence or warranted proof. Atheist scientists will never claim that they have discovered the absolute truth about natural phenomena, and of course, they can not prove or disprove the existence of God, the Unicorns or Santa Claus. They can only say that there is no reasonable evidence to warrant a belief that God, Unicorns or Santa Claus exist (but we all know that they do not exist). In science we do not prove anything unless we have justifiable claims that we can back up with evidence. Such evidence can ensure us that the Judeo-Christian God or Unicorns do not exist as much as we are sure that the Sun will rise tomorrow morning.

Since the last 150 years, following the first discovered Neanderthal cranium in Northern Germany, there have been a number of archaeological excavations seeking the origins of our species and ancient religious claims. Since the mid 1940's Israeli professional and amateur archaeologists have spend years digging the Sinai desert to find evidence of the Biblical God's existence, the Exodus, Moses and the 10 Commandments. They found none! A second attempt to confirm God's real estate brokerage and gift to the Jews was done in 1948 by orders of its first Israeli Prime Minister *David Ben-Gurion (1886 – 1973)*. He ordered archaeologists back to the Sinai Desert to find evident of the Jewish title to the land. None was found! All evidence discovered in fact, was that no evidence existed at all, and that the Judeo-Christian dogma was an organized delusion to spread fear and control over the un-ruling tribesmen of the Middle East during the Bronze Age. To paraphrase the British political philosopher John Locke, whose message to the ruling classes in 1600's was, *"give them [the people] subliminal thoughts [religious beliefs] for they can not think beyond hand to mouth."*

We turned religious faith into an untouchable or a taboo subject that exists beyond our daily concerns. Well we are wrong, for while we are ignoring it, faith has penetrated every aspect of our lives from politics to our sex lives. In USA election times every potential congressman, senator and even president must declare his or her religious belief if she or he is to be financially supported and eventually elected. I can assure you that no potential public servant from the president down would ever be elected if or when she or he declares and defends their atheism. The religious right is so powerful that the idea of atheist declaration is not even considered a viable electoral alternative. Yet, it takes one brave person among the 33% of America's agnostics and atheists, to take a stand and be engraved in the history of the USA. One of the most troublesome question that still lingers in my mind is about whether we fear other peoples' faith or we respect their faith. Are we talking about the faith of fanatics who fly planes into buildings or became suicide bombers, and whose beliefs are not part of humanist rationality? Are we having any reasons to think that the core essence of Judaism, Islam and Christianity, is not endorsing violence openly or otherwise? So why do we not take an anti-theist stand instead of tolerating religious faith?

Evidence has convincingly shown that the core philosophy of hatred in the Arabian Peninsula and the African Continent is the Muslim faith. We in the western world must claim the right to treat religions with ridicule and utter contempt. Those who hold to the notion of the absolute truth of their religious beliefs belong to the infancy of our human race. Can those infantile know that they are better off thinking for themselves and take the risks and rewards of new intellectual discoveries? The religious offers of certainty, the offers for a complete celestial security, the offers of a fixed faith that you can not escape from, an offer that a celestial power is watching you, is an offer not worth having. Part of our human creativity and our human curiosity is to take risks to discover applicable truths about ourselves and our cosmos. There are truths that we do not know yet, and knowledge that we can never have enough of it. Can the believers understand that human morality and decency did not derive from religion, they preceded it! Can you warn your decent family members to beware of the irrational, seductive and transcendent malware promoted by professionals of the industry of religion?

Why should we turn the *other cheek* and become religious moderates with faulty compassion, instead of preferring human decency for ourselves and our neighbours? You should know that religion can make a good and decent people, like your neighbour, act nasty and intelligent people to say stupid things. Do not be afraid of being militant anti-theist and expose obvious religious idiocies. Let the neon of self-delusion know that their idiocy of the "Intelligent Designer" confirms that their God was incompetent, callous, cruel, indifferent, self-declared jealous, capricious and bigoted, deceitful and genocidal, homophobic and insecure, irrational and malevolent, violent and anti-science, misogynistic, vindictive and a bully who demands a constant praise and adulation.

On a more personal level, militant atheism (to borrow Richard Dawkins' phrase) compels us to seek out reasons for our arguments and disputation rather than just be spectators of religious idiocies and unfairness. In a more poetic sense, your disputations metaphorically should reflect your favoured dance, for it is far more satisfying to be part of that dance rather than being a spectator. While you are alive do not stand by being reserved and quiet; for when you are in your grave, death will provide you with plenty of silence. We must increase and speak out our support of Charles Darwin's *Theory of Evolution and the Origin of Species* against the reactionaries of creationism. Darwin's *Evolution by Natural Selection* is the most profound theory ever presented by the human mind. His masterpiece on *The Origins of Species* in mid 19th century has changed the way and how we perceive our cosmos and our place in it. Briefly, what Darwin achieved is nothing less than a complete explanation of the diversity and complexity of all life forms on earth. His explanations make it possible, even for people who are not biologists, to understand his simplest ideas about how life evolved. The human evolution story is far richer, extensive and interesting than any religious faith of creation. This is why supporters of Natural Evolution are militant atheists and, because they understand the extraordinary reality of our world, therefore, they need to *"step up to the plate"* and be counted.

Evolution is a fact and it is supported by undeniable reasons and evidence. There is nothing whimsical about how nature's force drives evolution, for it is brutal and powerful in its impact. Darwin's theory of human evolution is also brutally honest and not at all veiling over the evidence. The evidence presented was in collision course with the dominant religious mythology of its day that each animal and each species had a unique place in God's creation and unchanging design. The world that God "created", with the entire small and large animal population, including the human race, was about 6,000 years old. Darwin's theory of evolution utterly dismissed that belief.

Yet, in the USA, 45% of the people still cling to the religious faith that God create the world in 6 days and that the earth is about 6,000 years old. I think it is scandalous that such high presentence of people pass on their religious delusions to their children, who remain unfamiliar with the biological science of evolution. Evolution is about our existence in the world, it explains a huge amount of evidence because everything about life is explained by it. The collision course takes place between Darwinian evidence of evolution and the biblical false pattern-faith explanations that are deeply rooted in the minds of those 45% believers. Their children were first taught these biblical myths at the time when they had no chance of comparison between evidence and religious indoctrination. These children were indoctrinated to believe, and they believe because they were brought up to believe. Their position is hopeless until later on; if they ever decide to look at the massive evolutionary evidence more closely.

Existing fossils collected, catalogued and investigated over the last 160 years from around the Ecuadorian Galapagos archipelagos of South America tell a far more interesting story than the Biblical nonsense. The discoveries of fossils are a big challenge to the religious orthodoxy of any faith believer who follows the dogma of creation. The biological discoveries confirmed that life forms were not fixed, they changed over time, and they must have evolved. It was important then, as it is important today, to understand why and how this happened. Briefly, hundreds of thousands of fossils collected have confirmed that different species shared remarkable similarities between skeleton structures; their limbs had the same bones, the same chromosome order, although reshaped and resized in order to adapt to different environments and ways of life. The end result of such enormous biological evidence collected over many years and studied by many scientists then and now, has confirmed that every single species is related to other species. Natural Selection, Adaptation and Evolution are the fundamentals of our existence and perpetuation of our species.

It should be noted, however, that nowhere in the faith-based books is there a reference to natural selection, adaptation and evolution under any terms of biblical reference. The concept of "intelligent design" is simply an intellectual dishonesty on the part of the promoters in the industry of religion. They have abandoned their primitive base of creation and ignorance of the world as described in their holy books, and have thinly veiled over the murderous assignments demanded of their followers. They cover their historical crimes against humanity records with declarations of niceties, peaceful existence, conveniently avoiding the truth of the origins of their barbaric religion. Any criminal person who hides his past does so because of ulterior motives; either because he plans his next criminal actions, or has un-repented shame that does not want to be known. When there is a political authority of religious nature, such authorities neither do nor operate in the void. They operate within the social structures of our communities; and because they operate in the *Polis* their core characteristics are of a political organization. Whatever they do, they do under the principle of controlling and perpetuating their immediate interests. This is the core principle of Social Darwinism, where the survival of the fittest is their only purpose of existence. This is the dark side of Natural Evolution seeing in the natural world, from the Arabian Peninsula to the Amazon Rainforest. Accumulation, not reasonable distribution is their *mode operati*. They are accumulating masses of believers and they are distributing gifts of submissive and blind faith.

The meek submitted to these religious organizations because they wanted to escape from freedom (to use Erich Fromm's term). They are citizens of their countries in name only, for they first obey their cultists' laws and rituals set for them by the religious autocrats. Their legions are with those who claim; and who have set themselves up, as God's representatives on earth. These weaklings have given up the right to think for themselves, the right to make their own mistakes and correct them as they see fit, to take a chance and achieve freedom, to discover reason and evidence rather than submit to a celestial dictatorial faith. This is the dark side of Social Darwinism, for the dominated weak to submit to the dominant. Yet, humanity has created civilized societies precisely to counter-balance Social Darwinism. Democratic laws were created for institutions to protect the under-privileged from raw-capitalism and provide social cushions for the poor and their dependant. Yet the educational institutions have failed to educate school children about how the reality of the material world works, how to dialectically think (not what to think), and have allowed the sanitized religiousness of faith-based schools to utterly indoctrinate their students

When it comes to children religious faith it is a dangerous and contagious virus. It is a virus partly transmitted by faith-based schools, by clergy and down through generations of grandparents and parents to child and grandchild. Without a doubt, children are most vulnerable to the infections of religious viruses. It is because children are biologically programmed to accept, and store in their memory, knowledge received from figures of authority. As such, a child's brain is set up in a Darwinian way to believe what it's been told by elders. Children quickly absorb knowledge because there is no time to experiment with warnings of "danger" or "don't go too near a fire," for if children who may apply a scientific scepticism to those warning they would be injured or dead. The child's brain would believe anything is been told; even if those are delusions, falsities, utterly idiotic, or children's fantasies such as Santa Claus and the Tooth Fairy, or Snow White and the Seven Dwarfs. When the child grows up it would pass the same delusions or fantasies to its own children.

The damage religion has done to humanity's mental faculties goes beyond praying at church on Sundays. Over the centuries, religion has implanted false pattern-explanations of how the world works, false pattern-meaning of linguistic-terms and to believe in pattern-subjects that do not exist and illusion and delusions that do with religious rituals. We are accustomed to believing in mental-things just because we have mentally-thought of them. We are mixing *reality-terms* as foundations to *delusion-terms* to make sense of what we are saying. If the clergy said to you that *"Moses heard God's voice coming from behind a burning bush"*, you may identify the reality-terms (the man, Moses, voice and bush) from delusion-terms (God and God's voice in relation to the burning bush). Do not trust everything that you thought as been true just because you thought of it! The physical world does not run in accordance to the sequence of your thoughts. By mixing the physicality of reality-terms with mentally delusion-terms, it is possible to conclude into any kind of believable delusions which creates fantastic worlds that do not exist. Political ideologies, commercial advertisers and our very own wishful thinking follow the pattern-style set by millennia of religiousness. It all began with the delusional story of Adam, Eve and the apple tree (all reality-terms) and mixed with delusion-terms such as the talking-snake and heaven.

Since our brains are biologically adapted to look for pattern-meaning in life, we have been adapted; by centuries of religious delusions, and we have transferred the essence of delusions, into other spheres of real life. There are many so called "atheists" who are angered at God for not delivering on their wishes so they "punished" God by no longer believing in him. But the criminality of pattern-delusions which humanity has suffered by the Nazi ideology (a mixture of reality-terms and delusion-terms) has caused the extermination of 20.000.000 "sub-humans" in WWII. The Stalinist, Maoist or the Khmer ideology in both China and Laos; the delusions of the martyrdoms' heaven with its 72 virgins available to ISIS Muslim suicide bombers, the delusional Papist offer of "resurrection" of all the Crusaders" who died in the Christians holy wars against the Muslims, and the list of delusional crimes against humanity can go on. All those who faithfully followed such delusions died or have indiscriminately killed men, women and children in concentration camps or in killing fields. Religious faith based indoctrination of countless human generations in accepting delusions in combination with our biologically programmed brains to look for patterns in life, has created a biological adaptation in our psychic make-up. Perhaps there is a historical statistical probability that needs to be further investigated to discover convincing evidence by natural scientists, biologists and neuroscientists.

It is beyond my own qualifications to offer scientific conclusions of the aforementioned subject. However, the idea was intriguing! This was when I was in a position of witnessing the dramatic effects between reality-based terms and delusion-based terms and the resulting consequences. In an adult education class, I presented an experimental story to my students that, I do not longer recall its origins. The point of this experimentation was to see if my students will accept---as reality or delusion---this 500 years old story on the subject of differentiating between material reality and delusion. If you accept this story as a possible reality based narrative, why? If you choose that this story is based on delusion and acting upon it will be a human tragedy, why?

The key reality-terms of this story are *the King, the Castle, the Soldiers, the Prince, the Cobbler, the King's Slippers,* and the illusion-terms are, *the Magician, the Magic-pill and Inter-changed Personalities*. The rest of descriptive and prescriptive terms are used as props. Let us begin with the classical, once upon time....

"In a far way city-state of Agnostos there lived a King in the hill castle over looking his subjects below. The King governed his subjects fair, but with a strict enforcement of his laws.

Within the King's family there was a very spoiled nephew the Prince who was in the habit of looking to cause any mischief in order to entertain himself. But the Prince was always careful not to break the King's laws which had severe consequences.

In the village below, there was the Cobbler whose special task was also to mend and make new Slippers for the King. It is so happens the Cobbler was about to finish the best Slippers he ever made for the King. He thought, "Today I shall deliver his Slippers and receive my payment of gold coins."

So far the story is told by using reality-based terms to support illusionary based terms of the *"city state Agnostos, the King, the Cobbler and the*

Slippers" which do not really exist. This also means that, in order for an illusion to make sense, it needs reality-based terms. In this way, the reality based terms will solidify the presentation of the illusion.

The same principle using *reality* based terms mixed with *delusion* based terms, applies to primitive Arabian theistic myths that are presented in the Qur'an or tribal legends in a logical way to naïve or self-deluded religious devotees. Let us continue…

"When the Cobbler had the King's Slippers ready, he began ascending towards the hill castle, eager to deliver them to the King. As it is so happened, the Prince was descending the hill and he and the Cobbler greeted each other as their paths crossed.

Curiosity got the best of the Prince who asked the Cobbler what was in his bag he was carrying. The Cobbler replied that he was carrying the King's Slippers about to deliver them. The Prince demanded to see them, and the Cobbler complied, not expecting that the Prince will keep them for himself. All the Cobbler's protests did not help him to retrieve the Slippers back. The Cobbler had no choice but to continue with his ascent and to inform the King that his Slippers were stolen by his nephew the Prince. The King was furious and sad at the same time because stealing a King's property carried the mandatory death penalty, that is, D E A T H with no chance of appeal."

Although the story is definitely a myth, it still makes sense because it is supported by reality-based terms and has a logical sequence to it. And so….

"The King immediately ordered his soldiers to seek and arrest the Prince in order for him to face the consequences demanded by law.

Here the Prince had two choices, either faces the death penalty for stealing the King's Slippers, or find some way of escaping punishment.

Choosing the best choice available to him, the Prince visited a famous Magician; who lived in the forest, and ask for his help. After listening to the Prince's story, the Magician decided to offer the Prince a powerful Magic Pill. Once this Magic Pill is swallowed there will be an inter-change of Personalities including all memories between the Prince and the Cobbler.

As soon as the Prince swallowed the Magic-Pill something extraordinary happened; he had now all the pass memories, hopes and aspirations, his wife and children, dreams and thoughts: but of the Cobbler.

This means that he was still looking like Prince but with Cobbler Personality (PCP). PCP physically looked like the Prince but had no knowledge about his past life as the real Prince. This PCP now knows how to make shoes and slippers, the location of his shop and the names of all his neighbours.

Simultaneously, the real Cobbler felt that there was a change taking place within him. He no longe recognised the shop he was in, who the people

655

around him were, and why every one was calling him Cobbler. He was in fact now the Prince. In fact, he had the Prince's memories of a comfortable living in the King's palace, with all the wealth and servants available to him. His appearance was of a poor man's clothes, but he physically still looked like the Cobbler. But in fact he now was the Cobbler with the Prince's Personality; He was the (CPP).

When the King's soldiers arrested PCP he protested that the soldiers had the wrong man. He said, "I am not the Prince, I am the Cobbler" but the soldiers still brought him before the King. The dialogue between them...

King: *Prince, you have stolen my Royal Slippers.*

PCP: *No my King, I did not steal your Royal Slippers, in fact I am the Cobbler who made them for you.*

King: *You are not the Cobbler, you are the Prince, with Prince's clothes, with Prince's looks and every one here can see that you are the Prince.*

PCP: *My King, I am telling you that I am the Cobbler, and if you take me to my shop, I can start making you a new pair of Royal Slippers. This will prove to you that; although I look like the Prince, in fact, I am the Cobbler.*

So, the King, the PCP and the soldiers descended the hill castle and through the villages' roads they finally arrived at the "Cobbler's Shoppe" as the wooden sign said. As they entered they found CPP sitting not knowing what the fuss is all about....

King: *Oh there you are my good friend Cobbler (CPP). This fellow (pointing to PCP) claims that he is the Cobbler instead of the Prince, but as you can also see, he looks like Prince, so he is the Prince.*

PCP: *I am telling you my King that I am the Cobbler, so let me tell you the names of all my neighbours, the names of my wife and children, and that if you lift that small wooden plank on the floor you will find some coins that I have been saving.*

These claims were proven correct.

King: *Cobbler (CPP) what have you to say about all this, who are you?*

CPP: *I am and I look like the Cobbler, and there is nothing more I can say. This is my home, my wife, my children and my Shoppe.*

So, the King, the CPP, the CPC and the soldiers went back to the Royal Palace. Once there the King gathered his advisers and places this direct question:

King: *Who is going to face the capital punishment (Death) for the capital offence that was committed? Who wast going to be CPP or PCP?*

The reader has 3 choices to make: A) the First is to find guilty CPP; B) the second choice is to find PCP guilty, and; C) the third choice is not to pass a sentence to any of the two. In each case the reader may offer reasons for his or her decision; for after all, a man's life is in your hands!

This is a just fictional story or an illusion which contains parts of reality-based terms and fictional-based terms. There is of course nothing wrong with fictional stories unless one believes them and acts upon those beliefs. If you believe that the story is possible, and act by administrating a capital punishment on one of the characters, you have just committed a crime against someone because of your beliefs. If your answer is that no punishment should be administrated against any of these characters, was it because realised that the story is just fictional (not real) or for some other reasons? If you take away the illusion-related terms such as the Magician, the Magic Pill and the Inter-change of Personalities, then you have no fictional story at all. On the other hand, if you were to administrate a legal punishment, it has to be based on reality, verifiable evidence and perhaps witness testimonies, but not based on personal beliefs.

Humanity has faced many tragic events that were initiated by the delusionary powers of non existent or delusional beliefs. Reading books based on fictional-based terms of the time, the Nazi ideology of the Arian Race, the Final Solution and medical experiments on victims are full of delusional-related terms. Upon such delusional (fictional) based terms, the Nazi believers based real administrated punishments in accordance to those believes. Religious Books of the Jewish, the Christian and Muslim faiths are full of delusion related-terms that people believe to be real and follow, but not once asking for evidence based on reality-based terms. Do they know the difference between reality-based terms and illusionary-based-terms, in the sense that something is real, and that something is delusional and does not exist?

Delusional terms such as Heaven, the 72 Virgins waiting for the suicide-bombers, Life after Death, Miracles, Resurrections, Born Sinful, Walking on Water, Holy Wars, Infidels, Apostates, Witches, Intelligent Design, Praying for Cures; the Second Coming of Christ, Mohammad's Flying-horse, The Split in half of the Moon, the Tablets of the Ten Commandments, the Archangel, the Resurrection of Lazarus, the Virgin Birth, all these terms contain delusional connotations of pure fiction, illusions or delusions. Yet, again and again religious people, for centuries have acted upon them, with tragic results against innocents and helpless people.

Most people that believe in the God delusion do so because they have been taught so from a very early age and because of their own intellectual inability to differentiate between reality-based terms and false conclusions based on delusion-based terms. This plays a profound role in peoples' lives, in the belief in the existence of God which is a delusion-based term.

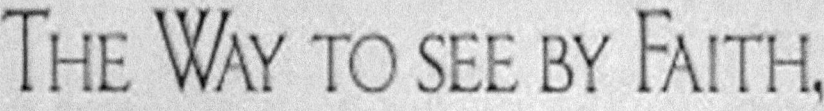

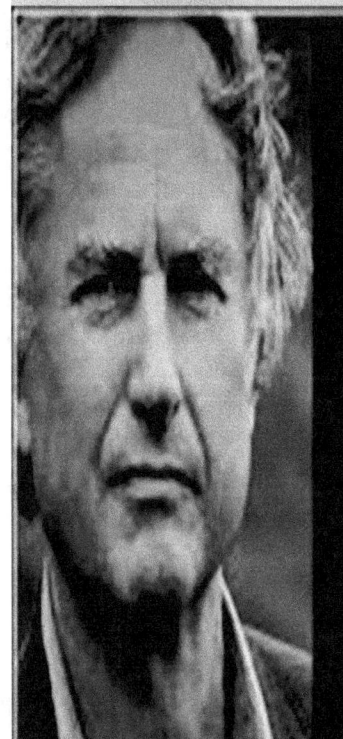

Destruction of Hellenistic civilisation by Christian mobs in Greece & Alexandria

RELIGIOUS FALLACIES

Let us begin with the age long question: is the coming end of the world true? The answer to this question is simply yes, the coming end of our planetary system, our galaxy, including our planet Earth, has been taking place for hundreds of thousand of millennia. This is a scientific conclusion, not a religious desire to end the world. It is estimated that the visual Andromeda will collided with earth in about 5.5 billion years in the future.

According to cosmic scientist Stephen Hawking, the *"Big Bang Theory"* states that our universe was not always in existence, for it was created by the "Big Bang" some 15 billion years ago. This is one of the most extraordinary discoveries of our modern cosmology. The estimated age of the Earth is about 4.5 billion years. The end of the Universe is certain to happen in 5 to 20 billion years as the Milky Way, our galaxy, will collide with our large spiralled neighbour, Andromeda. The galaxies, as we know them, will not survive. So go ahead and build your summer cottage, visit the Greek Islands, pay your bills or buy that new dress you always desired. If and when the end of the Universe comes, it won't be for at least another 5.5 to 20 billion years in the future. So relax and enjoy life, for you have plenty of time ahead of you!

This scientific theory does not contain any hateful motivation towards humanity or the physical world. It is not theistic, satanic or the Nostradamus kind of neither prediction, nor does it contain a pathological self-destructive morality that seeks the annihilation of the only home we have ever known. Biblical verses are schizophrenic and were written by people who felt no love for our magnificent nature, and who only wanted the end of the world to come sooner rather than later because we are all sinners. Those are ramblings of the godly, which are scaring the hell out of worshippers, especially the children who attend religious Sunday schools. The Jewish settlers of Palestine want to fill the land with the Jewish diaspora which would then entice the Messiah to return and cause the apocalyptic event for the destruction of the world. The Biblical prediction of Jesus' Second Coming means that humanity would die. Religious cults that support the end of the world want all of us to die, in order to have that messianic prediction come true. What about those who are not Christian or Jewish, who live in the Amazon Rainforest; the Hindus, the Buddhists and others who have nothing to do with the monotheist futuristic destructive predictions. Would they also die, along with the rest of us in the Jewish and Christian faith?

The plain truth is that none of us---atheist, humanist and theist---would ever get out of this world alive; that no special pleading, deliverance or appeals would ever suspend the Laws of Nature consisting of birth, growth, decay and death. No salvation, redemption or "supernatural" deliverance can produce more than a hollow and superficial appeal to the Sky-God. Only the force of humanity that endures would emancipate us from the chains of such deceptive superstition and religious delusions. It was our innate humanist solidarity which is now the source of morality and discovery from times immemorial. Those innate aspects belong to us and not to some despotic Sky-God.

The danger to our humanity is the theocratic enemy of fundamentalist Jews, Christians and Muslims. They have extended their octopus-tentacles from nuclear fanatics of the Israeli state to Mullahs' madrassas in the Arabian Peninsula, Pakistan, Iranian and Afghanistan. This theocracy includes the faith schools of the US and around the world. They are nothing more than religious bullies who make absurd claims that they have God on their side. These faith schools are brain-washing children with false-science to accept the biblical condemnation of nature and the end of the world. Students are literally bullied to surrender their reason to absolutism and to abandon their critical, dialectic and objective enquiry. This lethal and insane name is called religion.

Who will die the day the Jesus Second Coming? Let's assume that Christians are numbered at 1.2 billion strong. If 50% of them are devoted Christians of the "right-kind," then 600 hundred million will be saved into the bosom of Jesus. The remaining 600 million Christians and the rest of the earth's 6 billion people will die because they are not true Christians, for this includes all Muslims and Buddhists, India's religious cults, the Hindus and most of the indigenous population in the entire Amazonian Rainforest. You see, fundamentalist and right-wing Christians do not want heaven to be overcrowded, so others must die. They simply cannot wait for the end of the world, looking forward to humanity's final-solution because of its sinfulness, perhaps by the unleashing of an atomic war. In this case they are sure that God knows who's to live and who's to die and God's "chosen people," the Jews, would be first then to be saved. You and I will die wherever we are on that day; playing with our children in the park, going to work, taking care of an elderly person or flying a plane. In old Jewish mythology, achieving the end of the world would come when all the Jewry in the Diaspora returned to the Promised Land---which they are insisting of stealing from the Palestinians---and only when this happen would their Messiah appear. In the meantime, the crimes against the Palestinians are forgiven because those are committed in God's name.

Fundamentalist Christians are in agreement with the Jewish mythology that the earth is approximately 6,000 old. This was in fact been supported by the former Secretary of State of the US and twice presidential nominee, William Jennings Bryan, who gave court testimony in the 1930's that the Earth was created by God some 4,004 years BC on Saturday, October 22nd, at 6 pm. There are still fundamentalist Christians in the USA and Europe today who are helping the fanatical Israeli settlers to achieve the repatriation to ensure that the end of the world comes to its final Armageddon. They maintain the traditional religious contempt for the physical world in favour of their subliminal delusional idea of the second coming. In accordance with the biblical accounts, the "painful" and sinful living of human beings would come to an end, including all things humanity has accomplished. This includes medicine, science, art and letters, philosophy, theatre and poetry and all knowledge, including this book that you are reading at this moment. All would turn into scrap so that the cults of death, this hideous thing can be achieved by the fanatics. This is a fatalistic and an inescapable dilemma imposed upon the blindly faithful of all 3 monotheistic religions. Pakistani generals are not at all concerned with a nuclear holocaust, for they are sure that on that day, God would spare the devoted from the sinful. It is ironic that fanatic Muslims---who despise science---are looking forward to using science to achieve their hideous desire and sick dreams of the annihilation of the world.

The annihilation of this sinful world by the second coming of Jesus is a death wish which is shared by millions of Christians. To give you an example, in the 1999 millennia period, some of even the most educated people believed that the end of the world was coming at the turn of the year 2000. Some people sold their goods, some travelled to distant destinations to find refuge and others resorted to simply praying for salvation. This date was based on some primitive numerology and chronology which only existed in the Christian Calendar. The Chinese calendar, on the other hand, was far ahead of rest of the western world showing the year to be 4697-98.

We must understand what religion has done to our mammalian nature. It has encouraged the adaptation of our own natural predicament to look for false pattern-meaning. These patterns are relentlessly invented and re-invented by our brain and then pursued by us in order that we can govern our thoughts and behaviour. This also means that, when we cannot come up with any sensible explanation based on reason and evidence, we tend to come up with any false pattern-meaning rather than none at all. This is evident when we look at our historical development as a communal species.

We invent junk-science when we are ignorant of legitimate science or when it does not satisfy us or has not been discovered as yet. As such, we invented astrology before we had astronomy, junk-science before proven science, alchemy before chemistry, homeopathy or magical "cures" along medically proven drugs, benevolent-dictators before democracy and we had religious fallacies before we discovered evidence, reason and truth. Based on evidence of true pattern-meaning, reason and truth, we can now explain why one person gets sick and another does not, and it is not because of the false pattern-meaning that says God punishes the sinful i.e., the sick. As part of our biological evolution, we have been programmed to look for patterns in life, even when some false patterns attempt to suspend the Laws of Nature in favour of some obnoxious religious fallacy.

One of these obnoxious religious patterns is the coming end of the world which tries to suspend the Laws of Nature and explain it in non-scientific terms. The religious faithful believe that the Laws of Nature will be suspended if only they could pray louder, lighting-candles, offer promises and donations, help the Jewish to rebuild the Temple, and wish for God to destroy this world so they can finally go to heaven. A sequence to the religious pattern of humanity's Armageddon (the death of us) is the comforting religious delusion of *life after death.* There are a number of prophesies in the biblical texts which need to be analysed for their contradictory predictions and their desires for the end of the world. The bottom-line is that religiousness in the 1st century of Jesus was delusional, destructive and misanthropic, as it is today. Let us begin with a fundamental premise:

Deuteronomy 18:22
"When a prophet speaks in the name of the Lord, if the thing does not come about or come true, that is a thing that the Lord has not spoken. The prophet has spoken it presumptuously; you should not be afraid of him." We need to remember this verse, because many of Jesus' prophecies did not come true!

In Mark 13:1, Jesus admires the Temple in Jerusalem,
"wonderful stones and wonderful buildings" and in his next breath, he declares that the Temple would be destroyed,

Mark 13:2, *"Not one stone shall be left upon another..."*

Mark 12:3, Jesus was positioned *"opposite the Temple"*

Mark 13:4, When people ask Jesus when *"these things"* will be destroyed, they did not get an exact day and time, only that the destruction of the Temple would happen due to apocalyptic events, such as, the sun will stop shining, the moon will darken and stars will fall. These events will happen when Jesus returns, but he has not!

Mark 13:26, *"with great power and glory"* to gather his people. These are the apocalyptic events in according to the Gospel of Mark.

In **Mark 13:30,** *"Truly I say to you, this generation [40 years] will not pass away until all these things take place."* The delusional Jesus was sure of the destruction of the world during his life-tine, that is, before 33 AD. This message was also repeated, for the ill educated and ignorant, in

Mathew 24:34 and **Luke 21:32,** many Christians in the 1st century believed that the second coming of Jesus, and the end of the world were eminent, and will happen during their lifetime. These delusions were vastly propagated to 1st century religious communities resulting in mass expectations of these apocalyptic events, in where Paul states:

1 Corinthians 7:29 *"the time is short,"* and again Paul in

1 Thessalonians 4:17, *"we who are alive and remain,"* when Jesus returns. The author repeats Paul's declaration of the return of Jesus in,

Revelation 22:7, *"And behold, I am coming quickly"*

Revelation 22:12, *"Behold, I am coming quickly"*

Revelation 22:20, *"Yes, I am coming quickly"*

You may recall in **Mark 13:30**, that Jesus was very specific about his time of return from death, and his generation must have heard him saying these words. However, they have been dead for 2,000 years and not one of them ever came back to testify on Jesus' return. They died without seeing *"all these things taking place."* Here Jesus' false sayings, comes to mind according to the premise in **Deuteronomy 18:21&22,** the *"Lord has not spoken."* Was Jesus then, a false prophet? Was the "Jesus" a mythical man; or one the biblical authors created, in order to support their own delusions? **Does** it mean as in, **Mark 13: 26 -27**, that Jesus will not be *"coming in the clouds"* and *"gather together his elect"* and not *"all these things taking place"* during his own life time? In fact, this is exactly what did not happen. If one applies the specificity of **Deuteronomy 18:21&22;** the prophecy did not come true, and God did not said it, thus Jesus was not a true prophet. In the Gospel myths, the authors put Jesus' voice on them as if they were original sayings. Furthermore,

Matthew 16:28, continues by saying, *"Truly, I say to you, there are some of those standing here who shall not taste death until they see the Son of Man coming in his Kingdom."* The authors tells believers not to despair, and in

Mathew 10:23, *"But whenever they persecute you in this city, flee to the next; for truly I say to you, you shall not finish going through the cities of Israel before [or until] the Son of Man comes."*

You need to remember that Israel was a very small country with very few cities and to go from one city to the next on such a small real-estate will not take long. Thus, the end of the world was expected to take place soon, and within their lifetime before the end of the 1st century. Again Jesus speaking in,

Mathew 23:36, *"Truly, I say to you, all these things shall come upon this generation."*

The end of the world will come when, **Mathew 26:64**, *"[Y]ou will see the Son of Man sitting at the right hand of the Power and coming on the clouds of heaven."* To whom was Jesus was addressing *"you will see"* is no other than the *High Priest Caifas, 18-36 CE.*

For Jesus, the end of the world was a sure thing, **Mark 9:1**, *"Truly, I say to you, there are some of those who are standing here who shall not taste death until they see the kingdom of God after it has come with power."* A similar message is repeated in Mark **14:62** & **Luke 9:27**.

In 1**Thessalonians 4:16-17**, "For *the Lord himself will descend from heaven [and] we who are alive and remain shall be caught up together with [the resurrected] to meet the Lord in the air."*

The above prophecies are all referring to the imminent destruction of the world; the second coming of Jesus, the resurrection of the dead, the ascend in the air of the chosen people, the appearance of God's power through the clouds, the death of the rest of non-believers, the multi-theist Roman occupiers of Israel and the non-believer Jews were to be destroyed along with the earth. This was the ultimate exhibition of hatred and misanthropic desire expressed in these prophecies. None of these absurdities, delusions and hatred came true.

By the year 60 CE, the church leaders were concerned that Jesus' promise to return had not happened, and some cause had to be found to justify this fallen prophecy (or false pattern-meaning), in

2Peter 3:9, *"The Lord is not slow about this promise, but he is patient towards you, not wishing for any to perish but for all to come to repentance."*

When a prophecy fails, religionist groups, including all three monotheistic religions, turn to a centuries' old proven adaptation strategy to justify that failure. Among the things crucial to such religious survival is the quick, confident and innovative reaction of the groups' leadership to rationalise the failure of the prophecy. In **2 Peter 3:9,** we see an example of this: Jesus did not fail to return, it is a mere delay until the day when all people on earth (100%) *"come to repentance."*

The 1st century Christian believed the Jesus return was a sure thing and would take place within their (40 years) generation. This did not happen! So, how do believers deal with a fallen prophecy? It is important to know that believers have been dealing with failures of prophecies quite successfully, and Christianity has survived for all these centuries, by an array of adaptational strategies. Why is that? It is because its application of an array of adaptational strategies, including the spiritualisation of prophecies, a successful rationalisation, are the most important factors for contributing to the maintenance of beliefs in the event of a prophetic failure. All three large monotheistic religions have a broad and intricate ideological system. They include miracles and resurrections, hell and fire, repentance, heaven and afterlife, spirits, prophecies, saints, etc. The failure of prophecies is characterised as a test of faith, merely one component. Most of the time the failure of prophecies, is regarded as being a human error. It is the fault of others, rather than admitting their own self-delusion and false prophesies. Blaming others is evident in,

2 Peter 3:3-4, *"...mockers [who] will come with their mocking [will raise their voices and say] "Where is the promise of his coming?"* mockers are *"following their own lusts"*

As such, it is not Jesus' prophecy of return that has failed; rather it is the "mocker's" fault for spreading doubt among believers. The "blame others" rationalisation practiced by believers is a continual phenomenon since the early days of Christianity. Therefore, the adaptation of the "blame others" ploy is a well-versed and a major part of religious DNA, whether it is Christianity, Judaism or Islam. In fact, no one should be surprised to see the "blame others" ploy as often as in the religious activities of Baptist churches, televangelists and mega-churches. Christianity offers believers a broader and much more complex set of beliefs than any other religious group. It does not merely offer a prophecy "here and there," but an entire framed-system of comprehensive worldview, and a sense of personal and collective identity within its social structure.

There is an existing faith methodology—eschatology---which "helps" believers deal with the final catastrophic events of mankind with ease or comfort. Any fallen prophecy is still a part of a dense indoctrination and practice of significant beliefs and activities. This system is so broad that it is able to embrace and minimise all biblical religious contradictions. The gravity of belief's uncertainty or non-conformation is shifted upon the believers' mind, not on religious fallacies. The solution plainly lies in blind faith, for God is bigger than one's doubt and, in the end, it is the belief-system which the believer holds that entices him to devote himself to his religion. This blind faith is subsumed to renew his faith in prophecies, even when those prophecies or miracles have failed to come true. The broader mission within the Christian belief system is allowing adherents a certain amount fallacy without any significant negative affect on their religious faith. Blind faith, therefore, provides the kind of resilience, displayed by faith-based groups in the face of prophetic failures, which diminishes any doubting experience. The negative impact of prophetic failure is therefore, much less than any imagined by non-believers. Believers tend to easily adapt and even ignore evidence against the fallacies of their religious beliefs. For instance, if Jesus really meant what he stated in the above **Mark 13:30,** the prediction has failed the above **Deuteronomy 18:22** fundamental premise and test. Religious advocators offer believers a rationalisation in support of their false-claim: Jesus' prediction did not fail; it meant something other than what it declared. Again this prediction of Jesus return is clearly stated in, **Mark 13: 26-27,** *"And then they will see the Son of Man [Jesus] coming in the clouds with great power and glory. And then he will send forth his angels, and will gather together his elect from the four winds, from the farthest ends of the earth, to the farthest end of heaven."* But this event never happened nor did the predicted end of the world, even though in **Mark 13:23**, Jesus said to his followers, *"Behold, I have told you everything in advance"* of all the things he wrongly predicted would came true. I am not sure why Christians believe anything Jesus says, or others claimed that Jesus has said. Jesus was wrong and his prophecies fail!

Among the futuristic apocalyptic claims, one has to do with the creation of the State of Israel in 1948. Using various rationalisations, religious futurists ignore the fact that there is not a word in the bible about the creation of the modern State of Israel, yet they are still trying to insert this notion into **Mark 13**. They are trying to historicise the part of Jesus' words, in

Mark 13:28-29 *"Now learn from the parable of the fig tree: when its branches has already become tender and put forth its leaves, you know that summer is near. Even so, you too, when you see these things happening, recognise that He is near, right at the door."* Many Israeli and right-wing Christians are attributing this to Jesus talking about the creation of Israel in 1948. The great charlatan Hal Lindsey reads on his book, *"Late Great Planet Earth,"* that *"The figure of speech of the "fig tree" has been a historic symbol of national Israel. When the Jewish people, after near 2,000 years of exile, under relentless persecution, became a nation again on 14 May 1948, the "fig tree" put forth its first leaves."* This delusional right-wing Christian author is not so much a pro-Israeli, but rather he stands for the countdown to the world's Armageddon, starting on the day Israel was created in14 May 1948. In addition, the same author published another book *"The 1980s Countdown to Armageddon"* when he was sure that the 80's would be *"the last decade of history."*

One must remember that a Jewish biblical generation was 40 years, which means that by 1988 the world would have been destroyed, to the delightfulness of the religious delusionary. This catastrophic event did not happen, but thousands of believers bought his books, all awaiting the end of the world. Some gave away their possessions, and the author sold many books and got rich at the expense of the ignorant, the ill-educated and self-deluded. To assure the ignorant, ill-educated and idiots of his prediction, the author clearly stated that *"Within 40 years or so of 1948, all these things could take place."* Of course, here we are, a number of decades later in a new millennia and nothing has happened. As a charlatan of religiousness, the fraudulent author encourages his readers to keep buying his revived books in order to keep up with the latest updates. It should also be noted that in neither **Mark 13,** nor in the entire bible, is there a reference to a "Fig Tree" in relation to the State of Israel of 1948, nor is there any biblical reference mandating the restoration of Israel as a primary condition for the end of the world.

Aside from this primary condition, the right-wing Christians in the USA believe that their next popularised condition to meet, is the construction of the Jewish Temple on its traditional site in Jerusalem where the Dome of the Rock (built 60 years after Mohammad's death) is located. This is a core point of violent confrontation between Muslims and Jews. The Jews want to re-build the Jewish Temple so that their Messiah will appear which will cause the end of the world, a notion that is shared by right-wing Christians, of the USA and Canada. Again, this is the site on which the Muslim Dome of the Rock (built in 691 AD) is located.

Earlier, I noted that right-wing Christian fundamentalists fully support the settlers' aspirations for building the Jewish State of Israel. The question now is, why such devoted interest in the Jewish state of affairs? There are some crazy and incendiary ideas behind their approach which may potentially lead to the destruction of the real-estate where Israel and Palestine are located. The dream of rebuilding the Jewish Temple is one such potentially dangerous idea, unless someone simply believes that these ideas just silly ideas which merely exist in the minds of the zealots, but they are not. When you visit the site of *The Temple Institute*, an organisation that strives to rebuild the Temple for

"...the fulfilment of the Biblical prophesies that promise the reestablishment of the Holy Temple in Jerusalem,...seeking to...rekindle the desire and yearning for the rebuilding on the Holy Temple and [to] help to prepare as much as possible for the actual rebuilding." In actuality, The Temple Institute has employed people to prepare the various sectors of the Temple, with meticulous priestly garments in ancient style, and to follow particular

instructions in the biblical scriptures of the Jewish Bible.

In December 2007, the Institute announced that the completion of the headpiece of the Temple's High Priest is ready, and in accordance with **Exodus 22:26-27.** The Institute also announced that *"[W]e have begun work on architectural blueprints for the Third Temple, including cost projection, modern supplies, electricity, plumbing, computers, etc."* It should be noted that much of this work has been financed by the US fundamentalist Christians committed to this futuristic perspective. It should be noted that the whole building project places Christian, Jewish and Muslim on an apocalyptic collision course. Muslim religious leaders regard any attempt by Jews to take over the Dome of the Rock as a core sign of an impending Islamic apocalypse. According to the writer Rob Dreher's article *Red-Heifer Days*, appearing in the National Review Online in April 2002, there has been at least four plotting attempts to clear the space where the Temple Mount stood. Some of the plotters were part of the top leadership of the Israeli army and the police forces. Dogmatic faith in religious mythology does not allow for possible political compromise. In a piece of real-estate ownership that was promised by God to two different ethic groups there could never be peace. There is no room to negotiate between two dogmatic sets of belief; a Jewish and a Muslim. When one side believes that this is in the prophetic schedule, that this schedule is historical before it even happens, that this is how God favours one group over the other, and this is how events will bring about the final phase of human history; under those circumstances, both Jews and Palestinians cannot negotiate peace or anything else.

Fundamentalism in support for the end of days of the Dome of the Rock is a chilling prospect. The only real reason that fundamentalist Christians advance this futuristic idea is because they refuse to acknowledge Jesus' plain meaning of **Mark 13:30,** *"Truly, I say to you, this generation will not pass away until all those things take place"* was a faulty prediction for his contemporary generation. In fact, by the Bible's own standards set in **Deuteronomy 18:22**, warning about false prophecies which are not from God, Jesus was not a true prophet. Other apologists have taken the term "generation" to mean something other than *"people of this day"* or *"people of this time,"* yet there is not textual reason to translate the term "generation" in any other way. Jesus was wrong and his predictions were faulty and therefore he was not a true prophet.

MOTHER TERESA: LOVE OF SUFFERING

Was *Anjeze Gonxhe Bojaxhiu* (1910-1997), better known as Mother Teresa, not so saintly after all? Here, some of my readers may wonder why on earth I would go after the memory of shrinking old lady, who devoted her entire life to her religious calling? Well, I admit that I am guilty only of the fact that I am examining the influence and the motives of a woman who had openly boasted that she was operating more than 500 religious convents in more than 105 countries, not counting India. Was she chairing and operating a religious multinational corporation which main selling product was the "religious conversion to Catholicism" under the guise of charity and caring for the poor? **Her** zeal assumed the proportion between what is ordinary charity work and what religious dominance her convents excerpt in the countries they operate in. Her *Home for the Dying* resembled photos of Nazi concentration camps such as Dachau, with no chairs, just stretched mats (as beds) virtually no medical attention or painkillers beyond Aspirin. Yet her global institutional income was, and still is, more than enough to outfit several first class medical facilities in India. You see, the decision not to relieve the poor's pain and suffering was a deliberate one, for the aim was to follow "Jesus suffering," not to relieve of suffering but to prolong a vicious religious-cult based on death, suffering and subjection.

For instance, in the *Hospice for the Dying*, Mother Teresa's (MT) sisters will talk to the sick patients about their need to find Jesus in their last days on Earth. Sick, poor of Muslim and Hindi faith; who are mostly ill educated, perhaps even ignorant, have little understanding of the sisters' attempts to obtain their religious conversion to Catholicism. They agree to the conversion out of desperation for salvation or simply agree due to their apathy. The sisters then, baptised everyone to Christianity without them knowing the significance of the act of baptism. In according to MT estimates more than 29,000 terminally ill were baptised in 1996 in this manner. This scandalous act, of course, created a big scandal among the Muslim and Hindi religious sectors. For instance, *Mohan Bhagwat*, head of India's most powerful charity organisation, the *National Volunteers Corps*, has accused MT organisations of serving the poor in order to persuade them to convert to Catholicism. Mohan stated, *"[their] service would've been good, but it [has] one objective, to see that the person who was been helped felt obliged to become a Christian"* and that *"...our services isn't like Mother Teresa's."*

Was her care for Kolkata's, India, poor and sick dubious and her handling of millions of cash, received as donations, was at least suspicious? Let me begin by saying that Mother Teresa (MT) followed the long traditional right-wing fundamental Catholic values and practices of loving poverty, but never expressed love for the poor. In fact, the sick and poor were used as a means to an end: spreading the twisted side of right-wing Catholicism. In a 1981 press conference she was asked, *"Do you teach the poor to endure their lot?"* She replied, *"I think it is very beautiful for the poor to accept their lot, to share it with the passion of Christ. I think the world is being much helped by the suffering of the poor people."*

One may say that her belief and her idolising of the suffering of the poor is part of the popular right-wing theology which is misanthropic and full of absurdities and contradictions. Therefore, it can be safely affirmed that popular theology; practiced by MT's *Missionaries of Charities* and the *Hospice for the Dying*, can be prescribed to be vulgar, demonic and evil. When it comes to the practices of the right-wing popular religion, propagators like MT are guilty of every possible dishonesty, and inducement of their belief, on the poor, that they must endure their suffering just as Jesus endured his.

For 30 of the 45 years of MT charity work, was contacted under the influence of enormous—counting in millions of pounds and dollars--wealth from dubious sources; stashed away to serve other purposes, rather than helping the poor and the sick. Although millions of dollars were deposited in various banks accounts and financial institutions, most of these accounts were kept secret. Here, I hope to answer the question; where the millions of dollars for the poorest of the poor gone?

The Hospice for the Dying is a remote treatment facility for the poor and the sick of Kolkata, India. The facility is divided into large rooms where 50-60 plastic-gurney mattresses located in each room. The walls of the facility are unwashed and not painted to maintain the minimum standards of cleanness. Each room has a number of high up windows to provide a degree of daylight but they increase the sense of isolation from the outside world. The rooms for men are separated from the women's rooms. Mattresses are lying on the cement floor, one next to the other, with people on them who look like they could be in a picture of Nazi concentration camps. There are no bed sheets or pillows on them, just a thin plain plastic-mattress. The facility's large rooms have no chairs to sit, no tables to eat, no material to read or games to play, nor are there "companions" to keep the occupants active and mentally occupied. The longitudinal walking corridors between the mattresses are used by the nuns who walk up and down while correcting the sitting or laying positions of the occupants. There is no playground for the ill children to be entertained and no yard for the adults to walk and pass their time. Outside doctors visiting the facility have observed a significant lack of hygiene, unfit conditions, shortage of actual care, poor quality food and no painkillers. Volunteers and sisters with no medical training have to make their own decisions about the care of patients because of the lack of doctors or medically trained personnel, and they do not distinguish between curable and incurable patients. The volunteers' indifference towards the medical safety of the patients is evident when the same needles are used, over many times, but they are not sterilised, only rinsed in cold water.

So the curable poor who could otherwise survive will be at risk of dying from infection and lack of treatment. It should be noted that not all the sick are terminally ill, while others are "housed" in the facility, hoping for curative medical treatment that never comes. The occupants are men, women and children under the care of the untrained personnel of the facility. The Hospice for the Dying is therefore a miss-named, for not all of the poor occupants are terminally ill. For instance, a child may accompany its sick parent, sharing living space with their mother. When children are abandoned, or are mentally ill they maybe housed in the same kind of facilities.

In 1952, MT opened her first Home for the Dying in a building structure made available, free of cost, by the local government of Kolkata. With the financial assistance of local official and businessmen, she converted an abandoned Hindu Temple into a Home for the Dying. Her motto, which became very appealing to all those who were participating in her charity works, were to care for *"the hungry, the homeless, the blind, the crippled, the lepers, the unwanted and unloved, and people who became a burden to the society and are shunned by everyone."* By 1995, the original 13 members of her congregation in Kolkata had grown to more than 4,000 sisters running orphanages for victims of floods and mudslides, famine and epidemics. However, witnesses testified that, when the *Union Carbide* industrial disaster devastated the perpetually suffering local population, MT and her sisters were visiting the victims offering them icons of the Virgin Mary and exhorting them to pray instead of providing medical care, food, relief packages and blankets. Donations to support The Missionaries of Charities—before its fame--came from a number of local governments, businesses and private sources, and from multinational corporations located in India, such as the infamous *Union Carbide* operating in Bhopal area. Volunteers from local areas or foreign countries, with little or no experience in nursing-care, serve the inmates of the facilities in whatever was their need. In 1981, there were 200 charitable organisations operating in Kolkata, India and Mother Teresa's Missionaries of Charity assistance to the poor was numbered in the few hundreds, while the Assemblies of God charity organisation was feeding 18,000 people per day.

Following her reward of a *Nobel Peace Prize* in 1979, MT used the world's mass right-wing media and her celebrity status to propagate the Catholic Churches' condemnation of abortion, use of contraception and divorce. Her institutions continued to maintain the same ethos of her "love of suffering," for her views of the poor's suffering was that: the more they suffer the closer will bring them to Jesus. Human suffering had a spiritual value in the distorted world of her religious fanaticism. The support, recognition and the millions of donations she received have aroused suspicion of fabrication and criticism because she presented a degrading image of Kolkata in order to raise more donations and her fame around the world. Her particular false love for the suffering of the poor served her as a light-beacon of austerity ethos which her foundations still maintained, even after her death in 1997. MT vast expenditure of donated money was not used to alleviate the suffering of the poor people by establishing modern medical facilities in Kolkata or transforming the dreadful Home of the Dying into a much more modern hospice. Any modern care, such as systematic diagnosis and strong analgesics for the cared would have disrupted the religious ethos of the suffering of the poor, at her Home for the Dying. She always idealised a life of suffering which she imposed on the sick through lack of pain-relievers and illness combating medicine other than aspirins.

The Missionaries of Charity in both Bangladesh and India appear to run in a style of the British Poor Houses of the 18th and 19th centuries, a warehouse to store the ill and the poor. For the millions upon millions of donations the charity receives from around the world, a great deal more modern medical care for should have been available to the sick. The current administration (2017) of the world's Missionaries of Charity follows and acts on the delusional theories and practices of MT which maintains that *"we are a charity house not a medical facility."*

Everything that most of us have idealised about MT charity organisations; her beliefs and her practices, are basically false. It must be one of the most successful religious con-jobs or earth's greatest hoax amongst all other religious charity charlatans, and there many of them in the 21st century. MT was corrupt, nasty, cynical and cruel. Her legacy was embedded in the religious aspirations of her organisations in more that 105 countries around the world which bear her name and that of her organisations. These aspirations were built as institutions under "charity" status in order to promote the Catholic faith and convert indigenous people to Catholicism, not to assist the destitute and the dying. For instance, MT original institute still practices the same cruel attitude towards the poor and dying in India today. Under the cruel slogan and justification of, "we are not a medical facility," MT declared *"that we see Christ in [their] broken body, and we touch Him and that touch is [and] comes from the deep faith that Christ cannot deceive."* It was her obsession with her "love for suffering" and her obsession that people must suffer in order to come close to Jesus. MT and her institutions should be held accountable for creating a cult of suffering which definitely has a harsh side. Even in the Charities' environments there is the residents' pain and misery when dealing with strict instructions to imitate and to be "like Mother Teresa," to subvert every kind of human emotion. If one of the goals of the Missions is to love people, then the nuns serving are emotionally cut-off from loving people. Although the Missions are fraudulently in the business of alleviating "suffering" they do tend to strongly believe in the act of suffering, and it is very difficult to achieve both in the same time.

In fact in according to Bill Donohue, President of the Catholic League, *"Mother Teresa wanted people to live in impoverished conditions, so she can identify with the poor she was serving."* Does this mean that people must suffer so that MT can be enlightened? If so, this is a very twisted form of faith. In fact, MT was not the least interested in alleviating poverty and, with no exaggeration; millions of Third World poor died due to her "love for suffering" and millions remained poor and ignorant, more sick and more fearful. One means of keeping the faithful together, is the old-time deception of maintaining the status of the ill-educated and the ignorant.

In fact, the "Home for Dying" destitute in Kolkata, India, does not function as a hospital, does not provide medical attention; it is a place for victims to suffer and die under the rules of the Catholic faith. Those institutions use charities to "help the poor" from any oppressive states or individuals, that stole the money from the poor in the first place. How does the Catholic Church justify this kind of sleaze? As usual, it justifies by means of theft and deception and by taking from the "rich crooks to help the poor." This is a tolerance of crime against the poor by the rich and powerful. She raised more than $ 75 million during her last 20 years of her life. Even today, in 2017, the Missions of Charity still continue to refuse publishing their accounts of receivables and expenditures for the public to obtain them. Much of the international donations given to the Missions of Charity are kept in Vatican's "Bank of the Holy Spirit.

Most of the money MT raised was spent on religious activities, not for the poor. Now, more than 50% of the *Missionaries of Charity* around the world are nunneries and brothers' retiring in comfort homes, not what people thought they were giving money for. The money simply went to hire and indoctrinate a new bunch of complete obedient and illiterate India nuns, not for the poor and dying of Kolkata or around the world. They are indoctrinated in the concept of the "love of suffering" of the poor which justifies the lack of beds, lack of medical attention, the unsanitary communal toilets to defecate, and where the occupants are not allowed visits from friends or relatives. They must lie or sit on the bed all day long. The only ones that look after them are the non-qualified sisters and volunteers of the Missions. These sisters are up before daybreak and lead a life dedicated to prayer, service and simple living way of life, not at all unfamiliar to these women who come from India's impoverished village background.

Jean-*Claude Duvalier,* nicknamed *"Baby Doc,"* was the absolute power in Haiti from 1971-1986, when he was overthrown by popular uprising. During his reign of terror he maintained a notorious life style by getting involved in a multimillion dollar drug trade, selling body parts of dead Haitians, where thousands of Haitians were killed and tortured while hundreds of thousands fled the country. On May 27, 1980 he wed *Michele B. Pasquet* at the estimated cost of $2 million, though *The Christian Scientist Monitor* reported that the wedding *"was enthusiastically received by a majority of Haitians,"* by the poor and destitute people. In 1981, Mother Teresa (MT) flew to Haiti at the invitation of "Baby-Doc" to accept the *Legion d'Honneur* and millions of dollars donation from a corrupt politician who was found to have stolen millions of dollars from the improvised nation. Upon accepting the Legion d'Honneur MT praised "Baby-Doc" family as the Catholic *"who loved their poor"* and that *"their love was reciprocated."* MT knew that "Baby-Doc's" donations were stolen money from the impoverished Haitians, yet not once she offered to return the money.

***Ian** Robert Maxwell, (1923-1991)* was born *Jan Ludvik Hyman Binyamin Hoch* of a Yiddish-speaking Orthodox Jewish family from Ukraine. He became a British media mogul who built a successful publishing empire. He was a stern supporter of the Zionist occupation of Palestine and faithful to his religion. This, of course, did not prevent him from being a corrupt individual who stole money to support his extravagant life style. After his death it was revealed that he fraudulently misappropriated 450 million pounds from his employees' pension funds. MT received donations of millions of pounds from Maxwell; finding out afterwards about the embezzled funds, she praised him before accepting the stolen funds but was unwilling to return any of the stolen money.

Charles *Humphrey Keating Jr., (1923-2014)* was an American financier of the Lincoln Savings and Loan Association. Keating was a founder and activist of the anti-pornography organisation, *Citizens for Decent Literature,* and served as a member of the *President's Commission on Obscenity and Pornography*. In the early 1990s 23,000 people who invested 2 billion dollars of their money in Lincoln Savings lost their savings, and Keating was charged with embezzlement of millions of dollars. He was convicted and served 5 years in prison before he was released on legal grounds. He was praised, many times, by different religious denominations for his charitable work and moral standing against pornography. MT was one of his moral supporters who also received a hefty donation of 1.25 million dollars for her own, so-called, charitable work. During Keating's trial, MT was contacted, at the request of the persecutor asking her to return to the victims the 1,25 million she had received, but she refused to return any amount! During Keating's sentencing hearing, MT expressed her sympathy asking the US courts "to be lenient" towards Keating although he crossed the line between "business as usual" and fraud. The prosecuting attorney Paul Turley observed that *"No Church...should allow itself to be used as salve for the conscience of the criminal"* and pointed out that the donated money was stolen money: *"You have been given money ...that he has been convicted of stealing by fraud...do not keep the money [from those] that worked for it and earned."* Teresa never replied to Paul Turley's request and neither did the Vatican that has inherited the stolen funds following Teresa's death.

Enver Xoxha (1908-1985), during his rain as the Secretary of the Albanian Communist Party from 1941-1985, followed the repressive style of the *KGB* and *East German Stasi* and, at one point, more than one third of the population was either incinerated in labour-camps or interrogated by the Albanian repressive *Sigurimi*. The justice system regularly degenerated into *show-trials* in order to lessen dissidence. An estimated high number of political prisoners were executed; ranging from 5,000 to 50,000, during his regime. In August 1989, MT endorsed the violent regime of Enver Xoxha while visiting her home country of Albania. She was received by Xoxha's widow and a number of high officials and, subsequently, MT laid a bouquet on Xoxha's grave without ever commending against Xoxha's human rights abuse, including the persecution of Roman Catholic and Greek Orthodox clergy. But she did accomplish what she was out to accomplish: the regime's legal permission to acquire land property and material help to establish a number of her Missionaries of Charity.

Count Licio Gelli was born in Pistoia, Italy in 1919-2015. He was a financier, chiefly known for his role in the Vatican's Banco *Ambrosiano* financial scandal, and a well known Fascist "Black Shirt" volunteer sent by Italian dictator Mussolini to Spain in support of *Francisco Franco* Fascist regime. He was an Arch-Fascist and Grandmaster to the infamous P2 Fringe Masonic lodge, a *Third Reich* devotee with high level contacts including *Hermann Goring,* one of the chief architects of the Nazi regime. In 1996, Gelli was nominated as a candidate for the *Nobel Prize in Literature* supported by *Mother Teresa* and *Naguib Mahfouz* an Egyptian writer. Gelli's involvement with Banco Ambrosiano, an Italian bank whose main shareholder was the Vatican Bank, had to do with the bank's collapse in 1982, and later, it was revealed he was funnelling funds in support of the Somoza dictatorship and later to the *Contras* of Nicaragua and the *Solidarity* in Poland.

Mother Teresa did not serve the poor in India; she served the rich in the West. She helped them overcome their guilty conscience by taking millions of dollars and Euros from them. Some of her donors were dictators and convicted criminals who tried to whitewash their dirty hands. MT revered them for a price. I admit though that most of her supporters were honest people with good intentions who were deceived by her and succumbed to the illusion that the *"Saint of the Gutter"* was there for the poor, to wipe all their tears and put an end to their pain and suffering. Those who love their faith and illusion often refuse to see the material-reality. Do the poor of the world have to be grateful to the deceptive MT for the millions she collected in their name by her worldwide religious propaganda directed toward the honest and warm-hearted?

Mother Teresa may appear to some as an unfair target of the atheists but, rest assured, this is not the case because it is very important to expose the fraudulent nun. We all know that there are millions of poverty stricken people who suffer because it is nearly impossible to escape from poverty. This was also Mother Teresa's feigned concern. True enough, Mother Teresa was not the cause of people's poverty in Kolkata, India but she was a confirmed promoter of it because MT loved poverty but not the poor. For instance, human rights activists support women's rights for the empowerment over their reproductive system (i.e. the means to control the birth rate of unwanted children) instead of keeping them in the animal cycle of their biology (annual pregnancies). Add to this birth control, some limited financial seeds for start-up, small scale, women's enterprises, and success is proven. Mother Teresa's religious fundamentalism turned her against any kind of birth control---abortions or the use of condoms---due to her pseudo-morality indoctrinated by her Catholic faith. She claimed that abortion was murder and the use of condoms was against God's will, but preaching is not what women and the overpopulated and poverty stricken city of Kolkata needed.

It is very early in the morning and the sisters in Mother Teresa's Mission in

India are ready for their daily prayers. It is a life dedicated to simple living, a way of life not unfamiliar to many of the sisters who came from a poor village background. But the world's most extensive religious-based charity organization faced a loss of public trust from the very people that supported it financially. Despite all the devotion to serve the poor and the needy, the business of charity is under close scrutiny and financial accountability. More seriously, Mother Teresa's Missionaries is facing criminal charges of child abuse. Some of the babies under their care have been abandoned by single mothers and other children are cared for because they are mentally or physically challenged. Many of the care-staff come from overseas and are compassionate volunteers with little or no child-care experience. Some stay for a month and others stay a little longer because they realise that the Mission is short of staff and desperately needs their help. But it does not take long before deep reservations are felt. There are independent reports of sisters slapping and hitting children, bouncing their heads around, strapping children in chairs, keeping them unclean and neglected. These Sisters are illiterate, from remote backward villages, stupid and deluded, hysterical females who are afraid to express their ignorance of what is going on in the Missions in India. These hysterical girls take their frustrations out against the most vulnerable children in India, by being abusive and utterly punitive. **There** is a general neglect of medical attention and a lot more needs to be done with modern medical care. In short, the mission's is run in the style of the British poorhouse facilities of the 18th and 19th centuries. The Mission's defence has always been that *"we are not a medical order"* but they have never explained why people are not brought in to provide medical care since it does not appear the Missions are short of money.

Because of the likes of the overseas volunteers, the Missions are saving millions of dollars which it receives from all over the world. It is a genuine concern because the MT charity functions as a business monopoly and, because it receives an enormous amount of donations as well as large numbers of volunteers and monies from other charity organisations. Yet they provide little nutritious care, educational, emotional or outdoor activities. There is our social responsibility to debunk the myth of Mother Teresa. The mainstream media created an image of Mother Teresa that reflected our standard desire of perfect "motherhood" more than it reflected the reality of who Mother Teresa was. Above all she had that twisted logic of love for fatal suffering or a tangle view of love and pain based on a long discredited religious Catholic faith. To believe that suffering is the best sign of love demands the immolation of self for the beloved, which Mother Teresa was determined to follow all her life.

A deeper question should be asked about why the three monotheistic religions of the western world worship the fetishes of pain and suffering? This attitude of embracing pain and suffering is build not only in Judaism, Christianity and Islam, but also into other religions, especially in Buddhism. The tragic fact is that Mother Teresa's Catholic view of pain and suffering makes not distinction between avoidable and unavoidable suffering, and instead she cultivated a submissive acceptance of the twisted logic of love for pain and suffering. This is a dominant theme in the religion of Christianity and its church. A believer must endure things without attempting to change his condition, and it is their religious duty to suffer long. Such twisted logic does not permit the believer to take charge of his life and become master of his own destiny. They must simply surrender their well being, their dignity and their humanness to tolerate pain and suffering as long as possible. Thus, if they believe that their affliction comes from God and it is like Christ's, who are they to object God's demands? But let's not forget that the opposite is also true: believers, who willingly or unwillingly embrace this dreadful theology, encourage their friends and children to suffer, even taking it upon themselves to inflict it, not remove it, when they have the power to do so. You see, it is one thing to suffer well; it is another thing to invite it. In the case of the Mission, it is one thing to sit with sick poor people in their suffering, and it is another thing to let those poor people suffer because the Mission would not provide medical attention simply to meet the requirements of the Catholic religious dogma.

MT had, in many occasions, stated that *"there is something beautiful in seeing the poor accept their lot; to suffer it like Christ's Passion…the world gains much from their suffering."* Of course, the tradition of acceptance of pain and suffering has long been ingrained in religious theology. For example, the early Christians were fascinated by the concept of martyrdom; as it is also widespread and accepted in the Muslim world, the likes of St. Paul, Polycarp, Ignatius and the Jesuits of South America wanted to be martyred. It was such an honour for one to sacrifice, (an eternal reward) that they seemed to do anything in their power to accept pain and suffering--- even death---for their faith. They all took their examples from the Christian myth of Jesus' acceptance of his execution, and St. Paul who did his utmost to stay in chains which eventually ended with his execution---as legend has it. Anjezes Gonxhe's (Mother Teresa) ministry had a peculiar perception of suffering and death, suffering like Christ, and she viewed their dying as sharing in Christ passion.

She was known to wear a *cilice,* a steel-strap secured around her thigh that inflicts pain with inward-pointing spikes. Eyewitness, Sister Jeanne, confirms that MT participated in self-flagellation that turned her lower thighs red, then redder with white streaks, and that MT taught others that wearing spiked chains and self-inflicting pain allowed them to share Jesus work of redemption. This is simply the irrational hell of organised religion. Her use of fairytales to promote pain and suffering should be viewed with the utterly contempt it deserves.

In an overpopulated country like India, vilifying abortion and birth control is reckless at its worst. Refusing to a female cancer patient her pain killers, because the patient's *"suffering was like Christ on the cross, so Jesus must be kissing her."* This poor and terminally ill woman died a painful death, for the sake of a multi-millionaire, a religious, twisted fundamentalist. She used her fortune, which sat in bank accounts all over the world, to build religious institutions in her name, rather than purchase medical equipment and medicine for the poor under her supervision. She was essentially saying that, to extol the virtues of poverty, let the sick and the dying suffer, abandon medicine and birth control, all because that would take them closer to "Jesus." MT was so shockingly unreasonable, she bordered on being a repulsive, masochistic, misanthropic and psychopathic dwarf Albanian woman. How else can someone come to such positively dangerous conclusions, if not for religious faith? In all rationality, why would any sane person refuse pain killers to a dying woman in pain, other than for a belief in God? What an idiotic argument for an all loving-God that would be. This was a mentally insane and utterly sick nun who held water and bread out of children's reach so that they wallowed and kissed her feet, begging to be fed.

" WITHOUT SUFFERING OUR WORK WOULD JUST BE SOCIAL WORK, VERY GOOD AND HELPFUL, BUT IT WOULD NOT BE THE WORK OF JESUS CHRIST"
MOTHER TERESA

ILLUSTRATED

MEDALS AND HEFTY DONATIONS

BUT HER POOR & SICK STILL LIVED IN INHUMAINE CONDITIONS

THE POOR & SICK STILL LIVED IN INHUMANE CONDITIONS

ILLUSTRATED
YET, MT USED THE MILLIONS OF FUNDS SHE RECEIVED TO BUILD RETIREMENT HOMES FOR CATHOLIC CLERGY, NUNS AND RELIGIOUS SCHOOLS

THE POOR & THE SICK WERE TREADED WITH THE LOVE FOR SUFFERING

ILLUSTRATED
YET, MT USED THE MILLIONS OF FUNDS SHE RECEIVED TO BUILD RETIREMENT HOMES FOR CATHOLIC CLERGY AND NUNS AND RELIGIOUS SCHOOLS

THE POOR & THE SICK WERE TREADED WITH THE LOVE FOR SUFFERING

ILLUSTRATED
YET, MT USED THE MILLIONS OF FUNDS SHE RECEIVED TO BUILD RETIREMENT HOMES FOR CATHOLIC CLERGY AND NUNS AND RELIGIOUS SCHOOLS

ILLUSTRATED
YET, MT USED THE MILLIONS OF FUNDS SHE RECEIVED TO BUILD RETIREMENT HOMES FOR THE CATHOLIC CLERGY, NUNS AND RELIGIOUS SCHOOLS

THE PLIGHT OF CHILDREN

Atheist and Humanists are concerned over the spread of the indoctrination of children disguised as an education in religious or faith-based schools. Faith-based schools are the main source of spreading the virus of religiousness that distorts children's view of the world. Such distortion will perhaps affect them for the rest of their life and generations thereafter. Using the Holy Books as guides to their education, children are taught lessons from ancient biblical mythologies (of Hell and Fire, superstitions and damnation) as existing places and true historical events. Installing pattern-fear in the children's brains, faith-based schools are venerating biblical accounts of mass exploitation and murder of children,
Numbers 31:18, *"they shall kill every first born"* and the rape of young girls,
Samuel 15:3 *"kill all men and women, but keep unmarried girls for yourselves and do with them as you wish."*
This is clearly a brutish immoral and psychological abuse of children's innocence disguised as an education. They are taught to believe for the sake of believing and, because of such narrow scope, there is no encouragement for further or objective investigation and thus there is no advancement. They are taught the biblical myth of creation as a pseudo-science, of biology as an "intelligent design" and morality as exclusive accomplishment of religion. These arguments and claims are weak and can only be installed into the innocence of children's minds. With the assistance of the parents, faith-based schools are poisoning, with the virus of religion and indoctrination, the minds and lives of innocent children.
I grew up in the faith of the Orthodox Church. As a child attending elementary school, it was obligatory to listen to daily class of religious mythological-stories. Orthodox Christianity was gently imposed upon me by the cultural settings of the Greek society and, of course, my classmates. One of my earliest school memories was asking my teacher, during class assembly, with genuine curiosity; who was the creator of God? If God created the first people, Adam & Eve, and had two boys Cain and Abel, where did their wives come from? The teacher simply muttered something along the lines of: *"it does not work like that."* These questions may even have accelerated the process of my disbelief in religion. However, the final rejection of religion came about when I heard the teacher-priest proclaiming that; *"If a woman kills a "faggot" she will go to heaven."*
There is something bizarre about the virus of faith which leaves a terrible legacy. It divides future generations of children by giving them a faith-based

identity as Jewish or Christian, Muslim or Hindu the same as their parents' religion. Religious faith is thus a divisive force and children are divided from other children because they follow different rituals and because of their parents' religion. Such beliefs rob children of their own unique characteristics that define them as who they are individuals. Because such difference is constantly drilled into them in schools and at home, future generations of citizens are segregated from one another. Why is it allowed, to label children into such religious sub-categories as Catholic or Protestant in Ireland, Orthodox or Jehovah in Greece, Sunni or Shiite in Iraq, and Buddhist or Hindu in India? Don't parents know that their children are far too young to understand religious divisions; whether their God is better than the others' God? A visitor to the Middle East, India or Myanmar can witness how children of different faiths are separated and behave suspicious of one another. Children of different faiths do not play together; do not know anything about each other, which may eventually lead them to embark into future religious hostilities and social paths.

In the Orthodox Jewish groups inside Israel, Europe and North America, this divisive force is prominent in the sense that there are only inter-faith marriages taking place within the groups. This inter-breeding excludes the flow of new genes into Orthodox communities. For instance, long inter-breeding may result into low or poor pool-gene quality; as it appears in a number of children within the Orthodox Mennonite communities of Upper Canada, South America and elsewhere. In Orthodox communities' regardless of their social base, their faith is taken to its extreme. Their children are hoisted away from external influence and only attending segregated community functions and schools. Any entertainment function that involves the world beyond their segregation, such as TV or the Internet is strictly forbidden. None of the children of fundamental faith communities will ever have the chance to read my book, *Prisoners of Our Ideals,* Darwin's *Evolution and Natural Selection, the Origins of Life or the Ascent of Man,* and Richards Dawkins, *The Blind Watchman or Enemies of Reason* or the book by the late *Christopher Hitchings (1949-2011), God is not Great* nor will they ever read my book *The Moral Necessity of Atheism* nor will ever learn about the theory of the *Big Ban*g in the universe which took place 13.5 billion years ago.

Most of the faith-based school children will grow up believing that the universe is only 6,000 years old or about the age of the Agricultural Revolution in ancient Mesopotamia. They are victims of a distortive religious system of beliefs which they were born into, and of delusional traditions with roots lying in the biblical cultist mythology brought out of the desert by illiterate tribesmen of the Fertile Crescent and Arabian Peninsula about 4,000 years ago. The irony is that faith-based school students are innocent children who are fed proven falsehoods. Such imposing distorted traditional views are proven to be false by science, reason and evidence. Yet these children are not given the opportunity and freedom to choose for themselves their own views of the universe supported by evidence and not by false claims.

One of the core dynamics of organised religion is its adaptability to current political and social trends. In the last centuries, the religious industry has proven to be capable of re-inventing itself through myths, oppression and intentional distortion of human history. In the last part of the 20th century, religion in the Western World has shed its public authoritative image for a much more conciliatory attitude of spreading love instead of spreading authoritarian theism. This is a deliberate attitude, intended for public consumption, a trick which has a long history of success in organised religion. Such adaptability is also evident in the teachings of faith-based schools by downplaying the Adam and Eve story in Genesis. In their so-called science classes they teach children the "controversy;" their own title-description, of biology vs. a re-invented naturalism called "intelligent design" instead of the biblical Genesis or creation. Evolution and Natural Selection is still regarded as "controversy," a substitution term for pseudo-science called "intelligent design," implying that God created evolution in according to his design-schedule and will. The old mixture of gospel theocratic delusion is no longer capable of convincing even the most devoted of the faith followers of its legitimacy. These damages have yet to answer the question: if God is the Intelligent Designer of life on earth and of the stars of the universe, why do we have or need rabbis, clergy and imams to tell us this?

The menace of faith-based schools is a slow creeping make up of brainwashing of children during the most delicate state of their psychological development. These schools insist that faith matters. Parents of those faith-based schools also insist that they have the right to educate their children as they wish. Atheists and Humanists maintain that we should rethink what is best for children and the balance of the rights between them and their parents. Children must be placed on a *"First Thing First Priority"* to determine their own cognition and to approach the world with genuinely open minds and not through the narrow lens of blind faith and indoctrination. Schools with formal links to an organised religion are alarmingly increasing every year in Europe and North America. In Greece, Ireland as in South America, nearly every public or privately run school heavily indoctrinates students in obligatory religious studies, which is a deceptional by-product of general Pan-Catholic culture in every aspect of life. In some states and provinces in North America, a number of public funded schools became more and more secular. In such cases, the religious industry adopted free enterprise market strategies to entice parents to seek privileged schools of faith. Through a slue of legalisms, these religious based schools have held onto their privileged positions and the power to hire teachers based on their particular beliefs. They have achieved state-funding for construction of their buildings, operation of their establishments and to maintain the right to determine acceptance of pupils based on their parents' faith. So much for the hypocrisy of the *Separation of Church and State!*

It should be up to the parents to demonstrate their financial commitment to the values and ethos of Judaism, Christianity or Islam by supporting of those schools; their willingness to support the Synagogue, Church or Mosque through donations, along with their faith of frequent attendance at religious ceremonies. Only the correct faith is a pre-condition imposed upon parents in order for their children to be accepted in faith schools. In some South American faith-based schools, demanding monthly payments on time and in the full amount is a top priority. If and when a parent delays a single payment, their child is placed in a "chair of shame" in the school's front yard displayed before the rest of students, and is shamed in silence for their parent's financial difficulties. Imagine what this would do to a child's self-esteem or, closer to home, imagine your own child being in that position.

There is no evidence that students in faith-based schools are doing better in their subjects than in secular schools. Any claim to the contrary, is purely a market ploy. Then why do some parents make a hypocritical-bond with beliefs they do not hold in order to register their children in faith schools? Is it because those schools are better financed and have better equipped sports programs than secular schools? Do those parents know that by sending their children to faith schools they are contributing their hard-earned tax-dollars to their children's indoctrination that is difficult to shake-off?

Some parents may appreciate the school's teach casual religious indoctrination of their children, but faith schools do far more than teach the dogma of religion. Their indoctrination injects blind faith into children that are far too young to defend themselves. Children, in this case, do not experience the biological elegance of human life and the material-reality, the beauty and awesomeness of the universe. Instead they experience the daily ritual of dogma and a set of ancient mythological superstitions and delusions that are difficult to overcome. Children's brains are like sponges and they absorb real or false pattern-meanings of life that can last a lifetime. In this case, when a child imagines a false-pattern that in reality is not there; the child's brain attaches a meaning where none exists. For example, for every disappointment, a child may ask a dead-end pattern-question: "Why me all the time"? But does life return a reply, "Why not you"? Human beings' brains are biologically programmed to look for pattern-meaning in life. We interpret life on the basis of the kind of patterns we see in reality or imagination. Then, a pattern that our brain has invented, places a meaning whether a meaning exists or does not exist. Our brain is biologically programmed to see patterns in life, and we have no choice over their make-up. Only afterwards, we can make a choice over the truthfulness of the pattern-meaning that our brain has invented. Our brain makes hundreds of pattern-meanings per day, so it creates shortcuts in order to comply with the demand. Sometimes our brains get the pattern-meaning right other times it does not, and all these patterns are based on our own or others' past experiences, assumptions or recollections.

In the case of children in faith- based schools, their life experience is very limited. As they are bombarded daily with the dogma of religious superstitions, children's brains create pattern-meanings from those falsities where none exist. Any gap in their brain that still exists is filled with false pattern-meaning made up of illusions or delusions. Now the pattern-meaning of religion is completed, but it is made up of pattern-narratives that do not exist. This is a child's believing-brain at work. The daily ritual of dogma affects children's brains like a virus, that is, the virus of believing and not investigating.

Atheists and Humanists maintain that schools should be available to everyone, regardless of their religion, and that public taxpayers should not finance faith schools of any kind. The fundamental concept of "Separation of Church and State" must be held true and *State*-financing withdrawal from faith *Church*-schools. Take the faith out of the faith-schools in order to achieve a true social secularity. The concept "State" is the whole population, and the "Church" must be separated from the whole, and operate strictly for its own believers and not beyond. It is a pure hypocrisy to claim that there is a separation of Church and State while each one of us in the state is paying for their faith schools and institutions. No religious organisation or church is paying taxes to the state, but this is not a separation, it is a pure financial free market ploy. It is not right for the public to finance the teachings of "life after death" and other delusions which are purely religious fallacies.

There are 5 million African children that are dying of hunger and diseases every year. A religious claim, that at the end all such tragic events will make sense, does not alleviate the parents' pain. The promise of afterlife blankets pain with a false promise; that somehow, at the end of out existence, we will all be saved in another world! Those parents are the ultimate products of the industry of religion, such as Christians or Muslims who follow their daily faith based obligation to Saints, Prophets or God to protect their underage children from naturally occurring events. Their prayers to Sky-God to save their children go unanswered! This is because praying is like talking to yourself, and no one else!

Now, the afterlife delusion comes in the middle of this reality with no supportive evidence of this claim. This delusion is created as a substitute for real wisdom; for understanding our predicament that nature sometimes functions in dreadful circumstances and, through our medical science, we can find counter measures to protect ourselves. Atheists and Humanists have an ethical and moral responsibility to absorb this into our deepest essence and counteract the afterlife "happy-talk" that, at the end, all these children's deaths in Africa and among refugees running from war in Syria, Iraq, Somalia and Libya are all part of God's plan. Since there is no absolute truth, we cannot say one way or another whether faith-based schools are morally right or not for your children. We can only say that there is no persuasive evidence for or in favour of them or on their behalf. But we can confirm that what can be claimed without persuasive evidence can also be dismissed without persuasive evidence. The final decision as a responsible parent is yours and yours alone.

Residential Schools

In the 19th century, the Canadian government adopted a policy called "aggressive assimilation" into Christianity for aboriginal peoples of Canada. This policy lasted until early 1996. The best chance of diminishing aboriginal traditions was to take their children into residential schools where they would learn and adopt the Catholic and Protestant faith along with white men's English language and lifestyle. By 1931 more than 80 residential schools were operating across Canada, and by 1996 more than 150,000 aboriginal children were removed from their villages, their families, their language, their customs and traditional native lifestyle.

Students were forbidden to speak their first language or practicing their *Animist* spirituality. If and when they were caught, they experienced severe punishment. There are many accounts of aboriginal children being treated severely; physically including a cuff on the ear or being pulled by the ear or being dragged across the room by the ears or being thrown downstairs or shoved downstairs. Some of the staff were sexual predators, and many of the students were sexually abused. Missionary staff lavished time and attention on Christian religious rituals, often denigrating aboriginal traditions. Aboriginal spiritualism consists of complex social and cultural Animist customs related to nature and specific animal species, such as, the salmon, the eagle or the bear. The imposition of Christianity was a foreign influence through missionaries and religious societies. This resulted in the eventual replenishment of traditional spiritual practices entirely. But assimilation was not always smooth and students rejected early conversion attempts and generations suffered under destructive Catholic and Protestant religious policies.

The Christianisation of the aboriginal children was ostensibly a motive for the Christian churches and the indoctrination of the students was left largely to religious orders and societies such as the *Jesuits, the Recollets, the Capuchins,* the *Sulpicians* and the priests of the *Society of Foreign Missions.* To those societies, severe punishment and harsh treatment of students was deemed necessary for rearing, assimilating and educating them under the Biblical motive *"spare the rod, spoil the child."* Due to the extreme high level of physical and sexual abuse; committed by religious members of the institutions; which ran the residential schools, many students suffered from depression about living with the loss of culture. The living conditions of residential schools were geared to eliminate all aspects of indigenous culture. Aboriginal students had the hair cut very short, they were dressed in uniforms, and their daily routine was strictly regimented by timetables. Boys and girls were kept separate, and even siblings rarely interacted, further weakening family bonding relations. These boys had no idea how to interact with girls which did not help them in later life.

It should be noted that residential school children did not receive the same quality of education as the general population in the public or private school system, and the residential schools were chronically underfunded. Learning was primarily focused on practical not academic skills. For instance, girls were taught and were primed for domestic service such as doing laundry, sewing, cooking, and housecleaning. Boys were taught and trained for carpentry, tinsmithing, animal-farming and construction. Many students were attending classes part-time and worked for the school the rest of the time without pay. Girls did the housekeeping, cooking, laundry, general maintenance and vegetable gardening-production as well without pay. This work was done involuntarily and it was presented as practical education for the students, but the residential schools could not run without it. With so little time spent in class---taught by non-professional teachers—most aboriginal students had only reached grade 5 by the time they were 18 years of age. At this stage, they had to depart from the residential schools, and many were not qualified to pursue higher education.

Without exaggerating, the residential schools were nothing more than institutionalised pedophilia. Sexual abuse was widespread, and students were living under an oppressive environment where emotional and psychological abuse was constant. Survivors recall being beaten, strapped, shackled in their bed and raped. Some had their tongues pierced with needles as a punishment for speaking in their native language. Such abuses, along with poor sanitation, overcrowding, inadequate food and medical care, resulted in a shockingly high rate of death. In 1907, government medical record shows that 24% of previously healthy aboriginal children across Canada were dying in residential schools. Elsewhere, it was reported that 47% to 75% of students from the Canadian Prairies who were discharged from the residential schools died shortly after returning home. The extent, to which the officials and clergy of the Catholic Churches knew about the abuses, tragedies, and the alarming and horrific death rates, has never been fully disclosed. Among others, those who spoke out and called for reforms were met with silence and indifference and thus the deplorable conditions persisted. So much for religious morality and ethics!

Freedom from Religion

Religion in the public school system creates divisiveness, and awareness of religious differences between students often builds walls between them. It should be emphasised that we must teach child-students that there is no worse source and cause of strife, quarrels, fights, malignant hostilities and opposition, persecution, even war and all evil in the world, as religion. Let religion once enter our community affairs and our public schools, they would be destroyed.

So when I hear the question, *"Should we teach religion in schools?"* it makes me cringe. Why? The western world and more notably the Mediterranean countries---France, Spain, Portugal, Italy, Malta, Greece and Cyprus --are currently in the inevitable position of being at the bottom of the list of developed nations when it comes to teaching Natural Selection and Evolution in public schools. As a consequence, at least 50% of the adults outright believe in the religious myth of creation and reject Natural Evolution. As rejectionists of reason, these people remain scientifically ignorant, as they reject facts and accept fable. For example, in Greek public schools, Orthodox priests and professional theologians are taking advantage of their captive audience of students, as a ripe mission field for recruitment. When the minister of public education suggested that parents have the right to have their children not participate in religious classes or that it is up to the parents to instruct their children in religious beliefs of their choice, the priests and professional theologians reacted forcefully. This led us to the question about teaching religion in schools, for if we teach religion, whose religion? It is known that nearly always it is the dominant religion that is "taught," or rather propagated with brief reference to other religions thrown in. But, if there is a proposal to teach contemporary or ancient dead religions, it should include the teaching of atheism as well. Ultimately, the object of teaching school children in public or private schools is critical thinking skills. Are religionists willing to agree that, at their critical age, students must be allowed to question religion?

As an atheist myself (and like other atheists and humanists), I know more about religion and the bible than typical believers. They know so little about the history of their religion, and are often ignorant of the tenets of their religion. This makes their Sunday prayers purposeless, a devotional memorialising and parroting of passages from the bible. Do they know that there are hundreds of other religions and cults in the world, all claiming to be the *One True Faith* and having "insight" into God's mind? They can not all be right! Maybe, they are all wrong!

Poverty, Madrassa and Islam

Madrassa is an Islamic religious school which instructs child students in a particular austere and rigid form of Islam which is rooted in Saudi Arabia Wahhabi or Salafi Muslim tradition. Around the world, Saudi wealth and charities contribute to an explosive growth of madrassas in the Pakistan-Afghanistan region and East Africa where children from impoverished families are recruited to attend *Wahhabi* madrassas where all expenses are covered by Saudi networks of Islamist extremists disguised as charity organisations. Saudi money is fostering religious radicalism in once moderated regions of Africa and Central Asia. This has been documented by *Wiki Leaks* in official documents obtained clandestinely by the organisation.

The networks reportedly exploited worsening poverty in those regions in order to recruit children into madrassa seminary networks from which they will be indoctrinated into the jihadist ideology. Generally exploited families with multiple children; particularly those facing financial difficulties due to poor crop yields, are carefully identified and initially approached by "charity" organisations linked to religious political parties. A "teacher" (*maulana*) will generally be introduced to the family where he will convince the parents that their poverty is the direct result of the family's deviation from "the true path of Islam." The maulana will then suggest that the shortest way to return to "the true path of Islam" is to devote the lives of one or two sons to Islam. The maulana will then offer to educate these children aged 8 to 12 years old at the local madrassa and to eventually find them employment in the service of Islam. It is at that point that the myth of "martyrdom" is introduced and indoctrinates the family by promising that, in the event their sons are "martyred," they will obtain God's favour in the afterlife. Of course, an immediate cash payment is given to the family to compensate the parents for their "sacrifice" to Islam.

These madrassas are generally in isolated areas and are kept small enough; most under 100 students; so as not to attract significant attention from curious neighbours and authorities. At those madrassas, students are denied any contact with the outside world and are indoctrinated in sectarian extremism, hatred for non-Muslims and anti-Western liberal philosophy. Contact between students and their families is forbidden, although the maulana will periodically visit the families to report on their sons' excellent "progress" and, to offer them additional financial assistance, if needed.

It is pertinent to the issue of Muslim pedophilia to ask the question to sheer extend of *homosexual paedophilic* abuse within the Madraasas and the imams. This prompts my assumption that an extreme patriarchal monotheistic religion, combined with the governing and social requirement to keep the "purity" of women intact in a culture where men are perceived to be sex-starved, perhaps engenders a homoerotic institutional culture that attracts homosexual teachers and imams to the madrassas and mosques. However, those factors cannot alone explain the predominance of homosexual pedophilia. You see, most madrassas teachers themselves were students of village madraasas who entered madraasas at the young age of 12 – 14, and missed the critical passage to maturation of the first sexual experimentation with the opposite sex. Caught in a bind of stunted sexual growth, these young boys may be driven emotionally to claim their past unexplored adolescent territory that the teachers and imams placed out of bounds. In addition, the personal homosexual paedophilic experience; which madrassas teachers subjected them to, can simultaneously initiate innocent boys into homosexual pedophilia. Such abuse can also cause a student-victim to later appropriate (as a teacher himself) his former madrassas teacher's predatory behaviour to compensate for the same feelings he had during the time he was being sexually abused in the madraasa seminary.

Let's not forget that homosexual pedophilia predominates behind the madrassas's walls. Teachers and imams in madrassas have greater access to young boys than to young girls within the Muslim sex-segregated theocratic institutions. Imams and teachers take young boys (not girls) for private lessons and field trips where homosexual pedophilia takes place. It is true enough to assume that the generational encouragement of homosexual pedophilia within the madraassa hierarchy is partly attributed to the fact that the teachers themselves had been child victims of abuse.

I think a more crucial question is why this long history of a major part of Muslim institutional practice of homosexual pedophilia has not been exposed more vigorously. Why has institutional silence about an explosive open secret persisted for millennia among traditional imams and the faithful school children, yet no progressive Muslims---at least in the west---have even initiated and full exposure the sexual abuse that takes place within madrassas? What is happening in the Muslim world that is prompting imams to expose the criminal behaviour of the immoral western "unbelievers" (of apostasy or adultery) yet as custodians of their "true faith," they remain silent about their own homosexual pedophilia?

Israel's Shas religious based schools
It is a well known fact that extremely religious views; when central to the religious based school's curriculum, invariably dilutes the quality of the education. In the USA today, the education of fundamentalists' children is devalued by the indoctrination of "subjects" like creationism, while in the religious schools of madrassas the focus is on teaching the Qur'an to the exclusion of preparing children for the modern world. David Levy, of the *New America Foundation* writes that:

"[In Israel] the Haredi (ultra-orthodox) population has grown...from 3% of the population in 1990 to over 10% today...the rapid expansion of the state funded but independent education system established by the ultra-orthodox...Shas schools have come to trump the state-school system in the provision of certain services, such as transportation and hot meals."

This trend has great implications for Israeli society and its economy; the Shas system and other ultra-orthodox schools teach a narrowly religious curriculum that is less geared to providing students with the necessary skills to enter into a modern society. In their defence, the Shas claim that at least they are not producing suicide bombers. But what the Shas create is a social division between themselves and other religious schools, racism against other Jews – *Ashkenazim* do not enrol *Sephardim*--because the latter are regarded as inferior to the former. These are some of the scandals regarding ultra-orthodox schools not willing to be less dogmatic towards other Jews. It is not uncommon to name non-Jewish people as *"goyim,"* an offensive term that describes them as evil, in ultra-Orthodox Jewish schools. It is part of their prayers, teaching and their whole ethos. Students tend to become so afraid of the world "out there" after being taught how dangerous, bad and evil non-Jews are, that it makes it very difficult to overcome such psychological trauma. Ultra-Orthodox schools are actively teaching the students extremism, hatred and fear for the non-Jewish "other."

On a sunny afternoon in Stamford Hill, at the heart of London's Hasidic Jewish district, parents are waiting to pick up their children from pre-schools and primary schools. Scattered groups of teenage girls link arms and chatter together in Yiddish as they walk home from secondary schools. Strangely though, in a community where large families are a common phenomenon, there are no teenage boys to be seen anywhere in the streets. Nor are there any registered secondary schools for boys in the Stamford Hill area. Where do the boys go when, at the age of 12, they leave Stamford Hill area of independent primary schools? There is no secret about where the boys go, when from the age of 13, many boys in this Yiddish community attend religious *Yeshivas*, which focus is on studying the Talmud and the Torah. These schools tend to start early in the day and finish late at night. They do not teach the national curriculum of basic English or maths. In short, they deprive children of their basic right to education. An ex-student says that he barely spoke English when he left Yeshiva at the age of 19, and that he basically had to begin his education again after telling his parents their ultra-Orthodox lifestyle was not for him. The Yeshiva school clearly prevented him from receiving a broad and balanced curriculum, and he did not even know what the term "science" meant. Each Yeshiva school, with its own influential religious fanatics, is explicitly dedicated in ensuring that young earth creationists are not troubled by conflicting world views featuring the *Big Bang,* the chemical formation of the planetary system, and the possibility of pre-marital sex (without damnation), hostility towards homosexuality, all a major cause of social segregation.

But there are additional problems regarding most basic health, safety and child well-being checks in Yeshiva schools because most are operating illegally while providing some kind of boarding service which is also unregulated. Typically the Yeshivas are tucked away behind a small grid of streets or semi-detached houses or in a prefab or mobile single story structure. There is little or no sign that education is taking place within, though their addresses and services are known to the Jewish community, but the existence of illegal and unregulated Yeshiva schools is an open secret. In one case, in the London borough of Hackney there was an appearance of an abandoned building with boarded-up windows. But when you look closer, and listen to the noises that come from inside, or when you open the back door of the premises, there is a fully equipped commercial kitchen preparing the day's lunch. The Yeshivas are not subject to any health inspections and they do not adhere to any standards. They are simply places where kids are indoctrinated from dawn till dusk, and it is a scandal that ultra-Jewish parents send their children to Yeshivas to be brainwashed.

Much of the educational neglect in the ultra-Orthodox communities has also occurred in other places outside Israel, including child sex-abuse. In the ultra-Orthodox Jewish communities of New York, there is a collective silence towards reporting child molesters who are preying upon vulnerable children, while simultaneously projecting an image of caring and concern. The ultra-Orthodox molester Rabbi *Nechemya W.* tried, through a third person in 2015, to bribe a young woman and her boyfriend with $ 500,000 to drop the charges of sexual child abuse against him. The fight to protect child-victims of sexual abuse in Orthodox and ultra-Orthodox communities is difficult and daunting, and those brave men and women inside the community can pay a steep price for reporting a molester. One of these men in the ultra-Orthodox community, *Nuchum Rosenberg* forced the issue of the child sexual abuse by Rabbi Nechemya W. into the public square. For his bravery, Rosenberg became a victim when someone threw bleach in his face.

The most deplorable religious inspired ritual of the ultra-Orthodox faith is the risk imposed on infant boys who are subjected to the practice of MBP: the practice of following circumcision by a *mohel*---with a mohel engaging in oral suction on the wound. This primitive practice creates a foreseeable risk that the boy-infant will contract herpes, which at such an early tender age can be deadly or cause permanent disability. Prevent measures have failed miserably in their implementation because of the politics surrounding the issue, and the total abolition of such witchcraft practice has never been considered. The intent to protect these children at risk is at the level of "lip service" which the ultra-Orthodox community continues to ignore. In fact, any attempt to stop this barbaric practice was stopped by a lawsuit alleging a violation of religious freedom.

Northern Ireland

The majority 95% of Northern Ireland's schoolchildren are taught in schools that are primarily of the same religion. Detailed data obtained also found in Belfast 180 schools in the last academic years had no Protestant students attending classes, while 112 Protestant faith schools taught no Catholic pupils. The seriousness of the religious divide in the Northern Ireland educational system can be described as a benign form of apartheid which is fundamentally damaging the social fabric of Irish society. In July 2012, Secretary of State *Owen Paterson* said that 90% of public housing in Northern Ireland is segregated. This means that thousands of children are continuing to both live and learn with only others of the same religious background.

However, there is a new trend of balancing school enrolments by integrating Catholic, Protestant, other or no faith students in Northern Ireland. These schools are trying to build a historical base of integrated schools in order to serve the whole community. Most parents make a conscious decision to send their children to be educated together with other faiths. However, there is a twist to this story. These schools have adopted a belief system typical of faith-base schools. Some parents enrol their children while others do not, and in this sense, they are exclusively still Catholic faith-based schools but not exclusively for Catholics.

A World Divided

I think that the whole idea of an educational world in western societies is divided by two opposing domains, religious and secular. The original social theory once claimed that modernisation in the school system meant secularisation and, secularisation meant the declining of religiousness in schools. This also meant that religion was a private affair; the secular was public and political. Therefore, as societies modernised, their knowledge of Natural Selection and the Origins of Life would lead them to become more secular and religious myths and superstitions would gradually lose their remaining public hold. Until quite recently, this expressed hope was told by progressive biological scientists such as Richard Dawkins in Western social thought.

Sadly, the power of private money appears to be more powerful than reason and scientific evidence. A well-financed penetration of religion into education is attempting to solidify itself in Christian, Jewish and Muslim community schools. Yet, there are many secular voices calling for a single and all inclusive publically funded school system in Europe and the USA. The role of religion in our secular, pluralistic society will always generate intense debate. After all, schools are meant to represent ourselves and our society. Secular schools take the young and impressionable minds and teach them the values, ideas, identity and history we wish to transmit to the next generation. As such, a good and balanced education does not so much teach students *what to think* (a particular belief or ideology) as it teaches them *how to think*, by dialectical reason and verifiable science.

But, *how to think*, is exactly where a dispute is likely to be greatest. Does our way of thinking, our very approach to knowledge, stem from a world view based on a particular set of religious beliefs on our faith? How we answer this question says a lot about our desire for neutrality, free-thinking and openness to experimentation and exploration. This will be the foundation upon which we will build our educational system.

The reader should conclude by now that I'm an atheist speaking on the subject of religious education in general. This means that I have never believed, in any way, shape or form, in the existence of a Sky-God, an intelligent designer, a higher being or of a supernatural order to be included in the educational system. From an early age, I concluded that religion and its ceremonies are full of *illusionary-symbolisms* (not reality) and *linguistic-metaphors* (connecting two unrelated things) which are expressed in religious ceremonies in a strange language and with outdated meaning. I know from personal experience that religious indoctrination is damaging and I'm strictly an advocate for secular education. However, I think that religion should be treated and be taught as other Roman, Greek, Jewish, Persian or Arabian myths that are ancient man-made stories that do not pertain to modern times. One must remember that, *"Only sheep need a shepherd,"* and if you believe in a *"Sky-Master, you are then an Earth-Slave."*

Immigrant and Refugee Students

Many refugee families from Syria, Iraq, Libya, Somalia or Yemen arrive in Europe and North America after escaping an internal war conflict or political oppression and many face challenges along the way. Their situation can be stressful, as those school-age children often take time to familiarise themselves with the language of the host country and parents try to secure jobs and locate future housing. Some of these school-age children have been abused, neglected, or abandoned and who unification with extended family is of the utmost necessity for them. In contrast, many refugee families have fled from Afghanistan, Syria, Libya or Yemen arriving in refugee camps, crossing the Mediterranean Sea in unsafe boats for Italy or the Greek Islands, to be relocated to a safe nation. There are an estimated 6 million refugees fleeing conflict regions around the world who often have faced untold horrors such as rape, abduction and human trafficking. Many families have been lost at sea due to bad weather, unsafe boats or being thrown overboard by the traffickers.

Refugee students are often included within the general school population without proper counselling and preparation, making them more vulnerable than the children of immigrant parents. Refugee school children may have traumatic experiences and challenges adapting to a new culture and learning a new language which is important for their successful adjustment. In other words, refugee students suffer from the trauma of the pre-, trans-, and post-refugee periods in their lives. The lost of home, country, common language, safety, family and possessions continues as these school children adapt to the new country.

In addition, a family's level of adaptation and assimilation into the new social environment can also impact the refugee-students' functioning, in that, parents may struggle with religious and cultural beliefs that are incompatible with the mainstream culture and with what occurs when parents and their school children differ in their acquisition of the new culture and customs. This can impact a refugee student's adjustment to the new social environment, in that, the "uprooting" and lack of understanding of the new culture can significantly impact the student's self-concept. As an adolescent, the refugee student may struggle with balancing loyalty to a traditional set of family values with the newly acquired notion of western individualism.

Each refugee student arrives at school with characteristics that are as unique as the countries from which they originate. One level of social and academic barrier refugee student's encounter is their level of prior-education. In some cases, students arrive in schools to receive formal education for the first time, while in other cases their education was interrupted by their migration to the new country. Multiple psychic traumas have been cited as possibly hindering a refugee's ability to learn. However, early educational responses help to restore a sense of normalcy, hope and can also foster emotional and social well-being. Students who identify the school as the most significant influence in their assimilation and adaptation may gain self-confidence, resilience and the ability to overcome any previous trauma they experienced. This can result in caring, sharing and trusting; a sense of community environment created by the school. Secular education in private or public schools should consider the solving of the plight of the refugee students as essential to these children's well-being as food, shelter and water. The secular educational system can be responsive to those needs and can help to foster a caring environment, and help students to overcome an otherwise a lifelong trauma. This is also an opportunity for school directors, teachers and staff to show their humanity.

Amish religious communities

The Amish communities in North America live in a mysterious world, a place frozen in another time. The Amish live without automobiles, or electricity from the main grid, and life largely centers on farming, family and faith. Children's education ends at grade 8 with no option for intellectual advancement. The Amish emphasize the simplicity of life, the plainness of life. They have far fewer expenses than we have and have bought a lot of agricultural land over the years. They have no car or house payments to make, no insurance premiums, no jobs they hate, no retirement they are aching for, no nursing homes and no-extravagant health-care costs. This sounds like an ideal life style which most of us will never live. I was first very impressed by the Amish life style in the extensive time I spend working with an Amish communality members in Ontario, Canada.

What was most disturbing to see, however, were the biological effects of a long tradition of inter-breeding, resulting in a lack of any new gene pool entering the closed communities, resulting in autism in many Amish children. Over the years, I worked with Amish tradesmen and artisans, bought meat and fresh eggs, fruits and vegetables, honey and nuts. I was treated with respect but as a distant relative, and I was invited into their homes to share breakfast with the whole family. Still, what I saw was a disturbing number of autistic cases among Amish children, but I never raised the issue with any of them. I'm not sure why, maybe it was out of *respect* or perhaps because I was *too shy* or too *cowardly* to ask. Against all logic, reason and every shred of credible scientific evidence, their healthy living is the only confirmed evidence I have.

Secular societies neither can, nor expect, humanist attitudes from religious authorities or religious communities such as the Amish. Taking advantage of the USA Supreme Court, the Amish take their school-age children out of schools after grade 8 and move them into agrarian life without the option of continuing their schooling. This illusionary decision is based on the delusion of the unfailing goodness of the Amish. This decision is based on the delusional and foolish assumption that the isolated parents in Amish societies know what is best for their children. Is keeping their children ignorant of the events that are happening in the world the best there is for the Amish children?

Like all fundamentalist religious parents, the Amish gained an upper hand on refusals to adequately educate, and a route to incapacitate, their school-age children. Children in those Amish communities, as I have witnessed in Ontario, Canada, are virtually walled-off from the outside world, and the ones who do choose to leave have to suffer dearly for their lack of education. This marks the perils of extreme religious liberty for the proposition that children have no rights. Elected officials and community services have an obligation to ensure that the peril of extreme religious freedom is put under stricter scrutiny. It is time to rip off the pink-glasses and to treat children, in every sense, as humans with rights---even if religion is an obstacle to those rights.

Pedophilic Islamic Marriages

Bukhari 6:298, *Muhammad would take a bath with the little girl and fondle her.*

The Muslim or Islamic faith condones pedophilia; therefore contemporary pedophilic marriages are common practice around the world. Girls far below the age of puberty are often forced to marry a much older man (sometimes in their 50's or 60's) for various personal gains by the girl's parents or her guardians. Pedophilic Islamic marriages are most prominent in socially backward countries such as Kenya, the Middle East, Bangladesh,

Afghanistan, Pakistan and the Gaza Strip under the dominance of Hamas Muslim fundamentalists. This practice, of course, may also be prevalent to a lesser extent amongst a number of Muslim communities, and it is on the rise among the growing Muslim population in non-Muslim European countries. **Islamists** justify pedophilic marriages with tender aged girls using verses from the *Qur'an* that clearly advocate this primitive Arabian Peninsula practice. It should be noted that the Qur'an cannot be questioned or altered because it is the very word of Allah's eternal message to mankind, and it is regarded as being as relevant today as it was when the *revelations* were first proclaimed by Muhammad. In *pedophilia* in the Qur'an

Qur'an 65:4, *"And (as for) those of your women who have despaired of menstruation, if you have a doubt, their prescribed time shall be three months, and of those [girls] who have not had their **courses** [meaning menstruation or 'Yahidna], and (as for) the pregnant women, their prescribed time is that they lay their burden, and whoever is careful of (his duty to) Allah, He will make easy for him his affair."*

In fact, making mention of the waiting-period for the girls who have not yet menstruated, clearly demonstrates that it is not only permissible to give away the girl in marriage at this tender age, but it is also permissible for the husband to consummate the marriage with her. In accordance with the Qur'an therefore, no Muslim has the right to forbid pedophilic marriage which the Qur'an has held as permissible.

It is no secret that sexual abuse of children (pre-puberty) has serious implications whether the victims are Muslim or non-Muslim. It is also no longer secret that the Qur'an explicitly condones pedophilia, as do most Muslim scholars, Muftis and Imams. For Muslim believers to finally recognise the harmful effects of child sexual abuse, it becomes necessary, for those of us who care, to expose those effects through original or authentic Islamic sources. As such, we find *Aisha,* Muhammad's third and most favourite 9 year old child bride, to be the perfect example for assessing pedophilia and the harm on its victims.

***Aisha** bin Abu Bakr* entered Muhammad's house as a child bride at the tender age of 6 years old accompanied by her toys. At the age of 9 Aisha's marriage to Muhammad was fully consummated. There are so many things about the life of Aisha in Muhammad's household that Muslim apologists would rather have forgotten. A number of contemporary Muslim Scholars and political leaders justify pedophiliac marriages with under age girls – 9 to 12 years of age – using verses from the Qur'an that clearly promote this primitive practice.

In **Shahih Muslim 8: 333,** Aisha clearly confirms *"Apostle of Allah*

(Muhammad) married me when I was 6 years old, and I was admitted to his house when I was 9 years old." In fact, beside Aisha, Muhammad also preferred other young virgin girls to play with and fondle, and have adulterous sex.

In **Shahih Al Bukhari 7:62, 16,** Jabir bin Abdullah narrated an advice given to him by Mohammad *"to marry a young girl so that you may play with her and she with you"* and to allow enough time for *"that lady of unkempt hair [to] comb her hair... [*and to give enough time to*] the one whose husband has been absent may shave her pubic region."*

A positive disruption to these primitive customs is due to the western influence, social media and the western education of young Muslims. However, delaying the marriage of young girls in Muslim countries and the Gaza Strip under the Hamas fundamentalism is something new and contradictory to what the faithful have done over many centuries. It is also because of the influence and implication of western secular laws that a change in the understanding and the rituals of primitive Bedouin desert traditions is taking place. This applies also to the reactionary Muslim fundamentalist, such as the Taliban, Boko Haram, and Al Shibab, the ISIL and the Iranian and the Saudi Arabian theocracy. It is absolutely not permissible to consider changing Islamic customs and traditions in a Muslim country, by which people abide, and they must obey the sexual subjugation of women and the absolute power of the Shari'ah law. Yet, in some Muslim countries, the marriages of very young girls has been delayed by many years—beyond the age of puberty--because of the empowerment of women to choose their own socio-economic development and marriage status.

But in the Saudi and Iranian theocracy, primitive religious practices are hard to dismiss. For example, powerful Islamic leaders remain influential long after they are dead, such as the late Ayatollah Khomeini of Iran, the Supreme Leader of the Islamic Revolution. In his declaration to Muslim men, the Ayatollah stated,

"A man can marry a girl younger than nine years of age, even if the girl is still a baby being breastfed. A man, however is prohibited from having intercourse with a girl younger than nine (following Muhammad's example), other sexual acts such as foreplay, rubbing, kissing and sodomy is allowed."

Pedophiliac Marriages in Muslim Countries
Bangladesh

In September 2009, in Barisal, Mufti (high ranking cleric) *Faslul Haque Amini* threatened to deploy his 200,000 strong supporters and wage Holy War (Jihad) against the state if it passed any laws banning child marriages.

Indonesia

In August 2008, in the Central Java Province, a 43 year old Muslim cleric married a 12 year old girl. Not long after the marriage the police returned the girl to her parents. The cleric also announced his intention to marry two other girls aged 7 and 9, and argued that he had committed no crime because he intended to wait until the girls reached puberty before consummating sexual relation with them.

The Islamic Republic of Iran

The Chicago School of Professional Psychology, Los Angeles, August 2009, reported that in Iran a 13 year old is old enough to legally marry and is considered to be an adult at the age of 8 years and 9 months. Iranian gender biased laws favour men, where pedophiles are likely to prevail over the girls should they go to court. At the age of 8 years and 9 months, the girl is old enough to be convicted for a crime and be sentenced to flogging, stoning and hanging for adultery and fornication.

Malaysia

In February 2010, two girls aged 10 and 11 were wed to middle aged men in the sate of *Kelantan*. The 11 year old was found outside a Mosque suffering from internal bleeding and was taken to the hospital for treatment. The Prime Minister's office in charge of legal affairs about underage marriages stated that *"If the religion allows it, then we can't legislate against it."*

Pakistan

There are hundreds, if not thousands, of cases where girls were sold by their fathers in payment of overdue debt, most often for gambling, drinking and smoking illegal drugs. Forms of pedophiliac marriages are linked to tribal customs called *Vani* which is a common practice in the Punjab province and tribal regions bordering Afghanistan. The customs are tied to blood feuds among the different clans and tribes where the under-aged girls are forcibly married-off in order to resolve feuds. Another similar concept is called *Badal,* or revenge. This custom is strongly practiced in Pashtu province in the northern region of Pakistan with Afghanistan. This custom is used to settle disputes between clans in order to avoid bloodshed. An underage girl is send to be a bride to mend ties in a new family.

Saudi Arabia

A Saudi sheikh performed a marriage ceremony between a 10-year old girl and a 26-year old man. The reason for this? The girl's father said that he married-off his daughter, as he feared she would have pre-marital sex when she was older. The mother's plead to nullify the marriage was rejected by a judge who stricken down the plea on the basis of Shari'ah law. In February 2011, a 12-year old girl was fighting to divorce an 80-year old man who paid her father, who was under financial stress, a $22,000 for permission to marry her. The girl un-expectedly dropped her divorce case for reasons unknown.

In countries such as Yemen, Iran, Bangladesh and Nigeria, legal attempts at reforming laws and banning child-marriages have been vigorously opposed by Muslim clergy on the grounds that such a ban would be un-Islamic. In the case of Malaysia, popular pressure on the government has effectively turned back the clock of progress by passing new laws which allow for the practice of pedophiliac marriages in the Muslim majority nation. In short, without the religion of Islam, such practices would have long since been discarded as primitive, barbaric, immoral and anti-child.

Child Soldiers in Armed Groups
Being a child soldier is like being ripped from childhood and thrown into a violent adult world. The lives of innocents are decimated when watching other children playing and wishing that he (the child soldier) could join them in their childhood pastimes. Forceful recruitment at the age of 12 leads into decades of war and violence and into the most brutal civil and religious armed conflicts of our times. Rebel forces destroy the childhood innocence, forcing them to leave their homes and travel into the arid deserts of Arabia and the jungles of Africa. These child soldiers learn to shoot an AK-47 and hate anyone who is against their own rebel forces. It is very easy for a normal boy to transform into someone addicted to killing and to the opiates (Captagon-tablets) that the rebel forces provide to child soldiers.

The Islamic State of Iraq and the Levant (ISIL) is raising an army of child soldiers for future generations of religious radicals to fight against secularism or other religious faiths. Here we need to answer the question: why is the ISIL so determined to recruit, indoctrinate and arm child soldiers to fight on its behalf? This movement is using a "moment of strength" to prepare for a lengthy generational conflict in which young children will participate in major offences. Its aim is to create a militant force able to execute various acts of warfare on its behalf.

In November and December 2014, the ISIL released its social-media videos promoting the recruitment and indoctrination of children. The ISIL training facilities provide extensive programs that include weeks of religious indoctrination, radicalisation and military exercises. Programs such as *"The Cubs of the Islamic State"* are the vehicle for producing the next generation of fanatical child-soldiers to expand the ISIL influence and power base. The ISIL have already recruited child soldiers in suicide attacks and assaults against its rivals in Syria and Iraq. Children are depicted as merely props (with items like flags, guns and hand-grenades), as the next generation of soldiers performing executioners. Special attention is paid to the parental instincts of potential child-soldiers, creating the illusive impression of a utopia state where faithful Muslim believers can raise their children.

Videos depicting children soldiers in training and killing people send a very specific and chilling message and it is not difficult to top it with new videos that are more grotesque than the last. Its main objective is to demonstrate to the world that the ISIL is not made of a collection of thugs who beheads captives but a politico-military force that educates the population according to its beliefs, including the children. It actively recruits young boys, voluntarily or involuntarily, educates them in training camps, and assigns them roles in the group's attacks on infrastructure. In short, the ISIL is trying to raise children who will be thoroughly indoctrinated, fanatical, and with low threshold for committing acts of horrible violence. The ISIL believes the more children they can create in their image the better, and those children born into a violent religious ideology are usually the most committed to the course of being able to live by Islamic ideals.

Are those children-soldiers the next generation of terrorists? Its propaganda is aimed at showing the western world that they are so religiously devoted to the cause of re-establishing a Caliphate that they are willing to turn their children into warriors for generations to come. This desire to re-establish a Caliphate (which was abolished in 1924 by the Turkish secular leader *Kemal Ataturk (1881 – 1938*) is the ultimate objective of ISIL in Iraq and the Levant. It is meant to send a terrifying message to any religious or secular adversary. Their new generation of child-soldiers of the so-called Caliphate is viewed as a generational project. There are two notable differences about the use of child-soldiers by ISIL which differentiates them from those armed children of Uganda and Sierra Leone. First, the ISIL have exhibited an ability to recruit teenagers from foreign countries, including Britain, France, Australia and the USA. The second is the extreme reality of children being programmed, forced, or perhaps even encouraged to commit extreme acts of individual violence. These acts are both functional and propagandistic as to the purpose of using children in attacks and executions. As children, they are less likely to be under suspicion from security personnel, or the general population, until it is too late.

As part of their training, children are shown videos of actual executions, and are given a doll and a knife and ordered to practice beheading. In another case, the *Syrian Observatory for Human Rights* have released several videos showing children performing executions; in one, 25 children execute 25 Syrian soldiers by shooting them in the head. The SOHR also reports statistics indicating that at least 52 children died in 2015 fighting for the ISIL, including 18 who blew themselves up. The organization states that

711

dozens of foreign children who were indoctrinated and trained by the ISIL have also died. In addition, child-soldiers are inevitably doomed to grow up into violent adults, building a society with extreme violence in its core, creating a mental health crisis of epic proportions. The end results could be that former child-soldiers will face high levels of post-traumatic stress disorder, behavioural problems, anxiety and depression. Thus, to integrate them back into society, deprogramming them ideologically will be required. **Since** 2013, the ISIL has changed its nature as an armed group. It is no longer a mere terrorist group, but a well-organised army that can hold and administer large territories. It governs according to harshly interpreted Shari'a principles of Islamic laws, including the imposition of tax extortion on minorities—*dhimmi*—and the acceptance of second-class citizenship. Minorities under its governance, including Shia Muslims and Christians, are subjected to severe human rights abuses, mass executions, forced conversion and brutal acts of intimidation. Those acts have provoked shock and world wide condemnation for the brutal execution of foreign journalists and humanitarian aid workers, as well as captured combatants from opposing armed forces. The quality of its governance is extremely poor, but ISIL stated that the "improvement" of people's religion is far more important than improving the quality of their lives, and thus it continues coercing the people it governs. The danger is not limited to individual regions near the ISIL territories and flag. It has proven to be powerful attraction to young Islamists across the world by means of the adept use of social media, and slickly presented propaganda to entice teenagers to join its ranks. It is inevitable that some of these teenage recruits will return to their home base, taking with them their experience as members of the most brutal Jihadist armed group in the Middle East conflict.

Finally, I have tried to expose the plight of children around the world from a social, political and religious fundamentalist tradition embedded in our religious institutions and communities. I maintain that the plight of children is a global humanist moral issue; and it is viewed from Darwinian principles, not from theologically misguided points of view. Religious people get their morality from their holy scriptures; cherry-pick and choose, obey and adopt them, regardless of whether they are against the well being of their fellow humans.

Humanists and atheists get their morality from other sources than religious scriptures, symbolisms and traditions. Where the atheists and humanists get their morally about the plight of children is, of course, a complicated question. The bedrock of humanist morality comes from Darwinian heritage explaining the origins of humanist morality that comes from the ancient close kinship of clans; where each member knew one another, and had to stay in a mutual altruistic relationship for the benefit of all. These people were likely to meet again and again throughout their lives thus were more likely to be good and altruistic to each other. Since we no longer live in small bands, the same rule of thumb applies today in our modern urban society, that of the *Golden Rule: be nice to everyone as you want them to be nice to you.* Therefore, you and I are in a position to reciprocate the kindness.

This original Golden Rule has been re-defined in deeply theistic societies by superstition and religion, rituals and customs. But predominant humanist civilisations produced a much kinder and pleasant morality which included most facets of human relationships, human rights and positive moral expressions. True enough, it is really buffering to discover where our morality comes from, that it is innate in us, programmed in our brain as an innate instinct just like hunger or sex. When moral-philosophy is theologically inclined then morality is dictated to us by religiousness and religio-political agenda. The essence of the plight of children; who are damaged by religious morality, is the focus of our attention.

THE PLIGHT OF CHILDREN

ILLUSTRATED BRAINWASHING IN MADRAASAS MUSLIM RELIGIOUS SCHOOLS

ILLUSTRATED BRAINWASHING IN MADRAASAS MUSLIM RELIGIOUS SCHOOLS

AS YOUNG ADULTS THEY ARE READY TO OBEY THE DOGMA OF ISLAM

QUR'AN: 65:4, "YOU CAN RAPE, MARY AND DIVORCE PRE PUBESCENT GIRLS;

QUR'AN: 4:3, 4:24, 5:89, 33:50, 58:3, 70:30 YOU CAN ENSLAVE FOR SEX AND WORK

QUR'AN: 4:34, YOU CAN BEAT SEX SLAVES, WORK SLAVES & WIVES

GUIDED BY ISIL IMAMS, CHILD SOLDIERS

NONE OF THE CHILDREN LOOK UP, SHOWING THEIR ANXIETY THEY FEEL

CHILD KILLERS IN THE KILLING-FIELDS

QUR'AN: 9:29, KILL JEWS AND CHRISTIANS IF THEY DO NOT CONVERT OR PAY JIZYATAX

QUR'AN: 8:12, 47:4, CRUCIFY AND AMPUTATE NON-MUSLIMS

QUR'AN 9:111, YOU KILL NON-MUSLIM TO RECEIVE 72 VIRGINS IN HE AVEN

QUR'AN: 2:217, 4:89, YOU WILL KILLANYONE WHO LEAVES ISLAM

CANADIAN, IRISH AND AUSTRALIAN FAITH BASED RESIDENTIAL SCHOOLS

DESTROYING CHILDREN'S MINDS

PEDOPHILIA UNDER ISLAM

A SHAMEFUL PUBLIC DISPLAY OF AN IRANIAN IMAM

PEDOPHILIC MARRIAGES UNDER ISLAM

GIRLS AS YOUNG AS 9 YEARS OLD BECOME FULL TERM HOUSE WIVES

PEDOPHILIC MARRIAGES UNDER ISLAM

A MASS ISLAMIC WEDDINGS PROMOTED BY HAMAS IN GAZA STRIP

A CHILD SEXUAL VICTIM UNDER ISIL

LIFE AFTER DARWIN

Here, we must ask the question; what is it like to be an atheist since the days of Charles Darwin. Most of us started our lives as religious people, perhaps as Christian, Jewish or Muslim. Those of us who read Darwin were affected by a sense of discovering freedom, or at least changed our minds about the existence of God, the notion of intelligent design, or the notion of non-physical intelligence in the origins of things. Charles Darwin simply came along with a massively important biological theory of evolution which may or may not have had any effect on people's original sense of atheism or disbelief. Such people may have had no religious belief anytime in their life. This large constituency is made of people who have never had a religious belief, and to whom Darwin is yet another confirmation of their atheism.

Evolutionary theory has revolutionized the science of biology and has also had a big influence in people's lives. This influence is so large, that often it goes remarkably unnoticed. This influence is so pervasive that often we do not acknowledge it, such as, real natural selection. You see, the act of natural selection in our daily lives is permanent; we select products, friends, loved ones, a job or songs, and as such, we gravitate towards it. We select it from other choices, and such selection process we tend to make consciously during our daily lives. Darwin taught us how important selection is over our biological lives and transforms it into creative force.

Has this mode of selection affected our moral lives? My short answer is no, not really, not in any naïve way, and we certainly do not get our morals from Darwinism, not in any parable or allegorical sense. However, social-Darwinists did precisely that at in the end of 19th and beginning of the 20th centuries. They tried to inject a kind of poetic social-Darwinism into human affairs and morality. It was a mad fascist attempt to demonstrate that "the *weakest shall perish,"* and *"the strongest shall win"* which is the social-Darwinian way, in the state of nature. It makes it correct, in the sense that it's because it does exist in the state of nature. If we get any sort of morality from Darwin, it would come with a negative sign, and thus define the kind of society we do not want to live in as a "Darwinian society." Nevertheless, Darwinism makes us understand why we are "here," but we should be aware of the social-Darwinian consequences, the kind of society we ought to be living in, and the kind of morality we ought to practice with each other. Darwin, of course, can help us understand where our morals come from. We could ask questions such as: why are we helpful towards a needy person, why do we tend to care for a sick person who is unable to help himself, why do we donate blood, why do we help stranded refugees? Those are baffling questions, but it would be insulting humans to define the source of our morality to some celestial illusive non-existent "supernatural" entity. In fact, we have selected the basic rules of morality because it help us survive, for we are the products of "getting along," of ancestors who learned how to get along in society; and the ones who did not get along in society, were out-selected long ago. This does not mean we are perfect in our moral choices; nor does it mean we do not make mistakes, but that, in itself, is an aspect which shows that, through our selection, we have free will.

The traditional view of religion as being the source of our moral and ethics is proven false. I do not think that it is true that religion is moral or ethical, and certainly I do not think, of course, that any of its explanations about the origins of our species and cosmos or its destiny are true either. I think that most of these claims are conclusively and utterly discredited. I would submit also that the ecclesiastic dogma of *vicarious redemption,* by human sacrifice, is utterly immoral. *Compulsory love* is another sickly element of religious dogma. Both dogmas have their origins in the primitive Middle Eastern tribal societies and were called, *scapegoating.* In other worlds, you "piled" the sins of your society onto a goat, and drove it to the desert to die of thirst and hunger, believing that the tribe's sins have died along with it. The question is: is it moral to say that someone else's sins can be forgiven through the punishment of another person; whether Christ was sacrificed for "our sins" (not for his), or that our collective sins can be forgiven by piling them onto a goat? Is it ethical to believe and to propagate such a religious dogma?

For centuries, humanity has been indoctrinated, by religious dogma, to share the guilt of Jesus' sacrifice, although it took place long before we were born; you and I did not participate in it, nor did we have any say or control in the outcome of the event. I can now claim that, had I been present, I would have tried to stop the public torture and crucifixion of a self-delusional and eccentric Jewish rabbi (if he ever existed). Why then am I implicated in such a horrendous crime? Is it because of the "original sin" which you and I were conceived in and born of Adam and Eve, in Genesis 1? Even if you think this is an idiotic belief, it is nevertheless, a Christian belief.

Here we find a belief imposed upon millions of Christians without them having anything to say about it or the right to reject such dogmatic imposition. In political terms this is called an explicitly celestial totalitarianism. Millions of Christians were born under it, without having a choice of choosing whether they wish to live under its earthly government (the Church). This demonstrates something sinister about primitive monotheism, which is practiced in general. In most religions the engines of morality are driven by reward and punishment.

However, if there is no celestial authority watching us from above, if there is no eternal bliss and no damnation to follow, what then is the incentive for us to act morally? The short answer is that most of us want to behave and get along nicely with our co-workers, strangers and neighbours. People behave nicely to you if you behave nicely to them and life becomes convivial in its true sense. Living together, as in the case of family-members turns out to be an amiable pleasant way to carry on with your life. Every now and then, there are these catastrophic suspensions of conviviality. We have seen that we have the capacity not only to be nice, but also have the capacity for being nasty like no one else on earth. One of the things that we get struck by is that when the Thailand tsunami tragedy happened, people around the world were expressing their sympathy towards the 250,000 thousand victims of the tectonic plate movement. On the other hand, between 1900 and 2000 we, all of us, have killed more than 200.000.000 million of each other. It appears to me (without intentionally diminishing the victims' pain) that the movement of tectonic plates are very minor events in our lives.

Of course, there is something contemptible about the idea that we are only moral because of reward and punishment. The thought that most people would suddenly stop being moral, were not likely moral at all. Those of us who manage to be moral without being spied upon (in our imagination) are surely much more deeply moral than those who need the discipline of being spied upon. It is interesting to know that long before Darwin in 1859, Adam Smith (*1723 – 1790*) a Scottish moral philosopher identified this curious human capacity in his *Theory of Moral Sentiment* that we have to sympathize and feel of others' distress, to share their pain and to move towards others helpfully. The Cro- Magnon and the Neanderthal pre-historic relatives all actually knew that others suffer (due to hunting accidents), that the "others" who were moving around within the circumference of their vision, were in fact moved by the same sort of sentiments. These are the social boundaries that early human groups and contemporary societies we made of, and that is what makes us moral. Of course, ideas of morality tend to vary widely from one culture to the next, but there are common currents that we share within the "in-group" that perhaps are not shared between ours and outside cultures.

Evolution theory often invokes "human nature," a notion which may set limits on the changes we can make within our societies. This, of course, is a rather open question, one we ought to be working on. There are people who think that human nature is part of us, in the sense that change can come about through education and social engineering, while there are others who think that we are (in our core) very rigid and thus we can only make some superficial changes and adjustments. This is one of those historical controversies where fierce arguments go on back and forth for a number of centuries. Those arguments most often are based on what people would like to be true rather than what they know, to be true. Occasionally we do get disasters from socio-political groups, such as the Nazis, who were prompted by social-Darwinism (in the cruel sense), with a more sinister view that we could improve society by eliminating fallible gene-streams---by gassing to death the ones that do not measure up to our expectations. The German Christian Reformer, *Martin Luther (1483 – 1546)* in his treatise *On the Jews and Their Lies* (1543), set the ideological stage for the "improvement of society" by eliminating not only ethnic groups, but also a large number of fallible genes, because they were mentally ill or disabled. The eugenic gassing went on until 1941 but the genocide in concentration camps against ethnic groups continued until the end of WWII.

The Nazis were not the only authority which was experimenting with social-engineering. The Swiss have admitted that they too were practicing eugenics in the 30s, believing they could stop the procreation of "faulty-genes" by sterilizing the undesirables, in order to guarantee a health stream of genes they thought to be excellent. But for hundreds and hundreds of years, amongst the Germans, there was an idea that these "superior-genes" were in the "blood." Indeed, the metaphor *"in the blood"* (which is another way of referring to genes), invoked this idea of brutal "blood and earth." Germans were convinced they were excellent genetically, because they came from this "blood and earth" land. This was the metaphoric antecedent to biological gene theory.

Darwinism is an adaptable and dangerous idea for those propagators who invoke how the state of nature is (the strong survive and the weak fail), and apply it to the human principle about which societies ought to exist. Of course, Darwinism is a dangerous idea in many different respects. You see, any idea, if and when it's taken to the extremes, can be turned into a dangerous idea. Of course, here we are raising a general question about whether objective truth should ever be sacrificed for political reasons. Darwinism is much more important to objective truth than for it to be "bastardised" with politics. Even if Darwinism has exceedingly undesirable consequences, we still had to teach it to learn it because it is objectively true in a massively important way.

Most of the monstrous social-Darwinism committed by human beings is without scientific justification, or alluded to scientific justifications, and monstrous acts of massacres and genocide are committed by giving a cosmetic scientific justification because we have this, as yet, very difficult to explain "thing" within us which we may have inherited from our primate lineage (when humanity was in the state of nature), about what we do when "others" appear ethnically different from us. As a child, I happened to come across a book *"The Painted Bird"* whose author's name has escaped my memory. This story is based upon a bird-keeper who decided to take a canary out of a cage of similar birds. The bird-keeper placed the canary back after he painted it a different colour than the rest of the birds which were in the cage. The "painted-bird" was attacked and killed immediately by the rest of the feathered group because it was different than the rest. While I was living in the Amazon Rainforest, in Peru, I came across a group of flamingos crossing a muddy area. As it happened, a muddy-ball dried and hung from the chest of the chick-flamingo in a profoundly strange way. Because the muddy-ball altered the image of the chick-flamingo, the rest of the adult flamingos were attempting to drive this chick away from the group. Luckily, a day or two later, common occurring rain-storms melted away the chick's muddy-ball, thus once again, the chick-flamingo was accepted by the rest of the flamingos. This is the condition that animal-species live in the state of nature (a kind environmental social-Darwinism), where the life of the weak is "nasty, brutish and short." Looking at a certain segment of humanity's history, it does not appear that we have learned much!

Of course, the deep question is why this brutality recurs. Why is that the history of human beings? In addition to being a history of enormous cultural complexity, beauty, inventiveness, ingenuity and moral sophistication, which undoubtedly we have achieved, there is a parallel with monstrosity. Take, for example, the Christian life supporters who are curiously interested in saving embryos but curiously indifferent to saving living human beings. As if, somehow, embryos are subliminally innocent creatures which have a sort of greater right to protection than individuals we recognize and have relationships with. Right-wing Christian fundamentalists in the USA, in fact, are passionate supporters of the sanctity of life, but they are perfectly prepared to support the execution of very large numbers of people in death rows, regardless of their guilt or innocence (and, I must say, with a great enjoyment!)

The concept of relativism of morality in different cultures is worth investigating. It would be advantageous to learn more about different peoples' attitudes to morality. Anthropologists tell us about different customs where people differ enormously in dress codes, in the colour of the hats they wear or in their dances. But does this tell us something that applies or does not apply to moral principles? I assume that everyone agrees (as the Bible says) that we must not kill. However, does this mean that we must not kill humans, or that we must not kill members of our own tribe (Jews) rather than any other tribe? But, you see, the Old Testament's morality is all about you must not kill Jews, but you can kill everybody else with great gusto. Other religions do the same thing, and I suppose these killings become universal. The problem with this analysis is that we lack, from a comparative point of view, a comparison with the comparator, for we are products of societies that actually have survived. We actually need some examples from societies that did not survive, what their view of morality looked like, and have them explain their demise compared with our survival. More investigation needs to be done on that basis.

Within humanity's moral social make-up, we have concepts like "evil" and "virtue," which I think are baseless concepts. Evil, which is constantly invoked to explain some horrible things that occur to us, is made up as some sort of deep and crude force that lies at the base of our human nature which, when drilled and hit through, releases some sort of prime pew-substance called "evil" which gets things going destructively. I think it's not like that. What we have is the tendency to behave atrociously. We also have the tendency to behave in ways we all think are nicer to live by. But I do not think that "virtue" and "evil" are principles the way gravity might be or in the way that other "natural forces" could be. They are not forces in nature which somehow, if we are unfortunate enough, gush forth and make us do acts of evil. It is what we call certain forms of conduct which we broadly identify as not being nice.

On the other hand, this virtue and evil is bound up with the idea of right and wrong, which is part of our altruism and part of our cultural evolutionary heritage and a desire to see justice. We have erected this mythology about it, that there are certain abstract moral principles of "good" and "evil." There is a whole mythology built around it, and this is the way we, as primate social animals, have come together with structures that allow our survival and promote our flourishing. In primitive times morality was depended on pleasing God and atheists would be immoral because they do not follow God's morality. Atheists, of course, continue maintaining humanist-based morality that has been established long before monotheistic God was invented. As an atheist, I feel embarrassed that, as a pious-atheist, I must grant religion a developmental place theme or motif in human history; that it has been one of the channels through which poetic, and other extremely powerful means of expression have flowed because it invoked these principles we all adhered to; the notions of charity, of valuing the poor, the underprivileged, the meek and all the people mentioned in the Sermon on the Mount. It only came into the imaginations of people like the prophets that we owe to each other moral behaviour to each other because we are all God's children. Although, I think that is not true, it is however an undeniably poetic metaphor which has actually animated some of the most important moral developments in human history.

This, of course, could have been a *historical accident*, because throughout ancient history, literally everyone was religious, and thought in religious terms. Religion could also have been responsible for the rise of great art, music, literature and architecture, and I say, of course, the church leaders and clergy were the ones who had the knowledge and the money to patronize them. There is something about the poetic power of imagery and transcendentalism. But the thing that I find most objectionable is the transcendentalism of religion, which has been the source of some of the more powerful moral ideas. The idea that we must be the holders of a thing called "spirit" (I do not think we are), as a poetic metaphor, has actually empowered an enormous amount of moral activity. What I would like to see however, are more post-religious teachers of ethics, such as *Gandhi* and *Bertrand Russell*, whose moral philosophies lead us to ask why we should be good from a non-religious point of view.

The good news is that evolutionary progress in human civilization has taken a leap forward from the days of the Egyptian or Roman dynasties, and we are better-off than the early stages of human civilisation. As a society, the horrors of the 20th century WWI and WWII were more horrible than the horrors of medieval times only because the war technology was available to put the horrors into practice on such an enormous scale. Actually, as the centuries go by, we are steadily getting nicer in western societies. We have abolished slavery; we are on our way to abolishing religious, sexual and racial discrimination. We do not have to go very far back in history to see where slavery was taken for granted, where one's race just happened to be superior to any other. I think that we have made great strides, with lamentable steps backward, from time to time. But, on the whole, this trend is in the right direction.

The thrust of the question is about whether, on the whole, we are better in our fundamental attitudes and I think that things are definitely getting better. I think what has happened through the course of human history is the transformation and domestication of our primitive or savage mind. This domestication was because of literacy expansion and because people could now write things down and keep meticulous historical records. We have very complicated percussive attitudes towards our own thoughts which were not possible in pre-literate societies. Due to our widespread education, we have expressed extremely sophisticated judgments about the nature of morality itself. Philosophical and legal theories of justice have become unbelievably sophisticated from the 1800s on. This is not the result of religion but the inevitable result of literacy which creates a more much more elaborate series or form of social awareness which did not exist in primitive times. It is much more complicated and we hold elaborated debates about the nature of jurisprudence with a philosophical sophistication inconceivable in pre-literate society.

We differ from animals because of the fact that both our intellect and mechanical artefacts leap on forward from one generation to the next, thus we get better at doing certain things. Also, we are getting better at thinking ingeniously, both morally and technically, because of this capacity. In biological terms, this is called *extended phenotype* (from the Greek *phainein,* meaning *to show,* and typos, meaning *type*) which is related to all living organisms and is what determines their physical appearance. Those living organisms accomplish things (their mechanical artefacts) by virtue of their *genotype* (genes the body is made of). For instance, beavers are making beaver dams, exactly the way genes make the beaver and the dam. The genotype code is carried by all living organisms. Genes give instructions (inherited information) for metabolism, energy utilization, reflexes and behaviour which produce the *outward, physical manifestation,* or phenotype, of an organism. This means, that the things living organism make, by virtue of the genotype, determines their physical appearances (physiology) and also determines the artefacts which they make.

Intellect and artefact progress differ between living organisms. Some years ago, I watched wild honey-bees building their hives in various locations on my grandmother's farm. One after another, all hives built were the same in size and in honey-bee activities. Year after year, the hives were built the same way regardless of where they were built and, I assume that, a hundred years from now, the new hives will look the same. On the other hand, I walked from the outskirts towards the center of the town, *Serres,* Greece, where my grandmother's house was situated. As I was doing my walking, I noticed that the architectural style in the outskirts was different from that towards the center of the town. But I knew that it was the same species who built the suburban and the center of the town. This cultural evolutionary change took place without an alteration of species. I suspect that we are equally ingenious in this way, that there is a leap forward effect, i.e. the intellectual achievements of one generation (in the center of the town) alter and lead to the intellectual improvements of the next generation (in the outskirts of the town).

This is subverted in us by the things that remain the same, which we share with our primate ancestors, that all the streams of nastiness, of alliances and hostilities are in fact antecedents to all that we do both morally and immorally. This seems to remain the same, but we also have the same sophisticated ability to think ingeniously about morals better and better and even set up institutions to advance these moral improvements. Then, someone kicks them over with a vile desire to destroy them in order to rebuild them once again. There are unknown futures where we may again see Stalinism, Gulags, Hitlerites, concentration-camps, Pol Pot, Franco and new monstrosities could occur. Those would not be some momentary lapse; it's been going on since time immemorial in the conquests of the Mongols, the Vikings, the Bedouins, the genocide of the Armenian people of 1915 and the Belgian colonialists in Congo, where eight million black people were slaughtered in the name of oil, timber, minerals, rubber and cheap labour.

One thing that seems to occur, over which we have little control, are the sudden social ruptures among people who previously lived together closely yet are now prepared to commit hideous atrocities against one another. Take for example the Yugoslav Republic under Tito, where for centuries all its ethnic groups lived side by side in a relative peace. Following Tito's death, in May 1980, and the break up of the Yugoslavian unity, Christians and Muslims, friends and neighbours turned against one another with outrageous aggression. What we seem to have no control over, or we do not seem to be able to control, is the capacity to retread our violent impulse once we see the "other" such as, an immigrant, an asylum seeker, or another race. We do not seem to have the capacity to control our treacherous sadism when social arrangements are disrupted in some way.

What is described here is like declaring war on another country. It reminds me of WWI Christmas day where the British and the German troops met in "no men's land," shared drinks, wished each other Merry Christmas and played soccer. The next day both sides were shooting at each other once again. So, it is more general than the atrocities of Pol Pot, the Rwandan or the Belgian Congo massacres. It is something that decent people do to each other (or did to each other) once every twenty years throughout much of history because of political decisions made by each country. As such, conventional decency disappears and suddenly we turn into patriotic soldiers and the whole language changes as we move to war mode. I suspect this is what happened to ethnic friends and neighbours in ex-Yugoslavia, when they were deciding which group would be "theirs" and which group would be against another. Their own declaration of war was a very superficial artefact; the underlying motive was religious, and that is what created the atrocities between the

Croatians and the Serbs. You see, the Croatians were Catholic and the Serbs were Orthodox. The Croatians tested people in the way they crossed by themselves; if they crossed themselves inadvertently in the eastern way they were instantly shot or held over the edge of a cliff. It was their religious differences that created the spark for the atrocities, and the declaration of war, might only have formalized the structures of aggression. All that was required was to feel the simple "otherness," that Orthodox Christians were contemptible and invertebrate, and that Croatian Catholics were excellent and pure. Such discrimination against the "otherness" continues; today with Serbian Orthodox doing it to the Albanians; the Muslims are contemptible in the view of the Serbian Orthodox. Yet, all of them were ordinary people who held decent jobs and who were providers for their families.

We do not know why we are both "monsters" and "good-parents," and we do not know how to organize ourselves properly. We do have this extraordinary record of sophisticated improvement of moral sensibility; of literature which becomes increasingly sophisticated, which deals with justice, civil-rights and human-rights. All this rhetoric is completely contemporary with the most monstrous violations of the very standards that we have come up with. The reasons these violations happen, is that good-people simply allow it to, and do not opposed. The only hope is to communicate our social fears and to question ideologies that are propagated by political leaders. There are always people who are getting better at questioning but the fact is that many institutions embody the very sophisticated notions of justice and civil-rights, yet they have the worst possible averages. We must realize that we have this tendency to commit atrocious, monstrous acts which has killed millions of innocent people including the Armenian genocide in 1915. There are always people who speak on behalf of virtue but, ultimately, political or religious disruptions in otherwise unified communities, will always break out. My apologies for being somewhat pessimistic, my intent is to bring to my readers' attention our virtuous acts and crimes towards each other.

On a more optimistic note, we now see conscientious objectors who do not regard war as a glorious act, we now have anti-war demonstrations, exposing corruption, anti-economic slavery, uncontrolled massive surveillance, police-brutality, anti-militaristic takeovers, such as, on June 15, 2016, where thousands of people took to the streets in Ankara and Istanbul to prevent the renegade army from taking over political power in Turkey. Technology has promoted social-media; the citizens' "watchdog" those governments around the world attempt to suppress somehow. We still have wars but now we have the social-media which lionizes the "peoples' power" rather than being condemned and thrown in jail. In WWII the pilots who bombed cities in Germany were regarded as heroes, and now we are apologizing for the unnecessary act of war in Iraq. The decision to invade Iraq, taken by the British Prime Minister Tony Blair and US President Bush (both fundamentalist Christians) is still under review. Of course we are getting better, but we should not expect to a uniform or upward trend but with pockets of reversals, in rather piecemeal bits, "here and there." Some parts of the world would be getting better than other parts, for the time being.

Most of us would expect that the course of this progress would be somewhat quicker, but nevertheless, I do think however, that we see a general trend in the right direction. The reversals may seem as getting occasionally worse. This is because the technology for exposing these monstrosities is getting more efficient. We recognize that we are all humans; and this is right. Contemporary intellectuals would support the view that "we are all humans;" but two hundred years ago, only the white-race were regarded as being humans, the "others" were not. Given that culture and history can be viewed as our extended phenotype, is it proper to consider how we know about the social sciences, economies, and politics in order to discover the insights of evolutionary biology? For lack of a better word, I call human culture an "extended phenotype," for the same reason that, I contrasted the wild honeybee-hive structure with human architecture. The point of the wild beehive structures is that genes make bees build beehives to survive better, and as a result, they really are adaptations of the same kind. However, architects do not propagate genes as a consequence of building better buildings. This sounds a trivial thing to say; but this is precisely why human artefacts and human culture, are not (in a simple sense), 100% an extended phenotype.

It is now time to turn our attention to atheist morality. A popular question among fundamentalist Jews, Christians and Muslims is *"If morality did not come from God, where did it come from?* A very common answer is *"I don't know"* so religions deduce that God must have created morality. This argument leads to the *"God of the Gaps"* and to *"Argument from Ignorance"* which is not a good scientific answer to the question. The argument is not strong even if the complexity of morality cannot yet be properly explained. However, once a scientific explanation is available, the argument is completely disintegrated. It is no longer an argument at all. In the case of complexity in nature, the scientific theory, developed by Charles Darwin in 1859, is Evolution by Natural Selection. In the case of morality, the more recent scientific explanation (developed by Darwin's successors) is, still, evolution by natural selection. Altruism and other humanist moral behaviours can be explained by evolutionary theory which has been so successful that many surprising predictions have been verified. Of course, an alternative traditional religious dogma is to deny that atheists are moral, because, by their definition, atheists deny religious morality.

No doubt there are a number of different theories of humanist morality (without God) but, for our purpose, we need to consider only the main one: morality is built and is determined by our genes. For instance:

- We commonly agree not to steal because we accept that society functions smoother if people do not steal.
- We prohibit doing to each other what most of us would not like done to ourselves, a principle known as the *Golden Rule*, which was taught by ancient Greek moral philosophers before monotheism was invented by man.
- In cases of legal disagreements where interests conflict, we try to set a legal precedent as a solution that is acceptable to most people.
- In this view, "atrocities" and "virtue" are no more than convenient categories which we use to ease explanations.

Because of what Darwin said, that we are descendants of common stock which produced apes and humans, there are, in fact, genetically determinate factors or propensities to act in variously complicated ways that are analogous to but not identical analogies to ape behaviour. When such analogies are deformed, in the enforceable social arrangements, all sorts of enforceable behaviour tendencies get magnified and exacerbated under the peculiar conditions we have created for ourselves by being sociable in the way we are. You see, apes live in very small communities which actually behave badly with each other. We live with a vast number of other people in a very complicated urban civilization, where we conflict with one another (declare a kind of war on one another). The unspoken declaration of war with one another; sets the motion of thoughts on other things, which enables us to behave badly. These are not "pockets" of return or re-enactment of recurring conflicts; they are extremely re-calculated conflicts, perhaps because of linguistic or rhetorical technology. It was the rhetoric of *Nazism* and *Stalinism* which actually created the Gulag and the concentration camps. It was not the monstrous machinery which enabled the Gulag. The Gulag was an extremely primitive device with scarcely any machinery at all. What it was, it was an ideology for which there was no precedent. The idea of a millennial improvement in society which warranted the death of millions of people with the prospect of some sort of subsequent millennial improvement, after infinitely delayed the future.

One should also explain the phenomenal success of organized religious' phenotype; that it provides a false consolation upon our death. Does Darwin's evolutionary outlook provide us with any consolation in the face of mortality? Well, the world is divided into people who simply can not grasp this simple metaphorical point: *"that none of us would ever get out alive."* The idea of mortality is so consuming with people that seems obviously a preposterous notion. Personally, I find great consolation in knowing that, during the brief time that I have on this earth, I am privileged to have been born, to be allowed to understand rather a lot about the world I lived in, about the life-form of which I am a grateful part and that I acknowledged that my time is finite. I feel hugely privileged to have been granted a few decades in the sun during which I had to get to grips with understanding why I was ever born in the first place. I find this exhilarating, an exuberant thought, that life is finite, which makes me even more grateful to have it for the short time that I do. An understanding of evolution sets the context which personally I find quite profound and intriguing. If we all lived forever, then we would not value life; even though we do not seem to value life as much as we should. Knowing that we could not have it needs us, each in our own way, to make most of the time that we have.

Personally, the idea of not having a bodily existence (i.e., having a spirit) is logically incoherent for very interesting philosophical reasons. I actually think that what makes all of us feel that we are individuals and make us cherish our biological life, as we have it at the moment, is that there are all sorts of complicated pleasures and satisfactions, fears and dreads, which define our individuality and our physical existence, and this has to do with having a body. The idea of not having a body; but still being identifiable as being myself, seems impossible. I mean, how I would know that once it was me; walking, jumping, eating or having a temperature, is because a thing without a body can not do anything nor can it have indications that a given object is "here" rather than "there." The notion of continuing to be, without having a body, and still be identifiable, either to myself or to others, whom I expect to see later on, simply makes no sense at all.

When you associate this ludicrous kind of spiritualism with transmigration you have the making of third-class comedy. It is like having Jesus, on the way to the cross, saying to his followers, not to worry about him, because he knows that he is going to be transcending to Reverend Billy Graham, whoever he is. Of course, there is no space in Billy Graham's transcendental life because he simply can not entertain a lodger; particularly a disembodied lodger, who can thank Billy for putting him up for a while. The whole notion of "going to a better place" is tied to a system made up with ideas of upgrade reward. The problem is that one can not be rewarded if one is not embodied. This is a delusion that some people require in order to give them hope. It is rather pathetic the way some people get hope. The lives which supposedly Jesus drew attention to, asking them to come unto him, were the people who had no hope at all and for whom life was so ghastly because of political institutions. Inserting a "spirit" in the core of our spiritless existence provides people with an illusionary happiness rather than real happiness. It is only with the illusionary promise of an infinite diverse future that makes such illusion work for them. Fortunately they have not been introduced to theological incoherence; that your loved ones would be disembodied but you would still be happy. It just does not make sense, but it is a deflection of the monstrous social injustice of the bodied mortal world in which we live and that politics has screwed up the lives of 90% of the living population on the earth.

In this book, I went beyond religious beliefs. I have no beliefs to speak of and no faith; but dialectical-thoughts which consist of doing justice, holding dearly to the Golden Rule, and endeavouring to make my fellow humans see the truth, based on reason and evidence. I have shown in this work that I am atheist, my reasons for not being religious and the historical evolution of atheism from the first to the last chapter.

I was raised in the Greek Orthodox dogma until I started thinking for myself; with a little help from *Friedrich Nietzsche* (1844 – 1900). I was not aware of the cultural difficulties I would encounter from friends and family members for being an openly declared atheist. I must admit, however, that I was not as brave as I am today about being an atheist. I spent a number of years in "religious-closet," hiding my atheism, until I mastered enough courage to declare my convictions. My mother's concern was, *"Be whatever you want in life; a rebellious communist, a socialist or an anarchist, but please leave God alone."* I am none of the above, but I am an atheist who could not "leave God alone."

The circumstances in my life, took me to various countries in South America where I witnessed the national order of the Catholic priesthood, under a compulsive system of religion, a compulsive indoctrination of faith that only strengthened my determination and rendered my work in atheism exceedingly necessary. I have witnessed the wreck of religious superstition, of the false system of theology, of the babble of religious morality and the dehumanization of the ignorant but faithful peasantry. In the years past, I have read the creed professed by the Jewish-Greek Orthodox of the Old Testament, the Christian New Testament and most of the Qur'an, and they appear to me no other than badly written human inventions designed by ignorant tribal men to appease the ill-educated, the fearful and the terrified.

I do not condemn a person's individual beliefs, for he has the right to them, it is the institutions of the churches that monopolize power and profit.

It is nearly impossible to calculate the moral mischief mental delusions and religious lies, has produced in mankind. When a clergyman have dedicates his life to corrupt and prostitute his moral dignity for wages, and professes his professional "holiness," that man is prepared to commit every other crime including pedophilia. He takes the profession of a priest, rabbi or imam for the sake of power and profit (in order to qualify for the trade of priesthood) by lying to the self-deluded with his destructive sense of false morality.

Every religion, since time immemorial, has claimed itself by pretending that it has some special mission from God, communicated by means of revelation to certain patriarchs. The Jewish religion had Abraham and Moses, the Christians their *Messiah Saviour* or Jesus Christ and its saints, and the Arab-Bedouins of the Arabian Peninsula and their Mohammad, as if the way to God was open only to these men and no other. The revelation, when applied to religion, means that God communicated something to man. Here we have to admit that a "revelation" is a message that has been revealed to the first person and no other. For instance, when St. Paul revealed that Jesus' voice was calling him to dedicate his life to Christianity, and he tell this to a second person, a second to a third, a third to a fourth, and so on, it ceased to be a revelation and it becomes a hearsay or myth, or part of the ignorant' religion, which he is obliged to believe.

It is not difficult to account for the mythological premise that was given to the Messiah Saviour (Jesus Christ) being the son of God. He was born when the typological mythology was at its height and repute in the world of intelligentsia, and the past theological mythology had prepared the ill-educated desert people for belief in such a myth. In other words, it was not strange for the people to believe that an eccentric Jewish rabbi or a street orator in Bethlehem has been celestially begotten or was the son of God. This myth, therefore, had nothing new, wonderful or fantastic in it; it simply was on par with the dominant view of the period.

In a leap forward into the future, it is curious to see how Josephus' pacifist-mythology, of what is now called monotheist- Christianity, sprang out of the tail of pagan polytheism, such as:

a) the making of the central figure to be celestially chosen, like Mithras,
b) the three in one gods (father, son and the holy spirit) was nothing other than the actual reduction of the former plurality of gods, (which were counted in hundreds),
c) the statue of the Virgin Mary succeeded the statue of Diana of Ephesus,

d) the deification of mythological heroes changed into Christian Saints (for every reason and season),
e) the Church becoming the crowded Temple,
f) Rome being the place of idolatry of the new celestial myth, and accommodating the purpose of political-military power and revenue and
g) that similar systems of morality had been preached by Confucius and Greek moral philosophers, many years before.

You see, the Messiah Saviour (Jesus Christ) wrote no account of himself, of his birth, of his up bringing, of his parents, of his miracles, of the Apostles or anything else, not even a single line of the New Testament is of his own writing. The account of him is altogether the work of Josephus, the Roman Imperial Cult, the Jewish theologian Heron of Alexandria, and much later by Mark, John, Matthew and Luke. As for the account of resurrection and ascension, it was the necessary balance to the myth of Jesus' birth. The metaphors that brought Jesus into this world in a "supernatural" manner (Immaculate Conception) were obliged to take him out again in the same "supernatural" manner. But the resurrection of a dead Jesus from the grave and his ascension through the air, like the ascension of a balloon, is a thing which every Christian is required to believe, because the evidence never was given. It is cynical that a small number of persons claimed to have witnessed it and the rest of the world is called upon to believe it. The myth, as it relates to the supernatural acts of resurrection and ascension has every indication of deliberately distorting the Laws of Nature, because:
a) miracles violate the Laws of Nature,
b) the Laws of Nature cannot be violated, and
c) therefore, miracles are impossible.

The tale of the Sun standing still upon the mount Gibeon, and the Moon in the valley of Avalon, is one of the fables nearing the ridiculous. The subliminal message and the ridiculous often compliment one another, and it is difficult to class them separately. The atheists know that the Laws of Nature have never changed with respect to the principles of science, the properties of matter or the fundamental manifestations of the universe. Why, then, it is assumed that those Laws of Nature could change or be suspended on behalf of the blind faithful?

The faithful in general prefer to ignore the kind of wickedness there is in the pretended world of both the Old and the New Testament. Raised up in habits of superstition, they take for granted that the bible is literally true. Therefore, they permit themselves not to doubt it, and they have been taught to believe that it was written by god's authority. On the other hand, the Jews made God the assassin of other human species to make room for the Jews.

The Christians have made God the murderer of his Son-God, the founder of the new religion, in order to supersede and expel the Jewish religion. Islam's Qur'an was created on impositions, forgeries and plagiarism; deliberate distortions of the geographically desolate Arabian Peninsula and the perpetual propagation of warfare and violence as we witness today. In the words of *Baruch Spinoza* (1632 – 1677) in his *"The Theological-Political Treatise" (1670),*
"The greatest secret of [authoritative] rule is to keep men deceived, and to cloak in the specious name of religion the fear by which they must be checked, so that they will fight for slavery as they would for salvation, and will think it most shameful, but a most honourable achievement, to give their life and blood [so] that [the leaders] may have a ground for boasting"
Atheism is the oldest view in the world because it holds the absence of any deities. It is the oldest of modern and pre-historic man who appeared around 200,000 years ago. It predates the first religion by 190,000 years. It developed in Africa and spread throughout the continent and beyond. The first group of Neanderthals and Homo sapiens, sometime during the Middle Stone Age, used stone-tools for their hunting and defence. They knew that they have only themselves to thank for their survival, and possibly their ancestors, who showed them how to make and use them. None of them asked, *"where do we come from?"* They needed more complex language for that. Once they improved their ability to use articulate language, they had more important things to consider, such as organising their food supplies, safety for their families and co-ordinating and agreeing on the rules to live by.

As the millennia went by, they may have become curious of their origins, but we do not know at what millennia they started asking this question. From the evidence left in sites and graves, we know that they did not come up with any idiotic ideas or pseudo-answers relating to religion, not just yet anyway. A large number of humans began to migrate from Africa in their quest to find a more suitable environment, thus they started populating the rest of the world. In the places they settled many are burying their dead, and decorating the burial sites, signs of saying farewell to the loved ones. The question is, are they still atheists? I claim yes because their burials were not ritual, cloaked with *proto-spiritualism,* but a way of removing decomposing bodies from the community for health reasons. In other communities, where cremations where taking place, it served the same purpose.

Art forms of naked women begin to appear in figurines and cave-art and animals are depicted from their immediate environment, but the artists still have not invented the supernatural. They just enjoyed painting *symbolic* representations of whatever objects, from *reality,* appealed to their fancy and each to their own taste and ability. Some painted buffalo, some painted spirals and some did a hand print. As millennia continued to pass the cave-art and ceremonial burials became more symbolic in their meaning and gave a prominence to subliminal messages depicted in them. Cave-arts were given the kind of symbolism that satisfied both the artists and the community's emotional needs. Giant and powerful images of buffalo, tigers and lions represented a kind of *proto-animist* mythical symbolism of the natural world. By this time, our human cousins, the Neanderthals, vanished from the face of the earth and Cro-Magnon developed to fully human, as we are today.

The gravitational balance between symbolism and reality shifted in favour of symbolism, and reality was taken for granted as something that "is just there" that contains no magic and no mystery, no freedom of the imagination and no emotional expression. As communities grew larger, and individuals increasingly became marginalised, the only escape and entertainment from that reality was symbolism of every kind including natural storms, earthquakes, eclipses, the Sun, the Moon and the stars. The majority of the population were unable to distinguish between a *thing and a symbol of that thing.* This springs from several causes. The primary cause is that they were mentally isolated from the natural world, where the distinction between a thing and a symbol is more obvious. Another cause is their lack of knowledge which was the exclusive right of the priestly class and the powerful elite. The third cause is the vested interest to resist teaching people *how to think* (not what to think). This creates an intellectual laziness in communities in which symbolism is embedded; which does not appeal to reason but instead to emotions. If people could think creatively for themselves, it would be difficult to be governed. Read any account of ancient events; Homer, Iliad, Hercules, the Fall of Jerusalem, the Exodus, and you would be reading a typological mixture of symbolism (delusion-based terms) and reality (based-terms.) Distorting the reality of the natural world was the norm and the symbolism of religion became the greatest hoax ever propagated on earth.

Give or take 5,000 years of *proto-religious* process, the first recorded existence of organized religion comes from the first written scalped texts of the kill-game instruction of the *Egyptian Tahoe Tablet* pictorial records from about 5,000 years ago. This indicates that, by this time, society has been entirely religionized. This means that, for 195,000 years the sky-God was absent from human affairs. Archaeological evidence suggests that religion was created sometime during the Neolithic Era, from about 10,000 to 7,000 thousand years ago, as result of the Agricultural Revolution. During this period, human communities, for the first time, reach sizes in which the individuals don't personally know each other anymore. Up to this historical time, the Golden Rule applied to those who knew one another in close friendship and family quarters.

The desire to dominate such a large group must have been strong with many elites, although nobody ruled for a long period of time. Whoever came to power was replaced by someone stronger, shortly afterwards. A successful ruler would need something, or someone, to secure his power. Preferably, such a ruler would need to justify his authority by claiming his divine relationship with a Supreme Being that nobody can see and hear, apart from himself. Such Supreme Being is powerful enough to crush enemies, who coincidentally happened to be the ruler's enemies as well. As such, now religion is born! The idea of the existence of a Supreme Being and his earthly representatives spreads like a virus. Within a few thousand years, the world around the Mediterranean coast and the Fertile Crescent is entirely infected by religion.

Well, not entirely. Due to its geographical isolation by a current of interglacial, one small island community stays unaffected, because Tasmania was cut-off from all other humans of the African Continent and the Arabian Peninsula. So, Tasmania remains atheist until the first British settlement in 1803. Frankly, we do not know much about the early stage of the *proto-religion age*. However, since religion was created to justify political and celestial authority, we can be sure that, as a totalitarian system, it was strictly enforced from its very start; that is, during the period of the Agricultural Revolution. In a relatively short time, 190,000 years of global atheism is wiped out and is pretended to have never existed in the first place.

Since its beginning, all religions have survived and been spread by inventing, amending and discarding deceptions as a matter of convenience. For centuries, the low classes and the ignorant were terrorized by the clerical promise of eternal damnation. Abrahamic theologians (Jewish, Christian and Muslim) assured their believers that they would be crushed in giant olive-oil presses, torn to pieces by wild horses, fed with the gall of dragons, burned for eternity and tortured by demons. The Second Council of Constantinople in 543 AD, declared that

"Whoever says or thinks that the punishment of demons and of the wicked will not be eternal, that it has an end...let him be anathema."

The existence of God was held to prove of the existence of eternal hell, so the denial of eternal hellfire was interpreted as the denial of the existence of God. Contemporary theologians have now started to redefine Hell, because traditional teachings of hellfire and eternal torment have made God into a sadistic monster and have left deep psychological scars on many. According to redefinition of Hell, it is not a place at all, but only a condition of being distant from God.

Deception of the populous was always among the primary functions of religion. Deception was, and still is, the special trait of the Catholic Church (Mother Teresa, the pardonable sins of the dead, etc). Purgatory was the place where the sinful dead atoned for their pardonable sins and, for the right-price, the sinner's suffering could be reduced by the actions of the living. Sometimes the pardonable dead were permitted to return to the world of the living, but as *ghosts.* It was a common practice in the Roman Catholic Church to sell or exchange this merit in the form of an *indulgence,* where a Christian would pay or perform some service in exchange for a piece of paper letting the "spirit" of the dead off some punishment due to it after death. Indulgences are still part of the Catholic doctrine in a *modified form.*

It was known that in ancient Greece, its best known philosophers had been atheists. Most Roman philosophers were also atheists, and regarded religion, as man-made. People in the Arabian countries were also able to express their doubts about religion, in medieval times, until it became a crime. The blind Syrian poet, Abul 'Ala Al-Ma'arri *(973 – 1057 AD)* originally coined his scepticism and anti-religious views in his poetry of atheism; *"The inhabitants of the earth are two sorts: those with brains, but no religion, and those with religion, but no brains."* This remarkable eleven century Arab poet and freethinker, taught that religion was worthless except to those who exploit the credulous masses;

"Do not suppose the statements of the prophets to be true, they are all fabrications. Men lived comfortably till [the prophets] came and spoiled life. The sacred books are only such a set of idle tales as any age could have and indeed did actually produce."

Al-Ma'rri's poetry was renowned for unflinching religious scepticism:

The all err—Muslims, Jews,
Christians, and Zoroastrians:
Humanity follows two world-wide sects:
One, man intelligent without religion,
The second, religious without intellect.

Reason forbade me many things which,
Instinctively, my nature was attracted to;
And perpetual loss I feel if, knowing,

I believe a falsehood or deny the truth.

Had they been left alone with reason,
They would have accepted a spoken lie;
But the whips were raised to strike them,
Traditions were brought to them,
And they were ordered to say,
"We have been told the truth,"
If they refused, the sword was drenched with their blood,
They were terrified by scabbards of calamities,
And tempted by great bowls of food,
Offered in a lofty and condescending manner.

So, too, the creeds of men: the one prevails
Until the other comes; and this one fails
When that one triumphs; ay, the lonesome world
Will always want the latest fairytales.
And religious rites were a means of enslaving the masses:
O fools, awake! The rites you sacred hold
Are but a cheat contriving by men of old,
Who lusted after wealth and gained after their lust
And died in baseness—and their law is dust.

Al-Ma'arri's vision reveals the difficulty of living in the 10th century Arabian society without God. Modern humanism has its material roots in the ability of humans to transform their world, a world in which the great revolutions, philosophical, scientific, industrial and political, have provided concrete meaning of human driven progress. This was not the world of the 10th century Arabia and Europe, for it was a world in which life seemed forever static and immovable, in which the idea that humans could transform the world for the better would have seemed not merely hubristic but irrational and insane. A world without God seemed without a sense of meaning and no hope of recompense of life of pain and torment.

The blind atheist Syrian poet Abu al-Mar'arri

Religious Vandalism

Destruction of the statute of the Syrian atheist Abu al-Mar'arri 973-1058 AD

Nazi style religious propaganda

INDEX IV

Billy graham's, 736
Child soldier, 710
Greek public, 697
Inter-breeding, 706
Mother teresa, 670
Stephen hawking, 660
The origins of species, 637
Aboriginal spiritualism, 695
Abortion, 673
Abul 'ala al-ma'arri, 743
Abused, 704
Adam & eve, 690
Adam smith, 726
Adaptation, 651, 705
Afterlife, 648, 694, 699
Agricultural revolution, 691, 742
Aids, 646
Aisha, 707
Altruism, 734
Amazon rainforest, 652, 660
Amish children, 706
Amish, 705
Andromeda, 660
Animist spirituality, 695
Annihilation, 662
Apocalyptic, 660, 663
Arabian peninsula, 652, 692, 707
Armageddon, 662, 663, 667
Ascension, 739
Ashkenazim, 700
Assemblies of god, 672
Assimilation, 705
Astrology, 663
Astronomy, 663
Atheism, 698
Atheism, 740
Atheist morality, 734
Atheist, 648, 690, 703, 724, 642, 677, 695, 729, 739

Autism, 706
Baby doc, 675
Bangladesh, 708
Baruch spinoza, 740
Beliefs, 640
Big bang, 639
Birth control, 646
Blame others, 666
Blind faith, 693
Brainwashing, 692
British poor houses, 673
Bronze age, 640, 649
Brothers, 674
Cain and abel, 690
Caliphate, 711
Canada, 695, 697
Canadian prairies, 697
Catholic, 695
Catholicism, 670
Cave-arts, 741
Charlatan hal lindsey, 667
Charles darwin, 724, 650
Charles humphrey keating jr., 675
Child-soldiers, 712
Christian villain, 638
Christopher hitchens, 647
Church and state, 694
Cilice, 679
Compulsory love, 725
Concept-reality, 648
Condoms, 646
Contraception, 673
Contras, 677
Controversy, 692, 639
Count licio gelli, 676
Creation, 690
Cro- magnon, 726
Curable, 672
Curse of ham, 636

Dark age, 643
Darwin, 637
Darwinian, 712
David ben-gurion, 649
David levy, 700
Death, 679
Deceptions, 637
Dialectic, 661
Dialectical reason, 703
Dialectical, 636, 644
Dialectically think, 652
Dialectical-thoughts, 737
Disbelief, 724
Divisive, 691
Divorce, 673
Dome of the rock, 668
Enemy of reason, 638
Enver xoxha, 676
Epileptic, 638
Eschatology, 666
Ethics, 642, 697
Evolution, 651, 651
Extended phenotype, 734
Faith, 644
Faith-based schools, 690
Faith-based, 703
False claims, 692
False pattern, 662
False pattern-danger, 644
False pattern-explanations, 653
Faulty-genes, 727
Fertile crescent, 692, 742
Fictional-based terms, 657
Friedrich nietzsche, 737
Futuristic idea, 669
Galapagos, 651
Gandhi, 730
Generation, 669
Ghosts, 743
God of the gaps, 734

Golden rule, 638, 713, 735, 737, 742
Goyim, 700
Gulag, 735
Haitians, 675
Happy-talk, 695
Hasidic, 700
He society of foreign missions, 696
Historical accident, 730
Holy war, 708
Homoerotic, 699
Homosexual paedophilic, 699
Hospice for the dying, 670, 671
Human trafficking, 704
Humanist morality, 638
Humanist-reason, 640
Humanists, 690, 695, 712
Ian robert maxwell, 675
Ignatius, 679
Illusionary, 737
Incurable, 672
Indoctrination, 690, 693
Indonesia, 709
Intelligent design, 690, 692
Intelligent designer, 650
Inter-faith, 691
Intuition, 637
Irrational, 650
Islamic marriages, 706
Israeli, 700
Jesuits, 679, 696
Jesus suffering, 670
Jewish temple, 668
Jihadist ideology, 698
Jihadist, 712
Jihadists, 639
John locke, 640, 649
Junk-science, 663
Kemal ataturk, 711
Laws of nature, 661, 663, 739
Legion d'honneur, 675

Life after death, 663, 694
Lly insane, 680
Love for suffering, 674, 673, 675
Loved poverty, 677, 671
Madrassas, 699, 699
Malaysia, 709
Martin luther, 727
Martyrdom, 679
Martyred, 699
Masochistic, 680
Material-reality, 693
Maulana, 698
Mediterranean, 697, 704, 742
Meek, 645
Meekness, 645
Mesopotamia, 691
Messiah, 660, 668
Messianic, 640
Milky way, 660
Misanthropic, 665, 671, 680
Missionaries of charities, 671
Missionaries of charity, 674
Mohel, 702
Morality, 642, 661, 690, 697
Morals, 724
Mortality, 736
Mother teresa, 675
Mythological-stories, 690
National volunteers corps, 670
Native lifestyle, 695
Natural evolution, 697, 640, 651, 697, 703
Nazism, 735
Neanderthal, 648, 726
Neolithic era, 742
Neutrality, 703
Newton, 637
Nunneries, 674
On the jews and their lies, 727
Origins of life, 703

Pakistan, 709
Pattern-explanations, 636
Pattern-faith, 651
Pattern-fear, 690
Pattern-meanings, 693
Paul turley, 676
Paul, 679
Pedophiles, 709, 697, 699
Pedophiliac marriages, 707
Plight of children, 713
Polis, 652
Polycarp, 679
Polytheistic, 636
Predicted end, 667
Prophecies, 665
Prophetic failure, 666
Protestant, 695
Proto-animist, 741
Proto-religious, 741
Proto-spiritualism, 740
Proven science, 663
Pseudo-morality, 677
Pseudo-science, 690, 692
Psyche, 643
Psychopathic dwarf, 680
Qur'an, 707
Reality-based terms, 657
Reason to hope, 640
Recollets, 696
Red-heifer days, 669
Refugee families, 704
Refugee, 704
Relativism, 728
Religious fallacies, 694
Religiousness, 668, 690
Resurrection, 739
Revelation, 738
Richard dawkins, 703
Right and wrong, 729
Rob dreher's, 669

Saint of the gutter, 677
Salafi, 698
Saudi arabia, 709
Saudi arabian theocracy, 708
Scapegoating, 725
Schizophrenic, 638
Secularisation, 703
Segregated, 691
Sephardim, 700
Sexual predators, 695
Shari'a, 712
Shari'ah law, 708, 709
Shas, 700
Social bonding, 638
Social darwinism, 645, 652
Sohr, 711
Solidarity, 638, 677
Somoza dictatorship, 677
Spiritualism, 736
Stalinism, 735
State of nature, 724, 728
Stem cell, 646
Suffering, 678, 679
Sulpicians, 696

Superior-genes, 727
Superstitions, 636, 694, 703
Talmud, 701
Temple institute, 668
Terrorist, 712
The islamic republic of iran, 709
The painted bird, 728
Theory of evolution, 642
Totalitarianism, 725
Transmigration, 736
Turn the other cheek, 645
Typological, 648, 738
Union carbide, 672
Vicarious redemption, 725
Virgin mary, 672
Virus of believing, 694
Wahhabi madrassas, 698
Wahhabi, 698
Western individualism, 705
Wiki leaks, 698
Witchcraft, 702
Yeshivas, 701
Yugoslav republic, 732
Zionist, 675

www.ingramcontent.com/pod-product-compliance
Lightning Source LLC
Chambersburg PA
CBHW050320020526
44117CB00031B/1250